Learning From Practice

A TEXT FOR EXPERIENTIAL LEGAL EDUCATION

THIRD EDITION

EDITED BY

LEAH WORTHAM ▪ ALEXANDER SCHERR

NANCY MAURER ▪ SUSAN L. BROOKS

**WEST
ACADEMIC**
PUBLISHING

© West, a Thomson business, 1998

© 2007 Thomson/West

© 2016 LEG, Inc. d/b/a West Academic
    444 Cedar Street, Suite 700
    St. Paul, MN 55101 1-877-888-1330

West, West Academic Publishing, and West Academic are trademarks of West Publishing Corporation, used under license.

Printed in the United States of America

ISBN: 978-1-63459-618-3

To our students.
We hope your practice experience while in
law school helps you find fulfilling work
that is part of a life you love.

Table of Contents

Section I: General Topics

Preface—For Teachers

This edition of LEARNING FROM PRACTICE builds on the foundation of the first two editions. At the same time, it adds new value to the earlier texts. As you can see from the table of contents, we have expanded the scope of the topics covered and have reconceived the connections between those topics. We also have rethought how an externship teacher might use the text, while consciously offering material we think teachers in other experiential formats will find useful. The new subtitle reflects this change: A TEXT FOR EXPERIENTIAL LEGAL EDUCATION.

This Preface briefly reviews some history of the prior editions and describes the organization and coverage of this edition. It discusses different ways to use the text, including online resources. We address several new directions initiated in this edition that reflect both existing and emerging trends in legal education. We close with a statement of some of the values that underlie this edition: about our students, experiential learning, and law practice generally.

Changes in the Third Edition

The Acknowledgments section outlines this book's history. The first edition in 1998 offered resources for students to enhance their learning from an externship experience and for teachers to plan how best to help their students in that process. The second edition expanded the number and scope of those resources while preserving the book's focus on the externship experience. With this edition, we seek to create a more extensive resource by covering a much wider set of topics and by adding to the book's text more web-accessible links to on-line materials. We believe students and teachers will be able to use these materials in externship courses and other experiential courses in law school, especially those dealing with real world practice.

To that end, we have expanded the scope of coverage to include a broader range of topics relevant to students encountering real law practice. The new topics include effective communication, navigating cultural difference, professionalism, client relationships, collaboration, formation of professional identity, the future of the legal profession and legal service market, and several practice specific chapters. While still not comprehensive, the book's coverage now comes closer to providing resources for all aspects of experiential learning for law students in the wider world.

All previous chapters have been reviewed and revised, with many taking on new authors and undergoing major revisions. The chapters on professional development, supervision, bias, reflection and writing journals, lawyering, writing, and career development have been substantially re-envisioned. And all chapters reflect updated knowledge and scholarship, more closely connecting the text both to the student's experience and the teacher's needs.

With the significant increase in the book's content, we have reorganized the book into sections:

General Topics: This section includes chapters that deal with topics common to all externship courses and indeed many other experiential education courses. Here, you will find materials on student goal-setting, supervision, observation, communication, cultural awareness, the experience of bias, and reflective practice.

Professionalism and Ethics: This section groups together chapters from the prior editions that deal with regulation of lawyers generally, confidentiality, conflicts, and duties to third parties. It includes a chapter on professionalism, a many-sided topic that both overlaps with and contributes to discussions focused on ethical concerns.

Lawyering and Skill Development: Here, the book focuses on the development of lawyering competencies, ranging from practical judgment to client work to writing to making non-court presentations to collaboration.

Practice Contexts: Previous editions included a chapter on judicial externships, which remains in this edition in expanded form. In consulting our users, we received suggestions to include other practice-specific chapters. Chapters on lawyering in criminal justice, public interest, public service, and transactional practices are the result.

Your Future as a Lawyer: This section addresses issues related to the student's future as a lawyer . . . and as a person. Discussions of professional identity, work and well-being, and career planning focus on the student as an individual, while the discussion of the future of the legal profession and legal services market introduce the student to the winds of change sweeping through the profession.

Many chapters in this book refer to significant studies of lawyering and legal education over the last several decades. Appendix I contains brief reviews of these studies, including descriptions of their goals and a listing of some of their most significant aspects.

We have increased our emphasis on web-available resources throughout. Because the book will be available in electronic form, we have encouraged authors to embed links to other sources for students to follow. Since these links may become outdated over time, Appendix II provides permanently archived versions of these links, ordered by chapter and page.

We also have changed our approach to providing further resources. Most chapters include a short bibliography of sources, often including blogs and other resources beyond books and articles. Many also include endnotes to allow a curious student to follow a line of thought or become more aware of the scholarship relevant to this form of learning. The Teacher's Manual includes additional bibliographic resources.

How to Use the Book

The book was written in part to help busy teachers, often with multiple other duties, conceptualize a reflective component to accompany the students' experience. Since the first edition, a new best practice has developed: a substantial majority of externship courses and virtually all other experiential courses include a regular seminar session as part of the student's experience. New technology also makes possible other forms of reflective opportunities, including distance courses, tutorials, on-line case rounds, and more. Like our predecessors, the editors of this edition both assume and promote the value of a well-planned classroom session as a vital part of experiential education.

The book assumes many teachers will follow a "chapter-a-class" syllabus, and chapters have been written with this in mind. With 28 chapters, however, the new edition does not lend itself as easily to reading in its entirety within a single academic term. We recognize many courses will assign only parts of the book. Check with our publisher, West Academic, for current information on pricing for electronic purchase of individual chapters and groups of chapters, as well as custom-printing of hard copies of selected chapters.

You may wish to assign different chapters to different students within the class, especially in courses with a mix of placement types. Chapters vary somewhat in length. Some may be assigned for more than one class, including the judicial, criminal justice, and transactional chapters, which are among the longer chapters in the book. Finally, some teachers may ask student to choose among unassigned chapters as part of an independent review or separate assignment.

As did previous editions, the text has a Teacher's Manual available from West Academic with authors' comments on questions and exercises, additional ideas for class activities, and further bibliographic references. The Teacher's Manual also recommends segments of longer chapters a teacher may want to assign for particular teaching objectives. We encourage those new to experiential teaching to draw on these resources as well as this book.

Online resources also exist through which teachers can share materials and ideas about teaching, particularly suggestions about useful new multi-media materials they have created and have found. The bi-annual externship conferences that began in the year of this book's first publication have generated a wealth of resources in online form; indeed, in recent years, these conferences have been fully videotaped for later online viewing. Finally, the LEXTERN website, http://lexternweb.law.edu/, compiles materials, forms, and manuals used by externship teachers, and the LEXTERN listserv provides a forum for exchanging ideas.

Trends and Directions

This Preface already has identified one of the principal trends that shapes and structures the current edition: an emerging confidence in the value of well-designed and carefully delivered externship courses. The existence of this book by itself speaks to its potential use in an externship classroom. In addition, the wide range of topics in the book reflects the many distinctive features of externship courses, where law school faculty and on-site lawyers collaborate to expose the student both to a form of practice and a critical assessment of that practice.

The robust growth of externships since 1998 parallels an equally robust growth in experiential education generally. With this edition, the editors and authors worked to make this book useful for in-house clinical courses, experiential components of doctrinal courses, pro bono programs, transition-to-practice programs, and similar offerings. This book is valuable in any course where students engage in direct work on real problems, whether supervised by faculty or by lawyers outside the school.

The book also responds to changes in the market for law graduates that have been especially profound since the second edition in 2007. Chapter 27 in particular addresses these changes directly. It has a useful synthesis and introduction to the changes occurring in law practice, which we strongly encourage teachers to read and assign to their students.

The inclusion of chapters devoted to specific practice contexts also responds to the diversification of post-graduate placements for many students. "Big law" may no longer have the same dominant role for law students it did even as recently as 2007. With chapters on career planning, professional identity, and long-term well-being, this book seeks to equip students with tools to find their way through an unsettled and confusing market, both immediately after graduation and over the course of their careers.

Finally, while still written by U.S. authors, this edition takes into account that many students at U.S. law schools are involved in clinical experiences outside of their home countries and that their later careers likely will have global dimensions. The previous two editions have been shared with many law teachers and students outside of the U.S. as clinical education has spread around the world. This edition was written to be useful, perhaps with some adaptation, in externships and experiential courses globally.

Themes and Values

The editors and authors share many aspects of a teaching philosophy that pervades this book. These ideas emerge as themes and values that persist across most of the chapters, sometimes explicit, sometimes implicit, yet all moving in a similar direction. This final section makes them explicit.

We want students to become active participants in the development of their own lives and careers and to exercise **autonomy** and **self-direction** in their choices. We sometimes shorthand this goal as moving students towards being "actors rather than acted upon." Much of the book coaches students on how to take the initiative, make plans, and articulate and achieve specific goals.

We also believe in the inherent value of developing a capacity for **reflection** and **reflective practice**. Chapter 8 focuses on this idea explicitly, and virtually every other chapter stresses it as a key ability. These include topics as diverse as supervision, cultural difference, effective communication, professionalism, professional identity, work and well-being, and many, many others. One goal of the text and the exercises provided is to offer students content for reflection and specific prompts to do so.

Throughout the text, we stress the importance of **dialogue, communication**, and **collaboration** to law practice and life as a lawyer. Chapter 5 contains an important discussion of communication that stresses its nature as dialogue and encourages students to adopt a more conscious and self-aware approach to communication in all of their interactions. These themes also permeate other chapters, especially Chapter 16 on Collaboration.

This edition stresses **cultural competence** and the experience of **bias** in law practice. Chapters 6 and 7 deal with these issues explicitly. The themes these chapters discuss also are addressed in many other chapters, both explicitly and implicitly.

We have encouraged authors to promote **critical assessment of law practice** in the questions they pose about lawyering and about the political and social context within which lawyering occurs. Externships offer unique opportunities for such assessments, by separating law practice supervision by a site supervisor from clinical oversight by law school faculty. Chapters 19–23 offer students numerous avenues for critical appraisal of specific practice contexts, while many other chapters prompt equally sharp assessments of client relationships, professional identity, and the nature and future of the legal profession.

This book renews and extends an emphasis on **professionalism** as a key aspect of students' development as lawyers. Often dismissed as too vague or indefinite, the new Chapter 9 explicitly develops different ways students can understand the concept. Many other chapters address these themes both directly and indirectly.

Finally, we passionately want our students to find satisfaction and a sense of **well-being** in their careers as lawyers. Chapter 25 on Work and Well-being synthesizes considerable research on what helps people manage the responsibility with comes with being a lawyer and thrive. It emphasizes assessing and acting on one's intrinsic values—the sense of one's own authentic self—rather than extrinsic competitive pressures and perceptions of what others think, which studies have found create unhealthy stress and unhappiness.

In short, we continue to be dedicated to and energized by our work with students when we see how experiences in practice help them identify what will be meaningful for them in their life's work. The materials in this book can help students gain confidence they can become masterful practitioners doing work they find worth doing. The qualities of autonomy, relatedness, and mastery have been repeatedly validated as those most likely to support people's sense of well-being. We also believe developing habits of acting reflectively and intentionally are key to learning actively from experience and finding satisfying work.

Introduction—For Students

T his book is about learning from experience, specifically experience with law-yering. You can learn about lawyering in many courses including externships outside your school, clinics within your school, and in simulation courses such as drafting or trial practice. All of these offer the chance to work with clients, solve problems, and develop your sense of who you are and the kind of lawyer you want to become. This book, and the course in which you use it, can help you make the most of the present and plan for the future.

The many authors of this book share a passion for helping students get the maximum benefit from "learning from practice." We find it exciting when a student discovers satisfying work, builds confidence in the ability to practice, feels the pleasure and challenge of work that matters, and finds a path from lawyering experiences to a rewarding career. The chapters in this book share our years of experience teaching and learning alongside our students as they encounter the unique opportunities of life as a lawyer.

This book separates what we know into 28 chapters spread over five broad sections.

General Topics: The chapters here help you to set goals and plan your experience, work under supervision, observe carefully, communicate effectively, and reflect on your experience. You also will learn about how to navigate cultural difference and deal with the realities of bias in the legal system.

Professionalism and Ethics: These chapters alert you to the many ethical dimensions of law practice. They describe general ethical obligations associated with legal work and focus specifically on confidentiality, conflicts of interest, and your duties to tribunals and third parties. An introductory chapter introduces you to the complex, multi-sided idea of "professionalism," allowing you a better grasp of how to act and conduct your practice as a lawyer.

Lawyering and Skill Development: These chapters cover some of the important ways you can develop your abilities as a lawyer in this course. It includes discussions of key capacities: good judgment and legal decision making, client relationships, collaboration in teams, making presentations, and legal research and writing in a practice setting.

Practice Contexts: Some of you will take courses that include many different types of law practices, while others will focus on a specific type of practice. The chapters here introduce you to lawyering in some common and important practices: judicial chambers, criminal prosecution and defense offices, public interest organizations, government practices, and firms engaged in transactional legal work.

Your Future as a Lawyer: Your experience in your placement can have a powerful impact on your future as a lawyer and as a person. These chapters help you to appreciate the importance of a strong professional identity, opportunities to find well-being in your work, and ways to translate this experience into a job and a career. You also can learn about the massive changes sweeping through the legal profession in a chapter devoted to the future of law practice and the legal services market.

As editors and authors, we know you may encounter this book in bits and pieces, reading only selected chapters drawn from different places in the book. Some chapters are short enough for a single assignment, while your teacher may spread other chapters out over several assignments. Most chapters also offer you material for further exploration, both through endnotes and a Further Resources section at the end of the chapter. If you find yourself intrigued, confused, or excited by a discussion, we urge you to follow those pathways to more information.

We have increased the number of multi-media resources referred to in the text, about all of the topics in this book. As you see things on the internet and other media that could enhance your learning, please share them with your teacher. The editors are working on an internet-accessible resource for sharing teaching ideas and sources related to the topics here. Feel free to look for that and make your suggestions there as well.

Many chapters in this book refer to significant studies of lawyering and legal education over the last several decades. Appendix I contains brief reviews of these studies, including descriptions of their goals and a listing of some of their most significant aspects. In addition, many of the links in this book may become outdated over time. Appendix II provides permanently archived versions of these links, ordered by chapter and page.

Some common themes run through the book.

■ *Well-being*

We start from a common premise. We want you to find satisfying work that enhances your long-term sense of well-being. This view is not as widespread as you might think, nor is it simple to pursue. Many people believe that successful law practice demands an imbalanced life that involves undue personal sacrifice. We disagree. This book encourages habits that will help you to identify sources of satisfaction in legal work, think about your intrinsic values, and pursue a career path that aligns with both. Research described in Chapter 25 suggests that people are most likely to attain satisfaction when they act consistently with intrinsic values, gain mastery over work they find worthwhile, and feel a sense of relatedness to others and a community beyond themselves.

■ Autonomy and Active Learning

We also strongly favor active learning, with you as a planner and an active participant in your own learning process. This book stresses the value of acting rather than being acted upon, of planning and doing over reacting and responding. Throughout the book, exercises and questions will prompt you to take an active role in your own learning. Most chapters also highlight the importance of autonomy, that is, deciding and pursuing a path consistent with your personal goals and values.

■ Reflection

Finding well-being in work and life and pursuing your own path as a lawyer take careful thought and deliberation—a process of reflection. Virtually every chapter in this book prompts you to make the most of your experience through reflection. Reflection lies at the heart of self-directed learning and forms an essential part of law practice and legal problem solving. We urge you to slow down, give experience a second and third look, and assess what you learn with care and deliberation.

■ Dialogue and Collaboration

Both law school and popular culture sometimes paint lawyering as an adversarial, competitive, and above all individual practice, in which lawyers work separately from each other. We believe your work at your placement will paint a very different picture. In supervisory relationships, collaborative teams, disputes, negotiations, and transactions, lawyers work together far more often than alone. This book offers you new ways of understanding effective communication, as a dialogue that fosters relationships and encourages connectedness in all the activities of lawyering, and also as a framework for successful collaboration and teamwork.

■ Cultural Competence and Bias

The odds are good you already have encountered the related concepts of diversity and bias in your earlier life. This book offers focused discussion of how to navigate differences between people, including lawyers, clients, decision makers, and others. The increasing diversity of law practice has not led to the elimination of bias. This book offers you perspective and tools to deal with that bias, whether you experience it directly or observe it toward others.

■ *Critical Assessment*

In any course that exposes you to the real world of lawyering, you will encounter broader concerns, including intractable problems and issues. We think life as a lawyer requires you to be alert to these concerns. This book pushes you to question and think critically about how lawyering works and how law relates not just to individual problems but also to broader social, political, and cultural realities as well as how to make justice more affordable and accessible.

■ *Professionalism*

You surely will have heard someone talk about the importance of professionalism, yet you may not have considered the many dimensions of the term. This book separates these dimensions for careful exploration. It encourages you to consider professionalism not just as a set of rules or a way of dressing. To paraphrase one of our students, professionalism is more than something you do; it is instead a way for you to be, a subtle and pervasive way to live. It relates closely to your own values and to your sense of your role as a lawyer and your goals as a human being.

You will find much more in this book than we can hope to cover in a short introduction. As editors, we remain open to your feedback: your questions, comments, and suggestions for improvement. Feel free to email Leah Wortham at wortham@law.cua.edu, and she will pass your thoughts on to the other editors and to the authors if about a particular chapter.

As the dedication to this edition says, we hope this book will help in your journey to "find fulfilling work in a life you love."

About the Authors

ALEXIS ANDERSON is an Associate Clinical Professor at Boston College Law School, where she has taught since 1983. She currently teaches both experiential and ethics courses and supervises student attorneys in the Civil Litigation Clinic, an in-house legal clinic representing indigent clients in housing, family, and benefits matters. In addition, she regularly teaches Professional Responsibility seminars geared toward students in clinical courses. She also has designed and taught 1L experiential simulation courses and co-directed the externship program. Her scholarship frequently focuses on the intersection of clinical and ethical issues. Prior to joining the Boston College Law School faculty, Professor Anderson was a litigator in a large civil practice firm in Philadelphia. She received her J.D. and a M.A. in legal history from the University of Virginia and a B.A. from Wake Forest University.

JEFFREY R. BAKER is an Associate Clinical Professor of Law and the Director of Clinical Education at Pepperdine University School of Law. His role includes oversight of the school's legal clinics, externships, and practicum courses. He directs the law school's pro bono program and the Community Justice Clinic, which represents nonprofit and nongovernmental organizations in human rights, development, and justice work. After six years of private, civil trial and appellate practice in his home state of Mississippi, Professor Baker served from 2006-2013 as Director of Clinical Programs and Associate Professor of Law at Faulkner University Jones School of Law. There he directed the externship program and the Family Violence Clinic and designed and launched the Elder Law Clinic. Professor Baker is a mediator and has taught courses in constitutional history, pretrial practice, law and literature, and family law in addition to teaching negotiation theory and practice for Pepperdine's Straus Institute on Dispute Resolution. His scholarship addresses domestic violence and gender justice in families, including intersecting fields of moral philosophy, religion, legal history, social science, ethics, and multidisciplinary professional responses. He holds degrees in political science and ministry from Harding University and earned his law degree at Vanderbilt University.

LAURIE BARRON is the Executive Director of the Feinstein Center for Pro Bono & Experiential Education at Roger Williams University School of Law. In addition to overseeing the Center, she teaches the Public Interest Externship Program and the co-requisite Public Interest Lawyering Seminar. Her previous work includes representing children at the Juvenile Rights Division of the Legal Aid Society in New York City and working as a public defender and team leader at the Neighborhood Defender Service of Harlem. She also was a clinical teacher in an interdisciplinary Prisoners and Families Clinic at Columbia Law School, a school-based Legal Services Clinic at Rutgers-Camden School of Law, and a Juvenile Rights Advocacy Project at Boston College Law School. She received a B.A. from Yale University, a J.D. from New York University School of Law, and an M.S.W. from New York University School of Social Work.

MARGARET MARTIN BARRY is a Professor of Law and the Associate Dean for Clinical and Experiential Programs at Vermont Law School. In addition to her administrative duties, she teaches in the externship program, co-supervises the incubator project, and teaches simulation and doctrinal courses. Professor Barry spent most of her career teaching in the Families and the Law Clinic at the Columbus School of Law, The Catholic University of America. She holds a J.D. from the University of Minnesota and a B.A. from Luther College. Professor Barry is a member of the Vermont, District of Columbia, Maryland, and U.S. Virgin Islands bars.

STACEY BOWERS is an Assistant Professor of the Practice at the University of Denver Sturm College of Law, where she teaches in the law school's Corporate and Commercial Law Program. She teaches Corporate Drafting, Accounting for Lawyers, How to Read and Understand Public Company Financial Statements, and LLCs and Operating Agreements. Prior to coming to Denver Law, Professor Bowers practiced corporate and transactional law for over 15 years. She has a B.S. in Accounting from the University of Pittsburgh and received her J.D. and Ph.D. in Education from the University of Denver.

SUSAN L. BROOKS is the Associate Dean for Experiential Learning and a Professor of Law at the Drexel University Thomas R. Kline School of Law. She joined the faculty during the law school's inaugural year to develop and oversee all of the experiential and public service aspects of the curriculum. Professor Brooks spearheaded the development of numerous community partnerships where Drexel Law students can receive intensive hands-on training and do pro bono work. She also teaches Family Law and has developed innovative courses focusing on holistic representation, professional formation, effective communication and relational skills, and access to justice. Professor Brooks serves on the Executive Committee and is the Chair-Elect of the AALS Section on Balance in Legal Education. She received her J.D. degree from New York University School of Law in 1990, where she was awarded the Judge Aileen Haas Schwartz Award for Outstanding Work in the Field of Children and Law. Prior to attending law school, she practiced social work in Chicago. Professor Brooks received an M.A. in clinical social work from the University of Chicago-School of Social Service Administration (SSA) in 1984, and earlier earned a B.A. from the same university. She is a member of the Pennsylvania bar and maintains her social work certification.

STACY L. BRUSTIN is a Professor of Law and Co-Director of the Civil Practice Clinic at the Columbus School of Law, The Catholic University of America. She teaches and supervises law students who represent clients in family law, public benefits, employment, and other civil law matters. Professor Brustin has taught two externship courses: Becoming a Lawyer and Immigration/Human Rights Clinical Externship Course. She also has taught, conducted research, and written on professional responsibility, bias in the legal profession, access to justice, and multicultural communication. She formerly worked as a staff attorney and is currently on the Board of Directors of Ayuda, Inc., a legal and social services agency representing immigrants and refugees in the Washington, D.C. metropolitan area. Professor Brustin holds a J.D. from Harvard Law School and a B.A. from Tufts University.

CARMIA N. CAESAR is an Adjunct Professor and Director of the Externship and Public Interest Law Scholars Programs at the Georgetown Law Center. Prior to joining the Law Center, she was the senior attorney in the TeamChild Juvenile Justice Project at the Center for Children's Advocacy (CCA) in Hartford, CT, providing educational and mental health advocacy to children involved with the juvenile justice system. Professor Caesar is a graduate of Pomona College and Harvard Law School. Immediately following law school, she completed a graduate fellowship in public affairs with the San Francisco Office of the Coro Foundation.

LIZ RYAN COLE is a Professor of Law at Vermont Law School, where she has taught since 1984. That year she co-founded Vermont's Semester in Practice, the full-time semester-long external clinic she taught and directed until 2011. She built on her experience in private and legal services practice and training for local, regional, and national legal services organizations by applying lessons from practice to course design for law students and training and coaching their mentor judges and lawyers. Her interest in supervision and feedback is matched by her interest in understanding the brain science that underlies learning and legal ethics, the politics and economics that shape legal education, and the power of land use law in environmental protection. She received her J.D. from Boston University and her B.A. from Oberlin College.

TRACYE G. EDWARDS is an Assistant Teaching Professor at the Drexel University Thomas R. Kline School of Law. She develops innovative online curricula and teaches upper-level students within the Co-op Program and the Master of Legal Studies Program. Professor Edwards also delivers numerous presentations for clinical legal educators and co-op supervisors on creative teaching methods with an emphasis in technology applications. Her prior legal practice focused on commercial transactions, employment law, intellectual property, and corporate compliance for private and public entities. Professor Edwards served as counsel to ARAMARK Sports and Entertainment, an assistant solicitor to the City of Philadelphia Fairmount Park Commission, and an associate with Jennings, Strouss, and Salmon. She received her J. D. from Duke University and a B.A. from Goucher College.

DAISY HURST FLOYD is the Dean and the University Professor of Law and Ethical Formation at Mercer University School of Law. She received her B.A. and M.A. from Emory University and her J.D. from the University of Georgia School of Law. After graduating from law school, she practiced law in Atlanta with the firm of Alston, Miller, and Gaines and then served on the faculties of the University of Georgia School of Law and Texas Tech University School of Law before coming to Mercer Law School as Dean in 2004. Dean Floyd's teaching and research interests include Ethics, Legal Education, Civil Procedure, and Evidence. She regularly teaches Externship I and has been involved with the development of externship pedagogy that focuses on ethical formation. She has a particular interest in the ways in which higher education shapes students' ethical development and the possibilities for cross-disciplinary collaboration within higher education. Dean Floyd was named a Carnegie Scholar by The Carnegie Foundation for the Advancement of Teaching in 2001 in support of her research on the development of professional identity among American law students and participated in the Carnegie Foundation's 2007 study of legal education. She is a member of the American Bar Association Standing Committee on Professionalism.

TIMOTHY W. FLOYD is the Tommy Malone Distinguished Chair in Trial Advocacy and the Director of Experiential Education at Mercer University School of Law. His responsibilities include supervision of clinical and other experiential learning courses such as externships. He also teaches a variety of courses in criminal law and legal ethics. Professor Floyd has published two books and is the author of numerous articles in the area of legal ethics, law and religion, legal education, and criminal law and the death penalty. His service activities emphasize access to justice issues and lawyer professionalism. Professor Floyd has chaired the State Bar of Georgia Access to Justice Committee, the Advisory Board of the Georgia Council for Restorative Justice, and the Supreme Court of Texas Grievance Oversight Committee. He also has served on the Advisory Board of the Georgia Justice Project, the Supreme Court of Georgia Equal Justice Commission Civil Justice Committee, and the National Advisory Committee of Equal Justice Works. He received a B.A and M.A. from Emory University and his J.D from the University of Georgia, where he served as Editor-in-Chief of the GEORGIA LAW REVIEW. He began his career in legal education in 1982 at the University of Georgia School of Law, as Associate Director and then Director of the Legal Aid Clinic. He was on the faculty of Texas Tech

University School of Law from 1989 to 2004, where he was the J. Hadley Edgar Professor of Law and the Co-Director of Clinical Programs.

RUSSELL GABRIEL is the Director of the Criminal Defense Clinics at the University of Georgia School of Law in Athens, a position he has held since 1996. In that role he was the head of the public defender office in Athens until 2005, when the State of Georgia created a statewide public defender system. The UGA Criminal Defense Clinics are now externships through which students are placed in the state-level public defender office in Athens for up to four semesters. He also teaches criminal procedure, race and law, and capital punishment. Prior to the UGA appointment, he worked as an assistant public defender in state and federal public defender offices in Athens and Atlanta, Georgia and as an associate at the law firm of Lobel, Novins, Lamont, and Flug in Washington, D.C. He has been an active member of the Indigent Defense Committee of the State Bar of Georgia since 2001 and holds an LL.M. from Harvard, a J.D. from the University of Georgia, and a B.A. from the University of Michigan. He is originally from Wooster, Ohio.

MARIANA HOGAN is a Professor of Law and Director of the Advocacy Program and Externship Programs at New York Law School. She regularly teaches Trial Advocacy, Deposition Skills, and Evidence. Professor Hogan also administers the Law Office and Judicial Externship Programs, developing placements, advising students, and teaching related seminars. During her term as Associate Dean for Student Development, Professor Hogan developed and taught a Professional Development program for all first-year students. As an expert on advocacy skills, Professor Hogan is a frequent lecturer and teacher for the National Institute for Trial Advocacy (NITA), the New York City Office of Administrative Trials and Hearings (OATH), and the New York City Law Department. An active member of the bar in New York City, she serves on the Indigent Defense Organization Oversight Committee for the local Appellate Division and has served on the Mayor's Advisory Committee on the Judiciary and the Board of Directors of New York County Lawyers' Association (NYCLA). Before becoming a law professor, she was a public defender in state and federal courts in New York City. She holds a J.D. from Georgetown University Law Center and an A.B. from Brown University.

KENDALL L. KEREW is a Clinical Assistant Professor and Director of the Externship Program at Georgia State University College of Law. In addition to the Externship Program, she heads the law school's Academic Success Program, which she redesigned in 2013. Professor Kerew joined Georgia State's law faculty in 2005 and taught Research, Writing & Advocacy until 2010. Prior to joining Georgia State, she spent her first two years of practice as an associate with King & Spalding focusing on employment law and the subsequent five years as an Assistant Attorney General with the Georgia Attorney General's Office, representing the state in matters involving education, elections, local government, and employment law. Professor Kerew is Co-Chair of the AALS Clinical Legal Education Section's Externship Committee. She holds a J.D. from Vanderbilt Law School and a B.A. from Emory University.

INGA N. LAURENT is an Associate Professor and Director of the Externship Program at Gonzaga University School of Law. She is an active member of the national externship community, serving as Co-Chair of the AALS Clinical Legal Education Section's Externship Committee from 2013-2015 and as a member of Externship Committee of the Clinical Legal Education Association since 2011. Aside from her work with externships, Professor Laurent is engaged in advocating for racial equity with an emphasis on addressing racial disproportionality in the criminal justice system and diversifying the legal profession. Prior to working in an academic setting, Professor Laurent worked as a staff attorney with Southeastern Ohio Legal Services (SEOLS) under a grant from the Federal Violence Against Women's Act (VAWA). While at SEOLS, she provided holistic civil legal services to victims of domestic violence. Professor Laurent received her J.D. from Cleveland-Marshall College of Law and her B.A. from Westminster College.

LISA G. LERMAN is a Professor of Law at the Columbus School of Law, The Catholic University of America, where she has taught since 1987. Professor Lerman has taught professional responsibility, contracts, family law, and clinical and externship courses. Professor Lerman is co-author of ETHICAL PROBLEMS IN THE PRACTICE OF LAW (Wolters Kluwer 2005, 2008, and 2012) (with Schrag) and ETHICAL PROBLEMS IN THE PRACTICE OF LAW: MODEL RULES, STATE VARIATIONS, AND PRACTICE QUESTIONS (Wolters Kluwer 2015-2016) (with Schrag and Gupta). She has written many articles about lawyers, law firms, the legal profession, and legal education, including *Lying to Clients*, 138 U. PENN. L. REV. 659 (1990). Earlier work focused on domestic violence law. Professor Lerman was on the planning committee for the ABA National Conference on Professional Responsibility, a member of the Legal Ethics Committee of the D.C, Bar, and chair of the Professional Responsibility Section of the Association of American Law Schools. Professor Lerman serves as an expert witness on legal ethics issues, providing expert reports and expert testimony. She has been a consultant on legal education issues at law schools in the U.S. and in Europe. Professor Lerman received a B.A. from Barnard College, Columbia University in 1976, a J.D. in 1979 from New York University, and an LL.M. in Advocacy from Georgetown University Law Center in 1984.

LISA V. MARTIN is a Clinical Assistant Professor of Law at the Columbus School of Law, The Catholic University of America, where she co-directs the Families and the Law Clinic, a live-client, in-house clinical program and serves as the Director of the Experiential Curriculum, overseeing the externships program and the law school's external clinical courses. She also has taught courses on Gender, Law, & Policy and International Rights of Women. Her teaching, scholarship, and practice focus on issues relating to intimate partner violence; poverty; the relationships between children, parents, and the state; and access to justice. She formerly worked as a staff attorney and co-managed the Teen Dating Violence Program at Women Empowered Against Violence, an organization dedicated to providing holistic legal and social services to individuals subjected to domestic violence and sexual assault, and as a litigation associate at Arent Fox PLLC. Professor Martin holds a J.D. from the Georgetown University Law Center and a B.A. from the College of William and Mary.

NANCY MAURER is a Professor of Law and Director of Field Placement Programs at Albany Law School in Albany, New York. She teaches a variety of clinical, skills, and interdisciplinary courses including Field Placement, Negotiating for Lawyers, and Legal Issues in Medicine. Professor Maurer founded and for many years directed the Albany Law School's Civil Rights and Disabilities Law Clinic in which law students represented clients in discrimination, education, and other disability rights matters under faculty supervision. She co-developed Albany's Introduction to Lawyering program designed to expose first-year law students to essential research, writing, lawyering skills, and professionalism in context through a year-long simulation. She writes and lectures in the areas of legal education and disability law. She is co-editor and an author of the New York State Bar Association books on DISABILITY LAW AND PRACTICE. She received her J.D. from George Washington University National Law Center and B.A. from Middlebury College.

LINDA MORTON is a Professor and Associate Dean of Experiential Learning at California Western School of Law. The focus of her teaching, scholarship, and service has been on clinical pedagogy, creative problem solving, alternative dispute resolution, public health, interdisciplinary work, and community engagement. In addition to supervising students in the law school's Clinical Internship Program since 1989, she has co-taught a Mediation Clinic and a Public Health Clinic in collaboration with other professionals, and also taught various simulation courses. She helped create and supervised California Western's Pro Bono Program and the California Western Community Law Project, an interdisciplinary partnership that offers aid to the underserved. For the past two decades, she has trained students as well as community members in mediation, facilitation, conflict resolution, and teamwork, in addition to volunteering as a mediator for several nonprofit organizations. Professor Morton is the recipient of the Father Robert Drinan Award for her work in helping the local community of San Diego. She has a J.D. from Northeastern University School of Law and an A.B. from Princeton University.

J.P. "SANDY" OGILVY is a Professor of Law and the Director of the Office of Law & Social Justice Initiatives at the Columbus School of Law, The Catholic University of America. He was the Coordinator of Clinical Programs at the Law School from 1991 until 2006. Currently, he directs the Innocence Project Clinic & Clemency Project and teaches Civil Procedure. Professor Ogilvy is a past chair of the AALS Sections on Clinical Legal Education and Pro Bono and Public Service Opportunities. He is the recipient of the 2003 William Pincus Award and the 2013 Father Robert Drinan Award. He has been a clinical teacher since 1980, when he was a teaching fellow at Georgetown University Law Center's Administrative Advocacy Clinic. He has taught in client-based clinics, externship programs, and simulation courses. Professor Ogilvy has published in the areas of clinical legal education, legal pedagogy, and lawyering skills. He is the director of the National Archive of Clinical Legal Education and produced two documentary films on the early history of clinical legal education using materials from his Oral History Project on Clinical Legal Education. He hosts several listservs, including LEXTERN, the listserv for externship faculty and administrators. Professor Ogilvy holds an LL.M. from Georgetown University Law Center, a J.D. from Lewis & Clark Law School, and a B.A. from Portland State University.

MARK POPIELARSKI works as a Research/Reference Law Librarian at the University of Denver's Sturm College of Law. Specializing in Corporate & Commercial, Workplace, and Tax Law, he provides instructional, research, and reference services to institutional and public patrons. He earned his J.D. from the American University Washington College of Law, M.B.A. from the University of South Florida, and M.S.L.I.S. from Drexel University.

MARGARET (MEG) REUTER has a current faculty appointment in Brooklyn Law School's Civil Practice Externship Clinic. She served as visiting professor at Indiana University-Maurer Law School to teach its signature first year course, *The Legal Profession*, and is currently a member of the research faculty at Maurer's Center on the Global Legal Profession. During her tenure as Assistant Dean at New York Law School's Office of Professional Development and director of its Office of Academic Affairs, she focused on law school curriculum design, professional development, externship teaching, and student advising. Her research focuses on the relationship between experiential coursework and its value to law graduates' transition to practice, especially during their early careers. Previously, she was an associate in the litigation practice group of Schulte Roth & Zabel LLP in New York, served as

Special Counsel for New York City's Department of Transportation, and clerked for Justice Stewart Pollock of the New Jersey Supreme Court. She is a *cum laude* graduate of New York University School of Law, was elected to its Order of the Coif, and was Articles Editor of NEW YORK UNIVERSITY LAW REVIEW. She holds a B.A. from Douglass College, Rutgers University.

MICHAEL H. ROFFER is an Associate Librarian for Reader Services and a Professor of Legal Research at New York Law School. He regularly teaches a variety of legal research classes as well as a seminar on judicial externships. A member of the New York Bar since 1984, he served as a Law Clerk for Judge Roger J. Miner of the U.S. Court of Appeals for the Second Circuit. Prior to teaching, he practiced law for fifteen years at two major New York City law firms. He holds a J.D. degree *magna cum laude* from New York Law School, where he was a John Ben Snow Scholar and an Articles Editor for the NEW YORK LAW SCHOOL LAW REVIEW. He also holds a M.L.I.S. (Masters in Library and Information Science) from Rutgers, the State University of New Jersey. He received his B.A. degree *magna cum laude* with Honors in Economics from Brandeis University and is the author of THE LAW BOOK: FROM HAMMURABI TO THE INTERNATIONAL CRIMINAL COURT, 250 MILESTONES IN THE HISTORY OF LAW (2015).

AVIS L. SANDERS is the Director of the Externship Program at the American University Washington College of Law, overseeing the field placements and externship seminars for over 400 law students each year. She teaches the Externship Seminar and provides training and guidance to over 30 externship faculty members who teach in the Program. She served as the Co-Chair of the AALS Executive Committee on Externships for three years and is a regular presenter at national externship conferences. Ms. Sanders practiced employment discrimination law at the Washington Lawyers' Committee for Civil Rights and Urban Affairs from 1990 to 2002. She directed the Committee's EEO Intake Project and worked as a staff attorney on a number of its individual and class action cases. She also was responsible for training and supervising hundreds of law students and attorneys who provided pro bono assistance to the Committee on employment discrimination cases. She holds a J.D. from the Benjamin Cardozo School of Law, a B.A. from American University, and holds a third dan black belt in the Korean martial art of Taekwondo.

SUSAN B. SCHECHTER has been the Field Placement Program Director and Lecturer-in-Residence at University of California Berkeley School of Law since 2006. Each semester, she works with 60-80 students who extern in nonprofit, government, and judicial placements and has helped organize and co-teach the field placement companion courses with judges and attorneys. Over the past 25 years, she has held a variety of law school administrative positions and maintained a focus on helping law students interested in public interest or public sector careers and pro bono issues. She was a founder and has been an active member of BACE (Bay Area Consortium on Externships) and other relevant committees, including several AALS sections. She has been an organizer or presenter at numerous conferences including Externships, Equal Justice, AALS, and other national and regional conferences. Professor Schechter holds a J.D. from University of Pittsburgh School of Law and a B.A. from Washington University in St. Louis, Missouri.

ALEXANDER SCHERR is an Associate Professor and Director of Civil Clinics at the University of Georgia School of Law. He created and teaches in the Civil Externship program and teaches a poverty law counseling course called the Public Interest Practicum. Professor Scherr also has taught Dispute

Resolution; Evidence; and Interviewing, Counseling, and Negotiation. As Director of Civil Clinics, he has helped to increase the law school's clinics from 4 to 13 programs. He has served as President of the Clinical Legal Education Association, a member of the Executive Committee of the Clinical Section of the AALS, and as a member and chair of the AALS Standing Committee on Clinical Legal Education. Professor Scherr participates actively in organizing both national and regional clinical conferences. He is a licensed mediator. He writes on clinical legal education, lawyering theory, and mental health.

MARJORIE A. SILVER is a Professor of Law at Touro Law Center where she teaches the Civil Practice Externship seminar and other courses including Professional Responsibility and New Paradigms in Law and Lawyering. She is a contributing author and the editor of THE AFFECTIVE ASSISTANCE OF COUNSEL: PRACTICING LAW AS A HEALING PROFESSION (Carolina Academic Press 2007), and the forthcoming anthology, TRANSFORMING JUSTICE, LAWYERS AND THE PRACTICE OF LAW (Carolina Academic Press). She is a board member of the Project for Integrating Spirituality, Law, and Politics and sits on the Advisory Board of the Dave Nee Foundation, the mission of which is to fight depression and prevent suicide among adolescents, young adults, and law students. She was the 2011 chair of the AALS Section on Balance in Legal Education and remains active as an *ex officio* member of its Executive Committee. In 2010, Professor Silver was recognized by the American Bar Association's Commission on Lawyer Assistance Programs, which awarded her one of its five inaugural Law Student Wellness Awards. Professor Silver received her undergraduate degree from Brandeis University and her law degree from the University of Pennsylvania. She served as law clerk to U.S. District Judge Joseph S. Lord III, E.D. Pa. Prior to beginning her career in legal education in 1983, she served as the Chief Regional Attorney for the U.S. Department of Education, Region II.

HANS P. SINHA is a Clinical Professor at the University of Mississippi School of Law, where he directs the Externship Program. His previous work includes directing the Prosecution Externship Program at Mississippi, teaching in the Tulane Law School Criminal Defense Clinic, and serving as an Assistant District Attorney and a Deputy Public Defender in New Orleans, Louisiana. He holds a B.A. degree from the University of Pennsylvania, a J.D, from Tulane Law School, and an LL.M. in International and Comparative Law also from Tulane Law School.

CINDY R. SLANE, formerly an Assistant Clinical Law Professor at Quinnipiac University School of Law, now advises, teaches, and writes on issues of lawyers' professional responsibility, and serves (pro bono) as outside ethics counsel for Connecticut Legal Services, Inc. As Director of Field Placement Programs at Quinnipiac (1994-2009), she was the primary architect of the development of the law school's externship program, routinely teaching five externship courses: the Corporate Counsel, Criminal Justice, Judicial, and Public Interest Externships, and their sequel, Field Placement II. Before joining the Quinnipiac faculty, she was a trial-department associate with Day, Berry, & Howard (now Day, Pitney), in its Stamford, Connecticut offices. She also was a three-term gubernatorial appointee to Connecticut's Permanent Commission on the Status of Women, serving as treasurer, vice-chair, and chair, and several times representing PCSW before the Judiciary and Appropriations Committees of the Connecticut General Assembly. A member of the Connecticut Bar Association's (CBA) Standing Committee on Professional Ethics since 1998, she also is a member of the CBA's Professional Discipline Section, serving as treasurer as this volume goes to press. She has made numerous presentations on women's issues, legal ethics, and clinical law teaching before local, state, regional, and national audiences. She holds a J.D. from Yale University and a B.A. from Douglass College (Rutgers University).

NANCY M. STUART is a Clinical Professor of Law and the Associate Dean for Experiential Learning at U.C. Hastings College of the Law. Professor Stuart has responsibility for the array of experiential programs including in-house clinics, field placement clinics, and the judicial and civil legal externship programs as well as the pro bono program. A former member of the U.C. Hastings in-house Civil Justice Clinic Faculty (2000-2005), she also has taught the Judicial and Legal Externship Seminars and supervised students in these placements as well as teaching Legal Ethics, Problem Solving and Professional Judgment, and the Social Justice Concentration Seminar. Prior to U.C. Hastings, Professor Stuart was a staff attorney with the Lawyers' Committee for Civil Rights of the San Francisco Bay Area and with the Hawkins Center, now Rubicon Legal Services. She received her J.D. from U.C. Hastings and a B.S. from CA Polytechnic State University, San Luis Obispo.

ANN VESSELS is Professor of the Practice of Law at the University of Denver Sturm College of Law, where she is the Director of the Legal Externship Program. She teaches the Corporate Externship Seminar and the Semester-in-Practice Seminar. In addition, Professor Vessels is the Director of the Veterans Advocacy Project, a program in which students advocate on behalf of Veterans in disability compensation and discharge upgrade cases. Prior to coming to Denver Law, she was a partner in the law firm of Rothgerber Johnson & Lyons LLP (now Lewis Roca Rothgerber) where she practiced commercial litigation and employment law. Professor Vessels also served as the General Counsel and Senior Vice President of Human Resources for Junior Achievement, a global nonprofit organization that strives to educate and inspire young people to succeed in a global economy, and was the President of the Colorado Leadership Alliance, an alliance of academic leadership programs for outstanding undergraduate students at colleges and universities across Colorado.

JANET WEINSTEIN was a professor at California Western School of Law until her retirement in 2014. She served as the Director of the Internship Program and taught primarily interdisciplinary and problem-solving courses. She was involved in clinical legal education for over 35 years, beginning in 1978, when she directed one of the first environmental law clinics in the country. She taught a variety of courses including interviewing, counseling, and negotiation and mediation. She participated in the creation of the STEPPS program (Skills Training for Ethical Preventive Practice and Career Satisfaction) at California Western.

CARWINA WENG is a Clinical Professor of Law at Indiana University-Maurer Law School and the founder and director of Maurer's newest clinic, the Veterans Disability Clinic, representing veterans in proceedings before the Board of Veterans Appeals. She also has directed clinical students representing clients with Social Security and Medicaid disability benefit petitions. She teaches *The Legal Profession*, an innovative first-year course in attorney ethics and professional teamwork skills. Professor Weng taught at Boston College Law School's clinic, the Legal Assistance Bureau (2001-2006), and Florida Coastal School of Law, and co-directed the McCalla Children and Family Advocacy Center (1996-1999). Her writing focuses on clinical education and multi-cultural lawyering. Before bringing her talents and passion to teach law students, she practiced poverty law with Greater Boston Legal Services (domestic violence, abuse prevention, divorce), was a Skadden Public Interest Fellow at The Legal Aid Society of New York (housing and AIDS matters), and clerked for First Circuit Court of Appeals Judge Frank Coffin. Professor Weng holds an A.B. *summa cum laude* from Yale University and J.D. *cum laude* from New York University School of Law, and was elected to the Order of the Coif.

LEAH WORTHAM is a Professor Law Emerita at the Columbus School of Law, The Catholic University of America (CUA) in Washington, D.C. She created the *Becoming a Lawyer* externship course at CUA and has co-edited and co-authored the three editions of LEARNING FROM PRACTICE, which aspires to help law students get the maximum benefit from externships as a step toward work and lives they enjoy and find worthwhile. Her other primary teaching areas have been professional responsibility and criminal law. Beginning in 1996, she has worked with law teachers and students abroad on introducing interactive teaching methods, establishing clinical programs, teaching legal ethics, and strategies for legal education and legal profession reform. She has taught, conducted workshops, and consulted in 29 countries in programs with participants from many more. She has worked extensively with the D.C. Bar, the second largest bar in the U.S with more than 100,000 members, including the Rules of Conduct Review Committee (as chair); the Ethics Committee, which issues ethical opinions interpreting the conduct rules; and lawyer discipline hearing committees. She holds a J.D. from Harvard University and a B.A. from Macalester College in St. Paul, Minnesota.

Acknowledgments

Teh first edition of Learning From Practice (LFP) published in 1998 emerged from the sharing of ideas and materials at the monthly meetings of faculty at the Columbus School of Law of The Catholic University of America (CUA) who taught in the Becoming a Lawyer externship course. Seven CUA teachers with a colleague from Vermont Law School authored the first edition's 15 chapters. Eight additional authors from other law schools joined in the second edition, and 22 new authors have joined the third edition.

The third edition editors first acknowledge the tremendous contribution of J.P. ("Sandy") Ogilvy, the lead editor of the past two editions. His steady hand and hard work were critical in making this book a reality. Sandy also created and still maintains the LEXTERN website http://lexternweb.law.edu/, which compiles materials, forms, and manuals used by externship teachers as well as the LEXTERN listserv. Lisa Lerman and Leah Wortham also served as editors for the first two editions. With the publication of LFP's first edition, CUA hosted the inaugural Externship Conference in 1998. Coinciding with LFP's third edition publication, the Eighth Externship Conference will take place in March 2016. The externship conferences have grown from national to international events.

With 35 authors who have contributed, this third edition of Learning From Practice was a large collaborative effort over more than three years. Every chapter entailed several exchanges of drafts among editors and authors. Many represent cooperative efforts of co-authors, sometimes drawing on the work of a past author as well. The editors thank all participants for a harmonious process, which we believe has resulted in an overall product much richer and better than any of us could have produced alone.

As with the second edition, Carol Logie designed the cover and chapter headings and prepared the manuscript for publication. Many thanks also for the cheerful help and support of West Academic Editor, James Cahoy, throughout all stages of the production process. Finally we thank student research assistant Kayla Allgeier, Albany Law School, for her assistance in checking citation form in the Further Resources and Endnotes and research assistant Calvin Webb, University of Georgia, for his efforts in reviewing and conforming websites throughout the text and for a final review of citation form.

The following are the thanks of individual authors and editors for help and support they received.

Chapter 1, Alexander Scherr: I thank my externship students, whose skepticism about the externship seminar has pushed me to reflect long and hard about what such a seminar can do.

Chapter 2, Laurie Barron: I would like to thank my colleagues Cecily Banks, Suzanne Harrington-Steppen, and Eliza Vorenberg for collaborating with me each and every day. The ideas, concepts, and exercises I brought to this chapter are the collective result of that collaborative effort. I am so very lucky to work with such inspirational colleagues and friends.

Chapter 5, Susan L. Brooks & Inga N. Laurent: Many thanks to Carolyn Cunningham and The Human Potential Project and the faculty of the Haven Institute for contributing so much to the content of this chapter and providing information that can aid all of us in communicating more effectively. We are also grateful to our externship and clinic students who continually bring laughter, insight, and joy into our work.

Chapter 6, Margaret Reuter & Carwina Weng: We would like to thank our readers for their insightful comments and questions about our earlier drafts, including Sandee Magliozzi, Anne Kubisch, Lisa Robinson, and Indiana University-Maurer Law School students, Angela Andrews and Alex Bayrak.

Chapter 7, Stacy L. Brustin & Carmia N. Caesar: Thanks to Emily Black, CUA reference librarian and Emily Shinogle, student research assistant.

Chapter 8, Margaret Martin Barry: I would like to thank the wonderful Vermont Law School externs I supervised and whose reflections helped my thinking about this chapter. Alexander Scherr: I would like to thank the University of Georgia law students from whose journals I have learned so much over the years. More specifically, thanks to Raqketa Williams for her invaluable research assistance and more importantly, for her readiness to challenge assumptions on how to read and evaluate reflection.

Chapter 9, Nancy Maurer: I would like to thank Albany Law School's externship students for their stories and insights of learning from practice. Their experiences formed the basis for many of the exercises and much of the guidance for this chapter. In particular, thanks to research assistants Kayla Allgeier, Heather Davis, and Taylor Ferris and to my colleagues at the Law Clinic & Justice Center for generously sharing innovative teaching ideas.

Chapters 10 & 13, Lisa G. Lerman & Lisa V. Martin: Lisa Lerman: Thanks to the many student externs who educated me about ethical issues that come up during fieldwork. Lisa Martin: Thanks to David Koelsch, University of Detroit Mercy School of Law, who reviewed and provided helpful suggestions on Chapter 13.

Chapter 11, Alexis Anderson: Many thanks to Valle Nicole Hauspurg, my student research assistant. In addition, my thanks to the Boston College Law School externs and clinic students who have shared their ethical challenges through the years.

Chapter 12, Cindy R. Slane: Many thanks to Professor Arlene Kanter, Syracuse University's Bond, Schoeneck and King Distinguished Professor of Law; Laura J. and L. Douglas Meredith Professor for Teaching Excellence; Director, College of Law Disability Law and Policy Program; and Co-Director, SU Center on Human Policy, Law and Disability Studies, for her invaluable contributions as co-author of the 2d-edition predecessor to the Conflicts of Interest chapter in this volume and for allowing us to revise and include in this 3d edition of LEARNING FROM PRACTICE the conflicts inventory form she developed for the externship program at Syracuse.

Chapters 14 & 15, Alexander Scherr: I thank my clients. My work for them has led me to understand the value of good judgment and the importance of thoughtful client relationships. I also thank my colleagues in legal services and in the clinical community, whose many insights and critiques have shaped the way I understand and organize the work of lawyering.

Chapter 16, Linda Morton & Janet Weinstein: We want to acknowledge the outstanding research assistance of Carlos Armstrong and Turner Hopkinson. We also want to acknowledge each other for our harmonious, creative, and often humorous collaboration over many years.

Chapter 17, Kendall L. Kerew: I would like to thank my colleagues, Andi Curcio, Roy Sobelson, and Austin Martin Williams, and my research assistant, Niaa Daniels, for their thoughtful comments on earlier drafts of this chapter.

Chapter 20, Russell Gabriel: I would like to extend my heartfelt appreciation to Alice, Larry, and Rick. Thank you for your continued support.

Chapter 21, Susan B. Schecter & Jeffrey R. Baker: The authors wish to acknowledge the good work of the following U.C. Berkeley School of Law colleagues and friends: Dori Kojima, student, for her assistance with research and writing; Bryn Starbird, Pro Bono Fellow/SLPS Coordinator, for her cite checking and editing; and Kimberly Meyer, Field Placement Program Coordinator, for further cite checking, formatting, and reviewing. In addition, we wish to acknowledge the following practitioners for their insights and edits: Elizabeth Kristen, Director, Gender Equity & LGBT Rights Program and Senior Staff

Attorney, Legal Aid Society–Employment Law Center; Patti Prunhuber, Staff Attorney, Public Interest Law Project; and Bruce Budner for his contributions of exercises and questions for the Teacher's Manual.

Chapter 22, Jeffrey R. Baker & Susan B. Schechter: Thanks to Nancy Hunt, director of Pepperdine University School of Law's Washington D.C. Externship Semester, for her guidance and contributions to the chapter on public service placements.

Chapter 25, Marjorie A. Silver: My deep gratitude for the work of my research assistant, Kathleen Miller. I am indebted to the members of the AALS Balance in Legal Education Section and those of the Project for Integrating Spirituality, Law, and Politics (PISLAP) who have inspired me, and the myriad of lawyers, law professors, and others whose work has informed this chapter. A special acknowledgment to Dr. Amiram Elwork, whose premature death in 2014 deprived us of one of the most thoughtful voices dedicated to the well-being of lawyers.

Chapter 26, Avis L. Sanders: I would like to express my appreciation to the Externship Program faculty of the American University Washington College of Law. Their creativity, enthusiasm, and willingness to provide guidance to our students in all areas of legal education are an inspiration. I would particularly like to thank Professor Johanna Leshner and Professor Christopher Gowen who generously shared with me many of the innovative ways in which they have used externship pedagogy to help students leverage their externship experiences to develop meaningful and successful careers. I would also like to thank Meghan Gibbons, Samantha Strasser, and Stephanie Mediola for their tremendously helpful input and editing.

Chapters 18, 27, and help in my editorial role, Leah Wortham: Thanks as always for the invaluable assistance of the always amazingly helpful and resourceful CUA Senior Reference Librarian, Stephen E. Young.

Chapter 28, Susan L. Brooks: I am grateful to Ilene Wasserman for teaching me about Appreciative Inquiry and so much more, and for introducing me to the SOAR Model.

Multimedia Resources, Tracye Grinnage Edwards: For their unwavering IT support, I am eternally grateful to Jerry Arrison, Tab Edwards, Taye Edwards, Xavier Edwards, Andre Grinnage, Joan D. Grinnage, John W. Grinnage, Jr., and Dale Muggleworth.

COPYRIGHT ACKNOWLEDGMENTS

Excerpts from the following books, reports, articles, and materials appear with the kind permission of the copyright holders:

American Bar Association, *Trial Attorney Evaluation of Judge*, ABA Judicial Division/Judicial Division Lawyers' Conference. Reprinted with permission.

Cartoon, *"I wish my identity wasn't so wrapped up with who I am."* Bruce Eric Kaplan, THE NEW YORKER COLLECTION, The Cartoon Bank, Conde Nast. Reprinted with permission.

Chart, *Internal vs External WB Correlates in What Makes Lawyers Happy: A Data-driven Prescription to Redefine Professional Success*. Reproduced with permission of the authors and the George Washington Law Review.

26 Lawyering Effectiveness Factors in Predicting Lawyer Effectiveness: A New Assessment for Use in Law School Admission Decisions, CELS 2009 4th Annual Conference on Empirical Legal Studies Paper 18 (July 31, 2009). Reprinted with permission.

Learning From Practice

A TEXT FOR EXPERIENTIAL LEGAL EDUCATION

THIRD EDITION

CHAPTER 1

Introduction

ALEXANDER SCHERR & SUSAN L. BROOKS

Why This Book?

W elcome to your externship. This book will help you learn from what you are about to do. If you have had a temporary job before, you already know the drill: you feel you learn a lot as you go, but after the job ends, the learning fades. This fading happens fast if you turn quickly to other intense experiences—exactly the kind that can fill your time in law school. Using this book can make your learning more durable: by planning for what you do, engaging it more intensely, understanding it more fully, and fixing what you learn more permanently in your memory. This book gives you the tools to make your learning last.

In this chapter, we cover the basics of an externship course. We discuss the reasons to do an externship, how externships differ from other law school courses, and how externships help you become a lawyer. We identify the unique features of the externship experience and the impact this course can have on you as a lawyer. We talk about how to learn from experience in ways that recur both during the semester and beyond. As we go, we present a roadmap for the chapters to come.

Why Do an Externship?

You already have chosen to do an externship. So the question "why do an externship?" may seem obvious . . . and late. As Chapter 2 will discuss more fully, however, your goals for your externship have a huge impact on what you do, what you learn, and what you take away. In addition, hearing what others are learning from an externship helps you to identify goals that you have not yet considered.

In our work as teachers, we have seen people use the externship experience to learn any or all of the following:

■ *Learn About Law in the World of Real People and Problems*

Other classroom courses can teach you the law, legal process, and legal reasoning. Only practice can teach you how the law and lawyers solve real problems and make change for people in the real world. While you learn the topics of law in the classroom, you learn the function of law at your placement in ways that help to make sense of the doctrine you cover in other classes.

■ *Learn About How Lawyers Work*

Your externship exposes you to real lawyers at work and lets you work alongside them for a time. Both through observation and practice, you encounter the demands of their work directly and have the chance to sort out whether you like what you see.

■ *Learn How to Practice Law*

At your externship, you will do some or all of the work your supervising attorneys do. This experience gives you the chance to develop skills associated with that work. Chapters 14–18 of the book cover several of the core competencies of practice: exercising judgment, working with clients, working in teams, writing for practice, and making presentations. This list does not exhaust the possibilities for developing skills, although almost every lawyer has to develop skills in these core areas.

■ *Learn About the Role of a Lawyer and the Influences That Shape That Role*

Your externship will expose you to the distinctive roles lawyers play, as advocates, planners, judges, legislators, negotiators, leaders, and many more. In your externship, you will learn how the rules of ethics apply to and regulate that role. Chapters 10–13 talk specifically about the rules that apply to your role as an extern, while many other chapters discuss the ethical rules that apply to lawyers in a wide range of contexts. Finally, your experience will move you along the path of professionalism, in all of its various shades of meaning. See Chapter 9 on Professionalism.

■ *Learn How to Organize a Law Practice and Deliver Legal Services*

You can learn a lot about certain practice areas by assessing how your placement delivers its services. Chapters 19 to 23 introduce you to the structure and organization of law practices in particular settings: judges' chambers; criminal justice practices, both prosecution and defense; public interest and public service offices; and transactional practices.

■ *Learn How to Learn from Supervision*

As you work at your placement, you will work under the supervision of lawyers in active practice. Various chapters of this book talk about how to work with supervisors to build on your talents and address your weaknesses. See Chapter 3 on Professional Development Planning and Chapter 8 on Reflection and Writing Journals.

■ *Learn How to Work with People*

Law school can leave you feeling isolated and convinced all lawyers work in isolation. But lawyering happens within a rich network of relationships. Your placement will help you work out how to navigate the social and interpersonal aspects of law practice. The book offers you guidance on effective communication and professional relationships in Chapter 5 and on collaboration in Chapter 16. Chapters 6 and 7 focus on a critical aspect of relationships: dealing with people from different backgrounds, coping with your own biases, preparing for biases you might face, and considering how bias affects the practice of law. Chapter 15 discusses the relationships you form with clients and how your choices about clients shape you and your career.

■ *Learn How to Get a Job as a Lawyer . . . and to Identify the Job You Want*

Many students find externships valuable for their impact on job prospects. Although you may not land a permanent job at your placement, the value of an externship is still substantial: getting a reference, developing a writing sample, building marketable skills, networking in a practice area, among many other benefits. Chapter 26 discusses these advantages and highlights more indirect benefits: learning your preferences (or dislikes) for certain areas of law or practice; opening previously unknown possibilities for work; understanding what your supervisors value in new attorneys; integrating your own beliefs and values into your career goals.

■ *Achieving Health, Happiness, and Balance as a Lawyer*

You will work alongside lawyers who have struck their own balance between their commitment to work and their other life commitments. This allows you to ask whether you would want the same balance, and if not, how you would arrange your commitments differently. Chapter 25 discusses these choices and helps you start developing your own approach to life as a lawyer.

■ *Learn How the Law Is Practiced Now and in the Future*

Chances are many of your law professors have not practiced law in a while, and some may not have practiced at all. Your externship gives you a chance to observe how law is practiced now. It also introduces you to the changing face of law practice and allows you to assess how changes in the legal profession will affect how you practice law. Chapter 14 discusses how to learn about lawyering, while Chapter 27 discusses some of the changes now sweeping through the legal profession.

■ *Learn About the Kind of Person You Want to Be as a Lawyer*

You may have heard that law school and law practice can change you and make you into a different person. A more accurate statement may be that law school introduces you to new talents and opportunities and exposes you to unfamiliar challenges and risks. Chapter 24 discusses how you can make intentional choices as you respond to these new realities and gives you tools for forming your own identity as a person and a professional.

What Is Different About an Externship Course?

An externship class differs from most other law schools classes. Unlike classroom courses or seminars, you learn not from a text or a professor, but instead from experiences outside the law school while you engage in the activities of law practice. Unlike a simulation class like trial practice or negotiation, you work on problems and opportunities in the real world, where your work directly affects other people. Finally, unlike an in-house clinic, you work in a law practice focused on those problems and opportunities and not primarily on educating new lawyers.

Your externship course places you alongside attorneys to work on the same problems and issues on which they work. You have the opportunity to exercise or to observe a wide range of lawyering abilities: client interviewing, courtroom representation, negotiation of deals, counseling of clients, drafting of documents, and many more. You can gain exposure to a wide range of practices, including individual representation, government lawyering, judicial decision-making, and others.

You also have the benefit of learning from two different kinds of teachers: your supervising attorneys and your externship teacher. This separation of roles allows you two distinct perspectives on your experience and gives you the chance to observe and critique your work experience in ways that can strengthen what you learn and make it more permanent and useful.

Your externship experience offers other advantages:

- You identify and pursue your own goals and develop your own process for drawing conclusions and building on past work. Many people find they enjoy self-directed learning, in that it helps them to take better advantage of the other kinds of learning opportunities in law school.

- You learn to exercise independent judgment, both at your placement and in defining and pursuing your goals. This autonomy introduces you to the feel of law practice after you graduate and take on the long-term task of managing your own professional development.

- You become an active participant not only in work at your placement but also in identifying, assessing, and drawing lessons from that work. Many people find direct participation in work that matters in a real world context gives them a broader range of things to learn and a deeper understanding of what they are learning than sitting in a class or reading from a text.

- You have selected your workplace and the kinds of problems and opportunities on which you will work. The fact that you selected your placement can make what you learn more relevant and immediate than it might in other contexts, especially if it connects directly to your own goals for yourself.

- You learn how it feels for others to depend on you, giving you the sense of being of value to others and having responsibility for how cases turn out. Many people find doing work that matters (to them and to others) gives what they learn an intensity and strength that secures it in their memory more firmly.

- You have the chance to learn at your own pace and in your own style. Similarly, you have a chance to encounter different styles of teaching through supervision. This variety and flexibility broadens and deepens your knowledge of how to approach learning for the rest of your career.

How Does This Help Me Become a Lawyer?

Work at your placement puts you squarely in the role of a lawyer even as you continue to be a student. This fact alone draws many students to an externship. You shift from focusing on performance in school to performance that affects people and issues far beyond yourself. You encounter the unique demands of ethical awareness that come from serving as a legal representative. At the very least, you make your own time management tasks more complex, requiring you to balance work and other commitments in ways that foreshadow the time demands placed on practicing lawyers.

An externship also helps by putting you in the real world, working with real lawyers on real problems. This experience gives you the chance to deliver legal services under supervision and assume responsibility for the outcome of your work. You will practice core competencies including interacting with clients; writing for a practice audience; assessing practical problems in light of the law; developing and making choices; and implementing choices through advocacy, negotiation, or planning.

The seminar for which you are reading this book offers distinct advantages over other kinds of classes. Externship seminars can cover a range of topics: from long-term professional development to the performance of specific skills; from substantive law to ethical understanding; from solving problems as a lawyer to balancing legal work with other life commitments.

Whatever focus your class takes, you will find it both informs and responds to your learning at your placement. Most externship seminars give you invaluable perspective on what you can take away from your placement, strengthening both your insight and your ability to apply what you learn to your long-term development. In turn, your experience at your placement creates an invaluable context for the ideas posed in the seminar, sharpening your understanding and building your ability to apply classroom readings in practical ways.

Frequently Asked Questions About Externships

Externship courses prompt questions that recur almost every semester, in every externship course. These include the following:

- *How Is This Different From a Job?*

When you work for pay or volunteer for no credit, you focus primarily on delivering a service for the benefit of the organization and for its clients. You may learn as you go, picking up insight as you complete tasks and observe events. You could describe this as "incidental learning," that is "unintentional or unplanned learning that results from other activities."[1] This is learning on the go, without plan or intention.

By contrast, in an externship course, you learn by plan and by intention in ways that justify the award of credit. You have two sets of teachers: the supervising attorneys at your workplace and the externship teacher at your school. Each group, and especially your externship teacher, has your learning and development as a significant goal. You will find yourself encouraged to consider what you plan to get from your placement, what you actually learn, and how to fix your learning in place for the long haul. This more intentional approach to learning from experience helps you make the most of what you encounter.

■ *Why Do We Have a Class?*

The externship seminar plays a key role in developing what you learn from experience. Earlier in this chapter, we noted the various topics an externship seminar can address and described how your seminar and your experience interact to deepen and broaden your understanding and development.

The externship seminar has other effects. It can help you to become more effective at your placement by exploring workplace challenges and providing you with substantive law and practice training that improves your ability to perform with excellence. The seminar creates a small community focused on the experience of working outside the law school. Your relationships with faculty and fellow students can prompt unexpected insights and foster a sense of common purpose that helps you through the challenges of work.

Finally, the externship seminar introduces you to the practice of reflection, the organized and intentional habit of thinking about and learning from experience. The discussions in your externship class model and shape the kind of analysis and assessment through which you draw long-term lessons from your work on-site.

■ *Why Do I Also Have to Read?*

The readings in this book, along with others your faculty may assign, give you a structured frame of reference that fosters meaningful understanding during your semester at work. This structure contrasts sharply with the often unstructured messages of incidental learning. It is, in fact, possible to learn a fair amount at your placement from observing and thinking. You will learn more from the externship with the information these readings provide.

Consider this example. Imagine that you face an important task: say, buying a new car. You could drive to the dealership, walk the lot, talk with a sales person, discuss financing, and buy the car, all without reading and research. But you would benefit from reading: brands and models; prices, profits margins, and discounts; sales strategies and tactics; and financing, warranties, and legal rights. Reading provides useful information and offers a context in which to achieve your goals for the transaction and get the best long-term value from what you do.

We admit your work at your placement is not like buying a new car . . . at least, we hope not! Even so, you invest substantial effort in your externship with the idea of getting something of lasting value. The readings in your class serve the same purpose of orienting you to the experience. They provide you with multiple perspectives and increase your effectiveness in meeting your goals.

■ *What Role Does My Externship Teacher Play?*

Externship teachers can play several roles. Your teacher may help you identify and apply to the right placement, one that fits your goals and qualifications. The teacher can introduce you to the parameters of practice at your placement, including the ethical obligations and professional expectations at your placement. Your teacher can help interpret the lessons of the readings and classroom discussions in ways that can add value to your long-term learning. Your teacher can serve as a willing ear and a resource in dealing with unexpected challenges or difficulties at your placement. Finally, your teacher can prompt you to identify, reflect on, and meet your goals for your placement, assuring you get good value from the overall experience.

■ *Why Am I Being Asked to Reflect?*

Most externship courses ask you to reflect on your experience, in class, in conversation, and in writing. This book has a lot to say about reflection, both in a separate chapter and through regular discussion in other chapters. For now, consider reflection and reflective practice as a form of quality control. By talking and writing about what you do while you are doing it, reflection assures you know your own goals and make the most of your chances to meet them. By encouraging critique and analysis, reflection makes sure you hold your supervisors (and your teachers) to the task of giving you the experience you deserve. Finally, reflective practice gives you the chance to see clearly, assess accurately, draw conclusions reliably, and make effective plans for further learning. See Chapter 8 on Reflection and Writing Journals.

■ *How Will Any of This Help Me to Get a Job?*

In many ways; see Chapter 26 on Externships and Career Development. For now, consider the following. Externship practice exposes you to law practices you might not otherwise encounter, giving you a chance to network in that context. As an extern you develop competencies of real value to your employers. Your work also develops your self-confidence as a lawyer, confidence that has valuable side-benefits in talking with potential employers. Externship work gives you stories to talk about during interviews. Writing samples display your abilities in a practice context. References from people in the world of practice supplement those your professors might provide. Finally, an externship gives you the chance to reflect on what you do and do not want to do as a lawyer and offers real insight into practice areas you might want to pursue.

What Is "Experiential Learning"?

This introduction refers regularly to "learning from experience." All learning is, to some extent, experiential. Everything we learn comes from our experience in the world. Here, we focus on a more specific understanding of "experiential learning": learning grounded in a personal experience in an authentic setting. By an "authentic setting," we mean one similar to the setting in which you will later use what you learn.

Many jobs, even simple ones, rely on written materials and classroom instruction to teach employees some of what they need to know to perform the job. In a law school clinic or at an externship placement, you will apply and test the knowledge you have acquired in other law school courses or elsewhere.

■ *Making the Most of Experience*

We noted earlier that you should distinguish experiential learning from merely experiencing and even the incidental learning that arises from activity. Instead, experiential learning requires the active processing of experiences. This process is cyclical. Figure 1.1. You need to plan for the experience, have the experience, reflect on what happened, and integrate or synthesize what you learned with existing knowledge. This process—plan, do, reflect, integrate—accurately describes the act of learning from experience.

The cycle of experiential learning works at both a macro level over the course of a whole semester, and on a micro level, for particular tasks.

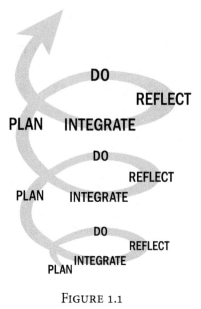

FIGURE 1.1

Plan, Do, Reflect—The Big Picture

On a macro level, you should begin your externship experience by planning for it. This involves setting realistic goals and objectives for yourself. What do you want to accomplish through the externship? What skills do you want to learn or improve? During your externship, it is useful to revisit your initial goals statement from time to time to reflect on and evaluate your progress toward meeting your goals and objectives and to revise, as necessary, your goals and objectives in light of your experiences. At the end of your externship, take some time again to reflect on the total experience, take stock of what you have learned, and integrate your new knowledge with your existing knowledge base as you prepare for your next set of experiences. Refer to Chapter 2 on Professional Development Planning for further information about setting goals for your experience.

Plan, Do, Reflect—Specific Tasks

The experiential learning cycle also works in the micro sense, for specific tasks and specific experiences during the semester. Consider as an example that you work in a judicial externship. Your judge has asked you to draft an order on a motion to vacate a default judgment.

■ *Plan*

Before you begin drafting the order, assess your personal goals for the project. For instance, you might want to use the order as a writing sample. Will this be possible, because ultimately the order will be signed by the judge? You might want to use this task to get feedback on your legal research and writing skills. What specific skills do you want to improve? What type of critique and feedback do you want? You might discuss the task and review your learning goals with your externship teacher and seek your teacher's input. After thinking about what you want to accomplish, you might devise a work plan that sets a timetable for accomplishing each research and writing task.

In addition to considering how the task will advance your goals, you also will find it useful to plan for how to do the task. Is there an existing model or template you can use? Can you map a research strategy before you start? Do you face deadlines that will alter how you work on the project? It can be useful to create a plan for how to complete the task efficiently.

■ *Do*

Next, you execute your plan. You reread the motion, the opposition, and the supporting memoranda filed by the lawyers. You reread the applicable rules of civil procedure. You review the cases that seem closest to the facts of the case before you. You check for models for this kind of writing such as examples of prior orders of this kind or on this kind of issue. Then you compose a draft and revise it several times before you present a polished draft to the judge suggesting she deny the motion to vacate.

The judge thanks you for your work. She suggests some changes in your writing style such as the use of active rather than passive voice. More surprisingly, she says she has decided to grant the motion even though your conclusion was appropriately supported by the cases you cited. She explains that case law in the area gives judges considerable discretion in deciding whether to vacate a default. She believes every defendant should have an opportunity to have a trial on the merits of the plaintiff's claim, barring extreme circumstances not present here. The preparation and drafting of your order and the judge's feedback are concrete experiences of "doing" in the model.

■ *Reflect, Analyze, and Integrate*

After meeting with the judge, you reflect on the experience. Revisit the plan you made at the start: how well did it hold up in practice? You could talk to the judge's clerk to get another perspective. You could write a journal entry about your experience. You could talk to other clerks or judicial externs or read articles about writing style or standards for reopening a default judgment. You could think about how to incorporate the judge's suggestions on your writing style in other writings you will do. On the standard for default judgment, you consciously or unconsciously will form theories, ideas, and concepts about the authority of judges, the uncertainty of the law, the discretion of judges, the process of judicial thinking, ways of presenting and opposing motions to vacate default judgments, and other matters. Although you might not think about all of these topics, and you might think of others, some reflection and analysis should lead you to integrate your learning from this experience with prior knowledge to create new knowledge, or modify existing knowledge.

▪ *Apply*

The next time you are asked to draft an order for the judge, you will use the ideas and impressions you developed in your earlier experience. By applying your new knowledge to another task, you begin a new cycle of learning. If you did not have a model as a starting point, you might decide you could work more efficiently if you had a model the next time. When you get your next assignment, you might decide to ask the judge or the judge's clerk if there is a model you can review. Or you might ask whether the judge is inclined to decide the matter one way or another. Some judges prefer that externs draft opinions without knowing the judge's inclination because the draft provides a fresh perspective for the judge. The process gives the student a chance to work out the problem independently. Other judges are willing to give some guidance at the outset based on their own reading of the papers or the oral argument.

Stay aware of this interaction between micro and macro levels of experience. Doing so can directly improve the quality of your experience, both as you do it and when you complete it. For example, you might set goals for a particular task that relate to goals for your whole semester, such as learning how to write more concisely and persuasively. As you complete each task, mark your progress toward your overall goal, increasing your satisfaction with each task. When the semester ends, you can chart the path you took and set goals for further progress or different goals entirely.

We offer one more suggestion about the value of conscious and intentional learning from experience. After you graduate, you may find that your supervisors are attentive and sympathetic mentors, guiding you well both on specific tasks and on your overall development. Nevertheless, we think the odds are good you will have to rely at least as much on yourself as on your supervisors to guide your own growth as a lawyer. Consciously practicing the learning cycle and reflecting carefully and in depth can ensure, regardless of the supervision you receive from others, you are the one to determine and shape your own development.

Summary

In this chapter, we have introduced the reasons for this book and the likely goals of your externship course. We have scanned the central task of learning from your own experience and have related it to the various parts of your course, including the seminar, the readings, the writing of reflection and the relationship with your externship teacher and your supervising attorneys. Whatever the contributions of your teachers and your fellow students, your externship remains yours to develop into long-term insight, growth, and satisfaction. We encourage you to take hold of your experience and make the most of the opportunities you will encounter.

ENDNOTES

1   Sandra Kerka, *Incidental Learning*, Trends and Issues 2000 Alert No.18, 2000 at 3–4.

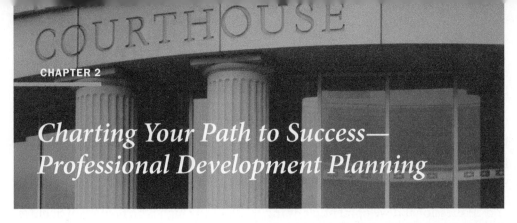

Charting Your Path to Success— Professional Development Planning

LAURIE BARRON & NANCY M. STUART

*Give me six hours to chop down a tree and
I will spend the first four sharpening the axe.*

—Attributed to Abraham Lincoln

P lanning is critical to achievement of your ultimate goals, and it is a dynamic process. You may have already identified your dream job and are on the path to landing there. You may know you want to do transactional work, for example, and are unsure of the setting: government, large or small firm, or non-profit organization. Perhaps you know you want to be a litigator and are uncertain whether civil or criminal law is a good fit. Whether your ultimate career goals are crystal clear or still coming into focus, your decision to pursue an externship will help you on your path.

Keeping focused on your ultimate vision is essential to success. Thinking about the skills that all lawyers need and about your own particular performance goals will give you more control over your learning process and will allow you to take full advantage of the opportunities at hand. Effective lawyers and law students invest the time to plan, to identify and articulate goals, to specify particular actions to accomplish those goals, to monitor their progress, and to revise their plan as they change and grow. Engaging in professional development planning in these ways will help you to sharpen your axe and ultimately become the lawyer you want to be.

Professional Development Planning—Sharpening the Axe

The pace of change in the legal profession requires lawyers to be nimble and adaptable in order to serve their clients effectively and to anticipate changes in the delivery of legal services. Effective lawyers engage actively in ongoing professional development and embrace responsibility for acquiring new knowledge and skills. Lawyers ideally engage in this process for themselves. Indeed, more and more employers in a wide array of settings expect their employees to engage in conscious professional development planning. Professional development planning may be linked to a lawyer's retention, promotion, or compensation. Lawyers who are committed to their own professional development are often happier and more satisfied with their careers.

Professional development planning is a tool through which you can acquire the knowledge, skills, and experience necessary to keep abreast of changes in your chosen area of expertise. This type of planning can take many forms, although it often includes two elements: assessing the big picture and creating your own Professional Development Plan.

Assessing the Big Picture

- Consider the reasons you came to law school. What were you hoping to do with your law degree? How has your vision changed since you started in law school? How does this externship align with your vision?

- Identify the knowledge and skills of effective lawyers. What are the essential lawyering competencies necessary for success in your externship setting?

- Assess your current knowledge and skillset. Where you are currently? What feedback have you received from prior supervisors? Identify the baseline of your knowledge and skills at the start of your externship so that you will be able to observe your growth.

- Identify the learning opportunities unique to your placement. Consider which experiences you will be able to use to benchmark your progress.

Once you have a good understanding of what lawyers do, what you want to learn, and what learning opportunities your placement offers, you can focus with precision on developing your plan of action.

Creating Your Professional Development Plan

- Set goals specific to your externship. You may want to include goals addressing knowledge, skills, networking, etc.

- Define action steps. For each goal, identify steps or actions you will take to achieve that goal.

- Monitor your progress. Measuring your progress increases the likelihood that you will meet your goals.

· Evaluate and revise your Professional Development Plan. Your plan should be a work in progress, a dynamic document that changes in response to feedback, new assignments and experiences, and insights gained.

· As with many new tools, professional development planning initially might feel cumbersome. However, walking intentionally through each element of the process will set the stage for a successful experience in your externship while demonstrating your commitment to becoming the professional you envision. The balance of this chapter explores these activities in detail.

Be not afraid of growing slowly;
be afraid only of standing still.

–Chinese Proverb

Revisiting Your Assessment of the Big Picture

■ *Exploring Your Vision*

We encourage you to review your long-term career goals, to recall what made you decide to attend law school, and to assess how this externship will help you to achieve those goals. This will help you to be successful both now and in the long-term.

> **Exercise 2.1** On a blank piece of paper, consider the following questions, and jot down anything that comes into your mind. You will refer back to these notes as you move through this chapter and the process of professional development planning.
>
> Think back to the reasons you came to law school.
> - What was your original vision?
> - What kind of lawyer did you intend to be?
> - If your vision has changed since you have been in law school, what is the current vision?
>
> Imagine yourself in 10 years in your dream job.
> - What do you love about it?
> - What do you do on a day-to-day basis?

- What is your reputation as an attorney?

Now think about yourself right now, today, preparing for this externship.

- How does your externship relate to your vision?

- What are the reasons you chose this externship?

- Are you committed to a specific type of practice and need experience?

- Are you trying to decide if this practice setting is a good fit for you?

- Do you already have a post-graduation job and want to explore a substantive area that you may pursue for your pro bono practice?

▪ *Knowledge and Skills of Effective Lawyers*

The critique of legal education that graduates are not prepared for the demands of practice has gained traction as the legal marketplace has changed. The current marketplace suggests that clients will no longer absorb the cost of training new lawyers. We are seeing more job openings for lawyers who are a few years out of law school and fewer entry-level positions across job settings. There are many views—from the bar, the bench, clients, etc.—about how lawyers should be taught, prepared, and trained, as well as about where this learning should happen.

Critiques of legal education are not new. In 1992, the ABA Task Force on Law Schools and the Profession conducted a study of the bench and bar that focused on identifying a shared vision of the knowledge and skills new lawyers should seek to acquire.[1] The report of the Task Force, commonly referred to as the MacCrate Report, acknowledged the common goal shared by law schools and the practicing bar, the "education and professional development of the members of a great profession."[2] The report included a list of the "Fundamental Lawyering Skills and Professional Values." See Appendix I for more on the MacCrate Report.

A more recent framework analyzing the essential skills required of effective lawyers was created by two researchers at the University of California Berkeley. Marjorie Shultz and Sheldon Zedeck conducted a multi-year study of several thousand law students and alumni, including practicing lawyers and legal employers, from UC Hastings and UC Berkeley resulting in a list of 26 "lawyering effectiveness factors."[3] See Appendix I for more about the Shultz and Zedeck study.

These reports and others included in Appendix I are foundational and form the basis for many of the calls to reform legal education. Some would say legal education has stood still, while others would claim change is happening, albeit slowly. What is important is that you have a sense of what you know and what you still need to learn, and that you begin to frame which skills and opportunities for professional growth you would like to focus on in your externship.

Exercise 2.2 Knowledge and Skills of Effective Lawyers: Consider the list of skills and attributes of effective lawyers in one of the reports in Appendix I. Your externship teacher may assign you a particular list. Has the legal profession changed in ways that the particular list of knowledge and skills does not reflect? Make a list of the skills that you think are missing.

Which of these skills do you think law school emphasizes in the courses you have taken thus far? Which are not emphasized in law school but are critical to success as a lawyer? When you think about your larger career goals, what additional gaps do you see in your development of professional skills?

What are the attributes, knowledge, and skills possessed by lawyers whom you admire? Consider the lawyers in your externship. What do you think is necessary for success in this particular office? Articulate additional research you might do to identify what you need to know to be successful in a particular practice setting, including your current externship and beyond.

With these lists in mind, make a list of the skills you see as critical to your success that you will be able to develop in your current externship.

Self-Assessment

> *Know thyself.*
> —Socrates

Now that you have a good sense of the range of knowledge and skills necessary to be an effective lawyer and have considered this information in the context of your current externship, the next step is to reflect upon your current skill set. You know yourself best. Most of us do not have a personal trainer in the law to assess our strengths and weaknesses and design the drills to help us improve. While you may have received detailed critiques in your smaller writing seminars or clinical programs, you have undoubtedly had other legal experiences where you did not receive comprehensive feedback.

It is up to you to think about the experiences you have had, the critiques you have been given, and your own understanding of your legal skills in an effort to understand yourself as a developing lawyer. You might long for a committee of legal coaches to provide a comprehensive assessment of your talents and challenges as a lawyer. But this evaluation is now your job, and the externship is a good place to begin or to continue the task of self-assessment. It will be incumbent on you to "know thyself" in this externship and throughout your legal career so that you are continually growing and improving as a lawyer.

> **Exercise 2.3 Know Thyself—Evaluating Your Current Skill Level:** Look back at the skills you identified in Exercise 2.2 as critical to your success and further development in your externship. Take a moment and consider the feedback you have received regarding your skills in your prior legal experiences—including pro bono work, legal research and writing courses, skills/simulation courses, summer internships, paid employment, clinics, and prior externships.
>
> - What do you see as your strengths and challenges within those particular skills?
>
> - What is the basis of your assessment? Did you receive feedback from a faculty member, a supervisor, or a client? Or is it based on your own self-assessment?
>
> - What skills have you not yet had a chance to develop?
>
> Perhaps you spent a lot of time screening clients for a legal services office but little time actually digging into the legal issues and planning a strategy to address the issues. Perhaps you wrote informal memos with an answer for your boss in the law firm but never wrote formal memos articulating your legal analysis and making a recommendation. Perhaps you were asked to review contracts for internal consistency but never drafted one yourself.
>
> How would you describe your level of competency in each of these skills? You may want to consult the evaluation tool your supervisor will be asked to complete to describe your performance at the end of the externship. How does this inform your assessment of your skills?
>
> With these reflections on your current skills and level of competency in each, begin to narrow your list of skills and focus in on the ones that you believe you can

learn in this externship setting. This free-write will form the basis for your Professional Development Plan.

Identify Learning Opportunities—Be Intentional

Identifying the skills you would like to develop during the externship as well as your individual strengths and challenges lets you identify the learning opportunities available to you. While you undoubtedly have a broad sense of the type of work you will be doing, in order to maximize the value of this experience you will need to have a deeper understanding of the range of work available to you and what the lawyers in your field placement actually do day-by-day. While you can learn about available opportunities by talking to your supervisor, you can also learn simply by being aware of all that is going on and being open to anything. Understanding that you may not have all the information you need as you begin your externship, it is still helpful to think about the following:

- How do the lawyers in your office keep up with the changing law? What do they read on a weekly basis—newspapers, blogs, practice guides, listservs?

- How do the lawyers in your office expand their own skill set? Do they moot arguments with their colleagues? Do they read each other's contracts, client letters, memos, or other written work? Do they attend trainings?

- What different types of work are available in this setting? Are there opportunities for client interviews, court hearings, investigation (informal and formal), research and writing, legal education workshops or community presentations, negotiation sessions, or observing other lawyers' work?

- How do the lawyers in your office collaborate with each other? Are there weekly case-crunching sessions to brainstorm cases, staff or team meetings, informal gatherings in the hallway or ad hoc?

- How does your supervisor get supervision? Does your supervisor have a mentor? Is there a hierarchy? What is the editing process before a document goes out the door? How much autonomy does your supervisor have?

- What can you learn from the non-attorney staff? What are the roles of the administrative staff, office manager, social workers, paralegals, investigators, or other staff? Are staff included in brainstorming sessions about cases?

· What can you learn from watching your supervisor interact with judges, opposing attorneys, co-counsel, clients, court personnel, and others?

> **Exercise 2.4 Learning Opportunities:** Make a list of the opportunities that you believe are available in your externship. Circle the ones that interest you the most and that are most directly connected to your concrete goals.

Creating Your Professional Development Plan: Drawing the Strands Together

Having considered the big picture—where you are headed, generally or specifically, as well as the knowledge and skills of effective lawyers—and having also studied the immediate picture—your current skill set, strengths and challenges, and the learning opportunities available in your externship—you are ready to craft your Professional Development Plan. Your responses to Exercises 2.1 through 2.4 will guide you as you draft your plan.

Choose a format that makes sense to you and that will be understandable for your supervising attorney. Your externship teacher may have a particular format for you to follow or may allow you to choose a format that appeals to you. Regardless, your plan should be clear, detailed, and reflective of who you are as a person and developing lawyer. It should be designed to build on your strengths, develop your challenging areas, and help you achieve your goals. Your plan should be so individualized that your faculty supervisor can recognize your plan without reading your name.

For each goal, it will be helpful to include the strategy or action steps that you will use to achieve that goal and a realistic way of measuring your progress toward that goal. The next three exercises provide a helpful framework and breakdown this process into three steps: Goal—Action—Progress.

■ *Set Goals*

Goals can be drawn from across the spectrum of knowledge, skills, and relationships you would like to build as you become the lawyer you envision for yourself. Your goals should be set at the right height for you, not so low that you are not pushing yourself but not so high that they are unattainable.

Exercise 2.5 Generate a list of possible goals. Try not to censor yourself initially and let your thoughts flow. Write down all the things that come to mind. Consider the following goals:

- learn how to conduct an effective client interview;

- gain experience with formal discovery, increase understanding of when, how, and which tools to use;

- develop professional relationships with attorneys and community members invested in public health issues and policy.

How are these examples useful as you think about articulating your goals? If a colleague shared these goals with you, what feedback would you offer to help improve them? How might you use these to improve upon your own goals?

From your goals list, choose three that are important to you and also are specific to your placement. Frame your goals positively, clearly, and concretely.

Articulate Action Steps

Working with the three goals you have chosen, the next step is to think about how to achieve them. What concrete steps, experiences, and observations will help you to advance toward these goals? What do you actually need to do to reach these goals? Refer back to your list of learning opportunities. The following questions may help you to articulate action steps tailored to your goals:

- Are there materials you should read?

- What or who do you need to observe?

- What experiences do you need to have yourself?

- What do you need from your supervisor or other attorneys in the office?

- What do you need from your externship teacher or fellow students?

For example, as a future civil litigator, you may want experience with formal discovery. While you might love to conduct a deposition, that may be unlikely in your externship. There are many action steps short of conducting the actual deposition, however, that still increase your discovery skills. Perhaps you can draft questions for your supervising attorney, help prepare the witness, take notes during the deposition, and debrief with your attorney at the end, or participate in some other way.

Think concretely about the action steps that might be involved in the goal of learning how to conduct an effective initial client interview.

Assume that you have chosen this goal because although you have done simulated client interviews in a law school class, you have never conducted an interview in person by yourself. In your first summer at legal services, you gathered information from clients over the phone and observed your supervising attorney conduct interviews and you occasionally chimed in, but you never had the opportunity to plan and conduct the interview yourself.

Action Steps or strategies might include the following:

- Think back to any critique you have received about your interviewing skills to remember your strengths and areas for improvement.

- Read about client interviews. Ask your supervisor for materials to read or watch.

- Plan to observe three client interviews by three different attorneys. Before each one, review the client file, ask the attorney the purpose of the interview and what the goals are, and take notes during the interview so you can debrief with the attorney about decisions that were made.

- Write out a plan for your own client interview by reviewing the referral sheet, the client's file, and other material you may have. Think carefully about the purpose of the interview and what you are trying to accomplish.

- Review your goals and strategies for the interview with your supervisor.

- Conduct an interview that you videotape or which is observed by your supervisor.

- Self-assess and then debrief with your supervisor.

- Incorporate your supervisor's feedback into the plan for your next interview.

- Practice, practice, practice.

For more on working with feedback, see Chapter 3 on Learning from Supervision. For more on client interviewing, see Chapter 15 on Client Relationships.

> **Exercise 2.6** For each of your top three goals, identify and articulate at least three action steps you could take: resources to review, activities, experiences, or mechanisms available to you through your placement to achieve the goal.

Monitoring Progress

The third and final step in the process of creating a successful Professional Development Plan is finding a way to measure your progress. This will likely include a timeline, perhaps tied to each of your action steps, as well as benchmarks by which you will be able to determine where you are on your path to achieving your goals. The reflective component of your externship may help you to evaluate your progress. For the example above, some ways to measure your progress for the one interview you conducted might include the following:

- comparing your outline to the notes you took during the interview;

- soliciting feedback from your supervisor;

- evaluating whether you needed additional meetings for follow up questions;

- observing the time it took you to complete the interview compared to prior interviews;

- finding a way to evaluate whether you are building an effective relationship with your client:

  – has your client been responsive?

  – was the second client meeting easier than the first?

In terms of timelines and benchmarks, you may want to think about how to measure your progress. You might chose a quantitative measure, such as the number of interviews you want to conduct by a certain point in the semester. You might also choose a qualitative measure, such as the thoroughness with which you gather information in an interview by a certain point in the semester.

> **Exercise 2.7** For each of your top three goals and action steps, identify the mechanisms that you will use to measure and evaluate your progress throughout the semester.

Professional Relationship Building with your Supervisor

- *Be Intentional—Again*

Sharing your Professional Development Plan with your supervisor is an important step in building the foundation of your supervisory relationship. After refining your plan with your externship teacher, you will ask for your supervisor's feedback. Presumably, you met with your supervisor when you interviewed for the position, but that may have been months ago during the preceding semester. You have grown as a professional since that interview and are now in a different posture. The first impression that you make on your supervisor is critical to setting you on a path to achieve your goals.

Think about your ideal supervisory relationship. What do you want this to be? Is this field placement somewhere you would like to work some day? Are you trying this placement out to broaden your experience base although you are not interested in it as a career? Are you looking for a life-long mentor? The more concrete you can be about what you want and need, the better your chances of creating the relationship you want. No matter what you want from this relationship, your supervisor will be in a position to evaluate you—not only for the law school program but potentially also for the Character and Fitness committee of the state in which you will eventually take the Bar Exam—and so it is a relationship that must be handled with care.

You may have decisions to make about whether or not to share certain personal information with your supervising attorney. Perhaps you have a learning difference that may require you to take more time on certain types of assignments. Perhaps you have a chronic medical condition that may require you to be out of the office on certain occasions. Whatever it is, your externship teacher is there to help you assess what to share, how to share it, and to create a plan for the meeting.

- *Discussing Plan With Your Supervisor*

You will interact with your supervisor on a daily or at least a weekly basis, but this meeting about your Professional Development Plan is a foundational one that requires careful planning. This meeting should enable you to show your supervisor that you are a professional who has put a great deal of thought into choosing this particular externship and what you want to learn while you are there. You want to ensure that your supervisor will customize this externship for you and tailor it to your individual strengths, challenges, and goals. This is your chance to distinguish yourself and to explore, together with your supervisor, the types of experiences that might be available to you. You want your supervisor to understand the experiences you have had in the past and what you are hoping to work on in the context of this placement. In order for your supervisor to give you appropriately challenging work, she needs to know where you have come from, your strengths and challenges, and where you would like to focus your work in the externship.

Exercise 2.8 Preparing for the Initial Meeting With Your Supervisor:

What do you want your supervisor to know about you?

Think about what you want to tell your supervisor about your background, your strengths and challenges, and life goals. How much do you want to share? Are you comfortable sharing all of your goals with your supervisor? Perhaps you have had a difficult time working with supervisors in the past and an explicit goal of yours is to create a productive relationship with your supervisor. Perhaps you have a learning difference. Is that something you want to disclose?

What do you want to know from your supervisor?

What do you know about her work style, background, or supervision style? What can you learn about her before this meeting from the organization's website? What do you need to know about her expectations of you? How will you be evaluated? What will the plan be for supervision going forward? Can you set up a weekly meeting? Do you have other questions about the organization, mission, funding, or priorities that you cannot learn from the website?

How will this meeting be most effective for you?

Think about the logistics of this meeting. How will you feel most comfortable discussing these issues with your supervisor? Do you want to share a draft of your Professional Development Plan? Would you rather just talk it through? How will you signal to your supervisor that this is an essential component of the externship for you and get her feedback but also buy-in to your plan? How can you talk about your plan in a way that is respectfully proactive and flexible without being demanding?

This initial meeting will lay the groundwork for a productive working relationship with your supervisor. You may need to refine your Professional Development Plan after this meeting to reflect your supervisor's input, and this Plan should be a dynamic document that you modify throughout the semester. It is a document that you will refer back to regularly to ensure that you are getting the experiences you hoped to receive. It can serve as a reminder or tickler for both you and your supervisor to keep you on track to maximize your professional growth.

■ *The Evaluative Process*

Your externship program may involve multiple evaluation processes: your own self-assessment, an evaluation by your supervising attorney, and an evaluation by your externship teacher of your performance in the seminar or program.

Although it may feel premature to begin thinking about the evaluation process when you have just begun, it is something that you can begin to prepare for in advance.

- Keep a list and a hard copy of all of the work that you do.

- Keep a list of all that you observe including client interviews, court hearings, etc.

- Keep track of any and all direct feedback you receive.

- Keep track of any indirect feedback. For example, you receive indirect feedback when you compare your draft to the final draft submitted by your attorney.

- Think about how long assignments are taking you and whether you are becoming more efficient and productive.

- Think about how you will obtain feedback from your supervisor, your professor, or other sources.

- Learn how you, as an extern, will be evaluated by your supervisor. How does the way you will be evaluated compare to the way the lawyers in your office are evaluated? Is there a list of competencies by which the attorneys are evaluated?

  – Will you be required to prepare a self-evaluation?

  – Will you have a formal mid-semester meeting with your supervisor and/or faculty member? If so, what will you be required to produce for the meeting?

    – How will you be evaluated at the end of the semester? Will you have a chance to review your evaluation with your supervisor?

    – What role will your externship teacher play, if any, in this evaluative process?

    – How can your externship teacher help you to prepare for this process?

You want to be prepared for any formal or impromptu meetings with your supervisor about how things are going and whether you are having the experience you hoped to gain. A law school semester goes by incredibly quickly and thinking about the issues bulleted above will prepare you to have that conversation with your supervisor whenever it might happen.

You will also have regular interactions with your supervisor about specific tasks and assignments. In Chapter 3, you will learn how to manage task-specific supervision. Each interaction about a specific assignment provides you with an opportunity to discuss how that task relates to your plan for the semester. You can make sure of this by considering each assignment as it relates to your plan and, if appropriate, by discussing the connections you see with your supervising attorney.

QUESTIONS TO CONSIDER

Think about how you will ensure that you are on track to achieve your goals and also are meeting the expectations of the program and your supervising attorney.

- Does your school require that you have a mid-semester meeting on-site with your supervisor and externship teacher?

- Are you asked to complete a mid-semester self-evaluation and share it with your supervisor and teacher?

- Is there any formal structure within your externship placement for your supervisor to evaluate you or give you feedback in the middle of the externship?

- If not, do you want to ask for such a meeting?

- Do you have a sense of what your supervisor thinks of your performance?

• How can you ensure that you are meeting your supervisor's expectations?

Remaining True to Yourself

Always be a first-rate version of yourself, instead of a second-rate version of somebody else.

—Judy Garland

Externships are wonderful arenas in which to hone your professional identity. Professional identity, in contrast to professional development, focuses on identification and internalization of the values and ideals you hold as you become the lawyer you want to be. Professional development helps you to prepare to be effective as a lawyer as you move along the continuum from novice to expert. Understanding your professional identity allows you to set standards in terms of ethics, morals, and values for yourself as a person and a lawyer. You can then draw upon them as you face challenging ethical and representational decisions in the practice of law. For more on these topics see Chapter 9 on Professionalism and Chapter 24 on Professional Identity.

Much of this chapter has focused on thinking about your legal skills. It is also critical that your lawyer identity remain true to who you are as a person. This developing professional identity is often not an easy transition though it can be easier if you remember who you are, what you value, and why you came to law school. While you might try on different lawyer personalities as a law student, ultimately you need to find a way to be a lawyer that fits with the person you want to be. While this might sound simple, in law school it may seem as if you are being taught that there is only one "correct" way to cross-examine, negotiate, make a closing statement, or interview a client. The skills you are learning will only work, however, if you can also be yourself while you are doing them.

For example, you observe an attorney yell at a client about a provision in a contract. Inside, you know that you would never be comfortable communicating with a client that way. You might watch your supervisor do a closing argument without any notes and assume that your goal must be to memorize all closing arguments. At the same time, you know that your comfort level will be much higher if you use notes. Perhaps your supervising attorney is aggressive and begins every negotiation with an adversarial opening offer or demand. Yet you believe that your personality is better suited to a problem-solving approach which seeks a collaborative result. It is important as you watch and learn from others that you think critically as you incorporate these lessons into your evolving professional identity.

Be cautious about reacting to what you see your supervising attorney do as "just a question of style." To be sure, all attorneys develop their own style or approach to the routine demands of practice. Before you dismiss a given approach as not suited to your own personality or values, consider the following questions: Why might the lawyer you observed have chosen to approach the task in the way that she did? What goals was she pursuing, and did her strategy achieve those goals? What alternative ways of handling the task can you identify, and how would those alternatives achieve the underlying goals in different ways? After you ask these questions, you may discover a different way to act while still staying true to yourself.

In any case, as you develop into the lawyer you hope to be, remember what your personal skills and talents are. What makes you unique? How can you build on your natural gifts? While there is no one way to be an effective lawyer or to practice law, be open to the feedback you receive, even if you do not always agree with it. Trust that with all kinds of feedback, you will continue to grow professionally.

Ongoing Professional Development—Beyond the Externship

While the shortest distance between two points may be a straight line, many lawyers find that the path to their dream job resembles the switch-backs you encounter when hiking to reach a mountain peak. As you complete your externship you may find that you are on a direct path to reach your peak and know how to continue to build upon the growth you experienced this semester. Others of you may find that what you thought was a direct route was actually a false summit, and the path ahead has more curves than originally anticipated. Effective professional development planning requires a willingness to reassess and adjust as you progress through your career. It can be valuable to learn that what you thought you wanted is actually not what you wanted at all.

Chapter 28 on Looking Back, Looking Forward is a great resource as you contemplate how to build upon your Professional Development Plan for this externship and create a plan for your next venture, whether that be choosing courses for next semester, preparing to maximize your growth in a summer placement, or anticipating your first job as a graduate. Some people like to develop a plan for the next year and also one for the next three to five years. As you work to develop a plan for longer-term goals, these may be broader than those you developed for your externship. Articulating short-term and longer-range goals acknowledges the dynamic nature of professional development planning, and will help you to evaluate the opportunities ahead and continue on your path to become the lawyer you want to be.

ENDNOTES

1   Legal Education and Professional Development: An Educational Continuum, Report of the Task Force on Law Schools and the Profession: Narrowing the Gap, A.B.A. Sec. of Legal Educ. & Admissions to the Bar (1992) (the "MacCrate Report.")

2   *Id.*

3   Marjorie M. Shultz & Sheldon Zedeck, *Predicting Lawyer Effectiveness: Broadening the Basis for Law School Admissions Decisions,* 36 Law & Soc. Inquiry 620 (2011).

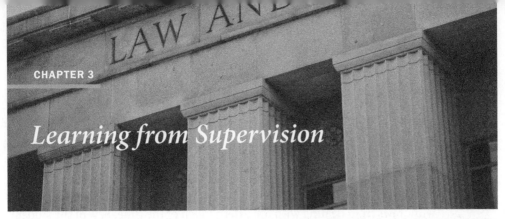

Learning from Supervision

LIZ RYAN COLE & LEAH WORTHAM

Those having torches will
pass them along to others.

— Plato

T his entire book focuses on learning from practice—learning while engaged in legal experience rather than in a classroom. Students do most of their best learning from practice when they work with experienced and dedicated lawyers. Sometimes, however, even fine, experienced, and dedicated lawyers are not good supervisors and teachers. In this chapter we focus on helping students elicit the feedback that will be most helpful to their learning. We concentrate particularly on assignment clarification and using the feedback you receive to help you gain the most from your interaction with your supervisors and colleagues. Learning how to take the most from both helpful and unhelpful supervision and feedback will help you maximize your learning, both during law school and after you graduate. In addition, if you think consciously about the feedback and supervision process as a student, you will very likely be a more effective supervisor when your turn comes.

What is the context within which law students enter into the world of learning from supervision? Many law student students and supervising lawyers seem to think that the process of supervision falls into one of three categories: the good, the bad, and the ugly.

■ *From the Student's Perspective*

· In a "good" supervision experience, the supervisor is a thoughtful, supportive mentor who takes the time to explain things carefully and enables the student to produce top-quality, highly-praised work.

- In a "bad" supervision relationship, the student is never quite sure where she stands—what she is to do, whether her work hit the mark, what needs to be improved for next time, and the supervisor's overall assessment of her work.

- In an "ugly" experience, the supervisor seems frustrated and impatient or withdraws from dealing with the extern much of the time. Few of the student's contributions survive in the final product, but the student never knows why.

■ *From the Supervising Attorney's Perspective:*

- In a "good" relationship, the supervisor and student are on the same wavelength. The supervisor gives several staccato instructions. The student nods intelligently, produces the work quickly and efficiently, and thanks the supervisor for permitting the student to work with her.

- In a "bad" relationship, the student creates a drain on the supervisor's time and requires handholding through each step of the process. The final work product is good, but the supervisor wonders if it would not have been faster and easier just to do it herself.

- All supervisors dread an "ugly" relationship. In an "ugly" supervision experience, the student does not "get it." The work product is late and has mistakes the supervisor can easily spot and probably others she cannot find without redoing the work. The supervisor cannot use the product and has to do it herself or look for someone else to do it but fears it is too close to the deadline to produce a quality revision. The supervisor is reluctant to tell the extern that the work is no good, worrying that the extern will be upset and argue—or the supervisor gives feedback and the student becomes defensive. Who needs this, the supervisor asks?

When externs and supervisors are asked to describe effective assignment clarification and effective feedback, they usually generate almost identical lists, and these lists normally match closely with the components education and management theorists identify as essential for productive supervision. These components include use of clear terminology, communication of clear expectations, selection of tasks appropriate to the supervisee's level, and making the supervisee feel valued and included. When, however, we ask students whether they receive effective assignment clarification and feedback in legal jobs, their responses are discouragingly negative. Whether in summer jobs or in other work settings, students often get neither clear task assignments nor helpful feedback on their work. Why might that be?

Whether good, bad, or ugly, supervisors and students regularly report that communication about work is difficult. Law schools, unlike graduate programs in fields like business, spend very little time teaching about effective communication, teamwork, or supervision. That loss is significant because our experience in practice and teaching shows us that effective communication can make a powerful and positive difference for supervisors and students. We believe the tools and lessons you will learn as you work through this chapter will provide you with a solid foundation for a life of learning from practice, help you make the most of this semester, maximize the value of the work you produce in the externship, and prepare you to be an effective supervisor yourself. Chapter 5 on Effective Communication and Professional Relationships and Chapter 16 on Collaboration and Teamwork provide additional insights. Chapter 17 on Writing for Practice gives further application of assignment clarification and feedback to externship writing assignments.

In this chapter we concentrate on strategies for externs as feedback receivers so you will have the information you need to advance your goals and take constructive advantage of the feedback you receive at work, in personal relationships, and the full spectrum of ways we interact with others. In THANKS FOR THE FEEDBACK: THE SCIENCE AND ART OF RECEIVING FEEDBACK WELL, Douglas Stone and Sheila Heen refer to this skill as "creating pull" in feedback receivers, thus helping them to be better learners, rather than concentrating only on a "push" strategy of improving the skill of feedback givers. Even though our focus is on students, we sometimes discuss supervision from the perspective of the supervisor so you can gain a better understanding of how and why your supervisor acts as she does. Our overall goal is to help you get the supervision you want and deserve. We agree with Stone & Heen, a "truth often ignored is that the key variable in your growth is not your teacher or your supervisor. It's you."

The Three Legs of an Effective Supervisory Relationship

A three-legged stool is an extremely solid, untippable construction. Macro planning/goal setting, micro planning/assignment clarification, and effective feedback create three legs of a steady supervisory structure, a solid foundation for productive supervisory relationships. When used in combination, these three practices help assure that supervisees are clear about what supervisors want them to do, about the assessment of their work, and what supervisors suggest for future improvement.

Macro planning means establishing long-term goals for an experience. For externs, this means identifying, articulating, and setting goals for the semester in your placement.

It also means communicating these goals to your supervisor and perhaps getting her perspective on which goals seem feasible. Macro planning gives you an overall structure within which to engage in micro planning and use the feedback you receive. See Chapter 2 on Professional Development Planning.

Micro planning is a method for "assignment clarification" that makes it possible to establish the best approach to, and desired outcomes for, each individual assignment. Micro planning provides the structure within which feedback can be most effective. As an extern you share your supervising attorney's goal of producing a quality product efficiently. You want to impress your supervisor, experience minimum frustration, and avoid time-consuming, wasted effort. Using assignment clarification increases the odds that you will submit a satisfactory product. By learning when and how best to seek clarification of assignments, you maximize the odds of producing the desired product the first time.

Feedback is the term for any process in which a system regulates itself by monitoring its own output. We have all heard the penetrating electronic sounds before a concert, the acoustical feedback that tells the musicians something needs adjusting. In the supervising and teaching context, we use the term feedback to describe communication about oral and written work. Once you establish both your long-term (macro) and your assignment specific (micro) goals, you and your supervisors must then communicate about the tasks you complete. Your supervisor's response, or lack of response, is feedback for you. You also will give feedback to your supervisor with your questions and reactions, even if you might not think of it in those terms.

We turn now to the two aspects of learning from supervision that we focus on in this chapter, micro planning/assignment clarification and strategies for getting helpful feedback and using whatever you receive effectively.

Assignment Clarification

Assume an extern receives this assignment at her placement.

Supervisor **(S)**: "I'd like to know what the requirements are in Vermont before a deeded septic easement can be deemed abandoned and if those requirements are different from those for abandoning other deeded easements."

What should the extern do?

Exercise 3.1 What does the extern need to know about the assignment in the example? What information generally is needed about an assignment to enhance the chances of producing what the supervisor wants? Jot down some ideas before reading further. This, and most other exercises in this chapter are appropriate for journal entries, if journals are part of your externship.

Optimally a supervisor's assignment will provide enough background for the extern to understand fully what she is to do and the standards against which the product will be judged, with opportunities for the extern to ask questions and get clarifications, to ensure there is mutual understanding and agreement on what is to be done. If a supervisor assigns a task without much explanation, an extern can fill in possible gaps and be sure there has been a "meeting of the minds" by summarizing the extern's understanding of the assignment and asking follow-up questions that address five points: What, How, Why, Who, and When.

In this easement assignment example, the extern might respond to the supervisor's request by asking questions such as the following:

- Would it be accurate to summarize the research question as Vermont law on septic easements? How/where do you want me to start?

- Are you interested in any law outside of Vermont?

- Do you want my conclusions only, or do you want a memo with cites?

- Do you want copies of the cases I've read? Links? An abstract? Only the relevant cases?"

- How much time do you think this should take me?

- Is there anyone other than you who will read what I give you?

- In general, how do you plan to use this information?

- When do you need this?

With this prompting from the extern, the supervisor may respond that the extern should begin her research with a particular legal encyclopedia and tell her to look in New Hampshire, Maine, Connecticut, Massachusetts, and New York, as well as Vermont. She may want a memo with cites, but may tell the student not to copy the cases because she easily can review them online. Finally, she may say she wants the memo tomorrow to use over the weekend as she drafts a brief. This expanded explanation would lead the extern to remind the supervisor that she has classes all day tomorrow and to ask if submitting the work by Friday would be all right. The supervisor might respond that she is in court on Friday morning but will be back after lunch, so by 2:00 p.m. would be fine.

Simple? Yes, but just because it is simple and quick, does not mean that is the way it usually plays out. Imagine instead what could happen without assignment clarification.

The scene is Thursday afternoon in the office: Supervisor **(S)** says, "Where is that student? I needed that memo today!" She asks her assistant to track down the student and rushes off to complete other tasks. S is frustrated.

On Friday morning, Extern **(E)**, having gotten an urgent message from the assistant, skips class and hurries to the office only to discover that S is in court. E now realizes that she did not have to skip class. **E** is frustrated.

When S returns from court the following conversation ensues:

> **S:** *"So, what did you find out about easements?"*
>
> **E:** *"I found that there are no cases in Vermont that distinguish septic easements from other easements."*
>
> **S:** *"Well, that's not exactly what I asked, but tell me, where did you look? What cases did you find?"*
>
> **E:** *"Oh, I didn't know you wanted the cases if the answer was that there were no differences."*
>
> **S:** To herself: *"Expletive!! Now I know what I'll be doing this weekend!"*

What a difference a few questions could have made!

Look back now at your answers to Exercise 3.1. How do the questions you thought of compare with the five areas of inquiry: What, How, Why, Who, When.

1. **What** you have been asked to do

This step involves getting clarity on what you are looking for, including what level of detail the supervisor expects. Asking about the depth of research the supervisor expects can be as helpful to the supervisor in refining what she expects as it will be to you the student.

Thus the student might say: *"I want to confirm my understanding: you want any case law I can find on easements created for purposes of disposing of septic waste. Are you interested in any law outside of Vermont? If so, what other jurisdictions might be important?"*

2. **How** you should go about the task

This step gives you a chance to ask both about research and presentation.

Are there any research tools or strategies the supervisor recommends you use? The answer to this seemingly simple question also may draw out more information from the supervisor on what the supervisor already knows but has not yet shared about resources, such as memo or research banks.

Thus the student might say,

"How do you suggest I start?" or

"I was thinking of starting with a Google Search using the words septic and easements. Do you think that is the right place to start?"

How does the supervisor want you to present what you find? Can the supervisor give you an example of a similar product she thought was very good? Her response might provide a more precise understanding of how the product will be used and also might reveal matters of personal preference and work style. Think about the variations in ways supervisors may want information returned and ways to ask about them. Would the supervisor find it helpful to have a log of your research trail to know what avenues you tried? Does she want copies of cases? Relevant pages? Does she like key phrases to be highlighted?

Thus the student might say, *"Do you want my conclusions only, or would you like a memo with cites? Do you want copies of the cases I've read? Links? An abstract? Only the cases I thought were relevant?"*

3. **Why** the supervisor is asking these questions in the first place

Understanding how something will be used—the context for the supervisor's assignment—can help you understand what to produce. It also is useful for the supervisor to provide this information so a student can learn more about the "big picture" parts of learning, for example, how specific components fit into a strategy and how legal research and fact gathering relate to building a theory of the case. The ideal supervisor would provide this context for its value in assignment clarification and enhancement of student learning, but many supervisors skip this step. Consider how you could ask questions that acknowledge respect for the supervisor's choices about how much information to give and the constraints on her time, but also provide you the needed information.

Thus the student might say, *"I think I can do a better job if I understand how you'll use this information. Who are the clients? What happened to them?"*

4. **Who** is going to use what you submit

This step can help the supervisor shape the task. If you ask this question when you are originally given the assignment, it may prompt your supervisor to tell you more about it before you begin, giving you context to help determine what is and is not important. It also may help you remain involved as the supervisor takes your work and turns it into something she will use.

Thus the student might say, *"Who is my audience? Is there anyone other than you who will read what I give to you? Are you going to be writing a letter? Having a client meeting? Drafting a contract or pleadings?"*

5. **When** the supervisor needs the task completed

Knowing the supervisor's deadline and how much effort the supervisor wants expended on the project will be helpful for you to schedule your work. It also will be helpful to understand how your deadline relates to the ultimate deadline because that information will help you understand how polished the product you turn in is expected to be. Finally, if you have bad news for the supervisor about the feasibility of her deadline against your other responsibilities, it is better to make this information known now instead of when a deadline is missed. The supervisor may or may not have her own deadline, and if she is experienced she likely will give you a deadline that allows her time to edit and build on what you submit.

Thus the student might say, *"When do you need this?"*

It also helps to distinguish between an externship in law school and your work as a young lawyer after law school. In the former, your work ought not to be billed to a client, while in the latter it will. When work is billed, the billing lawyer must take into account how much a client is willing to/has the capacity to spend on a project. Even outside this context, externs will want to consider the opportunity cost of putting too much work into one project. Too much time invested in one project means less time available for others.

Another factor is the importance of what the supervisor is looking for. If it does not matter much, then perhaps you should only spend an hour or two on the task, but if it is key to the theory of the entire case that the supervisor is developing, then it is worth more time. In addition, you likely have agreed to provide a finite number of hours in the externship. Your supervisor may have an opinion about how you should prioritize your work within those hours. Finally, supervisors sometimes forget that it takes law students a bit longer than it might take the supervisor to complete a task. Asking them about time to devote to a project can prompt them to think about the reasonableness of the tasks they have assigned.

Thus the student might say, *"How much time do you want me to spend?"*

Once you have gotten as much clarification as you can, write it down and share it with your supervisor for the project. Email is fine. What you write does not have to be long. Summarize. Reference the five points: What, How, Why, Who, and When.

1. **WHAT** *"I have been asked to . . . ."*

2. **HOW** *"I will begin the process by . . . (list books and other print and electronic resources if your assignment has a research component)."*

3. **WHY** *"It will ultimately be used for . . . ."*

4. **WHO** *"My audience for this assignment is . . . ."*

5. **WHEN** *"The date you need this by is . . . ."*

There is another good reason to send and keep a copy of your summary. Even if you and your supervisor are in perfect agreement about all aspects of the task when you begin your work, your supervisor may continue to think about it, developing her thoughts over time. By the time you submit your work, your supervisor may have forgotten exactly what she asked you to do. It is good practice to be able to refer to your initial memo in the event there are differences of understanding. If it is sent by email, it will be easy for your supervisor to check a couple of days later and reply with a change in direction or an additional suggestion.

> **Exercise 3.2** Reread the previous paragraphs. Ask yourself what some of the reasons might be that a supervisor may not give such guidance in the initial assignment? Jot down some of your ideas before reading further.

Here are some possible reasons for lack of clarity in a supervisor's assignment:

- The supervisor may forget how big the differences can be between a law student and an experienced attorney. The actual age difference in law students and their supervisors may be small, but the difference in law practice experience is likely to be significant. With practice, professional judgments become almost intuitive. It may require some thought for an experienced lawyer to break out the step-by-step process that a less experienced law student should pursue.

- As with a variety of day-to-day communication, we may come to know something well and forget that others do not have our level of knowledge. Have you ever worked so hard to research a paper that everything about the topic seemed "obvious" to you, and then a reader told you your points needed more explanation? How many times are we reminded that people cannot "read our minds"?

- The supervisor may be rushed and want to limit the time spent on explanation unless she sees, or you can help her see, that failure to give adequate explanation the first time can result in wasted time.

- The supervisor may not, in fact, have figured out exactly what she wants to know and why. In many collaborative relationships, the doer of the task ultimately may refine and develop what is to be done. This is a high-risk proposition for a new legal extern. If the supervisor does not know exactly what she wants, your question may help your supervising attorney clarify her thinking.

Thus far, we have given some examples of the kinds of questions that might be asked at the time of an assignment to clarify the task. It is wise to have a pad and pen or tablet, etc. at hand during every meeting with a supervisor so you do not have to trust your memory on what was said.

What if more questions come up once you have started the project? It may be useful to ask at the outset where you can go for help if something comes up during the project. The response may be, "Come back and ask me," or the question may elicit the information that the supervisor is going to be out of the office during the assignment period. She may suggest others who can help when she is unavailable. You also may want to ask your supervising attorney for permission to frame the question as a hypothetical so that you can get some help from your externship teacher at the law school, another professor in the field, or a classmate. Even if the supervisor is out of town or in court, she may suggest communication by email or voice mail.

Sometimes, getting clarification does not go as smoothly as you hoped. What might you do if, for example, your supervisor seems impatient with your questions? First, think back over your questions to the supervisor. Are they specific? Are they framed to communicate the reasons you asked the question and how the answer would be useful? As one example, it may be easier for the supervisor to respond to specific options like

"Do you want copies of important cases that I find?" than a more general "In what form would you like my research?"

Second, consider whether there are other ways to get clarification. Are there other people in the placement who work often with the supervisor and would have an idea about the particular assignment or at least about her general preferences? As mentioned earlier, you may be able to ask your supervisor or someone else knowledgeable for a sample of similar products. Are there previous experiences with the supervisor from which you have learned how she likes things to be done?

Third, you may be able to get some support from your school. Consider discussing a possible follow-up conversation with your externship teacher—perhaps role-playing how you might ask for clarification? Working on your own, with peers, or with your externship teacher, this could be a good time to consider whether you and your supervisor have the same approach to dealing with difficult conversations. If you think your approaches are different, consider how you can bridge these differences. Are you someone who is more comfortable thinking out loud about a problem, while your supervisor may prefer short, focused conversations and gets cranky when interrupted? Do you come to a halt when faced with a question you cannot answer? What strategies can you adopt to help yourself move forward without regularly interrupting your supervisor? If you find yourself with any of these issues, it can help to schedule a regular time to talk with your supervisor rather than having rushed conversations that happen sporadically during short interactions in passing.

Finally, a regular pattern of negative reactions to legitimate requests for clarification could be a signal that you need to discuss your situation with your externship teacher or program administrator. While your externship teacher may have suggestions about other ways to approach the field supervisor, the externship teacher also may need to take your supervisor's pattern of behavior into account in preparing other students for the placement or even in considering whether to continue the placement if your supervisor is not open to reasonable requests for clarification from an extern.

Exercise 3.3 Think of a recent assignment you were given. Write out the answers to these questions.

What was I told?

What did I discover I needed to know but was not told?

Which things might I have asked about? Were there things that came up that could not have been anticipated? How might I have handled the unanticipated questions differently?

If questions came up later, how did I decide what to do? What else could I have done to resolve them?

If I were going to take on this assignment again, what would I do differently?

Effective Feedback

Assume you were given an assignment, worked hard to ask the What, How, Why, Who and When questions, and submitted your assignment. Now you want to know how well you did, whether you provided what your supervisor was looking for, and whether you know what you should do differently in the future. Effective feedback should help you answer these questions.

What is feedback? Consider a rocket. A rocket going into space is guided by signals that bounce back to earth, where revised signals are then generated to modify the rocket's course. The revised signals are communicated back to the rocket as feedback. This feedback leads to changes in the rocket's trajectory in the same way you want feedback from your supervisor to help you make changes in your own trajectory.

Even if she does nothing at all when you submit work, your supervisor is giving you a form of feedback. Saying nothing does not, however, give you the information you need to make changes in your trajectory. No feedback at all may mean anything from "no news is good news," to, "I am too busy to review it right now," or even "your work is so bad I cannot even bring myself to discuss it with you." Leaving you to guess is not effective feedback. We begin this section with some brief thoughts about challenges to effective feedback and conclude with an approach to help you elicit the descriptive feedback you want and deserve.

Challenges to Getting Effective Feedback

Exercise 3.4 Earlier in the chapter we asked you to consider what obstacles you could think of in getting effective assignment clarification. Now we ask a similar question: What might be some of the reasons lawyers fail to give useful feedback to the people they supervise? Consider making notes of your answer before reading further.

Here are some common responses offered by lawyers for not giving feedback:

· They do not want to take the time because they fear giving feedback will slow them down, and they are simply too busy.

· They want to take the time but think their own supervisors will not value the time spent with students.

· They are afraid of hurting the extern's feelings or creating a tense working relationship.

· They do not know what to say and what it takes to motivate externs.

· They have difficulty explaining their thought processes to those they are trying to teach. As experienced practitioners, their standards and practices have become so deeply ingrained that they have purely intuitive reactions to a novice's product.

· They have never seen models of effective feedback applied and do not know what to expect and how to help make it happen.

Were there others on your list?

Exercise 3.5 Feedback is a conversation with give (push) and take (pull). What might students do to make it hard for feedback to be given and received?

Here are some common supervisor concerns about students:

· They give the impression that feedback from the supervisor is not welcome.

· They are afraid to confess ignorance.

· They do not make themselves available when the supervisor is free and interrupt her when she is not free.

· They have never seen models of effective feedback and do not know what to expect and how to help make it happen.

Were there others on your list?

Keeping these challenges in mind, let us consider one student draft of a memorandum with two different supervisor response scenarios.

Erica Extern works for a firm, one of whose clients is Harry Jones. Allison Gordon is suing Harry Jones. Erica has been assigned to write a brief in support of a motion to disqualify John Taylor, the lawyer who currently represents Allison Gordon, and who previously represented Harry Jones. The brief contends that, because Taylor formerly represented Jones, he should now be disqualified from representing Ms. Gordon in this matter against the firm's client Jones. The disqualification challenge rests on the argument that the previous and present matters are substantially related, thus meeting the test for disqualification in this jurisdiction's version of Model Rule of Professional Conduct 1.9 and the related case law. Erica has submitted a draft of the brief. First assume Erica's supervisor is Samantha, who writes the first memo below. Then assume instead that her supervisor is Simon who gives Erica the second memo below. Compare how you would react to each memo.

SAMANTHA'S MEMORANDUM

To: Erica Extern

From: Samantha Supervisor

Re: Draft Brief in the Jones case

Your draft brief reflected extensive and thorough research. I was impressed that you found the 1981 drafters' original research comments, but I decided not to use that part of the brief.

Your public policy argument on the construction of Model Rule 1.9 was nicely stated. I think it's better to start with the rules construction argument so I moved the policy argument to after the rules construction argument.

Your writing could use tightening. Say things clearly and succinctly.

It is helpful to give the reader a little better sense of where you are going. I dropped the point about "insight" into the client.

Thanks a lot for all your hard work. Your research was a big help to me in getting the brief done on time. Tightening your writing and doing more road mapping will help me to use more of your work as written, but this was a terrific first effort.

SIMON'S MEMORANDUM

To: Erica Extern

From: Simon Supervisor

Re: Draft Brief in the Jones case

You seem to have done a great deal of research. Your writing needs work in several respects. I made a number of comments on the brief, and you can see the changes I made in reworking the final draft. This summarizes some language patterns that I think need work.

You dilute the power of what you have to say in several ways

1. Strip out legalese expressions such as above-mentioned, aforementioned, henceforward, thenceforth, to wit, and so on.

2. Avoid passive verbs and surplus words. For example, substitute "Jones said" for "A statement was made by Jones to the effect that." "Bound" substitutes for "was binding upon." "When" can substitute for "at the time of." "Does not" is better than "does not operate to." I have marked a number of examples of passive voice and participles, infinitives, gerunds, and other noun or adjective forms denoting action when a finite verb would have done better.

3. A former professor of mine used to say, "Whenever you are tempted to say 'clearly' or 'obviously,' STOP. It must mean that your proposition is neither clear nor obvious." "Clearly" and "obviously" rarely strengthen an argument. Watch overuse of adverbs in general.

4. You need a clearer road map of your argument. Use a topic sentence at the beginning of an argument to forecast what a section will say. On page three, a topic sentence could make clear why you are reciting the facts. For example, "In Taylor's prior representation of Jones, confidences important to this litigation could have been divulged." Then identify the confidences that might have been shared in that representation. Sum up with a characterization favorable to our client's position. For example, "Effective representation in *Wadsworth v. Jones* required communication

of information about Jones's solvency. That information would be useful in Gordon's current claim against Jones."

Arguments should be listed in order of their strength and the ease with which a judge could adopt them. Our jurisdiction's version of Model Rule 1.9 has not been construed by the courts. We are asking the court to adopt the majority definition of "substantial relationship," which gives us a strong argument that the current matter and the previous matter on which Taylor represented our client fall within the definition such that our client's consent was required for Taylor to represent Gordon in this matter. It is a much smaller leap to ask the judge to construe the rule in line with the majority view than to ask for a decision based on public policy.

Make the arguments in this order: (1) Rule explication—this is what the Rule says. (2) Follow the majority—this is how they have construed the Rule. (3) Explain the public policy reasons supporting this view. I dropped the legislative history argument. The Model Rules went through too many revisions, and there has been too much case law to make the Rules' drafters' 1981 comments and other legislative history in the ABA of much relevance.

Use key terms consistently. You refer to the initial meeting, the first interview, the first client conference, and the first talk that Jones had with Taylor. I gather you mean all to refer to the same event: the initial meeting between Taylor and his then-prospective client Jones. Pick a single descriptive phrase and stick with it.

After you have gotten on paper the arguments you wish to make, it may help to outline the points and reconsider their order. In Section II, you seem to make four or five sub points in support of your argument. It is not clear where one starts and another ends.

I do not think our courts have found that general information providing "insight" about a client is relevant to a finding of substantial relationship. Review all the cases again and look at cases on this point from all over the United States. If you do not think your argument needs revision in light of that, print the cases on which you rely so I can read them.

> **Exercise 3.6** What would you think and feel if you received each of the memos above? These two exemplars have different strengths and weaknesses. Would you prefer one rather than the other? What are your reasons? What do you think was helpful and not helpful about each?

What Makes Feedback Effective?

If students cannot hear what supervisors are telling them, the feedback will not be effective. Both the specific language used and the context within which the feedback occurs are factors that affect what we can hear and understand. The following discussion includes some information on good practices in giving feedback for you to keep in mind when you react to your supervisor and to consider as you take on supervision tasks in your own career. It also describes ways you can make the feedback you receive most useful to you even if the supervisor's way of giving feedback is not optimal.

THANKS FOR THE FEEDBACK defines three primary types of feedback sometimes given and often desired by potential feedback receivers: appreciation (thanks and other forms of acknowledgment); coaching (comments directed toward learning and improving performance); and evaluation (information on "where one stands," e.g., a grade or rating, prospects for promotion). The authors posit that much of the angst and frustration surrounding feedback is mismatch and differing perceptions between the giver and receiver of feedback: (1) mismatch of what is given with what a receiver wants at a particular time; (2) differing perceptions between giver and receiver about what kind of feedback is being given and its purpose. Think about what those concepts mean with regard to the two feedback memos on an extern's first assignment you just reviewed.

The potential for mismatch in the content, perceptions, and intentions of feedback helps explain the different ways one might react to these memos. The first (Samantha's) memo is strong on appreciation of the extern's work. It also provides an evaluation benchmark: "[T]his was a terrific first effort." This gives feedback on "where the extern stands" against explicit or implicit standards regarding what the supervisor expects of a new student extern.

The second (Simon's) memo contains considerable coaching but not much appreciation.

Virtually everyone wants and needs evaluative feedback at some point, to "know where they stand," even if the answer is painful. People vary both in our need for expressed appreciation and how we find it most satisfying to receive appreciation. Some people want and need explicit words of praise before they can hear and understand the feedback offered. Others believe feedback that begins with appreciative statements is dishonest and of less value than feedback that provides immediate correction. Stone and Heen characterize evaluation as the "loud" type of feedback and cite to brain research explaining why "Bad news is emotionally louder than good . . . ." The emotional volume at which you hear the feedback offered affects your ability to hear and understand the points your supervisor wants to make.

Stone and Heen also observe that people's reaction to feedback varies a great deal based on differences in their **baseline**—the "default state" to which people generally gravitate after good or bad things happen; **swing**—how far they move up or down from the baseline after feedback; and **sustain** or **recovery**—the typical duration of someone's ups and downs. They cite to research finding that the amount of time people need to sustain positive emotion or recover from negative emotion can vary as much as 3,000 (!) percent.[1]

How important is appreciation to you? Everyone wants at least some appreciation, but people differ in how much they want or need to hear it in feedback. Similarly, almost everyone finds it useful to receive specific suggestions on what to do differently in the future, but people vary in what they can hear or absorb during feedback. We have heard multiple students say, "I would be devastated," by the second (Simon's) memo while other students react saying, "Hey this supervisor is telling me specifically what he wants; the first memo didn't really tell me anything useful that would help me to do better next time."

THANKS FOR THE FEEDBACK provides a number of recommendations for tempering one's emotional reaction to feedback so one can glean what is valuable from it even if, as a subtitle of their book says, "it is off base, unfair, poorly delivered, and frankly you're not in the mood." One strategy is to be explicit about the kind of feedback you want, e.g., that you value explicit coaching about what your supervisor thinks you should do differently but right now you are looking for an assessment of "how you are doing" overall. The authors point out that feedback receivers often distort and overreact to feedback meant as coaching because they understand it to be evaluation, i.e., hearing the supervisor's suggestions about what to change in the future as a conclusion of a "bad job" rather than just suggestions on how to improve given to a valued supervisee.

Stone and Heen suggest three practices to enhance the ability to grow from feedback. The first is "to sort toward coaching," to "hear coaching as coaching," and not leap to seeing everything as evaluation that drowns out any other message. The second is to acknowledge that, while evaluation of performance may have consequences for you and you generally have limited or no control of your supervisor's assessment of a past performance, the stories you tell yourself about what the feedback "means" are within your control. As you gain more legal experience, you can become more confident about assessing whether you agree with the rules and standards that underlie a feedback giver's judgment about your performance. And you can think about how to turn down the negativity of the story you are telling yourself about the importance of the feedback while still assessing the value of the substance. Third, give yourself an evaluation in addition to the evaluation you received from your supervisor: a "second score." The first score is what the evaluation said about your performance. The second is the score you give yourself on what you did with that evaluation, how you learned from it, and how well you avoided overreaction.

Consider whether you approach life with a "fixed" or a "growth" mindset. People operating from a fixed mindset perceive feedback as a "grade" that exposes weaknesses of fixed traits and abilities. To those who operate from a growth mindset, feedback can be seen as a helpful step toward growth and change. Chapter 25 on Work and Well-being provides more information on the usefulness of cultivating a growth mindset.

Finally, consider the language of feedback. One often hears people talk about positive and negative feedback. We prefer the terms affirming (what you may think of as a positive statement) and corrective (what you may think of as a negative statement). Affirming feedback affirms and reinforces behavior one would like to see repeated in the future. Corrective feedback suggests changes in behaviors that one does not want repeated in the future. Affirming feedback is equally if not more important than corrective feedback. Many people are able to hear and incorporate corrective feedback more effectively when it is combined with a sincere affirmation of things done right. Affirming feedback is more than saying "good job." And, just as with corrective feedback, it needs to describe performance with examples and specificity if it is to be effective.

What Externs Can Do About Getting More Useful Feedback

First—Be ready with your own critique. Once people have completed a talk, written a paper, or finished a race, they almost always have a lot of ideas about how to do "it" differently the next time. Supervisors often do not consider that asking a supervisee for their own assessment before commenting is usually a better place to begin than the supervisors' own critique and prescriptions. The supervisee already may understand what could be better. The assessment may reveal that the problem was a misunderstanding about the task. The supervisee's own thoughtful assessment can put the supervisor more at ease in giving critical feedback.

Even if your supervisor does not think to ask, offering your own critique is a way to take an active role in shaping the type of feedback you get. Letting supervisors know what you can see for yourself allows them to understand your openness to receiving feedback, allows them to focus on anything they see you have missed, and helps them make focused corrections in the area of improvement you have already self-identified.

As you think about setting up time for feedback, here are two possible scenarios to consider:

- *Scenario One:* You are working in a setting where more than one lawyer gives you assignments. You turn one in and are waiting for feedback. If a few days have gone by and you have not heard anything, send a follow-up email that says something along these lines: *"I enjoyed working on project x. I hope we can meet on (pick a reasonable time in the close future) to talk about how to improve my work for my next project. In the meantime, I looked over what I turned in and have a few ideas of my own about what I might do differently (and then describe them briefly)."*

- *Scenario Two:* You are working closely with one very busy lawyer. You have an agreement to meet once a week to review your work. The meetings are intense, and you often feel overwhelmed about all the things you should do better. Take control of what you can for the meeting. One or two days before the meeting, write to your supervisor saying something like this: *"I am looking forward to our scheduled meeting. I know we are going to review what I did on Projects A and B. To prepare for our meeting I have reviewed them myself and see some changes I would make the next time (then describe them briefly)."*

Second—Ask questions. When a supervisor decides to accept or revise a draft, the supervisor, at least implicitly, makes some judgments about what is acceptable to her. Even if you did not receive a copy showing and explaining the changes, you can compare your draft to the final copy and see what was changed. An experienced lawyer may make changes based on her experience and not even consciously articulate the reasons for the changes. If she did not explain revisions, think about the reasons she might have made them and ask questions to see if your assumptions are accurate.

Third—Look for ways to get timely feedback and keep reminding your supervisor that you want feedback. For feedback to be most effective it needs to be invited and timely given. By choosing to do an externship, you may be assuming that your supervisor knows you want feedback on your work. Your supervisor may assume that you, by virtue of your appearance at a work site, are inviting feedback. Remember that one of the reasons why supervisors may fail to give feedback is that they are not sure you want it, so it can be very helpful to invite feedback explicitly.

With regard to feedback being timely, if you get feedback so long after the event that it is no longer clear in anyone's mind, the feedback itself is generally of less value. Consider structuring a regular time for feedback, perhaps by setting up a weekly meeting with your supervisor. You can always cancel meetings, but it is hard to make new appointments on busy days.

Fourth—Try not read more than necessary into your supervisor's style. What can you do if your supervisor's style is to make critical global comments: "This brief is something I'd expect from a first year summer associate, not someone in their third year of law school," or it seems to you that her differences may be ones of style on which lawyers would differ?

It can help to practice, perhaps with a classmate or your externship teacher, receiving your supervisor's comments. Consider how to remove the defensiveness from your voice and body language. Think about the "sort to coaching" strategy described earlier: tell yourself to assume that feedback you are receiving is given to help you improve and grow, not a "grade" on a performance you cannot change.

Your supervisor's comments may reflect generally accepted standards in the legal profession or may instead reflect only an opinion or style preference of the individual attorney. Nevertheless, comments from a supervisor are opinions that "count." Even if they are not widely accepted, the supervisor's preferences set the standards for work done for her. Once, after a professor suggested that a student delete words like "aforementioned" and "heretofore" from his writing, the student responded that he had done so until he started working at a law firm where the lawyers all wrote that way. At the firm he might venture that his teacher suggested deletion of such terms, but ultimately, on matters of style—as opposed to ethics—"When in Rome, do as the Romans do."

Fifth—Ask for examples to make sure you understand your supervisor's comments. Ask for one or more examples so you can be sure you understand the feedback point being made. You might say, *"Can we look at an example of what you are talking about in this brief so it can help me understand how you want it done differently? I want to make sure I know what you are looking for."* You can mentally edit the comments you are hearing to remind yourself that these are only the opinions of the speaker. An absolute or global statement, e.g., "that was the worst movie ever!" leaves very little space to disagree. Mentally add, "I think," "In my opinion," or "I prefer."

Generally, people learn most easily from feedback—both affirming and corrective—when the feedback giver identifies the point being commented on specifically and non-judgmentally rather than in a global, conclusory statement. For example, the following statement comments specifically on a particular point: "You put the public policy argument first, before the rule construction analysis and the argument regarding how the rule has been construed elsewhere." A more general and less helpful version of statements might say, "You didn't put your arguments in an effective order."

If you get the latter type of response, try to step back, "edit out" any sting you feel, and ask questions to make sure you understand the specifics of what is being said and your supervisor's reason for favoring that approach. If may be helpful for you to share the assumption you were working from, e.g., on how to order arguments in a brief, so you can understand more fully competing approaches and the reasons your supervisor favors her position.

Sixth—Learn from the final work product. If your work product was a written draft, which was then finalized and sent out, but you did not get feedback on it, ask for copy of both the marked-up draft and the final as it was sent out. Compare the differences between what you wrote and the final. Are some conclusions obvious from the comparisons? If you are not sure about the reasons for some changes, prepare some questions for your supervisor. Of course these questions need to reflect an earnest extern seeking to improve her work and not to sound like a hostile opposing counsel.

What if, instead of discussing a written submission, you are seeking feedback on an "information memo," an assignment that asks for background information for the attorney or assignments to "find some cases" and provide copies or an oral briefing? If one of your externship goals has been getting feedback on writing, these can present a challenging situation for the student seeking feedback because there is no final copy against which you can compare your draft to glean patterns in the changes. With an information memo assignment, the supervisor often makes a much more general judgment that something is or is not "enough," or "okay". It also is difficult for the supervisor to know what you did not find if she does not already know the law on the point.

To get feedback on the adequacy of the research, you might say, *"I often have difficulty deciding when I have done enough research. How do you decide?"* or *"What do you look for in this kind of memo that will give you the confidence to rely on it?"* With regard to the writing you might say, *"I realize that the projects I have done have been background research for you. You were able to tell me whether I gave you adequate information, but it didn't make sense at the time to focus on how they might have been better written. Would it be possible now to assign me a project like a client letter or brief so we can focus on my writing?"* Or, if that does not seem possible, *"Could you take apart of one of the memos and give me some feedback on the writing?"*

Seventh—Share your learning goals and ask for your supervisor's help from the beginning. Assume for example that one of your primary goals for the semester is personal improvement in research and writing. Ask whether you can receive an assignment that would involve a draft of a final product that will be used in some way so you will be able to compare your drafts to a final product. *"I realize that there may not be any reason for you to critique my writing style and the logic of my arguments in a background memo, though critique of my writing is important for me. Could you take at least one memo and give me feedback on how you think it could be better written? That would really help me for the future."*

Using these seven approaches can help encourage your supervisor to give feedback from which you can learn and grow. They can help you get feedback on all kinds of performance, including performance that does not involve written work. For example, consider a situation in which you interview a client in the presence of your supervisor. The supervisor remains quiet during the interview. Because this is only your second client interview, you would very much like to get some insight into your performance. To do so, consider the following:

Critique yourself—After the interview, you might offer what you think were the strengths and weaknesses of your approach. For example, you might say, *"I thought that I gathered information about her lease thoroughly, but I felt that I missed something when asking questions about the condition of her apartment."*

Ask questions—Consider asking your supervisor questions about specific aspects of your interviewing approach. For example, you might ask, *"Do you have any suggestions about how I could have gotten more information about her landlord's reaction to her complaints?"*

Request timely feedback—You may notice that your supervisor is ready to leave right after the interview. Consider asking for some feedback then or at least setting a specific time when you can get the feedback. You might say, *"Before you go, I wanted to ask you a few questions about how this interview went. I have more clients to interview next week. It would help to get some feedback now."*

Don't (over)react to your supervisor's style—If your supervisor leads with critical commentary, pointing out things that did not work during the interview, listen carefully and do not get defensive. Instead, consider thanking your supervisor and asking follow up questions: *"How could I do that differently the next time? How would you have handled that problem?"*

Ask for examples—If your supervisor gives you a general or conclusory comment, follow up with a request for a specific example. For instance, if your supervisor says, *"Your questions often seemed too general and non-specific,"* you might follow up by asking, *"Can you give me an example of how I could ask a more specific question?"*

Learn from a similar performance—With non-written performance, there is no final product as there would be with a piece of writing. You can still compare your interview with others done by more experienced attorneys. Consider asking to sit in on other attorneys' interviews, both before and after you have a done a few yourself.

Relate specific performance to your overall goals—You may have identified "learning how to work with clients" as an overall goal for the semester. If so, remind your supervisor of this goal, and ask for comments on how this interview moves you closer to that goal and what steps you might take next time to continue moving in that direction.

Feedback for Your Supervisor

While students do not often recognize that they are in a position to give feedback to those supervising them, consider, perhaps in consultation with your externship teacher, using these principles to provide guidance in giving feedback to your supervisor on things that are working well for you as well as things you might like to change. If you would like to change some aspect of your experience, you may wish to describe the situation to communicate your reactions, to explain the reasons you would like things to be different, and propose the desired change. Here are some examples of what such a student might say:

- *"I understand you had a meeting with opposing counsel on the Jones case on Tuesday. I'm really interested in seeing what happens in informal exchanges among lawyers. Will there be other meetings with counsel or in chambers coming up that I could attend?"*

- *"For the last three weeks, the secretary has asked me to cover the phones for two hours each day while I am here. I'm happy to help out from time to time, but I am concerned I am missing being involved in legal work. In the alternative, you might also point out that 'the law school expects me to be involved more directly in the type of work that lawyers do.'"*

If the supervisor's response does not offer an acceptable alternative, you might propose one or pose a question to the supervisor:

- *"I'm wondering if there might be some alternatives for covering the phones."*

Remember too that when your supervisor does something you especially like or find useful, you can reinforce that behavior. For example, if your supervisor gives you effective feedback on your performance, be sure that your response communicates your appreciation. If you keep in mind that feedback's effectiveness is enhanced by specificity, you will be explicit about what you found helpful and why.

- *"I found it very helpful when you gave examples by line editing those three paragraphs to show what you meant about more active voice and succinct writing. I understand better how you want things done in the future, and I appreciate the feedback on my writing."*

Here the supervisor took the time to give examples and explanation. Unless the supervisor hears from the extern that it was useful, the supervisor may not be as motivated to take that time in the future.

> **Exercise 3.7** Think of something you would like to change about your externship. Write a plan of how you could improve the situation. Consider whom to talk to, what to say, when to initiate the conversation, and what reaction you are likely to get.
>
> Do not forget your school as a source of support. Talk about the situation with your externship teacher. Feedback from your externship teacher may assist you in conversations about improving your externship.

> **Exercise 3.8** Suppose your supervisor asks for feedback on her own performance in clarifying assignments, providing feedback, etc. Script the comments that you would give based on your experience with your supervisor thus far. See if you can apply the guidance provided in this chapter in your comments.

> **Exercise 3.9** Imagine your supervisor has just spent 30 minutes with you reviewing a significant written product. You are ready to revise your work and give her a finished product tomorrow. Her questions help clarify the portion of the analysis

that was somewhat confused, and her comments on your resources made you feel validated for the care you took with the research. How would you give feedback to your supervisor?

FURTHER RESOURCES

Alice Alexander and Jeffrey Smith, *A Practical Guide to Cooperative Supervision for Law Students and Legal Employers*, 29 Law Off. Econ. & Mgmt. 207–26 (1988–89).

Jeff Giddings, Professor of Law at Griffith University in Brisbane and supported by an Australian Office for Learning and Teaching National Fellowship, created The Law School Supervision Project. The resulting website provides resources for students, supervisors, and program coordinators to make the most of supervised practice courses including survey results of supervisors' perceptions of their experience, available at https://www.griffith.edu.au/criminology-law/effective-law-student-supervision-project.

Douglas Stone & Sheila Heen, Thanks for the Feedback: The Science and Art of Receiving Feedback Well (2014).

ENDNOTES

1   Douglas Stone & Sheila Heen, Thanks for the Feedback: The Science and Art of Receiving Feedback Well 153, 330 n.10 (2014) (citing Richard J. Davidson & Sharon Begley, The Emotional Life of Your Brain: How Its Unique Patterns Affect the Way You Think, Feel, and Live—and How You Can Change Them 41, 69 (2002)).

Observation

J.P. "SANDY" OGILVY

What really teaches man is not experiences,
but observation. It is observation that enables him to
make use of the vastly greater experience of other men, of
men taken in the mass. He learns by noting what happens
to them. Confined to what happens to himself, he labors
eternally under an insufficiency of data.

—H. L. Mencken

Watching others is a primary mode of learning. From birth, children are careful observers of their environment. They learn by observing and then imitating the behaviors of their parents, siblings, and others. Learning from observation does not end in childhood but continues throughout life. Learning through observation continues to be important even when you are spending much of your time in formal learning settings. Consider how you learn about someone you meet for the first time. You observe how the person dresses and with whom the person speaks. You listen to what the person says and also to how the person says it. Your initial, and perhaps final, impression of this person is formed through your initial observation.

Whether we are conscious of it or not, we constantly learn from our environment. In law school, whether in a classroom or in an externship, you are bombarded with a continuous stream of data from your observations. You learn information, behaviors, and values from observation of teachers, classmates, and supervisors.

In a typical law school classroom, the primary mode of teaching may take the form of a modified Socratic dialogue. You observe that the professor calls on the students in the row in front of you one after another. You detect a pattern and begin to relax a little, believing that the professor will not discover how unprepared you are. You make an observation, infer a pattern of behavior, and modify your emotional state in response to your observations and interpretations.

By listening to the dialogue between the professor and the students you also might discern a pattern in the nature of the professor's questions. Conscious reflection on the questions may better prepare you to answer the professor's questions when your turn comes. Understanding questioning patterns may enable you to focus your reading of the assigned materials as you prepare for the next day's class. For example, in Civil Procedure class, you might notice that the professor frequently asks what will happen in the case after this decision. As you prepare for subsequent classes, you note not just "who won" but also what happened next. To add another dimension, you may learn modes of behavior and values of which you are not aware or of which you become aware only years later. For example, the manner in which the professor relates to the students in the classroom provides a model that may affect the way you relate to clients after you enter practice. How does the professor respond to student questions? With enthusiasm? With impatience?

> *On one occasion I was in court observing students who, as part of their externship, were trying cases for the county prosecutor of a local jurisdiction. During a lull in the court's activities, I witnessed an interaction between a public defender and his client. The client, whose case was on the docket for a plea or trial that afternoon, was clearly anxious. On several occasions, he approached his attorney to inquire about the status of his case. At one point, his attorney told him sharply, "When I know something, you will be the first to know." I was struck by the tactlessness of the attorney's remark and by his demeaning tone. Waiting for a case to be called is a routine, oft-repeated event for the attorney, but is important and nerve-wracking for the client. Why did the attorney snap at his client? What had been the model for his behavior? Perhaps this lawyer had a professor who saw a faceless student who had asked the same, inane question every year for the past twelve years rather than the individual student asking a question that the student thought was important to his understanding. [J.P.O.]*

Much of your time at your externship will be spent in formal and informal observation of persons and events. Your externship will provide a golden opportunity to learn by observation. You will be flooded with information from your experience in the workplace. It may take some time to know what is important and how to interpret it. To make the best use of this information it is useful to have a framework to organize and interpret it. This chapter offers techniques for improving and using your observation skills so that you may use your observation time more effectively.

How can you learn to be a better observer? Lawyers often critique the observational skills of others—their clients, opposing parties, and both lay and expert witnesses:

> *At your deposition you said that the defendant was about 5'8" tall, but now you say that the defendant was over six feet tall. During your deposition, here on page 234, you state that the defendant was dressed in blue jeans and a tee shirt. Today your testimony is that the defendant was dressed in chino slacks and a long-sleeve shirt. You don't really remember what the defendant looked like, do you?*

Lawyers less often critique their own observational skills.

As a law student you will not find many books or articles that will help you to become a better observer and thus learn better from observation. Opportunities for observation abound, however, even in the regular routine of law school or legal employment. One of the most famous examples of a law student's observation of his environment is Scott Turow's book, ONE-L: AN INSIDE ACCOUNT OF LIFE IN THE FIRST YEAR OF LAW SCHOOL (1988), which describes his experiences as a first-year student at Harvard Law School. The readings at the end of this chapter offer critiques of institutions or legal systems based in part on law student observation. And some of you may have worked in a field, academic or otherwise, that developed your capacity for observation, including anthropology, psychology, sociology, or teacher education.

This chapter addresses a number of related topics: How should you plan for the observation? What are your purposes for the observation? Which events, subjects, and settings will be most useful for your purposes? Should you observe from the perspective of the participant observer or the outside observer? What are the differences between the two types of observers? When is the appropriate time for conducting your observations? How can you most effectively record your observations? How can you learn from reflection on your observation? What are some of the ethical issues involved in conducting observations?

Planning for Observation

Much of the learning that you do through observation is completely unplanned. Think about the last time you were in a group of people most or all of whom you did not know, for example overhearing the conversations of persons near you in a restaurant or theater or being introduced by a mutual friend to a group of strangers. Think about the conversation that was going on. You may have learned something about the setting in which the conversation took place. You probably learned some information from the conversation, and undoubtedly you learned something about the people involved in the conversation as well. Who seemed to be a leader in the group? Who used humor to achieve his goals? Who offered new alternatives? Even though you did not actually join the group or actively seek to learn information about the people or the setting, through your unplanned observations, learning occurred.

You can enrich and deepen your learning from unplanned observation by reflecting on your observations after they occur. Consider the last time you interacted with a group of people you did not know. If you recall the event and think about what you learned, you may increase your learning from the event. Now that the event is in your consciousness, you may generalize from the experience and explore what you have learned. This reflection can lead to additional learning. For example, if the group is one with which you will continue to have contact, such as a law school study group, your observations and initial reflections may lead you to plan how to help the group operate efficiently and effectively in pursuit of its goals.

Although you can learn from unplanned observations, you can learn more from planned observations. Because your experiences are so full of observations, you cannot attend to and evaluate them all. To avoid having data just flow by, we recommend that you build several planned observations into your externship experiences. By improving your observational skills, you will internalize the process. Even your unplanned observations will become richer learning opportunities. While pausing to observe attorneys in action when you are in the courthouse or other work setting has some value, planned observations can be much more intellectually stimulating.

We now turn to planning for observations and introduce you to the concept of the reflective observation cycle, which involves a continuing cycle of planning, observing, recording, reflecting, and sharing.

Planning for an observation involves asking familiar questions: why, who, what, when, where, and how: why to observe, meaning how is the data from the observation going to be used; whom to observe; what to observe; when to observe; where to observe; and how to observe.

In this situation, like every other in your externship, the cycle of learning starts with an articulation of goals. Why you are observing—what are your purposes for the observation? What do you want to learn? How will you use what you learn from the observation? Your answers to these questions will influence your answers to the other planning questions.

There are many purposes for which you might undertake an observation in an externship. You may want to improve your performance of a specific lawyering skill such as conducting a direct examination of an expert witness. To begin working on this skill, you may want to observe someone whom you regard as an expert conduct a direct examination. Or you may want to improve your skills in policy analysis by investigating how a court-annexed mediation program works for low-income people. You may wish to observe how the participants in the process are treated by judges, court personnel, mediators, attorneys, and opposing parties.

You may undertake planned observations to make concrete some abstract problem you are struggling to understand and, thereby, to provide additional information that can assist you in solving the problem. You may wish to observe others in order to step out of your own experience in an attempt to understand the values and assumptions others bring to a situation or problem. You may wish to compare information that you have acquired in textbooks and classroom discussions with information acquired in the field. Exercise 4.1 presents an opportunity to use planned observation to further one or more of your self-identified goals for your externship.

> **Exercise 4.1** Using your goals and objectives developed in Chapter 2 as a guide, make a list of topics for which focused observation could lead to the achievement of one or more of your learning objectives for your externship.

Use Table 4.1 on the next page to outline some of your major learning goals and objectives and then to identify some of the opportunities for learning from observation in your externship. Once you have decided on the purposes of your observation, you can answer the other questions. Table 4.2 provides an organizational tool for planning your observation.

■ *What Should Be Observed?*

Once you have identified topics or settings for focused observation, choose one or more of the topics for further reflection. Consider the complexity of the topic, how accessible the setting is to you, your time constraints in conducting the observation, and the extent of preparation required before you can begin your observation. Write down your concerns.

■ *How Many Observations Do You Need to Make?*

How many actors in the setting do you wish to observe? What is the time frame over which the observations will occur? How many different types of observations do you need to conduct? To what extent can the details of the events be observed and recorded? What questions do you want the observation to answer?

Table 4.1 Worksheet for Identifying Opportunities for Learning From Observation

Learning Goals	Learning Objectives	Opportunities for Observation
A. Improve interviewing skills	1. Establish client confidence and build rapport	a. Initial attorney client interviews b. Paralegal-client interviews c. Listen to phone interviews
	2.	a. b. c.
	3.	a. b. c.
B.	1.	a. b. c.
	2.	a. b. c.
	3.	a. b. c.
C.	1.	a. b. c.

	2.	a.
		b.
		c.
	3.	a.
		b.
		c.

Table 4.2 Planning for an Observation

What are my purposes for conducting this observation? (See Table 4.1)	1. Improve interviewing skills 2. 3.
What should be observed?	1. Initial meeting with a new client 2. 3.
Who should be observed?	1. Attorney Jones 2. Client Harris 3.
Where should I conduct the observations?	1. Attorney Jones's office 2. 3.
How should I observe? — as a participant — as a non-participant – directly – indirectly	If I am a participant, I may be more accepted by the client, although depending on my level of involvement, I may have fewer opportunities to make observations.
When is it best to I observe?	Whenever the initial client meeting is scheduled, I should try to observe several initial meetings to get a broader perspective of the behaviors I am interested in observing.

What ethical issues are involved?	I must be sensitive to protect the secrets and confidences of the client; I will certainly need the permission of Attorney Jones; Attorney Jones may wish to seek the permission of the client, depending on my role.
—Do I need special permission?	
—Are there confidentiality issues?	
—Other questions?	

■ *Whom to Observe*

Deciding whom to observe may be easy. There may be only one opportunity for an observation that involves just one person, e.g., the opening statement of the respected criminal practitioner you arranged to observe. If you are doing an investigation of a systemic problem, you may need to observe dozens of actors in the setting, for example, how each of the actors chooses to provide or to withhold information that may be useful to the other participants. It may be something in between. For example, you may want to observe how a particular drug is identified and placed in evidence in a prosecution for drug possession by attending several trials involving drug charges.

If you plan to observe only one person, then once the decision is made you move on to the other questions. It is rare, however, that your opportunities for observation are so limited. When several alternatives are available, you need to decide which of the alternatives to select. For example, there might be several attorneys at your placement you could observe doing the task you are interested in observing, but you have time only to observe one of them. As is true of most problems where the answer is not certain, you must decide what factors will influence your selection of the subject of your observation and then prioritize those factors in some fashion.

Think of a topic, situation, or problem from your externship experience you might want to investigate at least in part through formal observation. If you are an extern in a litigation setting, you might want to learn how the attorneys in the office prepare a witness to testify. If you are in a judicial externship, you may want to investigate how the judges in your court prepare for trial. If you work for a government agency, you might want to understand better how the hierarchical structure of the office affects the production of work. If you work for a solo practitioner, you may want to observe the assignment and flow of work within the office to learn about efficient administration of a small law office. What factors influence your choice of the person or persons to observe? Use Table 4.3 to list the factors you think would influence your decision. Then rank the factors according to their relative importance in your judgment.

Table 4.3 **Factors Influencing Decision of Choice of Person(s) to Observe**

Ranking	Factor	Comments

■ *What Factors Were Important to You? Here Are Some Possibilities:*

· When can you fit the observation into your schedule?

· When is the subject of the observation available?

· Do you want to observe a subject you believe is the best at the task or one whose performance is adequate?

· Which of several possible subjects is most likely to perform in a manner typical of the situation?

· Would the subject be available for questions after the observation?

· How accessible to you is your subject?

· Do you need to get permission for the observation?

· Do you need to disclose to the subject the fact that you are conducting an observation?

· How important to your observation is it that you be unobtrusive?

· Will a single observation suffice, or will you need multiple observations?

■ *Where to Observe*

If your subject can be found in only one place, the answer is easy. If the subject may be observed in more than one place, consider the following possibilities:

- **where** you are most likely to get close enough to the action to get the most data without being too intrusive;

- **whether** the time required to secure permission to observe in a particular setting outweighs the benefits to be derived from observing in that setting over an alternative for which permission is not required;

- **which** setting offers the most opportunities to observe the persons or activities that are of most interest to you; and

- **where** you will have the best opportunity to make contemporaneous notes of your observation.

For example, assume you want to observe the initial meeting with a new client to observe how an attorney conducts such a meeting. You may know that two of the attorneys in the firm use different settings for such meeting. One always meets the new client in her office, which is relatively small; the other almost always uses a conference room, which is larger. In the office setting, you would be seated very close to the new client. In the conference room, you could be seated several feet away from the client. If either attorney would be willing to allow you to observe a meeting, you could reflect on whether the more intimate or less intimate setting would best further your goals. For instance, if you are seated next to the client in the small office, you may have less opportunity to observe the demeanor of the client in response to the attorney's questions than you might in the larger room where you can possibly sit facing the client.

■ *How to Observe*

You may be a participant observer or a non-participant observer. If you are a non-participant observer, you may observe the situation directly by being physically present) or indirectly by viewing a videotape or listening to an audiotape of an event. A "participant observer" is involved in the activities that are being observed. For instance, your supervisor might ask you to participate in the deposition of a witness. The supervisor might ask you to take notes, evaluate the witness, and assist with the documents that will be shown to the witness during the deposition. This will provide an excellent opportunity for observation, but as a participant your ability to observe is constrained. Some constraints are physical; you cannot give your full attention to the tasks assigned to you and at the same time take detailed descriptive notes on the deposition. Other constraints are ethical; your obligation to perform the tasks assigned to you will limit your ability to concentrate on your personal learning goals.

As a non-participant observer, you may have fewer physical limitations on your ability to conduct your observations, but ethical constraints are still present. You may need special permission to observe some situations, for example an in-camera conference among the judge and attorneys. Your ability to report on your observations may be restricted, even if you have the necessary permission to observe. For example, your supervisor might invite you to sit in on a client interview just to observe. You have the necessary permission to observe, but you cannot report some of what you learn from your observation to third persons because you must protect the confidences and secrets of the client. When you are a non-participant observer, you want to be close enough to the action to hear the words spoken and to see the facial expressions and body postures of the actors, but not so close as to interfere with what is going on because they can see your facial expressions and body posture. Even the fact that you are taking notes will make some people nervous, so you may have to take notes unobtrusively or rely on memory and make notes after the observation.

Whether you are a participant or non-participant observer, you may want to interview some of the people you observed to clarify and deepen your understanding of the event you observed. For example, suppose you observed closing arguments in a non-jury trial. You made extensive notes and gave some thought to what elements of each argument you thought were effective or ineffective. After the judgment is entered, you might try to interview the judge, both counsel, the clients, the court clerk, or others about their perceptions of the effectiveness of the arguments. You might learn how the arguments affected the decision maker, what each attorney's goals were for her argument, and whether and how those goals were achieved. You can compare and contrast the perceptions of several participants with your own to more fully understand the event.

■ *When to Observe*

If your observation is part of a course, your instructor may impose a deadline. Schedule your observations well in advance of the deadline for turning in a written report to allow sufficient time to reflect on the observation, draft the report, and revise it. Your own schedule and other commitments will limit your ability to schedule observations. Your biorhythms also may influence the timing of your observations. If you are a morning person, you may want to schedule your observations before noon. If you need to observe a specific individual performing a task, then your observations will need to be timed to coincide with the time of performance by that individual. On the other hand, if you plan to observe a situation in which there are many actors, the timing of your observation may depend on such things as when the most actors are present, when the most representative sample of actors or events are present for observation, whether there is a need for repeated observations, and so on.

Recording Observations

Without some effective way to record your observations, the exercise, though perhaps entertaining, will be of minimal value as a learning experience. Our memories are too unreliable for anything more than general observations. You can use one or more of the following techniques to assist in recording your observations.

- **Narrative description** involves writing down what the observer saw and heard as field notes and then constructing a narrative report using the field notes to recall detail.

- **Time samples** are used to record information that is being observed at regular intervals. Through a time sample, you can take verbal snapshots of a subject's behavior over the course of the observation. To do this type of recording, write a short description early in the event, then wait a period of time and write another short description of the same subject: a witness; a juror; a party in the negotiation; the participants in a public hearing. Such snippets of description, when put together, will give you a relatively complete record of the observation without the need to be taking notes constantly.

- **Checklists** contain a series of behaviors the observer expects to see during the observation. The observer may want to note the frequency over time the subject performs the behavior. For example, how many times does an attorney object during the deposition, and what are the kinds of objections? In a negotiation session, you might record features of the interactions between the negotiators such as whether or not they maintained eye contact, whether questions were answered directly or the respondent seemed evasive, and the patterns of offer and counter offer. Post-session reflection on your observations should enable you to better understand what each negotiator did that was effective and what might have been counterproductive to a successful outcome.

- **Interaction reports** record what subjects say or do to each other. You might select one person as the focus of the observation and record everything the subject says or does for a specified time period.

- **Rating scales** require the observer to rate behavior, generally on the basis of frequency, for example, from always to never, along a continuum of values. One common practice is to evaluate conduct like eye contact or verbal habits: how often a negotiator looks away from or straight at the other negotiator; how often an advocate shows a verbal tic, like saying "ummm" or "Clearly . . . ." Another example could be trying to observe how effectively advocacy is organized by tracking when and how a speaker returns to a core theme.

Each of these techniques has strengths and weaknesses. For example, a time sample might require recording fewer events than an interaction report but would not generate as much data. Checklists may be easy to use if the behaviors being recorded are not complex, but they risk missing important interactions or events not clearly included on the checklist. Interaction reports provide very detailed data of the interaction being observed but require constant attention and very precise note-taking techniques. Rating scales have some of the same advantages as checklists but suffer from the same limitations. In addition, rating scales frequently add room for error through inter-rater inconsistencies. The technique or techniques you choose to use will depend on a number of factors, but most important are the intended use of the data and the amount of time you have to prepare for the observation.

In most cases you will use narrative description to record your observations contemporaneously or as soon after the observation as possible. Each narrative description may contain a number of features that can be noticed in the situation you are observing. Ethnologist James P. Spradley listed the following dimensions of observation in his book PARTICIPANT OBSERVATION (1980):

- **space**—the physical place or places where the observation occurs;

- **object**—the physical things that are present and used by the actors who are being observed;

- **actors**—the people involved; this may include the principals being observed and others who are present;

- **act**—single actions the actors being observed do;

- **activity**—a set of related acts the actors do;

- **event**—a set of related activities the actors carry out;

- **time**—the sequencing of the events over time;

- **goal**—the things actors are trying to accomplish; and

- **feeling**—the emotions felt by the observer and expressed by the actors and others present in the space.

Here is a sample narrative written by Spradley. In this excerpt from a set of field notes, Spradley describes the presentation of a witness to a grand jury on which he sat. Spradley first sets the scene in the grand jury where the members of the grand jury sat quietly waiting for the prosecuting attorney to begin. After searching through his files, the prosecuting attorney selected one file and then addressed the members of the grand jury.

> *"I've got two cases to present this morning. I'll have to rush. We have ten witnesses." He spoke fast and conveyed a strong impression that we would have to move quickly throughout the morning.*

> *"This is a case of felonious theft by retention. It means retaining property of at least $2500, retail market value on the date of the offense. Here is a summary of the case. One day in July a van was broken into and a revolver was stolen. Then later there was another robbery of stereo equipment from a stereo store. The police, making an investigation of a house, recovered the revolver, three Pioneer receivers, one Teac tape deck, two JBL speakers. There were three people in the house at the time, and the police found the prints of one of them on some of the stereo equipment."*

> *The prosecuting attorney spoke rapidly, and when he came to this point he looked up at a clerical assistant and motioned to him. He got up and left the grand jury room. I looked at the people on the grand jury and they were now whispering to each other, all looked very interested.*

> *"We now have our first witness," the prosecuting attorney said as the clerk returned with a middle-aged man dressed in a blue business suit. [The clerk seats the witness and administered the oath and the prosecuting attorney begins his examination of the witness.]*

> *"What is your name?" the prosecuting attorney asked. "Bob Johnson." "Would you spell your name and give your address?" "B-O-B J-O-H-N-S-O-N, 42 East Alder, Center City."*

> *"On July 14 did you report a theft?"*

"Yes, a .38 Colt was stolen from my van. I had purchased it in February of 1972, paid $118 for it. At the time I worked for the Center City Police Department and I have a permit to carry the revolver."

"As of July 10, do you have any opinion about the retail value of the .38 Colt?"

"Yes, about $140, because it had gone up about $20 more than the purchase price."

The prosecuting attorney turned abruptly to the grand jury and asked: "Any questions?" He paused for a total of three seconds, turned to the witness, and said, "Okay" and the clerk quickly ushered him out of the grand jury room.

This incident, and others he observed, led Spradley to reflect on the prosecutor's emphasis on speeding up the process of presenting cases to the grand jury. He sought to understand how the prosecutor sped things up, including techniques the prosecutor used to keep the jurors from asking questions and ways to hurry witnesses in delivering their testimony. He also noted events that can slow down the process, hindering the prosecutor's quest for speed. There are other reflections one might make as well. The prosecutor seemed to be skilled in moving the proceedings along. But is justice being properly served when the members of the grand jury are not encouraged to ask questions they might have of the witness and indeed seem to be discouraged from doing so? Is that proper?

> **Exercise 4.2** Review the excerpt and see how many of the items on Spradley's list you can identify in his recorded observation. Spradley's observation of the grand jury process was unplanned. Because he was called to grand jury duty like any other citizen, presumably, he did not set out with a research agenda to study a grand jury. Because of his training and interests, however, he was able to apply his skills of observation and analysis to a situation in which he found himself. As you become more skilled in observation, you also will be able to find more learning opportunities in unplanned events.

Because you cannot transcribe everything that occurs during an observation, detailed note taking is critical. Especially when you are a participant observer, your notes may be quite condensed. You can prepare for note taking by creating a template containing the nine dimensions described above with space near each dimension label for notes about it. The notes themselves may be no more than single descriptive words or short phrases that capture the observation. These can jog your memory when you later write an expanded narrative account of your observation. For example, if you were observing a pretrial conference in the judge's chambers, your notes might look like this:

- **actors**—Judge Brown, attorney Smith, attorney Jones, reporter, clerk

- **activities**—welcoming, setting tone, describing process, clarifying, giving instructions, outlining, cajoling

What you record depends on what you want to observe.

When possible, record conversations verbatim, especially when your goals include studying your subject's rhetoric. Use concrete descriptive words. Avoid generalization and characterization. For example, instead of saying the attorney appeared to be late for another appointment, record what she said about her schedule, such as, "she glanced at her watch repeatedly during the observation, and that she hurried from the room." Instead of saying the witness appeared nervous, identify the specific observations that led you to that conclusion. "The witness sweated profusely throughout the cross-examination, his eyes darted around the room, and he gripped the sides of his chair so hard his knuckles whitened." The key to recording data for later analysis is to expand, fill out, enlarge, and give specific detail. You can add interpretations of it later. Condensed notes should be expanded into a fuller account as soon as possible after the observation ends. Any delay in recording leads inevitably to a decrease in the details that can be recalled.

■ Reflection on Observation

The final stage in the observation cycle is reflection. In thinking about what you saw, refocus some attention on your learning goals and objectives. Reflection should lead to deeper, more complex learning about a skill, an event, or a system. It also can lead to asking more precise questions and making more focused observations. How completely you examine, analyze, and critique your observations can substantially determine how much real learning you will gain from your externship.

We recommend that some of your reflection on observation be done in writing, through the use of journals or reflection papers. The exercise of committing your reflections to paper permits you to write to learn. Perhaps you have had the experience of being asked to write on a topic about which you thought you had little to say (like an unexpected exam question), only to find that as you began to outline an answer, you were able to write your way to a good response. The process of writing focused your attention and assisted your recall of what you knew about the topic. Similarly, writing your condensed notes into an expanded version will trigger memories from your observation and provide more data for analysis and interpretation. As you review the material, you will perceive new connections. Rewriting your expanded notes into a journal entry or reflection paper provides an additional opportunity to recall more detail and to begin to analyze and interpret the data from which insights will occur.

Interpretation of data is never value free. As you try to learn from your observations, it is useful to try to check yourself frequently to try to avoid misinterpretation. If you have read Chapter 5 on communication, you will be aware that separating out your perceptions from your interpretations requires vigilance and lots of practice. Three areas for particular vigilance include observer bias, non-representativeness of the observation, and errors introduced by the mere fact that the subjects know they are being observed.

■ *Observer Bias*

As an observer you may have prejudged in some fashion the actors or events you will observe. For example, assume you have chosen to observe a particular defense attorney engage in plea negotiations with the prosecutor. You have been told this particular defense attorney frequently engages in conduct that is questionable ethically. Because of this information you may filter your observations of the attorney's conduct through a fine mesh that assumes unethical conduct when, in fact, none may be present.

A halo effect is a lingering effect of a particularly strong positive or negative reaction to something that occurs. It causes the observer to interpret more of the data from the observation favorably or unfavorably than is justified. Suppose you encounter one of your professors in the checkout line at the grocery store. The professor does not acknowledge your presence, even though you brush elbows as you set your purchases down. If you know this particular professor to be good-naturedly absentminded, you may attribute his failure to greet you to this idiosyncrasy, rather than to an attitude that students do not exist outside the classroom. The professor gets the benefit of your previous knowledge of the professor's personality.

Your interpretation also may be biased if the limits on your own frame of reference hamper your ability to appreciate fully what was observed. We have all had an experience in which what we thought we heard turned out to be quite different from what was actually said. Our minds try to make sense out of imperfectly perceived data and sometimes produce a logical, but inaccurate, picture of the actual communication. Suppose you just came out of a class during which you were engaged in a heated, yet friendly, debate with another student. In the hallway you overhear the student saying to a classmate your name and the word "unreasonable." You might assume the student was telling your classmate that you were being unreasonable during the debate. In fact, the student may have said, "knowing that's her position really makes me think twice; I have never found her to be unreasonable."

■ *Non-Representative Generalizations*

Another significant source of interpretive error is the effect of making generalizations from a small or non-representative data set. You probably would not make a career decision on the basis of the recommendation of a single family friend. Likewise, you should be cautious about drawing conclusions about actors, events, or systems from limited observations. Assume you are an extern in a government agency. You have chosen to investigate whether the agency is fulfilling its designated mission. During your observation of the work of the agency, you notice that a number of the staff attorneys leave their desks and go into a nearby conference room to talk and drink coffee. You wonder whether the attorneys are conducting personal business during work hours and neglecting their work. This interpretation may be correct, or it may reflect observer prejudgment. Perhaps you believe lawyers who work for the government do not work very hard. This may lead you to assume because coffee is being consumed, no work is being done. Even if the lawyers were gossiping and not working, you may have observed an atypical event and assumed it to be common.

What are some other examples of misinterpretation from a small or non-representative data set? Let us assume you come into the office a bit earlier than usual one morning and see a secretary making coffee you know everyone in the office will drink throughout the day. Based on this single observation, you may assume the secretary in this organization, being the low person in the hierarchy, is tasked with making coffee for everyone else. It may be the case, however, that the task of making coffee is rotated among the entire staff, including the attorneys, and on the day you observed the secretary making coffee it was simply his turn.

Similarly, you are scheduled to interview at a government agency at 4:00 p.m. on a Friday. When you arrive you notice that half of the attorney offices are unoccupied and dark. You may assume these government lawyers left early because it is Friday afternoon. The fact may be, however, that the occupants of the empty offices are on flextime and scheduled to work from 7:30 a.m. to 3:30 p.m.

■ *Subject Awareness of Observation*

You also should be cognizant that your subject's awareness of your observations may cause the subject to alter the behavior you are planning to observe so it is no longer typical. It is not uncommon for someone engaged in a task to alter the performance of the task when the person knows someone is observing. Performance could be enhanced; the subject might prepare more carefully to avoid errors that might otherwise be caused by inattention. Performance could be diminished; the subject's anxiety might disrupt the activity.

If it is important that the behavior you observe be unaffected by the subject's awareness, you will need to conduct unobtrusive observations or multiple observations of the behavior so the observation's effectiveness is not diminished by familiarity or a sense of trust between you and the subject.

Repeated observations greatly reduce the odds that the data are non-representative. Also, you can test the reliability of your observations by comparing them with those of others observing the same event. There may be possibilities for this in your externship seminar if several students observe the same event, record their observations, and compare the results.

Through a technique called triangulation, you can attempt to confirm your observations through informant interviews involving multiple perspectives and through the collection and use of artifacts (e.g., documents, pictures, physical objects) employed in the situation observed. Just as scientists can locate any spot on the surface of the earth by recording the point of intersection of the data streams from three satellites in high earth orbit, the technique of triangulation in reflective observation allows the observer to make interpretations more accurately than is possible from data drawn from only one perspective.

For example, a person in an appellate court judicial externship may wish to observe oral arguments in order to study how lawyers respond to the questions from the panel of judges. The extern could confer with the judge and her clerk before an argument and let them know the focus of the planned observation. After the argument, the three of them, judge, clerk, and extern, could share their observations of how the lawyers responded to questions from the bench and reflect on what was effective and what was not. By inviting the judge's and clerk's observations, the extern has two additional perspectives on the same event on which to base her reflections. If the court is one that records oral arguments, the audio or videotape of the argument may be another source of information that can be used during further post-event analysis and reflection.

Ethical Issues

Any activity involving interaction among lawyers and third parties may involve ethical conflicts. The observation by law students of lawyers at work is no exception.

Through observation you may become more sensitive to the ethical issues that arise in the situations you are observing and in relation to your role as observer. Watch for examples of the problems described as you learn through observation of lawyers at work.

See also Chapters 10–13 on ethical issues including confidentiality and conflicts of interest

■ *Confidentiality*

When you act as a participant observer, be aware of your obligation to protect the confidences and secrets of the clients on whose behalf you are working. Although you are not yet a lawyer and may not be subject to formal sanction by the licensing authority in your jurisdiction, your supervisor and the firm or organization for whom you work may be subject to sanctions if you fail to protect the confidences and secrets of clients. Moreover, you may jeopardize your admission to the bar if you fail to act in a professionally responsible manner. Before you share with others what you have learned from observation, consider whether your report would violate the client's trust. If you are observing otherwise private lawyer-client interactions, but you are not part of the lawyer's firm, your presence could effectively result in a waiver of the attorney-client privilege for communications between the lawyer and the client.

■ *Conflicts of Interest—Observer vs. Student-Lawyer*

Whenever you work on behalf of an externship placement, you provide service to the client or organization and provide a learning opportunity for yourself. At times these dual purposes may conflict. Consider this example: You have been asked to assist your supervising attorney with a meeting with lawyers from another firm as well as the client in a large real estate transaction. You are to assist in handling the documents that will be used during the meeting, take notes, and observe the general demeanor and credibility of the lawyers from the other law firm involved in the deal. This is the first client meeting you have ever attended, and you want to be able to make a detailed observation of the entire event. You want to be attentive to all of the dimensions of the observation opportunity, including space, objects, actors, acts, activities, event, goals, time, and feelings to learn as much as possible about handling a client meeting with a big corporate client. In this situation, your first obligation is to the client on whose behalf you are participating in the meeting. Therefore, you must subordinate your personal learning objectives to the discharge of your assigned tasks. This is not to say you should jettison completely your personal learning objectives. Because part of your assigned role is to observe the lawyers from the other firm, you probably can observe and record other features of the event at the same time without jeopardizing the client's interests. Unless your supervising attorneys asks for your recorded observations, you may never report your additional observations to because your observations are tangential to your assignment. You may simply use them for further reflection and learning.

On some occasions you might ask to observe persons or events even when you will not produce a product for the externship. For example, assume you have helped your supervisor prepare for the deposition of a witness. Observing the actual deposition would further your learning objectives, but your supervisor has not assigned you any responsibilities that would require you to attend. If permission is granted for you to attend, the balance between producing work for the externship and satisfying your personal learning objectives shifts markedly toward your objectives for the time you spend observing the deposition.

Some of your observations, done by you solely for your benefit, also could be made available to your supervisor who might learn useful things from them. I remember sitting in on a deposition for which I had helped collect documents that would be used when questioning the witness. I had no actual role or duties in the deposition so I was free to observe and learn from the attorneys. During a break in the questioning, I was able to share with my supervisor an observation I had made of the demeanor of the witness. I thought the witness, although an employee of the opposing party, was trying to be helpful to my supervisor who was questioning him, but the aggressive nature of the questioning was causing the witness to begin to hold back. After the break, my supervisor softened his tone and the witness again became more forthcoming.

In addition to the special ethical issues raised by the role of participant observer, there are other more general ethical issues you must consider when doing any type of field observation. Perhaps the foremost consideration in any observation is concern for the privacy interests of those observed. Before you share your observations with your externship teacher or classmates in your externship seminar, consider the privacy interests of the participants in any setting you observe. The more public the setting, such as an in-court observation of litigation not involving juveniles, the less of an expectation of privacy the participants will have. As you move your observations into a more private space, such as the meeting rooms of the organization for which you are doing your externship, the expectation of privacy by the participants in the settings you observe increases dramatically. The concern for the privacy interests of the participants should lead you to consider whether information, such as names, identifying characteristics, criminal charges, or relevant strategy issues about the participants or the setting should be withheld or changed in any report you make to third persons about your observations. Even if client confidentiality is not an issue because of the nature of the setting and events being observed, it is still worth considering the appropriateness of revealing specific information the participants may themselves consider private or confidential.

In any situation where you conduct an observation anonymously, consider whether you need special permission. Disclose your presence and your purposes for observation where possible. Although disclosure may cause participants to be more self-conscious and to change their behavior in response to your observation, disclosure will be critical if your presence or activities are looked into for some reason such as an inquiry into whether your presence resulted in the waiver of the attorney-client privilege for matters discussed during a meeting with the client. Participants will be less likely to feel that they were spied upon.

As ethical questions surface during preparation for your observations and during the observations, you are encouraged to share your concerns with your externship teacher and, when appropriate, with your supervising attorneys and resolve fully your concerns before you proceed.

Exercise 4.3 In order to prepare for field observation, take a few minutes to do one or more of the following observation exercises, and then reflect on your observations in your journal. Your journal entry should not merely be a rewriting or an expansion of the contemporaneous notes you took during the observation, even though you will find that you are adding detail to your notes as you revisit the observation. Your entry should contain a record of the experiences, ideas, concerns, mistakes, insights, and problems that arise during field observation. Use your journal to reflect on the personal side of externship, including your reactions to the persons and events you observe and your perceptions of the feelings of others.

- Observe a person engaged in an activity for two minutes. Take notes about as many dimensions of the situation as you can. Expand your notes into a narrative description of what you have just observed.

- Observe two persons interacting for five minutes. Take notes about as many dimensions of the situation as you can. Expand your notes into a narrative description of what you have just observed.

- Write a detailed description of a physical space (classroom, faculty office, attorney's office) you were in recently. After writing the description, return to the same room and conduct an observation. This time take notes of your observations. Expand your notes into a narrative description of what you have just observed. Compare and contrast the two descriptions.

- Pair yourself with a classmate and watch a short segment of a film or conduct a two-to-five minute observation of a situation. Compare and contrast your observations. What did your classmate observe that you did not? What did you observe that your classmate did not? What did each of you record the other did not? What might explain the differences in what was observed and what was recorded? If you are watching a film, first watch it with the sound muted and record your observations, then watch it again with the sound on. What were the differences you noted from each viewing?

An externship typically offers many rich and varied opportunities to observe the work of lawyers and legal organizations from which a great deal of learning may be derived, whether you are observing as a participant or a non-participant observer. Using the externship to refine your skills of observation and reflection will pay benefits throughout the rest of your career in the law. It is the nature of law and law practice that change is ever present, and you will continue to learn new information, skills, and practices as you move from novice to journeyman to skilled lawyer. By becoming a skilled observer you will have mastered one set of tools that you will continue to use as a life-long learner in the law.

FURTHER RESOURCES

Daniel Newman, Legal Aid Lawyers and the Quest for Justice (2013). This book examines the state of access to criminal justice in Great Britain by considering the health of the lawyer-client relationship under legal aid. In the largest study of its kind for some two decades, ethnographic fieldwork is used to gain a fresh perspective upon the interaction that lies at the heart of the criminal justice system's guarantee of a fair trial. The research produces two contradictory messages; in interviews, lawyers claim a positive relationship with their clients, while under participant observation there emerges the opposite reality. The lawyers treat their clients with wanton disrespect: making fun of them, talking over them, and pushing them to plead guilty despite protestations to the contrary.

Greg Guest et al., Collecting Qualitative Data: A Field Manual for Applied Research (2013). This book is designed for researchers and provides a practical and step-by-step guide to collecting and managing qualitative data. Although you are unlikely to be acting as a researcher in your externship placement, Chapter Three—Participant Observation—provides a good primer on some of the topics discussed in this chapter. Chapter Three is available online at http://www.sagepub.com/upm-data/48454_ch_3.pdf.

JAMES P. SPRADLEY, PARTICIPANT OBSERVATION (1980). Although first published in 1980, Spradley's book remains a classic text in the field of ethnography. It is written in an accessible style that makes it as useful to the novice as it is to the expert.

Susan D. Bennett, *"No relief but upon the terms of coming into the house" — Controlled Spaces, Invisible Disentitlements, and Homelessness in an Urban Shelter System,* 104 YALE L.J. 2157 (1995). The article was written from data collected by a group of community activists and law students who spent time in the waiting room of a municipal office that provided emergency shelter and support services to homeless persons. The observers were present to provide basic information and assistance to homeless families applying for overnight shelter and to note how these families were being treated in the application process.

Barbara Bezdek, *Silence in the Court: Participation and Subordination of Poor Tenants' Voices in Legal Proces*s, 20 HOFSTRA L. REV. 533 (1992). The article describes a court-watching project by law students. The students observed interactions among litigants, attorneys, and court personnel in landlord-tenant court.

Council for Court Excellence, *Community Observation of the United States District Court For the District of Columbia* (Aug. 2004). This publication reports the findings and recommendations of the Council for Court Excellence's third Court Community Observers Project. Appendix II contains a sample court observation form. The document is available on the Council's website: http://www.courtexcellence.org/uploads/publications/2004USDistCtFinalReport.pdf.

DC Coalition Against Domestic Violence, *DC Court Watch* (2006). This document reports on a project in which trained volunteers observed Civil Protection Order hearings in D.C. Superior Court's Domestic Violence Unit from January 2006 through September 2006. Data from 349 cases was collected on an instrument created for the project. The report (and the instrument) is available at http://dcsafe.org/wp-content/uploads/2010/10/Court_Watch_Report_Apr072.pdf.

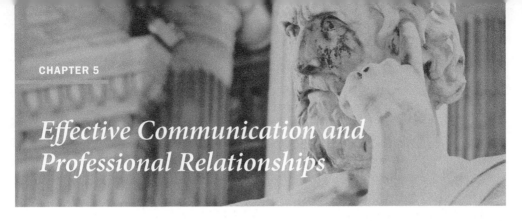

CHAPTER 5

Effective Communication and Professional Relationships

SUSAN L. BROOKS & INGA N. LAURENT

Communication is an act of courage

—Meg Wheatley

*When we change the way we communicate,
we change society*

—Clay Shirky

Introduction: Why Study Communication?

Effective communication with clients isn't something that most lawyers give much thought. And this trend starts in law school, where the focus tends to be on substantive law and legal theory. If communication is even mentioned, it's in the context of oral argument to the court or written memos of law. The importance of clear communication with clients isn't often discussed and the techniques for doing so are rarely fodder for classroom discussion or CLEs. And that's a damn shame, since in the absence of clear communication, lawyer-client relationships tend to disintegrate rapidly[1]

Most lawyers spend a lot of their time communicating, so whether or not they succeed in their work depends largely on the effectiveness of their communication. If you accept this premise, it may not surprise you that many of the topics covered in this book are linked to effective communication. Some have obvious connections, such as giving oral presentations. See Chapter 18 on Making Presentations. Yet, if you think about the many ways communication plays a role in your day-to-day life as an extern, you will realize that communication also includes giving and getting feedback from supervisors, navigating cultural differences, dealing with bias, working with clients, collaborating with others and working in teams, forming your professional identity, and achieving well-being. (See Chapters 3, 6, 7, 15, 16, 24, and 25 respectively.)

In this chapter, we approach communication with a broad lens by focusing on how you can use communication to create, sustain, and improve professional relationships. These ideas also will help you when faced with confusing or difficult moments that may arise in your placements, whether they occur with a supervising attorney, a co-worker, a client, a judge, a witness, an opposing counsel, or any other person you work with in the community.

Our approach to communication focuses on building relationships rather than viewing communication adversarially, as lawyers often do. Most law students have been exposed to communication in terms of how to be persuasive in making an oral argument or how to out-maneuver an opponent in a cross examination. This chapter envisions communication as a positive set of tools and techniques that can lead to more effective and successful accomplishments in your externship and in your future legal career, including, of course, work with clients. While the communication approach presented in this chapter may not address every issue that arises while doing legal work, if you take these practices to heart, they will help you navigate many of the challenges that arise in your externship and in your future professional life, and they will likely enhance your personal life as well.

> **Exercise 5.1** Choose a context in your placement where a lot of communication takes place. Envision the many ways that communication can occur there. Who is communicating? What is their tone of voice? Are they communicating solely with words? What is their body language? Now imagine a different legal setting where you have witnessed communication. How is the communication different in this setting?

As you consider communication with this wide scope in mind, you will find many resources created for lawyers, including books, websites, blogs, YouTube videos, commercial products, and workshops, such as those providing continuing legal education. The vast resources that are available to lawyers regarding communication reinforce the idea that communication is important and is a skill that can be improved. To analogize, consider what it means to learn the set of skills of direct examination. First, you need to know the underlying purposes of and concepts behind direct examination, which might include reading about different methods and their relation to theories of trial practice, and watching experienced lawyers' direct examinations. You then practice the skill and work to improve your technique through repetition and also through your own reflection and feedback from others.

Becoming more effective at the skill of building relationships through communication takes commitment and practice. While some of the ideas expressed here may appear simple, they are not necessarily easy to incorporate into your interactions with others, especially in tense or awkward situations. As you gain a more conscious approach to communication, you can begin to appreciate the choices you have in critical moments and try out new ways of responding. Over time, these new ways of responding will become a more natural part of your repertoire.

Roadmap for This Chapter

In this chapter, we discuss communication in a variety of ways, starting with foundational knowledge. First, we define communication and provide a brief historical overview. Next, we describe the various components of communication, including both verbal and nonverbal communication. In the second part of the chapter, we focus on how you can use communication to transform your relationships with others and at the same time gain greater self-awareness. We begin this section by describing how to combine the ingredients of an interaction into a dialogue. In the final part of the chapter, we provide specific guidance on applying these ideas to help navigate challenging conversations in your externship and beyond. The chapter includes questions and exercises throughout to help you process difficult concepts and practice the building blocks of effective communication.

QUESTION TO CONSIDER

What have you noticed/learned/experienced about communication during your externship so far?

Defining Communication

Here are a few standard definitions of communication:

WEBSTER'S DICTIONARY defines communication as "the act or process of using words, sounds, signs, or behaviors to express or exchange information or to express your ideas, thoughts, feelings, etc., to someone else." The OXFORD DICTIONARY defines it as "the imparting or exchanging of information . . . ."

While these definitions show that the act of communication can take many forms, they both describe communication as an exchange of information. You transmit information to me, and I transmit information to you, much like a tennis ball bouncing back and forth. In this chapter, we ask you to take a different, more relational view of communication. Communication is not talking at each other. Rather, communication is something we create together, and in doing so we can generate new ideas and possibilities, including strengthening our relationship.

Here is another definition of communication closer to this chapter's approach from the book COMMUNICATING EFFECTIVELY: "[A]ny process in which people, through the use of symbols, verbally and/or nonverbally, consciously or not consciously, intentionally or unintentionally generate meanings (information, ideas, feelings, and perceptions) within and across various contexts, cultures, channels and media." [2] As you read this chapter, we invite you to consider communication as a process that has many layers and dimensions, and we encourage you to use these tools to make more intentional choices about communication.

THE ASCENT OF COMMUNICATIONS MAN

A Quick History of Human Communication and Language

As is often said, we cannot move forward without an understanding of where we have been. The capacity for language is one of the most, if not the most, fundamental features of humanity; without it, humanity would not have evolved. Around 200,000 years ago, we lived a nomadic lifestyle among predators and prey that were often faster and stronger than we were.

Our survival depended on our ability to work collectively to outmaneuver other species. Language evolved to meet this need. Mark Pagel, a noted linguist, explains that language "is a piece of social technology for enhancing the benefits of cooperation, for reaching agreements, striking deals, and for coordinating our actions."[3] Language enabled us to become the dominant species through the coordination of action, collectively and across time. For an expanded version of the "History of Communication," take a look at this TED talk: http://www.ted.com/talks/mark_pagel_how_language_transformed_humanity

We communicate with others within our own communities, and, increasingly, we are able to communicate globally, transcending spatial, language, and cultural barriers that have existed for millennia. Some communication experts believe we are living at a critical juncture in time. The alphabet was the first major transformation, and the second was the printing press. The third has been the creation of electronic language.[4] Within the span of only a few generations, technological development of the telephone, radio, television, film, computers, cell phones, and the internet have altered the world dramatically.[5]

Understanding the important role language has played and will continue to serve in human development provides an impetus for learning how to use language and communication more intentionally and thus more effectively. Given the importance of communication to collaborative efforts, we turn next to examining communication from the standpoint of how the choices we make in a given conversation help shape our relationships. To do so, we will study the component parts of an interaction.

The Ingredients of an Interaction

By becoming more conscious of the elements of human interaction, we can slow down the process and make conscious choices in critical moments. In this section, imagine what a conversation would look like if you could observe it in slow motion and periodically freeze the frame. This slow motion analysis highlights the choice points that exist at each turn, allowing us to notice what is occurring and interrupt behaviors that get in the way of what we are trying to achieve in a particular conversation. This ability to notice and make well-informed choices will help equip us to create more positive relationships.

The core ingredients of an interaction are the following:

- Context,

- Intention,

- Perception,

- Interpretation,

- Feelings/Feelings About Feelings,

- Action.

Below is a visual depiction of the operation of these six ingredients when two people are interacting. The chapter then takes up a detailed description of the first five ingredients. Action, what people actually do, is essentially the sum of these five. An important dimension of action that falls outside of the other ingredients is non-verbal communication, which is also discussed in detail.

In the following graphic, each large circle represents a person in an interaction. Notice that most of the ingredients on each side are "swimming" in the circle that represents "context." Between the two people is a figurative "bridge" that represents the shared space they can create if they enter into a dialogue.[6]

Connection & Awareness with Communication

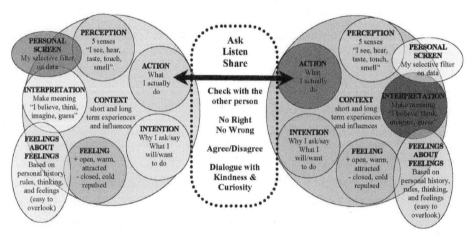

Adapted by Cathy and Ernie McNally from communication models developed by Bennet Wong, Jock McKeen, and Virginia Satir

This next section provides more detailed descriptions of the core ingredients, using two different field-placement scenarios as illustrations.

■ *Scenario #1*

A Federal District Court Judge is supervising the externship of a third-year student. The student's first assignment is to summarize the opposing parties' motions into a short memo to help prepare the Judge for the parties' oral argument on the motion. A few hours after the student turns in the assignment, the Judge pulls the student aside in the hallway and says "Listen, I want to say something to you about that memo. So, this is a good attempt, but you really need to focus more on brevity. Okay? Thanks. I need to run. We'll talk more later."

This interaction might sound like a simple and straightforward bit of feedback from a judge to a law student. At the same time, there are complex webs surrounding both parties that affect the judge's comment as well as how the student hears, interprets, and acts based upon the information he has just received.

Context

Context means all the influences that affect who we are in the present moment. These influences can include our family, neighborhood, community, and culture, as well as multiple identities reflected in the roles we play personally and professionally. At any given moment, a particular aspect may be more prominent, meaning that we are more conscious of its impact on the present. At other times, context can influence the moment quietly; its presence affects us without our knowing it.

In Scenario #1, imagine the student is a 24-year-old male who lost his father at an early age and looks up to the Judge as a mentor and father figure. Now imagine instead the student is a 40-year-old female, who has had another successful career prior to attending law school. Alternatively, what if instead the judge were female or 32 years old and the youngest on the bench? What about a judge and an extern who have different ethnic or racial backgrounds? A judge who was formerly a partner at a law firm compared with someone who was a former professor or maybe a public interest lawyer? For example, if we were to assume a twenty-something Latino male student and a very senior Latino judge whom the student admires and identifies with as a father figure, it is possible that the judge's remarks would be taken as more critical by the student, and the remarks might negatively affect the student's overall self-perception. This situation might play out very differently with that same judge if the student were older and had had a successful prior career or perhaps did not identify so strongly with the judge. Another way context might make a difference is even more immediate: maybe the student is having a bad day for personal reasons or is elated at having just received a permanent job offer. Maybe the judge is in the midst of a hectic week or is extremely tired.

In short, the student's immediate situation, age, sex, gender, ethnic and racial background, as well as similar aspects of the judge's situation and background, will influence how each of them participates in the communication and also how each interprets what has taken place in a given interaction. Developing a greater appreciation of our own context and learning about the context of others can help create deeper and more meaningful conversations that can lead to shared understandings. Conversely, ignoring another person's context or assuming information about that person's context, such as that it is the same or similar to our own, can lead to misunderstandings that impede relationship-building. For more on understanding how an understanding of context can help, see Chapter 6 on Navigating Cultural Difference.

> **Exercise 5.2** Draw a daisy with petals or a wheel with the hub at the center and spokes emanating from the hub. Now put the word "me" in the middle, and on each petal or spoke, write down some of the different contexts or roles you can identify when you think of yourself in law school and in your externship at the present moment. Similar to a daisy or a wheel, some petals or spokes will be more at the forefront and others will be further back. As you look at the various contexts in your current situation, which ones do you think are more prominent for you right now in your life? Which are less prominent? Consider which contexts seem to be within your control and which seem to be outside of your control? Are there any contexts you might be able to change or focus on differently to make your externship more successful?

Intention

Intentions are the often unspoken thoughts that underlie our words and actions. Sometimes when we speak our intentions may not be all that clear, even to ourselves. To improve communication, it is important to be clear with ourselves about our own intentions. It also may be helpful to share our intentions with the other person. This idea of stating our intentions out loud may be especially helpful when we think we need to say something that is likely to be hard for the other person to hear. If we begin by stating genuinely that our intention is, for instance, to do a better job at work or to be able to complete a particular task, then it may help the listener, for instance, a supervising attorney, to listen more openly.

Building positive relationships with others starts from positive or constructive intentions: "good will" or "generosity of spirit." Generosity of spirit has been defined as "living life from the inside out" and engaging others with an open mind. When these qualities are lacking, we often become mired in petty details, arguing about the exact words that were spoken. If your genuine intentions are less positive, for example if either of you is already angry, you may want to wait until another time for a conversation. Timing matters. On the other hand, there may be situations in which you choose to communicate in the midst of conflict. The important thing is to make intentional choices. Good will and disagreement can co-exist. In many legal situations there are good intentions on both sides and yet the parties' positions are far apart. As long as both parties approach the situation with good will, they may well be able to identify some shared interests, even if they are unable to resolve all of their differences.

With respect to the externship student and judge, consider how the conversation in Scenario #1 might have gone differently had the judge stated his intentions to the student in this way. "I'd like to give you some quick feedback about your writing. The thing is, I really want to help you progress from being a good writer to being a truly excellent writer, which I know you can be. I see a lot of potential in you—you remind me a bit of myself when I was a law student. I wish someone had taken the time to give me this kind of pointer." If then the judge had made the same remark about the need for the student's writing to be more succinct, the student likely would have had an easier time receiving the feedback.

Perception and Interpretation

Perception is the raw data: what you can observe or notice with your senses. By contrast, interpretation is what you make of perceptions: the story you construct from the data you receive. Perceptions and interpretations are "velcroed" together. Typically, we move rapidly and unconsciously from the raw data to the story we are telling ourselves to make sense of that data. For example, if you see flowers on a colleague's desk, you might jump to many different interpretations: it is her birthday, or maybe it is her anniversary, meaning she must be married, or she is newly dating someone, or a partner at the law office gave them to her for doing a good job on a case, or she just likes flowers. These interpretations will be influenced by other perceptions as well as other elements of the interaction, such as context. For instance, does she have flowers on her desk frequently, or is this the first time? What kind of flowers are they? Do you know anything else about her personal life, the status of her cases, or other aspects of her work-life? To be more effective in communicating, we need to work to become more aware of the transition from perception to interpretation. In other words, we can aim to separate what we perceive from the process of moving from perception to interpretation. It can be very helpful to "check it out," meaning to share our perception and interpretation with the other person. If we leave our interpretation unconfirmed, we are merely left with our own story, which may be largely based on our assumptions and judgments.

Returning to the example of a work colleague who has flowers on her desk, "checking it out" could mean commenting on how you noticed the flowers and sharing whatever story you might have formed about them with kindness and curiosity. You also might state your context and intentions: "I realize that we've been working together for a little while now and I hardly know you. I noticed these pretty flowers on your desk. Did I miss your birthday?" On the other hand, in some cases, we may choose *not* to check out our story with the other person. For instance, in this same situation you might simply choose not to inquire about the flowers, especially if you do not know your colleague very well. Not asking would be respectful of your colleague's privacy, and, as such, might be a more appropriate choice in that moment. Nevertheless, in many situations confirming perceptions and interpretations is often useful, particularly when it comes to navigating your way through issues you think may be critical to furthering your professional relationships.

Remember, perception is raw data: the information we register from our five senses without evaluation or assessment. Interpretation is what we make of the data: the meaning we make out of the raw data by creating stories to explain it. Often we move unconsciously from perception to interpretation and assume the interpretation to be "true," forgetting the interpretation is only what we constructed. Being more conscious of how we add meaning to raw data avoids mistaken interpretations of what we see and hear.

In slowing down the process, we can better distinguish our interpretations from perceptions. Another important benefit is that it allows us to consider other possible interpretations. This idea also can be thought of as "reframing," which is essentially the process described in Chapter 6 on cultural difference as "parallel universe thinking." If we are able to slow ourselves down, we can suspend our judgments so we can truly listen to another person.

■ *Scenario #2*

A student in a public interest externship is meeting in her supervisor's office to discuss a concern about a client the student has been asked to contact. The supervisor is moving around a lot and frequently glances toward the phone, the door, and her watch. The student perceives these actions and interprets that the supervisor is impatient with her, or irritated in some way, or possibly bored and disinterested in the issues the student is raising. She has jumped from perceptions to her interpretations without confirming them with her supervisor. Perhaps instead the supervisor is actually late for a meeting with the supervisor's boss. It is possible that the supervisor appreciates the student's work so much that she wants to stay and listen to the student's concerns, even though it will make the supervisor later than she is already.

QUESTIONS TO CONSIDER

Can you imagine one or two other explanations for the supervisor's behavior that are different from the student's initial interpretation? What might the extern say to check out whether her perception of what is going on with the supervisor is correct? How might the supervisor have clarified what was really going on for her to avoid this miscommunication?

Feelings

Feelings start with bodily sensations, such as coolness or warmth, relaxation or tightness. Our feelings can be an important source of information, although we may try to ignore or minimize them. Feelings also may set off a feedback loop, meaning we get caught up in our feelings about our feelings and lose touch with the actual feeling state.

Just as we have suggested the usefulness of conscious attention to context, intention, perception, and interpretation, we suggest developing awareness of your feelings about and in interactions with others. Felt experiences underlie the thoughts (interpretations) we make from our perceptions. The suggestion here is to identify and to locate feelings as bodily sensations. Feelings can be positive, such as experiencing a sense of warmth and closeness, or negative, such as experiencing coolness or distance.[7] Anger, sadness, happiness, and fear also arise from feelings, although they are harder to locate: saying I feel angry, for example, does not say whether I feel close or distant.[8]

Many of us can more easily identify our thoughts than our feelings, and law school often pushes us toward living inside our heads. As a consequence, we may try to ignore or simply not pay attention to our feelings, which lead us to miss an important part of communication. We also can ignore how we feel about having feelings. For example, imagine a situation in which a supervising attorney offers constructive criticism about an extern's research memo. If the extern is feeling hot and tight inside, he then also might feel embarrassed because he thinks he should not be having a reaction to constructive criticism. That sense of getting heated or tight is the feeling, and embarrassment is the feeling about the feeling. Importantly, a negative feeling is also information. If you are aware of the feeling, that awareness can contribute to greater clarity.

Returning to Scenario #2 with the fidgety supervisor, the student's interpretations were based on her own assumptions and judgments. The student assumed that her supervisor was irritated or disinterested, and then she quickly jumped to negative self-judgments: I am not smart enough; I am blowing this placement, and now the supervisor is unhappy with me. The student's actual feeling may be a lump in her throat or heaviness in the pit of her stomach. The feeling about the feeling—the negative self-judging—can turn into a negative feeling loop, where the student fixates on feeling badly and then feels worse for "beating up" on herself, all of which can get in the way of communicating effectively with her supervisor. To help unpack what is going on in this interaction, she would first need to acknowledge her own perceptions and interpretations, recognizing that her assumptions may be incorrect. Ideally, she would find a calm, kind, and respectful way to check out her interpretation with the supervisor. It may help if the students can hold onto a posture of curiosity. We will revisit these suggestions later in the chapter when we offer guidance for navigating challenging conversations.

Action—Non-Verbal Communication

Recall the Scenario #2 supervisor's non-verbal communication: moving around, frequently glancing toward the phone, the door, and her watch. We communicate an immense amount of information without ever opening our mouths.

Studies have shown that non-verbal communication, makes up over half, if not more, of the messages we receive and transmit.[9] Non-verbal communication includes eye contact, tone of voice, pace, facial expressions, touch, spacing, posture, and even smell.

Eye contact: One of the most important aspects of non-verbal communication is eye contact. It is important to bear in mind that how eye contact is approached varies greatly among cultures . In the U.S. context, one expert recommends thinking about eye contact using the story of the three bears: not too much and not too little. Too much becomes staring and creates awkwardness and discomfort. Too little may be interpreted as disinterest or a lack of confidence. "Just right" eye contact is often described as a kind of soft gaze or "soft eyes."

Body language—a particular way of thinking about non-verbal communication—has been the subject of a recent and highly influential study.[10] The study found that our own "feeling states" are closely linked to our posture and other aspects of our physical presence. By shifting our posture we can change how we feel about ourselves in the moment. Our own shift in feeling states in turn also has a significant effect on the perceptions and interpretation of others. For instance, if we sit in a hunched over position and fold our arms into ourselves, we not only make ourselves small, we are likely to feel clenched or tight inside and lose energy. The person observing these actions may interpret that we are meek and not self-confident or disinterested. If instead we sit up tall and literally make ourselves "bigger," we are likely to feel more open and powerful, and others will interpret our posture to mean we are more self-confident and energetic.

One important take-away, according to Amy Cuddy and her colleagues at Harvard Business School who conducted this research, is that we can all benefit from what they call "power posing." Before an important meeting or interview, they suggest finding a private space and adopting a "superhero" stance for a minute or two. For instance, think about that famous poster of "Wonder Woman" standing with her hands firmly on her hips, back straight, head held high. Their research shows that by adopting a stance such as this one for two minutes, even if you are faking it, you can *become* more confident. In other words, adopting a powerful pose can change your own feeling state, give you more confidence, and enhance your ability to succeed in whatever important situation you are facing.

To learn more, take a look at Amy Cuddy's TED talk: http://www.ted.com/talks/amy_cuddy_your_body_language_shapes_who_you_are.

Smiling is another example of how changing your body language—even the pure physiology of it—can change how you feel and affect how others respond to you. In Amy Cuddy's TED talk, she uses the example of forcing a smile by holding a pencil between your teeth. Studies have shown that even without having an intention to smile, if you force the physiology of a smile, you will begin to feel happier, meaning more relaxed and open. Smiling during interactions with other people often elicits a more positive response than might otherwise occur. For another take on the power of a smile, watch the TED talk by researcher Ron Gutman, who shares how smiling can improve your health, well-being and overall success in life: http://www.ted.com/talks/ron_gutman_the_hidden_power_of_smiling.

> **Exercise 5.3** Find a private space within your home or office, ideally where you can see yourself in a mirror. Take a few minutes and try out power posing. Now try the exercise where you put a pencil between your teeth. Take a minute to record your how you felt after posing and smiling.

Communication as Dialogue

With greater awareness of what is going on in your interactions—both verbal and non-verbal—and more intentional choices, you can aim toward creating a dialogue: a conversation in which people think together in relationships.[11] As law students working in various settings, you are engaging with a wide range of different professional relationships, including with supervising attorneys, externship teachers, administrators, and other staff members. Some of you also are creating relationships with clients, agencies, community partners, and witnesses. Doing legal work means you will need to navigate challenges that arise in interacting with others you encounter in your placements.

> **Exercise 5.4** Make a list of all of the professional relationships that are a part of your current externship:
>
> 1. Which ones are most important to the success of your placement? Can you put them in some kind of rank order?
>
> 2. Which ones are easier and which are more difficult? Jot down your immediate thoughts about what you think makes one easier and another more difficult?

Aiming toward a dialogue means sharing ideas in a way that gets beyond each person's viewpoint. Dialogues explore possibilities, even when there are fundamental differences, including different assumptions and strong positions. We are focusing on creating dialogue for several reasons: (1) you will be more successful in your efforts to communicate with a wide range of listeners; (2) the necessary skills for dialoguing generally are not highlighted and taught in law school; and (3) these skills are easily learnable and, with practice, can become more like habits.

■ *Scenario #3*

Assume two lawyers represent opposing sides in a civil, landlord-tenant dispute. Often when lawyers are discussing a case, each simply states their clients' position to the other lawyer. If instead the lawyers choose to engage in a dialogue, the goal would be to reach a shared understanding, which may be different than either of their original positions. So, for example, maybe a lawyer representing Mark, a tenant, offers the reasons his client missed two payments. Mark's child has been in and out of the hospital for the last two months while doctors have been trying to pin down a diagnosis for his illness. Mark had to pay the initial bills, leaving him short of cash, but now the deductible has been met so his cash flow is eased. The lawyer for the landlord, Sheila, explains how with the dip in the real estate market, she is also struggling with cash flow and Mark's missed payments have put her behind on making the mortgage payment. Mark and his family have been good tenants otherwise, so Sheila would rather not have to evict them. Now that the parties have shared with each other more about their contexts, Mark and Sheila also can identify their mutual interests, which are for Mark and his family to remain in the apartment and to figure out a way to catch up on rent. At this stage, the parties can talk through different options for addressing these shared concerns. Once each side has a better understanding of the other party's underlying circumstances, a different resolution can be created. Treating the communication as a dialogue instead of an adversarial exchange can help to surface alternatives and lay them side-by-side so they can be seen in context. Imagine how this situation could have played out if the lawyers solely presented the clients' original bottom lines. What would the cost have been to the clients?

Thinking together means each person no longer views his or her position as final. It requires relaxing each person's grip on certainty and listening to the possibilities that can emerge—possibilities that otherwise might not have occurred. So, a dialogue is not simply about reaching an agreement or "getting to yes." The purpose is rather to create a different and shared context from which new agreements might emerge. In the situation described above, the parties might agree Mark will pay Sheila a late fee to help offset her unexpected costs. Sheila will drop the eviction proceeding. Going forward, the parties might agree Mark will give Sheila at least a week's notice if he suspects he might not be able to meet his obligations in the future.

Moving toward dialogue requires emphasizing the goals of awareness and clarity rather than argument and persuasion. This approach requires a major shift in thinking for law students and lawyers, who are given the message repeatedly that our job is to persuade others by having the "best" argument. The key to greater awareness and clarity is through **curiosity**. If I am viewing a situation differently from you, I need to become curious about those differences, instead of simply digging my heels in and arguing more fiercely. Engaging in a dialogue can allow new possibilities to emerge and can allow people to know each other on a deeper level and learn more about themselves in the process. Importantly, in a dialogue, **no one is ever right, and no one is ever wrong. We can agree or agree to disagree**. And, even if we agree to disagree, we can improve our awareness and clarity, which will allow us to become more intentional in our communication.

Reflective and Creative Dialogue

■ *Reflective Dialogue*

Before anyone can have a genuine dialogue with another person, it is important to have a reflective dialogue within ourselves: a structured way of pausing to examine and reflect on our own underlying rules, beliefs, and intentions. The result may be that we see more clearly what we have assumed and taken for granted, and notice more about ourselves. Reflective dialogue requires letting go of our own tightly held positions and being willing to suspend our judgments.

QUESTIONS TO CONSIDER

Think of a time when you made a judgment about a person or situation. You then came to a different understanding (an "ah-ha moment") and realized that your judgment was mistaken or incomplete. Try to recall what led you to come to that realization. What was the process that occurred between your original judgment and your changed view?

Our ability to notice and to reflect on our own inner chatter helps us to know ourselves better. This self-exploration and the journey toward greater self-awareness begins with our core values. Chapter 24 on Professional Identity and Formation provides a framework for identifying and thinking about what you see as your core values. The research presented in that chapter as well as

Chapter 25 on Work and Well-being, indicates that lawyers and others who focus mainly on intrinsic values, such as finding meaning in their work and building and sustaining relationships, end up being happier and more satisfied with their careers than those who are more focused on extrinsic values, such as wealth and status.

As is discussed in Chapters 24 and 25, many law students describe law school as an experience of losing touch with these essential qualities about themselves. Studies such as those by Larry Krieger and Kennon Sheldon[12] have shown that factors including the intense competitiveness of law school as well as other stressors that have a negative effect on students' self-esteem contribute to this loss of self. For some students the disconnection from their core values is accompanied by depression or other emotional or psychological struggles.

> **Exercise 5.5** Take a moment now and think about the values that informed your decision to go to law school. You might consider the list of possible core values on the worksheet linked to below if it is helpful. As you will see, the worksheet offers a large list of possible values. For purposes of this exercise, see if you can identify the eight or ten values you see as most essential to who you are and want to be in the world. Now see if you can rank them, or at least choose your top five. http://www.virtusinc.com/wp-content/uploads/2009/11/core-values-worksheet.pdf

Dean Daisy Hurst Floyd, a co-author of Chapter 24, states:

[my students] recount losing the sense of purpose–their visions of what it means to be a lawyer–that brought them to law school. Not only have students been able to articulate the loss of this vision, but they have repeatedly described the loss as quick and traumatic, very much akin to a death, reinforcing the aptness of the grief metaphor.[13]

Dean Floyd goes on to say that it is equally if not more disturbing that legal education sometimes has a negative influence on students' perceptions of the law and its role in society. Students often arrive at law school full of excitement about how law can be used to further social justice. And yet, many of them leave law school cynical and disillusioned, perceiving the law as value-neutral and lawyers as not caring about the impact of law on society.

For these reasons, understanding who we are and who we fundamentally want to be in the world is essential to communicating more effectively.

> **Exercise 5.6 Reflections on the Journey of Vocation:** Take a few minutes and jot down 5 or 6 "stepping stones"—choice points, milestones, events, people—that brought you to where you are right now—at this point in your life. Draw a graph, a map, or any other image of your stepping-stones in a way that represents your journey. After you are satisfied with your depiction, write a sentence or two that captures that choice point, milestone, event, or person and its significance.
>
> • Observe the flow of choices and events, directions and detours that your career path, or vocation, has taken. Consider which ones seem more external, and which ones seem more internal.
>
> • Your list may include significant people along your journey, places, events that marked a change in direction, or ideas that gave you a new understanding of yourself.
>
> • Not all stepping-stones are happy moments. We often experience a crisis and then find a way to turn it into an opportunity. Consider whether there are experiences that were difficult at the time that you think are important to include.

■ *Creative Dialogue*

Connecting with your core values and what is important to you prepares you to have a creative dialogue, whi means using communication to find shared meaning and develop new possibilities. Being in a creative dialogue requires being fully present: bringing your attention to what is happening in this exact moment and minimizing distractions. You bring your context and intentions and interact with someone else who brings theirs. While you are interacting, you will be perceiving and interpreting certain things. You will have feelings and will likely have feelings about those feelings. The same is happening to the other person. Your perceptions, interpretations, and feelings will in some way determine your actions.

Once you have a general appreciation of what is going on during an interaction and how the components can be broken down and better understood, the trick is to see if you can use that understanding to shape your responses in real time while you are interacting with another person. This skill takes a huge amount of practice! Holding on to an awareness of what is going on for you while concentrating on another person—be that your client, supervising attorney, the judge in the courtroom, your classmate, or faculty supervisor—is hard. Another way of thinking about this process is trying to be both in the "first person" while observing yourself in the "third person" simultaneously.[14]

> Mindfulness can be a useful tool in trying to develop this level of self-observation. Here we are referring to mindfulness as a conscious effort to become aware of our thoughts and feelings—to notice and accept what is going on inside of us. By being mindful during an interaction, we allow ourselves to pause and to make more deliberate choices. Mindfulness is also essential to improving awareness and clarity. It is only when we slow down, and even pause for a moment, that we are able to notice the distinctions between our perceptions and our interpretations or between our thoughts and our feelings. Along with the specific practice of meditation, mindfulness has generated a rapidly expanding body of research across many disciplines and a tremendous amount of media coverage. For instance, a number of studies demonstrate the ability of meditation to alter brain chemistry in positive ways as well as other dramatic benefits, all of which lead to stress reduction and other favorable health outcomes.[15] One can imagine that other forms of mindfulness practice have similar positive benefits. Mindfulness is rapidly gaining followers among many sectors, including in professional education. A growing number of lawyers, judges, and law professors are integrating mindfulness and meditative practices into their work and their teaching. [16]

In order to shape a conversation into a creative dialogue, it is important to commit to four types of behavior: (1) listening, (2) respecting, (3) suspending, and (4) voicing.[17]

1. Listening

As discussed earlier, we often jump to conclusions based on our perceptions and interpretations about what we see, rather than what we actually hear. Consider that light moves far more quickly than sound: 186,000 miles per second compared with 1,100 feet per second. This means that we take in what we see much more quickly than what we hear. To listen effectively, we need to slow down and try to operate at the speed of sound rather than the speed of light.

All too often, we are barely listening, as we are focused on composing a response in our heads. To listen well, we have to attend both to the speaker's words and the non-verbal cues or silence between the words. This conscious, careful, open way of listening has been called generous listening. Listening in this generous way means quieting the natural flood of thoughts and feelings going on within us and giving our full attention to hearing the other person: placing your own story as much as possible to the side as you listen. In this way, you can try to **hold** the other person's story as something that is different from your own interpretation of the story.

2. Respecting

Respecting is aimed at seeing the other person as a whole being. It is not a passive act—it involves a sense of honoring or deferring to another person. Respecting is tied to a sense of "mattering." All of us have a basic human need to be seen and heard—to matter. The concept of "mattering" was developed over two decades ago through research on high school children and college undergraduates.[18] In the study, students throughout this age spectrum fared better academically when they experienced themselves as mattering to others. This included making a difference in the lives of other people and in their broader sense of their worlds.[19] "[T]he most important lesson is that, even with our differences, we are all connected by our need to matter and to belong."[20] These findings comport with the results of a new study of over 6,000 lawyers undertaken by Larry Krieger and Kennon Sheldon, whose extensive research on law student and lawyer well-being is discussed in depth in the Chapter 25.[21] The factors with the highest correlation to success and well-being were the lawyers' experiences of authenticity, doing work that they defined as meaningful, and their sense of connectedness through positive relationships. Similarly, in the book, THE HAPPY LAWYER, authors Nancy Levit and Douglas O. Linder report: "[t]he type of happiness that results from doing work that you find meaningful . . . is an especially resilient form of happiness."[22] All of this research supports the benefits of focusing on intrinsic rather than extrinsic values. External, extrinsically driven signs of success, which for law students might mean good grades and securing a spot on the law review and for lawyers might mean big salaries and prestige, have little to do with lawyers' own accounts of what contributes to their overall happiness and satisfaction.

One way of achieving a greater sense of mattering is to focus on strengths, meaning our own assets as well as those of others. This approach shifts our thinking toward identifying and building upon what already is working in our lives, rather than only avoiding risks or fixing problems.[23] In assessing a given situation, we can ask what went well, rather than what failed. We can choose to put our energy into generating more of what has succeeded rather than putting our energy into avoiding pitfalls or problems. Focusing on strengths ties into the importance of appreciation. Chapter 3 on Supervision discusses appreciation as an important type of feedback. Expressing appreciation toward others and accepting appreciation are important aspects of demonstrating to others that they matter.

This strengths orientation is at least novel, if not radical, in law and lawyering. Law students generally are taught to identify problems—to "spot the issues"—and to see the role of lawyers as fixing what is broken. This can create a kind of a hero complex, which might unintentionally lead to devaluing clients' and others' internal strengths, skills, and resilience: the opposite of client empowerment.

Additionally, in today's highly competitive legal market, it is understandable that law students often see themselves as starting out with deficits, in terms of debt loads and job prospects, rather than assets, such as their sense of hope, work ethic, commitment to social justice, or creativity. If you make a conscious choice to focus on your strengths and the positive qualities of other people, you may find that you begin to create more openings for positive change. Another way of thinking about this strengths-orientation is to see if you can adopt a "growth mindset" rather than a "fixed mindset." Mindset is covered in Chapter 3 on Supervision and in greater depth in Chapter 25 on Work and Well-being.[24]

> **Exercise 5.7** Make a list of the traits or practices you consider to be your strengths, even if they are not "legal strengths." Relate them to your experiences in your externship and consider this question: how do you think you might bring your whole self to your work as a lawyer?

QUESTION TO CONSIDER

You might recall the scene from the movie PHILADELPHIA where Tom Hanks and Denzel Washington meet for the first time. If not, see if you can find a clip of it to watch. How might the situation have been altered had the attorney, practiced "respecting"?

Appreciative Inquiry (AI) is a broad philosophy and also a specific approach to navigating challenges that applies a strengths orientation. AI originated in the Organization Development field and has grown to be a model that can be applied to improving one-on-one interactions as well as addressing issues that arise in large organizations. In general, AI asks the question: what is working well and how can I/we do more of it?

This positively oriented approach can be contrasted with a "problem-solving" approach, which focuses only on what is broken and how can we fix it. By focusing on what is working, AI can lead to the creation of new possibilities and, as such, can be another way to achieve a creative dialogue.

AI relies in part on techniques of appreciative interviewing, which tap into the assets of the interviewee. For instance, a lawyer doing an appreciative interview might ask the client about the last time he successfully navigated a challenging situation and what resources or people he was able to bring to bear on that situation, rather than only asking about the client's legal problem. Appreciative interviewing also requires listening in a way that respects and normalizes what is going on for the other person. Appreciative listeners are genuinely curious and acknowledge the speaker's best intentions.

> **Exercise 5.8 Appreciative Interviewing:** Think of a time when you successfully navigated a challenging situation in your placement (or in a past experience). Consider what it was about you, the people around you, or the circumstances, that allowed you to succeed in that moment. Make a list of these successful strategies.

3. Suspending

Suspending, stepping back and being willing to try to see things with new eyes, even as you are aware of your own point of view, is one of the biggest challenges to having a creative dialogue. It requires setting aside our position and often deeply-held judgments, at least temporarily. Suspending requires the difficult practice of "reflection in action," described in Chapter 8 on Reflection. To successfully "suspend," we need to increase self-awareness and awareness of others. Separating perceptions from interpretation and noticing feelings (and feelings about feelings) all contribute to the act of suspending. Practicing mindfulness also helps us to become more self-aware and aware of others. Yet another way of framing these skills and abilities is to refer to them as Emotional Intelligence (EQ).

> Emotional Intelligence ("EQ") has four major components: (1) self-awareness, (2) self-regulation, (3) social awareness, and (4) managing relationships. View: https://www.youtube.com/watch?v=Y7m9eNoB3NU (Daniel Goleman introduces emotional intelligence.)
>
> Take the EQ QUIZ: http://greatergood.berkeley.edu/ei_quiz/.

For instance, consider a lawyer who disapproves of a client's past behavior, such as a criminal record that includes an aggravated assault. Suspending would mean being able to hold the client's story as seen through the client's eyes, alongside the lawyer's interpretation and perhaps even disagreement, without having to resolve the differences. The lawyer who truly can hold, appreciate, and honor the client's story will allow for new possibilities to arise in that relationship. Pursuing a creative dialogue with a client is a vehicle for appreciating the client as a whole person, and it also can lead to generating new ideas and possibilities for approaching the client's legal matters that otherwise might not have emerged.

4. Voicing

Voicing is about speaking with your own voice, authentically, which may also be challenging at times. Finding your voice in dialogue means asking yourself the simple question: what needs to be expressed now? Finding our authentic voice is sometimes difficult, given the nuanced and layered messages we constantly receive. Speaking with your own voice takes courage. And yet, it also can be liberating and transformative.

For instance, suppose you are in a situation like the previous externship scenarios and you want to have a dialogue with your supervisor. You would want to start by asking permission. "Is this a good time to talk?" Then, you would set out your context and your intentions: "I want us to have a good working relationship," or "I want to make sure that I'm doing a good job and meeting your expectations." Voicing your questions and concerns usually means beginning sentences with the word "I" and speaking "from the heart." You would check out your perception and interpretation, with kindness, respect, and curiosity. "I noticed that you seemed a little uncomfortable when we were discussing my case earlier, and I'm imagining that maybe you're unhappy with my work somehow. So, I hope it's all right that I wanted to check that out with you." Or "I wasn't sure what you meant when you made that comment about my writing needing to be more succinct. I'm worrying that maybe you're really unhappy with my writing. I wanted to ask you about it, because I'm very willing to do whatever I need to do to improve."

Voicing sometimes means revealing ourselves in ways that lead us to feel a bit vulnerable. In doing so, we also create the opportunity for others to know us better and to demonstrate that they care about us and are invested in helping us learn. In this way, vulnerability and authenticity go hand-in-hand.

Applying the Lessons of Dialogue

In this final section, we want to offer more concrete guidance to help you think through how to apply these lessons to an important or a difficult conversation. Bear in mind that there is no exact recipe, and that conversations may unfold in many different ways.

Generally, you want to create a safe space for a dialogue, which means paying attention to the physical setting as well as the timing. Make sure you seek permission: invite the other person into conversation. For example, you might say: *I wonder if you might have a little time now to meet with me. I want to run something by you and get your input. Is this a good time, or is it better if we schedule it for another day?*

If the other person agrees, and I am the one who initiated the conversation, I can begin by sharing my context and my intentions and voice my concerns as authentically as possible. If I am voicing a concern to my supervisor, I need to be aware of the difference in our roles and to be respectful and appropriately deferential. Once you have finished asking and sharing, you want to invite the other person to speak and then try to listen generously. For example, you might say: *I have been struggling a lot with the assignment I received from you two days ago. I'm not sure if I really understand the assignment, and I'm afraid I may have gone off in the wrong direction with my research. I know you've been really busy, so I haven't wanted to bother you, though I don't want to spin my wheels and end up with something all wrong. I'm hoping we can go over the assignment again briefly, and I can get a little more direction.*

Whether the topic is a confusing assignment or maybe something more difficult to discuss, such as a personal matter, the conversation can move toward clarity when each of you has had the opportunity to share your perceptions, interpretations, and feelings and has listened to the other. You may end up agreeing to disagree, and you may even feel cool or distant, though you will be clearer. This clarity generally will lead to greater appreciation and at least allow the relationship to continue in a constructive manner. You also may be able to reach a shared understanding and agree on appropriate next steps or actions.

Even when people are trying to listen generously, they can fall into becoming defensive. Moving toward a creative dialogue also means becoming aware of defenses. For instance, when externs sometimes find it difficult to listen to their supervising attorneys, or maybe their clients or an opposing party, one possibility may be that they are being defensive. Although defenses serve people in some ways, when people are defensive they are not truly listening. They may be rehearsing a rebuttal or judging what they have heard. Thus, if people can become more aware of their defenses, they can use their negative feelings to gain a deeper appreciation of their own contexts. Another common example of defenses might be someone who says: "whenever I hear anyone talk about a particular subject, say 'Twitter,' I tend to shut down and not listen." The more any of us is able to become aware of our defenses, the greater the chance that we can remain open and gain greater clarity and self-awareness.

To summarize:

· Create safe space for a dialogue—seek/get permission.

· Be fully present—minimize distractions.

· Ask, listen generously, and share—listen openly while suspending judgments.

· Hold onto a posture of kindness and curiosity—try to avoid being defensive.

· Look for areas of agreement and accept—respect areas of disagreement.

· Be willing to pause—allow time for reflection.

Concluding Thoughts

Before you began this chapter, you probably had an idea of some of the important ways lawyers communicate—through client counseling and advising, oral argument, trial practice, perhaps even giving formal presentations. Now you also have some other ways of thinking about communication that will be useful in your current placement and in your future legal career. Reaching the goal of using communication to build and improve relationships can be a challenging task. Mistakes can and often do arise because we each have our own worldviews—contexts and intentions—as well as interpretations. We leave you with three words of advice and encouragement: Practice, practice, practice!

> **Exercise 5.9** Think of a scenario where an externship student has to counsel a classmate who is in distress over an interaction that happened at that student's placement. See if you can use the tools of creative dialogue and appreciative interviewing to coach your classmate.

FURTHER RESOURCES

CAROL S. DWECK, MINDSET: THE NEW PSYCHOLOGY OF SUCCESS (2007).

DANIEL GOLEMAN, EMOTIONAL INTELLIGENCE (1995).

SUE ANNIS HAMMOND, THE THIN BOOK OF APPRECIATIVE INQUIRY (2nd ed. 1998).

NANCY LEVIT & DOUGLAS O. LINDER. THE HAPPY LAWYER: MAKING A GOOD LIFE IN THE LAW (2010).

DOUGLAS STONE & SHEILA HEEN, THANKS FOR THE FEEDBACK: THE SCIENCE AND ART OF RECEIVING FEEDBACK WELL (2014).

ENDNOTES

1   Nicole Black, *How Can Lawyers Better Communicate with their Clients?* http://www.mycase.com/blog/2012/08/how-can-lawyers-better-communicate-with-their-clients/-(August 21, 2012) (last visited on 6/23/15).

2   SAUNDRA HYBELS & RICHARD L. WEAVER II, COMMUNICATING EFFECTIVELY 6 (9th ed. 2009).

3   Mark Pagel *How Language Transformed Humanity*, TEDGLOBAL2011, http://www.ted.com/talks/mark_pagel_how_language_transformed_humanity?language=en (last visited on July 1, 2015).

4   *Id., see generally* ITHIEL DE SOLA POOL, THE SOCIAL IMPACT OF THE TELEPHONE (1977); NICCO MELE, THE END OF BIG: HOW THE DIGITAL REVOLUTION MAKES DAVID THE NEW Goliath (2013).

5   THE HUMAN POTENTIAL PROJECT, NOTES ON LANGUAGE ACTION AND REALITY (2008).

6   This visual depiction of the Haven Communication Model was created by Cathy and Ernie McNally, and is reprinted with permission by the Haven Institute. The McNallys were and are highly accomplished and esteemed educators at the Haven Institute. Sadly, Ernie McNally died in March 2014. Their interpretation of the model is based on the work of Bennett Wong, Jock McKeen and Virginia Satir. Similar depictions and descriptions of the Communication Model can be found at the Haven Institute's website, http://www.haven.ca.

7   David Raithby, *The Haven Communication Model* (2013) (Handout, used with permission, on file with authors).

8   *Id.*

9   *See* SAUNDRA HYBELS & RICHARD L. WEAVER II, COMMUNICATING EFFECTIVELY 138 (9th ed. 2009) (citation omitted). Studies vary on the amount, some have shown the percentage to be as high as 93%.

10   Amy J.C. Cuddy, et al., *The Benefit of Power Posing Before a High-Stakes Social Evaluation*, Harvard Bus. Sch. Working Paper No. 13-027 (2012), http://nrs.harvard.edu/urn-3:HUL.InstRepos:9547823 (last visited on July 6, 2015).

11   Handout on *Dialogue* (Adapted by Ernie and Cathy McNally from William Isaacs, *Dialogue and the Art of Thinking Together: A Pioneering Approach to Communicating in Business and in Life* (1999) (citations omitted), unpublished materials (on file with authors).

12   *See generally,* Kennon M. Sheldon & Lawrence S. Krieger, *Understanding the Negative Effects of Legal Education on Law Students: A Longitudinal Test of Self-determination Theory*, 33 PERSONALITY SOC. PSYCHOL. BULL. 883 (2007); Kennon M. Sheldon & Lawrence S. Krieger, *Does Legal Education have Undermining Effects on Law Students? Evaluating Changes in Motivation, Values, and Well-Being*, 22 BEHAV. SCI. LAW 261 (2004).

13   Daisy Hurst Floyd, *Reclaiming Purpose: Our Students' and Our Own*, 10 THE LAW TEACHER 1 (2003).

14   Ilene C. Wasserman, *Strengthening Interpersonal Awareness and Fostering Relational Eloquence,* in DIVERSITY AT WORK: THE PRACTICE OF INCLUSION 128 (2014).

15   *See, e.g.,* Heidi Wayment, et al., *Doing and Being: Mindfulness, Health, and Quiet Ego Characteristics Among Buddhist Practitioners,* 12 J. HAPPINESS STUD. 575, 576 (2011) (reviewing the literature on key ways mindfulness training increased physical and mental health, including strengthening the immune system and reducing stress, depression, and anxiety); Denali Tietjen, *Mindfulness Meditation Benefits More Than the Mind*, BOSTON.COM (June 4, 2014, 3:37 PM), http://www.boston.com/health/2014/06/04/mindfulness-meditation-benefits-more-than-the-mind/crdobytPKLDVhfRcCWkZ2M/story.html.

16   *See, e.g.,* Charles Halpern, *The Mindful Lawyer: Why Contemporary Lawyers Are Practicing Meditation*, 61 J LEGAL ED. 641 (2012) (lead article in a symposium issue of the JOURNAL OF LEGAL EDUCATION devoted to Mindfulness in Legal Education; Rhonda V. Magee, *Educating Lawyers to Meditate?* 79 UMKC L. REV. 1 (2010).

17   *See* WILLIAM ISAACS, DIALOGUE AND THE ART OF THINKING TOGETHER: A PIONEERING APPROACH TO COMMUNICATING IN BUSINESS AND IN LIFE (1999).

18   *See* Gregory C. Elliott, et al., *Mattering: Empirical Validation of a Social-Psychological Concept*, 3 SELF AND IDENTITY 339, 339 (2004) ("Mattering is the perception that, to some degree, and in any variety of ways, we are a significant part of the world around us.").

19   Nancy Schlossberg, a professor at the University of Maryland, studied mattering in the context of her work with undergraduate university students. Her work was based on the work of Morris Rosenberg and his colleagues, sociologists who first developed this theory in the early 1980s around their study of adolescent behaviors. Schlossberg articulated five areas of mattering: (a) attention; (b) importance: (c) ego-extension; (d) dependence; and (e) appreciation. *See generally* Nancy K. Schlossberg, *Marginality and Mattering: Key Issues in Building Community,* 48 NEW DIRECTIONS FOR SOCIAL SERVICES 5 (1989).

20   *Id.*

21   *See* Lawrence S. & Kennon M. Sheldon, *What Makes Lawyers Happy?: A Data-Driven Prescription to Redefine Professional Success*, 83 GEO. WASH. L. REV. 554 (2015).

22   NANCY LEVIT & DOUGLAS O. LINDER, THE HAPPY LAWYER: MAKING A GOOD LIFE IN THE LAW (2010).

23   SUE ANNIS HAMMOND, THE THIN BOOK OF APPRECIATIVE INQUIRY 6–7 (2d ed. 1998).

24   *See generally,* CAROL S. DWECK, MINDSET: THE NEW PSYCHOLOGY OF SUCCESS (2007).

CHAPTER 6

Navigating
Cultural Difference

MARGARET REUTER & CARWINA WENG

Introduction

First impressions

Scene 1: Sandy Jansen received this email reminder of an upcoming meeting.

APPOINTMENT

Subject: Michelle Lee, potential new client
Location: Conference A-2
Start time: Mon Oct 11 3:30 PM
End time: Mon Oct 11 4:30 PM

Notes:

Michelle Lee called last Monday. Her husband is hospitalized at Metropolitan Hospital, and she is considering bringing a medical malpractice lawsuit. She mentioned that she will be accompanied by Jon Simon, her husband's former supervisor.

Ms. Lee's contact info:

- Tel: 333-121-2323

- Email: michelle.lee@rmail.com

- Address: 249 West Sunset, Metropolitan City

Trish
Executive Assistant
Trader, Linn & Wortle LLP

S andy is a partner in a ten-attorney firm in a mid-sized city, specializing in medical malpractice. Sandy knows nothing about Ms. Lee other than this memo. Ms. Lee's address and the hospital are in a middle-class neighborhood.

Quick Write: List at least three reasons why Jon might be accompanying Michelle. How might any of these reasons affect how Attorney Jansen approaches the new client? For the purposes of this exercise, do not be concerned with the impact of Jon's presence on attorney-client privilege. Complete this task before reading the next part of the exercise.

Scene 2: Michelle and Jon arrive at the lawyer's office.

Consider in turn each of the possible additional pieces of information below that the attorney observes about Michelle and Jon. Close your eyes and imagine the scene as you consider the added information. With your original list of reasons explaining Jon's presence, consider how your interpretation of Michelle might change if you observed any one of the following traits in your meeting with Michelle and Jon as compared to the others. How might those interpretations influence how the attorney should work with Michelle and Jon?

- When Attorney Jansen extends a hand to shake Michelle's, Michelle does not reciprocate but rather gives a quick nod and says, "Nice to meet you."

- Michelle looks like she is East Asian.

- Michelle is tall, with perfect posture, an energetic gait, and a very strong handshake.

- Michelle walks with a cane, and Jon is helpful.

- Michelle is Black, and Jon is white.

- Michelle answers all questions herself but ends each answer with a look at Jon, saying "Is that right?"

- Michelle says she and her husband know Jon from their synagogue.

Pause. Consider your reactions as you visualized each version of Michelle. As best you can, separate your impression in the first instant from your more considered impression. With which versions of Michelle and Jon did you feel more comfortable and have a clearer sense of how to engage her? Which versions of Michelle and Jon seem more distant, difficult, or uncomfortable? View the scenarios through Michelle's eyes. In which version do you think you (acting as her attorney) would seem most familiar, comfortable, or distant to her? Finally, consider how your impressions of Michelle and Jon changed as you read this example.

■ *Cultural Competence: Expectations of Lawyers*

As the scenarios above suggest, we interpret social situations through our own filters. (Throughout this chapter we generally write in the first person plural (we, our)—to signify that the authors and your externship teacher are on the same journey with you to develop progressively higher proficiency in cultural competence.) Our filters have developed over years of living in cultural communities. From our family and friends to the internet and other media where we live, we absorb cultural influences that shape our conscious and unconscious worldviews. Our ability to adjust our behaviors flows from what we already know (or do not know) about our own culture and the cultures of the people we encounter.

The exercise above illustrates a key skill for navigating cultural difference, namely the habit to view, interpret, and reinterpret the actions and words of other people to make sure we adjust our actions for effective culture engagement.

In your externship placement, you will encounter people from many cultures with whom you will want to interact fluently. The cultural identities of the supervising attorneys and judges, other attorneys and judicial clerks, your peers, other co-workers whether legal or non-legal, individuals in the courts or other offices with which you deal, clients—all are important for you to navigate well. An effective extern, lawyer, or other professional needs a healthy understanding of cultural differences and an ability to navigate them with finesse and humility.

The American Bar Association Section of Legal Education and Admission to the Bar and the State Bar of California are giving special attention to the need for cultural competence among lawyers. Both are in the midst of ramping up their standards for skills education for new lawyers. In August 2014, the ABA amended its law school accreditation standards to require each law school to set and publish learning outcomes for their graduates regarding "professional skills needed for competent and ethical responsibilities as a member of the legal profession." They specifically highlight cultural competence as one such skill.[1]

The State Bar of California (the second largest bar in the U.S.) is in the process of instituting a requirement for admission to the bar that every new applicant must have a minimum 15 experiential learning law school credits. The proposed rules specify the types of skill development that qualify as experiential learning, explicitly including training in cultural competence.[2]

■ *What Do We Mean by Cultural Competence*

Cultural competence encompasses several concepts and objectives. It is not simply appreciation for cultural diversity or the absence of racism or other discriminatory behaviors. Rather, it encompasses three inter-related concepts:

- actively and consciously developing awareness and skills to avoid acting with cultural ignorance or bias in dealing with others;

- deepening our powers of cultural observation and broadening our cultural vocabulary; and

- cultivating concrete skills to mitigate culturally ineffective interactions that we contribute to, observe, or experience.

To assist lawyers to navigate cultural differences with their clients, Professors Sue Bryant and Jean Koh Peters developed the *Five Habits of Cross-Cultural Lawyering*.[3] Originally introduced to assist law students in clinical settings, the Five Habits are now used widely by practicing lawyers as well to improve their representation of clients from diverse cultural groups. The Habits can be adjusted and applied to any cross-cultural relationship, not just with a client but also with anyone in your externship placement, like a supervising attorney, administrative assistant, judge, or other co-worker.

The basic premises of the *Five Habits* are that as culturally competent lawyers

- We should understand ourselves as cultural beings with biases, values, and perspectives that affect our relationships with people of different cultures, both our impressions of and interactions with others.

- We should endeavor to understand any communication or interaction as the speaker/actor intended, that is, to see the world through the eyes of the speaker/actor with his or her values, priorities, and cultural patterns.

- We should appreciate that cultural competence is a learnable skill–even though the learning never ends.

The Habits provide a set of processes that prime the lawyer to behave in an open and welcoming manner, to anticipate cultural differences, and to adapt deftly. Brief explanations of all five habits are included in the Appendix at the end of this chapter. For purposes of considering cultural competence in the externship setting, we will introduce and practice two of the Habits later in the chapter.

The approach of Bryant and Koh Peters to cross-cultural lawyering aligns well with approaches developed in other professional disciplines. In the health care profession, Dr. Josepha Campinha-Bacote is widely respected for her work on cultural competence. Her model of cultural competence lays out five constructs, represented by the mnemonic, **ASKED.**[4]

Awareness: Am I aware of myself as having a personal culture, at both conscious and unconscious levels? Am I aware of the opinions and biases, both subtle and overt, that I might hold toward other cultures and how they influence my interactions with others?

Skill: Do I have the skill to assess cultural difference accurately, and can I use such assessments respectfully?

Knowledge: Am I knowledgeable about different cultural and ethnic groups, especially in ways that matter to my professional life?

Encounters: Do I seek out face-to-face and other types of interactions with individuals who are different from me so that I can expand my knowledge of other cultures, moderate existing beliefs or assumptions, and mitigate stereotyping?

Desire: Am I genuinely motivated as a professional to seek encounters and to engage in the process to become aware, knowledgeable, and skillful in my interactions?

Law, like the nursing, medicine, and ministry professions, has an ethically-anchored responsibility to understand and serve its clients well in their own cultural context. Bryant, Koh Peters, and Campinha-Bacote center their work on the relationship of the professional to the client (and patient). We expand the circle in this chapter, to encompass our effectiveness with co-workers and others we encounter through work.

■ *The Roadmap for the Chapter*

1. **Motivation:** The chapter starts by tapping into the drive of emerging lawyers to appreciate and navigate differences among our many cultures. This effort aligns with Campinha-Bacote's construct, "Desire." Given the natural inertia

that flows from our comfort zones with people who share our cultures, active and sustained motivation is necessary to develop cultural competence.

2. **Cultural Awareness**: Cultural competence starts with self-knowledge. We first consider what we perceive and value in our personal identities and cultures. Part of understanding ourselves as cultural beings includes understanding the impact of the dominant culture on our own cultural identity. Such impacts include implicit or unconscious bias, invisible privileges of membership in a dominant culture, and the impact of negative and positive micro-messages that reinforce cultural hierarchies. (From time to time in this chapter, we use the term "dominant culture." The contours of the dominant or subordinate culture change with context. In a U.S.-based private law office, we would probably characterize the dominant culture as white, Eurocentric, male, and highly educated. Law offices in government and public interest organizations might exhibit greater variation.)

3. **The Journey of Cultural Observation, Interpretation, and Introspection**: We next consider the ability to recognize differences between ourselves and others and to develop skills to adjust our behaviors. Using specific practices, we strive to shift our cultural interactions from the reflexive, unconsciously-biased processing in our brains, which can be blunt and uninformed, to the conscious and deliberative processes that safeguard our egalitarian ideals.

4. **Pursuit of Cultural Knowledge**: Beginning with the recognition that each of us has blind spots regarding our own and other cultures, we consider how to approach the unknown and become more culturally fluent. We introduce a set of cultural markers that help us recognize where another person's cultural preferences and values might depart from our own. And we present a set of techniques to remedy incomplete or inaccurate cultural knowledge that can germinate the seeds of bias.

5. **Mistake and Repair**: Finally, through a closing exercise, we decode a series of micro-messages and devise a manner in which to proceed with more cultural finesse and fluency.

Motivation

Desire: Without desire and motivation to improve behavior and attitudes, valuing diversity is window dressing and empty platitudes. Being a good, well-meaning person does not mean that cultural competence follows naturally or reliably. We can easily risk falling into the trap of congratulating ourselves for our values of diversity and give short shrift to the need to develop the knowledge base (self-knowledge and world knowledge) and tools (emotional and cognitive intelligence) to become culturally adroit.

Our motivation—our readiness to adapt our actions—flows from many sources: from our personal values of diversity; from our sense of professional duty to serve our clients skillfully; and from the real sense that we (individually and collectively) can make the world a better, more egalitarian, and tolerant place.

Fortunately, the motivation of today's generation of emerging lawyers starts in a very good place. A recent MTV-commissioned study found that Millennials, i.e., the generation that includes most current law students, have commendable attitudes and aspirations about cultural competence.[5] Consider these findings and whether they ring true:

- 72% consider themselves more committed to equality than previous generations,

- Millennials are unsure whether to showcase or ignore cultural difference,

- 81% believe that celebrating diversity would improve society, but paradoxically,

- 73% put considerable stock in the value of color-blindness,

- 79% note that their friends have exhibited biased behaviors,

- 58% acknowledge that they personally have held biases, and

- 41% acknowledge that they may still hold some biases.

Importantly, the study shows high interest in improving one's ability to reduce bias:

- 80% want to know if they have biases of which they are not aware,

- 80% want to know if they have inadvertently shown bias toward another person, and

- 68% want tools to navigate through difference and bias.

But these beliefs and attitudes are not enough. For sustained motivation, we need three elements: (1) recognition of the problem, i.e., bias and intolerance stubbornly endure in society; (2) belief in our personal agency to make a difference; and (3) readiness to engage emotionally. The beliefs and attitudes expressed by Millennials in the MTV study suggest that the first two elements are in place. Emotional engagement can be harder. As Vernā Myers, a diversity consultant to some of the largest law firms in the world, explains,

> So many highly educated people tell me that they care about diversity and inclusion and want to learn more, but in the same breath they say, "But you're not going to get all touchy-feely with us, right?" [Her response:] It is hard to be culturally effective without feeling. So much about getting good with this work has nothing to do with cognitive intelligence. In fact, real progress usually begins when we develop emotional, social and spiritual intelligence—when we humble ourselves to learn what we don't know.[6]

Mutual support/Safe space: Humbling ourselves, especially in a group setting, can be risky and uncomfortable work. At some point along this journey, any one of us may stumble, say the wrong thing, or act in a culturally offensive or clumsy manner. Yet we cannot improve cultural competence without engaging others to share experiences, feedback, perspective, and support. This process requires trust and reciprocity, and so we need a positive, supportive space in which to improve our cultural tools and knowledge. We can make this class a safe space to discuss, ask questions, seek ideas, and reveal doubts. Here, we can share our own experiences to move the process forward. Be kind to ourselves, and be kind to our colleagues about missteps and naïveté. Focus on behaviors and consequences and not on the actor or speaker. And embrace responsibility for our collective growth in cultural competence.

Cultural Awareness

Often when we talk about difference we think first of stark delineations among social groups: Black. White. Asian. Latino. European. Jewish. Muslim. Christian. Female. Male. Straight. Gay. Differences that tend to be salient, visible, and categorized. We tend to think in terms of "us" and "them" or "the other." We are quite aware of the multi-layered, nuanced, and complex characteristics that animate our own identities, but we do not have the same depth of sophistication about the cultures of others. So, we will start our exploration of difference broadly, referring more fluidly to both culture and identity.

- *Culture*

Culture comprises the values and traditions learned through one's community. Members of a culture tend to share social rules of behavior, rituals, labeling and sorting systems, and language idioms, as well as perceptions regarding time and relationships with nature and history. The attributes of a culture are developed over time and generations. Subcultures develop among socio-economic levels, gender, region, ability, etc. The members of some cultures or subcultures may share a very detailed and unified definition of what it means to be a part of that culture. Other cultures might be much more disparate, and their members might have a less specific or less unified definition of what it means to be of those cultures. With such a broad-ranging definition of culture, we realize we are all part of many cultures.

■ *Identity*

When we speak about our identities, we expand on the sociological or anthropological definitions of culture. Our identities include a vast array of traits that describe us personally. So we can easily understand that people might self-identify by their politics, their community role or family role, their occupations, their avocations, and the like. Each of these identities might represent its own subculture with a set of patterns, preferences, and values. An extern's identity as a law student, for example, comes with a culture.

■ *Archetype and Intersectionality*

Our **personal cultures**—traditional culture and other identities— and that of classmates and co-workers, include two important and complementary concepts. First, none of us actually fits the archetypal definition of our culture—each of us has a personalized version of our nominal culture. Second, each of us represents the intersection of multiple cultures, subcultures, and identities.

Consider a client who has a Spanish surname. This fact might lead you to think there is a good chance her family came from Latin America, and she is Catholic. Rather, her family is from the Philippines, and she was raised in the Jewish faith. Despite those traditional cultural attributes, she sees herself more as a world citizen, a professional tennis player on the international circuit, and she happens to need a will drafted.

With this framework of cultural identity, we turn to examine our personal cultures. Self-understanding is a critical first step to developing the capability to perceive, observe, and interpret the cultural complexity of our clients, supervisors, and co-workers.

> **Exercise 6.1 Naming Your Identities**
>
> 1. List three identities or cultures that you think best describe you.

2. Write a short, general definition for each identity, a word or phrase and no more than one line.

3. Write a second definition, personal to you, of one to three sentences that explains how the identity fits you.

4. Pause. Re-read your generalized definition of each of your identities. Now write two to five alternate definitions that others in the broader society use for each identity.

Example:

Identity:	Mother
Quick, general definition:	Mother means a woman who has given birth to a child.
Personalized definition:	I am the mother of Jack; I raised him as a single parent; I will move heaven and earth to help him become the most successful person he can be.
Alternate general definitions:	Mother means to raise a child, whether biological, adopted, or other relationship.
	Mother is the glue for a family—whether a birth mother, sister, aunt, or grandmother.
	Mother is the person who shops, cooks, and cleans for us.
	Mother is more of a verb—to nurture one's own child or another person outside the family.

---

5. Reflect: How did it feel to give voice to your identities and what they mean to you? How do your personal definitions align or not with the definitions generally held in society? What definitions would have excluded you? Would it be possible to think of yourself with only one identity?

Exercise 6.2 Personal Culture In Social Context

Our membership in a culture also comes with a set of positive and negative traits, with privileges and burdens. Some of these might flow from our personal experience, or from the cultural community's own definition, or from the views of outsiders to the culture.

1. For each one of your three identity groups, list three positive traits, privileges, or benefits that are attached to membership in that group. You may include ones that you have experienced personally or that you know are typical of what others with the same identity tend to experience.

2. Now list three negative traits, burdens, or challenges that might be associated with membership in each of the identity groups.

Examples:

Identity:	Mother
Positive traits/privileges:	Unconditional love for her child, pride for her child's accomplishments, parental leave without losing job, life-long mutual support relationship.
Negative traits/burdens:	Blamed for every anti-social behavior or failure of the child as an example of her poor parenting, expected to handle both career and family fully, will likely shirk work responsibilities for family priorities.
Identity:	Differently Abled
Positive traits/privileges:	Tenacious, creative problem solver to maximize one's abilities, gets the best parking spaces.
Negative traits/burdens:	Selfishly demands accommodations, uses disability as an excuse, not very smart, probably is depressed.
Identity:	New Yorker
Positive traits/privileges:	Goes to the theatre and concerts regularly, politically liberal, lives with the rich and famous.
Negative traits/burdens:	Rude, greedy, arrogant know-it-all, amoral, politically liberal.

---

3. Reflect: How many of the traits emerge from your view of your culture, or the culture's view of itself? How many reflect views of people outside your culture? Are some of the traits you see as positive considered negatively by others (or vice versa)? Have you personally done anything to warrant either the positive or negative traits associated with any of your identities?

These exercises reveal several important tenets to consider about ourselves and about others:

- We are not simply one cultural label: "The woman." "The African." "The Evangelical Christian."

- No one else can be reduced to one cultural label either.

- Every cultural label comes with a complex bundle of characteristics and traits.

- While we may possess many of those traits, there are traits we do not possess and traits that we may affirmatively reject. We are not cookie cutter versions of our cultural identities.

- Our sense of our own culture and of other cultures is not limited to our personal experience. It is informed by the people and media of the places we live.

While these ideas are intellectually simple, we state them affirmatively because they are quite easy to forget in practice.

Why does cultural competence require so much self-awareness? Our personal cultures create a lens through which we view the world—our communication preferences, hierarchy of values, sense of time, and the like. We are steeped in our own cultures. At times we are so thoroughly inculcated with our culture's set of rules and norms that we are oblivious that others do not share their "rightness" at all. As Blaise Pascal, the 17th century French logician, wrote, "There are truths on this side of the Pyrenees that are falsehoods on the other."[7]

Only when we pause do we realize the impact of the lens. Consider these easy examples. Why would people from the U.S. say that drivers in London or Sydney drive on the "wrong side" of the road, rather than the left side? Why are most world maps drawn with the United States and Europe at the top? Why are some books written "backwards"?

We are steeped in the dominant cultures of the places where we live—whether we are members of the dominant cultures or of subordinate cultures. In our media-saturated world, the views held by the dominant culture about itself or about any subordinate culture are part of our awareness. So awareness of our cultural lens includes understanding how the dominant culture has laid its imprint on each of us.

■ *Implicit Bias*

One imprint that flows from the dominant culture is that we each bear implicit biases representative of that culture. Individually and as a group, we exhibit biased assumptions and behaviors even when we have firmly held beliefs and values of equality and fairness. Researchers in neuroscience and cognitive psychology help explain such contradictions.

UCLA Law Professor Jerry Kang has written extensively on this topic and has translated the vocabulary of these researchers for us.[8] "Schema" is the term used by cognitive psychologists for the categorizing function our minds perform. Think of schemas as mental shortcuts, also called heuristics, that allow us to sort things—objects, processes, and people—quickly and effortlessly. When using schemas involving people we assign an individual to some social categories based on visible traits such as appearance, gender, race, role, etc.

We see a balding man with white hair and wrinkles moving gingerly and categorize him instantly as elderly. Such a schema is reflexive and unconscious. By contrast, our explicit cognitive thinking (observations and interpretations) might prompt us to view the man and estimate his age, consider whether his shuffle is due to Parkinson's disease or other cause, or assess whether he needs assistance.

Schemas come from our direct, personal experience. But mostly schemas are built over time vicariously through layers and layers of cultural inputs—stories, books, TV, movies, magazines, advertising, news, internet, and digital media.

The social schemas we employ—every waking minute and unconsciously—comprise our **implicit assumptions** about people. When we articulated the definitions of our identities and characterized the positive and negative traits in Exercises 6.1 and 6.2, we were tapping into these implicit assumptions. These assumptions are valuable to interacting with the world with ease. They can also be an unwitting source of discriminatory impulses, opinions, and actions.

The schema of the elderly man may seem benign. Other schemas are not. For instance, a potent schema in the U.S. in the 2010's is that a young Black man wearing a hooded sweatshirt is seen as threatening. Even when we know and believe the schema is discriminatory, wrong, and shameful, it will be one of the things our mind processes unconsciously when we see a young man dressed this way. Cultural competence techniques help us not to act based on the schema.

Like any schema, people who are members of such a culture or bear those traits may well have a different view of the schema, and may not track the schema of the dominant culture at all. For instance, teenagers who wear hoodies are not likely to interpret each other as threatening.

> **Terminology**
>
> **Stereotype:** Value-neutral; simply traits or characteristics we associate with a cultural group.
>
> **Bias:** Positive or negative values or attitudes attributed to a stereotype. Ascribing those attributes was the core of Exercise 6.2.
>
> **Prejudice or discrimination:** Believing in or acting on bias. Mostly we think of prejudice or discrimination in negative terms, but positive discrimination (favoritism) is just the flip side of negative discrimination. Discriminatory behavior ranges from blatant acts to subtle, even unconscious behaviors.

Another way to think about schemas comes from Nobel Laureate Daniel Kahneman. In his book THINKING, FAST AND SLOW, Kahneman characterizes our mental processing as System 1 and System 2.[9] System 1 is always operating, it is involuntary, and it is fast. It works by creating associations of observations with one's repertoire of reference points. System 1 seeks to create a coherent explanation of an observation, as quickly as possible, without concern that it does not have enough "facts" to make a valid explanation. Kahneman notes, "System 1 is more influential than your experience tells you, and it is the secret author of many of the choices and judgments you make."[10] System 1 is where our schemas for categorizing people in social groups exist and operate—like the elderly man, the hoodie-wearing teenager, etc. In contrast, System 2 is our conscious, deliberative mind, where we will assess conflicting information, seek more information, and make complex judgments. System 2 is where our carefully considered aspirations for egalitarianism and tolerance exist. As Kahneman states it, "The attentive System 2 is who we think we are."[11] Our pursuit of cultural competence often requires that we move our cultural interpretations from System 1 to System 2.

■ *Measuring Our Implicit Assumptions and Biases*

How do we start this move from System 1 to System 2? First, we need to experience the embedded implicit biases in our System 1 minds and observe the degree to which they influence our behavior.

Researchers have devised a tool, the Implicit Association Test (IAT), to measure what a person is unconsciously thinking (System 1), rather than what is said or valued (System 2). The methodology used by the IAT is to measure an individual's reaction time in associating good words and bad words with different pictures, usually of peoples' faces, e.g., of different races or ethnic groups. In video-game style, the test-taker is asked to use computer keys to sort the pictures and words into different categories.

Provocatively and disturbingly, the researchers have learned that everyone, members of both the dominant and the subordinate culture, will identify the dominant culture with the positive words more quickly than the subordinate culture with the same positive words. And conversely, they will sort the bad words with the subordinate culture more quickly than with the dominant culture.

These results have been mirrored in every country tested, tracking each country's general social hierarchies: German over Turk (in Germany), Japanese over Korean (in Japan); white over Black; men over women regarding leadership matters; women over men regarding family matters; light-skinned over dark-skinned; youth over elderly; straight over gay, etc. The time differentials for test takers in each country occur pervasively, systematically, and with statistical significance.[12]

To recognize that we all carry implicit biases does not mean we all carry them to the same degree or we cannot take actions to revise our implicit associations and adjust our behavior to conform with our consciously-held values. Indeed, recognizing our implicit biases empowers us to take steps to bring our implicit associations more in line with our consciously held values.

Exercise 6.3 Examining Our Implicit Biases

1. Visit the IAT site https://implicit.harvard.edu/implicit/ and take at least two tests (about ten minutes each). The tests vary, covering topics including weight (fat-thin); disability (disabled-abled); gender/life roles (career-family, male-female); sexuality (gay-straight); age (young-old); and race (Black-white; Native American-white; Asian American-European American; Arab Muslim-Others). Choose at least one that is race- or religion-based.

2. Consider your results. What were your thoughts and feelings as you were taking the test? What is your reaction to your own results? In what ways might your test results inform your approach to developing cultural competency?

Note: The IAT is an educational tool designed to develop awareness of implicit preferences and stereotypes. It does not measure whether you accept, agree with, or act in furtherance of any implicit bias. Your results are personal and confidential. This Exercise asks for your reactions to the instrument; there is no expectation that you disclose your results.

■ *Case Study: Cultural Lens for Choosing Ideal Litigators*

Recognizing how our implicit associations can affect our personal behavior will help us reorient them in line with our consciously held values. Kang and a team of researchers conducted a series of three experiments to assess whether implicit or explicit biases about whites and Asians as successful litigators could predict the way in which study participants evaluated white and Asian lawyers in practice.[13] The results underscored the potency of implicit bias in how we make decisions.

First, in a questionnaire the study participants were asked whether whites and Asians have the traits necessary to be successful litigators. On average, participants reported that white and Asian Americans possess litigator-related characteristics to an equal degree. But they thought "most Americans" considered Asians less likely to have the litigator traits. Second, the study participants took a specially-created implicit association test in which they were asked to associate white and Asian faces with personality or work traits that are typical of litigators (e.g., eloquent, charismatic, verbal, assertive, persuasive) and work traits of scientists (e.g., analytical, methodical, careful, mathematical). The participants associated whites more with litigator traits and Asians more with scientist traits. Third, in the capstone experiment, the participants listened to audio recordings of two depositions by lawyers regarding similar personal injury cases, but with the white and Asian lawyers' faces and names shown as introduction. Both lawyers used typical vocal range and spoke with a standard U.S. accent. The participants were asked to evaluate the lawyers' performances regarding competence, likeability, and willingness to hire. They were not limited to choosing one as the "best."

What did the study reveal? The study participants were more ready to hire and recommend the white litigator. Implicit biases and explicit biases independently led to this same result, but through different routes. The more participants had **implicit biases,** the more competent they thought the white deposing litigator was, the more they liked him, and the more willing they were to hire him personally and recommend him to friends and family. Conversely, the more the participants explicitly and personally endorsed the belief that the qualities required to be a successful litigator are more prevalent among whites than among Asians (i.e., **explicit bias**), the less competent they judged the Asian-American deposing litigator to be, the less they liked him, and the less willing they were to hire him personally or recommend his services to friends and family. The subtle implicit and explicit cultural assessment of litigator traits and Asian lawyers ultimately lead to evaluations that undervalued the performance of the Asian deposing litigator compared to the same performance of the white litigator.

- *Implicit Assumptions and Micro-Messages*

Recognizing how our implicit associations affect our behavior helps us to adjust them in line with our consciously-held values. Kang's study showed a concrete and substantial impact of implicit biases on a willingness to hire or recommend as a lawyer, even if the prejudicial actions were neither intentional nor mean-spirited. Many of the impacts of implicit bias, however, are more subtle and come in the form of micro-messages. These are small, ephemeral, and frequently unrecognized by the sender of the message as having the potential to convey bias and naïveté.[14] They can be in the form of verbal, non-verbal, behavioral, or environmental messaging. Consider this example:

> In a large urban housing court that handles eviction proceedings, a Latina law extern walks into a courtroom with her supervising attorney, who is white. She opens the bar, enters the well, and approaches the court clerk. The clerk tells her tenants have to wait on the other side of the bar. The implicit assumption from the clerk is that this Latina woman was a tenant; not a lawyer or law student. Let us assume the clerk does not adhere consciously to a socio-economic stereotype that Latinos in housing court are likely to be renters facing eviction and in fact knows Latina lawyers and law students, but the implicit assumption kicked-in unconsciously and resulted in sending this apprentice lawyer a negative micro-message.

Typically, we send and receive between 2,000 and 4,000 micro-messages daily. Consider these examples of micro-messages one might experience in an office meeting:

- whether you are acknowledged upon entering a room, and, if so, whether it is quickly or not, or comes with a smile, greeting, or scant emotion;

- whether you are welcomed into a conversation that is underway;

- whether you are introduced by name, with positive attribution, or not introduced at all;

- whether your name is pronounced fluently, mispronounced, or even forgotten;

- whether you are mistaken for another person from your cultural group; or

- whether your opinion is solicited or not.

Messages that are positive, supportive, and affirming of one's value are termed micro-affirmations. Others, called micro-inequities and micro-aggressions, are negative, exclusionary, and antagonistic in impact, like the one described above with the Latina law student. Most of us are unaware we are sending such messages. Indeed, often a sender would deny any biased intent. The sender might see a lapse in courtesy, but hardly a sign of ill-will or bias toward another by virtue of that person's culture. As Kahneman notes, System 1 will automatically search for and substitute a "presentable" explanation for the slight, and the person will believe the explanation is true. Otherwise, the sender will recognize the slight's potential as a biased message, but lament that "you have to be so careful, so PC [politically correct] all the time." [15]

This blindness occurs in part because most of us define discrimination as intentional, blatant acts of prejudice or unfairness. Micro-inequities and micro-aggressions are the manifestations of inclusion-exclusion, superiority-inferiority, normality-abnormality, and desirability-undesirability. They layer on and reinforce society-wide inequities that can be blatant. The subtlety of micro-messages can make their impact all the more insidious. Members of subordinate cultures are more likely to experience a greater volume of negative micro-messages than are members of the dominant cultures.[16] Such negative messaging causes the recipients to question whether the content was discriminatory, intentional, neutral, or benign. They question themselves about being overly sensitive or thin-skinned.[17] The potent combination of reinforced discrimination and increased uncertainty often causes clients and colleagues who receive negative micro-messages to diminish their self-worth and question their readiness to sit at the table.

■ *Case Study: Micro-Aggressions and Implicit Bias in the Law Office*

Being highly educated does not immunize us from implicit bias. A recent study of 53 law firm partners involved blind evaluations of a memorandum written by a third-year associate.[18] One of two identical memos was provided to each participating partner. Each sample was purportedly authored by "Thomas Meyer," who was identified as an NYU law school graduate. The two documents were identical with one exception: for one memo, Thomas Meyer was identified as African-American and, for the other, as Caucasian. The partners were asked to review the memo for factual, technical, and substantive errors and rate the overall quality of the memo, as part of a study on the "writing competencies of young attorneys." Of the participating partners, 24 received the memo of the African-American associate, and 29 received the memo of the Caucasian associate. The group of partners was roughly one-third racial or ethnic minority and two-thirds Caucasian.

On every measure of these identical memos, the African American associate's work was rated, on average, more harshly.

EVALUATIONS OF ASSOCIATE MEMO WRITING	AFRICAN-AMERICAN	CAUCASIAN
Overall quality (1–5, 5=extremely well-written)	3.2/5pts	4.1/ 5 pts
Average number spelling or grammar errors identified	5.8 errors	2.9 errors
Average number of technical writing errors identified	4.9 errors	4.1 errors
Average number of factual errors identified	3.9 errors	3.2 errors

The study did not test whether any single partner would judge the Caucasian associate's writing more favorably than the African-American's work. That would be an example of direct discrimination.

Rather these results show that African-American associates can expect to receive harsher evaluations (on average) from dozens of partners, including from racial/ethnic minority partners. Would those partners consider themselves overtly racist? Highly unlikely. Would they believe they conscientiously treat all associates equally? Highly likely. This kind of differential evaluation is another example of micro-aggressions and implicit bias experienced by persons of non-dominant cultures, like our hypothetical African-American associate, Thomas Meyer.

■ Blindness Inside a Dominant Culture—Invisible Privileges

A force similar to implicit negative bias is in-group favoritism. We tend to trust or like members of our own social/cultural groups more than members of different groups. We presume our life experience is typical and our preferences and values are commonly viewed as legitimate or appropriate by most everyone. For those of us who are members of the dominant culture, it can make us blind to many of the privileges that benefit our daily lives.

Wellesley College Professor Peggy McIntosh created a list of dozens of benefits she enjoys daily (or nearly daily) by virtue of her membership in the dominant American group, a.k.a., white people.[19] Embedded in this laundry list of privileges are examples of micro-aggressions endured by racial minorities and micro-affirmations enjoyed by white persons, like McIntosh. They illuminate the impact of explicit and implicit biases.

Here is an excerpt of just ten from her list of invisible privileges that benefit white people.

- I can, if I wish to, arrange to be in the company of people of my race most of the time.

- If I should need to move, I can be pretty sure of renting or purchasing a house in an area which I can afford and in which I would want to live.

- I can be pretty sure that my neighbors in such location will be neutral to pleasant to me.

- I can go shopping alone most of the time, pretty well assured that I will not be followed or harassed.

- I can be pretty sure of having my voice heard in a group in which I am the only member of my race.

- I can be pretty sure that my children's teachers and employers will tolerate them if they fit school and workplace norms; my chief worries about them do not concern others' attitudes toward their race.

- I am never asked to speak for all the people of my racial group.

- I can swear, or dress in second hand clothes, or not answer letters, without having people attribute these choices to the bad morals, the poverty, or the illiteracy of my race.

- I can be late to a meeting without having my lateness reflect on my race.

- If I have low credibility as a leader, I can be sure that my race is not the problem.

The power of McIntosh's list is how easily she identified a multitude of ways people in the dominant culture can be naïvely oblivious to the ease with which they navigate the world, avoiding a seemingly relentless litany of indignities and difficulties members of subordinate cultures experience.

We all come with cultural advantage of some sort—albeit some far more advantageous than others. McIntosh's list can be reconceived and written from the perspective of any advantaged position—speakers without foreign accents, people whose names are easy for others to pronounce and spell, people without disabilities, people who are among the religious majority for their area, people who have advanced degrees or are studying for an advanced degree, etc. The important value to recognize is that when we are in the advantaged group, we enjoy privileges that allow us to move through life with less friction and to sidestep impediments the disadvantaged groups have to hurdle. These privileges are often invisible to us unless we work consciously to reveal them to ourselves.

Acknowledging and accepting our unearned privileges is an act of humility. It should not be a cause for guilt but a catalyst for greater awareness. A well-respected professional league coach once quipped about folks whose lives have few burdens: "That guy was born on third base, and he went through life thinking he hit a triple."[20] None of us wants to be that guy.

- *Takeaways: Cultural Awareness*

  · Recognize and acknowledge our personal culture.

  · Recognize that we come with blind spots.

  · Appreciate that we are all steeped in the dominant culture—whether as a member of the dominant culture or subordinate culture.

  · Understand the lens through which we view others. It is formed by our personal culture, our blind spots, and our unconscious biases.

  · Anticipate how others might perceive us as cultural actors.

  · Be aware that micro-inequities may not embody ill will, but they can be demoralizing and they can aggregate in destructive ways for persons of a subordinate culture.

  · Our unconscious biases and blind spots are malleable, not immutable.

We can alter our cultural lens by refining our observational skills and expanding our knowledge base. Both are covered in the next two sections.

The Journey of Cultural Observation, Interpretation, and Introspection

The next stage in developing cultural competence requires becoming an astute observer of cultural norms and developing the aptitude to consider multiple interpretations of the potential cultural factors at play in our interactions.

When working with others, we reflexively make some estimation of "who" they are and adjust our interactions accordingly. Some of those interpretations take place in our unconscious; some are more conscious and explicit. To develop cultural fluency, we should anticipate possible interpretations, observe, check our reflexive assumptions, and develop more refined and accurate interpretations. Closely observing and interpreting culturally the manner in which a person presents, keeps us from falling into reflexive, unthinking System 1 behaviors.

> **Thought experiment:** Do you engage in active cultural observation currently? Think about people with whom you have worked in any context, including neighborhood, school, employment, church, or volunteer service. Identify three individuals with whom you worked well and three with whom you had more difficulty. Analyze both groups: What commonalities do the members of each group have? What commonalities do you have with the members of each group? What aspects of the positive or negative experiences have cultural roots?

■ *Cultural Mapping*

Both commonality and difference present challenges to working across cultures. Professors Bryant and Koh Peters devised the Habits of Cross-Cultural Lawyering to provide helpful guidance in navigating both. Habit One—called **Degrees of Separation and Connection**—helps sharpen our powers of observation of others. By close observation, we will naturally see and have a more nuanced and individualized awareness of the people with whom we are dealing. That awareness will also help us to anticipate where the other person's preferences might depart from ours.

In Habit One the lawyer identifies commonalities and differences with the client to explore how culture might influence their relationship and the lawyer's ability to work effectively with client, e.g., fact gathering, decision making. The cultural mapping exercise is both graphic and narrative. First, the lawyer draws a quick graphic representation of her relationship with the client—two circles that overlap only to the extent that the lawyer feels connection or shared cultural identity and experience with the client, i.e., a Venn diagram. Second, the lawyer builds a list of traits or characteristics common to and different from her and her client. The lawyer can compare the circles to the lists of attributes to see how close her impression of cultural overlap is to specific information about herself and her client. The lawyer uses this comparison to look for cues to facilitate the lawyer-client relationship and to identify barriers that might impede a productive relationship.

One of the benefits of Habit One is to check our reflexes for doubting and believing. Is the client so similar to us that we believe his story instinctively and fill in the gaps with our own experience/expertise, perhaps inaccurately? Is the client so different from us that we doubt his story as implausible and require supporting details in order to trust it? Do we assume commonalities or differences that might not exist? Do we make judgments based on our commonalities or differences?

A reconsideration of the scenario at the beginning of the chapter with the prospective client, Michelle Lee, using Habit One may open new insights for how you would interpret and approach your interactions with such a client.

The Myth of the Virtue of Color-blindness (or Culture-Blindness)

Attempts to practice "color-blindness" put us at greater risk of the implicit bias traps of the associative System 1.

When we treat everyone the "same" without acknowledging color or culture, we tend to expect everyone to conform to and meet the standards and values of the dominant culture.

Without the tailwind-power of the privileges of the dominant culture (both visible and invisible), it is naïve to expect or assume that most members of subordinate cultures will meet those expectations.

Each time members of a subordinate culture diverge from our expectations, we reinforce the dominant societal opinions about difference, e.g., inferiority, undesirability. It creates and perpetuates systemic discrimination.

The more we notice cultural difference, pause, reserve judgment, and reinterpret our reactions to diverse individuals (including checking our privileges), the more we move our categorizations of social cues to the deliberative System 2.

Exercise 6.4 Cultural Mapping—A Few Good Men

Several scenes from the movie, A Few Good Men (1992), illustrate significant cultural differences and similarities among the lawyers assigned to a court-martial defense team, and between the lawyers and their clients. Watching video clips from the movie provides a useful way to practice Habit One.

Background: In the movie, Lance Corporal Harold Dawson and Private Louden Downey are arrested for the death of a fellow Marine, Private William Santiago, at the Guantanamo Bay Naval Station, Cuba. Dawson and Downey stuffed a rag into Santiago's mouth as part of an unofficial "Code Red" ordered by the commanding officer on the base to bring the wayward private back in line. The assault brought on respiratory complications that lead to Santiago's death. As portrayed in the movie, Code Red is a deeply-honored tradition in the Marines, but it is officially denounced. Lt. Daniel Kaffee was selected to represent Dawson and Downey. Lt. Sam Weinberg was assigned to assist him. Lt. Cmdr. Joanne Galloway was the original investigator of the death of Santiago and eventually became the third lawyer on the defense team.

- *Scene 1:* The first meeting of Kaffee, Weinberg, and Galloway, in which Galloway briefs them about her investigation.

- *Scene 2:* The following day, an encounter between Galloway and Kaffee at which she expresses concerns about his approach to the representation of the defendants.

- *Scene 3:* Kaffee and Weinberg's first meeting with Dawson and Downey.

- *Scene 4:* Kaffee and Galloway's reinterview of Dawson and Downey.

- *Scenes 5 and 6:* After one of the trial days, Weinberg and Galloway exchange views of their feelings toward the defendants.

1. Watch the video clips. Your externship teacher will tell you where they are available. Consider the cultures and identities of Kaffee, Weinberg, Galloway, Dawson, and Downey. What cultures are represented? How do the characters act in accord with what you know or assume about their cultures (or not)?

2. Apply Habit 1 to Kaffee and Galloway. Repeat the exercise mapping Kaffee with Dawson and Downey. How do the cultural differences impact the relationships among these five characters—considering first their effectiveness as legal counsel for the two defendants and second their effectiveness as a team of lawyers?

3. Next critique Kaffee's interactions from a cultural competence perspective. How well does he observe, note, and adapt his interactions vis-à-vis the cultural dimensions of his clients? What biases does he seem to hold about them? What micro-messages does he convey? What information does he need to work better with his clients?

■ *Encountering Difficulties and Reinterpretation of Cultural Indicators*

Bryant and Koh Peters explain in Habit Three, **Parallel Universe**, the vital need to reserve judgment when a lawyer cannot make sense of a client's behavior. Rather than react negatively, the lawyer brainstorms multiple explanations for a client's words or actions—especially those with which the lawyer has a strong reaction or disagreement.

The brainstorming helps the lawyer to move her approach from System 1 to System 2 functions.

Habit Three reminds us that different cultural norms can ascribe different meanings to the same words or behaviors. By identifying other explanations—benign, harmless, and/or cultural—a lawyer can develop an open-minded interpretation of puzzling or vexing behavior. Such disciplined naïveté allows the lawyer to reserve judgment before making lawyering choices.

In Exercise 6.4, Attorney Kaffee would have been well served to use Habit Three with Dawson, Downey, and Galloway. The Habit can readily be applied with anyone we are dealing with in our workplaces. Consider this example of **Parallel Universe** practice in action:

> David, an attorney supervisor, is late to every meeting with Maria, an extern, and it appears he is always late to meetings with anyone in the office. Maria is unfailingly punctual. Maria reacts by assuming that the supervisor's lateness indicates a lack of respect and an unprofessional sloppiness.

> By pausing for reinterpretation, Maria may consider that the supervisor's tardiness might be an indication of his personal culture, stemming from his ethnic or regional roots, that he is present-oriented. He will give priority to anyone in his presence. For instance he will avoid ending a meeting at an arbitrary time if they are working productively. His tardiness might reflect an office cultural norm that a scheduled time always includes at least a 15-minute grace period. Or it might stem from his sense of the privileges of being a senior manager, reflect his overloaded schedule, or illustrate his lousy time management skills.

Reserving judgment does not require that we ignore our preferences and values. Maria might consider that a commitment to punctuality is more professional and respectful of other people's time. However, by suspending or reserving judgment, Maria has the time and openness to figure out how to be effective (and culturally attuned) in her relationship with David.

How might Maria work through this? Here are a few possibilities:

- She can reflect that her own sense of punctuality is based on her upbringing and recognize that punctuality is not a universal norm.

- As illustrated above, Maria can consider the various reasons that might explain the supervisor's lateness. Is there one consistent reason or multiple causes?

- With these possible interpretations, Maria can decide how to deal with the issue—directly, indirectly, or adaptively.

- Maria can devise a plan to use her own time productively while she waits for the supervisor to become available.

- Maria might question whether the lateness matters for reasons other than her personal preferences, e.g., timing of subsequent meetings, difficulty coordinating with necessary parties. Would the supervisor want to know the reasons the lateness matters in order to adjust his actions?

- Maria might consider possible communication with her supervisor or others. Should the conversation be with the supervisor or should Maria seek the advice of another staff member first? If so, consider how the issue can be raised without being accusatory or impertinent, e.g., word choice, timing, solutions offered.

Maria's status as a temporary extern likely will limit how direct she will be with her supervisor. If her role were different, e.g., a peer or supervisor of David, or David were her client, she would likely consider a broader array of options, perhaps even negotiating an agreement about what kinds of meetings should start at the agreed time and which have more leeway.

Habits One and Three compel Maria to pause and recalculate whether and how cultural differences might be at play in her annoyance with David. Is punctuality a shared value, so that both she and David consider his lateness a lapse even if he frequently violates the norm? Or do schedule and punctuality have different cultural meanings for each of them? The point is that Maria can become far more effective as a professional if she acknowledges her culture's imprint on her opinions and brings her cultural navigation skills to bear.

Exercise 6.5 Cultural Mapping in Your Externship

1. Choose a relationship in your externship that challenges you—whether a client, supervisor, co-worker, or another person. Identify one or more aspects of the relationship that might be the source of your difficulty.

2. As with the example of Maria above, brainstorm various interpretations of the person's behaviors. Think broadly about personal, cultural, and social traits and experiences each of you has that might affect your ability to work

or communicate effectively. Consider also office dynamics or priorities that might contribute to the challenging circumstances.

3. Now contemplate ways in which you might be able to address the challenges. First brainstorm possible remedies, without judging their efficacy or your ability to implement them. Only when you have multiple interpretations, review and assess which options you can reasonably implement, whether direct, indirect, or adaptive.

■ *Takeaways: Cultural Observation, Interpretation, and Introspection*

· Taking the time to check our reactions to our interactions with others will allow us to surface some of our implicit assumptions and to revise our own behaviors and expectations.

· Taking the time to reinterpret a difficult relationship or interaction will give us the opportunity to devise a more culturally congruent response with the person.

· Each of these pauses gives us the opportunity to move our cultural response from the unconscious, impulsive System 1 to the deliberative System 2 and to allow for more finely tuned judgments and fluent actions.

Pursuit of Cultural Knowledge

The risk factors for cultural insensitivity can be characterized in two ways. One is cultural naïveté or ignorance. The second is cultural bias.

With the first, cultural naïveté, we assume that everyone shares our norms about communication and professional behaviors or at least that they should be treated as though they do. This risk factor reflects our failure to perceive and understand that the other person may have different cultural norms that are just as valid as our own. If the extern Maria above knows nothing about the variations of cultures in scheduling and time priorities, how could she possibly consider alternate cultural explanations for her supervisor's conduct? In such circumstances, her cultural development tasks are to learn about other cultures and to respect the legitimacy of their methods and preferences.

A second set of risk factors for cultural insensitivity stems from biases such as racism, sexism, and the like that flow from inaccurate and incomplete cultural knowledge.

Unlike the examples above, where we homogenize and presume that other people are just like us, in these cases we tend instantly to see and categorize the other person as "different." And through the function of System 1 implicit biases, we instantaneously ascribe negative stereotypes that pervade the dominant culture. Such stereotypes are the byproducts of limited, erroneous, and misapplied cultural knowledge. The cultural development task is quite different. It is to learn how to recognize and re-write the stereotype with greater accuracy and nuance.

- *Cultural Markers*

Cultures have many points of difference—foods, life rituals, values, etc. While it is fascinating to learn about the breadth of other cultures, our focus is on the differences that impact our professional responsibilities—namely, differences that affect communicating and working with others. By knowing a bit about how cultures, including our own, work, we can plan for interactions with tentative generalizations and with disciplined naïveté.

The descriptions below of cultural traits of one ethnic group or another come from the research of social scientists. While the descriptions of these traits may have validity in the aggregate, all members of any ethnic group certainly do not exhibit them uniformly, and some members may reject specific traits of their cultural group. For example, recall our individual responses to Exercises 6.1 and 6.2 in the early part of the chapter. That is where "disciplined naïveté" comes in. Knowing something about a culture helps us observe with greater acuity. But we consciously avoid assuming a person fits the generalizations and preferences identified by social scientists.

Professor Paul Tremblay has gathered several examples of cultural markers that help us to understand how many differences in cultural preferences can be misinterpreted easily.[21]

- *Eye Contact and Facial Expressions*

When researchers characterize the communicative potential of non-verbal communication, eye contact and facial expressions are key elements. In white American culture, "looking someone in the eye" suggests confidence and honesty. When someone averts his eyes, it is interpreted as uncertainty, weakness, and perhaps lying. Smiling and meeting one's eyes is one of the most common ways to welcome or connect with another. Smiling and nodding are seen as indicators the listener understands and/or agrees with what the speaker is saying. Social scientists have documented that Black Americans will tend to maintain eye contact more when speaking than when listening; while white Americans have the reverse preference and maintain eye contact more consistently when listening and less when speaking. In Chinese and Japanese cultures avoiding eye contact is a sign of respect, and masking emotional reactions, such as refraining from outward expressions like smiling, is an indication of maturity and wisdom. These traits have lead white observers to misconstrue Black Americans as inattentive and East Asians as mysterious or unemotional.

■ *Proximity/Physical Nearness*

Cultures tend to have closely-observed preferences regarding personal space, especially talking distance. Many cultures, including Latin American, African, Black American, Indonesian, and Arab, tend to prefer speaking much more closely to another than white American culture finds comfortable. British culture tends to prefer greater distance between conversants than white American culture.

■ *Sense of Time and Priority*

Dominant American culture holds that punctuality is important and that once a meeting is scheduled, participants will organize the rest of their days to attend the meeting on time. Deadlines are honored. Any deviations should be accompanied with as much advance notice as practicable and suitable apologies for the inconvenience. We all know many transgressors of the dominant cultural norms of punctuality. Yet other cultures, e.g., Hispanic and Caribbean, simply do not have the same literal sense of time or mutual commitment to a schedule. Such cultures tend to consider relationships more important than schedules.

■ *Direct/Indirect Communication Styles; High and Low Context Communication*

White American, Western European, and Israeli cultures are frequently featured as having the most direct communication style, with particularly heavy value in the explicit meaning of words and a preference for resolving things by discussing and airing issues fully. Cultures that favor indirect communication do not believe everything ought to be specifically verbalized. When dealing with conflict they prefer to avoid open dissent and strongly believe in sparing embarrassment of another. Such cultures use context and non-verbal elements of communication much more sensitively than direct communicators. Cultures of Asia, the Middle East, Africa, and South America are generally characterized as indirect communicators.

Direct communicators think indirect communicators

- are evasive and dishonest,

- cannot take a stand, and

- increase tension by not dealing with issues directly.

Indirect communicators think direct communicators are insensitive, have no tact, are boorish and insulting, and increase tension by dealing with issues in a blunt, direct manner.

■ *Labels and Hot-Button Terminology*

Labels can be more than tags; they can convey powerful imagery. So proposing, imposing, and accepting labels can be a political exercise.[22] Almost any application of a racial or ethnic label is not wholly accurate and will be under- and over-inclusive given the variety of humankind. Labels also change over time, and some labels are reserved only for insiders. Respecting how members of the group prefer to be labeled, whether to be definitionally accurate or nuanced (e.g., Latino/Hispanic, Chinese/Taiwanese) or to recognize a preferred phrasing (e.g., Black/African-American/Afro-Caribbean), demonstrates cultural competence.

■ *Sources of Cultural Knowledge*

The cultural markers above are hardly comprehensive and not necessarily applicable to the people we meet from a particular culture. So we will need to pursue greater cultural knowledge on our path to cultural competence. As we encounter someone from a different culture, sometimes the difference is readily apparent, and we actually have the opportunity to do a little research—whether in anticipation of the meeting, as for a new client, or once we have met the person and learned a bit about his background. Research takes many forms, from formal academic to informal internet research. Of course, human intelligence gathering—talking to friends, classmates, neighbors, and colleagues—can be our most vital source.

When we seek better understanding through talking to others, we need to show genuine interest, respect, and humility. Some cautions and suggestions we should keep in mind:

- Admit our ignorance, and ask for help. Ask the person with whom we are working for information that will help us to work together or for an explanation of behavior that we do not understand. Or ask for guidance from a third party who is a member of the other culture.

- Be mindful that the person we ask may not want to serve as a spokesperson, interpreter, or exemplar of his or her cultural group.

- Avoid flooding the person with questions and give a buffer of privacy.

- Recognize certain important or sensitive information will not be shared until the person trusts us and our motives.

- Consider how micro-messages we personally convey, whether micro-inequities and micro-affirmations, will build or impede others' trust in our motives.

- Do not make our friend or co-worker from the "other" culture do all the work to educate us; we have to educate ourselves too, e.g., engage in active observation.

- Broaden our media sources. Beware of overconsumption of information from limited media sources, especially ones that might reinforce our current set of biases and cultural myths.

- Expand our work and social circles to include people of many cultures.

- Remember, knowing something about a culture is informative; it should not be determinative of how we should interact with members of that cultural group.

- Notice whether and how individuals might be typical of a culture, may be from a subculture, or actually may reject some or all of the norms of their nominal culture.

- Practice active listening and close observation of the patterns and practices of others.

- Recognize the importance of context for any cultural observation. Characteristics of a culture that might be relevant at any one time are heavily dependent on context.

- Stay conscious about how we are responding to the new information.

- Notice that someone's foreignness may be reciprocal. We may be just as unfamiliar to them. Make it easier for them to ask questions too.

■ *Re-Writing Stereotypes That Flow From Limited and Imperfect Cultural Knowledge*

In our pursuit of greater cultural competence, we also need techniques to interrupt and neutralize the harmful impact of embedded negative implicit biases (e.g., ethnic, religious or sexual orientation discrimination, racism, sexism) that are based on incomplete, erroneous, or misapplied cultural knowledge. For example, the cultural stereotype and implicit bias that women do not have the "right stuff" for intellectually demanding jobs or that Asians do not have the traits necessary to be successful litigators will inhibit us from promoting or accepting women and Asians in those career paths. These are biases the culturally sophisticated professional actively wants to rework. Consider and apply techniques like the ones below.

■ *Seek Counter-Stereotypical Examples; Reassess the Measure of Success*

When we search out examples of people acting or performing in a manner that is contrary to our biases, we broaden our cultural encyclopedias and recalibrate our implicit assumptions. Thus, regarding women, we notice instances where women perform in decisive roles, lead challenging teams, or achieve substantial accomplishments. We avoid reinforcing simplistic views of women as less penetrating and perceptive than men. Similarly, with Asians, we recognize Asian lawyers who are charismatic and persuasive, rather than limit ourselves to a view of Asians as quiet, cooperative, and methodical. Not only do we want to be able to visualize such incisive women leaders and assertive Asian trial lawyers, but we want their achievements and characteristics to feel familiar, not anomalous.[23]

We also want to open our minds to the possibility that success in intellectually demanding work like lawyering can be achieved in more than one way. Women or Asian lawyers may choose different methodologies to be effective in their work (e.g., leading from behind, disarmingly subtle persuasion techniques).

■ *Meet More People and Observe More Cultures*

Professors Thomas Pettigrew and Linda Tropp reviewed over 500 separate studies that concluded that having more direct personal contact with people of other cultures reduces prejudice. The most vital elements of the salutary impact were (1) enhanced knowledge about the other group; (2) reduced anxiety about contact with others from the different culture; and (3) increased empathy and understanding of the other group's perspective.[24] Similarly, researchers in teamwork theory have shown that prejudicial stereotypes are reduced in work groups that have members of varied cultures, with similar status, and who are tasked to achieve a common goal.[25]

▪ *Be Ready for Positive Impressions*

Expect to learn something enjoyable and useful from people who differ from you. The more people we know from a culture, the less we will blend them into one opaque group. Is sharing pleasantries enough? Of course, cordiality helps. Go further; expect to find value in getting to know others. A favorite story comes from a well-traveled lawyer who volunteered for a park cleanup project on a team with a man from the local parks department, attired in work gear. Over the course of their day, the man helped the volunteers distinguish different birdcalls, pointed out special features of the park, and described a water-cleaning process they implemented that he had learned about while working on a project in Africa. The lawyer was chagrined. She had presumptively categorized him in a box: "blue-collar, limited education, and probably likes sports and beer." She now saw him as "worldly, intellectual, and can teach me something." She had surely been respectful of him, in a cordial casual way. But she lamented that she had sold him short; she had not respected him in the sense that he could and would bring value to her life and awareness.[26] Elitism was her blind spot.

▪ *Find Ways to Eliminate/Reduce Homogeneity*

"They all look alike." "I can't pronounce their names." Both things might be absolutely true for someone who has little contact with people from a particular culture. Where someone's group identity is prominent, individual identity can be obscured, which can make us more prone to common micro-inequities: mistaking one person for another in the same cultural group, mispronouncing someone's name, and avoiding saying someone's name. Developing the skills to individuate members of a cultural group will help us avoid seeing "them" as an opaque, undifferentiated group. It is one way to "check our privilege." Correct pronunciation may take practice, but it will be a substantial help to building rapport and trust.

Researchers have found that when people improve their ability to distinguish among faces of individuals of a different race, prejudice risk factors decrease. Brown University and University of Victoria researchers implemented a training program for Caucasian subjects to recognize different African-American faces. The Caucasian participants showed decreases in their implicit racial bias, increased their positive associations with African-American faces, and showed fewer negative associations with African-American faces.[27]

■ *Identify Our Personal Risk Factors*

Studies have shown that we will revert to our implicit biases, and behave in accord with them, when we are stressed, distracted, or doing repetitive work. The National Center for State Courts was concerned enough about the effects of implicit bias in the courts (from both judges and staff) that they conducted extensive studies and trainings. Here are a few of their findings about risk factors:

- When time pressures require decision makers to make complex judgments relatively quickly, they are more likely to make stereotypic judgments than decision makers whose cognitive abilities are not similarly constrained.

- When standards are vague or ambiguous, implicit biases creep into decision-making and evaluations.

- When someone is engaged in low-effort information processing (routine, repetitive work), attention and memory favor stereotype-confirming evidence.[28]

Consider these examples and reflect on our own tendencies. Identify situations that create red flags for us individually. Then plan correctives.

■ *Be Culturally Conscious; Avoid Color-Blindness*

Avoid assuming that everyone is the same. The color-blind or culture-blind approach will miss critical cues for cultural effectiveness. The direct communicator will think the indirect communicator is evasive. The people who need extended personal space will think those who speak at close distances are aggressive and rude. When we try to practice color-blindness, we tend to have hidden assumptions about privileges, opportunities, and burdens others experience, which have limited or no validity. The more we pause, reserve judgment, and reinterpret our reactions to diverse individuals, the more we move our categorizations of social cues to the deliberative System 2 where we can be more discerning and less reflexive.

Cultural consciousness does not equal special treatment or pity for a member of a subordinate cultural group, but it does mean respect, awareness, and adaptation.

Mistake and Repair

Part of becoming more culturally aware and fluent is working through the inevitable flops, mistakes, and offenses that we commit along the way. Self-recrimination is not helpful. Self-reflection is.

The MTV survey of Millennials shows some of the risks that people see along this path toward cultural confidence.[29] Only 20 percent are comfortable having a conversation about bias!

- 48% believe it is wrong to draw attention to someone's race, even in a positive way.

- 54% agree that it is hard to have a respectful conversation about bias in person or online.

- 61% agree that it is easier to see the risk of calling out bias, than it is to see the immediate benefit.

- 79% worry that the biggest concern of addressing bias is creating a conflict or making the situation even worse.

Recovering from a gaffe or interrupting another person's micro-inequity takes courage. It is easy to see how the incident might be worsened or to question the validity of your interpretation of the micro-message. When we anticipate or fear our attempts will be judged or rejected, understandably we develop a form of racial anxiety that might exacerbate the situation. But recovery or interruption is worth the effort. We become more artful with time and practice.

It may well be that a quick, sincere apology for a misstep is the best cure. Apologizing is not a sign of weakness. It is an indication of respect for others and of our own high self-regard for living up to egalitarian standards. However, if the recipient of our gaffe does not accept the apology, we need to try not to resort to defensiveness or blame the person for being too thin-skinned.

An examination of micro-inequities and micro-aggressions is a fruitful place for us to consider how to be more skillful in identifying mistakes and repairing their impact. We will view these from three vantage points: the actor, the recipient, and a nearby observer.

Exercise 6.6 Noticing and Responding to Micro-Messages

1. Read the full list of micro-messages below. Which would you see as conveying a neutral, affirming, or negative message?

2. Choose one category of micro-messages to examine more deeply. Using techniques like those offered in the previous section, identify tactics or strategies you might use in these instances. Consider the strategies from these vantage points:

   - recipient (as someone in that person's culture),
   - actor/speaker (as someone of your culture),
   - observer (as yourself).

   What would you hope to do in response? What would you most likely do?

3. Practice some responses with a classmate. In light of the ideas presented in this chapter, which responses were more effective?

■ *Racial and Ethnic Micro-Messages:*

· Two mid-level lawyers, Tim who is white and Shaquille who is African-American, completed a challenging assignment extremely well. A few senior lawyers discussed their work. One mentioned that Tim has shown promise from day one, and another wondered about the extent of Shaquille's contribution.

· An East Asian American, born and raised in the United States, is complimented for speaking English "so well."

· A Latina attorney is asked how she finds the firm's South American practice group. In fact, she is a member of the firm's intellectual property group.

· Three different people over the course of a few weeks asked a tall Black associate why he has yet to join the office basketball team.

· A Korean female lawyer was directed by her supervisor, "Tell me what you think about the brief. Look me in the eye. Give it to me straight."

■ *Gender Micro-Messages:*

- A female senior lawyer is labeled as pushy and difficult to get along with, whereas her male counterpart is described as forceful and someone who sets high standards.

- A female associate is asked to take notes at a department meeting.

- A female associate is advised to wear a dress or skirt suit to court.

- At a celebration dinner to congratulate a female lawyer and her team for execution of a major deal, the client gave a toast spending half the time talking about the lawyer's great new haircut.

■ *Sexual Orientation Micro-Messages:*

- An extern uses the term "gay" to describe a movie she disliked.

- When lunch conversation turns to judicial developments in gay marriage, everyone turns to the single gay man, asking him to explain what gay parents believe about child rearing.

- The girlfriend of a lesbian attorney joins her for the office party. They are told that their hand-holding is too much PDA (public display of affection).

■ *Religious, Disability, and Social Status Micro-Messages:*

- A firm that handles DUI defense asks the new Latino client to pay the firm's retainer in cash, a policy the firm has for all clients.

- The lead attorney for the opposing party comes to your firm for a settlement conference. He starts to speak more loudly and more slowly when an attorney for your office enters the conference room in a wheel chair.

- A lawyer is meeting with a client who is deaf and has a child who is also deaf. The child is the subject of a custody dispute with the other, hearing parent. The lawyer says to the client, "You really should agree to the cochlear implant for your daughter."

- A Muslim paralegal who wears a hijab is passed over to work on a high profile matter that may attract media coverage, in favor of a more junior paralegal.

- An extern who attends a law school from the lowest tier of US News rankings, completes a research assignment quickly, finds very useful on-point cases, and writes a beautiful memo. The supervisor remarks that she cannot believe the extern attends such "a lowly school."

Conclusion and Takeaways

Even when we are well intentioned about cultural difference, we all manifest bias because we are humans who live in cultures with preferences and biases about our own cultures and about other cultures. Our lawyering is necessarily affected because these biases operate at an automatic, unconscious level. Because we develop these biases over a lifetime, undoing their effects is not easy or quick. Nonetheless, our commitment to cultural competence will allow us to develop behaviors to overcome unconscious biases and to develop more inclusive and effective lawyering.

- Cultural competence begins with understanding our personal culture, including frankness about how it forms a cultural lens for how we personally view and interact with others.

- Our personal culture also comes with the baggage we carry from being immersed in the dominant culture where we live, play, and work. This holds true whether we are members of the dominant culture or members of a subordinate culture.

- The baggage, with all its stereotypes, is the product of our media saturated world—from literature, television, film, news, digital media, etc. These comprise our reference points, our encyclopedia. They are part of our unconscious mind that cannot be turned off.

- We can train ourselves to overcome these assumptions and biases, whether conscious or unconscious.

- Practicing the Habits of Cross-Cultural Lawyering will enable us to observe, interpret, and reinterpret our encounters, especially ones with uncomfortable dynamics.

- Reserving judgment and practicing disciplined naïveté shows the humility that our perspective is neither logically inevitable nor universally held.

- We can actively expand and deepen our cultural knowledge—our repertoire of reference points.

· We can anticipate how other people might perceive us, avoid negative micro-messaging, and be culturally open.

· We can recognize that we will make missteps, but should avoid self-recrimination. Do not let missteps make us shy away from engaging meaningfully with people very different from us.

ENDNOTES

1   AM. BAR ASS'N SECTION OF LEGAL EDUC. & ADMISSIONS TO THE BAR, STANDARD 302(D) & INTERPRETATION 302-1 (2014). Standard 302(d) and Interpretation 302-1 were approved by the Council of the Section of the Legal Education and Admissions to the Bar on June 6, 2014 and approved by the American Bar Association's House of Delegates on August 11, 2014.

2   *Task Force on Admissions Regulation Reform: Phase II Final Report*, September 25, 2014 (Jon B. Streeter, Chair; Patrick M. Kelly, Vice Chair) recommended a new requirement that an applicant must have taken 15 credits of experiential learning coursework in law school. The Task Force recommendation was adopted unanimously by State Bar of California Board of Trustees, November 7, 2014.

3   SUSAN BRYANT, ELLIOTT MILLSTEIN & ANN C. SHALLECK, Chapter 15, *Reflecting on the Habits: Teaching about Identity, Culture, Language, and Difference*, in TRANSFORMING THE EDUCATION OF LAWYERS (2014).

4   JOSEPHA CAMPINHA-BACOTE, THE PROCESS OF CULTURAL COMPETENCE IN THE DELIVERY OF HEALTHCARE SERVICES: THE JOURNEY CONTINUES (5th ed. 2007).

5   *DBR MTV Bias Survey Summary* (2014). MTV Strategic Insights partnered with David Binder Research in 2013 on a study designed to understand and measure how young people are experiencing, affected by, and responding to issues associated with bias. The study is based on in-person focus groups, online discussion panels, and one-on-one interviews between December 2013 and April 2014 with U.S. millennials (14–24 years old) representative of the U.S. population at large. *See also* Look Different, MTV, www.lookdifferent.org (last visited Dec. 27, 2015)

6   VERNĀ MYERS, WHAT IF I SAY THE WRONG THING? 25 HABITS FOR CULTURALLY EFFECTIVE PEOPLE, at 116 (2013).

7   GEERT HOFSTEDE, CULTURE'S CONSEQUENCES: INTERNATIONAL DIFFERENCES IN WORK RELATED VALUES (1980). As originally written by Pascal, "Vérité en-deçà des Pyrénées, erreur au-delà," PENSÉES.

8   Jerry Kang, *Implicit Bias: A Primer for Courts* (2009), prepared for the National Campaign to Ensure the Racial and Ethnic Fairness of America's State Courts.

9   DANIEL KAHNEMAN, THINKING, FAST AND SLOW (2011).

10   *Id.* at 13.

11   *Id.* at 415–17.

12   Kang, *supra* note 8, at 3.

13   Jerry Kang, Nilanjana Dasgupta, Kumar Yogeeswaran & Gary Blasi, *Are Ideal Litigators White? Measuring the Myth of Colorblindness*, 7 J. EMPIR. LEGAL STUD. 886–915 (2010).

14   Mary Rowe, *Micro-affirmations & Micro-inequities*, J. INT'L OMBUDSMAN ASS'N (Mar. 2008).

15   KAHNEMAN, *supra* note 9, at 415.

16   *See* MTV survey, *supra* note 5. When commenting on micro-aggressions, 25% of white millennials indicated that they had been personally hurt by them, 28% said that when added up, they have a serious effect on them; and 38% said that micro-aggressions were a problem for them personally. The people of color who were study participants had quite different experiences. Some 45% indicted they have been personally hurt, 49% indicated that the cumulative impact has had a serious effect on them; and 58% that micro-aggressions are a problem for them personally.

17   Derald Wing Sue, *Microaggressions: More than Just Race*, Psychology Today (Nov. 17, 2010), https://www.psychologytoday.com/blog/microaggressions-in-everyday-life/201011/microaggressions-more-just-race https://www.psychologytoday.com/blog/microaggressions-in-everyday-life.

18   *Written in Black & White: Exploring Confirmation Bias in Racialized Perceptions of Writing Skills*, in Yellow Paper Series, Nextions (Apr. 2014).

19   Peggy McIntosh, "White Privilege: Unpacking the Invisible Knapsack," (excerpted from Working Paper No. 189 *White Privilege and Male Privilege: A Personal Account of Coming to See Correspondences Through Work in Women's Studies*, Wellesley College Center for Research on Women) (1988).

20   Tom Shatel, *The Unknown Barry Switzer: Poverty, Tragedy Built Oklahoma Coach Into A Winner*, Kansas City Star and Chicago Tribune, Dec. 14, 1986 (reporting interview of Barry Switzer, football coach, University of Oklahoma and Dallas Cowboys).

21   Paul R. Tremblay, *Interviewing and Counseling Across Cultures: Heuristics and Biases*, 9 Clinical L. Rev. 373, at 386–95 (2002).

22   Ben L. Martin, *From Negro to Black to African American: The Power of Names and Naming*, 106 Pol. Sci. Q. 83 (1991).

23   A group of Twitter activists in the U.S. started a campaign to overcome the "hoodie = danger" schema, precisely to help people appreciate counter-stereotypical imagery. They posted side-by-side photos of themselves in street-casual attire and in "success" clothing to help people broaden their knowledge base and mitigate their implicit assumptions. Tanzina Vega, *Shooting Spurs Hashtag Effort on Stereotypes*, N.Y. Times, Aug. 12, 2014 (describing the Twitter campaign #IfTheyGunnedMeDown that emerged in response to the police shooting of Michael Brown, an unarmed black teenager, in Ferguson, Missouri on August 9, 2014).

24   T.F. Pettigrew & L.R. Tropp, *How Does Intergroup Contact Reduce Prejudice? Mseta-analytic Tests of Three Mediators.* 38 Eur. J. Soc. Psychol. 922–934 (2008).

25   *See* G.W. Allport, The Nature of Prejudice (1954); *see also* Lu Hong and Scott E. Page, *Groups of Diverse Problem Solvers can Outperform Groups of High-Ability Problem Solvers*, Proceedings of the National Academy of Sciences (2004); *see also* Scott E. Page, The Difference: How the Power of Diversity Creates Better Groups, Firms, Schools and Societies (2007).

26   Myers, *supra* note 6, at 45–46.

27   S. Lebrecht, L.J. Pierce, M.J. Tarr & J.W. Tanaka, *Perceptual Other-Race Training Reduces Implicit Racial Bias*, PLoS ONE 4(1): E4215. DOI:10.1371/JOURNAL.PONE.0004215 (2009).

28   Kang, Helping Courts to Address Implicit Bias: Strategies to Reduce the Influence of Implicit Bias, 2–4 (National Center for State Courts 2009), http://www.ncsc.org/IBstrategies.

29   MTV, *supra* note 5.

APPENDIX 6.1

Five Habits of Cross Cultural Lawyering

Professors Bryant and Koh Peters introduced the Five Habits in 2001 and have revisited and refined the habits in later articles and books. These short explanations of the Five Habits are extracted from their latest work, *Reflecting on the Habits: Teaching about Identity, Culture, Language, and Difference,* Chapter 15, in TRANSFORMING THE EDUCATION OF LAWYERS.

Habit 1, "Degrees of Separation and Connection," asks lawyers to identify and map the overlap between the lawyer's and the client's worlds, creating an inventory of the differences and similarities that the lawyer perceives. Examples include ethnicity, race, gender, age, economic or social status, role in the family, and time orientation. Appreciating these traits will assist the lawyer's interpretation of the client's body language, behavior, and statements.

Habit 2, "The Three Rings; or Forest and Trees", adds a third dimension—an analysis of how the client's and lawyer's cultural identities overlap with the cultural identities of others in the legal process, including judges, opposing party, opposing counsel, etc.. For instance, a judge may have a sympathetic or antagonistic view of the client and her story not only based upon a legal analysis of a claim, but on cultural impressions of the client, whether explicit or implicit. The list can then be analyzed to refine and strengthen the presentation of the client's matter.

Habit 3, "Parallel Universe; Not Jumping to Conclusions about Behavior," guides lawyers to explore multiple alternative interpretations of any client behavior and thereby avoid leaping to quick and perhaps inaccurate assumptions based on insufficient information. For example, a client's tardiness or failure to heed her lawyer's advice may not have anything to do with her attitude towards her case, but rather may be connected to a cultural habit or attitude.

Habit 4, "Red Flags and Remedies," directly addresses client interaction and being alert to incipient communication difficulties. The lawyer identifies ahead of time what she will look for to assess whether her comments and questions are being accurately received and understood by the client. Habit 4 accustoms the lawyer to reflect on communication while communicating and in between client encounters. For example, the lawyer can observe whether the client appears bored, disengaged or uncomfortable; the client has not spoken in many minutes and the lawyer is dominating; the client is angry; the lawyer is judging the client negatively; or the lawyer is distracted, bored, or is mechanically performing a common routine. If a red flag is spotted, a lawyer adjusts and redirects the conversation.

Habit 5, "The Camel's Back; the Sadder but Wiser Habit," addresses the inevitable moments when the lawyer blunders cross-culturally, and guides the lawyer to identify the factors, e.g., stereotypes, implicit biases, personal distractions or stressors, that lead to cross-cultural mishaps. This Habit encourages lawyers to monitor consciously for biased thinking by identifying potential stereotypes that might apply to the situation. As Bryant and Koh Peters remind us, "a[n] intentional approach to eliminating bias versus one that tries to ignore difference is more likely to result in decisions based on fact."

CHAPTER 7

Bias in the Legal Profession

STACY L. BRUSTIN & CARMIA N. CAESAR

Personal Reflections

I n 2003, on a spring afternoon, I took the train from Washington, D. C. to Manhattan to attend a friend's wedding reception. It was before I had children, so I remember feeling like my attire was flawless—a lovely dress, matching shoes, perfect hair, jewelry, and make-up. No purse because I was carrying a change of clothes that I had worn on the train in a small black satchel. I arrived a few hours early to spend time with some law school friends at their brownstone in Brooklyn. They had just had their first son, and I was newly pregnant with mine. The two or three hours passed quickly. It is amazing how close we had become in the three years that turned us into lawyers. Common suffering, civil procedure, and cold winters in Boston can do that, I suppose.

An hour before the reception was scheduled to begin, I changed and called a car for the ride into the city. I remember feeling excited to be in New York, a feeling that I used to get in the back of my grandparents' station wagon when we would cross into Manhattan from Queens to attend services at the Convent Avenue Baptist Church in Harlem. On this day, however, I was driving through Central Park to the Upper East Side to a museum housed in the Henry Clay Frick House on Fifth Avenue between 70th and 71st. It never occurred to me as I stepped out of a sleek Lincoln Town Car and walked up the flagstone path that I did not look every bit the part.

I remember crossing the terrace and seeing Sunny chatting with a security guard, as she waited for the first guests to arrive. Our eyes met, and I was flooded with warmth and the comfort that comes from knowing someone since the 4th grade. We began walking toward one another, both of us smiling ear to ear, but suddenly the moment ended. The guard stepped in front of my friend as if to protect her from some threat. "Can I help you?" she asked. "No," I responded, not quite realizing what was happening, wondering why someone was protecting one of my best friends from me. But I was guilty, guilty of forgetting my blackness, not remembering that I am not experienced as me, but as a black[1] person/woman/threat who does not belong.

"I'm sorry. The museum is closed for a private event." I was speechless for a moment, but only a moment, because then I understood. Even this other black woman, in her capacity as a security guard, did not think that I belonged at The Frick Collection, and certainly not at a function of the magnitude of this reception.

"I'm here for the party," I explained. "I didn't know," she said. "You're carrying that bag." I carried a small, black bag over my shoulder. Just big enough for a wallet, makeup bag, clothes for my ride home. I couldn't even fit my paperback book inside. Was it really my small, black bag or my big black self? Sunny rushed around the guard and assured her that it was okay to let me in, her green eyes sparkling with excitement, gushing about the evening, and all of the old friends who were due to arrive at any moment. I would like to say that I brushed it off, or that it did not bother me, but that would be untrue. It made me angry; it made me feel powerless; it was a reminder not only of how other people felt about me as a black woman, but also of how other people had successfully made us feel about ourselves. [C.N.C.]

I had been out of law school for about a year. I spent most of my days in the local trial court and was just beginning to feel like a lawyer, albeit an inexperienced one, when I had my first professional encounter with bias.

I was sitting in a settlement conference and the judge hearing the case was attempting to broker a settlement between my client and the other party. Every time my opposing counsel addressed me, she referred to me as young lady. "Listen young lady," "what do you mean young lady," "now, young lady . . ." She was not saying it in the good-hearted, encouraging way older people sometimes refer to those who are younger. She was using it to make me aware of my status and it was working. "Why does she keep saying 'young lady'?" I thought to myself, trying to keep my focus on the issues at hand. Finally, I could not stand it any longer. "Would you please stop referring to me as 'young lady'?" I asked. The judge looked up and the other attorney calmly replied, "Okay, older lady, what about this proposal?" The judge did not say a word. I was fuming inside, but did not want to let the other lawyer know it. I ignored her comment and continued with the negotiation.

That same year, I was appearing before a different judge in a family law matter. The courtroom was packed. My co-counsel and I (one white and one Latina) were presenting arguments to the judge on a procedural issue. When we finished, the judge turned to the other attorney and asked for his response to our arguments. While arguing his point, the opposing attorney referred to us as "lovely young ladies." The judge interrupted him in mid-sentence and ordered him to approach the bench. Although the judge tried to make her comments inaudible to the rest of the courtroom, everyone heard the admonishment. She fumed "while your opposing counsel may be lovely and may be young, you better not ever use that kind of inappropriate language again in my courtroom."

In both situations, as soon as the attorneys uttered their comments, I felt unnerved. The comments seemed inappropriate, but, I thought to myself, maybe I was being too sensitive. Perhaps the attorneys did not mean anything by what they were saying. Yet, it seemed they were trying to use their status to intimidate and belittle me. As a white woman, I felt that this inappropriate behavior did not rise to the level of something as serious as racial bias, but it was problematic. The one thing that was clear to me was that my legal education had not prepared me to deal with these issues. [S.L.B.]

The initials C.N.C. and S.L.B. refer to the authors Carmia Caesar and Stacy Brustin. Later in the chapter, when we tell our own stories, we refer to ourselves by our first names.

Why Do We Have This Chapter Anyway?

This is the 21st Century. A black man has been elected to our nation's highest office—twice! And there are not two, but three women on the Supreme Court, and one of them is a woman of color. Surely, we are in post-racial America in which those of us in the legal profession are aware of bias and have made corrections.

So, why do we have this chapter anyway? We believe this chapter is important because external progress does not erase bias within the profession. As discussed in Chapter 6, what we profess to believe and how we aspire to live and interact with our colleagues, clients, professors, and peers is no match for how we unconsciously process information, read situations, and initially react to people around us. Certain types of people scare some of us while some of us look at those same people and experience a sense of relief and familiarity. Certain types of cars, certain types of music make some of our hearts race with panic while some of us see the same cars or hear the same music and our hearts race with excitement and fond memories. MacArthur Award-winning psychologist, Jennifer Eberhardt, has been widely cited for her work, SEEING BLACK: RACE, CRIME, AND VISUAL PROCESSING, which examines how individuals process race and how those processes effect perceptions of other objects, particularly objects associated with crime.[2]

We have this chapter because even if you are of a generation committed to diversity and inclusion, you will be supervised by lawyers, collaborate with police officers, represent clients, and appear before judges who may not share your perspective or be aware of their own biases. This reality is reflected in a story posted by one of the author's black, female colleagues in 2014:

> I had a senior person interviewing for a job "working for me." The letter inviting him to interview was over my signature. He'd been working with my secretary for details of flights and hotels and what not. The day of the interview, he called me [by] my secretary's name, assuming that I had to be her, as he tried to blow past me into the room ahead of schedule to say hello to Dr. Jones.

We have this chapter because hiring, retention, and promotion are still influenced by structural bias embedded in the profession. Joe will get hired before Jose, even if they are the same guy. See http://www.huffingtonpost.com/2014/09/02/jose-joe-job-discrimination_n_5753880.html?ncid=fcbklnkushpmg00000047&ir=Black+Voices.

While the 2014 MTV study referenced in Chapter 6 found that millennials believe their generation is post-racial, race still plays a significant role in how each millennial experiences the world. For example, in responding to the statement "I am often asked about my ethnic background," nineteen percent of white people answered affirmatively, while sixty percent of persons of color answered affirmatively. MTV Look Different, MTV Strategic Insights, 2014 http://cdn.lookdifferent.org/content/studies/000/000/001/DBR_MTV_Bias_Survey_Executive_Summary.pdf. We are writing this chapter in the wake of the tragic police shootings of unarmed African American men in Ferguson, Missouri, New York City, and Baltimore. These incidents are painful reminders that there is still work for those in the legal profession to do.

Fortunately, as this chapter discusses, there has been progress. States have adopted laws and ethical rules prohibiting explicitly biased and discriminatory conduct. Younger lawyers expect and clients are demanding diversity in the profession. These changes, however, have not eliminated the longstanding patterns of discrimination that continue to impact present day law practice and the administration of justice.[3] In addition, as the narratives in the next section suggest, subtle, and sometimes not so subtle, forms of bias continue to pervade the legal profession.

At least 65 state and federal courts have published reports on bias. These reports have documented racial, ethnic, gender, disability, and sexual orientation bias in law practice throughout the United States. Studies conducted of law schools suggest that students perceive similar bias in the law school environment.

Concern about bias has caused many jurisdictions to adopt rules of professional conduct prohibiting judges and attorneys from engaging in biased behavior. These rules vary in scope, but they are designed to hold lawyers and judges accountable for their behavior in and out of the courtroom. For example, ABA Model Rule 8.4(d) on Misconduct & Maintaining the Integrity of the Profession states that it is professional misconduct for a lawyer to "engage in conduct that is prejudicial to the administration of justice." The comment to this rule clarifies that ". . . [a] lawyer who, in the course of representing a client, knowingly manifests by words or conduct, bias or prejudice based upon race, sex, religion, national origin, disability, age, sexual orientation or socioeconomic status, violates paragraph (d) when such actions are prejudicial to the administration of justice . . . ." These rules supplement existing state and federal laws that prohibit sexual harassment, employment discrimination, and tortious behavior.

Some behavior does not rise to the level of actionable discrimination or violation of a professional conduct rule, yet it is still inappropriate. How will you respond if, in a professional setting, someone makes an inappropriate comment to you based on your age, race, ethnicity, gender, disability, sexual orientation, socioeconomic status, or religion? What if the comment is directed toward a colleague? Will you have an ethical obligation to report the behavior? If not, will you make clear your disapproval, or will you let the comment slide?

The legal workforce increasingly reflects the diversity of the larger workforce. In practice, you will be supervised by or work alongside judges, attorneys, administrators, support staff, and clients whose race, gender, physical abilities, mental health, age, religion, sexual orientation, or socioeconomic class differ from yours. How will you develop solid professional relationships? How can you be certain that you are not inadvertently engaging in behavior or making decisions based upon negative stereotypes or internalized, biased assumptions?

What happens when you become a supervisor or managing attorney and you bear the responsibility for ensuring that neither you nor your institution tolerates discriminatory or biased behavior? Will you know how to protect your organization? Will you be able to supervise a diverse group of employees? Even if the law office or organization you manage is free of illegal, discriminatory practices, is that sufficient? How can you foster a positive, inclusive work environment in which all employees are productive and feel that they are part of the team?

This chapter encourages you to grapple with these issues during your externship—before you officially enter the legal profession. If you have not previously considered the issue of bias, then an externship provides an excellent opportunity to develop your awareness. For those of you who are all too familiar with the personal impact of biased or discriminatory behavior, an externship offers an opportunity to explore and refine how you will address these issues, as lawyers, in a professional setting.

We have this chapter because in 2014, partners at large law firms uniformly critiqued the exact same memo more harshly when they were told that the authoring associate was not white.[4]

Experiences of Bias in the Legal Profession

The concept of bias in the legal profession and its subtleties are best understood in the context of real life stories. The following excerpts explore bias from the perspectives of lawyers who have directly experienced it. The first excerpt was written in 2000 but, as the rest of the narratives demonstrate, the reality that Thomas Williamson Jr., a partner at Covington and Burling in Washington D.C. and former president of the D.C. Bar, describes is not a thing of the past.

Thomas S. Williamson, *Transcript of the Boston Bar Association Diversity Committee Conference: Recruiting, Hiring and Retaining Lawyers of Color*, 44 B.B.J. 8, (May/June 2000.)

> . . . Often there are no other blacks in your entering class of associates; there may not be others in the whole firm, or, at best, there will be a token scattering. Depending on which floor in the firm you're on, you may not see any black professionals for weeks or months at a time. Many firms have no black partners, and those that do only have one or two. The people of color who work in these firms are concentrated in support positions, at secretarial desks, in the mail room, pushing the carts around with audio/visual equipment, or in janitorial services. The firm's clientele rarely, if ever, include any black organizations or any black individuals.

> It may be an overstatement to say that this is a culture shock, but it is a particularly stressful entry experience. New black lawyers who have gone to these predominantly white firms understand the unwritten law that says you must be an expert, an expert in making white people feel comfortable, and, from the first, you are expected to act delighted and pleased that you are in such a "great firm." If you fail to follow that rule, fail to adhere to that law, there will be severe repercussions for your professional career. . . .

Partner critiques and supervision of black lawyers are awkward, at best. Partners are the authority figures in law firms. They hand out the assignments; do the evaluations; decide who will become a partner. Minority lawyers, especially black lawyers, understand that many white partners at the large law firms have low or skeptical expectations about the abilities of minority lawyers. Those low expectations inevitably affect the types of assignments and the types of evaluations black lawyers receive. . . .

White partners are generally very uncomfortable critiquing black lawyers for fear that aggressive criticism will be interpreted as racial animus. Even when a black lawyer does well, white supervisors are reluctant to push the good black lawyer to excel further, fearing it might be viewed as some kind of racial bias. This, of course, is very important for one's partnership prospects. Most firms expect their lawyers to be good, but the associates who want to make partner must show they can be excellent. Thus, black lawyers are shortchanged at the very time in their careers when they are most open to learning and most in need of advice and guidance. . . .

. . . The success mantra at law firms today is that you have to learn how to find clients and serve the clients if you want to get ahead. Minority lawyers face special obstacles in making their mark developing client relationships. Although a firm might provide a positive and nurturing environment for black lawyers, there's no assurance that the clients are eager to entrust their problems to people of color. . . .

Partners, of course, have to be realistic and business oriented and make careful calculations about how to foster client confidence. Will a client think a white partner is giving his company's problem top priority if the partner assigns an African-American lawyer to handle the matter? Some clients are reluctant to believe that black lawyers are smart enough to handle a difficult and sensitive problem. I have had personal experience with this "business sensitivity" in my own career, and my unpleasant experiences have not just been limited to my associate years.

I had been a partner for two or three years when a client telephoned another partner and said, "We're going to have a very sensitive board meeting and I know Tom is supposed to be there. But there are a couple of white southerners on the board, and I don't think he would be the right person to do this." The partner made it clear to the client that if Covington & Burling was to continue representing his organization, I would be the lawyer at the meeting. . . .

My examples of the special burdens and challenges of being an African-American lawyer in a large law firm are not intended to be comprehensive, but simply illustrative of the fact that racial integration in the law firm setting is not simply a matter of white people opening doors with good intentions. . . .

Maria Chavez, *The Rise of the Latino Lawyer: A New Study of Hispanics in the Legal Profession Reveals Inspiring Successes and Lingering Obstacles*, ABA JOURNAL (Oct. 2011) at 36–37.

There are dozens of different reasons why someone would choose to go to law school and become an attorney. Some may want to go into politics or trial work. Others may want to work for social justice, a nonprofit or a cause they are passionate about, such as the environment. Some view it, like many others, as a stylish path to making money.

. . . For some, however, the motivation that drives them to become attorneys is a bit different, motivated by a sense of feeling they have experienced wrongs in their lives. For many Latinos, the decision to become a lawyer can be very personal.

This was the experience for Anna, who grew up the youngest daughter of Mexican immigrants who earned a meager living as farmworkers in Burley, Idaho. As Anna recalls the experiences that motivated her to go to law school, she notes they weren't all pleasant. She hated that her parents weren't treated fairly when they worked in the fields of sugar beets, beans or potatoes. She recounts the grueling, often illegal, conditions they endured in the fields. . . . Her dad was always especially cautious when it came to the ranchers or bosses because he had no power and no conception of having rights. And it was his experience—her family's experience—that made her decide to go to law school.

Feeling wronged is also what drove Tony, a man now in his late 50s, to become a lawyer. His high school teachers suggested that he set his sights on becoming an auto mechanic. This made him so angry, he recalls, that he was determined it was the last thing he would become. Perhaps they thought that by guiding him into a trade, they were actually doing this young Latino a favor. And in a way they did.

. . . One of the main findings in my study is that Latino lawyers still face an astounding amount of racism and discrimination in their professions and in their communities. This experience does not end once Latinos have become professionals. . . .

In the survey, I asked Latino lawyers whether their ethnicity has caused them difficulties in their profession . . . . Although 46 percent of the respondents answered yes, a significant number of those who answered no included comments that echoed the experiences of those who perceived race-based professional problems.

Many of the comments included strong statements reflecting negative experiences with stereotypes and discrimination. The following examples are representative of their written comments:

"Societal stereotypes are very common in the legal profession. Most people believe you are a clerk/bailiff or interpreter."

"Having to overcome other people's prejudice; feeling different due to different values."

"Only to the extent that persons of color must be better than others to succeed. I truly believe this."

"Difficult to do jury trials because majority of jurors are retired white people."

"Not treated the same as my counterparts by courts, colleagues." "Do not fit in with the big-firm culture."

"Only initially with other lawyers. Anglo clients rarely contact me, but Latino clients constantly do."

"Latinos are not well-regarded in this country and other professionals do not know how to interact (threatening?)."

"I was not considered a good 'mix' for certain firms; looked upon as unqualified or undesirable."

"The primary difficulty being Latino/Hispanic has caused [me] has been in the interview process as I was seeking my first job. . . .

"People don't take you seriously."

"Presumption of incompetence."

"Negative stereotypes: lazy, affirmative action."

. . . But perhaps the most durable theme that emerged from the survey was the notion often cited by other minorities—that Latino lawyers needed to be "10 times better" as professionals than their non-Latino counterparts. This subtle, pervasive sense—that throughout the day, every day they are being held to a higher standard by their colleagues, clients, and even community members—is difficult to grasp in a personal sense, unless one has experienced it.

G.M. Filisko, *Just Like Everyone: Inclusiveness Efforts Seek to Make GLBT Lawyers—And All Others—Feel at Home*, ABA JOURNAL (Feb. 2010) at 40.

Like many in the gay, lesbian, bisexual and transgender community, Liza Barry-Kessler has never been sure of the reaction she'll get when potential employers, supervisors, co-workers and clients learn she's a lesbian. In the early 2000s, while working at a small lobbying firm in Washington, D.C., on issues of education, technology, and the Internet, many of Barry-Kessler's colleagues knew she was gay. But the issue was never discussed, and she sensed it was best not to mention it to clients. . . . "That wasn't something anyone ever said—the people I worked with weren't homophobic. But there was an additional level of hypersensitivity to the possibility that it would look somehow off-putting to the clients."

In 2003 with new employer AOL, then based in Dulles, Va., Barry-Kessler got an entirely different reception when she returned from her honeymoon after a non-state-sanctioned wedding. "It blew my mind," Barry-Kessler says. "My co-workers did whatever they'd have done for anybody else getting married. They decorated my cubicle, everybody contributed to a gift, and they had a cake for me. It was better than I'd hoped for. It was treated as normal."

. . . GLBT lawyers have come a long way . . . but many still make individual calculations about how much personal information they can safely reveal at work. "One of the most obvious places where issues arise concerning sexual orientation is at the recruiting stage," [another lawyer] says. "It somewhat frequently arises when recruits have done work related to their GLBT status as a law student or been involved in a leadership role at their college GLBT organization, and the entity might provide a reference. That's something you'd normally put on a resume, but frequently that's a concern if they don't know whether the firm is going to discriminate."

These challenges are compounded by the fact that many firms simply don't discuss GLBT issues, making it difficult for these attorneys to know whether the firm believes it's honoring their privacy or it simply wants the issue to go away. "Firm management who may feel they're being appropriately respectful of the privacy of gay lawyers by not asking them personal questions such as 'Do you want to bring your domestic partner to this client dinner?' are instead sending a signal that GLBT lawyers are supposed to be closeted, that the families [of heterosexual lawyers] have value, and the gay lawyers are supposed to just be lawyers," says Kelly Dermody, a partner at Lieff Cabraser Heimann & Bernstein in San Francisco. "If the leadership never uses the terms *gay, lesbian* or *GLBT*, or if the firm is completely silent, there's a certain message being sent." . . . Whatever the reason for many firms' palpable silence, the result is that gay, lesbian, bisexual, and transgender lawyers must use detective-like skills to root out whether potential employers are GLBT friendly.

. . . The *T* in GLBT represents transgender individuals, a minority within the minority facing a kind of discrimination and disrespect that few, even within the gay and lesbian community, have considered. M. Dru Levasseur faced challenges few other students encounter when he transitioned during law school. "People met me as female and under a different name," says the 2006 graduate of Western New England College School of Law, "and there was no way for me to have a different way to come out."

One of Levasseur's biggest challenges was how to address his gender identity during the hiring process.

. . . "During an interview, one person asked, 'Do you really think it's a good idea to tell people you're a transgender attorney?' I said, 'Yes, I do. In fact, I think it's a strength that I've gone through the challenge of transitioning, and I'm still a great attorney and have achieved in spite of all the extra stress.'" He got a job offer there. Levasseur also faced outright discrimination. "I was on a second interview [at a Northeastern office of a national firm], and the partner asked, 'What's transgender?'" he recounts. "I started telling him, and he interrupted and said, 'There are no gay people at the firm. If you wanted to start a gay group, you'd be the only one in it.'"

Kristin Choo, *Walking the Tightrope, Muslim Women Who Practice Law Are Asserting Themselves in Efforts to Reconcile Traditional Beliefs with Modern Secular Society*, ABA JOURNAL (Feb. 2013) at 38.

Amina Saeed, a co-founder and president of the Muslim Bar Association of Chicago and an estate planning attorney in suburban Lisle, says she started studying Islam independently with a group of other Muslim students in college. It was shortly after the first Gulf War in 1991, and for the first time, she was hearing ethnic slurs against Muslims on campus and elsewhere. At the same time, she learned that some Muslims were upset that she, a woman, had been elected president of her university's Muslim students' association.

. . . [W]hen Saeed announced her intention to study law, her parents were dismayed. That was hardly surprising, Saeed acknowledges, because in general, Muslim-Americans were slow to embrace the law as a profession. First-generation immigrants often were suspicious of the law and lawyers, who they viewed as functionaries of the government. "In the countries that they came from, anything associated with government was looked on with suspicion," she says. . . . But it took the traumatic events of Sept. 11, 2001, for the Muslim community to recognize the important role lawyers can play in American society. Suddenly, Muslims across the United States were facing intense scrutiny and suspicion from both law enforcement and the larger society. "What we were seeing was a real void in the community in terms of understanding their legal rights," says Farhana Khera, the president and executive director of Muslim Advocates. "There was also a void in terms of an effective advocacy voice for the community." . . . But with few older lawyers to turn to, Muslim communities had no choice but to seek out some young, newly minted lawyers.

. . . Perhaps nothing more dramatically illustrates the conflicts that female Muslim lawyers are navigating than their choices about whether to wear a simple cloth garment: the hijab, or headscarf. The hijab is fraught with meaning in almost every society with a significant Muslim population, and those controversies play out in many different ways—often reflected in government policies or cultural expectations. . . .

Female Muslim lawyers in the United States who choose to wear the hijab say they are not immune from these conflicting reactions. But they add that wearing the hijab also can work to their advantage. "I wear it because I believe my faith prescribes it, and it's part of being modest," says [one lawyer]. "It's a way of having people's attention focus on my actions and accomplishments and not on my physical attributes." But wearing the hijab also provides a means of engaging both Muslim and non-Muslim communities, [this lawyer] says. "It allows me to not only identify myself outwardly as a Muslim, but it enables me to challenge stereotypes and misconceptions about Muslim women and Islam," she says. She believes that if Muslims and non-Muslims encounter a well-educated American professional like herself whose hijab identifies her as a Muslim, it might challenge preconceived or traditional ideas about a "proper" Muslim woman's roles and capabilities.

Saeed says she wore a hijab from the time she started practicing law in 1996. But as she walked into the court, people often mistook her for a translator—sometimes even after she identified herself. "It made it more nerve-wracking because I felt I had to perform better than anyone else just to be considered an equal," she says. "But I honestly believe that that experience made me a better lawyer." But the hijab also has made her the target of discrimination, Saeed says. Last February, when she flew to Dallas for a family weekend with her husband and three children, she was singled out for extra security checks on both the outgoing and return flights.

———————————

The final excerpt examines obstacles that those in the legal profession have to overcome and the challenges they continue to face on account of disability and gender.

Carrie Griffin Basas, *The New Boys: Women with Disabilities and the Legal Profession* 25 Berkeley J. Gender L. & Just. 32, 33–37 (2010).

I was born with a rare genetic syndrome affecting my joints and connective tissues and necessitating forty-some odd surgeries on my hips, knees, and feet, but I did not feel disabled until law school. My health declined around that time and, rather than walking everywhere, I began to use a scooter—not a mint vintage Vespa, as the cool kids might imagine, but one of those orthopedic scooters . . . . Even then, while I seemed more obviously disabled to the outside world, the reflections of other people's attitudes toward my physical appearance—their quick summaries and sizing up of my abilities and weaknesses—always surprised me. When fellow students at Harvard Law waited patiently some fifty yards ahead of me to push the blue button on the automatic door, I wished they would slam the door in my face as they had done with other students. I wanted the same level of rudeness in order to feel as if I had received the same level of kindness. Equality meant no deviations from the norms of law school behavior.

These daily events, while having a cumulative effect, did not serve as my initiation into the profession as a woman with a disability as much as one professor's reaction to my disability. Our class was originally slated to be held in a building on campus that did not offer an accessible door and, therefore, left me to cast aside my scooter in the elements of Cambridge in January. The ADA coordinator moved the class to another building with an automated door, and during the first class, the professor went on for a few minutes about why the class had been relocated. He could not understand what happened because his "class was always in that other room," and he suggested that the registrar may have made a mistake. I went up to him after class and explained my situation. The next day, he was waiting at the door to the classroom building to hold it open for me. Our paths had not crossed without some serious intervention on his part; he had obviously been waiting a long time to hold the door—minutes, an hour?

. . . [I]n the classroom, I was also a delicate object to praise and pat on the head. I would get the easy questions, and he would gush publicly about how well I had done. . . . [On the last day of class] . . . [a]s [the professor] provided the customary adieus, he deviated from norms of any kind when he began to talk about a "special person" in class who would go far, "serve on the Supreme Court," and "has helped so many unfortunate handicapped people." That person was me. And he had kept our class several minutes over to tell them how special I was and how proud they should be of me. Of course, everyone fled when discharged and said nothing to me. If I had not been the target of that speech, I would not have known what to say to a peer either.

I do not blame my peers for leaving me alone or even the professor for highlighting me as a heroine of sorts. I understand the incredible discomfort surrounding disability—people tripping over themselves to say the right thing, parents pulling their staring children back into the grocery line, classmates treating the "asexual" female classmate with a disability as more an object of study than a potential friend or partner. I sound disenchanted, but at that moment, it was resignation to being terribly alone in a way that I had never experienced in other mainstream settings. Granted, the social element was one detail of law school that may not work for many people, but being singled out in the classroom for being different and being treated as less than my peers—in being heralded as more than them—created this divide that had reduced my entire being to two words: disabled and woman.

. . . Only months earlier, I had done the on-campus recruiting process for summer jobs. Hiring partners reacted negatively to seeing me totter into the room with a cane and an unsteady (and at that time painful) gait. Unlike my peers, the questions that I received were about Casey Martin, the disabled golfer, and the comfort of my chair—"just fine, thanks." Fifteen minutes were routinely wasted on asking me if I could "keep up with the work" and understood "what it entailed." Yes, I know law firm work takes energy, stamina, intellect, perseverance, and a general ability to put up with a caste system. When I smiled and reassured them that I was capable, they nodded and suggested that I go into disability law....

Exercise 7.1: Record your reactions to the above readings. Identify examples of explicit, implicit, and structural bias from the readings. What do you believe is motivating the biased behaviors? Why, in the 21st century, are such experiences still prevalent? Is the bias that these legal professionals describe different in any way from bias that occurs to non-lawyers or those not involved in the legal profession? Are the conflicts and frustrations that the law students and lawyers describe attributable, at least in part, to stresses intrinsic to the practice of law regardless of race, ethnicity, gender, religion, socioeconomic status, sexual orientation, or disability? Do any of these excerpts, though intended to illustrate bias, inadvertently perpetuate stereotypes as well? What is your reaction to some of the lawyers' comments that experiencing bias fueled their drive and made them better lawyers?

QUESTIONS TO CONSIDER

As you read, did you identify with the subjects of the narratives, the individuals who have experienced bias? Alternatively, did you identify with the other people in the story, and wonder if you have unwittingly done something to offend someone in the classroom, at your externship? Consider the kinds of bias discussed in these excerpts, as well as the legal contexts in which bias occurred—the law school classroom or job interviews, courtrooms, conversations with associates or partners, client meetings, etc. As you work at your externship, keep alert for these contexts and evidence of bias transpiring. Have you seen or experienced bias in the legal environment(s) you encounter in your placement?

Defining and Assessing Bias in the Legal Profession

What is bias, and how does it impact the legal profession? There are many different definitions of bias found in statutes and rules prohibiting discrimination, reports studying bias, and scholarly articles. Bias generally can be defined as intolerance, prejudice, differential or disparaging treatment toward an individual based on stereotypes, or perceptions of inferiority related to the individual's race, ethnicity, gender, age, sexual orientation, socioeconomic status, religion, disability, or other cultural characteristic or trait. The Final Report of the Task Force on Gender Bias for the District of Columbia Courts gives examples of biased behavior in the gender context:[5]

- · when people are denied rights or burdened with responsibilities on the basis of gender;

- · when stereotypes about the proper behavior, relative worth and credibility of men and women are applied to people regardless of their individual situations;

- · when men and women are treated differently in situations because of gender where gender should not make a difference; and

- · when men or women are adversely affected by a legal rule, policy, or practice that affects members of the opposite sex to a lesser degree or not at all.

Although these examples are in the context of gender bias, the concepts apply to other forms of bias as well. Bias may be manifested in the behavior of individuals or may have become institutionalized in an organization's policies and procedures.

Some forms of discrimination are obvious and illegal. Firing an employee when she becomes pregnant, for example, or refusing to promote an associate in a firm because he has a foreign accent are obvious forms of illegal employment discrimination. Bias also comes in more subtle or elusive forms. While one person might interpret an incident as clear-cut bias, another person viewing the same situation may not see it at all.

Research on bias in the legal profession, distinguishes among three types of bias—explicit, implicit, and structural.

Explicit biases are attitudes and stereotypes that are consciously accessible through introspection and endorsed as appropriate. If no social norm against these biases exists within a given context, a person will freely broadcast them to others. But if such a norm exists, then explicit biases can be concealed to manage the impressions that others have of us. By contrast, implicit biases are attitudes and stereotypes that are not consciously accessible through introspection. If we find out that we have them, we may indeed reject them as inappropriate . . . . Besides explicit and implicit biases, another set of processes that produce unfairness in the courtroom can be called "structural." Other names include "institutional" or "societal." These processes can lock in past inequalities, reproduce them, and indeed exacerbate them even without formally treating persons worse simply because of attitudes and stereotypes about the groups to which they belong.[6]

Rather than relying on anecdotal tales of individual and institutional exclusion, bar associations, courts, trade organizations, and scholars have taken a more systematic look at the issue. These reports compile revealing statistics, capture perceptions of those who interface with the justice system, and measure the degree to which bias permeates the profession.

In 2014, the National Association of Women Lawyers (NAWL) issued a report measuring the progress of women in the country's 200 largest firms. According to this report, women are significantly underrepresented in leadership positions in large law firms despite the steady stream of women graduating from law school. "Since the mid-1980's, more than 40% of law school graduates have been women. Therefore, by now, one would expect law firms to be promoting women and men at nearly the same rate. Such parity has not been achieved, with the typical firm still counting less than 20% of its equity partners as women."[7] When broken down by race, women of color in big law firms fare far worse than white women in terms of leadership status and somewhat worse than men of color. In the top 100 firms, 2% of equity partners were women of color, whereas 6% of equity partners were men of color.[8] The NAWL survey notes that "[v]arious reports over the past 10 years show that virtually no progress has been made by the nation's largest firms in advancing minority partners and particularly minority women partners into the highest ranks of firms."[9] In terms of representation in the judiciary, women fared better but still lag significantly behind their male counterparts. As of 2012, women held 27% of all state court judgeships[10] and as of 2014, 33% of federal district court judgeships.[11]

Studies have found that racial/ethnic minorities, regardless of gender, perceive bias in the legal system more frequently than those in majority groups. In 2003, the National Center for State Courts issued a report entitled *Perceptions of the Courts in Your Community: The Influence of Experience, Race, and Ethnicity.*[12] This report released results of a national study, which found significant differences in perceptions of unequal treatment in courts. African American and Latino respondents were more likely to believe that unequal treatment occurs frequently in courts than white respondents. All groups agreed, however, that low-income individuals from all racial or ethnic groups receive the worst treatment in the courts.

The National Association for Legal Placement reported that the "overall percentage of openly gay, lesbian, bisexual and transgender (LGBT) lawyers reported in the NALP Directory of Legal Employers (NDLE) in 2012 increased to 2.07% compared with 1.88%

in 2011. . . . Over half (56%) of employers reported at least one LGBT lawyer."[13] However, senior lawyers were less likely to identify as LGBT (1.4% of partners compared to 2.4% of associates), and 60% of the openly LGBT lawyers live in one of four cities: New York, Washington D.C., Los Angeles, and San Francisco.[14] Reports on the state of the courts and judiciary found that fourteen percent of all of the judicial employees and nearly half of LGBT workers heard derogatory remarks or jokes about a person in the office who was perceived to be a member of the LGBT community.[15]

The numbers of attorneys with disabilities reported in surveys such as the National Association of Law Placements survey is very low. According to NALP, "[o]f the approximately 110,000 lawyers for whom disability information was reported in the 2009–2010 NALP Directory of Legal Employers (NDLE), just 255, or 0.23%, were identified as having a disability . . . . Only a handful of firms reported employing at least one summer associate with a disability. Out of more than 9,000 summer associates, only nine were reported as having a disability . . . . The numbers reported are very low and percentages are about 0.25% overall."[16] Many law firms do not collect this data and many individuals, particularly those with disabilities that are not readily apparent, are reluctant to disclose. According to NALP, law graduates with disabilities experienced lower rates of employment than other law graduates. For the class of 2009, 80.7% of graduates with disabilities were employed, whereas 89.2% of non-minority graduates and 84.8% of minority graduates were employed.[17]

Scholars have conducted research using the Implicit Association Test (IAT), which is discussed in Chapter 6 on Navigating Cultural Difference, to measure whether and to what degree bias permeates the legal profession and justice system. One such study conducted in 2010 suggested that unconscious gender bias was widespread among law students. In tests measuring implicit attitudes a diverse group of female and male law students associated males as judges and associated women with home and family.[18] Another study of jury-eligible individuals from Los Angeles measured participants' explicit and implicit beliefs about the ideal lawyer. This study, discussed in more detail in Chapter 6, demonstrated that individuals who subconsciously held implicit stereotypes associating litigators as being Caucasian, as opposed to Asian, were more likely to rank white lawyers as more competent, likable, and deserving of being hired.[19]

Bar associations, courts, scholars, and policy makers have offered varying causes for these concerning statistics, perceptions, and findings. Some suggest that implicit biases and stereotypes lead to the continued subordination of traditionally marginalized groups in the legal profession.[20] These biases permeate the culture of legal institutions causing disparities in promotion to leadership positions and causing lawyers subject to biases to leave these legal settings. Others suggest that biased criteria and "in-group" bias or preference for hiring or promoting someone of the same gender, race, or background explain the disparity.[21] Still others argue that structural barriers such as poverty and lack of educational opportunities blocking access to college and legal education,[22] lack of affordable child care, unreasonable work demands, lack of a critical mass of attorneys from one's affinity group(s), historically rooted challenges generating clients and business, and lack of understanding about accommodations lead female, disabled and individuals from other traditionally marginalized groups to part-time, public sector, or non-legal work.

Some skeptics argue that bias is not at the root of these disparities and that the passage of time will remediate the differentials. Given historical trends regarding admission of traditionally marginalized groups to law schools, they suggest it will take time for these groups to reach the leadership ranks of the profession. Some simply attribute the disparity to individual choices regarding career paths and work/life balance. In our view, however, the lack of progress despite the significant increase in the admission of diverse law school students as well as the studies on implicit bias are compelling and raise serious questions as to whether time or choice are responsible for the disparities in the legal profession.

Courts, bar associations, and legal scholars have issued wide ranging recommendations for addressing the problems of explicit, implicit, and structural bias including:

- changing hiring and promotion policies to ensure equal opportunity;

- adopting institutional measures for strengthening diversity within law firms such as tying compensation to diversity initiatives;

- enhancing mentoring programs;

- conducting multicultural training for court personnel, attorneys, and judges;

- improving communication between workers and managers;

- increasing the number of employees who speak languages other than English;

- enhancing the data collection and research conducted on diversity within the legal profession;

- instituting flexible work schedule policies;

- ensuring diversity in law school admissions as well as in law faculty hiring and promotion;

- incorporating discussions of the history of exclusion in the legal profession into the law school curriculum; and

- improving disciplinary proceedings for attorneys and judges.

While court bias studies and reports have been lauded for recommending needed institutional changes, they have also generated criticism.[23] Critics argue that some of the task force recommendations threaten judicial independence and free speech. Some believe, for example, that the desire to bring about racial or gender equality is being used as a justification for changing substantive outcomes in civil and criminal cases. There is also concern that the enactment of disciplinary rules prohibiting biased conduct may prevent lawyers from expressing their personal opinions outside of the courtroom or inhibit lawyers from zealously advocating on behalf of their clients inside the courtroom. Other critics suggest that outgrowths of these studies such as mandatory continuing legal education courses on diversity infringe upon lawyers' free speech rights because the government cannot coerce individuals into speaking or listening to messages with which the individual disagrees and constitute thinly veiled attempts to fulfill an agenda of liberal political correctness.

Whatever your views of these reports and studies, you will likely observe and experience changes in court practice, personnel policies in the private and public sectors, judicial decision-making, and disciplinary rules brought about as a result of these initiatives.[24]

QUESTIONS TO CONSIDER

How should the judicial system cope with the effects of bias that are prevalent in the culture at large? Should reforms be implemented based upon the **perception** of bias? How does one account for the differences in perceptions between minority groups and majority groups? Are there situations in which zealous advocacy on behalf of your client requires you to appeal to stereotypes or engage in biased behavior?

Things That I May Take for Granted That Some of My Law School Colleagues Cannot (Inspired by the Work of Peggy Mcintosh:

1. I am not repeatedly asked for my ID or credentials to demonstrate that I am a law student.

2. My fellow students or externship colleagues do not assume that I am an administrative assistant rather than a law student.

3. No one assumes that any of my educational or professional accomplishments were bestowed upon me because of the color of my skin or my disability.

4. I am able to observe major religious holidays because the law school or externship where I work closes on these days.

5. If I make a mistake, no one projects my mistake onto the group(s) to which I belong.

6. No one asks to touch my hair, is surprised that I wear sunscreen, or asks personal questions about my physical abilities.

7. I am not told to smile more so that I appear "less intimidating" or told to act "more feminine" or "more masculine."

8. I do not need to worry that my being honest will make people around me feel guilty and uncomfortable.

9. I do not receive harsher or more lenient feedback on my work on account of my race, ethnicity, or other affiliation.

10. If I invite my spouse or partner to a law school or office event, he or she feels welcomed.

11. No one at a law school or office social gathering mistakes me for a waiter and asks me for a cup of coffee or a glass of wine.

12. No one is surprised when I mention that my parents are professionals and my grandparents were professionals.

13. No one asks me, having been born and raised in the U.S., what country I am from.

14. No one is impressed by my command of the English language, "complimenting" me for being so articulate and well spoken.

15. Colleagues do not look to me for comment or reaction when an abhorrent act is committed by someone from my ethnic, racial, or religious group.

16. Others consider my race, gender, sexual orientation, or other affiliation neutral and thereby view my opinions or decisions as arrived at objectively.

Strategies for Dealing With Bias

During the course of your legal career you may witness or become the target of biased behavior. How do you respond? You may not be certain that what you are seeing or experiencing is bias, but you perceive that something is not quite right. A comment an associate at your firm makes bothers you. A reaction of a judge to lawyers or litigants takes you by surprise. A policy of the organization in which you are working seems to disproportionately hinder the progress of certain groups of attorneys.

In some circumstances, the bias or discrimination you experience may be so severe and blatant that you decide to resort immediately to formal channels of redress such as reporting an ethics violation to the court or bar, requesting that a judge impose sanctions, lodging a grievance with an employer, or filing a discrimination or harassment lawsuit against your employer. There are federal laws, state laws, and company policies designed to address egregious forms of discrimination or abuse. In many instances, however, the bias is more subtle, making it difficult to determine how to respond. It is important to develop strategies for addressing biased behavior whether you are on the receiving end, a witness, or a supervisor who becomes aware of a particular problem. This section discusses a variety of informal and formal ways to do so.

First, a few personal experiences:

During my first year of practice, I was representing a client in a divorce and custody hearing in the local trial court. My client's first language was Spanish and she was testifying with the assistance of a court-certified interpreter. At one point in the trial, a new interpreter came in to replace an interpreter who was about to take a break. The opposing counsel jumped up and asked for a sidebar with the judge. She told the judge that according to her information (which she did not specify),the interpreter, who was Hispanic, had been through a messy divorce from an African-American man and could not be trusted to interpret the proceedings accurately because our case also involved a Hispanic woman seeking a divorce from an African-American man. I was outraged. I objected strenuously to the attorney's comments. I suggested that she was simply trying to disrupt the proceedings and deflect the court's attention from the substantive issues at hand. I waited patiently for the judge to chide the attorney for bringing such biased, unsubstantiated claims into the proceeding. Instead the judge asked personal and somewhat humiliating questions of the interpreter until he was assured that she was capable of interpreting in a neutral fashion.

Although the comment was not directed at my client or me, I felt that what had happened was wrong. I did not know exactly what to do; I did not want to react in a way that would anger the judge and potentially hurt my client's case. The main target of my outrage was the judge. While I believed the opposing attorney acted in an inappropriate, offensive manner, I was particularly troubled that the judge condoned her behavior. I was not sure, however, that there were grounds to file a formal complaint.

I spoke with several colleagues and they advised me to try to find a less risky way of addressing the situation. I eventually decided to take an informal route. One of my colleagues had been asked to participate in an upcoming judicial training on cultural sensitivity. All trial court judges were required to attend. I described the incident and my colleague used it as a hypothetical during the training. The judge in question was sitting front and center. Other judges reacted with harsh criticism to the response of the "hypothetical" judge. [Stacy]

QUESTIONS TO CONSIDER

What do you think about the judge's response? How should the judge have responded? Should Stacy have made a formal complaint? What do you think of Stacy's decision to use the incident as a hypothetical case at the training session? What other options might she have considered? What were the risks in taking the action she did?

In 2010, I was working as a TeamChild attorney, providing educational and mental health advocacy to children in the juvenile justice system. My work supported the cases of juvenile public defenders, and I would often come to court at their request to provide status updates to the judges about legal interventions that had resulted in academic or behavioral progress.

One morning, I happened to be walking through the parking lot toward the front door of the juvenile courthouse at the same time as the executive director of my office. Like many juvenile courthouses, this one was small and informal, and the floor that I regularly visited had only one courtroom on the delinquency side, and one on the child protection side. I imagine that the design was intended to both separate the two sides, and provide access in a system that is not supposed to be as adversarial as the adult criminal courts. In spite of its location in a large northern city, the courthouse felt like it belonged in a small town—proceedings featured repeat players who passed the time in between hearings exchanging second tier small talk, sharing highlights of fishing trips, First Communions, and karate tournaments.

*After two years in this practice, I was familiar with all of them. Yet as my boss and I entered the lobby, we parted ways. She kept walking and talking, and I very deliberately, slowed to put my briefcase on the x-ray conveyer belt and walk through the metal detector. She had made it through a couple of sentences before she realized that I had stopped, and when she turned to look for me, a look of annoyance came over her face. Annoyance, it seemed, that was directed at me. "You don't have to do that," she quipped. "You're an attorney. You need to tell them." "No," I explained, "**You** don't have to do that. They don't stop you, but they stop me. Every week. Do you really think that I haven't told them who I am?" "That's ridiculous," she countered. "You need to tell them who you are, so that you don't have to stop." I did not respond.*

More than once I had been confronted by the guards when I made the mistake of acting like an attorney, and walking past security. In fact, even after I told them that I was an attorney, they routinely instructed me to place my briefcase or case files on the x-ray belt. In addition to appearing in court, I had a monthly meeting with the Juvenile PDs. I regularly conducted trainings for the probation officers. Yet two years into my practice with that project, the strongest projection of my identity was my race.

In other courthouses around the state, I was routinely told upon my arrival that I was standing in the attorney line, and needed to wait someplace else. Clerks asked my name when I entered courtrooms to locate me on the party list in a housing case, a parent in a delinquency proceeding. Occasionally, I was given the professional boost of being asked if I was the social worker, having to explain to every person who entered a negotiation room that I was an attorney.

I don't consider this to be anything other than a first-world problem. I don't equate this inconvenience with the use of deadly force by the police, or global suffering. I do, however, equate it with a lack of control.

I often wonder when I will own the indicators that communicate who I am. At what point can I wear a black suit to a reception and know that I will not be mistaken for the wait staff? Is it reasonable for someone to think that the only reason that I should be in certain places is as an employee? Is it a mistake, or is it an unconscious communication to me that I do not belong? Is it really that big of a deal to have to say, "I'm sorry, I don't work here," or "I'm an attorney?"

*Part of my professional routine has been to breathe deeply and assume a modern incarnation of Butterfly McQueen, the lovable mammy who is happy with her station in life and never judges the foolishness of her mistress. The role still exists, but now she is played by Whoopi Goldberg and Queen Latifah. My reaction to these slights is to tactfully help the offenders feel unembarrassed by their ignorance and deflect the racism implicit in their statements. I presume the absence of malice. Like most people who are experienced as other, I am exhausted by the amount of energy I exert to make other people comfortable with **their** biases that emerge as a result of my blackness.* [Carmia]

QUESTIONS TO CONSIDER

What did the Executive Director "not get" at the juvenile courthouse? Should Carmia have continued the conversation with her boss? Have you witnessed incidents when good, well-intentioned people seem to miss incidents of bias, either explicit or implicit? Is Carmia compounding the problem by "tactfully help[ing] the offenders feel unembarrassed by their ignorance and deflect[ing] the racism implicit in their statements?" What role should bystanders to this type of conduct play? Does how you experience yourself professionally collapse into how you are experienced by others in professional settings? For example, if you think of yourself as smart and capable, is that how you think others are seeing you as well?

As a law student, what can you do ahead of time to prepare for dealing with issues of bias that will arise during your legal career? The following exercises are designed to help you envision responses and develop individual techniques for coping with explicit and subtle forms of biased behavior.

Exercise 7.2 Reactions to Bias in a Legal Setting: Break into small groups. Generate a list of possible responses for how the target of bias in the following scenarios might respond and how a bystander to the bias might respond. Identify the pros and cons of taking different courses of action and determine what you would be likely to do. Each group should pick one individual from the group to report back to the class on the lists generated.

1. Two recent law graduates, one a white male and one an Asian male, are clerking for a trial judge. They have become friends and during the course of their conversations, one of the clerks, the Asian male, discloses to the other clerk that he is gay, but he makes it clear that he has not discussed his sexual orientation with the other law clerks in the court, nor does he plan to do so. The two clerks are in the court cafeteria eating lunch with a few other law clerks. One of the clerks for another judge starts to tell a joke that disparages gay men. A few people laugh, some look embarrassed. No one says anything.

2. A female, thirty year old attorney appears before a middle-aged, male judge who comments on her physical appearance in open court, telling her he likes her blouse, immediately prior to the start of a hearing on her motion for summary judgment.

3. An attorney in a small law firm, who has been out of law school for about two years, is negotiating a settlement for a client. The opposing counsel is approximately twenty years older. Opposing counsel repeatedly refers to the junior attorney as "young man," interrupts him, asks when he got out of law school, and continuously references his inexperience: "When you have tried as many cases as I have, you will understand . . . ."

4. A partner in a medium-sized law firm is currently helping one of the firm's most important clients negotiate a commercial lease. The partner selected a talented associate in the firm to assist in the negotiations. When the client meets the associate and learns that she is blind, he calls the partner and expresses concern that the associate is "not right for the project" because she might be viewed as vulnerable rather than as a tough negotiator.

5. Six lawyers have been asked to participate on a bar association committee to plan an annual conference. Two of the lawyers are Latina women, two are white women, and two are white males. During the first committee meeting, one of the white women takes charge, proposing a number of workshops for the conference. One of the Latina lawyers suggests that they do a survey of bar members to gauge interest before planning the workshops for the conference. There is no response to her suggestion. A few minutes later, one of the white women suggests that the group distribute a questionnaire to bar members to obtain feedback before deciding which workshops to

offer. The other white lawyers nod in assent, one of them commenting that a questionnaire is an excellent idea.

Exercise 7.3 Using the same scenarios, record your responses to the following questions: Do you have an ethical obligation to respond to any of these actions? Even if you determine that there is no ethical imperative to respond, would you have a moral or personal responsibility to act?

Suppose you want to object to the judge's comments in scenario #2, but are afraid that the judge will take it out on your client by ruling against you. Do you have an ethical obligation **not** to object?

You are the senior partner of the law firm where the associate from scenario #3 works. The associate has just complained to you about opposing counsel's behavior. What do you suggest? Also assume that you the partner in scenario (4)How do you respond to the client?

As an observer to the acts of bias described in #1 and #5, how do you determine whether and how to intervene?

The race or ethnicity of the attorneys/judge in scenarios #2-4 is omitted. Would it affect your response if the subordinate lawyer in the scenario was a person of color? What if the more senior attorney or judge was a person of color?

Informal Strategies

There are many ways to address an incident involving blatant or subtle bias. How one responds will often depend upon the forum in which the conduct takes place and one's role in the system. For example, in the courtroom an attorney can choose to confront the offending party directly—whether it be judge, attorney, or clerk; ignore the behavior; seek a sidebar with the judge and ask the judge to address the issue; or communicate with the offending party by letter following the hearing or trial, provided that as an attorney you do not engage in ex parte communications with the judge.

Much of the biased interpersonal conduct that takes place during the course of litigation or transactional matters occurs outside of the courtroom, in depositions or negotiations. One can address this conduct in a variety of ways. In a deposition, an attorney might decide initially to ignore offensive behavior or use humor in response to a comment intended to intimidate. In cases of more egregious behavior, a lawyer in a deposition can attempt to preserve offensive comments as part of the transcript of a deposition by ensuring that all discussions are "on the record." The lawyer can also note the behavior on the record and, if necessary, halt the proceeding and bring the conduct to the attention of the judge or bar.

Bias may also take place among colleagues or peers in the office, in a law school classroom, or in the hallways of a court. One might choose to discuss the issue directly with the offending party or to seek out a supervisor, a professor, or a trusted colleague who can intervene. Others may try to use humor to alert the person to the offensive nature of his or her behavior. In some situations, one might simply ignore the conduct if it appears that a reaction is exactly what the offending party intended to elicit. Rather than directly confronting someone about the issue, one can adopt a more indirect approach, such as organizing or participating in an office training on multicultural competence and using real life examples that put the offending party on notice that certain behavior is unacceptable.

Another powerful way to address bias is to support a co-worker or colleague who has been treated inappropriately. Vernā A. Myers, an attorney who practiced corporate and real estate law before becoming a nationally recognized expert on diversity and inclusion in the legal profession, calls this "interrupting bias."[25] If, for example, you are a male and you witness a male co-worker making disparaging, sexist remarks to a female colleague, you may be able to influence your male co-worker's future conduct by demonstrating your disapproval of his behavior. This is often not an easy thing to do. As Myers notes, "[s]ometimes, we are reluctant to stand up because we see how people in the target groups are treated, and we fear we will suffer ourselves if we intervene."[26] Nonetheless, interrupting bias is a necessary step toward strengthening the profession.

The goal of "interrupting bias" is not to teach or change the other person's viewpoint. As Myers explains,

> . . . [p]eople might be changed through the process, but that isn't your focus at the moment you are interrupting. What you are trying to do is to stop the troubling behavior and get people to think, to pause. Maybe your interruption keeps an unfair policy from being passed, prevents someone's promotion from being denied, or helps the offended party hang in there because he knows he is not alone.[27]

Myers offers some suggestions for successfully interrupting bias:[28]

- Use a non-judgmental tone of voice orally and in written comments. This will decrease the likelihood that the person will respond with defensiveness. *I'm not sure what you mean by that reference.* Treat the individual you are interrupting with respect, do not adopt an attitude of moral superiority. *I may be misunderstanding the proposal, but it seems that your plan will exclude associates who are parents since the trainings are scheduled to take place after 6:00 p.m.*

- Engage in a conversation if possible and let the other person know you are listening. *It seems that you were focusing on cost which is understandable since it is less expensive to rent the training space in the evening. However, this may have unintended consequences.*

- Ask open-ended questions to gain a better understanding of what the person meant and give them a chance to clarify or correct an unintended gaffe. *What is it about Gerry's work that makes you concerned he is not ready to handle misdemeanor trials?*

- Explain why you are concerned about the comment or conduct and make clear this is your opinion: you are not speaking for others. *I'm troubled by the reference to Mimi as bossy when, in my view, she is exhibiting the same assertiveness that we have praised Roger and Dominic for displaying.*

- Offer a counter example or another perspective. *I've met several of the community leaders from that neighborhood, and I have found them to be open-minded and flexible.*

- Practice intervening so that you can more easily react in these situations. Develop a ready set of comments or responses.

Opportunities to interrupt bias in a legal context can take many forms. There may be opportunities to let colleagues know that terminology they are using in their writing or oral advocacy is inappropriate or could be considered offensive. Most colleagues would rather hear this information firsthand, even if the exchange is a bit awkward, than risk harming their client's case or tarnishing their own reputation.

The manner in which someone confronts offensive conduct and the timing of such response depends upon a number of factors. This includes your own personal style; do you feel comfortable using humor or do you prefer a more serious, straightforward approach? Your choice of approach also includes your analysis of whether raising the issue or failing to raise the issue will negatively impact your client, your credibility, or your case. You may decide to wait and raise the issue in a more indirect way at a later date, as Stacy did in the example with the judge and the accusation about the interpreter.

It can be particularly difficult to confront bias in an externship. The power imbalance between the extern and attorneys or staff members at the organization can limit an extern's options for interrupting bias, and law students may reasonably question whether taking the risk is worthwhile given their transient status at the organization. Many externs fear that that they have to ignore or go along with troubling behavior in order to receive a favorable recommendation or, possibly, a job offer. The following exercise encourages you to practice responding to and interrupting bias in the externship setting.

> **Exercise 7.4** Either in writing or in small groups, generate a list of possible responses to the following scenarios for the extern who is the target of bias and for the extern who is a bystander. Identify the pros and cons of taking different courses of action and determine what you would be likely to do.
>
> 1. Four law students are working as externs at a government agency. Two are white women, one is an African American male and one is an Asian male. The four law student colleagues are sitting together in the office cafeteria discussing their assignments when the African-American extern comments that it seems that he is receiving much less challenging work than the others. Indeed, everyone agrees that most of the projects he is receiving seem more administrative or secretarial than legal.
>
> 2. Two law students working as externs in a medium size law firm are invited to sit in on a deposition. One of the externs is a male of Indian heritage who was born and raised in New Jersey. He is an adherent to the Sikh religion and wears a turban. The other extern is a white woman. When they enter the conference room where the deposition is to take place, the deposing attorney (a partner at the firm) walks over and introduces himself. He turns to the Sikh student, asks where he is from and, smiling, asks whether wearing a turban makes it difficult for him to get through airport security.

There is no fool-proof recipe for responding to bias in these tricky situations. One option is to model positive behavior, using culturally appropriate language or references in the presence of the offending person to demonstrate a more competent response. At other times, you may decide to use one of the more direct techniques suggested above. Sometimes an immediate response is not feasible and you will need to discuss the situation with your field placement supervisor or law school externship teacher to consider more formal courses of action.[29]

Formal Strategies

There are circumstances in which the biased conduct is so egregious that informal responses are inadequate and more serious, formal action must be taken. Or it may be that informal mechanisms have failed to alleviate the problem. One avenue may be to register a complaint against a co-worker or supervisor with an internal or external grievance committee set up by the organization, agency, firm, or court in which you work.

If the conduct takes place during litigation, one can seek sanctions. State and federal rules of civil procedure authorize the imposition of sanctions against attorneys, law firms, or parties who engage in improper conduct designed to harass another party during the course of litigation. In a New York case, for example, the court granted an attorney's motion requesting that the court supervise all further depositions because of opposing counsel's inappropriate behavior. During the deposition, the plaintiff's attorney made derogatory and insulting remarks about the deposing counsel's gender, marital status, and competence.[30] In its decision, the court referenced an earlier decision in which the Court imposed sanctions against an attorney who, during a deposition, referred to opposing counsel as "little girl" and made other gender-biased, derogatory statements.[31]

Another option may be filing a complaint with the local board that licenses and regulates attorney conduct. Rule 8.4 of the ABA Model Rules of Professional Conduct prohibits lawyers from engaging in conduct that is "prejudicial to the administration of justice."[32] The comment to this rule clarifies the rule:

A lawyer who, in the course of representing a client, knowingly manifests by words or conduct, bias or prejudice based upon race, sex, religion, national origin, disability, age, sexual orientation or socioeconomic status, violates paragraph (d) when such actions are prejudicial to the administration of justice. Legitimate advocacy respecting the foregoing factors does not violate paragraph (d). A trial judge's finding that peremptory challenges were exercised on a discriminatory basis does not alone establish a violation of this rule.

All states have adopted a version of Model Rule 8.4. For example, according to Rule 8.4 of the Washington Rules of Professional Conduct,

It is professional misconduct for a lawyer to:

(g) Commit a discriminatory act prohibited by state law on the basis of sex, race, age, creed, religion, color, national origin, disability, sexual orientation, or marital status, where the act of discrimination is committed in connection with the lawyer's professional activities. In addition, it is professional misconduct to commit a discriminatory act on the basis of sexual orientation if such an act would violate this rule when committed on the basis of sex, race, age, creed, religion, color, national origin, disability, or marital status. This rule shall not limit the ability of a lawyer to accept, decline, or withdraw from the representation of a client in accordance with RPC 1.15;

(h) In representing a client, engage in conduct that is prejudicial to the administration of justice toward judges, other parties and/or their counsel, witnesses and/or their counsel, jurors, or court personnel or officers, that a reasonable person would interpret as manifesting prejudice or bias on the basis of sex, race, age, creed, religion, color, national origin, disability, sexual orientation, or marital status. This rule does not restrict a lawyer from representing a client by advancing material factual or legal issues or arguments.

State rules differ in scope. Some prohibit lawyers from engaging in biased behavior generally, while others proscribe employment discrimination or other biased conduct while the lawyer is engaged in professional activities or during the course of representation of a client.

Courts impose a variety of sanctions for violations of these rules ranging from warnings to disbarment. The Supreme Court of Indiana, for example, imposed a public reprimand of an attorney for making racially derogatory comments during a divorce hearing in violation of Indiana Professional Conduct Rule 8.4(g).[33] The court noted

. . . [l]egitimate advocacy respecting race, gender, religion, national origin, disability, sexual orientation, age, socioeconomic status, or similar factors does not violate Prof. Cond. R. 8.4(g), but our decision here is based upon the parties' agreement that race was not relevant in this case; there was no legitimate reason underlying the comments made by respondent. Respondent's misconduct is a significant violation and cannot be taken lightly. Respondent's comments only serve to fester wounds caused by past discrimination and encourage future intolerance.[34]

The Supreme Court of Washington upheld an eighteen month suspension imposed on an attorney for, among other things, having sent two ex parte communications to the trial judge which included disparaging remarks about the opposing party's national origin.[35]

In addition to specific rules prohibiting biased conduct, many jurisdictions have more general ethical rules requiring attorneys to conduct themselves in a professional manner and refrain from behavior designed to harass or interfere with the administration of justice. See Chapter 9 on Professionalism. The Minnesota Supreme Court, for example, upheld the Lawyer's Professional Responsibility Board decision to impose an admonition against an attorney who filed motions seeking a new trial in a personal injury suit in which he argued that the first trial was prejudiced by the presence of the judge's law clerk who was physically disabled.[36] The South Carolina Supreme Court imposed a six month suspension for a lawyer who, among other things, asked improper and irrelevant questions regarding a witness' sexual orientation and HIV status during a deposition.[37]

During your legal career, you may decide, after reading the rules of your particular jurisdiction and consulting with colleagues or local bar counsel, that you have an obligation to report an attorney who has engaged in biased behavior. In other circumstances, you may believe you have a moral responsibility to do so even if you are not legally obligated to report.

If the problem you are having involves a judge, then you will need to refer to the standards of professional conduct imposed upon judges as well as to the rules of civil or criminal procedure and determine whether you have a basis for filing a complaint or seeking other remedial action. The American Bar Association adopted a Model Code of Judicial Conduct in 1990 which was revised in 2007 & 2010, that addresses bias. Canon 2, Rule 2.3(A) & (B) provide

(A) [a] judge shall perform the duties of judicial office, including administrative duties, without bias or prejudice.

(B) A judge shall not, in the performance of judicial duties, by words or conduct manifest bias or prejudice, or engage in harassment, including but not limited to bias, prejudice, or harassment based upon race, sex, gender, religion, national origin, ethnicity, disability, age, sexual orientation, marital status, socioeconomic status, or political affiliation, and shall not permit court staff, court officials, or others subject to the judge's direction and control to do so.

The comment to this rule gives concrete, detailed examples of the types of conduct that constitutes bias, prejudice, and harassment. Under the Model Code, judges are prohibited from engaging in biased or prejudiced behavior, and they also are required to ensure that lawyers refrain from such conduct when appearing in legal proceedings. According to Rule 2.3 (C),

> A judge shall require lawyers in proceedings before the court to refrain from manifesting bias or prejudice, or engaging in harassment, based upon attributes including but not limited to race, sex, gender, religion, national origin, ethnicity, disability, age, sexual orientation, marital status, socioeconomic status, or political affiliation, against parties, witnesses, lawyers, or others.

At least 47 states and the District of Columbia have adopted Model Code 2.3 or similar rules prohibiting judicial conduct based on bias or prejudice. In addition, many federal trial courts, bankruptcy courts, administrative tribunals, and local courts have promulgated rules prohibiting judges from engaging in biased conduct based on race, ethnicity, gender, sexual orientation, or other personal characteristics or background factors. For example, Rule 1000-1 of the Local Rules governing the United States Bankruptcy Court in Arizona and Rules of Practice of the U.S. District Court for the District of Arizona, LRCiv 83.5, state that

> [l]itigation, inside and outside the courtroom, in the United States District Court for the District of Arizona, must be free from prejudice and bias in any form. Fair and equal treatment must be accorded all courtroom participants, whether judges, attorneys, witnesses, litigants, jurors, or court personnel. The duty to be respectful of others includes the responsibility to avoid comment or behavior that can reasonably be interpreted as manifesting prejudice or bias toward another on the basis of categories such as gender, race, ethnicity, religion, disability, age, or sexual orientation.[38]

Judges have been overruled, removed from cases, censured, or removed from the bench as a consequence of engaging in biased behavior. The Arkansas Supreme Court, for example, upheld a judge's removal from office, in part, resulting from derogatory sexist, racist, and homophobic remarks the judge posted on an electronic forum.[39] The South Dakota Supreme Court issued a six month suspension of a judge based, in part, on racist and sexist jokes the judge made to court employees.[40] The New York Court of Appeals upheld a decision of the State Commission on Judicial Conduct to remove a judge from office based, in part, on the fact that the judge used derogatory racial epithets and ethnic slurs. The court noted that " . . . such language, whether provoked or in jest, manifested an impermissible bias that threatens public confidence in the judiciary."[41]

Every jurisdiction has a board or committee that reviews the conduct of judges. Many courts and bar associations also routinely conduct surveys of the bar seeking information on judges currently sitting in local courts. These surveys provide opportunities to inform the bar and the judiciary about problems of bias in local courts. Similarly, whether judges are elected or appointed to the bench, individuals in the community often have an opportunity to comment on a particular individual's fitness to serve as a judge. One can report incidents in which the judicial candidate has previously engaged in biased behavior.

In addition to rules that govern judicial behavior, there are codes regulating the conduct of mediators and arbitrators. While these codes, unless adopted by a court or other regulatory body, do not have the force of law, they may be used to demonstrate or establish a standard of care. For example, the Model Standards of Conduct for Mediators were developed and approved by the American Bar Association, the American Arbitration Association, and the Association for Conflict Resolution. They require mediators to conduct mediations in an impartial manner. Standard II.B.1 specifies that "[a] mediator should not act with partiality or prejudice based on any participant's personal characteristics, background, values and beliefs . . . ."[42]

Depending on the offensive behavior, one also may choose to file a claim with the local Human Rights Commission, the Equal Employment Opportunity Commission, or file a discrimination lawsuit to remedy the situation. Filing an administrative claim is usually a prerequisite for filing lawsuits seeking remedies for an employer's discriminatory conduct. Note that the individual whose conduct is at issue and the individual's employer may be liable under discrimination statutes. In addition to civil rights statutes, tort law may provide a remedy if the behavior constitutes invasion of privacy, intentional infliction of emotional distress, assault, or battery.

The decision whether to utilize formal mechanisms to combat a situation of bias is a difficult decision to make. In many cases, you will not have an ethical obligation to report the conduct. Instead, you will have discretion about which course of action to take. If you are a new attorney, for example, you must weigh the likelihood of obtaining a favorable result through formal channels against the impact that taking formal action will have on your career. It is also important to think ahead to the time when you, as an attorney, may become an employer. As an employer, it is imperative that you establish policies and procedures for dealing with complaints about biased or discriminatory behavior in your firm or organization.

QUESTIONS TO CONSIDER

Reflect on the following questions in your journal or in class:

- Should lawyers, as officers of the judicial system, be held to a higher standard of conduct than other individuals when it comes to engaging in biased behavior?

- Can one readily distinguish when a lawyer is acting in his or her capacity as a lawyer as opposed to speaking or acting in an individual capacity?

- How would you counsel a friend who is considering formal action against a judge or another attorney? What are the pros and cons you would want your friend to consider?

- Some raise concerns that disciplinary rules prohibiting biased conduct prevent lawyers from expressing their personal opinions outside of the courtroom or inhibit lawyers from zealously advocating on behalf of their clients inside the courtroom. What is your view of these critiques?

- Are there any formal or informal office policies or grievance procedures in place at your externship organization to address concerns about bias and discriminatory behavior?

- Are there times when an attorney who has witnessed or been the victim of bias or even egregious actions by another attorney or judge may justifiably elect to do nothing?

Eliminating Bias and Creating Inclusion in the Legal Profession

The last section of this chapter focuses on steps that law students, lawyers, and legal institutions can take to eliminate bias—explicit, implicit, and structural—and to ensure inclusion in the legal profession. Building off of the research and strategies discussed in Chapter 6, we identify concrete techniques that law students can use in practice to counter internal bias and develop culturally competent communication and advocacy skills. We end by suggesting ways to create institutional change and foster inclusion in the profession.

Developing Effective Communication, Decision-Making, and Advocacy Skills: The Culturally Competent Lawyer

For law students and lawyers, eliminating implicit bias and developing the capacity to communicate effectively with individuals of varying backgrounds and abilities serves several important purposes. First, and most importantly, lawyers have the obligation to remedy injustice and ensure that laws are applied and enforced fairly. Lawyers who remain unaware of their own assumptions and internalized biases cannot effectively carry out their responsibilities. Failure to recognize these biases may translate into ineffective client interviewing or counseling, imprecise and inaccurate use of language in oral or written advocacy, incomplete legal analysis, offensive interpersonal communication, and faulty decision making. The American Bar Association recognized the importance of these skills when it adopted Rule 2.4 on Cultural Competence in the ABA Standards for the Provision of Civil Legal Aid, August 2006.[43] For additional communication ideas and techniques, see Chapter 5 on Effective Communication and Professional Relationships.

Second, cultural competence makes business sense. As the United States evolves into an increasingly multicultural society, an ability to work effectively with individuals of differing backgrounds enables majority lawyers[44] and law firms to attract clients, appeal to diverse juries, retain talented lawyers, and develop more creative, comprehensive solutions to complex legal problems.[45] As one study demonstrated, clients who perceive their lawyers as culturally sensitive are more likely to view their lawyers as competent.[46] Corporate and other organizational clients are increasingly seeking lawyers with a broad range of skills and experience. In addition, firms comprised of culturally competent lawyers are at less risk of incurring liability due to harassment or discrimination claims.

As discussed more fully in Chapter 6 on Navigating Cultural Difference, our view about people and the categories into which they fall are shaped by our parents, the media, teachers, peers, and a host of other external sources. From these experiences, we develop lenses through which our perceptions are filtered. The exercises in Chapter 6 encourage you to examine your own experiences, beliefs, and assumptions. Without conscious recognition that one's own culture is a filter through which information is channeled, a lawyer may not be able to recognize that someone else has a valid, yet different interpretation or reaction to the same set of facts, law, or circumstances.

Common sense is not enough. As Professor Bill Ong Hing points out,

. . . [c]ommon sense, without training, is dangerously fashioned by our own class, race, ethnicity/culture, gender, and sexual background. What we think of as common sense may make little sense or even be offensive to someone of a different identification background. Thus, the opportunity to learn and discuss different approaches with the help of different perspectives from readings, the opinions of others, and self-critique is unique.[47]

Exercise 7.5 Consider the following scenario and record your responses: A woman calls your law office seeking legal assistance. She is a grandmother interested in custody of her grandchild because she believes her daughter, the nineteen-year-old mother of the child, is too young to make responsible decisions for the child. The grandmother understands that her daughter is legally considered an adult, but she worries that her daughter is not mature enough to raise a child. The mother works full time and the grandmother cares for the child during the day. The grandmother believes that the mother uses her paycheck to buy unnecessary, frivolous items rather than saving money for an emergency or for the child's education. The grandmother is also very concerned that the mother is an atheist and does not plan to provide the child with a religious identity. You set up an appointment to determine whether you will take the case.

You are not familiar with the standards for custody or the rights of grandparents in your jurisdiction. If you decide to take the case, you will have to do more research on the legal issues.

What are your initial impressions of the factual situation? As you read the account, did an image come to mind of the grandmother and mother? In your mind's eye, how old is the grandmother? What were the racial and socioeconomic backgrounds of the grandmother and mother as you imagined them? Sexual orientation? Physical abilities? What initial assumptions did you make about the educational background of the grandmother or the educational status of the mother? Have you begun to develop views or concerns about the custody issue based on the little information you have received? How do your own values concerning money, work, family, and religion influence your initial views? Would your initial impression have been any different if the parent in the scenario was male and the grandmother was seeking custody from her son rather than her daughter? What questions would you ask to identify the grandmother's values and interests?

QUESTIONS TO CONSIDER

Is it appropriate to use your own cultural views or perspective when assessing a legal problem or fashioning legal advice? Do the ABA Model Rules or your state ethical rules give guidance on whether this is appropriate? How can you ensure that your own cultural values do not interfere with your ability to give sound legal advice—advice based on the potential client's values or objectives?

A lawyer is more likely to consider cross cultural differences when representing a client or interacting with a colleague who was born in another country or who does not speak English as a first language. However, cultural competence skills come into play whenever a lawyer interacts with a client, colleague, opposing counsel, court clerk, or judge whose background differs from the lawyer's in a significant way because of race, religion, education, socioeconomic status, gender, sexual orientation, disability, and/or age. As professors Lorraine Bannai & Anne Enquist point out,

> [r]ealizing that words are the tools of their trade, [law students and lawyers] . . . need to be particularly attentive to their spoken and written language and examine it for imprecision, stereotyping, and any potential for unintended offense. Realizing that legal analysis and legal argument are the professional services they will offer, they need to probe for cultural bias that leads to faulty reasoning.[48]

As discussed in Chapter 6, it is important to recognize that a person is not wholly defined by one characteristic or trait and may be significantly influenced by a confluence of factors, such as race and gender. Similarly, there are tremendous differences within cultural groups. Individuals who identify themselves as Latino or Asian, for example, hail from a host of countries that have unique histories, languages/dialects, foods, religions, and customs. "A broad definition of culture recognizes that no two people can have exactly the same experiences and thus no two people will interpret or predict in precisely the same ways."[49]

So, what concrete techniques can you use as a law student and legal extern to help ensure that you are communicating and making judgments in a culturally competent way? Like many other lawyering skills, the ability to interact and communicate with individuals from a variety of backgrounds takes practice and conscious effort. An externship offers opportunities to hone these skills. Building on the strategies developed in Chapter 6, the following is a list of concrete methods to use with colleagues, clients, court personnel, or others you may interact with during your externship to uncover your own assumptions; determine whether an assumption is accurate; challenge negative judgments; identify others' priorities, concerns and values; communicate clearly; and correct mistakes that you inadvertently make:

- Stay in information-gathering mode longer, listen carefully, ask questions rather than making statements or coming to conclusions prematurely.

- Try to identify or imagine circumstances under which an assumption or conclusion you are about to make is not true or does not hold up—if you can identify such circumstances, then do not make judgments until you have gathered more information.

- Before commenting or reacting, repeat back or summarize what you have understood the other person to say in order to ensure that you accurately received the intended message; make a concerted effort to capture the words and meaning of the speaker rather than putting your own spin on what was said.

- Be aware of your own cultural beliefs, values, customs, and biases.

- Question your own objectivity rather than assuming that you will assess a situation fairly simply because you have a desire to do so.

- Do not assume the normativity of your life. Do not measure a client's reaction, a court employee's comment, or a colleague's decision using your own beliefs, customs, and values as a yardstick.

- Do not assume that all people from a particular cultural group are the same or share the same values and priorities. Ask questions. Listen. Reflect before reacting.

- Before making a negative judgment about someone, try to come up with at least three or four possible, well-intentioned explanations for the other person's reaction or behavior.

- If you find yourself making negative assumptions about individuals from a particular cultural group, discipline yourself to identify examples of individuals from that group or situations that counter that bias or stereotype so that you can make better judgments.

- Identify areas of commonality you have with those you determine to be different from yourself and use these similarities to build rapport.

- Identify areas of difference and try to anticipate where areas of miscommunication might arise. Plan to ask more questions or gather more information.

- Recognize when you are under pressure to make a quick or less than fully informed decision and find ways to give yourself more time to consider the issue so that you do not reflexively resort to biased decision making.

- Be extremely careful with humor; ensure that jokes do not rely on inappropriate bias or prejudice. If you are not sure, do not tell the joke.

- Consider your choice of language in face to face interactions and in writing—reflect on which titles and terminology you should use to address or describe individuals of varying ages, races, ethnicities, and gender. If you are not sure, check.

- Clarify that your view or opinion is your individual view, specify using phrases such as "I think," "I believe," "My view is ... " rather than making global statements suggesting that there is only one reasonable position or view on an issue.

- Apologize if you make a mistake. If it is not appropriate or possible to apologize or correct the mistake immediately, then find the next available opportunity to do so.[50]

Creating Inclusive Environments Within the Legal Profession

In order to ensure that the legal profession reflects a diversity of perspectives, talents, life experiences, and skills, the institutions which comprise the profession must be inclusive. This is not simply a numbers game in which a law firm, government agency or public interest organization hires lawyers from traditionally marginalized groups and expects that an environment of inclusivity will inevitably follow. Instead, an inclusive environment is one in which attorneys of all races, ethnicities and backgrounds are acknowledged and have the same opportunity to acquire skills, develop professionally, and lead the organization.

Law student leaders, supervising attorneys, managing partners, bar leaders, and judges can take concrete steps to counter the effects of explicit, implicit, and structural bias and make the profession accessible and relevant to those who join its ranks. One of the difficulties is that many of the leaders of firms and legal organizations are well-intentioned managers who affirmatively eschew any type of bias and do not believe that bias has permeated the organizations that they lead. As Vernā A. Myers explains,

> I know "racism" feels like a harsh charge; it is, especially for many of my clients [her clients are law firms] who believe deeply in equality and fairness. When I use the term here, I am not talking about intentional racism, or people behaving out of racial animus. I am really referring to a more modern form of racism—unconscious biases and assumptions rooted in notions of racial superiority and inferiority that affect the way people behave and are embedded in the way organizations operate. This type of contemporary racism, sometimes called "aversive racism" or "implicit bias," is perpetuated by good, kind, well-meaning white people. [footnote excluded] It is subtle and mostly unintentional, and yet it is as concerning as old-fashioned forms of intentional and conscious racism.[51]

Myers suggests that it is necessary to "biasproof" a legal organization's policies and practices because "[o]ur organizations will never reflect our deeply held values of fairness and equality or experience the many benefits that inclusion can bring, unless we account and adjust for how the organizations' practices can hinder black people and non-majority groups from getting into the flow of the party, the lifeblood of the business."[52]

The narratives at the beginning of this chapter illustrate policies and practices that negatively impact attorneys of color, LGBT attorneys, attorneys with disabilities and others who have been marginalized from the profession. These include (i) obstacles at the recruiting stage such as vague interview criteria that give broad discretion to hiring attorneys to determine who will be able to "handle" the demands of the job and "work well" with clients; (ii) obstacles at the newly hired stage including arbitrary systems for distributing work assignments and loose processes for evaluation that result in attorneys not receiving challenging assignments or constructive feedback; as well as (iii) obstacles at the retention and promotion stage including a lack of mentoring and professional development programs that lead attorneys to experience isolation and diminishes opportunities to learn to network, generate business, and achieve other hallmarks of success in the profession.

At the heart of many of these practices is what Myers and others refer to as an implicit "bias in favor of" rather than against a particular individual or group.

It is . . . important to remember that biases run in favor of as well as against people. Sometimes the problem is not that some white people have biases against black people; it is that they unknowingly favor white people. They don't notice that they have a positive bias toward whites with whom they agree about so many principles and rules regarding appropriate performance, behavior, and ways of being. So when judging who the best person is for the opportunity, they unconsciously prefer candidates with whom they feel a greater level of comfort, a sense of familiarity.[53]

There are a number of strategies for fostering inclusion.[54] Research suggests that one initial way to counter the effects of implicit bias in legal settings, including in courts, is to diversify the pool of judges, attorneys, and staff working in these environments. Such diversity offers counterexamples to the negative images of members of racial, ethnic, and other minority groups that are perpetuated in the media and United States culture at large. Such exposure can counter the biased attitudes or stereotypes that members of the bench or bar unconsciously hold about litigants, colleagues, or others with whom they come into contact in their professional lives.

Given that efforts to diversify take time as well as financial and political resources, research also suggests that an additional, albeit less effective, method of countering implicit bias is through vicarious exposure. Using counterexamples in posters, videos, artwork, screen savers, or office trainings that project positive images of a diverse group of individuals may help mitigate the internalized bias that has seeped into the thinking of partners, managers, judges, attorneys, and other staff of an organization. These efforts also ensure a more inclusive environment in which individuals of various backgrounds and abilities feel welcomed rather than isolated.

Another way in which to mitigate bias is to improve the conditions under which important decisions are made. As the authors of the article, *Implicit Bias in the Courtroom* (one of whom is a federal judge) have suggested, " . . . [t]he conditions under which implicit biases translate most readily into discriminatory behavior are when people have wide discretion in making quick decisions with little accountability." Therefore, " . . . [e]ven if we cannot remove the bias, perhaps we can alter decision-making processes so that these biases are less likely to translate into behavior."[55] The authors refer to ways to mitigate bias in the courtroom, particularly among judges and jurors, but several of their recommendations as well as the recommendations of experts such as Vernā Myers are equally applicable to other legal settings. Methods for improving the conditions under which decisions are made include:

· Training leaders and managers in an organization to question their objectivity and educating them about unconscious bias and negative messaging.

Research suggests that those who believe themselves to be objective tend to behave in ways that are more susceptible to bias, whereas those who learn about the subtle ways in which implicit bias works and question their ability to be objective can decrease their susceptibility to such bias;

- Reducing vagueness of criteria as well as unbridled discretion and clarifying standards for making significant decisions such as hiring and promotion;

- Creating mentoring as well as professional development programs, and ensuring quality feedback so that everyone has an understanding of how a particular organization or business works as well as an opportunity to shine;

- Reducing time pressure under which important decisions have to be made in order to minimize the extent to which automatic "bias in-favor of" or other forms of implicit bias influence one's behavior; and

- Enhancing accountability so that supervising attorneys, managers, and others with leadership responsibility justify their decisions.

As a law student, it is not too early to identify and practice using strategies that will help create a more inclusive environment in the law school where you study, the externship where you work, and eventually, in the firm or institution where you practice, supervise, or manage other legal professionals. The following exercise encourages you to consider how to foster inclusivity.

Exercise 7.6: Record your answers to these discussion questions in your journal.

Take a critical look at the student organizations or law journals to which you belong or which you lead:

- Is there a diverse membership? Even if the organization is one designed to address issues of particular relevance to ethnic, racial, or other affinity groups (i.e., BALSA, LALSA, Women's Law Caucus), is there a diverse membership?

- Is there a process in place by which leaders in the group ensure that they are receiving perspectives from different constituencies in the organization or community? If not, are there obstacles preventing certain groups from joining or sharing their views?

- Does the organization have a process for ensuring that the group is addressing issues, selecting articles, or prioritizing projects that are of interest to different groups of students? Is there a process in place for gauging whether members are feeling engaged or alienated?

- Is there a mentorship program?

At your externship,

- How would you describe the work environment at the office or organization where you are doing your externship? Are there educational programs or other approaches used by the organization to address the issue of multicultural sensitivity?

- Are there any initiatives to ensure diversity and cultural competence of staff and managers?

- Are there certain positions in your office that seem to correlate to race?

- Do members of different groups interact with one another outside of their professional roles?

- What, if anything, have you noticed about the policies or environment at your externship that promotes or discourages inclusion?

Conclusion

An interesting empirical study was done to assess whether gender bias within the legal profession might be responsible for the low numbers of women in law practice leadership positions despite the nearly equal numbers of men and women entering law schools. The researchers evaluated whether law students have integrated gender bias and, if so, whether this implicit bias affects their decision-making. The results were somewhat alarming and yet, at the same time, optimistic. The study demonstrated that unconscious gender bias was widespread—in tests measuring implicit attitudes, a diverse group of female and male law students associated males as judges and associated women with home and family. At the same time, the law students were able to counter their internalized biases and make gender neutral decisions. The law professor and psychology professor who teamed up to conduct this study concluded,

Taken together, the results of the study highlight two conflicting sides of the ongoing gender debate: first, that the power of implicit gender biases persists, even in the next generation of lawyers; and second, that the emergence of a new generation of egalitarian law students may offer some hope for the future.[56]

This study gives reason for optimism that those entering the legal profession are better equipped to counter internalized bias and make decisions in a more considered, egalitarian way. However, the evolution to a bias-free profession will take time and effort. We hope that the strategies and techniques suggested in this chapter will guide you as you experience or witness acts of bias and as you become responsible for managing and "bias-proofing" legal institutions.

An externship provides a unique opportunity to start developing these skills. Will you recognize bias when you are confronted with it? How will you respond? What steps can you take to develop cultural awareness and improve your cross-cultural communication skills? How will you deal with bias in a profession that does not always keep pace with society? How will you interact with colleagues and superiors who may have joined a bar and practiced in a community that looks very different from the newly minted lawyers of today? You will grapple with these difficult questions throughout your career. Let your externship be one vehicle through which you devise and practice strategies for countering individual and institutional bias in the legal profession.

FURTHER RESOURCES

Diversity in the Legal Profession: The Next Steps. REPORT AND RECOMMENDATIONS, RACE AND ETHNICITY, GENDER, SEXUAL ORIENTATION, DISABILITIES, (ABA Presidential Diversity Initiative, Commission On Diversity, 2010), http://www.americanbar.org/content/dam/aba/administrative/diversity/next_steps_2011.authcheckdam.pdf.

National Center for State Courts: Gender and Racial Fairness State Links, http://www.ncsc.org/Topics/Access-and-Fairness/Gender-and-Racial-Fairness/State-Links.aspx?cat=Gender%20Fairness%20Task%20Forces%20and%20Reports.

Visible Invisibility, Women of Color in Fortune 500 Legal Departments, American Bar Association Commission on Women in the Profession, 2013, http://www.americanbar.org/content/dam/aba/administrative/diversity/Convocation_2013/CWP/visible_invisibility_fortune500_executive_summary.authcheckdam.pdf.

NATALIE HOLDER-WINFIELD, EXCLUSION: STRATEGIES FOR IMPROVING DIVERSITY IN RECRUITMENT, RETENTION AND PROMOTION (ABA, 2014).

Daniel Landis, Janet M. Bennett, and Milton J. Bennett, *Handbook of Intercultural Training* (3d. ed. 2003).

Vernā A. Myers, Moving Diversity Forward: How to Go From Well-Meaning to Well-Doing (ABA Ctr. for Racial and Ethnic Diversity & General Practice, Solo & Small Firm Div., 2011 ed.).

L. Song Richardson & Phillip Atiba Goff, *Implicit Racial Bias in Public Defender Triage*, 122 Yale L.J. 2626 (2013).

Yassmin Abdel-Magied, Beat Your Bias, Question Your First Impression, (TEDxSouthBank filmed January 2015), https://www.youtube.com/watch?v=vbHkh_faQu8.

Melody Hobson, Color Blind or Color Brave, (TED Talk filmed March 2014), http://www.ted.com/talks/mellody_hobson_color_blind_or_color_brave.

Jerry Kang, Immaculate Perception, (TED Talk San Diego, 2013), https://www.youtube.com/watch?v=9VGbwNI6Ssk.

Vernā Myers, How to Overcome Our Biases? Walk Boldly Toward Them, (TED Talk filmed Nov. 2014), https://www.ted.com/talks/verna_myers_how_to_overcome_our_biases_walk_boldly_toward_them.

Jay Smooth, *How to Tell People They Sound Racist,* July 21, 2008, http://www.illdoctrine.com/2008/07/.

Human Rights Campaign, Lana Wachowski Receives the HRC Visibility Award, YouTube (Oct. 24, 2012), https://www.youtube.com/watch?v=crHHycz7T_c.

Stella Young: I'm Not Your Inspiration, Thank You Very Much, (TED Talk April 2014), https://www.ted.com/talks/stella_young_i_m_not_your_inspiration_thank_you_very_much.

ENDNOTES

1   In this chapter we have elected to capitalize neither black nor white since both are racial constructs rather than ethnic categories. You will notice that ethnic references including Latino, African-American, and Native American are written with capital letters.

2   Jennifer L. Eberhardt, et al., *Seeing Black: Race, Crime and Visual Processing*, 87 J. Personality and Soc. Psychol. 876–893 (2004). "Using police officers and undergraduates as participants, the authors investigated the influence of stereotypic associations on visual processing in 5 studies. Study 1 demonstrates that Black faces influence participants' ability to spontaneously detect degraded images of crime-relevant objects. Conversely, Studies 2–4 demonstrate that activating abstract concepts (i.e., crime and basketball) induces attentional biases toward Black male faces. Moreover, these processing biases may be related to the degree to which a social group member is physically representative of the social group (Studies 4–5)." *Id.* at 876.

3   This chapter will largely focus on explicit and implicit bias. For a more thorough discussion of structural bias see Jerry Kang, et al., *Implicit Bias in the Courtroom*, 59 UCLA L. Rev. 1124, 1133 (2012) (*citing* Michelle Adams,

Intergroup Rivalry, Anti-Competitive Conduct and Affirmative Action, 82 B.U. L. Rev. 1089, 1117–22 (2002)) (applying lock-in theory to explain the inequalities between blacks and whites in education, housing, and employment); John A. Powell, *Structural Racism: Building Upon the Insights of John Calmore*, 86 N.C. L. Rev. 791, 795–800 (2008) (adopting a systems approach to describe structured racialization).

4   Arin N. Reeves, *Written in Black & White: Exploring Confirmation Bias in Racialized Perceptions of Writing Skills*, Nextions (2014), http://www.nextions.com/wp-content/files_mf/14151940752014040114WritteninBlackandWhiteYPS.pdf.

5   Special Committee on Gender to the D.C. Circuit Task Force on Gender, Race and Ethnic Bias, Final Report xiv–xv (January 1996).

6   Kang, *supra* note 3, at 1132–33.

7   Stephanie A. Scharf, Roberta Liebenberg, & Christine Amalfe, Report of the Eighth Annual NAWL National Survey on Retention and Promotion of Women in Law Firms (February 2014), http://www.nawl.org/p/bl/et/blogid=10&blogaid=56.

8   *Id.* at 6.

9   *Id.* at 16.

10   Am. Bar Ass'n. Comm'n on Women, A Current Glance at Women in the Law (Feb. 2013), http://www.google.com.au/url?sa=t&rct=j&q=&esrc=s&source=web&cd=2&ved=0CCIQFjAB&url=http%3A%2F%2Fwww.americanbar.org%2Fdam%2Faba%2Fmarketing%2Fwomen%2Fcurrent_glance_statistics_feb2013.authcheckdam.pdf&ei=g_XuVJbbKI_q8AWttoH4Bw&+usg=AFQjCNFshK0ILzdpbwxdHAEynldhlA8hJw (citing National Association of Women Judges State Court Statistics (2012), http://www.nawj.org/us_state_court_statistics_2012.asp).

11   Nat'l Women's Law Ctr., Women in the Federal Judiciary: Still a Long Way to Go, (July 2015), http://www.nwlc.org/resource/women-federal-judiciary-still-long-way-go-1. *See also* Judicial Facts and Figures, U.S. Courts (2013), http://www.uscourts.gov/Statistics/JudicialFactsAndFigures/judicial-facts-figures-2013.aspx.

12   Perceptions of the Courts in Your Community: The Influence of Experience, Race, and Ethnicity, National Center for State Courts 4–5 (Mar. 2003), https://www.ncjrs.gov/pdffiles1/nij/grants/201356.pdf.

13   Nat'l Ass'n for Law Placement, *LGBT Representation Up in 2012*, NALP Bulletin (Jan. 2013), http://www.nalp.org/lgbt_representation_up_in_2012.

14   *Id.*

15   Todd Brower, *Multistate Figures: Sexual Orientation Visibility and Its Effects on the Experiences of Sexual Minorities in the Courts*, 27 Pace L. Rev. 141, 186 (2007) (citing New Jersey Supreme Court, Final Report of the Task Force on Sexual Orientation Issues (Jan. 2001)).

16   *Reported Number of Lawyers with Disabilities Remains Small*, NALP Bulletin (Dec. 2009), http://www.nalp.org/dec09disabled.

17   ABA Commission on Mental & Physical Disability Law, ABA Disability Statistics Report 6 (2011) http://www.americanbar.org/content/dam/aba/uncategorized/2011/20110314_aba_disability_statistics_report.authcheckdam.pdf (*citing* NALP 2009 study)

18   Justin D. Levinson & Danielle Young, *Implicit Gender Bias in the Legal Profession: An Empirical Study*, 18 Duke J. Gender L. & Pol'y, 1, 3, 28–29, (2010).

19   Jerry Kang et al., *Are Ideal Litigators White? Measuring the Myth of Colorblindness*, 7 J. Empirical Legal Stud. 886 (2010).

20   *Id.*

21   Elizabeth H. Gorman, *Gender Stereotypes, Same-Gender Preferences, and Organizational Variation in the Hiring of Women: Evidence from Law Firms*, 70 Am. Soc. Rev. 702, 705–06 (2005).

22   The 2011 American Bar Association Disability Statistics Report notes that the scarcity of lawyers with disabilities in the profession is attributable, at least in part, to a pipeline problem. " . . . [T]he Center reports that only 12.3% of

working-age persons with disabilities held a Bachelor's degree or higher, compared to 30.6% of non-disabled persons, an 18.3 percentage point gap. This education disparity helps explain why so few persons with disabilities become lawyers, as many individuals with disabilities lack the educational background and academic prerequisites to apply to law school." ABA Comm'n on Mental and Physical Disability Law, Disability Statistics Report (2011), http://www.americanbar.org/.../aba/.../2011/20110314_aba_disability_statistics.

23   *See, e.g.,* Laurence H. Silberman, *The D.C. Circuit Task Force on Gender, Race, and Ethnic Bias: Political Correctness Rebuffed,* 19 Harv. J.L. & Pub. Pol'y 759 (1996); Kari M. Dahlin, *Actions Speak Louder than Thoughts: The Constitutionally Questionable Reach of the Minnesota CLE Elimination of Bias Requirement,* 84 Minn. L. Rev. 1725 (2000).

24   *See, e.g.,* ABA Comm'n on Diversity, Diversity in the Legal Profession (2010), http://www.americanbar.org/content/dam/aba/administrative/diversity/next_steps_2011.authcheckdam.pdf.

25   Vernā A. Myers, ABA Comm'n on Diversity, Diversity in the Legal Profession: How to Go From Well-Meaning to Well-Doing (2010).

26   *Id.* at 156.

27   *Id.* at 158.

28   *Id.* at 160–163.

29   The ideas and techniques discussed in this section are taken from a number of useful sources including: Jerry Kang, Judge Mark Bennett, Devon Carbado, Pam Casey, Nilanjana Dasgupta, et al., *Implicit Bias in the Courtroom,* 59 UCLA L. Rev. 1124 (2012); Vernā A. Myers, ABA Ctr. for Racial and Ethnic Diversity, Moving Diversity Forward: How to Go From Well-Meaning to Well-Doing (2011); Jonathan A. Rapping, *Implicitly Unjust: How Defenders Can Affect Systemic Racist Assumptions,* 16 N.Y.U. J. Legis. & Pub. Pol'y 999 (2013); L. Song Richardson & Phillip Atiba Goff, *Implicit Racial Bias in Public Defender Triage,* 122 Yale L.J. 2626 (2013).

30   Laddcap Value Partners, LP v. Lowenstein Sandler P.C., 859 N.Y.S.2d 895 (N.Y. Sup. Ct. 2007).

31   Principe v. Assay Partners, 586 N.Y.S.2d 182 (N.Y. Sup. Ct. 1992).

32   Model Rules of Prof'l Conduct r. 8.4 (Am. Bar Ass'n 2011), http://www.americanbar.org/groups/professional_responsibility/publications/model_rules_of_professional_conduct/rule_8_4_misconduct.html.

33   *In re* Thomsen, 837 N.E.2d 1011 (Ind. 2005).

34   *Id.* at 1011.

35   *In re* Disciplinary Proceeding Against McGrath, 280 P.3d 1091 (Wash. 2012).

36   *In re* Charges of Unprof'l Conduct Contained in Panel Case No. 15976, 653 N.W.2d 452 (Minn. 2002).

37   *In re* Hammer, 718 S.E.2d 442 (S.C. 2011).

38   Rule 1000-1 of the Local Rules governing the United States Bankruptcy Court in Arizona, http://www.azb.uscourts.gov/rule-1000-1; Local Rules of Practice for the District of Arizona, LRCiv 83.5, http://www.azd.uscourts.gov/sites/default/files/local-rules/LRCiv%202014.pdf.

39   *In re* Judicial Discipline & Disability Comm'n v. Maggio, 440 S.W.3d 333 (Ark. 2014). *See also* Press Release, Ark. Judicial Discipline & Disability Comm'n (Aug. 6, 2014), http://www.state.ar.us/jddc/press_releases.html.

40   *In re* Formal Inquiry Concerning Judge A.P. Fuller, 798 N.W.2d 408, (S.D. 2011).

41   *In re* Mulroy, 731 N.E.2d 120, 121–22 (N.Y. 2000).

42   Model Standards of Conduct for Mediators Standard II.B.1 (Am. Bar Ass'n, Am. Arbitration Ass'n, & Ass'n Conflict Resolution, 2005), http://www.americanbar.org/groups/dispute_resolution/policy_standards.html.

43   Standards for the Provision of Civil Legal Aid Rule 2.4 Cultural Competence (Am. Bar Ass'n 2006).

44   The term "majority lawyers" refers to lawyers who are members of one or more of the following groups in U.S. society: white, heterosexual, male, Christian, able-bodied, under seventy, and/or born in the United States.

45   G. M. Filisko, *Just Like Everyone: Inclusiveness Efforts Seek to Make GLBT Lawyers—And All Others Feel at Home,* 96 A.B.A. J. 40 (Feb. 2010); Cheryl L. Anderson, *The Business Case for Disability Diversity in Legal Employment,* 102 ILL. B. J. 132 (Mar. 2014).

46   *See* ROBERT F. COCHRAN, JR., JOHN M.A. DIPIPPA & MARTHA PETERS, THE COUNSELOR-AT-LAW: A COLLABORATIVE APPROACH TO CLIENT INTERVIEWING AND COUNSELING 25 (1999).

47   Bill Ong Hing, *Raising Personal Identification Issues of Class, Race, Ethnicity, Gender, Sexual Orientation, Physical Disability, and Age in Lawyering Courses,* 45 STAN. L. REV. 1807, 1810—11 (1993).

48   Lorraine Bannai & Anne Enquist, *(Un)examined Assumptions and (Un)intended Messages: Teaching Students to Recognize Bias in Legal Analysis and Language,* 27 SEATTLE U. L. REV. 1 (2003).

49   Susan Bryant, *The Five Habits: Building Cross-Cultural Competence in Lawyers,* 8 CLINICAL L. REV. 33, 41 (2001).

50   These suggestions are adapted from the following: Stacy L. Brustin, *Cross Cultural Communication,* in *The Impact Of Domestic Violence On Your Legal Practice: A Lawyer's Handbook* 70 (Margaret B. Drew, Lisae C. Jordan, Donna J. Mathews & Robin R. Runge, eds., 2004); Susan Bryant, *The Five Habits: Building Cross-Cultural Competence in Lawyering,* 8 CLIN. L. REV. 33 (2001); Jerry Kang, Judge Mark Bennett, et al., *Implicit Bias in the Courtroom,* 59 UCLA L. REV. 1124, 1172 (2012); VERNÃ A. MYERS, ABA CTR. FOR RACIAL AND ETHNIC DIVERSITY, MOVING DIVERSITY FORWARD: HOW TO GO FROM WELL-MEANING TO WELL-DOING 2 (2011); Paul R. Tremblay, *Interviewing and Counseling Across Cultures: Heuristics and Biases,* 9 CLIN. L. REV. 373 (2002).

51   Myers, *supra* note 25, at 2.

52   *Id.* at 141.

53   *Id.* at 122.

54   *Diversity in the Legal Profession: The Next Steps, supra* note 24.

55   Kang, *supra* note 3, at 1142, 1172.

56   Levinson, *supra* note 18 at 3, 28—29.

Reflection and Writing Journals

ALEXANDER SCHERR & MARGARET MARTIN BARRY

What is Reflective Lawyering?

Reflective lawyering is a process in which you evaluate your work as a lawyer to develop professional expertise. It is a skill that helps you identify successful actions, avoid prior mistakes, adjust current conduct based on past learning, and apply current lessons to future practice. This chapter describes reflection: what it is, why it matters, and how to develop your capacity to learn through reflection.

Every semester of law school you read cases, discuss them in class, create outlines, and demonstrate your comprehension of the substantive law you have covered through an examination or paper. You also may have applied what you have studied to hypothetical problems or simulations. In an externship the substantive law takes on new meaning. The problems are real; the facts less certain and more critical; and the challenges new and potentially disorienting. Reflection helps you to give form to what you do and what you observe. With practice, reflective lawyering becomes a habit that moves you along the path to expert lawyering.

Outside of law school you largely rely on your own assessments of what you are learning. Reflection is the core tool for this process. You analyze what you know, what you need to add to that knowledge, how you apply what you know, and the results of that application. It involves assessing what you have done in a structured, productive way.

At the outset you may resist the task of reflection altogether. Or, you may obsess over performance without processing it constructively. You may question the value of spending time to build the skills of self-assessment. We encourage you to be aware of these doubts, but not to give in to them. Remember that the process of reflection is a natural and useful way of developing your professional capacity.

The Cycle of Reflection

Donald A. Schön, a leading scholar on the issue of reflective professional practice, described it as the conscious process of naming what you have observed or experienced and connecting it to the professional identity you are forming.[1] As you reflect, you

- act;

- observe what happens after you act;

- analyze those observations—often seeking input from others about your assessment;

- identify what you have learned as the basis for new knowledge; and

- use the new knowledge as basis for future actions.

Think of reflection as a cycle:[2]

- *Experience* is an event or task done or observed during your placement. As the experience happens, you will want to focus on the event, place it in relation to your prior knowledge and experience, and focus on understanding your role, performing well, achieving your goals, and remembering things.

- *Reaction* is becoming aware of what happened during the experience. Reactions come from events that interest, puzzle, confuse, amuse, or anger you. They often relate to specific events or occurrences and may also come from noticing a connection between events: an "AHA!" moment when "this" has something in common with "that" and you make a connection. These reactions may not add up to much and may disappear as quickly as you notice them. They may also lead to . . . .

- *Theory* is interpreting the experience to identify lessons, make generalizations, or see it in a larger context. Theory often develops as reactions and events build on each other and patterns emerge that connect different events, or school with work, or events now with events in the past. Theory is more permanent than reaction, because you root it in more data and develop it over time.

- *Application* is understanding how theory will work when you encounter a similar experience again and changing your behavior accordingly. Application entails a critique of a theory's accuracy and reliability and an assessment of how to use theory in the future.

For example, assume on your first day at your externship your supervisor asks you to draft a complaint in a personal injury case for a client who slipped on a banana peel in a grocery store. What knowledge do you draw upon? You draw on what you know about banana peels, grocery stores, and people. You draw on what you learned in torts, procedure, and legal writing. You make your way to the sample pleadings files. You prepare a draft. You pause to review what you did and the steps you took to get there. You consider what worked and what you are not so sure about. You submit your draft and seek feedback from your supervisor. You develop a theory about what to do next based on your supervisor's feedback and what you have drawn from the experience of developing the first draft. You use your supervisor's comments and your observations about what your supervisor changed and what she left unchanged to improve the next draft and your overall approach. You use what you have learned to draft your next complaint, hopefully taking your own reflections and the feedback from others to a higher level.

You engage in reflection to develop familiarity with successful responses. In doing so, you build a foundation for managing inconsistencies or surprise. A novice who sees lawyering as a series of tasks that benefit from careful reflection can advance more rapidly to become a seasoned practitioner than the novice whose reflective skills are ill-formed or underused. It is not easy to reflect in practice—the seasoned practitioner just makes it look easy. Think of the 1984 movie THE KARATE KID. Instructed by his sensei to wash and wax the sensei's cars, the kid, initially frustrated, was surprised to discover how the complex movements of karate could grow out of that simple, repetitive motion. When you look at the response to a problem by a lawyer you admire, the actions can often seem reflexive, unconscious. If you ask how the lawyer knew to use the particular response, the lawyer may have difficulty identifying the process—wax on/wax off. The knowledge—initially pursued consciously—has become tacit. That tacit knowledge for the professional forms the basis for understanding new developments in law, procedure, factual development, and other aspects of practice.

Reflection in Your Externship

This process of experience, reaction, theory, and application happens from the very start of your externship and continues, consciously or not, until the end. You fluctuate between concrete experience and abstract thought, between quick, immediate expression and careful, extended critique. The process happens for specific, time-limited events: an interview, a cross-examination, a negotiation, a writing project. It also happens for more extended experience: your work with a client, your relationship with a supervisor, your encounter with a type of practice over a whole semester. In either case, the cycle allows you to do, see, connect, and critique in ways that produce learning.

This cycle will occur naturally, without your conscious attention. However, you can also engage in it consciously, intending to make the most of each phase. In fact, you can and usually do choose when and how you will engage in conscious reflection. In some areas of life, you will go on without consciously trying to learn, while in others you will pay attention, keep track, and put effort into learning.

Clinical reflection asks you to engage in this cycle consciously and cultivate the habits of reflective lawyering. In your externship, clinical reflection focuses on your developing understanding of law, law practice, life as a lawyer, and your identity as a lawyer. Reflective assignments ask that you become intentional and attend to the learning that is already present and available in your experience at your placement.

Why Reflection Matters

Reflection happens constantly. A moment's pause brings to mind times when you have stepped back and worked through a situation, a problem, a relationship, or a goal in a disciplined way and in search of better understanding. In the simplest sense, reflection serves our basic need to make sense of what we encounter and apply what we learn to the future.

This description also suggests other reasons to engage in organized reflection: as a personal practice, as a professional skill, and as a key to effective problem solving and a core component of good judgment.

Thinking back on her externship experience, Professor Suzanne Darrow Kleinhaus put it this way:

When I was a student in the externship, writing the journal required me to think about what I had learned over the course of my placement assignments in a way that just completing those assignments would not have let me do—nor would it have allowed me to recall them quite as vividly. This is true despite the variety and novelty of the research and writing assignments, negotiation and arbitration sessions, and attorney and client meetings. It was the reflection process that both ingrained the memory of these activities and caused me to consider their larger significance.[3]

As a Personal Practice

Reflection starts with your own experience, so it makes sense to start by talking about how reflection matters in personal terms. The practice of reflection affects most of the routine aspects of learning:

- *Clarifying Insight*—Reflection asks that you articulate the subject on which you mean to reflect with accuracy. In doing so, you should find that you see that subject more clearly, identify it more concretely, and discuss it in greater depth. You may also find that you begin seeing other subjects related to your starting point, improving your ability to distinguish what is important from what is not, and placing your experience in context.

- *Training Observation*—Reflection involves an effort to see events or ideas or emotions with greater clarity and precision. Repeated reflection prompts you to sharpen your focus and, in so doing, strengthen your ability to observe in the first place.

- *Strengthening Memory*—While reflection can and does occur while you are acting, it also occurs after the fact. In this way, reflection trains and sharpens your recall of experiences and your ability to organize your recollections for later access. Given this reality, it often makes sense to make note of your insights soon after the related experience. In doing so, reflection can reduce biases that often intrude between past events and present memory, permitting you more even-handed assessments of your experience.

- *Expressing and Integrating Emotion*—We usually have emotional responses to the things that we encounter, from mild curiosity to intense engagement. These responses pervade both experience and memory. Reflection lets us relive those responses to understand their import and absorb more fully how events have affected and taught us. Some say emotions trace the outline of our strongly held values. Reflection thus gives you room to explore the values that may inform your responses. Others note that emotion can distort perception and assessment. Reflection can help to counteract distortion and encourage more balanced assessment.

- *Assessing Relationships Between People*—Reflection permits you room to understand important relationships, ask how they work, and understand their impact. When it occurs while you are alone, through writing journals or just sitting thoughtfully, reflection gives you the distance to step back from social influences to assess your own role. Other kinds of reflection occur in groups, through conversations in supervision or classes. Such shared reflection allows you to "crowd-source" your insight, giving you access to ideas or responses you may not have considered on your own.

- *Uncovering Context*—Important events often have many layers of context or meaning to them. Reflection gives you time and space to understand this context. For example, a conversation with a supervisor may leave you dissatisfied, even upset: were your concerns imagined or real? Was your supervisor inappropriate or offensive, or merely unskilled with feedback? Or both? Using reflection to reframe an incident can help you be clearer in similar situations in the future.

- *Correcting Errors*—Reflection plays a critical role in processing your mistakes and weaknesses. It allows you the privacy and the freedom to assess mistakes on their merits: identifying their scope, specifying their causes, and strategizing to work differently the next time.

- *Improving Plans*—Reflection looks to the future as much as to the past and present. It allows you to imagine how a current plan may play out in different ways, and evaluate and adjust accordingly. Reflection thus strengthens your ability to think strategically: gauging how plans may match upcoming events; assessing your ability to respond; and making clear choices among the variety of goals you may want to pursue.

- *Developing Confidence*—Finally, reflection has a natural tendency to improve and deepen your understanding and to increase your grasp of what you see and know and plan to do. To that extent, reflection tends to increase your confidence: in what you know and understand about the past; in how you see and process what is happening now; and in how you plan for the future.

These personal benefits of reflection directly affect your abilities as a lawyer. A lawyer must be able to observe, describe, and remember events with clarity and precision. A lawyer needs to handle strong emotions and deeply held values with poise and understanding. A lawyer has to navigate a web of relationships thoughtfully and effectively. A lawyer needs to assess complex, multi-layered problems with alertness to their broader context. All lawyers make mistakes and must learn how to learn from them. Finally, a lawyer is also a planner and should have the ability to correct, adjust, and strategize as events unfold.

As a Problem-Solving Skill

The process of legal problem-solving involves a wide range of quite different activities. Lawyers actively engage with the world of conflicts and opportunities and also engage in dispassionate, even scholarly assessments. Lawyers build stories out of uncertain facts and research and analyze law, with each deepening understanding in response to the other. Lawyers plan and strategize, always in response to client needs and concerns, including limitations on time and resources. Lawyers advocate persuasively while fostering opportunities for settlement.

All this activity happens while moving forward toward results that may or may not occur. To hold this all together requires a presence of mind and the capacity to manage very different kinds of insight and behavior, often under great pressure. The ability to reflect on and integrate these activities represents a core competency of lawyering.

As a Central Feature of Good Judgment

Lawyers are valued for the quality of their decisions and their ability to exercise good judgment in accomplishing tasks. Developing a habit of good judgment over the course of a full career poses an enormous challenge. Good judgment for a particular case requires awareness of the law and of legal process, and also the influences and contingencies that contribute to a desirable outcome. Good judgment over a full career requires a routine practice of alertness and responsiveness to the context of each case. Your capacity to learn from both failures and successes will be invaluable, as will your ability to inform future decisions with the lessons of past work.

There are other reasons to engage in reflection. Later in this chapter we introduce you to many of them as we describe the topics you might discuss in written reflection. These topics will suggest different ways for you to use your capacity for reflection to develop your abilities as a lawyer and as a person.

Where and How Reflection Happens

The typical externship course asks you to do at least some reflection in writing. Externship courses can also provide opportunities for strengthening your reflective capacity in ways that may seem more natural for you than written work. These other methods give you room to strengthen your reflective capacity in ways that may prove more natural for you than written work. For example, your course may include:

- *Classroom Discussions*—Externship seminars provide room for group reflective process. One student describes an experience, other students ask questions about it, and others start to generalize, with differences of perspective about the accuracy of a conclusion or its application in other settings. These discussions can address cases, simulated exercises, or reading material for a particular class. Even classes focused on substantive law and process give room for reflection: how the law applies to a particular problem; how a particular process serves to achieve a particular goal; and how to manage pragmatic problems specific to your practice area.

- *Readings*—Many externship classes ask you to read as part of your overall experience. As you might imagine, the range, scope, and focus of reading assignments varies between different types of externship courses, even between courses at the same school. In many courses, the readings focus on knowledge specific to and necessary for your particular type of law practice. In others, the readings discuss skills, or practice realities, or social or political realities. These readings usually have at least two goals. They give you new knowledge and new perspectives that can touch off a new round of reaction, theory, and application for your experience.

- *Conversations with Your Law School Supervisor*—Your externship teacher will most likely have contact with you over the course of a given semester, outside of class, in one-on-one in meetings, emails, or phone calls. At the very least your externship teacher will ask you about your placement and push you to describe and assess your experience: another kind of reflection. In these conversations the externship teacher prompts you to reflect and suggests questions and assessments that model the kind of reflection the teacher will expect during the course.

- *Conversations with Your Supervising Attorney*—By contrast, your relationship with your supervising attorney may seem to involve little or no reflection. Instead, this supervisor may focus wholly on the task at hand: giving an assignment, answering questions, reviewing work product, and giving you feedback. Even this process has reflective aspects to it, if it prompts you to learn new abilities or improve existing ones. See Chapter 3 on Supervision. In many courses, your externship teachers and supervising attorneys will meet with you at the mid-point in conversations that reflect on the semester to date and plan for the remaining time. See Chapter 2 on Professional Development Planning. Finally, your supervising attorney may form a mentoring relationship with you: sharing insight into practice choices and realities, discussing career goals and professional development, even helping you to network and find a job.

- *Time Sheets and Time-keeping*—Most externship programs will require you to track and report your time and work. Time-keeping itself offers a small yet distinct opportunity for reflection. Recording hours and activities inventories how you are spending time: tasks and activities, subject areas of focus, and your integration into the practice. This process provides an outline for you to assess how your activities help you learn, how they relate to your goals, and what changes you might need to make.

Some occasions to reflect occur privately, others one-on-one, and others in groups. Taken together, they offer a context rich in opportunities for self-guided learning. And they interact. A discussion in class may spark a theme for a written journal. An early journal may lead to comment from your externship teacher, which in turn leads to further development in a later journal. Feedback from your supervising attorney may remind you of a particular reading, leading you to change how you approach the same task next time. The chances for reflection permeate every aspect of your externship experience.

Do not wait to use these chances. Reflection works best if you do it actively and with curiosity. Ask your externship teacher to explain what is expected in written reflection. Work to relate the subject matter of the class and the readings to your experience on site. Prompt your supervising attorney to give you perspective; ask questions, from the simple, "what just happened?" to the assertive, "what did you think of that lawyer?" or "what are the reasons you think that happened?" or "what led you to make that choice?" Listen and respond to other students when they offer insight and opinion in class or on a listserv. The more you do, the more opportunities to reflect will happen and the more you will learn.

Confidentiality

As valuable as it is to seek out the insight others can offer, you must protect your client's confidences when you do so. This topic is discussed in greater depth in Chapter 11 on Ethical Issues in Externships: Confidentiality. We also raise client confidentiality here because sharing your experiences is an important aspect of the reflective process. Those experiences are drawn from the work you do for clients.

Client confidentiality is at the core of the trust and candid dialogue that allows attorneys to get information from clients in order to effectively counsel and represent them. So what does the prohibition on "revealing information relating to the representation of a client" under Rule 1.6 mean in the context of creating a journal and sharing all or part of that journal with your externship teacher? What can you discuss in your externship class?

Of course, you can discuss client issues with other members of your firm, or government, or judicial office. There are also exceptions to maintaining confidentiality that reflect a balance between preventing harm and fostering candor, including the reporting of serious bodily or economic injury, but these speak of circumstances that do not usually result in disclosure in student journals or class discussion. If such emergency circumstances come to your attention, they should be discussed with your supervising attorney and, possibly, your externship teacher.

Since your externship teacher and your classmates are not part of your firm, organization, or judicial chamber, if you write about or discuss client-related issues in your externship seminar, with your externship teacher, or in your journal, you run the risk of disclosing confidential information. Given the importance of maintaining confidentiality, it would seem that confidentiality concerns cancel out any benefits that may come from seeking input from your externship teacher and externship colleagues. But that is not so. Lawyers need to discuss their work. They need to do so in order to optimize their service to their clients and generally to grow as professionals. While it is possible to contain such exploration within the law office, expertise often lies beyond such protected confines and effective practitioners seek it out.

You can generally protect client confidences by not stating the client's name, address, or other details about the case that could lead to connecting the information discussed to your client. You must remain alert to any basis for recognition. There are high profile cases where what you can reveal is even more constrained. If, for example, your client is a famous basketball player who is charged with sexual assault, it will be difficult to reference the case without revealing confidences. The charges will be in the papers, and even if you say "an athlete" it would be hard to argue that the client's confidences have not been breached by discussion outside your office.

Your supervising attorney bears the risk of your failure to understand ethical obligations, including client confidentiality. If you believe what you plan to discuss sufficiently protects client confidences, you should consult with your supervising attorney nonetheless prior to discussing any information gained as a result of your relationship with the office. Your externship teacher is a resource if you want to explore how to approach your supervising attorney with regard to disclosures. The supervising attorney can guide such a discussion with attention to preserving client confidences, but you should be careful in talking with your externship teacher to sufficiently identify the confidential nature of the information to be discussed.

Thus, one key is to understand the basic obligation to protect client confidences, err on the side of protection, and seek input when uncertain. While you should seek guidance from your supervising attorney and your externship teacher, you will also want to have a good idea of these parameters so you are alert to the possibilities for breach. The other key is to recognize that, alongside the need for care, you grow and your clients benefit from the efforts you make to broaden your insight.

Writing Journals

This section focuses on journals, by far the most common reflective task in externship courses, though also used effectively in law school clinics. We detail different types of journaling requirements and describe different styles and topics for written journals. We delineate a difference between journals along the way and end-of-semester, summary journals. We offer some thoughts on helpful and unhelpful journaling and, more generally, on how to evaluate your own reflective writing. We talk about faking it and making it: is it possible to fake a journal? Finally, we talk about how you can get better at journaling with practice.

Before we start, we want to note that journal assignments that you encounter often differ between externship teachers and courses. Journal assignments can vary in several ways:

- *Frequency*: You may have journals due as often as once a week or as rarely as once a semester.

- *Length*: You may be asked to write journals as short as a page or as long as 10 to 15 pages. More frequent journals often have shorter length requirements, while less frequent journals generally require more length.

- *Format and Formality*: Your externship teacher may ask for formal analytical journals with footnotes and citations, or may encourage a more personal, informal style.

- *Focus*: Some externship teachers assign particular topics to discuss in your journals, while other leave it to you to choose and develop a topic.

- *Feedback*: You may receive feedback from your externship teacher in several ways, including in-person conversation, written comment, or brief response.

All of these variations in journal assignments will affect how you approach writing a particular journal. As you consider the advice that follows, make sure to translate it into terms that make sense for your particular assignment.

Approaches to Reflective Writing

When you first consider the reflective writing task, you might think there is no single approach to reflective writing: each journal is personal, shaped by the experiences and insights of the writer. Yet, distinct styles of reflective writing do exist. Drawing on the cycle of reflective learning described above suggests the following:

Experience = narrative: Most students use journals to tell stories; in fact, story-telling usually dominates early journals. Good narrative not only informs the reader; it also helps the writer to organize and assess the experiences he or she describes. Editorial choices permeate good story-telling: selecting a story to tell, deciding what parts of the story deserve to be stressed, choosing when to end, and, especially, deciding the point of the story. Consider the stories that you write with an eye towards these choices and an ear for the points that your story makes. This will help you get a better sense of why that event mattered to you and what lessons you might learn.

Consider the following excerpt as an example of **story-telling**:

[The deceased man] was a twenty-eight year old bass player for a rock band . . . he was driving . . . on his way to Athens for a "gig". He was involved in an automobile accident, the details of which are unknown to me. He was rushed to [the] Hospital where he died. . . The dispute between Michael's divorced parents was over who would get his body and how it would be disposed of. Michael's father wanted his body buried in Florida where he and his second wife live. Michael's mother wanted the body cremated and the remains given to her. She had no definite plans for the remains, but wanted to take them back to her home in South Carolina. A great deal of information concerning this family came out at the hearing . . . Michael's father is a devout Catholic and was opposed to cremation in general, and the prospect that his ex-wife, if given the remains, would not provide for a "proper Christian burial" in particular. The cremation issue became moot when the parties agreed that it would be necessary due to the amount of time that had elapsed since Michael's death. So the issue then became who would get the ashes and what would be done with them. Michael's mother and younger brother offered the father a 2/3 to 1/3 division, which he adamantly refused.

So the testimony of witnesses as to what Michael would have wanted began. Michael's mom testified that she was not a Christian, but that she believed in some form of

"Supreme Being". She testified that based on her discussion with Michael, he did not believe in God at all. She felt strongly that Michael would have wanted her to have all of the remains, but she was willing to give the father one-third anyway. [Others testified about his lack of belief in any form of God, and his belief that he would want his mother to have his remains].

Michael's father testified that it would be unbearable to him if his ex-wife were allowed to scatter their son's ashes into the wind. He testified further about his son's Catholic upbringing. He recognized that Michael had drifted away from the Church, but that in the last couple of years has shown signs of renewing his Catholic faith. He thought that it was very common for young people to drift away from the church, but to come back to it once they started families of their own. He testified that he had followed that very pattern himself.

Exercise 8.1 The previous excerpt and those that follow offer examples that display both strengths and weaknesses. Think critically about these as examples of different types of journal writing.

Consider the following questions about the previous excerpt:

How well did the writer observe the events he describes?

How well did the writer organize and describe the story he tells?

The story ends without the student stating an explicit point or reaching a clear conclusion. Does this matter? Why? What reactions do you have to this story? If you had written this story, what would you say next?

Reaction = expression: Journals give you the freedom to say what you think, to express insights, feelings, objections, concerns—anything that has arisen out of your experience that touched you or moved you and is worth your conscious notice. These ideas may or may not relate to the stories you have told. They are typically short bursts of prose where you take the time to speak your mind without trying to abstract or generalize. The heart of this writing lies in sentences beginning with "I". . . I saw. . . I think . . . I feel . . . I wonder . . . I dislike . . . or I'm puzzled. Think of expressive writing as the vehicle for getting down short-term insight, without any special effort to detail it through stories or generalize it for a broad conclusion. Expressive writing helps you to notice things that may later provide valuable learning and starts you on the path to more general lessons and critical analysis.

Consider the following excerpt as an example of **expressive writing**:

I first observed court on x/x/xxxx, and saw a variety of cases. There was a criminal sentencing (a problem with coordination and bureaucracy in action, waiting for prisoner to be transported, also there was some question about a study J had ordered), a dispute about condo parking, and a contempt proceeding against an attorney. It seems like the most interesting stuff happens at sidebars with the attorneys and the judge conferring at the bench. Very mysterious! A lot like legal language and procedure —not very accessible to the public. The contempt hearing was an example of what not to do: the attorney had missed court and then missed his hearing! He basically threw himself on the mercy of the court. I wondered about what kind of personal problems were involved and hope he works it out. From overhearing conversations, it appears that there is a lot of time spent gauging the judge's mood, etc. The choice of attorneys for the person in contempt was apparently a good one as he has a good relationship with the judge. I learned a lot from listening to others and asking about their jobs. I talked with the court recorder and learned about what she did and saw her equipment (they save it to disk now, she prefers civil work, interesting that they usually work with the same judge). Also spoke with the court clerk and found out her job. She is not interested in being a lawyer, but she preferred the procedural side of things! In just one day of court I observed many of the things you said to look out for; substantive law, . . . legal practice, lawyering skills and ethical values.

> **Exercise 8.2** Consider the following questions about the previous excerpt: What do you think of the writing in the last excerpt? What problems do you see with the writing, if any? Is it too informal?
>
> How would you improve the writing? How well did the writer observe the events she describes? How important are the events she chooses to describe? What changes could the writer make to improve her reflection? In particular, this excerpt contains an almost stream of consciousness recounting of a series of reactions. What can the writer do to make these reactions more pointed and forceful?

Theory = generalization: As stories and reactions accumulate and you start to notice patterns, it becomes easier to identify and state the lessons you have learned or conclusions you have reached. These lessons or conclusions typically focus more broadly than short-term reactions and involve generalizations that emerge over time and in response to repeat experiences. Even as you write them, you may realize their limits. Noticing a weakness or a flaw in a conclusion should not deter you from describing it. The effort to state a lesson clearly is an important step toward making it stronger and more useful.

Consider the following excerpt as an example of **generalization**:

The truth is that I came to law school because my mother told me I had to. I thought that I was in the minority, that most people came to law school because they had a burning desire to be a lawyer. The discussion during our last class proved me wrong. From the tone of the discussion, it seemed to me like most of the class came to law school because they didn't have anything else to do. It also sounded like they didn't really want to be lawyers.

After [all this time in] law school I can think of nothing else that I would rather be, but it sounded like the majority of the class had traveled the exact opposite path. Perhaps that could explain the record numbers of addicted attorneys. If you don't like what you are doing, you look to something else to dull the pain, so maybe most of those addicted attorneys became attorneys simply because they went to law school; maybe they felt like they had to follow that course and were miserable doing it so they turned to drugs or alcohol. Who knows what the reason is, but one thing that I took away from that discussion was discovering that I really do have a passion for this profession.

I was angered when one of my classmates said that she had talked to older practicing attorneys and that none of them were happy practicing law. Later, upon some reflection, I realized that this was a good thing. My lack of direction was what led me to law school, but now because of law school I have direction. I just hope it's a good one.

> **Exercise 8.3** Consider the following questions about the previous excerpt: At one point, the writer suggests that "now because of law school I have direction." What does she mean by that? In which direction does she say she is headed?
>
> What are the experiences that lead her to that conclusion? How tightly does she relate experience to the conclusions she reaches?
>
> What suggestions would you make for this writer to improve the conclusions she reached in this excerpt?

Analysis = critique or application: The most useful reflective writing happens when you discover new lessons in assessing your experience. This kind of writing starts with questions: Is a story really accurate? Is a reaction really valid? Does this conclusion really apply to other situations? How might I use this lesson next week, next semester, next year, in my next job? Asking and answering these kinds of questions and trying to see the different possible answers leads to very useful reflective prose.

Consider the following as an example of **critical assessment**:

I guess that the last thing I need to discuss is my supervisor's managerial method. This is a difficult area for me because I am not sure what I really think. Her method is harsh, sometimes demeaning and very microscopic, but it would be hard to say that it is not effective. The attorneys in the office get the job done, and they do it very well. I had thought that a clear indicator that her methods were not very effective was the recent amount of turn-over among the attorneys. . . All of the attorneys, except for two, have been with the office for less than two years, and most for less than one year. After meeting the old staff at the luncheon the other day, I realize that this is not necessarily the case. Two of the workers that had left retired, and they had worked in the system for quite a few years. One left to be a judge . . . and I only met one lady who quit because of a general distaste for the work.

I think that whether or not a person can handle working under this supervisor will come down to their personality type. I am pretty easy going and I take criticisms all right. With her, you learn to take everything she says with a grain of salt. I have also learned to stand up to her when I know I am right. That is not to say that I get rude, I just explain to her my reasons. She does not always agree, but at least she hears my side.

What I have come to understand is that although it is easy to criticize her method, I am not sure that there is a more effective way. She is in charge of 6 attorneys and 2 paralegals, not to mention all of the support staff. She works very long hours, is always on top of everything. I do think that she could stand to be more approachable (she is kind of like a law professor in that everyone is scared to ask her questions), and could probably stand to be a little less first grade teacher harsh. But I cannot really argue with good results.

Exercise 8.4 Consider the following questions about the previous excerpt:

What questions does the writer try to work out in this excerpt? Do her questions relate solely to her supervisor? Do any relate to the writer herself?

How does the writer develop her critique of the supervising attorney at her placement? What questions does she ask? How balanced is her assessment?

How does this journal entry help the student prepare for further experiences as a lawyer?

No one approach to reflective writing will suit every reflective assignment. A good reflective journal easily could incorporate any or all of these approaches. As your experience and understanding of your placement develops over time, you may find yourself shifting your approach from narrative or expressive writing to more conceptual and analytical writing. Be conscious of the style and approach you have chosen, and try to use each one effectively. Recognize that narrative and expressive prose can have as much point and power in developing your ability to reflect as can conceptualization and critique. Consider using all four approaches in different journal assignments, for different topics and for different points. If you have doubts about your ability to reflect, the use of these different approaches can start to stretch and strengthen your ability to write and think reflectively.

Topics for Reflection

When asked to write reflectively, you might ask: what should I talk about? What should I avoid? If your externship teacher assigns you set subject matter for reflective writing, you will have your answer. But you will often have leeway to choose your own topics and develop them as you see fit. This section offers some suggestions about what those topics could be.

We start this list with an important question: do journals have to be only introspective or can you write about the world around you? Some people have a preference for seeing, reflecting, and writing about their inner life, emotions, intuitions, talents, self-critique, goals, preferences, values, and the like. They prefer introspection. Other people prefer to write about the world around them, in an effort to observe accurately and to assess critically the scope and complexity of that world. We could call this a preference for extrospection.

You might think reflective writing must only be introspective and the best reflective writing must focus on one's inner life. This impression may arise from the relatively common practice of personal journal-writing, in which many engage for self-insight, inner clarity, or emotional expression. Especially for someone new to a particular discipline or practice, the benefits of introspection can be distinct and powerful.

An exclusive focus on introspection does not match the realities of professional practice. Law practice engages intensely with external realities: clients, other lawyers, courts, businesses, institutions, culture, politics, society, and all of the intense dynamics between them. Extrospection is essential to the lawyer's reflective practice, as an important pathway to balanced assessment of the world in which lawyers work.

In truth, the distinction between introspection and extrospection is a false one. Your inner life both responds to and influences the world around you and vice versa. We do not exist in isolation but are thoroughly and deeply connected to the "outside" world. The effort to learn about yourself through experience includes an accurate appraisal of the world. Similarly, the effort to learn about a new and unfamiliar context prompts awareness of your own reactions. Reflective practice encourages both self-awareness and awareness of the world you encounter. The two go hand in hand.

We suggest you look both ways in your reflective writing: each focus requires a capacity for the other. Writing about your inner life almost always prompts discussion of the realities to which you are connected. Similarly, writing about the world means you will make choices about what to describe, how to describe it, and what "points" to make. These choices say much about your thoughts, preferences, values, and emotions. Consider whether an introspective or extrospective approach best suits a given topic, in light of your own preferences as a reflective thinker.

We turn to suggesting a range of possible topics for reflection.

- *Class Readings and Discussions*: The readings assigned by your externship teacher and the class discussions about those readings should help you gain perspective on your experience. They may also give you an analytical structure for writing with greater precision and in greater detail. Not all of the discussions or readings may help you. But, if you find yourself short of material to discuss in your journals, turn to the readings for the course and ask which ones help you make sense of your placement.

- *Substantive Law or Legal Process*: Your work often will lead to conclusions about the law and how it works. This understanding can evolve either from specific cases or resolutions, or from a series of similar cases. Write about a particularly difficult analysis, or a thorny research problem. Discuss how the law produced a result that was correct but unsatisfying. Consider both the written and unwritten rules that lead to particular decisions. In some cases, you will find the law does not provide a clear answer, or you must exercise judgment in assessing how to apply the law to the situation at hand. Write about this experience when it happens; you will be developing habits for how to handle similar situations in the future.

· *The Non-legal Realities of Legal Work*: Lawyers work with realities other than the law, realities that have as much influence on outcomes as the law itself. Lawyers deal with the goals, interests, and risk tolerances both of clients and other participants. Lawyers operate within a fabric of existing relationships; these relationships in turn have a history and trajectory that strongly influences the outcome. Lawyers work with the scope and limit of their clients' power, including limitations on time, money, and other resources. Lawyers work with the emotion and psychology of all those involved in disputes. Lawyers handle hard problems: situations where the law and non-legal realities intersect and conflict in ways that require the lawyer's specialized talents. And finally, lawyers often work in crises or situations where they must deliver as much bad news as good to those with whom they work.

   To work effectively with all of these pressures, you will need the ability to see and understand the human condition that underlies the legal issue. A steady habit of reflection can help you to see these influences, understand their effects, and work within them to forge a solution to the task at hand.

· *A "Practice Audit" of Your Placement*: You can also assess your workplace as an organization delivering a service: a non-profit handling particular kinds of cases; a government agency focused on a particular subject matter; a judge's chambers engaged in the business of resolving disputes; and many others. How is your placement organized? Who makes the important decisions? What process does it use to manage and move the work forward? See Chapter 14 on Learning about Lawyering.

· *Relationships Among Lawyers*: You can assess how lawyers work with each other, what connections seem important, and what culture of practice the lawyers have. How often do the lawyers you see work together and how effectively? How often do they work alone? How do the lawyers work with the other side: opponents in litigation, negotiators in transactions, and lawyers in other settings? What relationships do lawyers have with judges and vice versa? In all these settings, how big of an impact does a lawyer's reputation have, and how did the lawyer establish that reputation in that community? How large a role does collaboration play in the practice of law? See Chapter 5 on Effective Communication and Professional Relationships and Chapter 16 on Collaboration and Teamwork.

- *Relationships With Clients*: Lawyers almost always work in relationship to a client or a cause or a mandate or a web of interconnected duties and obligations. To whom are the lawyers at your placement responsible and accountable? How do they structure that relationship? See Chapter 15 on The Client Relationship. If you work for an agency or an organization, who does the lawyer go to for decisions and how is the process of decision-making handled? See Chapter 21 on Public Interest Lawyering. If you work for a judge, what does your judge see as her primary role: to manage the court docket efficiently; to make decisions that comply with applicable law and will not be reversed; to make decisions that lead to closure for the parties before the court? See Chapter 19 on Judicial Externships.

- *Standards of Practice*: You will most likely have the chance to appraise both good lawyering and bad, and in doing so, start to develop your own standards of practice. Keep track of your reactions to the quality of the lawyering you observe. If you see high quality work, consider what makes it high quality. If you see bad lawyering, work out why you thought it was bad and what you would have done differently; and again, ask others whether they agree. In articulating these reactions, you are developing a set of standards for how you would do the same task in the future.

- *Supervising Attorneys as Mentors and Role Models*: Chances are you will find much to admire, or to critique, or at least to comment on in how your supervising attorneys do their work. Do you see yourself using any of your supervising attorneys as a role model? What are the qualities you want to emulate, and which might you avoid, if any? Your supervising attorneys will also make choices about how they relate to you. While some may stay focused on the tasks at hand, others may take the time to engage you more personally, as a mentor. What have you learned from this mentoring relationship? What kind of supervision and mentoring might you want to replicate in your future practice? See Chapter 3 on Learning from Supervision.

- *Defining and Negotiating the Lawyer's Role*: Watch the different roles that you see lawyers playing and ask whether you might want to occupy similar roles in your practice. Are the lawyers you see primarily advocates, reserving their most important activities for the courtroom? Are they negotiators, focusing most on finding agreements? Are they planners and relationship builders, working out deals and transactions for others? What other roles do you observe in your placement?

Ask about the connections between lawyers' roles and their personal values, beliefs, and preferences. Lawyers experience their work both as individuals and as "professionals." Personal identity and professional persona often fit together easily and may never cause tension. At the same time, it can be challenging to learn your professional role and navigate those situations in which the personal and the professional come into conflict. The task requires you at once to maintain the integrity of your values and satisfy your commitments to clients and the legal system within which you will work. A steady habit of reflection increases your alertness to this task and sensitizes you to the conduct and choices a professional role can require.

- *Ethical Awareness, Ethical Action and Ethical Decision Making*: Lawyers work within a structure of ethical rules, with both ethical mandates and ethical aspirations to understand and apply. The demands of ethical conduct are often clear and easy to apply. But just as often, it may be hard to spot or act on an ethical concern. In these cases, recognition starts as a sense or an intuition: that something is off, or a particular path feels wrong. In these situations, noticing and naming your intuition can be half the battle. Once alerted, you will have to develop and assess your concern accurately within the framework of ethical rules. Finally, you will have to decide on a course of action, which often calls for difficult choices: withdrawing from representation, confronting a colleague, or asking for critical feedback from others.

  You will frequently encounter ethical questions at your placement. Some will relate to the practice in your office; others will arise from your own work. You can focus your journals on these dilemmas and the process through which your office handled them. How do your lawyers recognize an ethical issue has come up? How do they frame the issue and consult the relevant sources of authority? Does your office have an internal mechanism for handling ethical concerns; if so, how and how well does it work? If your office handles an ethical issue while you work there, what did you think of how it was handled?

- *Critical Assessment of Power and Politics*: You could critically assess the political and cultural values that inform your practice as well as their impact on others. What are the power relationships displayed in your office, between lawyers, between lawyers and clients, and between lawyers and the outside world? Who is privileged; who is not? To what extent do unwritten rules control what happens in your office, as opposed to the formal rules of law and procedure? How do the lawyers in your office implement their political values, and how closely does their actual conduct match those values? How much do lawyers' values, sense of privilege, and sense of normalcy control the lawyers' actions, and how do these factors affect those with whom lawyers have contact?

- *Identity and Bias*: You can also assess the diversity of identities at your placement, both for individual lawyers and the practice as a whole. Identity in turn relates to bias and includes questions about how to work in situations where the participants come from strongly different backgrounds and cultures. How do lawyers at your placement relate to others who identify differently? Do differences in self-identification lead to differences in the treatment of clients, other attorneys, judges, or anyone else? Have you observed the effects of bias towards others or experienced them towards yourself? See Chapter 6 on Navigating Cultural Difference and Chapter 7 on Bias in the Legal Profession.

- *Personal Talents and Abilities*: Your placement will give you the chance to practice one or more lawyering skills: interviewing, investigation, research, analysis, problem solving, counseling, advocacy, negotiation, planning, even judging. How well are you doing what you have been asked to do? What strengths do you notice? What weakness have you discovered? How can you develop the former and counteract the latter?

- *Personal Preferences and Aversions*: You will like some and may dislike other parts of your experience in your placement. Which parts of your work do you enjoy, and which do you shy away from? What is it that attracts you to things you enjoy, and what kinds of practices might permit you to continue to do those things in the future? What are the reasons you dislike the work you dislike, and how does that insight influence your thoughts about your career?

- *Intuitions and Feelings*: You can use your journal as a way of sorting out your thoughts, or articulating new intuitions, or expressing strongly felt emotion. Intuition and emotion in particular have a powerful connection to our values; we often have the strongest reactions and insights in situations where our values come into play. Articulating emotion can help you become more aware of your beliefs; or it can simply be a useful way of letting off steam, working out a problem, or gaining some distance from a hard situation.

- *Relating Work to Your Values*: Lawyers can easily lose sight of whether what they do matches what they think they should be doing. Many lawyers become absorbed in achieving what is expected of them without stopping to evaluate whether those objectives and approaches are consistent with their values and professional goals. Does your placement engage you in work consistent with your own values? How or how not? Some people find that new and unfamiliar experiences make them aware of values they did not know they had or can strengthen or change values they already held. What new beliefs or values do you find yourself identifying and developing at your placement? How does that realization help you understand your identity as a lawyer and the path that you may take going forward? See Chapter 24 on Professional Identity and Formation.

- *Life Balance and Career Satisfaction*: Lawyering is fascinating work, absorbing and challenging in its own right. Lawyering is also busy and demanding work, capable of filling your time with endless tasks. The economics of practice can lead to serious time commitments, whether you work in the for-profit world or not. Commitments to legal work can thus come to dominate other life commitments. It can take awareness, restraint, and patience to reorient yourself toward a broader balance of activities for work and family, community, spirituality, or even personal health.

  Wherever you work, you will have the chance to observe how the lawyers at your placement balance work with other life commitments: family, recreation, community, church, political beliefs, and many others. How do lawyers at your placement strike this balance? What trade-offs do they accept in achieving this balance? Reflecting on balance can also raise questions about the satisfaction and even the happiness those lawyers experience in their work. How happy or satisfied are the lawyers with whom you work? Are these the same thing? What do you think may account for the level of happiness or satisfaction you observe? See Chapter 25 on Work and Well-being.

- *Career Opportunities*: Most of you have chosen placements that might benefit your career. Your placement may match a personal interest or involve an area in which you want to practice. You may simply be curious and want to rule your kind of placement in or out of your career planning. Finally, you may see your placement as a chance to network, gain a useful reference, or get yourself known in a particular community. Your journal gives you the chance to reflect on your job search and connect your career goals to what you are learning on site. See Chapter 26 on Externships and Career Planning.

- *Criticism:* We sometimes have students who assume that they must be relentlessly positive and affirming in reflection. However pleasant this approach might be, you may find that your placement or your class does not meet your expectations. Complaints about work or supervising attorneys, questions about the relevance of the externship class, concerns about the multiple demands of the program—all of these are legitimate and useful topics for reflection. A good critical entry can help you identify what is wrong, articulate an alternative, and express a standard of judgment. If you engage in such critique, you will have benefitted from one of the great advantages of reflective assessment.

This list of potential topics by no means exhausts the possibilities. You can use this list as a springboard to other topics not listed here. Be careful to avoid the temptation to write about everything. This notion can lead you to write too much, producing a lot of text without much reflection. Given the time demands on a law student, we know this to be implausible: but we have seen it happen. Instead, pick and choose those topics that relate to the real value you experience at your placement. Narrowing your focus in this way can help you make the most of the reflective task.

Summary Journals

Your course may ask you to write several journals over the course of a semester. Whether it does or not, your course may also require you to write a journal at the end. These summary journals often ask you to review and discuss what you have learned over the course of the semester. Enough differences exist between journals during the semester and a summary journal to make it worth talking about the special demands of summarizing your experience.

In-process journals and summary journals have much in common. In both you write about your own experience. In both, you can take advantage of the possible kinds of writing that can help good reflection: narrative, expression, generalization, and critique. Both look at the past and can include introspective and extrospective assessment.

Summary journals differ substantially from their earlier cousins. We suggest at least three major differences:

- *Time Coverage*: In earlier journals, you tend to write about what has just happened or what you have noticed over the time period since the last journal. By contrast, a summary journal covers the whole semester, not just the time since you last wrote. The assignment pushes you to assess changes and developments from the time you started the course to the time you write the closing journal.

  To make this assessment, remember who you were at the start of the semester. Consider your goals for the course at that time and what you expected and hoped to get from the experience. Now, return your mind to the present:

what has changed? What do you know now that you did not know then? What can you do now you could not do then, and how have your abilities become stronger? Have you reached decisions or conclusions that were still unsettled at the start of the semester? Thinking about the entire semester allows you to trace your professional development over the entire time period in ways that help you to identify topics for the summary journal.

· *Range of reference*: In other journals you write during the semester, you tend to focus your topics more narrowly: on what is happening with clients, with tasks, with your placement's practice, or with the class. You do not usually consider all of the course content. By contrast, the summary journal asks you to review and synthesize all of what you have encountered: work, class, performance, observation, conversations, and even prior journals. Summary journals usually ask you to make a more conscious effort to synthesize and to generalize than journals in-process.

Consider the following comparison: In a class on substantive law such as Property or Evidence, you may go to class regularly, read steadily, and process and integrate as you go. At the end of the semester, you are tested; and to prepare for that test, you may outline the substantive material you have been assigned in a way you can use effectively during the test itself.

By contrast, most externships do not give you a final exam on your experience and thus do not usually require you to outline the course or to fix it in your mind for future use. A summary journal serves that function, asking you to gather together all of the components of the course in one mental space and ask: how do these fit together? What are the patterns? What have I learned?

· *Past and future*: With in-process journals, you tend to focus primarily on things that have already happened: stories, reactions, thoughts, and critiques, all with reference to what has gone on before you write. The summary journal prompts you to identify how your experience will affect you going forward. You get to ask exactly how useful the course was for you and in what ways.

This future orientation has both personal and editorial value. On a personal level, looking ahead allows you to relate this semester's experience to your next steps, your plans for your future legal work, and your goals for your career. A summary journal can help you step out of this semester's experience and fit it into the flow of your professional development. On an editorial level, looking ahead can allow you to narrow the range of topics you will discuss to those you know to be most important. You can ask what parts of your clinical experience had the most real value for you going forward and thus pose the best topics for reflection.

We can capture the three distinct features of a summary journal concisely: think about the whole semester; think about all that the course has brought you; and look forward to what you will use out of what you have learned. Notice that asking these questions encourages two kinds of reflective writing described earlier: generalization and critical analysis. While you may tell stories or express brief reactions, you are far more likely to formulate conclusions and assess their usefulness with a critical eye.

Be sure you understand exactly how your externship teacher wants you to handle the summary journal. You may be asked to focus on particular questions, or discuss particular readings, or engage in a particular kind of self-assessment. Whatever the assigned focus for your closing reflection, the features we have described give you useful tools for achieving an overview and securing in place things you most want to remember going forward.

You may encounter a major risk of summary journals: reflection fatigue. Some students report having run out of new things to say by the time they reach this closing assignment. What can you say you have not already said before? If you feel you suffer from reflection fatigue, the summary journal can seem like an insurmountable hurdle.

If so, we encourage you to back up and start over with the closing task. Reread your previous journals. What did you write about then? How do those topics look now, in light of your overall experience and your future? Alternately, take out a blank sheet of paper or bring up a blank screen and start listing answers to the question: what did I get out of doing this? Reorganize that list in ways that make sense to you, and consider how you would move from one topic to the next. These exercises can help you toward a summary that matches the experience as you lived it, and identifies the things you most want to remember. See also Chapter 28, Looking Backward/Looking Forward for a description of the Strengths-Opportunities-Aspirations-Results or SOAR method for closing assessment.

Evaluating Reflective Writing

Your externship teacher may or may not grade your reflective writing. The externship teacher will pay attention to what you write and will evaluate how well you are handling the task. The bare minimum standard for a "good" journal is the fact of completion.

If that is the case for your course, you will satisfy the requirement simply by turning in a journal.

If your externship teacher asks more than that, make sure you understand what that teacher expects. This may seem like an obvious point, although surprisingly few students ask what teachers expect out of reflective writing. Some externship teachers state clear requirements: page length, topics covered, deadlines to meet, and the like. This approach gives you clear benchmarks for completion to the designated level.

Your externship teacher may also assess your work for the quality of your reflection, an assessment that poses hard questions. Reflective writing focuses on you and your experience. That experience and what you see in your experience will differ from the experience and insight of other students. Moreover, you might write about a research task, while another student might write a reaction to a particular client, and another might choose to respond to the readings or talk about career choices. These topics may also differ in terms of their potential for depth of assessment. Finally, for whatever reason, you may have had a bad experience at your placement, in the very specific sense you got repetitive work or meaningless work, or never observed anything beyond your cubicle. How can you be expected to generate deep thought from a shallow placement? In short, is evaluating reflective writing subjective, style-driven, and random? We think not.

Bad Journal Writing

We mean to persuade you that, in fact, one can assess reflection and reflective writing for quality and distinguish bad reflective writing from good. Let us start with the bad. Here are some examples of what, in our view, constitutes bad journal writing:

- *Trivial Pursuits*: A student spent half of his closing journal reviewing the restaurants near his placement. The reviews were well-written; each had a little story, with good description. He articulated his reactions to the food and the service. He drew a broader lesson: "It's important to eat well in the midst of a demanding law practice." He engaged in critical thought and expanded his range of culinary preferences as a result. And, as it happened, the reviews proved accurate and useful.

  And yet, this student worked for a federal district court judge. He wrote a handful of proposed orders on complex issues and observed over 30 hours of hearings and trials. He had several conversations with the judge and his clerks about law practice and professional life. His choice to write restaurant reviews ignored all of that experience. He would have been better served by writing on other topics.

- *The Postcard Journal*: This kind of writing involves brief, uninformative assertions, together with expressions of gratitude for the experience. These sound something like: "Dear Prof: I'm here at work. This is great! I'm really enjoying it. Wish you were here! Thank you so much for the chance! Goodbye!" It's surprisingly easy to spend 5 or more pages writing like this.

  The postcard journal may in fact offer some taste of reflection. You could write "I really learned a lot from watching my judge interact with attorneys at sidebar" and feel like you have covered some ground. Other than identifying sidebar conversations as interesting, however, this sentence says almost nothing. It fails to identify what the writer learned or why the writer thought it was of interest. It does not connect the observation to any broader context: how the student might handle sidebars as a litigator, or what the judge's conduct says about her approach to judging, or other topics.

- *The Annual Report Journal*: Some journals contain a list of every event, no matter what, reported evenly and accurately. "Day One: I arrived at the office. I found my desk and sat there . . . Day 24: I arrived at the office. I found my desk . . . I wrote 7.35 pages of text on the following issue. I had lunch." This kind of journal lacks any editorial, critical or analytical thought; it lists facts, without telling a story, articulating a reaction, looking for a lesson or thinking critically. See "time sheets" above.

- *The Xerox Journal*: Some people write the same journal several times, up to and including their closing journal. As an extreme example, one student wrote an early journal and received feedback on it. For the next journal, he turned in the same text as the last, with two sentences added. After additional feedback, he turned in the same text as the last journal, with a paragraph added. When asked, the student said that he has said everything he had to say in the first journal and felt no need to add anything more.

  We will talk a bit later about getting stronger as a reflective writer. For now, consider the argument that everything worth writing about occurs in the first few weeks of the semester, and no further opportunities for learning occur after that. This may reflect a weakness in the placement itself. But we strongly believe good faith efforts to work and observe over the course of a full semester will almost always produce an increase in insight, learning, and critical assessment.

Remember reflective writing should help you strengthen the habit of reflection, which in turn develops your ability to deal with new learning challenges and complex problems. The examples above show students who spent time on writing but not on reflection. They missed the chance to practice this habit.

Writing a Good Journal

Other kinds of bad journals exist. These examples just scratch the surface. But they also help to identify by contrast some of the qualities of a good journal or a good series of journals. You can use the following questions to help assess whether your journal entries will produce a good impression:

- *Is it relevant?* The trivial pursuit journal fails this question. While the student acted reflectively, his topic did not relate either to his experience working at this placement or to any other aspect of the relevant course. In your own reflective writing, ask whether the topics you have covered relate to your experience at work, your class, the readings, or the assigned questions. If you are in doubt, contact your externship teacher and ask whether a given topic would be appropriate.

- *Is it informative?* The postcard journal fails this question. Consider what point or conclusion you want to reach in your journal, and ask whether you have given your reader enough information to understand how you got there. This information could consist of more narrative information, a series of brief reactions, a sequence of concepts, a well-worked out critique, or a combination of all of these. Make sure by the time you reach the end of a particular discussion, you have given your reader enough information to follow along with you.

- *Do you have a point to make? Do you reach a conclusion?* The annual report journal fails this question. Even if you are recounting facts, review what you have written to make sure the reader knows what point you are trying to make. You will have less difficulty with this if you are stating reactions, identifying lessons learned, or engaging in critical assessment. Reread your journal after you have completed it to see whether you have made the points you wanted to make and have not drifted in ways that can confuse your reader.

- *Does your insight change and develop as you write?* The xerox journals fail this question. While the first journal might have stated interesting and useful insights, simply copying and resubmitting those insights means the writer has abandoned any effort to see new things or deepen his insight into familiar things. Reread your journal after you have written a draft and ask two questions. Did your thinking change over the course of this journal? And does this journal add to or develop insights from past journals?

- *Have you tried out different styles of writing?* We discussed earlier several ways of writing a journal: narrative, expressive, generalizing, and critical. Try thinking about your experience in these different ways: as a story, an expression of thoughts and feelings, a source of lessons and generalizations, or the subject matter of a critique. Try out these different ways of thinking and writing, if not in a single journal, over the course of several journals.

- *Is your journal well-written?* You can write your journal in a much more informal style than, say, a piece of academic writing or a persuasive brief. Unless instructed otherwise, you can use the first-person singular, discuss personal reactions, and assess a wide range of realities in addition to formal law and legal process. However, do not mistake informality for permission to write badly. Writing reflectively means thinking reflectively, and, if your prose shows a lack of attention to detail, your reader may conclude that your thinking does as well. Proofread your journals. Review them for grammar, spelling, and punctuation. Your externship teachers may not let what they notice affect an assessment either of the journal or of your professionalism, although it is possible and perhaps even likely that they may.

- *How has this journal helped you become a better lawyer?* The point of reflective writing in an externship, just like the point of your work at your placement, is to help you become a better lawyer. This can mean several things: did writing the journal help you understand a skill that you wanted to strengthen? Did your discussion help you make better choices about your career? Did your analysis sharpen your insights into better and worse practices and help develop your standards of practice?

Note that all of these criteria suggest a process for improving your reflective writing: write and leave time to review and edit. Faced with the task of writing a journal, many people treat the task the same way they would treat a personal journal: write once and leave it alone. In the average law school schedule, this approach usually means that journals are written the night or even just a few hours before the deadline, leaving virtually no time to go back and think about what you have written. Develop a habit of writing journals that lets you step away and then return for at least one thorough session of reconsideration and editing. This process can go a long way to assuring the quality and depth of what you submit.

Faking Reflection: The Value of Authenticity

Students sometimes conclude that journals are so subjective and so subjectively evaluated that doing well on journals requires little more than scoping out what the externship teacher is looking for and saying the magic words.

Doing well with reflective writing does involve scoping out the task asked of you; however, as this chapter should persuade you, there are no magic words. More to the point, most externship teachers keep regular contact with you, in different ways. They will encourage you to write about experience they have heard you describe or they know that your placement usually provides.

Consider what your externship teacher may know about you and your work. If you have a seminar, your externship teacher will have had the chance to hear about your work there. Your externship teacher will know the readings that were assigned, the questions asked, and the discussions that happened in class. Your externship teacher will also likely have had meetings with you one-on-one and have had contact with your supervisor about your work. Your externship teacher will receive some form of evaluation of your work from your workplace. Finally, unless you work at a completely new placement, your externship teacher will also likely know about the work other students have done and the kinds of topics other students have discussed in journals in previous semesters.

Given all this information, it is probably easier to write authentically and reflect on your real experience and real conclusions. As with truth-telling generally, writing authentically will be more efficient, easier to track and remember, and likely be more interesting than anything you might make up. In this sense, authenticity has real value in your reflection: it offers you the benefit of your real goals and plans as motivators to write with the range and depth that more meaningful reflection requires.

Getting Better at Reflection through Writing

How can you use reflective writing to develop your reflective ability? We have already suggested ways to write a good journal. Following that advice will improve your reflective writing, journal by journal, and will also improve your capacity to reflect more generally. Yet, getting better at reflection involves more than writing one good journal, or even a series of good journals.

To improve reflection, approach your journals as a series of exercises, each building on the last. In your early journals, just try to find your balance as a reflective writer. Try not to reach for broad generalizations. Gather and present your data, using narrative or short reactions to interesting events. Focus on clear articulation of your reactions and telling stories that lead to a clearly identified conclusion.

As you work longer and write more journals, you will have time to develop more settled conclusions or develop a more critical and balanced assessment of a situation or an event. Use your later journals to try out generalization and critical analysis. You can continue to tell stories or express reactions, but you may find that you can link these together in longer discussions that develop a more general idea or dig more critically into what you have encountered at your placement.

Use all the opportunities to reflect made available to you by your externship course to expand your capacity for reflection. Listen to the topics your externship teacher raises in your seminar, and consider how the externship teacher raises them: the questions she asks, the discussion she prompts, and the way in which she articulates and frames what is at issue. Use the readings for the course as a source of ideas for things to look for at your placement. Then write a page or two on how what you read relates to what you experienced. Use conversations with your supervising attorneys or with your externship teacher to ask questions, pose problems, and create context for your experience. These activities can give you specific topics for your writing, and also help you exercise your reflective muscles in ways that will strengthen how and what you write.

As you approach the end, give way to the impulse to find closure and look forward. Ask hard questions about your experience: how have you or your insights changed over the course of the semester? What ideas or topics or themes seem to have mattered the most? What effect is this experience likely to have on you in the future? How have you developed as a lawyer over the course of the semester? These questions help you secure the learning you most want to remember and give you excellent material for a closing or summary journal.

Approached with good faith and good energy, this sequence of reflective activities should leave you in better position to reflect on other experiences going forward. Even if you never write a journal again after you end your externship or leave law school, as a lawyer, you will often encounter the need to think and act reflectively. You may find that reflection becomes a life-long practice.

Reflection as a Lifelong Practice

You are moving into that professional role where knowing how to evaluate the quality of your own work becomes an essential skill for professional survival and success. You cannot simply act; you need to develop greater understanding as to the reasons you acted in a certain way, whether your actions were effective, and whether they were warranted under the circumstances. The responsibility for making that assessment rests with you, the professional.

Your externship is designed to help instill a process that makes each of these steps intentional and habitual. The goal is to assure you approach your legal career as a lifelong process of professional development.

In addition to being a tool for developing expertise, reflective practice helps you build self-awareness, which can lead to greater resilience. Because the work lawyers do often brings them to the center of intense conflict, many lawyers suffer from high levels of psychological distress. Reflective practice provides important coping skills. By taking control of what you are experiencing as a lawyer and evaluating what the experiences mean, you can harness anxiety over the effect of what you are doing and turn it into positive energy that connects your desire for professional expertise with other personal values.

Indeed, it is not much of a leap to consider that such practices can serve other aspects of your lives. Some of you are married, parents, in relationships, musicians, dancers, athletes, and so on. By taking the time to reflect on and to assess these roles, you may gain insights into what is and is not working well in your life and whether you need to explore new approaches.

Everyone thinks about their experiences in some form. Many of us reflect only in response to important, intense, or painful events to come to grips with them and place them in the context of our lives. We suggest that the capacity for reflection can be learned, that it can be learned through practice, and that doing so allows you to get better at the task. Making the process of reflection a habit with regard to your professional development will help you to become a better lawyer, and it may well improve other aspects of your life.

ENDNOTES

1   *See generally* DONALD A. SCHON, EDUCATING THE REFLECTIVE PRACTITIONER: TOWARD A NEW DESIGN FOR TEACHING AND LEARNING IN THE PROFESSION (1987).

2   The diagram of reflection as a cycle is based on David Kolb's experiential learning cycle: concrete experience; reflective observation—where the learner reflects back on the concrete experience; abstract conceptualization—where the learner attempts to conceptualize a theory about what was observed; and active experimentation—where the learner tests the theory by incorporating it into the plan for a future experience. DAVID A. KOLB, EXPERIENTIAL LEARNING: EXPERIENCE AS THE SOURCE OF LEARNING AND DEVELOPMENT (1984).

3   Suzanne Darrow Kleinhaus, *Developing Professional Identity Through Reflective Practice*, 28 TOURO L. REV. 1443, 1447–8 (2012).

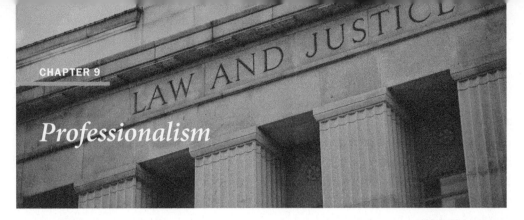

CHAPTER 9

Professionalism

NANCY MAURER

> *More civility and greater professionalism can only*
> *enhance the pleasure lawyers find in practice,*
> *increase the effectiveness of our system of justice,*
> *and improve the public's perception of lawyers.*
>
> — Justice Sandra Day O'Connor

Introduction

A s an extern you will have opportunities to observe and participate in the practice of law and consider those lawyering qualities you most admire and wish to emulate. You will begin to forge your own professional identity and reputation. Think back to your decision to go to law school—likely your reasons included helping others, solving problems, and being part of a noble profession.

Unfortunately, lawyers are not uniformly admired in our society and are often reviled in popular culture. Some attribute the bad reputation of the legal profession to a loss of civility and a lack of ethics and professionalism in our adversarial system, which is mirrored in society generally. Some blame the prevalence of lawyer advertising. Others fault law schools for failing to teach professionalism and values adequately, or suggest this problem is a natural result of lawyers advocating for client interests. Whatever the truth in any of these ideas, you may find yourself at the observing or receiving end of conduct you find disturbing or unprofessional. How will you respond? What strategies will you use to build professional competence and maintain a positive reputation as a lawyer?

This chapter looks at themes of professionalism in law practice, including expected norms of lawyer behavior in dealing with clients, courts, legal adversaries, and others. It explores various concepts of professionalism, the values attached to being professional, and how lawyer conduct affects reputation, clients, the legal system, and the profession in general. First, the chapter discusses what professionalism means and the reasons it matters. The chapter then explores ideals of professionalism based on civility and considers whether rules of civility make a difference and whether such rules should be mandated. Next, the chapter examines professionalism in relation to Rules of Professional Conduct and considers how ethical duties to clients, and in particular zeal in advocacy, at times may conflict with duties toward third parties, opponents, and tribunals, or with expected norms of conduct related to court efficiency and the administration of justice. The chapter additionally looks at professional reputation and offers tips for practicing professionalism. Finally, the chapter considers professionalism as incorporating concepts of individual and collective moral good.

On a practical level, this chapter considers specific issues that may arise in an externship and in practice, and identifies some strategies for building positive professional habits and for responding to unprofessional behavior you might encounter. How do you respond to rude, insulting, or inflammatory conduct directed at you or others? Are there risks to your reputation as a lawyer depending on your response or lack of response? How do you balance the demands of diligent client-centered representation with systemic expectations of professional collegiality and the public good? Is there a conflict?

With your personal reputation and the reputation of the legal profession in the balance, it is incumbent on each of us to form a vision of how to be "professional." Doing so personally can help to preserve the integrity of the legal system and perhaps improve the public's perception of the legal profession.

What Professionalism Means and Why It Matters

> *Attorneys must be held to a higher standard of conduct as "a lawyer is a representative of clients, an officer of the legal system and a public citizen having special responsibility for the quality of justice."*[1]

Lawyers rank among the least trusted of the professions—behind bankers, business executives, and nursing home operators—in Gallup Polls of Honesty/Ethics in Professions. http://www.gallup.com/poll/1654/honesty-ethics-professions.aspx. Only advertising executives, state office holders, car salespeople, members of Congress, and lobbyists fared worse. Nurses ranked highest as the most honest and ethical of the professions.

Jokes portraying lawyers as sharks, vermin, bottom feeders, or worse, are part of our culture. There is the often-repeated story of audiences applauding during the movie JURASSIC PARK when the T-Rex eats the lawyer as he cowers in an outhouse.

Real life examples of unprofessional conduct in the legal profession abound in the media, aided by technology that is able to capture and immediately disseminate instances of rude, uncivil, and occasionally outright belligerent behavior on the part of lawyers, judges, and law students. For example, after an assistant public defender in Florida verbally sparred with a judge while refusing to waive a client's right to a speedy trial, the judge challenged the lawyer to "go out back and I'll just beat your ass." The lawyer and judge left the courtroom, and the judge apparently then did as threatened, returning to applause in the courtroom. The verbal exchange and sounds of fighting in the hallway were captured on videotape and shown widely on television and the internet (http://www.usatoday.com/story/news/nation/2014/06/03/judge-attorney-courtroom-fight/9901631/.) An angry judge reprimanding a second-year law student for rude behavior on *The People's Court* also has garnered a number of YouTube views (https://www.youtube.com/watch?v=vO4G55uTMvM).

The legal profession is largely self-regulated in the United States with states and bar organizations administering various rules of practice, codes of ethics, and other standards of behavior—some mandatory and others advisory. For the system to work, the profession demands lawyers' actions comport with certain behavioral standards. What those standards should be, however, is subject to some debate. One lawyer's zealous advocacy may be considered overly aggressive behavior by another lawyer (or judge). One lawyer's strategy to gain an advantage for a client by refusing to accommodate an opponent's scheduling needs may seem to another like a failure to extend a common professional courtesy. Because much lawyering takes place outside of the view of courts or judges, sanctions for bad behavior are imposed only after the fact and may be applied inconsistently.

Professionalism is sometimes described as an "I know it when I see it" quality. Definitions vary. Lawyers are expected to dress appropriately and behave civilly, but most would agree that professionalism embodies more than proper appearance and good manners. It goes beyond compliance with the Rules of Professional Conduct and other statutory or regulatory standards and means more than simply avoiding legal malpractice and law breaking. Such rules set the floor below which lawyers must not venture, yet leave a great deal of room for lawyer discretion. By contrast, professionalism encompasses more than the mere minimum and includes good judgment, effective problem solving, and leadership. Professionalism contemplates being part of a learned profession that serves the public and contributes to societal good. To be truly professional requires developing both the educational background and the moral, ethical, and behavioral framework for a satisfying career and a life of value to society.

Some may question whether the legal profession has in fact become more uncivil in recent years. Changes in technology and communication may have just made bad behavior more visible across society. As lack of civility, or the appearance of it, becomes commonplace in politics, the media, and in courtrooms, and threatens to overshadow the more positive images of the legal profession, it is worth examining what professionalism means and what is expected of lawyers. Are there behavioral norms, separate and distinct from legal and ethical rules, from which we should not deviate? What are the consequences of professionalism or a lack of professionalism for us as lawyers, our clients, or the legal system?

The "professionalism" movement has its critics who argue that the rules governing lawyer behavior are unnecessary and elitist. Some propose lawyers be sanctioned solely for ethical violations rather than be held to new sets of behavioral rules that may conflict with the lawyer's ethical duties to clients or diminish client advocacy. Some critics question professional regulation altogether. For example, Professor Amy Mashburn suggests that as the legal profession grows more diverse, the rules of professional conduct and rules of civility may be seen as discriminatory attempts by an increasingly isolated elite group to impose customs and values on diverse and less prestigious attorneys.[2]

Others find that ethics rules themselves can lead to amoral behavior. Professor Richard K. Greenstein states "professionalization in general generates incentives for its members to behave inconsistently with sound moral principles."[3] As professional regulation pushes lawyers to simplify ethical requirements by focusing on protection of client interests to the exclusion of other interests, this pressure encourages moral simplification and creates what Professor Greenstein calls a "no remainder" principle[4] in which a lawyer fully satisfies professional obligations by advocating for client goals regardless of personal values, the interests of others, or society as a whole. In other words, having prioritized client interests, the lawyer may assume all ethical obligations are met. There is no moral remainder. As Greenfield notes, however, ethical decision-making is complex, and there will often be conflicts between client interests and the interests of others—a moral remainder. This disconnect between ethical obligations and personal values, in turn, may lead to lawyer dissatisfaction with the profession.

Professionalism is not defined in the Rules of Professional Conduct. The ABA established a Standing Commission on Professionalism in 1984 that attempted to define the profession, and its 1986 report, "*. . . In the Spirit of Public Service:" A Blueprint for the Rekindling of Lawyer Professionalism*, came up with the following:

The term refers to a group . . . pursuing a learned art as a common calling in the spirit of public service—no less a public service because it may incidentally be a means of livelihood. Pursuit of the learned art in the spirit of public service is the primary purpose. http://www.abanet.org/cpr/professionalism/Stanley_Commission_Report.pdf.

Twenty years later, in response to increased public mistrust of lawyers and changes in the profession brought about by technology affecting the way lawyers communicate, the ABA Standing Committee on Professionalism revisited the question of what professionalism means. In *Reviving a Tradition of Service: Redefining Lawyer Professionalism in the 21st Century*, the Committee refocused the definition on concepts of support of the legal system, access to justice, and the value of service to clients and society using the acronym "**SERVE**:"

S—Support the Legal System.

E—Exemplify professionalism through enhanced teaching, technology and training.

R—Reaffirm access to the Legal System, promoting justice through a dispute resolution system that is available to all.

V—Value our place in society, integrating our core values of professionalism in each representation to provide our clients with real value while ensuring that we and our associates maintain professional values and act with integrity.

E—Embrace professional Excellence while establishing balance and Equilibrium in lawyers' lives.[5]

Other bar associations, centers, or committees have proposed guidelines for professional conduct and have similarly attempted to identify core concepts of professionalism. Still, there is no single official definition.

Exercise 9.1 Defining Professionalism: Spend one to two minutes thinking of a lawyer, real or fictional, who embodies your ideal of "professionalism." List the characteristics of that lawyer. Take another one to two minutes to identify why those characteristics are important. What values do they reflect?

Defining Professionalism as Civility

> *[G]ood manners, disciplined behavior and civility—*
> *by whatever name—are the lubricants that prevent*
> *lawsuits from turning into combat. More than*
> *that [civility] is really the very glue that keeps an*
> *organized society from flying apart.*
>
> —Chief Justice Warren E. Burger

Professionalism is linked to civility and the terms are sometimes used interchangeably. You may find that conversations you have with supervising attorneys about professionalism focus on civility, good manners, collegiality, politeness, and a sense of decorum in behavior toward lawyers, courts, clients, and other participants in the legal system.

■ *Codes of Civility*

States, bar associations, trial lawyers, and other lawyer organizations have responded to the perceived lack of civility, especially in litigation, by enacting Codes of Civility or Tenets of Professionalism, or by requiring new attorneys to sign Pledges of Courtesy or Professionalism as a requirement of admission to practice. Most states' civility codes provide guidelines. The Preamble to New York's Standards of Civility, for example, says they are "intended to encourage lawyers, judges and court personnel to observe principles of civility and decorum, and to confirm the legal profession's rightful status as an honorable and respected profession where courtesy and civility are observed as a matter of course." A number of states, however, including Florida, South Carolina, Arizona, Michigan, and part of Texas have enacted mandatory civility codes or pledges under which lawyers may be sanctioned.

A study of civility codes and pledges across jurisdictions by Donald E. Campbell identified ten common obligations that are quoted below:

1. recognize the importance of keeping commitments and of seeking agreement and accommodation with regard to scheduling and extensions,

2. be respectful and act in a courteous, cordial, and civil manner,

3. be prompt, punctual, and prepared,

4. maintain honesty and personal integrity,

5. communicate with opposing counsel,

6. avoid actions taken merely to delay or harass,

7. ensure proper conduct before the court,

8. act with dignity and cooperation in pre-trial proceedings,

9. act as a role model to the client and public and as a mentor to young lawyers, and

10. utilize the court system in an efficient and fair manner.[6]

These obligations of professionalism might seem obvious. Why would a lawyer act otherwise? Yet in charged situations one can easily become swept away by the circumstances. This loss of civility can occur in hotly contested transactional or litigation settings. The ethics of client loyalty and the demands of the competitive marketplace to win at all costs may further encourage some to engage in "scorched earth" tactics in order to succeed. Whatever the reasons, we are inundated with visions of lawyers who cross the line from client loyalty and advocacy to uncivil or unprofessional behavior.

The consequences of a lack of civility can be quite real. Judges have attributed increased litigation costs to lawyers' unreasonable or abusive discovery demands or responses, frivolous motion practice, and refusal to consider reasonable adjournments or settlement proposals. Uncooperative or obstructionist lawyer behavior that requires judicial intervention wastes court time and creates system-wide delays. These behaviors ultimately diminish the professional image of lawyers. Lack of civility also can diminish the pleasure of practicing law.[7]

Courts increasingly are willing to sanction lawyers for uncivil behavior, particularly but not exclusively if there are ethical violations. The Eleventh Circuit, for example, upheld a denial of prevailing party attorneys' fees due to the failure of the lawyer to contact the defendant law firm as a common courtesy prior to filing suit. As the court stated:

> As the district court saw it, this conscious disregard for lawyer-to-lawyer collegiality and civility caused (among other things) the judiciary to waste significant time and resources on unnecessary litigation and stood in stark contrast to the behavior expected of an officer of the court. The district court refused to reward—and thereby to encourage—uncivil conduct by awarding Plaintiff attorney's fees or costs. Given the district court's power of oversight for the bar, we cannot say that this decision was outside of the bounds of the district court's discretion.[8]

The Fifth Circuit allowed sanctions to stand against a lawyer for "obnoxious and abusive behavior" against an opposing lawyer.[9] Among other uncivil behaviors, the lawyer in the case referred to an opposing attorney as a "stooge," "puppet," and "weak pussyfooting 'deadhead,'" who "had been 'dead' mentally for ten years," and an "underling who graduated from a 29th-tier law school." The court concluded:

> His attitude and remarks toward opposing attorneys, opposing parties, and the bankruptcy court were—to understate his conduct—obnoxious. Although incivility in and of itself is call for concern, what is most disconcerting here is the rationale [the lawyer] gives for his behavior. [He] asserts that his deplorable and wholly unprofessional conduct helps him recover more money for his clients. Unremorsefully and brazenly, [he] contends that his egregious behavior serves him well in settlement negotiations and is therefore appropriate.[10]

In such disciplinary situations, lawyers typically defend their behavior as zealous advocacy and argue sanctions designed to conform their behavior interferes with the client's rights as well as the lawyer's own free speech rights.

▪ *Should Civility Standards Be Mandatory? Are Civility Rules Necessary?*

Critics of the civility movement argue codes and pledges are unnecessary because behavior is already controlled sufficiently through the disciplinary process, and courts and bar associations already have authority to control bad attorney conduct through sanctions, fines, and discipline. Further, critics point to the inherent conflict between civility rules that ask lawyers to cooperate with opponents and courts for the good of the system, and the Rules of Professional Conduct that demand diligent client-centered advocacy within the bounds of the law without reference to broader public good. As the ABA observed:

> Admittedly, the effectiveness of these codes and pledges remains a subject of debate. Many of the codes are nonbinding, and thus may be of limited effectiveness. More importantly, values such as civility and professionalism are often viewed as antithetical to lawyers' obligation to represent their clients zealously. Resolving this fundamental conflict between professionalism and zealous advocacy—or, more precisely, convincing lawyers that there is no such conflict—remains an important but elusive goal.[11]

Consider the balance between client expectations and the role of lawyer as advocate with rules governing lawyer behavior as you address the following problems:

Exercise 9.2 Tom is an extern with Legal Aid who is assisting a tenant in a dispute with his landlord. Tom's client was served with an eviction notice after withholding rent for the last three months due to the landlord's refusal to repair or replace essential appliances. After making an initial appearance in court, Tom received the following email from the landlord's lawyer: "I am tired of baby lawyers coming into court and trying to get free rent for their freeloading clients. How much can he pay?"

What does this email make you think of the lawyer who sent the email? Would you advise Tom to ignore the statements and focus only on answering the question? If Tom does not ignore the statements, what should he say? If this email were sent to a lawyer rather than an extern, would you expect the lawyer to respond differently?

Exercise 9.3 Katherine is an extern in judicial chambers in a state trial level court. Her supervising law clerk assigned her to review a pre-hearing brief in a contentious divorce and child custody case involving allegations of sexual abuse of a child with developmental disabilities. Aside from the fact that the brief is lengthy and poorly written, Katherine is appalled and offended the lawyer representing the father in this case refers to the child in such disparaging terms. The lawyer states that the child's disabilities make the child "more akin to broccoli," and she belittles the child's complaints of sexual molestation by characterizing them as "versions of her story, worthy of the Goosebumps series for children, with which to titillate her audience." Katherine thinks the lawyer who wrote the brief should be sanctioned. Her supervising clerk, however, downplays the problem, excusing it as hyperbole. He instructs Katherine to stick to the legal issues.

What are the possible consequences of the lawyer's behavior in this case? Did the lawyer violate any rules of professional conduct? What can Katherine do? What should the judge do?[12]

Defining Professionalism as Compliance with Ethical Rules

Professionalism means more than compliance with Rules of Professional Conduct. Most lawyers would agree compliance with the applicable ethics rules is a part of professionalism. The Rules of Professional Conduct themselves, however, present some competing considerations between loyalty to clients and duties to others in the system. Judgment is required in balancing client interests and zeal of advocacy with fairness to opposing parties and others. Acceptable conduct is often determined by reasonable efforts and reasonable beliefs consistent with client interests under the circumstances.

Loyalty to clients is central to the U.S. regulatory scheme. For example, Model Rule 1.2 on Scope of Representation and Allocation of Authority Between Client and Lawyer provides that the client has the ultimate authority to determine the purposes the legal representation within the limits of the law.[13] Rule 1.3 on Diligence further requires a lawyer to act with "reasonable diligence" in representing clients. This guidance means the lawyer needs to pursue a client's interests "despite opposition, obstruction or personal inconvenience," and the lawyer is supposed to act with "zeal in advocacy."[14]

The Model Rules also place some limits on lawyers as advocates. See Chapter 13 on Ethical Issues in Externships: Duties to Third Parties and Tribunals. Rule 3.1 on Meritorious Claims and Contentions, for example, prohibits lawyers from bringing or defending frivolous claims. The lawyer has a duty to use legal procedure for the fullest benefit of the client's cause, but "also a duty not to abuse legal procedure."[15] Rule 3.2 on Expediting Litigation requires a lawyer to make "reasonable efforts" to expedite litigation consistent with the interests of the client."[16] Rule 3.4 on Fairness to Opposing Party and Counsel requires, among other things, that lawyers use "reasonably diligent efforts" to comply with proper discovery requests, but not "allude to any matter that the lawyer does not reasonably believe is relevant. . . ."[17] Rule 3.5 on Impartiality and Decorum of The Tribunal prohibits the lawyer from engaging in conduct intended to disrupt a tribunal.[18] Rule 4.4 on Respect for Rights of Third Persons prohibits a lawyer from using means in representing a client that have "no substantial purpose other than to embarrass, delay or burden a third person. . . ."[19] Finally, Rule 8.4 on Misconduct states that a lawyer shall not, among other conduct, "engage in conduct that is prejudicial to the administration of justice." A lawyer who "manifests . . . bias or prejudice . . . violates [this rule] when such actions are prejudicial to the administration of justice. **Legitimate advocacy** respecting the foregoing factors does not violate [the rule] (emphasis added).[20]

Discretion and judgment are required in order to manage competing responsibilities to clients and to the system. The line where legitimate advocacy ends and unprofessional behavior begins, however, is not always clear. This is especially so in non-litigation contexts outside of the courts' view. Where you draw the line should be guided at least in part by your sense of professionalism. You must be familiar with the ethics rules and have an understanding of the legal system and how it is meant to function. You need to understand your role is as lawyer, advocate, officer of the court, and public servant in the system in order to make judgments between competing interests. It is your sense of professionalism and your internalized understanding of what it means to be professional that can help you navigate the bounds of advocacy.

In the cases cited earlier in this chapter, the lawyers who were sanctioned for unprofessional conduct asserted they were acting ethically in accordance with their clients' wishes and interests. The courts, however, found their behavior was extreme and unjustified. Unprofessional behavior will not always be so obvious. In the following exercise, consider the bounds of advocacy and how client wishes, expectations, and interests affect lawyer conduct. Are there situations in which ethics rules related to client loyalty and client-centered representation conflict with other rules regarding lawyer conduct or with your views of professionalism? Are aggressive or offensive tactics justified when in the service of a client or when directed by a client?

Exercise 9.4 Daniel is an extern with a not-for-profit organization who has been assisting the parents of a six-year-old boy with disabilities in a long-standing dispute with their school district over their son's educational program. The parents had requested a formal hearing to challenge the district's proposed educational placement, but agreed to meet with the school Committee on Special Education (CSE) to see if the differences could be resolved. The CSE is an interdisciplinary committee charged with recommending and implementing programs and services for pupils with disabilities. The parents are members of their child's CSE and must be invited to participate in all meetings. The clients ask Daniel and his supervisor to join them at the meeting, telling Daniel this is not the first time they have disagreed with CSE recommendations for their son and the school views them as trouble-makers. Because the parents are bringing a lawyer, the school district asks their lawyer to be there as well. Unbeknownst to Daniel or his clients, the school district instructed its lawyer to be adversarial in the meeting, to "teach those parents a lesson" and to give them a taste of what to expect if they go forward with a hearing.

It is a short meeting. After introductions, Daniel presents a written proposal for a modified educational program on his clients' behalf. The school district's lawyer belittles the parents' concerns calling them frivolous and makes a show of ripping up the proposal. With that, the CSE chair closes the meeting and declares the hearing will go forward. Daniel and his supervisor are dumbfounded. The clients are visibly upset.

After the meeting, however, the school district's lawyer pulls Daniel aside and assures him he intends to recommend that the district implement at least some of the parents' suggestions and he thinks they can still negotiate. The adversarial approach was just for the district's benefit. "They asked me to give you and the parents a hard time. That's what my client expects. That's what I get paid to do."

What do you think of the school district's lawyer? Was his behavior at the meeting unprofessional or unethical? How might you account for the lawyer acting one way in front of clients and another with lawyers? Did the lawyer have other options? How might Daniel have responded during the meeting? After the meeting? How would you advise Daniel to address the situation with his clients?

Professionalism and Lawyer Reputation

If you once forfeit the confidence of your fellow citizens, you can never regain their respect and esteem.

—Abraham Lincoln

As lawyers in the digital age, our actions are potentially accessible and observable around the clock, and what we do can reflect on our clients, colleagues, and communities. In other words, a lawyer's professional reputation may be affected by all of the lawyer's actions, not just his legal work. As you assume the role of a lawyer in an externship, you will be expected to act professionally with regard to dress, demeanor, diligence, cell phone use, email etiquette, timeliness, confidentiality, and other matters at your placement. Your behavior outside of the workplace, on social media and in the public, also may be judged by others, and may impact your reputation and future job prospects in addition to your relationships with clients and co-workers. Your behavior, positive and negative, reflects on your field placement and your law school.

Exercise 9.5 Jane is an extern with the Office of the County Attorney. It is a collegial work environment in which the attorneys and support staff work hard and also socialize together outside of the office. Jane was delighted to be invited to attend a birthday party celebration for one of the assistant county attorneys at a local restaurant bar. After a number of free drinks, Jane felt tipsy. A friend who happened to be in the bar that evening told Jane she saw her stumble to the ladies room a few times and she could hear her laughing from across the room. Although Jane did not feel great the next day, she dragged herself to her placement as scheduled. She was embarrassed to overhear the County Attorney who had attended the party comment in a staff meeting that "our intern had a bit too much fun last night and she sure looks out of it today."

Jane is embarrassed and fears she has jeopardized any chance of ever getting a job with this office or a recommendation for employment elsewhere. Is there anything she can do to ameliorate this situation? Would you advise her to speak with her supervising attorney or externship teacher? Do the attorneys at Jane's placement share any responsibility in this situation?

Even excellent lawyers sometimes behave poorly. Lawyers with particularly stressful and time-pressured responsibilities such as district attorneys or public defenders may engage in a bit of "gallows humor" to blow off steam. You may be warned you need a thick skin to survive and thrive. Like any other workplace group, lawyers also may gossip about other lawyers or professional colleagues. If you hope to network and develop professional relationships within your office, do you join in or listen? As an extern, how do you respond when you observe lawyers in your office, including your supervisors, acting disrespectfully toward colleagues, opposing counsel, or judges?

Consider the following problems:

Exercise 9.6 Matthew is an extern with a county prosecutor's officer and has a student practice order. His supervising ADA has just assigned him to handle a trial in a misdemeanor robbery case against a defendant accused of stealing a pair of sneakers from a sporting goods store. The ADA tells Matthew, "The case is a slam dunk because the lawyer on the other side is an idiot. He is just this solo practitioner trying to take on all these cases to make money, but he doesn't know how to do anything. I cannot waste my time and energy dealing with this loser." Matthew plays along adding that he has heard that attorney is "the worst" and he is "happy to handle the cases where defendants are represented by incompetent counsel." Matthew is thrilled to be given the responsibility to handle a trial, and he wants his supervisor to like him and to continue to give him interesting assignments and a good reference at the end of the semester. On reflection, however, Matthew feels badly about participating in a negative conversation about a lawyer he does not even know.

What could or should Matthew have done differently in this situation?

Exercise 9.7 Megan is an extern with the public defender and is representing a young mother in a child neglect petition in family court under a student practice order. Family court tends to be informal, and Megan's supervisor has warned her the lawyer representing the largely absent father is known to be a loose cannon. Nevertheless, Megan is taken aback when the lawyer yells at her in court: "The only reason you are even representing this woman must be because you grew up in a disgusting home with drug-addicted, trash parents so you don't have the capacity to see this parent is unfit to care for the children and is neglecting them." Megan's supervising attorney is with her in court, but remains silent.

What can Megan do in this situation? Should she respond? Should she ask the judge to hold the lawyer in contempt or just let the judge handle it? What about the client? Should Megan reach out to the other lawyer? If Megan were already an attorney, would her response options or her responsibilities be different?

As an extern, you may witness or even be the target of unprofessional lawyer behavior. The more prepared you are to recognize, understand, and respond to inappropriate behavior, the better your externship experience will be. Anticipate how you might respond to office gossip about other lawyers or judges and consider how your response might reflect on your own reputation. Do you ignore the gossip or join in and try to steer the conversation in a more positive direction? What if a friend or fellow extern is the subject of negative comments at your placement? At what point should you alert your externship teacher to issues of professionalism you witness in your externship?

Exercise 9.8 Consider the following interaction referred to earlier in this chapter between a judge and public defender in a Florida courtroom. As this scene unfolds, a judge in criminal court is calling cases and setting matters for trial. The defendant whose case has just been called is represented by a lawyer from the public defender's office. The lawyer has refused to waive his client's right to a speedy trial. This means the judge will have to set the case for trial, filling the court's already busy calendar— something the judge was hoping to avoid. The transcript does not convey the tone or inflection of the lawyer's or judge's statements below. For purposes of this exercise, assume the lawyer speaks in a sarcastic manner and the judge responds in kind:

Judge:	You're Mr. Runkles?
Defendant:	Yes sir.
Judge:	Two charges assault and resisting. You have the public defender. Public defender, what do you want to do?
Lawyer:	Have they filed?

Judge:	They have.
Lawyer:	[in a sarcastic tone of voice] I'm not waiving.
Judge:	Alright. What do you want to do?
Lawyer:	[shrugs] What do you want to do? I'm not waiving. You want to set it for trial? Set it for trial.
Judge:	Alright.
Lawyer:	[interrupting] You want to send it for docket sentence? Send it for docket sentence. I'm not waiving in any case. This is an emergency created by the state . . .
Judge:	If I had a rock, I would throw it at you right now.
Lawyer:	You know . . . [gets cut off]
Judge:	Stop pissin' me off. Just sit down. I'll take care of it. I don't need your help. Sit down.
Lawyer:	As a public defender, I have a right to be here and I have a right to stand here and represent . . . .
Judge:	I said, sit down. If you want to fight, let's go out back and I'll beat your ass.
Lawyer:	Let's go right now.
[Judge and lawyer leave the courtroom; shouting and fighting are heard.]	
Judge:	You want to [expletive] with me?
[More shouting]	

Assume you are observing court that day. What are your thoughts about this situation? Who do you think is at fault? How would you describe the lawyer's behavior? If you think he was unprofessional, should his behavior be excused because he is advocating for his client and asserting his client's legitimate constitutional right to a speedy trial?

What about the judge? How would you characterize his behavior? How might you account for the behavior? Is there anything that could have been done to avoid or minimize this situation?

Consider, too, that there may be underlying causes for some unprofessional behavior. In some instances, the behavior in question may be caused wholly or partly by bias—whether implicit or explicit. See Chapter 7 on Bias in the Legal Profession. In other cases, certain kinds of behavior may be caused in some respects by illness or addiction. Are there health issues causing emotional distress that interfere with a lawyer's ability to act professionally? It may be worth considering whether the bad actor is battling a problem, be it anger management like the judge in this exercise or other health problems. See Chapter 25 on Work and Well-being.

Unprofessional behavior may have several different causes, and you may find it difficult to discern what they are and how much each contributes to the conduct. A hurtful remark may be the result of bias, or of "gallows humor," or other reasons. Observe and reflect before jumping to conclusions. There may be times when you need to take a moment to collect your thoughts. Give yourself the opportunity to stop, think, and evaluate the situation before your respond. See Chapter 5 on Effective Communication and Professional Relationships and Chapter 8 on Reflection and Writing Journals. Greater understanding may assist you in processing, if not excusing, objectionable conduct. If you conclude, for example, an offensive remark is an expression of bias, you may want to file a formal complaint or take other informal action with your law school or placement. See Chapter 7 on Bias in the Legal Profession. If, upon reflection, you believe there is a health issue, you may choose a different response. You may find it easier to empathize and dismiss an isolated rude remark. If you experience recurrent comments from the same lawyer that seem out of order or make you uncomfortable, however, it is important to consult your externship teacher.

By developing strategies for addressing some problem behaviors, you may be able to navigate around some touchy situations and avoid knee-jerk reactions that could affect your office relationships or professional reputation. Again, it is often useful to consult your supervising attorney or externship teacher to come up with strategies to address challenging situations.

The goal of this chapter so far has been the identification and development of tools and strategies to respond to questionable behavior of others. There are also steps you yourself can take to practice professional best practices. A few guidelines and additional exercises are provided.

Tips for Practicing Professionalism

For every instance of a lawyer acting badly, there are thousands more examples of lawyers acting professionally, and often selflessly, in practice. While instances of good behavior do not tend to go viral, you will find stories, articles, and living examples of professional behavior worth emulating. The New York Law Journal, for example, devoted a 2014 issue to "lawyers who lead by example" in lifetime achievement, public service and pro bono: http://nylawyer.nylj.com/adgifs/specials/101414LifetimeAchievers/2014_1014ssLifetimeAchievers.html?et=editorial&bu=New%20York%20Law%20Journal&cn=20141014&src=EMC-Email&pt=Special%20Report. And see, http://www.

bestcollegesonline.com/blog/2012/03/20/12-true-legal-heroes-law-students-should-look-to/, which invites students to learn about "some inspirational legal heroes that will remind you why you wanted to go to law school in the first place."

Judges, bar associations, lawyers, and law students have much to say about professionalism. Here are a few basic tips for ensuring you meet the expectations of the profession. Consider the characteristics of lawyers you admire, and add to the list of professional practice tips below:

- *Observe and Emulate the Best*

Review Exercise 9.1 and make note of what good lawyers do. You will likely find the lawyers with the best reputations treat all people with respect—clients, opponents, office personnel, staff, judges, and courts.

- *Be Prompt—Use a Calendar*

As one judge observed, "[An] aspect of incivility common in litigation today is simple tardiness . . . lack of attention to promptness is rude. It manifests a lack of respect for the court and a lack of consideration for the needs of other counsel, jurors and litigants."[21] Promptness is required for court and for all meetings and obligations. You may find yourself juggling a number of responsibilities at your externship placement and at law school. Use a calendar to help you manage your time so you are always prompt and prepared.

- *Communicate*

Treat your commitment to your externship like a job. As long as you communicate in advance and are otherwise able to meet your placement responsibilities, most offices will understand if you are occasionally and unavoidably unable to be at your placement at regularly scheduled times due to job interviews, illness, or other important law school or personal matters.

- *Turn off Cell Phones*

Ask your supervisor about office policies regarding the use of smart phones and personal computers generally. Even if there is no policy, cell phones and other electronic devices can be a distraction in the workplace, and it is best not to have them on. Discuss exceptions with your supervisor (e.g., you are expecting an emergency call from your physician.) If you need to accept a personal call, make a call, or send a personal text or email, step outside to take care of it.

Exercise 9.9 Laura is an extern with the District Attorney's Office who works in city police court. It is a high volume court offering opportunities to observe and assist with hearings and misdemeanor trials. This is where most of the new Assistant DAs start their careers as prosecutors. Laura reported the following in her externship seminar class: "All of the Assistant DAs constantly use their smart phones in court. It is not always work related. I saw one lawyer checking email and Facebook in between witnesses in trial. Yet my supervisor criticized me for checking my messages when I was only observing in court the other day. Is there a double standard?"

What do you think? Does the fact other lawyers do it make it acceptable for the extern? How might judges, witnesses, defendants, or others in courtroom view this behavior?

■ *When in Doubt, Go Formal*

Email—Treat email like a letter. Use proper salutations, and closings. Avoid using abbreviations and other shorthand you may find in an informal text message. Keep the audience in mind.[22]

Exercise 9.10 Joe, an extern with the United States Attorneys' Office has developed a friendly working relationship with his supervising attorney, Assistant United States Attorney Michael Smith. Joe is about to forward a memorandum to his supervisor. His cover email reads:

> Hey Mike,
> Here's the memo.
> Hope to review it with you l8tr.
> Joe

How might you redraft the cover email?

■ *Appearance—Dress (and Act) the Part*

Be prepared in your appearance so you are able to attend court, meet lawyers in formal settings, or participate in activities or events requiring business attire even on "casual Friday." When in doubt about appropriate dress for your workplace, choose conservative over trendy and err on the side of formality.

> **First Impressions Matter**
>
> *If you think that no one is watching, you are truly mistaken. Everyone in the office is examining the new person, especially the legal intern . . . . It was my goal to relay the message that [my law school] is training individuals to be professionals in their appearance and work product. Therefore, every time I was in the office, I looked my best and followed through with every assignment as if I were being evaluated at the end of the day. Half way through the semester, my supervising attorney . . . shared with me how [the] attorneys were impressed with my professionalism and attention to detail in assisting them with research. On the days when I thought no one was watching or playing close attention, they were, and it started on the very first day.*
>
> —Externship Student

■ *Manner of Communication*

Again, err on the side of formality: Judge Smith, Professor Jones, or Mr./Ms. Brown.

It is unlikely that people with whom you work will be offended by use of a title in addressing them. But some may be put off by instant informality and especially by uninvited informality. When in doubt, ask your supervisor directly—judge, counsel, or others in the field how he or she would like to be addressed. Alternatively, ask a colleague in the office about such protocol so that you use the preferred form of address.

■ *Step Back*

Make a habit of reflective practice and reflective communication by allowing yourself to step back from heated situations. Take a breath or take a break in order to consider you response, if any, to challenging situations.

Defining Professionalism as Conduct Consistent with the Common Good

Professionalism also can mean practice consistent with your personal values and with ideals of the common good. In this sense, professionalism means being a "good lawyer," meaning both working skillfully and effectively, and advancing a set of moral beliefs, such as justice, fairness, and compassion.

Your externship experience can help you figure out your identity and values—the professional characteristics you will strive to embody. Chapter 24 on Professional Identity and Formation discusses the importance of developing professional habits that integrate personal and professional values, and the challenges of taking moral action.[23] Chapter 25 on Work and Well-being discusses studies that show greater levels of career satisfaction among lawyers who practice consistent with their own values and beliefs. See also Chapters 10–13 on ethical issues encountered in externships. This section discusses the public dimensions of the lawyer's role, identifies several widely shared values that can motivate a legal career, and assesses some of the capacities necessary for this kind of professionalism.

In figuring out who you want to be as a lawyer, keep in mind that being a lawyer necessarily has a public dimension. You work under a license granted by the public, subject to public regulation. You work with tools that are themselves public: rules of law and legal procedure created for public use. Society grants lawyers authority to self-regulate as a profession in exchange for serving clients and the public good. Finally, no matter how private your practice is, your work will virtually always affect people other than yourself and your client. The choices you make about how to handle difficult situations will define how you relate to others and will also define how your work affects the world around you.

As a lawyer, you are expected to promote access to justice and maintain the integrity of the legal system as well as represent clients with competence and diligence. What will you do if your personal and professional interests conflict? What if a client or employer instructs you to take certain action that, although within the bounds of law, conflicts with what you think is right or fair to others? Suppose you are asked in your state agency externship to draft a policy to enforce an initiative with which you disagree: for instance, automatic employee dismissal for marijuana use which you think should be legal; or limiting sales of weapons at private gun shows which you think interferes with constitutional rights? What if your good intentions to engage in public interest or pro bono work interferes with other work demands and your desire for financial comfort and security? These questions have no easy answers, and your own answers may change as you grow as a lawyer and develop the personal insights and maturity to make difficult decisions and take appropriate action in such situations.

Many scholars writing about professionalism and professional formation include in the definition an essential "internalized moral core" centered on responsibility to others—clients and society.[24] Professionalism is characterized by the motivation and moral maturity necessary take action even when it conflicts with self-interest.[25] According to scholars and ethicists, moral maturity, like other essential qualities of professional lawyers, can be taught, fostered by mentors, and learned through practice, self-evaluation, and reflection. It is part of the pursuit of excellence. As an extern, you are beginning the developmental process of becoming a professional.

The final exercise in this chapter is intended to help you think about the professional lawyer you want to become. As you engage in this exercise, consider the following: What do you need to know to be prepared to act ethically and feel good about yourself and your life as a lawyer? How do you address the tension between what may be the best outcome for a client and your own sense of fairness or public good? How do you know what is the right thing to do in a given situation? Is behaving well or civilly the same as doing the right thing? Is it the same as being professional? What resources are available in your externship to try to answer these questions, and how can you use your externship to begin to form your vision of yourself as a professional?

> **Exercise 9.11** Final Journal Assignment: Imagine you are being honored after 20 years of legal practice and a colleague has been asked to talk about you for five minutes. How would you like to be acknowledged with regard to (1) your professional accomplishments, (2) your personal accomplishments, and (3) your character?

Conclusion

I think it is important for each person to think about who they want to be in this profession. When I think about that and develop words to describe it, they are all attributes of professionalism—civility and being ethical.

>   —Externship student

Becoming a lawyer is more than a job choice—becoming a lawyer will be an important part of who you are. Your externship offers an opportunity to consider further your vision of the professional you want to be—to reflect on what you value, the characteristics of people you admire, and those you do not. Exercises in this chapter, like many situations that arise in lawyering, do not have simple answers. Thinking ahead about how you will deal with troubling conduct you encounter or observe, moral ambiguity, ethical conflicts, and confronting injustice, will help you to cultivate habits of professionalism for your future career.

FURTHER RESOURCES

A.B.A. Center For Professional Responsibility, http://www.americanbar.org/groups/professional_responsibility.html.

Paul A. Haskins, Ed., *Essential Qualities Of The Professional Lawyer*, A.B.A. Standing Committee on Professionalism, Center for Professional Responsibility (2013).

David B. Casselman, *Civility Matters: Why Civility and Why Now?*, American Board of Trial Advocates, 2011, www.abota.org.

Neil W. Hamilton & Verna Monson, *The Positive Empirical Relationship of Professionalism to Effectiveness in the Practice of Law*, 24 Geo. J. Legal Ethics 137 (2011).

Muriel J. Bebeau, *Promoting Ethical Development and Professionalism: Insight from Educational Research in the Professions*, 5 U. St. Thomas L. J. 366 (2008).

The Center for the Study of Ethical Development, University of Alabama, http://ethicaldevelopment.ua.edu/.

Social Media Ethics Guidelines, Commercial And Federal Litigation Section, N.Y. St. B. A. (2015), https://www.nysba.org/Sections/Commercial_Federal_Litigation/Com_Fed_PDFs/Social_Media_Ethics_Guidelines.html.

ENDNOTES

1   David A. Grenardo, *Making Civility Mandatory: Moving from Aspired to Required*, 11 Cardozo Pub. L. Pol'y & Ethics J. 239 (citing Att'y Griev. Comm'n of Md. v. Sheinbein, 812 A2d 981,998 (Md. 2002).

2   Amy R. Mashburn, *Professionalism as Class Ideology: Civility Codes and Bar Hierarchy*, 28 Val. U.L. Rev. 657 (1994).

3   Richard K Greenstein, *Against Professionalism*, 22 Geo. J. Legal Ethics 327, 328 (2009).

4   *Id.* at 329.

5   Ronald C. Minkoff, *Reviving a Tradition of Service: Redefining Lawyer Professionalism in the 21st Century*, A.B.A. Standing Committee on Professionalism, (2009), http://www.americanbar.org/content/dam/aba/migrated/cpr/professionalism/century.authcheckdam.pdf.

6   Campbell proposes that civility is distinct from legal ethics and suggests that the professionalism lawyers owe to one another, clients, and courts should be treated as a "unique obligation of professional responsibility." Donald E.

Campbell, *Raise Your Right Hand and Swear to Be Civil: Defining Civility as an Obligation of Professional Responsibility*, 47 GONZ. L. REV. 99, 109 (2011 / 2012).

7   Carolyn E. Demarest, *Civility in the Courtroom from a Judge's Perspective*, 69 NYS BAR J. 24 (1997).

8   Sahyers v. Prugh Holliday & Karatiner, 560 F3d 1241, 1245–6 (11th Cir. 2009).

9   *In re* First City Bancorporation of Texas, 282 F.3d 864 (5th Cir. 2002).

10   *Id.* at 865.

11   Minkoff, *supra* note 4.

12   The case facts in this problem are based on the following: *In re* S.C., 138 Cal. App. 4th 396, 41 Cal. Rptr. 3d 453 (2006).

13   MODEL RULES OF PROF'L. CONDUCT r. 1.2 (1983) Unless otherwise noted, reference will be made to the Delaware Rules of Professional Conduct rather than the ABA Model Rules of Professional Conduct, which are copyrighted.

14   *Id.* at r. 1.3 cmt 1

15   *Id.* at r. 3.1 cmt 1.

16   *Id.* at r. 3.2.

17   *Id.* at r. 3.4.

18   *Id.* at r. 3.5.

19   *Id.* at r. 4.4.

20   *Id.* at r. 8.4 cmt. 3.

21   Carolyn E. Demarest, *Civility in the Courtroom From a Judge's Perspective*, 69 Jun. NYS BAR J. 24 (May/June 1997).

22   Gerald Lebovits, *The Legal Writer, E-Mail Netiquette for Lawyers*, 81 NYS BAR J. 64 (Nov.-Dec. 2009).

23   Chapter 24 on Professional Identity and Formation discusses the four components of moral action identified by psychologist James Rest. Rest described four distinct but interactive components to moral action: moral sensitivity, moral motivation, moral reasoning, and moral implementation. The development of these four characteristics help us to be able to recognize ethical issues, work through alternative courses of action with an understanding of their conflicts and consequences, make intelligent and thoughtful judgments, and have the motivation to ultimately take moral action. This chapter offers a number of examples of lawyers taking moral action to align personal values with client expectations.

24   Professor Neil Hamilton summarizes his studies of professionalism or professional formation noting that nearly all agree on the following characteristics:

Ongoing solicitation of feedback and self-reflection;

An internalized standard of excellent at lawyering skills;

Integrity and honesty;

Adherence to the ethical codes;

Public service (especially for the disadvantaged); and

Independent professional judgment and honest counsel.

NEIL W. HAMILTON, THE QUALITIES OF THE PROFESSIONAL LAWYER, ESSENTIAL QUALITIES OF THE PROFESSIONAL LAWYER, at 9.

25   Muriel Bebeau, *Promoting Ethical Development and Professionalism: Insight from Educational Research in the Professions*, 5 U. ST. THOMAS L. J. 366 (2008) (discussing the importance of identity development and the development of "other-directed values" for professional success).

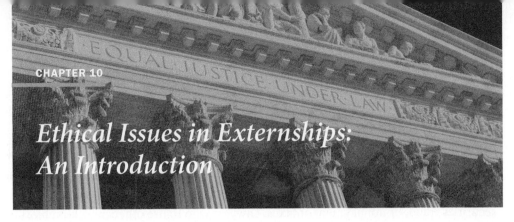

Ethical Issues in Externships: An Introduction

LISA G. LERMAN & LISA V. MARTIN

A Regulated Profession

T
he state supreme courts have a significant role in the governance of the legal profession. The high courts or their delegates decide who should be admitted to practice; also they adopt ethics codes to govern the conduct of lawyers. In most states, these rules are based primarily on the American Bar Association's Model Rules of Professional Conduct.

In most states, admission to the bar requires graduation from an accredited law school, obtaining a passing score on the bar exam, and being found to possess the necessary "character and fitness" to practice law. Upon admission to the bar, each lawyer agrees to comply with the state rules of professional conduct. Violation of these rules can result in a disciplinary proceeding and can lead to disbarment, suspension, reprimand, or some other sanction.

Law students who work as externs need to read the applicable state ethics rules at the beginning of the field experience. Even though law students are not formally subject to discipline unless they are licensed under student practice rules, study of your state's ethics rules is an important part of orientation to professional life. Also, if a law student engages in conduct that violates the ethics code, the supervisor could be subject to discipline, and the student's bar admission might be jeopardized.

> Students licensed under student practice rules may appear in court on behalf of clients. Some states allow admission under the student practice rule only of law students enrolled in clinical courses taught by full-time instructors representing indigent clients. Other states allow some supervised externs to be admitted under the student practice rules. You should make sure to check with your externship teacher about how these rules apply to your experience.

Civil and Criminal Liability for Lawyer Misconduct

Lawyers, like other people, are bound by a whole array of statutory and regulatory laws. Lawyers who commit crimes may be prosecuted under general criminal statutes; a surprising number of lawyers have gone to prison for crimes such as mail fraud, securities fraud, or nonpayment of taxes. Lawyers who injure others may be subject to civil liability. A lawyer who harms a client by conduct that is dishonest, incompetent, or otherwise violates accepted professional standards might have to pay civil damages or endure criminal penalties. A client who suffers harm as a result of the lawyer's conduct might sue his lawyer for legal malpractice, breach of fiduciary duty, or breach of contract. If the client prevails, the lawyer might be ordered to pay money damages. Most lawyers carry malpractice insurance, which offers indemnification for some civil liability.

In addition to the law that governs the general public, lawyers are bound by more specific legal rules. Lawyers who litigate, for example, may be sanctioned for filing frivolous suits, for withholding documents in discovery, or for other violations of the rules adopted by each court. Government lawyers are bound to comply with stringent conflict of interest statutes. Securities and banking lawyers must comply with various statutes and regulations that govern those industries.

Law students working as externs should be aware that the law that governs any given practice area may extend far beyond the rules of professional conduct. While reading the state ethics code is a good place to start, there is much more to learn about the law that governs lawyers. Externships provide opportunities to interact with and learn from experienced lawyers about this body of law. When you encounter a professional dilemma as an extern, it is critically important that you discuss the problem with your supervising attorney and/or with your externship teacher. In addition, the following sources may assist you in understanding the applicable law:

■ *American Bar Association, Model Rules of Professional Conduct*

The Model Rules of Professional Conduct are drafted and approved by the American Bar Association and are revised periodically. After adoption by the ABA, the Model Rules are then reviewed by a state bar committee for each state supreme court, which is free to adopt the recommended proposals or to vary from them. The Model Rules provide a good general reference, but when seeking guidance on particular practice issues, **always** refer to the applicable state ethics code rather than to the Model Rules. The Model Rules are published on the website of the ABA Center for Professional Responsibility at http://www.americanbar.org/groups/professional_responsibility/publications/model_rules_of_professional_conduct/model_rules_of_professional_conduct_table_of_contents.html.

The American Bar Association maintains a copyright on its Model Rules and imposes stringent restrictions on their quotation in works published by anyone other than the ABA. For example, the ABA requires that any rule be quoted in its entirety and accompanied by all of the comments that follow the rule. The ethics codes as adopted by the states, however, are not copyrighted. Like other legal rules, they are in the public domain. The Delaware Rules of Professional Conduct are nearly identical to the Model Rules, so in this book, we quote from the Delaware Rules. If a quoted Delaware rule differs from the corresponding Model Rule, the difference is explained in an endnote.

■ *American Law Institute, Restatement (Third) of the Law Governing Lawyers*

The American Law Institute produced this excellent synthesis of the body of law that governs lawyers. The Restatement includes information about ethics codes, rules of civil liability for legal malpractice and breach of fiduciary duty, bases for court sanctions against lawyers, rules on attorney-client privilege, protection of attorney work product, and other statutory, regulatory, and case law.

■ *ABA/BNA, Lawyers' Manual on Professional Conduct*

This manual provides a comprehensive and up-to-date reference source on the whole range of law regulating lawyers. Its scope is as broad as the Restatement, and its coverage is more detailed.

■ *Advisory Ethics Opinions*

The ABA and the state and local bar association ethics committees write advisory opinions for lawyers who seek guidance on ethical questions. These opinions are published on the Internet, in bar journals, and elsewhere. When you encounter an ethical dilemma, you can seek guidance in the advisory ethics opinions in your jurisdiction. Alternatively, you can call or write the bar ethics committee in your jurisdiction to seek guidance. Some ethics committees provide informal telephone guidance as well as formal or informal written advice on ethics issues.

The Unmet Need for Legal Services

As a member of the legal profession, you will share a responsibility to use your legal training to serve the community. It is estimated that low-income people in the United States are able to secure help from lawyers to address only about one of every five legal problems they experience. The recent recession has increased significantly the number and exigency of legal needs experienced by low-income families and also the number of families who qualify for free legal services. At the same time, reductions in funding have eroded the ability of civil legal services organizations to meet this demand. The distribution of labor across the legal industry adds to this gap. In 2003, Professor David Luban estimated that the ratio of lawyers available to meet the needs of non-poor people was about 1:240, but the ratio of lawyers available to serve the needs of the poor was nearly 1:9,000. Lawyers from all segments of the legal profession can help address the justice gap by providing pro bono services.

Rule 6.1 encourages lawyers to devote at least 50 hours per year to providing pro bono legal services. In 2012, the New York State Bar Association instituted the first pro bono service requirement as a prerequisite to admission. Through various initiatives, the organized bar is attempting address the overwhelming unmet need for legal services among the poor and middle class. Lawyers can satisfy their responsibility to provide pro bono services in a number of ways. Rule 6.1 recommends that "a substantial majority" of such services should be provided to "persons of limited means" or organizations that serve people of limited means, such as homeless shelters, food pantries, churches, and domestic violence programs. Pro bono services may include "individual and class representation, the provision of legal advice, legislative lobbying, administrative rule making and the provision of free training or mentoring to those who represent persons of limited means." Lawyers also may provide services to "individuals, groups or organizations seeking to secure or protect civil rights, civil liberties or public rights, or charitable, religious, civic, community, governmental and educational organizations in matters in furtherance of their organizational purposes" and "participate in activities for improving the law, the legal system or the legal profession." Many bar associations have developed organized programs to support pro bono service by providing hotlines for people who need pro bono counsel, screening the cases and referring them to volunteer lawyers, and by providing training, mentoring, and technical assistance to those lawyers.

Lawyers often find pro bono service to be some of the most rewarding work they undertake. With such a wide range of possibilities, you consider how you will do your part to serve the community as a member of the legal profession. What causes, issues, or problems are you passionate about addressing? What areas of law do you believe are in need of reform? Given your talents and interests, how can you best meet the legal needs of low-income individuals and the organizations that support them?

Exercise 10.1 Investigate pro bono policies and practices at your externship placement. What types of pro bono cases do the lawyers take? Is there a policy in place encouraging pro bono service by attorneys? If the placement is a law firm, do pro bono hours count toward an annual target or minimum? Are there institutional barriers or problems that prevent or complicate the completion of pro bono work? If you are working at an organization that provides civil legal services to the poor, what challenges does your organization face in meeting the demand for legal representation? Does your organization use pro bono services to augment its impact?

Ethical Duties in the Workplace

This section concerns ethical duties related to the supervisory structure of the workplace itself, lawyers' duty to report serious professional misconduct of other lawyers, and restrictions on practice by law students.

Dilemmas that arise in the course of an externship can be awkward and intimidating, especially if they involve decisions or conduct of others in the work-place. The extern often is a relatively inexperienced, temporary worker who hopes to make a good impression, make contacts, get a good recommendation, or even get a job at the placement after graduation. Depending on the nature of the ethical issue, the extern may confront a conflict between these goals and a professional duty or moral obligation to turn down an assignment, question a supervisor's judgment, consult another lawyer (in or out of the office), blow the whistle, or resign. The following scenarios raise some examples of these difficult issues. Although we hope scenarios of this sort will be uncommon, it is worthwhile to consider these problems in hypothetical form because they tend to arise in situations that are emotionally charged and require a timely response with significant risk if an improper decision is made. Being prepared by having thought through the issues in advance will reduce that risk.

Supervisors, Subordinate Lawyers, and Law Students

Lawyers must abide by the state rules of professional conduct in the jurisdictions where they practice. Lawyers also must ensure that law clerks, secretaries, paralegals, and legal externs follow the rules. For example, employees in law firms should be trained to protect client confidences. Rules 5.1 and 5.3 explain that lawyers who have managerial authority should supervise, set policies, provide training, or take other measures to assure that all employees, both lawyers and non-lawyers, comply with the rules. If a subordinate employee (lawyer or non-lawyer) violates a rule, the supervising lawyer may be held responsible by the disciplinary authorities if the supervisor directed the conduct or knew about it and failed to intervene.

The rules require your supervising attorneys to help you to understand the requirements and prohibitions of the ethics rules. For law students with little prior legal experience, this requirement may sound reassuring. As a practical matter, however, you should assume responsibility for your own professional conduct by reviewing the relevant rules and by seeking guidance when you need it. If you are authorized to practice under a student practice rule, you have an independent personal duty of compliance. Even if you are not admitted under a student practice rule, you soon will be admitted to practice and be bound by the rules, so it is advisable to conform your work to the ethics code while you are in law school.

What if your supervisor directs you to do something that you know is improper? Consider an extreme example. Suppose a supervisor directed an extern to forge the signature of the firm's managing partner on a check? The rules would not insulate the extern from the consequences of doing what the extern was told to do. First of all, forgery is a felony. Many people are prosecuted and punished for crimes they committed at the direction of another person. The rules of professional conduct apply in addition to, not in place of, other law. An act of forgery, for example, is a criminal offense and, if committed by a lawyer, would be a serious violation of Rule 8.4's prohibition against misconduct. The student forger could be denied admission to the bar based on past conduct like forging a signature on a check even if she was not criminally charged. The rules obligate your supervisors to guide you, but you must keep your moral compass by your side at all times and take responsibility for your own compliance with the law.

What if your supervisor tells you to do something that seems wrong, but you are not sure? Do you follow the instruction or not? The rules provide guidance on this question. Rule 5.2 emphasizes that each lawyer is responsible for her own conduct, but if the lawyer "acts in accordance with a supervisory lawyer's reasonable resolution of an arguable question of professional duty," then the lawyer is not in violation of the rules and will not be subject to discipline. If you are asked to do something that might be unethical or unlawful, try to do some research and be sure to get professional advice from someone you trust. If there is a reasonable basis for thinking that the conduct is proper, you may defer to the judgment of your supervisor. If not, then you have a true workplace dilemma, which you should be sure to discuss privately with your externship teacher.

■ *Duty to Report Misconduct*

Every lawyer is considered to be "an officer of the court" and has a responsibility to protect our legal system. To some extent, the legal profession is "self-regulated." This means that lawyers are expected to have sufficient professional integrity to police our own profession. A central feature of this system of self-regulation is the duty imposed on lawyers in nearly every state by Rule 8.3(a), which requires that "[a] lawyer who knows that another lawyer has committed a violation of the Rules of Professional Conduct that raises a substantial question as to that lawyer's honesty, trustworthiness or fitness as a lawyer in other respects, shall inform the appropriate professional authority." The rule does not require that a lawyer report every violation of a rule. A lawyer who sees misconduct must report the misconduct only if the other lawyer's behavior is so serious as to raise a substantial question about her honesty, trustworthiness, or fitness. Also, reporting is required only if the lawyer "knows" that such a violation has occurred. Rule 1.0(f) explains that "knowledge" means "actual knowledge" that "may be inferred from circumstances." Rule 8.3(c) explains that in reporting misconduct, a lawyer is not required to disclose client confidences. Does this exception excuse lawyers from reporting misconduct by lawyers in their own firms? Usually not, because much misconduct relating to another lawyer's work on a client matter can be disclosed without revealing client information, even if the reporting lawyer is employed by the same law firm.

Legal externs are not obliged to report unethical conduct to the bar counsel; however, lawyers are under this obligation. This onerous duty is worth some advance consideration. An extern who encounters what may be serious misconduct by a lawyer needs to think through how to respond as if he or she were bound by the rules. This thought process is an excellent way to understand better the duty to report professional misconduct. It is also useful to talk with an experienced professional about the matter. A law firm or government agency may have an ethics counsel or an ethics officer who could be consulted. If the supervising attorney is not the lawyer whose conduct is at issue, an extern might be able to discuss this issue with the supervisor. Often, an extern might prefer to discuss the matter with his or her externship teacher or with a professor who teaches professional responsibility. Before consulting someone outside of the organization, an extern should think through whether the conversation can occur without revealing client confidences. If the conversation might require revelation of client confidences, she needs to start the conversation by asking whether the faculty member is willing/ able to have a confidential lawyer-client conversation with the extern about the issue. If the answer is yes, the extern may speak openly with the professor. Rule 1.6(b)(4) allows lawyers to reveal confidences to seek advice about their ethical obligations, so the rule would likely be read to permit such consultation by law students as well.

■ *Restrictions on Law Practice by Students*

Law students may not engage in the practice of law unless they are granted a limited admission under student practice rules. "Practice of law" is defined by state common law.

While definitions vary, most states define the term to include representation of clients in court cases, administrative proceedings, or in transactions; drafting legal documents such as wills and contracts for clients; giving oral or written legal advice to clients; or any other work that calls for the professional judgment of a lawyer. "Giving legal advice" is commonly understood to involve explanation of how the law might apply to a particular set of facts. A non-lawyer may give information to others about the law—for example, explaining to a victim of domestic abuse how to get a civil protection order—but if a non-lawyer explains to another person how the law might apply to a particular set of facts, this advice might cross the line into unauthorized practice of law.

Most states have specific rules that allow limited licensing of law students to appear in court, usually only if they are in law school clinical courses and if they represent indigent clients. Students who are not licensed under student practice rules may work on client matters under the supervision of lawyers, but they may not sign pleadings or speak in court proceedings. Many administrative agencies, such as the Social Security Administration, allow both lawyers and non-lawyers to appear as advocates, so law students are allowed to handle some administrative hearings without being authorized under the student practice rules.

> **Exercise 10.2** Fitz MacMillan is a second year law student. He hopes to become a prosecutor and eventually to go into politics. This semester, he is an extern with the county attorney's office. About a month into the semester, Fitz's supervisor, Sam Galway, told Fitz that he was impressed with his work and had decided to let him try some misdemeanor cases. Fitz was amazed and flattered. Also, he realized that this experience would be invaluable, and that if he did a good job, it might improve the odds of his being hired after graduation. Even so, he was a little uneasy.
>
> Fitz mentioned to Sam that he was not admitted under the student practice rule, which he thought only allowed court appearances by students supervised by professors. Sam said, "Don't worry about it. I know you'll do a good job. When you stand up in court, just introduce yourself by name. This office is so big that the judges don't know all the lawyers. They'll just assume that you are new."
>
> What should Fitz do?

■ *Practical Guidance on Unauthorized Practice*

If your externship involves work on client matters or giving legal advice, read the rules on unauthorized practice in your state. If you are not admitted under a student practice rule, any legal work that you do, such as interviewing or advising lay people or drafting documents, must be supervised by a lawyer. Apart from the obvious usefulness of having the guidance of a more experienced person, your supervisor's oversight will protect you from crossing the line into unauthorized practice of law.

As a general matter, you should avoid giving even the most casual legal advice to friends and family members until after you are admitted to the bar. Although your friends and family are unlikely to report you for unauthorized practice, you might give advice that is incomplete or incorrect and the person you are advising could suffer harm as a result.

Workplace Dilemmas

■ *Competence and Diligence*

A lawyer who represents a client must provide representation that is both "competent" and "diligent." Competence, under Rule 1.1, "requires the knowledge, skill, thoroughness and preparation reasonably necessary for the representation." This rule requires that a lawyer who takes on a matter in a particular area of law must possess the necessary skills and knowledge before undertaking the matter, or the lawyer must obtain the relevant skills and knowledge through study or through affiliation with a lawyer who has experience in the type of work involved. Rule 1.3 explains that a lawyer also must be diligent in pursuing a matter on behalf of a client. The lawyer must devote the time and attention needed to learn the facts and to research the law and must then pursue the required analysis, drafting, negotiation, and advocacy in a prompt and professional manner. These broad standards are interpreted to require of each lawyer at least the level of competence and diligence that would be exercised by an ordinary member of the profession.

What are the ingredients of competent and diligent representation? The ABA's MacCrate Report identified ten fundamental lawyering skills and four core lawyering values "with which a well-trained generalist should be familiar before assuming ultimate responsibility for a client." The listed skills include problem solving, legal analysis and reasoning, legal research, factual investigation, oral and written communication, counseling, negotiation, litigation and alternative dispute resolution procedures, organization and management of legal work, and recognizing and resolving ethical dilemmas. Consider (if you know enough about your future professional path) which skills are likely to be important to your performance as a lawyer. You can use this process to identify "holes" in your legal education and then look for simulation or clinical courses that will help you to acquire the needed competencies. See Chapter 14 on Learning About Lawyering.

An externship in a practice setting offers a law student the opportunity to observe practicing lawyers and to consider what is required to become a competent and diligent lawyer. Often the best way to understand competence and diligence is to observe law practice by lawyers whose work exemplifies competence and diligence and by lawyers whose work falls below these standards.

> **Exercise 10.3** You may have opportunities to observe court proceedings as part of your externship. If not, take yourself on a field trip. Spend a few hours in your local courthouse. Most court proceedings are open to the public; courtrooms hearing juvenile delinquency, child abuse and neglect proceedings, and other family law-related proceedings typically are closed to the public. Often you can learn from one of the court clerks what is happening in each courtroom and which proceedings may be observed. In general, you simply may walk into a courtroom and sit quietly in one of the seats behind the bar and watch whatever is going on. If you wind up in a courtroom where the proceedings are boring or difficult to understand, usually you can just slip out and try another courtroom. You may find it interesting to observe proceedings involving criminal, landlord-tenant, or small claims cases. In many jurisdictions it also is possible to observe lawyer disciplinary hearings. You can call your local bar counsel's office to ask whether you might sit in on a hearing.
>
> You have two primary tasks. First, observe and evaluate the performance of the lawyers and the judges. Because you will not have read the pleadings, you may not fully understand the substance of the matters being heard. Even so, you can observe how the lawyers and judges do their work. Are they well-organized? Well-prepared? Is their conduct professional? If you were the client of each lawyer you observe, would you feel satisfied with the representation? Allow yourself to observe any and all aspects of the proceeding. You might become interested in the role of a law clerk, the reactions of people in the audience, or the informal interactions that take place in the hallway.
>
> Second, observe the parties and consider what the process was like for them. Approximately what percentage of the parties you observed had legal representation? How did proceedings involving unrepresented parties compare to those in which

lawyers were involved? Did the absence of a lawyer seem to impact the progression or outcome of the proceedings? How did the judge's interactions with unrepresented parties compare to those with lawyers? What did you notice about the race, gender, age, class, and nationality (as you perceived them) of the lawyers, judges, and parties? Did you notice any relationships between the demographic characteristics of the actors and their behavior toward one another?

Note-taking is permitted in some but not all courtrooms. If you are permitted to take notes, record your observations during the proceedings. Otherwise, take a break between observations, and find a place to sit and write down what you have seen and what you think about it. After your court observation is completed, you might want to write a journal entry about the most interesting things you saw and your reactions. Consider the implications of your observations for your own professional development.

Many law students who complete court observations are surprised that some of the lawyers they observe do not exhibit even minimal standards of competence or diligence and are struck that many if not most parties proceeding pro se could benefit from legal representation. By recording your observations about the conduct and circumstances that concern you, you may gain perspective on law practice. For many students, this experience is a great confidence-builder and motivator. As a new lawyer, whatever you may lack in knowledge and experience, you can make up for with careful preparation.

Although most legal externs do not see professional conduct at their placements that falls below minimum standards of competence and diligence, there are some who do. Consider what you would do in the following situation.

Exercise 10.4 Rebecca Bromberg accepted an externship with Mishkin & Cowle, a small firm that represents clients in estate, probate, and real estate matters. Rebecca was to spend Tuesdays and Thursdays at the office, mainly working with Samantha Cowle.

When Rebecca came in to the office, Samantha often was not there but left assignments for Rebecca on her desk chair. The assignments tended to be cryptic, things like "Read the Gonzales file and write a complaint," or "Write a summary judgment motion for the Unger case." Rebecca tried to do as she was asked, but most of the time she felt like she had no idea what she was doing. She had no prior experience drafting actual legal documents.

When Samantha came to the office, she tended to show up around eleven in the morning, rush around for a couple of hours trying to catch up, and then leave for lunch. Rebecca initially thought that Samantha was just terribly busy. She was frustrated because she could not get time to talk with Samantha about her assignments, and she got no feedback at all on the work that she turned in. Rebecca wondered if her own work was so bad that Samantha could not afford to take time to help her to do better.

After a few weeks, Rebecca began to realize that something was really wrong. She often heard Samantha's secretary, Ernie Kemp, on the phone with Samantha's clients, saying things like "No, I'm sorry, Mrs. _____, Ms. Cowle is not in today. . . . Yes, I gave her your messages. . . . Yes, I will be sure to let her know that you called again." One day when Samantha came back to the office after a long lunch, she smelled of alcohol and left again after an hour. The next week, when Rebecca opened a file drawer in Samantha's office looking for a client file, she found a large bottle of gin.

Once Rebecca was in the office and Ernie was out sick so Rebecca was asked to answer the phone. That day Rebecca talked to a number of Samantha's clients. All of them were angry and frustrated that they could not reach their lawyer. One woman was facing a hearing scheduled for the following day, and she had no idea if Samantha would appear. She said that she had not had any contact with Samantha since an initial interview two months before, when she had told Samantha her story and given her a check for $5,000.

If you were in Rebecca's shoes, what would you do? Consider when you would seek advice and insight from others, including your externship teacher.

■ Substance Abuse

Lawyers are afflicted with addiction to drugs and alcohol at rates significantly higher than the general population. According to the American Bar Association's Commission on Lawyer Assistance Programs, one out of every five lawyers is addicted to alcohol—a rate that is twice the national average. Lawyers also abuse illegal drugs at higher than average rates. Alcohol and drug abuse are major factors in the vast majority of serious disciplinary cases and in many civil and criminal cases brought against lawyers. Alcohol and drug abuse and their consequences also can raise issues during the bar admission process. Substance abuse negatively impacts lawyers' health, and their relationships with family members and friends. It also may erode lawyers' professional competence and lead to complaints of misconduct, malpractice claims, and lasting harm to a lawyer's professional reputation. See Chapter 25 on Work and Well-being.

Alcoholism and Alcohol Abuse

Alcoholism is a progressive disease that causes over 88,000 deaths per year in the United States. People who abuse alcohol have greatly increased risks of many cancers, liver disease, heart disease, dementia, and stroke. The disease is thought to be caused in part by genetic factors and in part by environmental, mental health, and other factors. One symptom of the disease is denial; most people who drink excessively deny to themselves and to others that they have a problem with alcohol.

What is "excessive drinking" for increased health risk purposes?

1. Binge drinking: more than 4 (women) or 5 (men) drinks during a single occasion.

2. Heavy drinking: Average consumption of more than one (women) or two (men) drinks per day.

Lots of binge drinkers and daily drinkers are not alcoholics, but some of them will become alcoholics.

For more this on data, see National Institute on Alcoholism and Alcohol Abuse, Alcohol Facts and Statistics, http://pubs.niaaa.nih.gov/publications/AlcoholFacts&Stats/AlcoholFacts&Stats.htm and Centers for Disease Control and Prevention, Fact Sheet, Alcohol Use and Your Health, http://www.cdc.gov/alcohol/fact-sheets/alcohol-use.htm.

Substance abuse also is a problem in law schools. In 1993 the Association of American Law School's Special Committee on Problems of Substance Abuse in the Law Schools surveyed 3,400 law students at nineteen law schools. Twelve percent of the respondents said they abused alcohol during law school. Within this group, 3.3 percent said they needed help to control their substance abuse. Many people think that the number of students abusing alcohol and drugs has increased during the last twenty years.

In recent years, abuse of Adderall, a prescription stimulant and Schedule 2 controlled substance intended to enhance attention and concentration for people with Attention Deficit and Attention Deficit Hyperactivity Disorders, has become increasingly common among law students seeking a boost in focus and productivity, especially during exam periods. The benefits some students experience from what one commentator has called "brain-doping" are offset by significant costs, including the risks of addiction and, for those who lack a prescription, criminal prosecution. Misuse of Adderall also causes decreased confidence and creativity and deprives the brain and the body of opportunities for relaxation and renewal. In addition, applicants for bar admission may be required to disclose use of non-prescribed prescription drugs. This unlawful activity, if disclosed or discovered by the character and fitness evaluators, can pose problems for bar admission.

> **Exercise 10.5 A Self-Assessment on Substance Abuse:** Excessive consumption of alcohol is so widespread on college campuses across the United States that many students are not aware that their alcohol consumption is too high or that they may be at risk of developing alcoholism or of other problems. To take a look at your own consumption of alcohol, fill out the self-assessment questionnaire of the National Council on Alcohol and Drug Abuse, Inc. (NCADA), at https://ncadd.org/learn-about-alcohol/alcohol-abuse-self-test. Answer the questions honestly. After you complete the questionnaire and review the results, write a journal entry (for yourself only, if you prefer) about your thoughts about your alcohol consumption. If the questionnaire indicates that your alcohol consumption may be problematic, we urge you to take action to address the problem. Do some reading; talk to a friend, a family member, or a counselor; or contact the state bar's Lawyer Assistance Program. If you use illegal drugs or take prescription drugs without a prescription or in larger than prescribed amounts, complete the NCADA questionnaire at https://ncadd.org/index.php/learn-about-drugs/drug-abuse-self-test to assess your drug use. If your answers reveal a problem, write a journal entry and take action, as suggested above.
>
> If you are having problems with substance abuse or dependency or suspect that a colleague or friend is struggling, contact your state Bar Association's Lawyer Assistance Program (LAP). LAPs provide confidential, expert advice and support and can help lawyers and law students to address various problems including substance abuse, depression, and other mental health problems.

▪ *Truthfulness*

Under Rule 8.4(c), lawyers are obliged to avoid all "dishonesty, fraud, deceit or misrepresentation." While there are some circumstances in which a lawyer engaging in advocacy on behalf of a client might withhold information from an opposing counsel or might select what information to present or not to present in court, lawyers owe their primary loyalty to clients and are expected to be honest in dealings with their clients. Rule 1.4 mandates communication and consultation with clients. Rule 7.1 prohibits any "false or misleading communication about the lawyer or the lawyer's services." Despite the requirements of these rules, sometimes lawyers are not entirely candid with their clients. A lawyer who lies to or deceives a client or another person can sometimes present another workplace ethical dilemma.

Exercise 10.6 Some Questions About Billing Practices: Tim Connolly works as an extern at Goldberg & Lamont, a small general practice law firm. Tim spends about half his time on a pro bono case in which the firm is representing a group of patients in a public psychiatric hospital in a lawsuit demanding improved services and living conditions. The other half of his time, Tim works on various matters for paying clients. Tim's supervisor, Corey Lamont, asked Tim to keep careful records of all of his time, noting which matter he is working on and what he is doing. This is relevant even for the pro bono case, because the firm will file a fee petition if its clients prevail. The firm does not bill clients for Tim's time, but it asks him to use the firm's time-keeping software to make it easier for them to verify his hours at the placement.

Several weeks into the placement, Elham Bolton, the firm's bookkeeper, comes to see Tim to go over his time records. She points out that Tim recorded 4.4 hours for the day he observed Corey taking a deposition in a child support matter. Elham said that Corey had recorded 7.6 hours for the same deposition. She wondered if Tim had made a mistake in recording his time.

"No mistake," Tim told her. "I'm new to this timekeeping business so I'm extremely careful."

"Okay," said Elham, "but I already asked Corey, and he confirmed that the deposition went on for over seven hours."

"That's weird, because I was there the whole time," Tim replied. We started just after nine and ended between 1:00 and 1:30."

"Perhaps he added some hours to compensate for some time he hadn't billed," Elham suggested. "In any event, I can't send the bill to the client listing Corey as billing 7.6 hours if I have reason to know that he didn't."

Tim is concerned about this news. He is concerned that he has done something wrong and also worries that his supervisor may have committed an ethical violation. Evaluate Tim's concerns and identify what he might do about them. What would you do if you were in Tim's situation? Consider when you would seek advice and insight from others, including your externship teacher.

▪ *Abuses of Power*

Many students have placement supervisors who are wonderful professional role models and good mentors. Most lawyers, however, have various personal and professional strengths and weaknesses. Occasionally, lawyers' behavior toward their subordinates turns abusive or predatory. The following problem invites exploration of possible responses to such conduct.

Exercise 10.7 An Uncomfortable Workplace: Gwen Ormond was an extern in the United States Senate, working for Senator Boyd. She was having a mixed experience: some interesting work on a judicial confirmation, a couple of good research assignments, but too much time answering phones and responding to constituent letters. Usually, Gwen did not really mind pitching in with the administrative work; it seemed logical because she was the most junior person in the office. One day, however, she came to class feeling really upset by her experiences on the Hill. She explained what happened.

I feel like a baby for complaining about this, but Nancy Shaw, my supervisor, is just a b**** sometimes! She's always in a rush, and often she gives me assignments with virtually no explanation of what I'm supposed to do. I try to figure it out, and I do the best work I can, but today she came to my desk as soon as I arrived and started screaming at me because I'd distributed a "Dear Colleague" letter that had two typographical errors in it to all the other senators. This was my fault, because I had proofed the letter, printed it, run it through the autopen machine, and sent it out. But it was just two small typos! She yelled at me for about ten minutes in front of all the other staff. I don't think I've ever felt so humiliated in my life. I mean, I know that Nancy has a bad temper, but she called me a stupid cow! It was just so insulting.

After I came back from a good cry in the ladies' room, I settled down and made some progress on a research project. I was searching the web for ammunition that Senator Boyd could use to oppose a judicial nominee. About three that afternoon, John Chapman, the senior legislative assistant, called me into his office and said that "the senator" wanted me to show up at this fundraiser tomorrow night. John said, "He asked me to give you this message personally—he really wants to see you there." Then, get this! He said, "Just wear a silk dress or something—the senator likes silk."

Well, for one thing, I don't own a silk dress. For another, I don't want to go to this party. I told him I was busy. He said "Cancel your other engagement, whatever it is. This is important." John wouldn't take no for an answer!

What should Gwen do? Should she say or do anything about Nancy's temper tantrum? Should she go to the party? In considering Gwen's dilemma, evaluate whether either Nancy or John, the lawyers on the senator's staff, have engaged in professional misconduct.

See Chapter 3 on Learning from Supervision and Chapter 7 on Bias in the Legal Profession.

Conclusion

This chapter is meant to introduce you to some of the common ethical issues that arise in legal practice and encourage you to be mindful of how your ethical obligations and those of others should guide your professional conduct. We hope that you will not encounter any issues as serious as those raised in the problems presented in this chapter, although it could happen, and if so, we want you to be prepared. Many of the exercises in this chapter are based on true stories. Law students sometimes are faced with very difficult dilemmas. This chapter and those that follow on specific ethical issues, as well as many others in this text, aim to assist you in sorting through both minor and major ethical dilemmas.

FURTHER RESOURCES

A.B.A. Section on Legal Educ. And Admission to the Bar, Report of the Task Force on Law Schools and the Profession: Narrowing the Gap (Robert MacCrate ed., 1992).

Report of the AALS Special Committee on Problems of Substance Abuse in the Law Schools, 44 J. Legal Educ. 35 (1994). For a useful resource for law students, see *Substance Abuse and Mental Health Tool Kit for Law Students and those Who Care about Them*, a collaborative effort of the ABA Law Student Division, the ABA Commission on Lawyer Assistance Programs (CoLAP), and the Dave Nee Foundation, http://www.americanbar.org/content/dam/aba/migrated/lsd/mentalhealth/toolkit.authcheckdam.pdf (last visited Nov. 4, 2015).

Know Your Rights: Workplace Sexual Harassment, Strategies for Victims, Am. Ass'n. of Univ. Women, http://www.aauw.org/what-we-do/legal-resources/know- your-rights-at-work/workplace-sexual-harassment/#strategies (last visited July 13, 2015).

ABA Comm'n on Lawyer Assistance Programs, http://www.americanbar.org/groups/lawyer_assistance.html.

Alexis Anderson, Arlene Kanter & Cindy Slane, *Ethics in Externships: Confidentiality, Conflicts, and Competence Issues in the Field and in the Classroom*, 10 Clin. L. Rev. 473 (2004).

Todd Essig, *When Study Drugs Kill (Part 1)*, FORBES (Feb. 10, 2013, 1:31 p.m.), http://www.forbes.com/sites/toddessig/2013/02/10when-study-drugs-kill-part-1-how-ambition-becomes-adderall-addiction/.

Todd Essig, *When Study Drugs Kill (Part 2)*, FORBES (Feb. 10, 2013, 1:33PM), http://www.forbes.com/sites/toddessig/2013/02/10when-study-drugs-kill-part-2-reducing-the-risks-from-brain-doping/.

Peter Joy & Robert Kuehn, *Conflicts and Competency Issues in Law Clinic Practice*, 9 CLIN. L. REV. 493 (2002).

LEGAL SERVICES CORP., DOCUMENTING THE JUSTICE GAP IN AMERICA: THE CURRENT UNMET CIVIL LEGAL NEEDS OF LOW INCOME AMERICANS (2009).

Lisa G. Lerman, *Professional and Ethical Issues in Legal Externships: Fostering Commitment to Public Service*, 67 FORDHAM. L. REV. 2295 (1999).

LISA G. LERMAN & PHILIP G. SCHRAG, ETHICAL PROBLEMS IN THE PRACTICE OF LAW (3d ed. 2012).

David Luban, *Essay: Taking out the Adversary: The Assault on Progressive Public-Interest Lawyers*, 91 CAL. L. REV. 209, 211 (2003).

DEBORAH RHODE & GEOFFREY HAZARD, JR., PROFESSIONAL RESPONSIBILITY AND REGULATION (2d ed., 2007).

Ethical Issues in Externships: Confidentiality

ALEXIS ANDERSON

- Can I use some of the memos I wrote at my placement as writing samples?

- Can I connect with friends on Facebook/LinkedIn and share my experiences this term?

- Do I have to sign the confidentiality agreement that my placement gave me?

The Scope of the Confidentiality Obligation

Your externship training begins with learning the professional duties owed to your workplace. Confidentiality, i.e., dealing with sensitive information responsibly, is at the heart of those duties. Lawyers promise it; clients rely on it; state disciplinary boards demand it. If you extern in an organization that represents a client or clients, you become part of the legal team obligated to protect information related to the representation of clients. In addition, whether or not your placement engages in direct client representation, you will become privy to other sensitive information that your employer will want you to protect. This Chapter is designed to help you navigate the ethical puzzles related to confidentiality, including those posed above.

A natural corollary to attorney loyalty, confidentiality helps ensure client candor and trust, which are keys to effective lawyer-client relationships. In addition, the duty to maintain client confidences and workplace secrets is integrally related to an attorney's need to prevent conflicts of interests. See Chapter 12 on Conflicts of Interests. Therefore, it will be incumbent on you, with guidance from your supervising attorney and externship teacher, to safeguard all confidential workplace information.

Confidentiality issues arise not just at your placement. New technological innovations are not only shaping what lawyers can do and how they can do it in their offices, but also what and how attorneys can conduct themselves outside the workplace. During your externship, you will encounter ethics challenges related to new technology as it transforms how you conduct business remotely, use social media, transfer data, and more generally, practice in a "virtual" world.

You are embarking on practice at a time when American lawyers are thinking globally. The question of how to protect client secrets is very much an ethical norm that transcends state and national borders. While different legal systems have resolved the line between disclosures and confidences in distinct ways, the policy questions about client loyalty and system integrity are similar in discussions around the world. Take, for example, France, where a lawyer's lips are sealed even if a client consents to a disclosure, but where communications between lawyers are confidential even as to one's client. In China, client communications that involve potential crimes against state security or against public safety are exempt from protection. Given these distinctions, developing the good habit of learning the ethical rules applicable to your practice setting and jurisdiction early in your career is critical.

This chapter provides an overview of the ethics rules related to maintaining confidences in different practice settings. In addition, it contains exercises designed to help you implement those standards. Reviewing those problems with fellow students will help prepare you for the confidentiality challenges that will arise during your externship. When ethical issues develop, consult with your externship teacher and supervising attorney.

Protection of Confidential Information

Rule 1.6(a) establishes a broad and mandatory rule: "A lawyer shall not reveal information relating to the representation of a client" unless the lawyer is permitted to do so by one of the exceptions listed in Rule 1.6 or by another rule.[1] This duty of confidentiality attaches when an individual consults a lawyer for legal advice, even if the lawyer does not accept that individual as a client. The duty protects communications between lawyer and client and all other information related to the representation, regardless of its source. The duties under Rule 1.6 apply even if the client has diminished capacity. Further, a lawyer is obliged to protect as confidential information learned from witness interviews, research, discovery, and even information that is in the public domain.

Balancing the confidentiality duty to clients with other important public policies has been one of the most contentious issues in the adoption of the ABA Model Rules. This controversy often has been replicated in the states as they decide whether to adopt the Model Rules provisions on confidentiality or modify them. From their original enactment, the Model Rules gave lawyers discretion to reveal confidential client information if necessary to prevent a client from committing a crime that poses a threat of imminent death or substantial bodily harm. That approach differed from the broader language of the earlier ABA Model Code, which had permitted lawyers to disclose confidential information to prevent any type of client crime.

Since then, the ABA several times rejected proposals to add an exception for serious economic injury flowing from a client crime or fraud. In August 2003, after publicity surrounding Enron and other corporate scandals, and in the face of Congressional action on the Sarbanes-Oxley Act, the ABA adopted recommendations from its Corporate Responsibility Task Force to include such an exception. By that time, more than forty states' rules allowed for disclosure of a crime or fraud that would result or had resulted in serious economic injury.

Here is the current text of the Delaware Rule 1.6, which includes two new provisions, 1.6(b)(7) and 1.6(c), enacted in 2012. As Chapter 10 explained, the American Bar Association is the copyright holder of the Model Rules and imposes stringent restrictions on quotations of the Model Rules. All quotes to rules of professional conduct are to the Delaware rules, which are almost identical to the Model Rules with any difference explained in an endnote.

■ *Rule 1.6 Confidentiality of Information*

(a) A lawyer shall not reveal information relating to the representation of a client unless the client gives informed consent, the disclosure is impliedly authorized in order to carry out the representation, or the disclosure is permitted by paragraph (b).

(b) A lawyer may reveal information relating to the representation of a client to the extent the lawyer reasonably believes necessary:

(1) to prevent reasonably certain death or substantial bodily harm;

(2) to prevent the client from committing a crime or fraud that is reasonably certain to result in substantial injury to the financial interests or property of another and in furtherance of which the client has used or is using the lawyer's services;

(3) to prevent, mitigate, or rectify substantial injury to the financial interests or property of another that is reasonably certain to result or has resulted from the client's commission of a crime or fraud in furtherance of which the client has used the lawyer's services;

(4) to secure legal advice about the lawyer's compliance with these Rules;

(5) to establish a claim or defense on behalf of the lawyer in a controversy between the lawyer and the client, to establish a defense to a criminal charge or civil claim against the lawyer based upon conduct in which the client was involved, or to respond to allegations in any proceeding concerning the lawyer's representation of the client;

(6) to comply with other law or a court order; or

(7) to detect and resolve conflicts of interest arising from the lawyer's change of employment or from changes in the composition or ownership of a firm, but only if the revealed information would not compromise the attorney-client privilege or otherwise prejudice the client.

(c) A lawyer shall make reasonable efforts to prevent the inadvertent or unauthorized disclosure of, or unauthorized access to, information relating to the representation of a client.

Exceptions to Confidentiality

As you see, Rule 1.6 contains a number of express exceptions to the otherwise comprehensive duty in Rule 1.6(a) to protect client information relating to the representation. Other rules place further limits on a lawyer's duty to maintain confidences. For example, Rule 1.13 establishes another discretionary exception to Rule 1.6. A lawyer who represents an organization may disclose otherwise confidential information to prevent injury to the organization if the lawyer knows that a constituent of the organization has done something illegal or for which the entity may be held liable, if the action or omission will seriously damage the organization, and if the organization's highest authority refuses to act after the matter had been "reported up" to that authority. Rule 1.14 provides another type of exception for clients with diminished capacity. While the information relating to representation of these clients must be protected as confidential communications, their lawyers are impliedly authorized to reveal information to the extent necessary to protect client interests. Rule 1.14(c).

Rule 1.6 does not explicitly identify situations in which a lawyer must disclose confidences, but a careful reading of the rules as a whole reveals this obligation. Rule 3.3 specifies some additional exceptions to Rule 1.6, when disclosure of otherwise confidential information may be required because of an overriding duty of candor to a tribunal. See Chapter 13 on Ethical Duties to Tribunals and Third Parties. In some instances, a lawyer's duties to third parties likewise could require revelation. Rule 4.1(b) provides that a lawyer shall not knowingly "fail to disclose a material fact when disclosure is necessary to avoid assisting a criminal or fraudulent act by a client unless disclosure is prohibited by Rule 1.6." Because Rule 1.6 allows disclosure to prevent, mitigate, or rectify a fraud, Rule 4.1(b) requires disclosure if silence would assist a fraud.

In an externship in which a student is assisting a lawyer rather than serving as the frontline lawyer, the supervising attorney will decide whether a disclosure is permitted or required. Your own judgment will more often be concerned with honoring basic confidentiality duties. A careless comment or action by an extern could reveal information protected by Rule 1.6 and even could constitute a waiver of attorney-client privilege, discussed more fully below. Conversely, if a supervisor fails to make a disclosure required by the rules, an extern will be faced with the decision whether to challenge the supervisor's decision or to report the supervisor's conduct within the organization or to the disciplinary authorities. Consultation with your externship teacher will be particularly important as those ethical challenges arise.

Balancing Technological Innovation With Confidentiality Duties

Technological advances have recently prompted the ABA to revisit the confidentiality rules. In 2012, the ABA's Commission commonly known as Ethics 20/20 released its final report, which contained proposals designed to help the profession adapt to these new innovations. While technological developments offer significant advantages in terms of access to legal assistance, the ABA was mindful that these changes also raise confidentiality concerns. Therefore, the ABA adopted new provisions requiring attorneys to make "reasonable efforts" to protect information covered by Rule 1.6 regardless of the type of communication tool being used, e.g., cloud computing, smartphones, and other remote access devices. Rule 1.6(c) and Comments 18–19.

As lawyers and externs use new methods to transmit data, the professional duty to prevent unauthorized access or inadvertent disclosure of data becomes heightened. Gone are the days when lawyers could satisfy their duties of protecting client files merely by limiting key access to the client file room. Now, client information is commonly stored not in hard copy, but rather in electronic format. Furthermore, your placement may not house its data servers on-site but rather rely on third-party vendors who manage remote storage of client data. Cloud computing necessarily means that third parties have access to confidential information; therefore, appropriate protocols need to be in place to ensure that data remains appropriately protected. Your placement will have determined what procedures and tools it will adopt.

Your confidentiality duties during your externship are twofold: to abide by the placement's security protocols and to conduct yourself consistent with the professional obligation to protect client information and workplace secrets. You may be asked to sign a confidentiality agreement; at a minimum, you need to learn and then comply with your placement's confidentiality procedures. Practice settings will vary as to whether you can access workplace files remotely depending on their data security procedures. Placements also will differ on how to talk shop responsibly. Your supervising attorney is responsible for ensuring your compliance and should be your primary resource as questions arise regarding confidentiality.

Comment 18 to Rule 1.6(c) lists a number of factors designed to ensure that lawyers make "reasonable efforts" to protect client data. These elements include sensitivity of the data, likelihood of disclosure if additional safeguards are not employed, and cost and difficulty of employing those additional measures. The efficacy of additional safeguards must then be balanced against any adverse consequences to the lawyer's need to provide competent representation.

In addition to ensuring the protection of client secrets, workplaces often have rules to safeguard other types of sensitive information. For example, a corporation may have procedures in place to protect proprietary information. Specific clients may request heightened protections, e.g., password-protected emails. Judges have internal rules designed to maintain the integrity of the judicial process and protect confidential matters within their chambers. The new amendments to Rule 1.6 explicitly recognize that certain clients and practice settings may trigger the need for greater security measures, which would raise the bar of what constitutes "reasonable efforts." As you embark on your fieldwork, you should consult the ethical rules of your jurisdiction and ask your supervisor about the confidentiality rules at your placement. Then you must learn to conduct yourself in a manner that complies with those rules.

Relationship Among Confidential Information, Attorney-Client Privilege, and Work Product Immunity

Lawyers' ethical duty to protect confidences is related to, but distinct from, the rules of evidence that establish the attorney-client privilege and work-product doctrine. See Rule 1.6, Comment 3, (noting the broader scope of confidentiality duties). Confidential communications between a lawyer and a client relating to legal advice or legal services are protected by the attorney-client privilege. The RESTATEMENT OF THE LAW GOVERNING LAWYERS §§68–86 and PROPOSED FEDERAL RULE OF EVIDENCE 503 provide useful summaries of the basic doctrine of attorney-client privilege, although state law varies on some points. To trigger the privilege, the communication, which can be oral, written, or electronic, must be made between privileged persons, which include the lawyer's staff, in private, and for the purpose of seeking or providing legal advice or legal services.

The scope of the evidentiary privilege has been such a contentious issue that Congress did not include the proposals on the various privileges when it enacted the Federal Rules of Evidence. However, the proposed rule on attorney-client privilege has been adopted as law, on a district-by-district basis, by many federal districts. The proposed rule also has had considerable influence on state law. While Rule 1.6 concerns the ethical and fiduciary duty of lawyer to client, the privilege rule concerns whether matters within its scope are admissible in court. When the privilege applies, neither the lawyer nor the client can be compelled to testify regarding the protected information.

Information prepared for, or in anticipation of, litigation likewise may be protected from disclosure by work-product immunity. Rule 1.6, Comment 3; RESTATEMENT OF THE LAW GOVERNING LAWYERS §§ 87–93; FEDERAL RULES OF CIVIL PROCEDURE 26(b) (3). Generally, the information shielded by either the attorney-client privilege or the attorney work-product doctrine is a subset of the larger category of information protected by the ethical rules on confidentiality.

Application of Confidentiality Rules to Externships

Given the broad sweep of the ethical rule requiring confidentiality and the professional duty to protect workplace secrets, one approach could be to keep completely mum about what you are doing at your externship. To adopt such a blanket prohibition, however, would undermine your ability to learn from practice and limit your opportunity to reflect on your externship experience. If you cannot talk about your work at all, how can you complete journal entries, participate in seminar discussions with externs placed in other settings, or seek guidance on supervision matters and other ethical issues from fellow students or your externship teacher? A "gag rule" would deprive you of an important opportunity to learn about when and how you may talk about your legal work without running afoul of confidentiality duties.

If you participate in an externship seminar, your discussions with your externship teacher and with other students, as well as your submission of journal entries, connect you and your supervisor and, by extension, the clients, organization, or chambers you serve, to your law school community. This connection can be a source of ethical tension because neither your fellow students nor your externship teacher is part of the attorney-client relationship or the legal staff at your placement. Hence you will face the following challenge: if you are to extract maximum learning from your externship experience by sharing those experiences with your externship teacher and seminar classmates while honoring your professional obligations as a lawyer in training, you will have to learn how to "talk shop" without disclosing confidential information.

To determine how best to navigate the confidentiality waters at your placement, you should seek guidance from your supervising attorney and externship teacher before you discuss any aspect of your work with someone outside of your externship organization. Should you confront a situation in which you are unsure of your ethical duty, you should first consult your supervisor, who is best positioned to instruct you in the proper handling of confidential information. You and that attorney can then have a nuanced discussion about the specific ethics question, taking into account the particular workplace demands and culture. In addition, consider consulting with your externship teacher. Many states permit confidential consultations with externship teachers who are admitted to practice in that jurisdiction. Rule 1.6(b)(4). It is much easier to resolve confidentiality dilemmas before any disclosure has occurred. Do not wrestle with confidentiality issues alone!

The following exercises will help you learn and manage your confidentiality duties during your externship.

> **Exercise 11.1 Learning the Ropes:** Keeping in mind the material in this chapter, prepare a journal entry[2] covering the following issues:
>
> 1. To whom do you owe the duty of confidentiality at your placement?
>
> 2. Are there any workplace secrets that must be maintained, in addition to client confidences?
>
> 3. What are the sources of those requirements?
>
> 4. What are your placement's data security protocols?
>
> 5. What workplace information, if any, can be shared with your externship seminar classmates and teacher?

If you wish to keep copies of your own work product from your externship, consult your supervising attorney about workplace rules, and what, if any, information must be redacted. If you are interested in using sanitized versions of your work product as writing samples for prospective employers, ask your supervisor for permission. If your externship teacher requires that you turn in copies of your work product, be sure that your supervisor understands this requirement and permits you to do so. Learn what the ethical rules in your jurisdiction require and what workplace procedures must also be respected.

If your placement has given guidance on confidentiality, evaluate the relationship between the directions you received and the obligation imposed by the state confidentiality rules. Are the boundaries articulated by your supervisor more restrictive or less restrictive than the relevant rules? If there is a discrepancy between your supervisor's instructions and the state rules, what accounts for it? Which binds you?

One of the best ways to ensure that you understand the confidentiality mandate is to analyze the confidentiality rules in context. To that end, consider the scenarios presented below.

> **Exercise 11.2 Talking Shop Outside the Workplace:** The evening after her first day at her externship, Meredith Blackburn posted the following on her Facebook Wall: "Working for the Mayor!" In addition, she sent out the following message to her friends' group:
>
> *Just started working at Harmon, Guerney & Brown. Grabbed the chance to extern at the firm because it's such a great resume builder (even if no money). They told me not all the work would require major brainpower; I told them I'm on it.*
>
> *Anyway, you wouldn't believe what I got for my first assignment! They asked me to proofread our client's new will. You won't believe who the client is! Mayor Virginia Wood! Okay, all I was doing at this point was reading stuff in her file, but it sure was interesting reading. Of course I can't tell you what is in her will, but I'll tell you one thing. There are going to be a lot of angry relatives when everyone finds out how she decided to dispose of her money!!*
>
> 1. Did Meredith violate Rule 1.6 in her use of Facebook? If so, which of her comments are improper? Do you have enough information to answer that question? What else do you need to know? If Meredith's client had not been a public figure, would your analysis change? Does the nature of the legal work matter, e.g., a juvenile case, a highly publicized criminal prosecution, a private business transaction?

2. Apart from whether Meredith's conduct violates an ethical rule, what do you think about what she said? Can you articulate a principle from Meredith's conduct about what constraints lawyers or law students should impose on themselves in discussing client matters?

3. Assume that Meredith posts again later in the semester, recounting her experiences working on a different matter. Her second case assignment involves her work with a criminal defense lawyer at her firm on a matter that has received significant media attention. Meredith is careful not to use the client's actual name, but describes the new client as a suspected terrorist known as the "Boston Marathon Bomber." Is that precaution sufficient to avoid violation of Rule 1.6?

4. Change the scenario again. Assume Meredith has just begun a placement at a local prosecutor's office and she has been assigned to assist with the prosecution of the "Boston Marathon Bomber." Is she permitted to refer to her plum case assignment in a text to her roommate? Who is the client of the prosecutor, and by extension, Meredith? Is there any problem if Meredith mentions that she is working on the prosecution of the "Boston Marathon Bomber" case? See Chapter 15 on Client Relationships.

5. Assume Meredith is externing with the local federal district court judge who has been assigned to preside in the "Boston Marathon Bomber" case. Judges do not have "clients." To whom does Meredith owe her loyalty? What, if any, confidentiality concerns are involved here? May she text that she is working on the "Boston Marathon Bomber" case?

A good starting point in protecting client confidences is to refrain from mentioning the names of clients to anyone except your co-workers. More may be required to avoid revelation of client confidences. Context is very important. What might constitute appropriate safeguarding of client information in a big city may not be adequate in a small town setting: compare, one of many criminal prosecutions in a major city with the marquee trial in a rural community. Therefore, even if you do not use client identifiers, sharing details about your work in some situations may not satisfy your duty to protect client confidences.

Exercise 11.3 "What Merger?" At the beginning of each meeting of an externship seminar for students working in corporate general counsel's offices, the externship teacher asks students for an update on placement activities. Georgia Anastas, who works in the in-house legal department of a large, publicly-traded company, responds to the teacher's inquiry in a despairing tone: "Things have been pretty awful for the last two weeks." "What's the problem?" the teacher asks. "It seems as though no one has any time for me," Georgia responds. "They're all too busy working on the merger." "Is the merger public knowledge?" the teacher asks with trepidation. Georgia hesitates as she begins to grasp the significance of the question. "No, it isn't," she replies.

1. What, if any, ethical considerations are involved in this problem? Do the same restrictions apply if you are talking about your work with a roommate, a fellow extern, or your externship teacher? How might disclosures impact her fellow students? Would your concerns be any different if Georgia had only written about her malaise in a journal rather than describing it in seminar?

2. How should Georgia proceed now that the proverbial cat is out of the bag?

Exercise 11.4 What You Can Take Away: Before law school, Rick Mendez was in a band that made some recordings. His placement this term is with the in-house legal department of a major record label. Since his band days, he has frequently blogged on a prominent music site for R&B recording artists. Last week, he blogged the following:

> *I now understand the fine points of negotiating a music deal—the issues on which artists have some flexibility to negotiate and the issues on which they do not. Those key points affect the label's decision as to when to give a better deal. Now I can see the stupid things I did with my own band, and I can't wait to share this expertise with my friends to help them get the best deals possible. I bet some of them will be negotiating with the same label for which I just externed.*

1. What, if any, ethical questions are raised by Rick's desire to use his on-the-site training for his and his friends' advantage?

2. If Rick does not tell anyone the name of the record company for which he externed, can he share the business tips he learned?

Suppose you want ethical guidance from your externship teacher or from the other students in your seminar. They are not part of the lawyering team at your placement and, therefore, cannot become privy to workplace secrets. The most effective way to obtain advice without breaching confidentiality is to avoid disclosure of information that could identify the client and to pose your dilemma as a hypothetical. Comment 4 to Rule 1.6(a) encourages consultation to ensure compliance by condoning the use of hypotheticals "so long as there is no reasonable likelihood that the listener will be able to ascertain the identity of the client or the situation involved."

This problem also raises questions about whether Rick's loyalty to his client may be compromised by his self-interest. See Chapter 12 on Conflicts; see also Rule 1.8(b) (regarding use of information relating to representation of a client to his disadvantage).

Exercise 11.5 The Email Attachment That Went Away: Alex Tanner, who is externing at a firm downtown, has just written the following journal entry for his externship teacher, but he is unsure whether he should send it.

> *During my externship, I received a copy of an email that my supervisor, Duane, had sent to a client. The email referred to an attached memorandum offering advice on a particular legal issue I had researched. I opened the document with pride, assuming I would find a copy of the memo I had produced. I was shocked to discover that Duane had mistakenly attached the wrong document. In fact, the attached memo contained legal advice for another client. I brought the matter to Duane's attention. He was quick to express regret for the error. He asked me to send the correct attachment to the client. I questioned whether additional remedial steps needed to be taken. Should we request that the client destroy the erroneously forwarded document? Should we tell the client whose information had been leaked that the accident had happened? Duane basically rebuffed my questions and made clear that I should not press the matter further. This whole situation is still bothering me, though. I'm upset that we made this mistake and about my supervisor's response to it. I really think more needs to be done.*

1. What, if anything, would you recommend that Alex do? Should he tell his externship teacher? If so, how? Can he seek advice from other students in the seminar or from other attorneys at his placement?

2. If he were to seek guidance from others, what repercussions might result—to him, to Duane, to his externship teacher or to the externship program?

3. Would Alex's legal memo still be protected from disclosure if an adverse party were to demand its production?

Exercise 11.6 The Metadata That Got Away: A month later, Alex faces another ethics challenge at his placement. This time, he is the one on the hot seat. He and Duane had been negotiating a settlement in a highly contentious civil case that was coming to closure. The opposing attorney had sent over a draft Agreement which Duane and Alex had reviewed with their client, a tenant. Then Alex was tasked with revising the Agreement to try to get a more favorable deal from the landlord's attorney. Alex did so, but also left margin comments to remind Duane that the client had given them authority on several points to accept less than the revisions indicated. Here are the relevant provisions of the draft Alex sent to Duane for his final review before sending it to the opposing counsel:

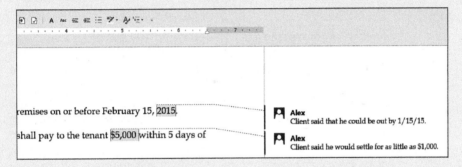

Duane called Alex later in the day, thanking him for his work, and advising that Alex should send the draft to the opposing counsel, "after you delete the margin comments." Alex followed those instructions to the letter. He deleted the two comments and then forwarded the Agreement by attachment to the opposition.

The next day the opposing counsel sent the Agreement back, with a cover email stating, "Your position in Paragraph Two is unrealistic. Our client will not pay $5000 and we suspect your client knows that."

Alex reports that he was initially dumbfounded as to how the opposition could have intuited the authority given Alex and Duane by their client. Then Duane guessed the error: while Alex had indeed deleted the comments, he had not taken the extra step of stripping the revised Agreement of metadata.

1. Duane asks Alex what he recommends they do, given that the client's interests have likely been prejudiced. What should Alex propose that they do?

2. What if any duty did the opposing counsel have to bring the error to Duane and Alex's attention?

Exercise 11.7 The Emotional Strain: Rosaline Watson, who is externing at a local Victim Rights Center, submitted the following email to her externship teacher:

My client, I'll call her Sue, is in a terrible situation. She is worried that her estranged husband who is father of her two children could become abusive. After hearing some of the threats he's made, I counseled her to go into court immediately and seek a restraining order (RO). But she said she was really scared to do that given how small her town is. She's worried that her husband's brothers will find out and come after her. She's also concerned about how the local families will react when they hear about the RO. Her kids are old enough that some of their peers might make life hard for them at school. I told her to think about her options and let me know if she'd like us to help her get a restraining order.

Nearly a week has elapsed and I have remained very concerned about Sue's safety. Yesterday, she called back and said she wanted our assistance in getting a RO. Evidently, her daughter's teacher had just called to advise her that the school had filed a report of possible abuse by the father with the Department of Social Services. I talked to my supervisor, and together we consulted with the Social Worker on staff at the Victim Rights Center, Nila, who provided information on domestic violence family shelters, which I relayed to my client. Unfortunately, Sue decided not to move out lest the whole problem become more complicated for the children. Sue authorized us to help her obtain a RO, so my supervisor and I got an ex parte order the same day.

Legally, it was a great result, but I'm still worried about Sue because the father and his family still know where to find her. My supervisor suggested I call the local police to warn them that Sue and her family might need their help. The duty officer said the department already knew the father all too well. I also reminded Sue to keep a cell phone with her at all times. But I can't help worrying about her safety. What if she and her children suffer because I didn't do enough?

1. Do you see any confidentiality issues in Rosaline's decision to share her emotionally draining case with her externship teacher? Did she properly sanitize her description of her client's confidential information in her email?

2. Is there any difference between sharing the information with her teacher and sharing it with other students in the externship seminar? How might Rosaline get support and ethical guidance from her externship teacher?

3. Given the report to the government agency and the subsequent issuance of the restraining order, are Sue's revelations about the father's conduct still confidential?

4. Are the professional duties that govern the teacher and the police officer or other helping professionals, like social workers, different than those that govern lawyers?

Conclusion

Taken literally, Rule 1.6 bars lawyers from revealing any "information relating to representation of a client" absent exceptions or client consent. Workplace secrets, too, require protection. Now that you have had opportunities to study the confidentiality rules, analyze the exercises presented in this chapter, and discuss the issues with your peers and externship teacher, you are ready to make the hard, but necessary, judgments that will allow you to "talk shop" respectfully, professionally, and consistent with all applicable confidentiality obligations.

FURTHER RESOURCES

MODEL RULES OF PROF'L CONDUCT, r. 1.6, 1.13, & 1.14 (and counterpart rules from the jurisdiction in which you are externing).

RESTATEMENT (THIRD) OF THE LAW GOVERNING LAWYERS §§ 68-s86 (AM. LAW INST. 2000).

ENDNOTES

1   Unless otherwise noted, reference will be made to the Delaware Rules of Professional Conduct rather than the ABA Model Rules of Professional Conduct, which are copyrighted.

2   Increasingly, externship programs are using online features, such as discussion boards, as the vehicle to communicate extern reflections. Our references throughout to "journals" are intended to encompass any type of reflective writing undertaken by externs as part of their externship requirements.

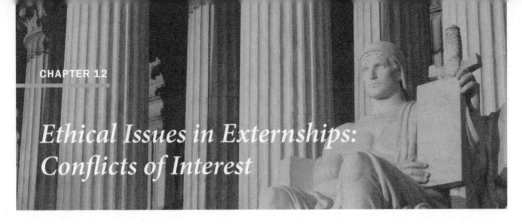

Ethical Issues in Externships: Conflicts of Interest

CINDY R. SLANE

Being Jamie: A Cautionary Tale

J amie's spirits were high as he hung his jacket on the hook on the back of his office door that Tuesday morning. It was his second day as a soon-to-be-bar-admitted, first-year associate at Ranken and Rome, L.L.C., the now-five(!)-person firm at which Jamie had worked first as a summer law clerk a little more than a year earlier. He spent most of yesterday afternoon observing his new colleague, Margarite Krikorian, argue a motion for summary judgment in state court, and while he was walking from the train station to the office this morning, he received a text message from another of the firm's lawyers, Matt Goldberg, asking Jamie to stop by his office at 10:00 so Matt could bring him up to speed on an interesting new case that recently came into the firm. Life was good.

Cheryl Ranken and Ed Rome, the firm's founding—and so far only—partners, were victims of the market pressures that had forced many large law firms to contract several years earlier: both were passed over for partnership at the 225-lawyer firm where they had begun their careers after their respective clerkships. Though there was some discussion with the managing partner of them remaining on as "of counsel" after the disappointing partnership vote, Cheryl and Ed had decided instead to seize the opportunity the universe had thrust upon them and set to work turning lemons into sorbet. They left the firm without burning any bridges, incorporated their new enterprise as a two-member L.L.C., rented office space, ordered business cards, contracted with Westlaw and a professional liability insurer, recruited an administrative assistant, hung out a shingle, reached out to their former corporate clients, and since then had been developing what they were confident they could build into the best commercial-litigation boutique in the area.

Cheryl and Ed were very capable lawyers, and it did not take long for them to secure a modest yet steady stream of work from the clients they had represented at their former firm. Former colleagues at the firm, too, referred work to them from time to time when conflicts of interest precluded the firm's taking particular matters. Ranken and Rome had enough business to hire a lateral associate at the *end of year one, and a second lateral midway through year two. By October of the same year, it seemed fairly certain that the firm would be able to support another associate by the end of year three; this time, though, Ed and Cheryl concluded that hiring at the entry level made sense and decided to go with a known commodity.*

Jamie was over the moon to receive Ranken and Rome's offer letter; he called Cheryl and Ed immediately to thank them and signed and returned the letter to indicate his acceptance only a day later. What a relief—a decent salary, the promise of interesting work, no more resume drops, no more inquiry letters, no more late nights spent scrolling through job postings on the career services website and Craigslist! Assuming he passed the bar—a condition precedent, to be sure, but one Cheryl and Ed said they were certain would not be an issue—Jamie would begin his new job the Monday after the bar results were announced.

Matt was on the phone when Jamie knocked tentatively on his open office door just before 10:00 that Tuesday morning but motioned him in, quickly ended his call, and said that he had asked Jamie to stop by because he and Cheryl wanted him to start work immediately on a very important matter that had come into the firm six weeks earlier—a matter, he said, which was going to require a significant commitment of firm resources for the next year at a minimum.

Matt began to describe the case in general terms. It was unbelievably good timing for Jamie, an opportunity for him to be involved in a major commercial case almost from its inception, a factually and legally complex matter in which the firm's clients were asserting a challenge to a corporate acquisition, and a high-profile case with very big legal guns certain to be arrayed on the other side.

Although Jamie managed somehow to remain composed through Matt's recitation, on the inside he was almost giddy with excitement: this was just the kind of experience he had hoped he would eventually have at Ranken and Rome, but he had never dreamed he would be involved in something so big, so soon.

Jamie had been lucky enough to do some M&A work at his Corporate Counsel Externship at Global MarketShare during the spring term. He had attended a number of strategy meetings with his field supervisor and their client-constituents, and, as part of due diligence in connection with Global's acquisition of Griffin & Dunne, a mid-sized advertising agency, had spent 35 or 40 hours reviewing contracts that would be assigned to Global via the transaction. Though the contract review had been tedious at times, Jamie had thrived on the work. He also had been the envy of many of his Corporate Counsel classmates, but he had figured it might be years before he got to work on a merger or acquisition again.

Then Matt flipped the file in front of him across his desk and around to face Jamie. "Why don't you start by reading through this," Matt said. "The draft complaint is in there; it's almost final. We're representing the members of Griffin & Dunne, L.L.C., in their lawsuit against Global MarketShare, Inc. We'll be filing next week in the district court. When you're done, come back with any questions, then you can start helping Cheryl and me with interrogatories and requests for production."

Jamie's eyes fell to the label on the folder. He stared at it, unblinking, for what felt like an eternity. "I don't think I can work on this," he said finally, his stomach rolling as though it had just done a double rotation with a twist in the pike position off a ten-meter board. "I think I have a conflict. I did an externship in the general counsel's office at Global MarketShare last spring. I did some work on this deal before it closed. I had no idea it ended up in litigation."

Matt looked as though he had just received breaking news of some sort of international calamity. "Oh, s#%t," he said, "we have to tell Cheryl and Ed right away."

Two hours later, Jamie sat across from Cheryl in her office, his jaw clenched. Ed perched, grim-faced, on the corner of Cheryl's desk; he and Cheryl both looked as miserable as Jamie felt. "First, Jamie," Cheryl said, "please know that we're both incredibly grateful that you brought your conflict to our attention. We're very impressed—that most definitely was the right thing to do—but we're also very sorry; we wish as much as you do that the situation were different. We hope you can understand. We're a small operation and this case is extremely important to us—we expect it to generate at least $250,000 in fees for the firm. With the other work we have, though, we won't be able to staff it if the entry-level person we bring in this fall can't work on it.

"We're sure you remember that the offer we extended to you last November was subject to the resolution of any conflicts of interest," Ed added. (Had that been in the letter? Jamie could not remember.) "We had no idea you had worked at Global MarketShare during your externship last semester; in fact, we didn't even know you had done an externship until a couple of hours ago. We'll be giving you two weeks of severance pay, of course, and both of us will do all we can to help you find another job, but unfortunately, the firm just can't afford to hire a sixth lawyer right now and we have to have a junior person who can work on this case."

O kay. Now that I have your attention . . . what are you feeling? Shock? Empathy? Apprehension? Vague nausea, both in solidarity with Jamie and at the realization that his situation at some point could be yours?

Sadly, although the names and other identifying details have been changed, Jamie's story is all too real. And Cheryl was right: in immediately disclosing that he had worked on the acquisition the preceding spring, Jamie did exactly the right thing under the circumstances. If he had kept silent, crossed his fingers, and begun work on the case, Global almost certainly would have filed, and quite likely would have won, a motion to disqualify Ranken and Rome when it learned of Jamie's participation in the matter. The firm probably would have had to disgorge its fees to date, whether in resolution of a claim by Griffin & Dunne for malpractice or as restitution per an order of the lawyers' disciplinary authority in the jurisdiction.

Under other circumstances, though—say, if Jamie had informed his prospective employers about his externship when his placement was confirmed, such that they were aware of the very real possibility that he would arrive in September with a conflict when Griffin and Dunne's principals first approached the firm about representation in July—perhaps the story would have had a much happier ending.[1]

What can students learn from imagining themselves in Jamie's shoes? Most importantly, conflicts of interest are serious business for both lawyers and their clients and can arise by virtue of the legal work law students perform—in volunteer positions in externships, in summer and academic-term employment—even before they are admitted to practice.

This chapter is designed to help you to develop your conflicts competence and thereby avoid "being Jamie," in three ways. First, it will offer an overview of the legal ethics rules on conflicts and examine situations in which conflicts issues typically arise in externship practice. Second, it will invite you to engage with the conflicts rules by presenting a number of hypotheticals, each drawn from the experience of externs much like yourself and designed to provide you with practice in recognizing and avoiding or resolving the sorts of conflicts you may encounter by virtue of your externship participation. Third, it will offer guidance as to how you can discharge your personal and professional responsibility to avoid representation that would result in conflicts of interest, not only during your externship semester, but also during the rest of your legal career.

Conflicts in Context

Even though they are not licensed lawyers, law students—including those participating in externship programs—must be alert to and avoid representations that would give rise to conflicts of interest. A potential or actual conflict of interest exists when a lawyer's ability to fulfill her professional responsibilities to one client may or will be impaired by the lawyer's responsibilities to another current or former client, the lawyer's duties to a third party, or the lawyer's own interests.

Concerns about lawyers' conflicts of interest have a long history. As early as 1280, a London ordinance forbade attorneys from engaging in a variety of activities that presented conflicts of interest, including representing parties on both sides of an action. That tradition notwithstanding, in 1770, John Adams, then a 34-year-old lawyer practicing in Boston, represented all nine defendants charged with murder following the incident widely known as the Boston Massacre: Captain Thomas Preston, the officer of the Crown who led seven soldiers to the aid of a sentry at the scene of a disturbance on King Street and was alleged to have given an order to fire, and the soldiers who were alleged to have fired into the crowd.[2]

Key issues in the case were certain to be whether the soldiers had been ordered to fire, and if so, by whom, as well as which of the defendants fired the shots that killed five people and left six wounded.

The soldiers understood the risk they would face if Preston, who was to be tried first, persuaded the jury that he had not issued an order to fire. The court, however, refused the soldiers' petition that it try Preston and the soldiers together.

By all accounts, Adams and his co-counsel Josiah Quincy, Jr., performed admirably at both trials. Preston and six of the soldiers were acquitted of all charges; the two soldiers not acquitted were convicted not of murder, but of manslaughter.

Adams' representation of more than one of the Boston Massacre defendants, however, plainly would have run afoul of modern conflicts doctrine from the outset. While courts in several jurisdictions have blessed representation of co-defendants by different lawyers in the same public defender's office where adequate safeguards are in place to protect confidential client information,[3] both courts and ethics committees in a number of other jurisdictions impute conflicts among defenders in a single office.[4] Consequently, in these jurisdictions, lawyers associated in a single office do not represent more than one co-defendant, and rather represent only one, referring his or her co-defendants either to lawyers in other public defender offices or to outside counsel.

The RESTATEMENT 3D OF THE LAW GOVERNING LAWYERS, too, imputes conflicts among associated public defenders ("The rules on imputed conflicts and screening of this Section apply to a public defender organization as they do to a law firm in private practice in a similar situation," RESTATEMENT 3D OF THE LAW GOVERNING LAWYERS § 123, Comment d(iv)), and notes that, absent informed consent from all affected clients, a lawyer in a criminal matter is prohibited from representing "two or more defendants or potential defendants in the same matter" or "a single defendant, if the representation would involve a conflict of interest." Id., §129. It is difficult to imagine that any modern court would sanction a single lawyer's representation of multiple criminal co-defendants with interests as divergent as those of Preston and the soldiers.

Modern rules regarding conflicts of interest are grounded in the lawyer's duty of undivided loyalty to each client he represents and the lawyer's obligation to safeguard confidential client information. See Chapter 11 on Confidentiality. They address the obvious conflict of interest that would arise if a lawyer represented opposing parties in the same matter. They also address other situations in which a lawyer's professional independence or the lawyer's ability to honor his duty of loyalty to an existing or former client may be compromised.

Many relationships and circumstances can give rise to actual or potential conflicts of interest. Conflicts may arise directly, for example, as a result of a lawyer's representation of two current clients, a current client and a former client, a current client and a prospective client, or a prospective client and a former client. Conflicts may arise indirectly, too, when an individual lawyer's conflict is imputed to other lawyers associated in practice with that lawyer. In other words, sometimes a conflict for one lawyer is a conflict for her law firm colleagues as well. Finally, conflicts may arise between the interests of a client and the personal or financial interests of the lawyer. As law firms have grown larger, as lawyers have become more mobile, and as liberalized joinder rules have produced more cases involving multiple litigants, the frequency of conflicts of interest has increased.

Some conflicts of interest can be resolved by obtaining the "informed consent" of the affected client(s). Securing a client's informed consent to representation burdened by a conflict requires explanation of the risks posed by the conflict and the choices presented. Once fully advised, clients can waive such conflicts. Other conflicts are so serious that they cannot be resolved by obtaining waivers; these conflicts preclude representation of one or more clients.

Violation of conflicts rules can have serious repercussions for both lawyers and clients. In fact, conflicts of interest are among the most common grounds for disqualification motions and civil malpractice suits by clients against their attorneys and give rise to many habeas corpus petitions asserting ineffective assistance of counsel claims under the sixth and fourteenth amendments to the United States Constitution.

The majority of allegations of conflicts violations play out in disqualification motions, habeas petitions, and civil suits asserting claims sounding in professional negligence. Some conflicts violations—most often those that involve lawyers' taking advantage of clients, whether in business transactions or other relationships—result in professional discipline.[5] Violation of specialized conflicts rules can expose lawyers to significant financial penalties as well.

A particularly painful example of the latter involved Spencer Barasch, the former head of enforcement for the Fort Worth Office of the Securities and Exchange Commission (SEC), who left government service for private practice in 2005. Without SEC consent, Barasch later represented Stanford Financial Group in a matter before the SEC, despite having had substantial involvement in the Stanford Financial Group investigation while at the SEC. As a result, Barasch himself became the subject of an SEC and Justice Department investigation, for alleged violation of federal conflicts of interest rules. The NEW YORK TIMES reported on April 13, 2012 that Barasch had billed Stanford Financial Group approximately $6500 for the legal work that gave rise to the civil enforcement action. According to a Justice Department press release issued the same day, Barasch settled the conflicts allegation—without admitting any wrongdoing—by agreeing to pay a $50,000 fine, the maximum civil penalty for violation of the federal conflict of interest rules.

Lawyers' conflicts can be costly for clients as well. For example, in the ten months between former Democratic Presidential candidate John Edwards' 2011 indictment on charges that he violated federal campaign finance laws and his trial on those charges in April 2012, eleven attorneys represented him. Only four, though, emerged from the blizzard of conflicts challenges that each new appearance generated to sit with him in court as his trial began.[6]

Being required to begin again—and sometimes again and again—with new lawyers when a conflict of interest surfaces is understandably difficult for clients facing criminal charges or litigating civil claims. Few relish having to change proverbial horses in the middle of storm-swollen streams. Ironically, though, clients facing criminal charges that carry prison sentences—even indigent clients—are among the more fortunate where conflicts are concerned, for "[w]here a constitutional right to counsel exists, our Sixth Amendment cases hold that there is a correlative right to representation that is free from conflicts of interest." *Wood v. Georgia*, 450 U.S. 261, 271, 101 S. Ct. 1097, 67 L. Ed. 2d 220 (1981) (citations omitted). The consequences of conflicts for clients in the civil legal services context are often far more dire. For an indigent client, the civil legal services lawyer who must decline or terminate representation because of a conflict of interest may well be the last lawyer in town.[7]

The Devil Is in the Details

Conflicts of interest issues, like most issues of lawyers' professional responsibility, generally do not arrive neatly packaged and labeled with the operative facts set out in orderly fashion as they might be in an appellate opinion or law school examination. Far more often, conflicts are buried in case files archived in storage facilities and on law firm servers, within reams of documents produced in discovery, or on witness lists shared by opposing counsel, sometimes only shortly before trial.

In order to become adept at recognizing, avoiding, and resolving conflicts, students first must master the conflicts rules, which are among the most complex of the Rules of Professional Conduct. The reality that so many requests for guidance on conflicts issues reach state bar ethics committees comes as no surprise to anyone who has tried to navigate these challenging ethical waters. A single conflicts rule, Rule 1.7, which—in just two paragraphs—sets forth the general provisions governing concurrent conflicts, requires no fewer than 35 paragraphs of explanatory and illustrative commentary for clarification.

Although nearly all state ethics codes follow the ABA Model Rules format, most state rules vary to some degree from the Model Rules, and those state rules govern lawyer's professional conduct in each jurisdiction. The divergence among conflicts provisions is particularly notable. See THE ABA CENTER FOR PROFESSIONAL RESPONSIBILITY *State Rules Comparison Charts*, http://www.americanbar.org/groups/professional_responsibility/policy/rule_charts.html.

Lawyers practicing in federal, state, county, or municipal offices or agencies (e.g., the SEC, the office of the state attorney general, the office of the city attorney, or the department of children and families) face additional professional responsibilities. They must comply with the ethics codes of general application in their jurisdictions, and also with the particular rules—including the conflicts rules—that govern lawyers working in those settings. See, e.g., N.Y. General Municipal Law §§ 809–809, Conflicts of Interest of Municipal Officers and Employees, available at https://www.osc.state.ny.us/localgov/pubs/gmlposter.pdf (last visited April 8, 2015), and Supplemental Standards of Ethical Conduct for Members and Employees of the Securities and Exchange Commission, 5 C.F.R. § 4401, http://www.gpo.gov/fdsys/pkg/CFR-2012-title5-vol3/pdf/

CFR-2012-title5-vol3-part4401.pdf (last visited April 8, 2015). All students who plan to seek bar admission in a U.S. jurisdiction need to master the conflicts provisions in that jurisdiction. Students enrolled in international externship programs and assigned to work with lawyers in countries other than their own must also become familiar with the conflicts provisions, both general and particularized, that govern the lawyers and non-lawyer assistants in their host jurisdictions and at their placement sites.[8]

In sum, although the focus here and in the other ethics chapters in this text is on the Model Rules provisions,[9] mastery of the Model Rules will not be enough to ensure the ethical competence required by Rule 1.1. Rather, externs must become familiar with the conflicts rules in force in the jurisdictions in which their externship placements are located, as well as any additional rules of particular application to lawyers in the practice settings in which they work.

The Rules Governing Conflicts of Interests

Rules 1.7 through 1.12, Rule 6.5, and parts of Rule 1.18 set forth the requirements governing conflicts of interest. As mentioned in previous chapters, the American Bar Association maintains a copyright on its Model Rules and imposes strict restrictions for their quotation. Unless otherwise noted, quotations in this book are to the Delaware Rules, which are almost identical to the Model Rules, and any differences in text are noted. Rule 1.7 addresses concurrent representation conflicts, which are conflicts between two current clients, one current client and one prospective client, or a current or prospective client and the lawyer's personal interests or duties to third parties. Rule 1.8 addresses conflicts that may arise in other situations in which the lawyer's personal interests and a client's interests may differ, such as when a lawyer and a client become business partners. Conflicts between duties to current and former clients are addressed in Rule 1.9. Rule 1.10 prohibits lawyers from representing clients if other members of their firms have conflicts that are imputed to them. Rule 1.11 addresses conflicts that involve government lawyers, offering guidance for lawyers who leave government practice to work in the private sector and vice versa.

Rule 1.12 prohibits lawyers who formerly served as judges, mediators, arbitrators, and judicial law clerks, from representing clients who appeared before them, unless they receive informed consent from all parties involved.

Rule 1.18 addresses conflicts arising from a lawyer's duty of confidentiality to prospective clients who do not subsequently become clients.

Finally, Rule 6.5 establishes significantly relaxed conflicts-checking obligations and limits imputation of conflicts when lawyers participate in nonprofit or court-annexed limited legal services programs.

All of the conflicts rules serve the overarching goal of promoting public confidence in the outcomes produced by our judicial system. We will consider each of these rules in turn.

Concurrent Conflicts

▪ *Rule 1.7: Conflict of Interest: Current Clients*

Rule 1.7 outlines a number of circumstances that give rise to concurrent conflicts of interest and establishes the conditions upon which representation may continue notwithstanding the existence of such a conflict.

> (a) Except as provided in paragraph (b), a lawyer shall not represent a client if the representation involves a concurrent conflict of interest. A concurrent conflict of interest exists if:
>
> > (1) the representation of one client will be directly adverse to another client; or
> >
> > (2) there is a significant risk that the representation of one or more clients will be materially limited by the lawyer's responsibilities to another client, a former client or a third person or by a personal interest of the lawyer.
>
> (b) Notwithstanding the existence of a concurrent conflict of interest under paragraph (a), a lawyer may represent a client if:
>
> > (1) the lawyer reasonably believes that the lawyer will be able to provide competent and diligent representation to each affected client;
> >
> > (2) the representation is not prohibited by law;
> >
> > (3) the representation does not involve the assertion of a claim by one client against another client represented by the lawyer in the same litigation or other proceeding before a tribunal; and
> >
> > (4) each affected client gives informed consent, confirmed in writing.

▪ *Rule 1.8: Conflict of Interest: Current Clients: Specific Rules*

Rule 1.8 expands upon Rule 1.7(a)(2)'s prohibition of representation where a lawyer's own interests will affect adversely the lawyer's ability to provide competent, diligent representation to a client. It governs, for example, where a lawyer enters into business transaction with a client, such as a loan or a sales transaction, including the sale of law-related goods or services, such as the sale of title insurance to a real estate client and the purchase of property from an estate the lawyer represents. Rule 1.8 Comment 1. The rule's safeguards work to ensure that a lawyer's superior knowledge and bargaining power will not give the lawyer an unfair advantage in such a transaction.

Rule 1.8 also identifies a number of other circumstances in which a transaction or relationship may compromise a lawyer's duty of loyalty and independent professional judgment. This includes, for example, situations where a third party—such as an employer or an insurer operating under a duty to defend— pays the lawyer's fee for representing the client, or where a lawyer contemplates beginning a sexual relationship with a client. In some such cases, Rule 1.8 restricts the lawyer's conduct, for instance, by requiring informed client consent,[10] recommending or requiring that the client secure independent representation in connection with the transaction,[11] or both. In others, it imposes an outright ban on the transaction or relationship.[12]

▪ *Rule 1.12: Former Judge, Arbitrator, Mediator, or Other Third-Party Neutral*

Rule 1.12(b) addresses a final set of circumstances in which a lawyer's personal interests may conflict with her professional obligations—the obligations a lawyer undertakes as a neutral. Absent informed consent from all parties, confirmed in writing, the rule prohibits a lawyer "serving as a judge or other adjudicative officer or as an arbitrator, mediator or other third-party neutral" from negotiating for employment with a party in a matter in which the lawyer, as neutral, is "participating personally and substantially." It does permit "[a] lawyer serving as a law clerk to a judge or other adjudicative officer [to] negotiate for employment with a party or lawyer involved in a matter in which the clerk is participating personally and substantially" without informed consent of the parties, "but only after the lawyer [serving as a law clerk] has notified the judge, or other adjudicative officer."

Successive Representation Conflicts

■ *Rule 1.9: Duties to Former Clients*

Rule 1.9 addresses situations in which lawyers' responsibilities to former clients conflict or may conflict with their responsibilities to current or prospective clients. In doing so, it endeavors to balance a number competing interests and duties: the lawyer's duty of loyalty to both former and current clients, the former client's interest in the ongoing protection of confidential information, the current client's interest in representation by counsel of his choosing, and the lawyer's interest in professional mobility.

Note that while Rule 1.9 guides the analysis of such a conflict with respect to former clients, Rule 1.7 guides the analysis with respect to current or prospective clients. Rule 1.7, which addresses concurrent conflicts, is "client-based": it prohibits representation adverse to a current client—even in a wholly unrelated matter—without informed consent, confirmed in writing, from all affected clients. Rule 1.9, by contrast, is "matter-based": absent informed consent, confirmed in writing, from the affected former client, it prohibits representation adverse to that former client only in matters that are "the same as or substantially related to" a matter in which the lawyer represented the former client, and only where the new client's interests are "materially adverse" to those of the former client.

Rule 1.9(b) limits the circumstances under which lawyers who leave a firm take the firm's conflicts with them to situations in which departing lawyers themselves have acquired confidential information material to a matter that is the same as, or substantially related to, a matter in which the former firm provided representation to a client. It provides as follows:

> (b) [a] lawyer shall not knowingly represent a person in the same or a substantially related matter in which a firm with which the lawyer formerly was associated had previously represented a client
>
> > (1) whose interests are materially adverse to that person; and
> >
> > (2) about whom the lawyer had acquired information protected by Rules 1.6 and 1.9(c) that is material to the matter[,]
>
> unless the former client gives informed consent, confirmed in writing.

Rule 1.9(c) requires all lawyers to protect the confidences of former clients. A lawyer may not use such information to the disadvantage of the former client or reveal such information unless permitted to do so by the rules.

■ *Rule 1.12: Former Judge, Arbitrator, Mediator or Other Third-Party Neutral*

Rule 1.12(a), too, addresses successive-representation conflicts, specifically prohibiting lawyers from undertaking client representation in "a matter in which the lawyer participated personally or substantially as a judge or other adjudicative officer or law clerk to such a person or as an arbitrator, mediator, or other third-party neutral" without the informed consent of all parties, confirmed in writing.

Imputed Conflicts

■ *Rule 1.10: Imputation of Conflicts of Interest: General Rule*

Rule 1.10, the general imputed conflicts rule, makes lawyers' conflicts "contagious" in some circumstances. Comment 2 explains that the rule flows from two related premises: first, that lawyers working together in a firm (see Rule 1.0(c)) are "essentially one lawyer for purposes of the rules governing loyalty to the client," and second, "that each lawyer is vicariously bound by the obligation of loyalty owed by each lawyer with whom the lawyer is associated." The rule also assumes that lawyers who work together, for example, in a legal aid office, private law firm, or government law office, ordinarily have access to confidential information regarding every matter in which any lawyer associated with the office is involved. Whether they are "essentially one lawyer," or "vicariously bound" by their colleagues' obligations of loyalty to their clients, all lawyers associated with the office are obliged to safeguard that information.

Rule 1.10(a), therefore, imputes the conflict of one lawyer to all of the other lawyers associated in the office,[13] prohibiting all of them from

> knowingly represent[ing] a client when any one of them practicing alone would be prohibited from doing so by Rules 1.7 or 1.9, unless the prohibition is based on a personal interest of the prohibited lawyer and does not present a significant risk of materially limiting the representation of the client by the remaining lawyers in the firm.

Comment 4 following Rule 1.10 offers at least some comfort to legal externs; it notes that paragraph (a) of the rule does not bar representation if the lawyer is prohibited from acting because of events before the person became a lawyer, for example, work that the person did while a law student. Such persons, however, ordinarily must be screened from any personal participation in the matter to avoid communication to others in the firm of confidential information that both the non-lawyers and the firm have a legal duty to protect.

This comment suggests that, in most instances, a lawyer may resolve successive-representation conflicts acquired during an externship semester by screening, without notice to or consent from the affected former client.

Preventing the imputation of conflicts when lawyers move between firms is somewhat more complicated. After a number of unsuccessful attempts to persuade the ABA House of Delegates to bless screening to prevent the imputation of conflicts when lawyers change jobs, proponents of a rule change to that effect finally prevailed in 2009, when the House voted first to amend Model Rule 1.10 to permit screening without client consent (February 2009) and subsequently to clarify that the new screening provision applies only to lawyers moving between firms (August 2009). Per Model Rule 1.10, as amended, laterally transitioning lawyers can prevent the imputation of conflicts to colleagues at a new firm as long as the incoming lawyer is "timely screened from any participation in the matter" and "apportioned no part of the fee therefrom[.]" Model Rule 1.10(a)(2)(i). However, such screening will be effective only if, per paragraphs (a) (2)(ii) and (iii) of the Rule,

> (ii) written notice is promptly given to any affected former client to enable the former client to ascertain compliance with the provisions of [the] Rule, which shall include a description of the screening procedures employed; a statement of the firm's and of the screened lawyer's compliance with these Rules; a statement that review may be available before a tribunal; and an agreement by the firm to respond promptly to any written inquiries or objections by the former client about the screening procedures; and

> (iii) certifications of compliance with these Rules and with the screening procedures are provided to the former client by the screened lawyer and by a partner of the firm, at reasonable intervals upon the former client's written request and upon termination of the screening procedures.

Conflicts Rules for Government Lawyers

- *Rule 1.11: Special Conflicts of Interest for Former and Current Government Officers and Employees*

Rule 1.11 addresses conflicts encountered by lawyers moving between private and government practice. Although it expressly binds former government lawyers to Rule 1.9(c) and current government lawyers to Rules 1.7 and 1.9, in some respects it is less restrictive than the rules that apply to lawyers who move between other practice settings.

In the absence of informed consent from the appropriate government agency, Rule 1.11(a) prohibits a former government lawyer from representing a client "in connection with a matter in which the lawyer participated personally and substantially as a public officer or employee." Rule 1.11(b), however, permits the former government lawyer's firm to undertake representation of such a party without consent of the government client, as long as

(1) the disqualified lawyer is timely screened from any participation in the matter and is apportioned no part of the fee therefrom; and

(2) written notice is promptly given to the appropriate government agency to enable it to ascertain compliance with the provisions of this rule.

Rule 1.11(c) bars a former government lawyer from representing a client if the lawyer, in the course of the representation, could make use of confidential information that the lawyer acquired about a person while in government service to the material disadvantage of that person. A former U.S. Attorney, for example, could not undertake representation in which she could make adverse use of information acquired during a criminal investigation. Rule 1.11(c), however, approves of screening to prevent the vicarious disqualification of other lawyers in a former government lawyer's firm under these circumstances.

Rule 1.11(d) prohibits a current government lawyer from "participating in a matter in which the lawyer participated personally and substantially while in private practice or nongovernmental employment . . ." unless the relevant agency consents.

An extern who is engaged in federal or state government service, including executive, judicial, or legislative placements, or who hopes to work in a government practice setting after graduation needs to pay particular attention to the iteration of Rule 1.11 in force in the relevant jurisdiction, as well as any other statutory or regulatory conflicts provisions that apply to lawyers or non-lawyer assistants while they work in those settings and after they leave government employment.

Potential Conflicts

The rules that govern conflicts situations apply to actual conflicts of interest, meaning conflicts that exist at present or will exist from the outset if a lawyer undertakes representation of a particular prospective client and also to conflicts that may arise in the course of representing a prospective client. Whether a lawyer may undertake representation despite a potential conflict depends on the likelihood that a conflict will materialize in the future, and on how adversely the conflict could affect the representation. A lawyer who faces a potential conflict and concludes that such representation is permissible may proceed with the representation, but only after receiving informed consent from all affected clients.

Positional Conflicts

Comment 24 following Rule 1.7 addresses another category of conflicts of interests: conflicts that arise where

> there is a significant risk that a lawyer's action on behalf of one client will materially limit the lawyer's effectiveness in representing another client in a different case; for example, when a decision favoring one client will create a precedent likely to seriously weaken the position taken on behalf of the other client.

Such conflicts, referred to in ethical shorthand as "positional conflicts," can arise if a lawyer accepts representation that will require the lawyer to make an argument on behalf of one client to a particular tribunal and shortly thereafter make a contrary argument to the same tribunal on behalf of another client.

Very few situations in which lawyers propose to advocate in different settings on behalf of clients with conflicting interests give rise to authentic Rule 1.7 concerns. However—notwithstanding Rule 1.2(b)'s assurance that "[a] lawyer's representation of a client, including representation by appointment, does not constitute an endorsement of the client's political, economic, social, or moral views or activities"—some clients may perceive a conflict and therefore strongly object to activities plainly permitted by the rule. Even if the representation does not violate Rule 1.7, a lawyer needs to address such client concerns as a matter of good client relations.

For example, Rule 1.7 would not prohibit a lawyer who represents a business client in its environmental matters before state and federal regulatory bodies from engaging in advocacy in a different forum on an issue unrelated to the client's environmental matters. However, if the activity involves an issue about which the client has strong, opposing views, and the client learns of the lawyer's involvement on the "other side" of the issue, the client could decide to take its legal business elsewhere, rendering any Rule 1.7 blessing irrelevant.

In one particularly troubling example of an attempt to persuade corporate clients to use this sort of economic leverage over their lawyers to pressure them to abandon politically unpopular clients, Charles D. Stimson, then Deputy Assistant Secretary of Defense in charge of military detainees suspected of terrorist activities, said during a January 11, 2007 interview on Federal News Radio that the fact that lawyers from many of the country's major law firms were representing prisoners at Guantanamo Bay, Cuba, was "shocking." He went on to name more than a dozen of the firms included in a report provided to him by a conservative talk show host, and then opined, "I think, quite honestly, when corporate [C.E.O.s] see that those firms are representing the very terrorists who hit their bottom line back in 2001, those [C.E.O.s] are going to make those law firms choose between representing terrorists or representing reputable firms . . . ."

An outraged profession reacted swiftly and vocally to condemn Stimson's remarks. Commentary appeared in newspapers, periodicals, and online forums, and as of January 16, 2007, more than 130 law school deans had signed a statement decrying any encouragement by government officials in a free and democratic society of "intimidation of or retaliation against lawyers who are discharging their professional obligation to provide pro bono representation" and "urg[ing] the Administration promptly and unequivocally to repudiate Stimson's remarks." *Statement of Law Deans Concerning Stimson Remarks*, BALKINIZATION (January 17, 2007 2:05 p.m.), http://balkin.blogspot.com/2007/01/statement-of-law-deans-concerning.html. Within three weeks, Stimson had resigned. Thankfully, this story had a positive ending, albeit not for Stimson. The episode also serves as an important reminder of the professional and personal risks sometimes undertaken by lawyers who represent unpopular clients or causes and also of the U.S. legal profession's strong commitment to equal access to justice and embrace of its pro bono obligations.

Relaxed Conflicts Provisions for Lawyers in Certain Limited Legal Service Programs

Some externship programs assign students to work with lawyers in nonprofit or court-annexed legal services organizations that provide short-term, limited-scope representation to clients in their communities, e.g., elder-law clinics held weekly or monthly in area senior centers, family-law clinics held in space provided by libraries or community centers, or temporary restraining order assistance programs based at local courthouses. Externs assigned to such placements need to pay careful attention to Rule 6.5, which governs the conflicts analysis in these settings.

- *Rule 6.5: Nonprofit and Court-Annexed Limited Legal Services Programs*

Added to the Model Rules of Professional Conduct in 2002, Rule 6.5, exempts a lawyer working in nonprofit and court-annexed limited legal services programs from certain of the provisions of Rules 1.7, 1.9, and 1.10, unless the lawyer "knows" either that the representation involves a conflict of interest for the lawyer (Rule 6.5 (a)(1)) or "that another lawyer associated with the lawyer in a law firm is disqualified by Rule 1.7 or Rule 1.9(a) with respect to the matter." Rule 6.5(a)(2). Per paragraph (b) of the Rule, "except as provided by paragraph (a)(2), Rule 1.10 is inapplicable to representation governed by [Rule 6.5]."

The Comment to Rule 6.5 explains the rationale behind the relaxed conflicts provisions: first, a recognition that "[s]uch programs are normally operated under circumstances in which it is not feasible for a lawyer to systematically screen for conflicts of interest as is generally required before undertaking a representation" (Rule 6.5, Comment (1)), and second, a recognition that "the limited nature of the services significantly reduces the risk of conflicts of interest with other matters being handled by the firm." Rule 6.5, Comment (4). Consequently, again per Comment (4) "a lawyer's participation in a short-term legal services program will not preclude the lawyer's firm from undertaking or continuing the representation of a client adverse to a client being represented under the program's auspices. Nor will the personal disqualification of a lawyer participating in the program be imputed to other lawyers participating in the program."

Duties Arising from Consultations with Prospective Clients

- *Rule 1.18: Duties to Prospective Clients*

Rule 1.18 addresses a final category of conflicts—those arising from consultations about the possibility of forming a lawyer-client relationship with prospective clients who ultimately do not become clients. The rule prohibits both the use of information obtained by the lawyer in that context, "except as Rule 1.9 would permit with respect to information of a former client." Rule 1.18(b). Where that information could be significantly harmful to the prospective client in a particular matter, it also prohibits the representation of a client with interests materially adverse to the prospective client's interests in that matter. Rule 1.18(c). Rule 1.18(c) also imputes the disqualified lawyer's conflict to other associated lawyers, though Rule 1.18(d) permits representation in such matters with informed, written consent from both the affected client and the prospective client (Rule 1.18(d)(1)), or if the conditions set out in Rule 1.18(d)(2) are met.

The Usual Suspects: Common Conflicts Scenarios in the Externship Context

We turn now to a discussion of the conflicts that students are most likely to encounter while participating in externships. Conflicts related to an extern's prior, current, or future legal employment, or her personal views or activities, may arise early on during the application process. Suppose, for example, that a law student is considering an externship with a judge who is presiding in a murder case in which the prosecutor is seeking the death penalty. Suppose the student is a vehement opponent of the death penalty and a regular participant in demonstrations and vigils at the prison where the defendant is incarcerated during trial. This law reform work might affect the extern's ability to work on the matter or might create an impermissible appearance of impropriety for the prospective supervising judge.

Conflicts also can arise during the externship semester or after the semester ends. For instance, a conflict might arise in connection with an extern's legal work at a placement, during discussions in a seminar, in journal entries submitted for teacher review, or when a former extern seeks employment or pursues pro bono activities.

Conflicts of Interest in the Externship Placement Process

The avoidance or resolution of conflicts of interest identified during the placement process and prior to the externship will govern whether a student will be able to work in a particular placement. As Comment 3, Rule 1.7 explains, "[a] conflict of interest may exist before representation is undertaken, in which event the representation must be declined, unless the lawyer obtains the informed consent of each client under [certain] conditions." Some conflicts may be fairly obvious. For example, it is unlikely that a law student employed part-time as a social worker for the Department of Children and Families could extern at a legal services organization that has filed a lawsuit against the Department. Other conflicts are harder to detect. For example, even a careful conflicts inventory may not disclose that a client on whose family matter a student worked extensively as a summer law intern at a legal services office will be a witness against a client represented by a prospective externship supervisor in an eviction proceeding. Identifying and avoiding or resolving all such conflicts, though, is imperative.

Externship programs vary considerably in their application requirements and placement procedures. Some programs encourage or require eligible students to find their own placements. Others place students at established placements in law offices or judges' chambers. Still others arrange interviews for students at pre-approved placements, with faculty supervisors matching selected students to placements based on the outcome of those interviews.

Where students arrange their own placements, the responsibility for identifying and avoiding or resolving conflicts falls primarily on supervising attorneys and externs. If the externship teacher or administrator makes placement decisions, she plays a significant conflicts-checking role. In every circumstance, identifying and avoiding or resolving existing and potential conflicts is essential. Doing so protects clients and spares all of the externship players the time, distress, and embarrassment of dealing with later-discovered conflicts that could have been detected and addressed before the semester began.

> **Exercise 12.1** In preparation for participation in your law school's externship program, conduct a conflicts inventory of your own. A form for this purpose is provided as Appendix 12.1 to this chapter. List your previous employers, legal and non-legal, paid and volunteer positions, as well as all of the business and legal matters, whether litigation-related or transactional, in which you have had substantial personal involvement at each of your previous jobs. Suppose, for example, you worked part-time last year at a law firm. You need to include on your list any matters on which you did enough work that you learned some client confidences.
>
> For each matter you list, include the names of all of the parties involved. For example, if you worked at a small company before beginning law school, and that

company merged with another company—whether before or after you left—include in your inventory your employer, the company with which it merged, and the new entity. Remember what Jamie's experience teaches. Ordinary business transactions sometimes evolve or devolve into legal disputes. Corporate acquisitions may go off track. Sellers may have second thoughts or buyers may be seized by remorse. Creditors in a bankruptcy proceeding may mount retrospective "fraudulent transfer" challenges to the sale of business assets, even though the transactions at issue may have raised no red flags at all prior to the bankruptcy filing.

Include in your inventory all of your organizational memberships, for example, in the Sierra Club, the National Rifle Association, the Boy Scouts, or Students for Choice. List, too, any other responsibilities, associations, activities, and/or strong personal views that could give rise to conflicts: "I work weekends as a per diem registered nurse, so I am a mandated reporter of child abuse and neglect"; "My wife is a lawyer who appears in federal court in this jurisdiction"; "I own three national sandwich-shop franchises in my home state"; "I could never be a zealous advocate on behalf of a defendant if I believed she intentionally harmed a child."

Discuss your completed inventory with your externship teacher and prospective supervising attorneys during the externship placement process. Update it as your externship semester progresses. Make careful notes on the matters in which you are involved at your placement. Keep your inventory handy, though not accessible to others, for it almost certainly will contain confidential client information. You will need to update it during your externship semester and refer to it as you search for post-externship legal employment.

Concurrent Representation Conflicts

Among the conflicts that students involved in externships must identify and avoid or resolve are concurrent representation conflicts. For example, because the state—the "client" of every extern in a prosecutorial placement—is an adverse party to every defendant facing criminal charges in a particular jurisdiction, a student who works in a part-time job at a local criminal defense firm during his externship semester almost certainly will be barred from working as an extern at the local office of that jurisdiction's district attorney.

This extern cannot accept a prosecution placement unless he can avoid or resolve the actual or imputed conflicts that would result from his contemporaneous law firm employment during the externship semester. Although Rule 1.7(a)(2) and (b)(2) establish client consent as a means for resolving concurrent conflicts, consent is unlikely to be available here. The student's desire to work for the prosecutor probably would make the clients of the criminal defense firm worry about the student's loyalties. Those doubts would undermine the clients' trust in the student and therefore materially—and thus impermissibly—limit the student's ability to provide them with competent representation.

In this instance, the extern can avoid the concurrent conflicts by declining the prosecution externship placement or by giving up the part-time job at the law office. However, even if the student elects to avoid the concurrent conflicts by giving up his part-time job, he and his fieldwork supervisor will have to be alert to any successive representation conflicts the student may bring to the prosecution placement by virtue of his previous employment.

> **Exercise 12.2** Steven has applied for an externship at the District Attorney's Office. He has been working for the past year at a family law firm in the jurisdiction and plans to continue his part-time job at the firm while he is participating in the externship. He does not believe that this plan presents any conflicts issues because his firm does not represent clients in criminal matters. Is Steven correct? Explain your conclusion.

Consider another example of a possible concurrent conflict. Suppose a law student working at the public defender's office has applied for a contemporaneous externship with a judge who hears criminal cases in the public defender's jurisdiction. The extern would not be representing clients with conflicting interests because, as a judicial extern, the student would not be representing clients at all. Yet her duties to the supervising judge could conflict with her duties to clients represented by the public defender. Suppose, though, this extern is screened at both practice settings from involvement in public defender cases assigned to her supervising judge. Would screening resolve the conflicts? Perhaps not, because the student's ex parte access to a judge who presides over cases litigated by the public defender's office might give rise to an appearance of impropriety of the sort banned by the Code of Judicial Conduct. See Model Code of Judicial Conduct, Canon 2. In view of the student's conflict, the prosecutor's office might even request that the judge recuse herself from all cases in which the public defender's office has a role.

Suppose another extern seeks placement with a judge who currently is presiding over a case in which the student's spouse, partner, or other close family member is representing one of the parties, or with a judge who will preside over a case in which the a party is represented by lawyers at the student's current or future employer. Although screening might resolve some such conflicts, these conflicts generally will not be apparent from a student's resume. Consequently, the student must bring them to the attention of her teacher and supervisor.

Externship participants also must identify and avoid or resolve a final subset of concurrent conflicts—positional conflicts—during the externship placement process. Consider the dilemma presented in the scenario that follows:

Exercise 12.3 Adrienne, a 3L enrolled in a fall term externship program, has been volunteering for almost a year at a not-for-profit legal services organization that advocates on behalf of clients with psychiatric diagnoses. Of particular concern to the organization and some members of the population it serves is a restrictive new gun control law enacted by the state legislature in response to a horrific school shooting in a small town in the northwestern corner of the state. The shooter, who had lived in the community since childhood, had a long history of mental illness. The new legislation prohibits ownership and possession of certain classes of firearms and all high-capacity ammunition clips and requires a satisfactory background check as a condition of the issuance of any gun permit. It denies gun permits to any person convicted of a felony and any person who is the subject of a criminal or civil restraining order and requires any police officer who serves a restraining order immediately to confiscate all weapons registered to or in the possession of the person who is the subject of the order. The law also denies gun permits to any person with a medical history that includes certain mental health diagnoses, including schizophrenia.

Over her second-year summer, Adrienne worked extensively on a brief that the organization has since filed in the state appellate court on behalf of a client who was denied a permit to own a firearm based on a thirty-day hospitalization for a schizophrenic episode following his ingestion of LSD in 1996. Among the issues on appeal is whether the new law's restriction on gun ownership based on psychiatric diagnoses violates the right to bear arms articulated in the second amendment to the United States Constitution. Adrienne's supervisor credited her as "law student intern on the brief" in acknowledgment of her significant contribution to the final product. Adrienne has committed to continue volunteering at the organization, at least until she graduates from law school in the spring.

Because she is interested in working for the government after graduation, Adrienne has applied for an externship placement at the state Attorney General's Office. She receives a phone call inviting her to interview for a position in the unit that represents the state's Department of Youth Services. Adrienne does not disclose her association with the advocacy organization during her interview with her prospective externship supervisor. She sees her pro bono work as purely a personal matter, unrelated to the work she will do as an extern at the AG's Office. Adrienne's interview goes well; her placement is confirmed.

When the externship semester begins, the legal services client's case is still pending before the appellate court, with oral argument scheduled for mid-December. In late September, Adrienne's supervising attorney calls her into his office to give her a new assignment. He tells her that he would like her to begin work on an amicus brief the Department will file in a case brought by five members of the local chapter of the NRA to challenge the constitutionality of the state's new gun control law. Her supervisor says that even before the tragedy three years ago, the Department was well aware of the risks posed to children and families when firearms are readily available in their homes, particularly when anyone with access to them is mentally unstable. In fact, the Commissioner of Youth Services testified before the legislature in support of the bill after it was introduced and wants the Department to do all that it can to make sure none of its provisions are overturned. The case has just reached the state appellate court.

Reread Rule 1.7 and Rule 1.10 and their respective comments. Identify the provisions that are relevant in this scenario. List all of the actual or potential conflicts of interest that Adrienne's concurrent activities present. How might these conflicts cause problems for Adrienne, for the advocacy organization and its lawyers, for the Division of Youth Services and its lawyers, for the externship program, and for Adrienne's externship teacher? Would the situation be any different if Adrienne had contributed research and drafting assistance on the brief challenging the new law, but her supervisor at the advocacy organization had not acknowledged her as contributing to the brief? If the appellate court already had heard oral argument and taken supplemental briefs on the case? If it already had ruled on the case?

What steps could Adrienne, her supervising attorney, or both, have taken to identify and avoid or resolve Adrienne's conflicts during the placement process? What policies and procedures should the externship teacher or the administrator of an externship program implement to help avoid the kind of dilemma in which the parties in the problem find themselves?

Finally, what would you advise Adrienne to do now?

Successive Representation Conflicts

Actual or potential successive representation conflicts often come to light during the externship placement process because many externs come to an externship with at least one summer's legal work experience. Because a lawyer's duty of loyalty runs both to current clients and to former clients, an extern's prior legal experience may give rise to a conflict with respect to the clients of the extern's prospective placement.

Rule 1.9 allows resolution of some successive conflicts by obtaining informed consent from the former client. Even without the consent of the former client, a law student whose previous legal employment includes a summer at a local law firm may accept an externship placement at a nonprofit organization that represents a client who is adverse to a client of the law firm in a matter that is the same as or substantially related to a matter in which the student was involved during her summer at the firm. She may do so, however, only if the advocacy organization timely screens her from any involvement in the matter, and both she and the advocacy organization are careful to safeguard all confidential information she acquired during her former employment. See Rule 1.10, Comment 4.

Likewise, because externs are law students, where an extern previously has worked in a general practice firm and subsequently applies for an externship placement in an in-house legal department at a corporation the firm opposes in litigation, any resulting conflicts may be resolved by screening. However, if an extern whose placement is in the in-house legal offices of a corporate client works concurrently at a general practice law firm, both the student and the lawyers at each office may be barred by Rules 1.7 and 1.10 from undertaking representation adverse to the clients of either practice without the informed consent of all affected clients.

> **Exercise 12.4** Rebecca has applied for an externship at the U.S. Attorney's Office. Last summer she worked as a summer associate at a law firm, and she has accepted an offer to return to the firm following graduation. Rebecca became interested in the position at the U.S. Attorney's Office after she observed an attorney from that office argue a motion in a case on which she was working for the firm. She is not sure if the case is still pending.
>
> May Rebecca work as an extern at the U.S. Attorney's Office? Explain your conclusion.

Conflicts of Interest That Arise During the Externship Semester

Even if a careful pre-placement conflicts check discloses no actual or potential conflicts, a conflict may arise after the student begins working at the externship site. These late-blooming conflicts might spring from an extern's activities at the placement, or they might involve the extern's participation in the academic component of the externship program.

Conflicts That Arise From Placement Activities

Perhaps the most frequent conflicts confronting law students involve those who work in two legal practice settings during a single semester. A student, for example, might have a paid job with one office and an externship at another. A careful pre-placement conflicts check may identify such conflicts, but a lawyer who supervises an extern who holds another legal position also must conduct ongoing cross-checks to identify conflicts that arise from the student's duties to clients of either office.

If a student works only on a single matter or a discrete set of matters at her job and has no access to confidential information about other matters, both the supervising attorney at the externship and the legal employer may be willing to assume this ongoing responsibility. If, however, a student proposes contemporaneous association with two law offices, checking for conflicts could be quite burdensome.

A student who works in only one practice setting during the externship semester also must be alert to conflicts. An extern placed at a prosecutor's office, for example, may be surprised to see the name of a classmate, relative, friend, or even law school faculty member, on the court docket at his placement. Worse still, the extern may receive an evening phone call from a friend or family member scheduled for a court appearance the next morning. If the caller knows that the extern is working in the prosecutor's office, he may be hoping that the student can use his influence to secure a reduction in a fine or a dismissal of a charge. In such a situation, the extern's perceived or actual responsibilities to the caller, or the friendship or family loyalty involved, is in conflict with the extern's duty as a member of the legal team at the prosecutor's office. The student must explain to the caller that it would be inappropriate for him to be involved and needs to consider reporting the contact to the supervising attorney.

In all such interactions, of course, the student must be mindful of the provisions of Rule 4.3 (lawyers' dealings with unrepresented persons) and Rule 3.8 (special responsibilities of prosecutors) and be alert to the dilemma that would result if, during the conversation, the caller discloses information that might incriminate the caller.

Another type of conflict could arise because of a mid-semester job search or an offer of part-time, summer, or post-graduation employment. As Rule 1.7, Comment 10 notes, "when a lawyer has discussions concerning possible employment with an opponent of the lawyer's client, or with a law firm representing the opponent, such discussions could materially limit the lawyer's representation of the client."

Rule 1.12(b), by contrast, expressly authorizes lawyers serving as law clerks to judges or other adjudicative officers to "negotiate for employment with a party or lawyer involved in a matter in which the clerk is participating personally and substantially, but only after the lawyer has notified the judge or other adjudicative officer." Students externing in other practice settings also should advise their supervisors of the particulars of ongoing job searches and of any job offers so that the supervisors can identify and remedy any potential conflicts.

Conflicts That Arise From Seminar Participation and Journaling

Participation in an externship seminar likewise may give rise to conflicts as externs working in diverse practice settings share observations about their placement experiences in seminar meetings, tutorials, or journal entries. These academic activities are among the defining features of externships, setting for-credit externships apart from most other "real world" legal experiences available to aspiring lawyers.

Although students learn much from conversations with seminar colleagues and exchanges with externship teachers, they must approach these activities with some caution to avoid discussion that would reveal confidences or create conflicts of interest. The extent to which students in an externship seminar may discuss client matters in class depends on the structure of the particular externship program.

In what some refer to as hybrid programs, all seminar participants work in the same off-campus placement under the direct supervision of a supervising attorney who also teaches the externship seminar. In such programs, all seminar participants are members of the same firm, and therefore can speak freely in class about confidential client matters.

In other programs, however, the students in an externship seminar work at a diverse array of placements. Two externs in such a seminar may work with lawyers who represent clients who are adversaries in litigation. Similarly, two students may be placed at organizations that take opposing positions in a public policy debate. May externs assigned to the local district attorney's office report on placement activities in a seminar attended by externs working in the public defender's office in the same courthouse? May an extern assigned to a national anti-death penalty advocacy organization participate in an externship seminar with students from a local district attorney's office if that office seeks the death penalty in selected cases? May an extern for a local federal judge participate in a seminar with students externing at the local Office of the United States Attorney? The answer is a resounding YES! With some careful attention, externship programs can manage these issues, and, in fact, students can benefit greatly from exposure to the ideas and experiences of students working on "the other side."

It is indeed the case that the general conflicts of interest rules prohibit a lawyer from representing a client if such representation will be directly adverse to another client and impute conflicts among lawyers practicing together. If the common seminar were a law firm, and if the students in the class were practicing together, the resulting conflicts might be insurmountable. But an externship seminar is not a law firm, so the participants in a common seminar do not, by virtue of their seminar participation, become part of the lawyering teams at one another's placements. Rather, as long as seminar participants take appropriate measures to safeguard confidential client and chambers information in discussions with teachers and classmates, they can avoid any potential ethical problems.

Most externship programs—even those with no seminar components—require students to submit journal entries about their field experience. These narratives may both reveal and give rise to conflicts of interest. For example, suppose a student is concerned about what he believes to be a serious violation of a rule of professional conduct by a supervisor and discusses that conduct in a journal entry submitted for teacher review. If the student asks for guidance as to his own ethical obligations in the situation, his journal entry may be protected as a confidential lawyer client communication.[14] Suppose, though, that the student does not ask for advice but makes this disclosure in reliance on his teacher's general assurance that she does not share student journal entries with others without student consent.

If the ethical breach is as serious as the student thinks it is, the conflict in this situation is apparent. The student's self-interest in completing the externship and securing a favorable reference from his supervisor conflicts with the duty to report lawyer misconduct set out in Rule 8.3.[15] Even if he may not be formally bound to comply with the rules, the student, soon to be admitted to practice, must grapple with this obligation. In addition, if the student's externship teacher is admitted to practice, the student's disclosure would give rise to a conflict between her promissory obligation to keep student journal entries confidential and her own professional reporting obligation under Rule 8.3.

Disclosures in journal entries also may give rise to conflicts and confidentiality concerns when teachers unexpectedly find themselves in possession of information about the strategies of parties opposed to one another in litigation. A student assigned to a busy, urban, prosecution placement, for instance, while taking care not to disclose what she believes might be identifying details about a case, may discuss in a journal entry her discomfort with her supervisor's decision to pursue very serious charges against a young, female defendant who has asserted a claim of self-defense in response to those charges. A student working in the public defender's office in the same jurisdiction may submit a journal entry recounting his discomfort with the "pushing the envelope" tactic his supervisor used midway through an initial interview to suggest what the student fears may be a baseless "battering-and-its-effects" defense to a young, female client who had made no mention of spousal abuse. ("I can't say yet what the prosecutor is thinking about this case, but I can tell you one thing: jurors don't like to convict a young woman like you of murdering her husband if we can convince them that the husband had it coming—that she didn't see any other way to get out of an abusive relationship.")

In this situation, even though both students have been careful not to disclose the defendant's name or anything more than broad characterizations of the case, the teacher may deduce that both students are working on the same matter. If the teacher is not admitted to practice in the jurisdiction, of course, she may not offer legal advice to either student without engaging in the unauthorized practice of law. If she is locally admitted, though, the question becomes whether she may assist either of her students as they struggle with the ethical issues presented by their case-in-common or whether, in doing so, she herself would be engaging in activity prohibited by Rule 1.7.

There are no easy answers in such challenging situations, yet externs and their teachers need to attend to and discuss these issues. They can work together to develop appropriate guidelines to ensure protection of placement information, both in the classroom and in journal entries.

> **Exercise 12.5** Tony and Sonja are enrolled in the same externship seminar. At the beginning of the semester, neither has selected a placement. Both interview for externships during the first week of classes. Tony accepts a position with the local Social Security Administration office. Sonja accepts a position in a disability rights advocacy organization that handles appeals for individuals with disabilities who are challenging the Social Security Administration's decisions denying their applications for disability benefits. Tony's and Sonja's law school requires that all externs participate in the externship seminar. This semester, there is only one section of the seminar.

During seminar meetings, the externs discuss various aspects of their experiences. Each student also is required to make a presentation about the student's placement and to turn in journals detailing placement activities and reflections on the externship experience.

What ethical issues are presented by the students' placement in offices that routinely are adversaries in litigation? Does their externship teacher need to restrict Tony and Sonja's discussions of their placement activities in the seminar? In their journal entries? Are any other special precautions required given their placements? If so, what precautions would you recommend, and why?

What if Tony is assigned to assist in the defense of a case in which Sonja is involved on behalf of the petitioner? How do they and their teacher need to handle this situation?

Externship Conflicts and the Post-Externship Job Search

Conflicts of interest issues related to externship participation may arise weeks, months, and even years after both the application process and the academic component of an externship program are over. The duty to protect the confidences of former clients is not extinguished when an externship ends but follows externs into all subsequent job searches. Whenever a former extern proposes to accept a new legal job, she must check for possible conflicts with previous legal employment, including externships. This task will be infinitely easier if each student keeps a careful list of the names of all client matters in which she was involved.

Exercise 12.6 Michael is a summer extern at the city law department. Michael's supervisor includes him in a series of meetings at which city lawyers discuss strategy for an ongoing case. His supervisor tells him that the litigation has been extraordinarily contentious and that the outcome is very important to the city government. In fact, the city views this lawsuit as the most significant problem that the city has faced in the last decade.

When the externship ends, Michael begins a job search and lists his externship experience on his resume. He participates in an on-campus interview with the law firm that represents the plaintiffs in the litigation involving his former placement, receives a job offer from the firm, and begins working part-time at the firm during the spring term of his third year, then full-time once the bar exam is behind him. He does not disclose his new job to his former externship supervisor. Instead, the supervisor learns of Michael's employment at the firm when, six months after Michael's admission to the bar, the two run into one another at a bar association function.

The city's lawyer plainly is concerned. Michael reassures her that he has not been involved in the case at the firm, and that he has not discussed the work he did on the case during his externship with anyone since his externship concluded. Three days later, the city's lawyers file a motion to disqualify the firm, alleging that through Michael's employment at the firm, the firm's lawyers have violated Rules 1.9, 1.10, and 5.3 of the Rules of Professional Conduct.

In what way(s) is Michael's situation distinguishable from the situation in which Jamie found himself at the beginning of this chapter? Is there any support for the City's motion in the facts and the Model Rules? Can you marshal support for the firm's opposition to the motion from the same sources? What other sources should you consult as you research the conflicts issue here? What policy considerations would you urge the court take into account in ruling on the motion? And finally, if you were the judge, how would you rule?

An Action Plan: Protocols for Identifying and Avoiding or Resolving Conflicts

Identifying Actual and Potential Conflicts

The best way for an externship program to avoid conflicts is to develop an effective conflicts-checking process, one that will gather as much information about the extern's work and personal history as early in the application process as possible, and thereby facilitate the identification of both actual and potential conflicts that might require client consent or preclude representation of one or more clients.

As noted, the crucial first step in such a process is a requirement that each prospective extern conduct a detailed conflicts inventory. Although some potential or actual conflicts will be apparent from a prospective extern's resume, a resume ordinarily will not list the individual matters in which a student has been involved in the course of her prior legal employment, nor will it itemize every organization to which the student belongs nor catalogue the student's strongly-held personal beliefs. Therefore, identifying all actual and potential conflicts will require that students share both their resumes and the results of their conflicts inventories with their externship teacher or administrator and supervisors. Because responsibilities to non-legal employers also may present prohibited Rule 1.7 conflicts, careful conflicts checking will require that students disclose all contemporaneous non-legal employment as well.

Given the mandate of Rule 1.6 that lawyers keep confidential all information related to the representation of clients, the prospective extern is presented with a dilemma: how much information about prior or contemporaneous client representation may a student disclose in the course of a conflicts-checking protocol? Although the rules are silent on this issue—even the circumstances under which a client's name may be protected as confidential remains an open question under the rule—several ethics advisory committees and most commentators agree that lawyers may disclose the names of clients in order to check for conflicts. In successive representation situations, they also may identify the matters in which they provided representation to those clients.

The ABA Standing Committee on Ethics and Professional Responsibility issued a formal opinion on this topic shortly after the ABA House of Delegates amended Rule 1.10 to permit screening without client consent to prevent the imputation of conflicts when lawyers move between firms. The opinion concludes that although "conflicts information" (generally, the identity of the parties and issues involved in a matter on which the transferring lawyer worked) is protected by Rule 1.6 as information related to representation, because both a lawyer moving between firms and the lawyers at his or her prospective firm have a duty to detect and resolve conflicts of interest, the migrating lawyer ordinarily may disclose such information. Disclosure, however, normally should not take place until the lawyer and the new firm have had substantive discussions about a future association, and even then only subject to certain other limitations.[16]

As to requests for personal information from the extern, the rules likewise offer little guidance. It is advisable, therefore, for students who are applying for externships to discuss this issue with their teacher and to provide at least enough information to allow the teacher to determine if further investigation regarding any actual or potential conflict is warranted.

> **Exercise 12.7** Imagine that you and two classmates have decided to form your own law firm after your law school graduation. How would you go about setting up a conflicts-checking system for the new firm? Where would you turn for guidance as to how to design and implement such a system? What information would you have to gather with respect to your work history as law students? What information would you have to gather from prospective clients in order to identify all actual and

potential conflicts that might arise from their representation? Ask a member of your law school's clinical faculty or a lawyer in a law office in which you have worked about the conflicts-checking system employed in that practice setting. Compare that system with the recommendations of at least one legal ethics or law practice management resource, such as a law review or bar journal article, materials published by the Practicing Law Institute of New York or an opinion by the ethics advisory committee in your jurisdiction.

Avoiding or Resolving Conflicts

If a student's careful pre-placement review of her conflicts inventory with either the externship teacher or a prospective supervising attorney, or both, discloses an actual or potential conflict of interest, or if a job search or an offer of contemporaneous or future employment gives rise to such a conflict, both the student and the supervisors must take appropriate steps to avoid or resolve the conflict.

Avoiding Conflicts—Declining Representation

Avoiding a conflict that is certain to arise in a particular placement generally requires either that a student accept an alternate placement or relinquish plans for the contemporaneous employment or activity that gives rise to the conflict. While such "conflict avoidance" is appealing in its simplicity, its consequences may be harsh for a student who is committed to completing an externship at a particular placement and who is equally committed to maintaining other employment or continuing particular categories of volunteer work during the period of the externship. Unfortunately, in many cases, these activities will be mutually exclusive.

Resolving Conflicts—Informed Client Consent

In other cases, informed consent from all affected clients, confirmed in writing (i.e., consent provided after disclosure of the conflict and consultation with respect to its possible impact on the representation), may resolve, or "cure," a conflict. However, if even one affected client withholds consent, or if the conflict will limit the student's ability to provide competent and diligent representation to an affected client, the student will not be able to work as an extern at the prospective placement.

Resolving Conflicts—Screening

In some situations, screening without notice to or consent from clients may be available to address conflicts of interest that students bring with them to their externship placements or that develop during an externship semester. Where representation giving rise to a conflict of interests may proceed only with informed client consent, that consent frequently is conditioned on a promise that the conflicted lawyer or law student will be screened from any involvement with the matter that gives rise to the conflict.

Rule 1.0(k) defines "screened" as "denot[ing] the isolation of a lawyer from any participation in a matter through the timely imposition of procedures within a firm that are reasonably adequate under the circumstances to protect information that the isolated lawyer is obligated to protect under these Rules or other law." The Rule 1.0 commentary emphasizes that the implementation of screening measures must be timely to be effective, Rule 1.0, Comment 10, and notes that

> [t]o implement, reinforce and remind all affected lawyers of the presence of the screening, it may be appropriate for the firm to undertake such procedures as a written undertaking by the screened lawyer to avoid any communication with other firm personnel and any contact with any firm files or other information, including information in electronic form, relating to the matter, written notice and instructions to all other firm personnel forbidding any communication with the screened lawyer relating to the matter, denial of access by the screened lawyer to firm files or other information, including information in electronic form, relating to the matter and periodic reminders of the screen to the screened lawyer and all other firm personnel. Id., Comment 9.

Screening, however—whether with or without client consent—is not available in all jurisdictions, and even where it is, externship teachers often are reluctant to approve placements conditioned on it. Although screening may be a desirable means of resolving at least some of the conflicts of interest faced by lawyers, it is less appropriate when the individual to be screened is an extern. Because a primary goal of most, if not all, externship programs is to expose students to as broad a range of lawyering styles and professional experiences as possible, teachers encourage externs to develop professional relationships with as many members of the legal team at their placements as possible and to work on as diverse an assortment of matters as possible. They urge students to talk with their placement colleagues about other matters on which the students will not work directly and to seek guidance from them with respect to the extern's own developing legal skills and career aspirations. To screen a student from involvement in a particular matter, or from contact with one or more members of the legal team at the placement, is necessarily to limit the extern's exposure to some subset of the lawyering experiences available at the placement site, cutting the student off from potentially rich learning opportunities.

Avoiding Conflicts—Withdrawal From Representation

Where a non-consentable conflict arises during an externship semester or a consentable conflict arises after the semester is underway and an affected client withholds consent to the representation, the conflicted student may be required to discontinue work at the externship placement. In that case, the student's options may be limited to forfeiting some or all of the fieldwork credit the extern would have earned or scrambling to make arrangements to complete the requisite fieldwork at another placement site.

Conclusion

One of the advantages of externship participation is the opportunity it offers students to "practice" at practicing law while they are still in law school, under the guidance of capable mentors and supervisors. With the privilege of practicing law as a law student comes the responsibility to become aware of and to conform one's conduct to the applicable rules of professional conduct in the placement jurisdiction.

Among the most important of the rules that govern the conduct of lawyers and the legal externs who work under their supervision are those addressing conflicts of interests. As the Preamble to the Rules of Professional Conduct aptly notes at paragraph (13) "[v]irtually all difficult ethical problems arise from conflict between a lawyer's responsibilities to clients, to the legal system and to the lawyer's own interest in remaining an ethical person while earning a satisfactory living." Violation of the conflicts rules can carry serious consequences for clients, for law students and their teachers and supervisors, and, by extension, for the externship program itself. We hope that this chapter has helped you both to become more familiar with the rules that govern in conflicts situations and more attuned to some of the ways conflicts of interest arise, so you can recognize and respond appropriately to the conflicts issues you will encounter as a law student extern and as a practicing lawyer.

FURTHER RESOURCES

On the personal and professional consequences of perceived conflicts created by the representation of unpopular clients: Steven Jones, *The Case for Unpopular Clients*, WALL ST. J. (March 13, 2010), http://www.wsj.com/articles/SB100014240527487036 25304575116250512434096.

Alexis Anderson, Arlene Kanter & Cindy Slane, *Ethics in Externships: Confidentiality, Conflicts and Competence Issues in the Field and in the Classroom*, 10 CLIN. L. REV. 473, 544 (2004).

Peter A. Joy & Robert R. Kuehn, *Conflict Of Interest And Competency Issues In Law Clinic Practice*, 9 CLIN. L. REV. 493, 504 (2002).

ENDNOTES

1   "Wait," you may be thinking, "not so fast! Ranken and Rome had extended its offer, and Jamie accepted it, prior to the firm's engagement on the matter giving rise to the conflict. Ed and Cheryl—lawyers with managerial responsibilities at the firm—apparently made no subsequent effort to determine whether Jamie might have acquired one or more conflicts by virtue of his activities as a 3L. Given these facts, couldn't Jamie assert some sort of claim against the firm?" Good thinking (you must have paid attention in Torts and Contracts!), but not likely to bring Jamie much comfort as he heads back in his office to pack up the few personal items he unpacked just a day earlier. It is only the very rare new law graduate who would count as a win trading a promising job for a promising breach of contract or wrongful-termination claim before the ink is dry on his certificate of bar admission.

2   For an engaging account of the Boston Massacre trials and the events surrounding them, *see* John F. Tobin, *The Boston Massacre Trials*, N.Y. ST. B. Ass'N J. 10 (July/August 2013).

3   *See, e.g.*, Anderson v. Comm'r of Corr., 308 Conn. 456 (2013) (affirming denial of a habeas petition asserting ineffective assistance of counsel based on petitioner's representation by a lawyer in the same public defender's office as the lawyer representing petitioner's co-defendant); State v. Bell, 447 A.2d 525 (N.J. 1982) (holding representation of clients with conflicting interests by public defenders from the same office not per se prejudicial); State v. St. Dennis, 358 Mont. 88; 244 P.3d 292 (2010) (holding that, because protocols to protect confidentiality were in place and adhered to in this instance, no conflict of interest occurred when attorneys from different offices of the Montana Office of Public Defender represented both defendant and co-defendant).

4   *See, e.g., In re* Formal Advisory Opinion 10-1, 741 S.E.2d 622 9 (Ga. 2013) (affirming advisory opinion and holding that where a single lawyer in the public defender's office of a particular judicial circuit has a conflict of interest with respect to the representation of co-defendants, that conflict is imputed to all lawyers working in the same office), http://www.gabar.org/barrules/handbookdetail.cfm?what=rule&id=557 (last visited Apr. 8, 2015); Scott v. State, 991 So. 2d 971, 972 (Fla. App. 2008) (noting that "a public defender's office is the functional equivalent of a law firm [such that] [d]ifferent attorneys in the same public defender's office cannot represent defendants with conflicting interests" (citation and internal quotation marks omitted)).

5   *See, e.g.*, ABA STANDARDS FOR IMPOSING LAWYER SANCTIONS section 4.3, (approved Feb. 1986, amended February 1992) (recommending sanctions ranging from reprimand to disbarment for failure to avoid conflicts of interest). *See also* Chief Disciplinary Counsel v. Zenas Zelotes, 152 Conn. App. 380 (2014) (affirming imposition of a five-month suspension from the practice of law for the defendant's violation of Rules 1.7(a)(2) and 8.4(a) of the Connecticut Rules of Professional Conduct by engaging in an intimate relationship with a divorce client).

6   Brian Baxter, *John Edwards, a Man of Many Lawyers, Shuffles Legal Team Once Again*, AM. L. DAILY (March 23, 2012), http://www.amlawdaily.typepad.com/amlawdaily/2012/03/Edwards-legal-team.html.

7   David H. Taylor, *Conflicts of Interest and the Indigent Client: Barring the Door to the Last Lawyer in Town*, 37 ARIZ. L. REV. 577, 626 (1995) (reporting survey results indicating that the most common consequence where conflicts preclude representation in the legal services context is that the client goes without representation, and advocating a shift from a "zero tolerance" standard to an "actual prejudice" standard for evaluating conflicts in such settings).

8   *E.g.*, *Charter of Core Principles of the European Legal Profession and Code of Conduct for European Lawyers*, (Jonathan Goldsmith, responsible ed., The Council of Bars and Law Societies of Europe, 2013), http://www.ccbe.eu/fileadmin/user_upload/NTCdocument/EN_CCBE_CoCpdf1_1382973057.pdf (last visited Apr. 8, 2015). For a helpful exploration of the challenges involved in regulating lawyer's conflicts of interests, in particular, in international practice, *see* Janine Griffiths-Baker & Nancy J. Moore, *Regulating Conflicts of Interest in Global Law Firms: Peace in Our Time?*, 80 FORDHAM L. REV. 2541 (2012).

9   Unless otherwise noted, reference will be made to the Delaware Rules of Professional Conduct rather than the ABA Model Rules of Professional Conduct, which are copyrighted.

10   r. 1.8(b) (requiring informed client consent for use of information relating to the representation to the disadvantage of a client), (f) (requiring informed client consent where compensation for representing a client will come from one other than the client), and (g) (requiring informed consent from all affected client prior to making an aggregate plea agreement or settlement of claims for two or more clients).

11   r. 1.8(a) (governing business transactions with or acquisition of ownership, possessory, security or other pecuniary interest adverse to client) and (h) (governing agreement prospectively limiting lawyer's ability to client for malpractice or settling claim or potential claim for such liability).

12   *See, e.g.*, Rule 1.8(c) (banning preparation of instruments conveying substantial gifts from clients to lawyers), (d) (banning negotiations and agreements for media or literary rights prior to the termination of representation), (e) (banning certain types of financial assistance to clients), (i) (banning acquisition of a proprietary interest in the cause of action or subject matter of litigation), and (j) (banning initiation of sexual relations with clients).

13   *Supra* note 2.

14   *See* r. 1.6(e), (authorizing disclosure of otherwise-confidential information "to secure legal advice about the lawyer's compliance with these Rules").

15   r. 8.3(a) (requires a lawyer who has knowledge of another lawyer's violation of the Rules of Professional Conduct giving rise to doubts about the other lawyer's "honesty, trustworthiness, or fitness as a lawyer in other respects" to report the misconduct to "the appropriate professional authority").

16   ABA COMM'N. ON ETHICS & PROF'L RESPONSIBILITY, FORMAL OP. 09-455 (2009) (concerning disclosure of conflicts information when lawyers move between law firms), http://iardc.fastcle.com/EdutechResources/resources//bytopicid/24414/ABA%2009-455.pdf (last visited Apr. 8, 2015). The opinion limits disclosure to that reasonably necessary to detect and resolve conflicts, prohibits disclosure that compromises the attorney-client privilege or otherwise prejudices a client or former client, and prohibits the lawyer or law firm in receipt of conflicts information from revealing it or using it for any purpose other than identifying and resolving conflicts.

APPENDIX 12.1

EXTERNSHIP PROGRAM CONFLICTS OF INTERESTS INVENTORY

Name:

Externship Course: Semester:

Prospective Placements(s):

The information you provide here will help you and your faculty and field supervisors to identify any actual or potential conflicts of interests that would jeopardize the confidentiality and loyalty you owe to your prospective externship placement. Please take your time to answer these questions thoughtfully and completely. (Attach additional sheets if necessary). PLEASE NOTE: You have an obligation to update this form to reflect any change in circumstances prior to your beginning work at your externship placement and/ or during the semester(s) in which you are enrolled in the Externship Program.

1.   Are you now working or volunteering, or have you worked or volunteered for a law firm, legal services office, corporation legal department, governmental agency, judge, hearing examiner, or in the securities industry (in a legal or non-legal setting) prior to enrolling in the Externship Program?

   YES [ ] NO [ ]

   If yes, where are you working/have you worked? [List all, starting with most recent and providing dates and locations.]

   On what type(s) of cases did you work at each location?

2.   Are you planning on being employed or volunteering at any office in any of the categories listed in question #1 during your externship semester?

   YES [ ] NO [ ]

3.   Are you planning on maintaining any other non-legal employment, board affiliation, or volunteer activity during your externship semester?

YES [ ] NO [ ]

If yes, where will you be employed, serving as a board member, or volunteering?

What type of work will you be doing?

4.   Please list any entities to which you have applied for future employment, including law firms, legal services offices, corporation legal departments, governmental agencies, judges, hearing examiners, or employers in the securities industry (legal or non-legal). You need not include a prospective employer from whom you have received either a "no thank you" letter or an offer of employment which you have declined. If, between now and the completion of your externship, you contact any other prospective employer not listed on this form to explore a potential employment relationship, or if any prospective employer contacts you for that purpose, you must update this form to include that prospective employer.

5.   Please identify any other personal, financial, or family interests that could present conflicts of interests for you at your proposed placement(s).

6.   Have you been enrolled in the Law School's Externship Program or in an In-house Clinic before?

YES [ ] NO [ ]

If yes, please indicate the semester(s) in which you were enrolled (including summer sessions) and identify your clinic and/or externship program and placement below.

*Please Note: You have an obligation to update this Conflicts of Interests Inventory if any of the information you have provided changes between the date you submit this form and the end of the semester in which you are enrolled in the Externship Program.

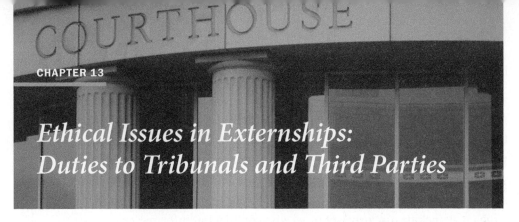

Ethical Issues in Externships: Duties to Tribunals and Third Parties

LISA G. LERMAN & LISA V. MARTIN

S ome legal externs work in law offices that represent clients in litigation or work for judges who are overseeing litigation. Ethical questions arise in all arenas of law practice; litigators, however, can scarcely walk across a room without stumbling over an ethical question. Some litigation ethics issues involve duties to clients, of course, but many dilemmas that arise in litigation involve conflicts between a lawyer's duty toward a client and the lawyer's duty toward a judge, an adversary, or a witness.

The pace of a busy litigation practice may not allow much time for explicit discussion of ethical issues. An experienced litigator may have encountered so many issues in the past that he or she can process the problem and think through the options without even having a conversation about it. A law student encountering an ethical issue for the first time, on the other hand, may learn a great deal from an explicit and detailed discussion of the nature of the problem presented, the options available to address the issue, the ethical and legal boundaries on action, and the strategic and practical considerations that must be taken into account. Legal externs may find it useful to discuss questions and concerns about ethical issues in an externship seminar or in journal entries. Chapter 11 on confidentiality provides guidance on how to explore these issues while also safeguarding client confidences. In this chapter, we introduce some of the ethics rules that govern lawyers in litigation settings and present some problems for your consideration.

Duties to Tribunals

Lawyers admitted to practice often are referred to as "officers of the court" even if they are in private law practice. Every lawyer has a duty to protect the integrity of the system of justice by showing respect for law and the legal system and by maintaining high standards of professional conduct. For more information on lawyers' duties related to professional conduct, see Chapter 9 on Professionalism.

Lawyers have a duty to be truthful in presenting evidence and arguments to tribunals. For the court system to produce fair and accurate decisions, judges must receive accurate information about the facts of each case and the applicable law. American judges rely on lawyers to present facts and typically are precluded from conducting their own investigations to locate evidence relating to the cases before them. Judges simply review what is presented to them by the lawyers and parties in the case. Therefore, lawyers are prohibited from presenting false information about facts or law to finders of fact. In some situations, lawyers may have an affirmative duty to disclose information to judges, which may include disclosure of otherwise confidential information.

Notwithstanding these duties to tribunals, a lawyer's primary responsibility is to her client. A lawyer must protect client confidences except in a narrow range of circumstances. Wherever the rules require or permit the lawyer to reveal confidential information, she should limit what is revealed to the minimum disclosure that will suffice to meet the purpose of disclosure. Lawyers are mainly advocates, not judicial officials or law enforcement officers. They often possess information about criminal or fraudulent acts of clients. Unless disclosure is permitted or required by the ethics code, the lawyer must protect this information.

Any time a lawyer does not reveal information about a client's misdeeds to a judge or an opposing counsel, the lawyer is withholding information. From one perspective, this is deliberate deception. On the other hand, if a lawyer were to reveal all that she knows of her client's doings, the lawyer would fail in her duty to advocate on her client's behalf within the bounds of the law.

One way to address this tension would be for a lawyer to avoid acquiring adverse information about a client to the extent possible. By maintaining deliberate ignorance, the lawyer would avoid knowing things that might need to be disclosed. But if the lawyer follows this approach, she might miss learning information that is critically important to her representation of the client and may make mistakes or be surprised in litigation when previously unknown information emerges.

This tension between a lawyer's obligation to the client and to the justice system is the unavoidable product of our adversary system. The tension is highest when a lawyer is representing an indigent client in a matter in which the client's life or liberty is at stake, such as in criminal cases, immigration matters, or child abuse and neglect cases. A person with no resources who faces deportation or the loss of liberty, life, or children at the hands of a well-resourced government arguably deserves the undivided loyalty of counsel. Yet all litigators must walk a fine and nuanced line between advocacy and truthfulness. Rule 3.3 and the comments that follow it offer guidance for litigators in a variety of situations. The profession is far from reaching a full consensus on when a lawyer's duty to the tribunal needs to trump the duty to protect confidences, but the rule and its comments reflect a synthesis of the collective wisdom of many experienced lawyers. As noted in previous chapters, the American Bar Association holds the copyright on the ABA Model Rules of Professional Conduct and imposes stringent restrictions on their quotation. All quotations to Rules of Conduct in this book refer to the Delaware Rules of Professional Conduct, which are in the public domain and are almost identical to the Model Rules. Any differences in text from the Model Rules are noted.

- *Rule 3.3. Candor Toward the Tribunal*

(a) A lawyer shall not knowingly:

> (1) make a false statement of fact or law to a tribunal or fail to correct a false statement of material fact or law previously made to the tribunal by the lawyer;
>
> (2) fail to disclose to the tribunal legal authority in the controlling jurisdiction known to the lawyer to be directly adverse to the position of the client and not disclosed by opposing counsel; or
>
> (3) offer evidence that the lawyer knows to be false. If a lawyer, the lawyer's client, or a witness called by the lawyer, has offered material evidence and the lawyer comes to know of its falsity, the lawyer shall take reasonable remedial measures, including, if necessary, disclosure to the tribunal. A lawyer may refuse to offer evidence, other than the testimony of a defendant in a criminal matter, that the lawyer reasonably believes is false.

(b) A lawyer who represents a client in an adjudicative proceeding and who knows that a person intends to engage, is engaging, or has engaged in criminal or fraudulent conduct related to the proceeding shall take reasonable remedial measures, including, if necessary, disclosure to the tribunal.

(c) The duties stated in paragraphs (a) and (b) continue to the conclusion of the proceeding, and apply even if compliance requires disclosure of information otherwise protected by Rule 1.6.

(d) In an ex parte proceeding, a lawyer shall inform the tribunal of all material facts known to the lawyer that will enable the tribunal to make an informed decision, whether or not the facts are adverse.

The application of this rule raises many questions. For example, what is a false statement? Does this category include statements that are literally true but incomplete or misleading? How do you distinguish a material fact from a non-material one? How sure about "falsity" must a lawyer be to "know" that she has offered false evidence? You can find guidance on these and other questions in the comments that follow Rule 3.3 in your state ethics code and in court opinions and advisory ethics opinions that interpret or apply the rule. Reading the comments that follow Rule 3.3 with care is a good start to understand these issues and to see the variety of litigation situations in which these issues may be presented. What follows is an excerpt of some of the notable passages in the comments, with some key words and phrases in bold. All bold text has been added by the authors.

> [1] This Rule governs the conduct of a lawyer who is representing a client in the proceedings of a tribunal. It also applies when the lawyer is representing a client in an **ancillary proceeding** conducted pursuant to the tribunal's adjudicative authority, **such as a deposition.** Thus, for example, paragraph (a)(3) requires a lawyer to take reasonable remedial measures if the lawyer comes to know that a client who is testifying in a deposition has offered evidence that is false.

> [2] This Rule sets forth the special duties of lawyers as officers of the court to avoid conduct that undermines the integrity of the adjudicative process. A lawyer acting as an advocate in an adjudicative proceeding has an obligation to present the client's case with persuasive force. Performance of that duty while maintaining confidences of the client, however, is qualified by the advocate's duty of candor to the tribunal. Consequently, . . . [t]he lawyer must not allow the tribunal to be misled by false statements of law or fact or evidence that the lawyer knows to be false.

> **Representations by a Lawyer**

> [3] An advocate is responsible for pleadings and other documents prepared for litigation, but is usually **not required to have personal knowledge of matters asserted** therein, for litigation documents ordinarily present assertions by the client, or by someone on the client's behalf, and not assertions by the lawyer. . . .However, **an assertion purporting to be based on the lawyer's own knowledge, as in an affidavit by the lawyer or in a statement in open court, may properly be made only when the lawyer knows the assertion is true or believes it to be true on the basis of a reasonably diligent inquiry.** There are circumstances where failure to make a disclosure is the equivalent of an affirmative misrepresentation. . . .

Offering Evidence

[5] Paragraph (a)(3) **requires that the lawyer refuse to offer evidence that the lawyer knows to be false**, regardless of the client's wishes. This duty is premised on the lawyer's obligation as an officer of the court to prevent the trier of fact from being misled by false evidence. . . .

[6] If a **lawyer** knows **that the client intends to testify falsely or** wants the lawyer to introduce false evidence, the lawyer should **seek to persuade** the client that the evidence should not be offered. If the persuasion is ineffective and the lawyer continues to represent the client, the **lawyer must refuse to offer the false evidence**. If only a portion of a witness's testimony will be false, the lawyer may call the witness to testify but may not elicit or otherwise permit the witness to present the testimony that the lawyer knows is false.

[7] The duties stated in paragraphs (a) and (b) apply to all lawyers, including defense counsel in criminal cases. In some jurisdictions, however, [DC and Massachusetts] courts have required counsel to present the accused as a witness or to give a narrative statement if the accused so desires, even if counsel knows that the testimony or statement will be false. . . .

[8] The prohibition against offering false evidence only applies if the lawyer knows that the evidence is false. **A lawyer's reasonable belief that evidence is false does not preclude its presentation** to the trier of fact. . . . Thus, although a lawyer should resolve doubts about the veracity of testimony or other evidence in favor of the client, the lawyer cannot ignore an obvious falsehood.

[9] Although paragraph (a)(3) only prohibits a lawyer from offering evidence the lawyer knows to be false, it **permits the lawyer to refuse to offer testimony or other proof that the lawyer reasonably believes is false**, . . .Because of the special protections historically provided criminal defendants, however, this **Rule does not permit a lawyer to refuse to offer the testimony of such a client where the lawyer reasonably believes but does not know that the testimony will be false. Unless the lawyer knows the testimony will be false, the lawyer must honor the client's decision to testify**. . . .

Remedial Measures

[10] Having offered material evidence in the belief that it was true, **a lawyer may subsequently come to know that the evidence is false.** Or, a lawyer may be surprised

when the lawyer's client, or another witness called by the lawyer, offers testimony the lawyer knows to be false . . . In such situations or **if the lawyer knows of the falsity of testimony elicited from the client during a deposition, the lawyer must take reasonable remedial measures.** In such situations, **the advocate's proper course is to remonstrate with the client confidentially, advise the client of the lawyer's duty of candor to the tribunal and seek the client's cooperation with respect to the withdrawal or correction of the false statements or evidence. If that fails, the advocate must take further remedial action. If withdrawal from the representation is not permitted or will not undo the effect of the false evidence, the advocate must make such disclosure to the tribunal as is reasonably necessary to remedy the situation, even if doing so requires the lawyer to reveal information that otherwise would be protected by Rule 1.6.** It is for the tribunal then to determine what should be done—making a statement about the matter to the trier of fact, ordering a mistrial or perhaps nothing.

[11] The disclosure of a client's false testimony can result in grave consequences to the client, including not only a sense of betrayal but also loss of the case and perhaps a prosecution for perjury. But the alternative is that the lawyer cooperate in deceiving the court, thereby subverting the truth-finding process which the adversary system is designed to implement. . . .

Preserving Integrity of Adjudicative Process

[12] Lawyers have a special obligation to protect a tribunal against criminal or fraudulent conduct that undermines the integrity of the adjudicative process, such as bribing, intimidating or otherwise unlawfully communicating with a witness, juror, court official or other participant in the proceeding, unlawfully destroying or concealing documents or other evidence or failing to disclose information to the tribunal when required by law to do so. Thus, paragraph (b) requires a lawyer to take reasonable remedial measures, including disclosure if necessary, whenever the lawyer knows that a person, including the lawyer's client, intends to engage, is engaging or has engaged in criminal or fraudulent conduct related to the proceeding.

Duration of Obligation

[13] A practical time limit on the obligation to rectify false evidence or false statements of law and fact has to be established. **The conclusion of the proceeding is a reasonably definite point for the termination of the obligation. A proceeding has concluded within the meaning of this Rule when a final judgment in the proceeding has been affirmed on appeal or the time for review has passed.**

Ex Parte Proceedings

[14] Ordinarily, an advocate has the limited responsibility of presenting one side of the matters that a tribunal should consider in reaching a decision; the conflicting position is expected to be presented by the opposing party. However, in any ex parte proceeding, such as an application for a temporary restraining order, there is no balance of presentation by opposing advocates. The object of an ex parte proceeding is nevertheless to yield a substantially just result. The judge has an affirmative responsibility to accord the absent party just consideration. **The lawyer for the represented party has the correlative duty to make disclosures of material facts known to the lawyer and that the lawyer reasonably believes are necessary to an informed decision.**

Withdrawal

[15] Normally, a lawyer's compliance with the duty of candor imposed by this Rule does not require that the lawyer withdraw from the representation of a client whose interests will be or have been adversely affected by the lawyer's disclosure. The lawyer may, however, be required by Rule 1.16(a) to seek permission of the tribunal to withdraw if the lawyer's compliance with this Rule's duty of candor results in such an extreme deterioration of the client-lawyer relationship that the lawyer can no longer competently represent the client. . . . In connection with a request for permission to withdraw that is premised on a client's misconduct, a lawyer may reveal information relating to the representation only to the extent reasonably necessary to comply with this Rule or as otherwise permitted by Rule 1.6.

If a lawyer has offered false evidence or knows that someone else has engaged in criminal or fraudulent conduct related to the proceeding, the lawyer must take remedial action. What must she do? When is disclosure necessary?

"Remedial action" means that the lawyer must take steps to ensure that the finder of fact is not misled. The rules encourage lawyers to carry out this duty without disclosing client confidences, if possible, and if a disclosure is necessary, to disclose as little as possible. See Rule 3.3, Comment 11. If a client has made a false statement in court or in a deposition, a lawyer first needs to try to persuade the client to make a statement correcting his own testimony. If the client refuses to correct his testimony, the lawyer might seek to withdraw from representing the client and explain to the court that the lawyer is withdrawing because continuing to represent the client would require the lawyer to engage in unethical conduct. This is known as a "noisy withdrawal." Such a statement often is sufficient to alert the judge to a problem in the evidence that has been presented. If withdrawal is not possible or would not put the court on adequate notice of the problem, the lawyer may need to make a direct disclosure to the judge.

None of this is easy or fun, of course, but the rules in most states are clear that a lawyer may not sit by and watch her own client or a witness present what the lawyer **knows** to be false information in court. The integrity of the judicial process is so important that, in some cases, it takes precedence over a lawyer's duty to a client.

What is a "tribunal"? At first glance, Rule 3.3 appears to apply only to lawyers presenting information in courts. In fact, the rule applies whenever a lawyer is presenting information to any finder of fact, whether the proceeding is in a court, an administrative agency, a legislative hearing, or an arbitration proceeding. See Rule 1.0(m).

Most people assume that Rule 3.3 applies only to court, administrative, or arbitral adjudicative proceedings. In fact, the rule extends to legislative and administrative proceedings that focus on consideration of proposed statutes or other rules. Rule 3.9 explains that except for ex parte proceedings, **the duties articulated in Rule 3.3 apply even if the lawyer is representing a client in a non-adjudicative proceeding before a legislative or administrative agency.** This means the duty of candor toward "tribunals" would apply, for example, to a lawyer submitting comments on behalf of a client in an agency rulemaking proceeding and to a lawyer representing a client who is providing testimony on proposed legislation. Legislators and administrative officials depend to some degree on the accuracy of information presented to them. They cannot make good policy decisions if they are misled about the facts. Therefore, lawyers are asked to assist in implementation of rules barring presentation of false information in those settings.

> **Exercise 13.1 Conflicting Duties:** Lauren Nielsen emailed her externship teacher and requested an emergency meeting for advice about a situation at her placement. Lauren had been thrilled when she was offered a position at Immigration Legal Services. She was pleased when she was assigned to work on the case of Paola Fuentes. Because Ms. Fuentes's U.S. citizen husband had abused her, Ms. Fuentes was able to file a "self-petition" for legal status under the Violence Against Women Act ("VAWA"). At the time Lauren began working at her placement, they had just learned Ms. Fuentes had become eligible to seek a "green card" and become a lawful permanent resident as a result of her approved VAWA self-petition. Lauren was asked to assist Ms. Fuentes to apply for lawful permanent resident status. Such applications are adjudicated through an administrative process that requires

the submission of a detailed application and an interview with immigration officials. If the application is denied at the administrative level, then Ms. Fuentes could be placed in removal proceedings before an Immigration Judge and, unless other relief is available to Ms. Fuentes, she could be deported.

When Lauren arrived at her professor's office, she was distraught. She explained that she had met with Ms. Fuentes that day to finalize the application. Lauren explained to Ms. Fuentes that her supervisor had asked them to review a portion of the application to ensure the answers were correct. Something Ms. Fuentes had said to the supervisor in the past made the supervisor think that Ms. Fuentes might have been involved with bringing her mother to the U.S. The application asked whether Ms. Fuentes had participated in alien smuggling, in other words, in helping someone to enter the country unlawfully. Lauren asked Ms. Fuentes to tell her more about how Ms. Fuentes's mother had traveled to the United States. Ms. Fuentes explained that she had become fearful for her mother's safety after she learned there was no one looking out for her in Guatemala, so she paid a coyote (someone who helps people to cross the border illegally for a fee) to bring her mother to her in the United States. Lauren thanked Ms. Fuentes for the explanation. Lauren told Ms. Fuentes that the facts required that they check "yes" in answer to the alien smuggling question. She told Ms. Fuentes that her supervisor believed that checking this box would not have adverse consequences, as Ms. Fuentes could apply for a waiver that would allow her to obtain her green card despite her having assisted her mother to come into the United States unlawfully.

Lauren reported that after this last part of the conversation, Ms. Fuentes's demeanor changed completely. Ms. Fuentes began shouting at Lauren and accused her of tricking Ms. Fuentes into telling the story so she could sabotage the application. She told Lauren to keep the story to herself and not to tell anyone else. Ms. Fuentes stormed out of the office. Later that afternoon, Lauren's supervisor emailed Lauren saying that he had received an angry message from Ms. Fuentes, who had said that Lauren was incompetent and she never wanted to see her again. She had asked that her case be assigned to someone else. The supervisor asked Lauren to meet him the following morning.

Lauren is panicked that she has made a bad impression on the supervisor by angering her client. She also feels for Ms. Fuentes and realizes how vulnerable she is. If Lauren discloses this information to her supervisor, her supervisor may insist that Ms. Fuentes disclose the matter and apply for a waiver. If things go this way, the application might be denied, and Lauren would bear responsibility. Lauren wonders if she should pretend that the conversation never happened. If Lauren does not tell the supervisor about Ms. Fuentes's payment to the coyote, it is possible that no one would ever find out about it.

1. Should Lauren report Ms. Fuentes' payment to the coyote to her supervisor? What ethical rules are at issue?

2. Assuming Lauren informs her supervisor, what will her supervisor's obligations be under Rule 3.3? What options must the supervisor present to Ms. Fuentes? If the supervisor wants Ms. Fuentes to disclose the information and she refuses, what should the supervisor do?

3. Was Lauren too thorough in questioning Ms. Fuentes about her mother? Would it have been better not to ask for details about her mother's arrival in the United States?

4. If Lauren does not inform her supervisor and does not insist that Ms. Fuentes disclose the payment to the coyote, could the supervisor be disciplined or sanctioned for her nondisclosure?

Prosecutors are a special category of lawyer and have additional responsibilities to the courts and the defendants whom they prosecute. These extra duties are explained in Rule 3.8, parts of which are presented below.

- *Rule 3.8 Special Responsibilities of a Prosecutor*

The prosecutor in a criminal case shall:

(a) refrain from prosecuting a charge that the prosecutor knows is not supported by probable cause; . . .

(d) make timely disclosure to the defense of all evidence information known to the prosecutor that tends to negate the guilt of the accused or mitigates the offense . . . .

[(h) When a prosecutor knows of clear and convincing evidence establishing that a defendant in the prosecutor's jurisdiction was convicted of an offense that the defendant did not commit, the prosecutor shall seek to remedy the conviction.][1]

Comment 1 after Rule 3.8 explains:

A prosecutor has the responsibility as a minister of justice and not simply that of an advocate. This responsibility carries with it specific obligations to see that the defendant is accorded procedural justice, that guilt is decided on the basis of sufficient evidence, [and that special precautions are taken to prevent and to rectify the conviction of innocent persons.] . . .

> **Exercise 13.2 False Testimony:** Isaiah Goodwin told the following story in his externship seminar:
>
> *I'm working at the prosecutor's office, mainly working for this one guy named Steve Charney. Yesterday I went with him to court to watch him try a case in which the defendant, a twenty-four-year-old man, was charged with possession of cocaine. It was a pretty straightforward felony case, except for one thing.*
>
> *The arresting officer got on the stand and testified that when he searched the suspect, he found a large bag of white powder, which turned out to be cocaine, in the suspect's right jacket pocket. The bag of powder was introduced into evidence. The defendant did not testify. He was convicted, of course. A sentencing hearing was scheduled. The defendant had one prior drug conviction, so he probably will go to prison for a long time.*
>
> *After this case was concluded, Steve stayed in the courtroom to prosecute another case, but I left to go back to the office to work on a research memo. I stopped at the water fountain in the hallway outside the courtroom. I noticed that the officer who had testified was chatting with another policeman a few feet away. So I took a long drink and listened.*
>
> *The arresting officer was boasting to his friend about how this guy was going away for years, for sure, and that it was about time, because everyone knew he was a dealer. "Of course I didn't really find anything when I searched him, but no one will ever know that now. It's about time that guy got taken off the street."*
>
> *I felt like I had just stumbled onto the set of Law and Order. I couldn't believe it. When Steve got back to the office, I went in to see him and told him everything I had heard. I expected that he would jump out of his skin when he heard what had happened. But he just listened, and smiled. He said something like this: "Well, Isaiah, welcome to the real world. These things happen all the time. It's just part of law enforcement." I tried to argue with him, but he became incredibly patronizing. He said something like, "Last time I checked, I was the one with nine years' experience as a prosecutor, and you were the law*

student volunteer. I suggest you try to learn a few things instead of telling me how to do my job."

To be honest, I'm pretty freaked out. For one, my boss now thinks I'm a total idiot and the rest of my semester is probably shot, not to mention my chance of getting a decent reference. For another, I was planning to become a prosecutor, but now I'm wondering how often this happens and whether this sort of attitude is typical. Maybe I was naïve in believing that police and prosecutors play by the rules. Wow, if this guy really had nothing on him, then anyone could be arrested, charged, and jailed for no good reason.

Maybe I should be a defense lawyer instead. Or maybe the criminal justice system is just too messed up, and I should go do something tamer, like trusts and estates.

Another thing is really bothering me. What about this guy who is about to get sent to prison based on false testimony? My boss seems unconcerned. Maybe I should tell someone else, maybe the district attorney (Steve's boss), or maybe even the judge. To sit silent makes me complicit in this, doesn't it?

1. What if any obligations does Steve have under Rule 3.3? What about under Rule 3.8? In doing this analysis, assume that Isaiah is telling the truth about what he heard and that the police officer was telling the truth in his comments to the other officer.

2. What do you think Isaiah needs to do in this situation? What if he writes a memo to Steve memorializing the conversation he overheard and explaining his concerns about it, and Steve continues to turn a blind eye to the problem? What then?

3. Was it improper for Isaiah to eavesdrop on the conversation between the police officers? Was it improper for Isaiah to report the conversation to Steve? Was it improper for Isaiah then to report the whole story to his externship seminar?

Exercise 13.3 Adverse Authority: Annette Sanderson is an extern at the Employment Law Center. She works for Micah Portman, who handles employment discrimination cases. Micah received a motion to dismiss one of his cases. The motion argued that the statute of limitations had run. Micah drafted a response to the motion, citing the relevant statute of limitations and a case that supported an interpretation of it favorable to the Center's client. He asked Annette to take his draft response and check whether any other authorities needed to be cited.

Annette's first step in her research was to look for cases that cited the opinion Micah had cited. Immediately she found a just-published opinion by the intermediate state appellate court that overturned the decision Micah relied on and interpreted the statute of limitations the same way as the lawyer who filed the motion to dismiss. This decision was on appeal to the state supreme court.

Annette checked the defendant's motion to dismiss to see if this new case was cited. It was not. Annette reported to Micah on her research. Micah said, "I'm glad you found this case, but I don't think I'm obliged to cite it. We'll let the defendant's lawyer do his own research."

Is Micah correct? How do you think Annette needs to respond to his analysis?

Duties Toward Opposing Counsel, Witnesses, and Others

As you have seen, lawyers have an array of ethical obligations toward their clients and toward the justice system. In addition, lawyers are required to be truthful and to conduct themselves in a professional manner in their dealings with opposing counsel, witnesses, and others.

Truthfulness

The ethics rules are organized into sets of duties lawyers owe to clients, tribunals, and others. As you read in the previous section, Rule 3.3 addresses the duty of truthfulness toward tribunals. Other rules (including Rule 1.4 on advice and Rule 7.1 on communication about legal services) address the lawyer's duty of candor to clients. Rule 8.4(c) prohibits any and all "dishonesty, fraud, deceit or misrepresentation." Rule 4.1 articulates a lawyer's duty of candor toward adversaries and third parties.

■ *Rule 4.1. Truthfulness in Statements to Others*

In the course of representing a client a lawyer shall not knowingly:

(a) make a false statement of material fact or law to a third person; or

(b) fail to disclose a material fact to a third person when disclosure is necessary to avoid assisting a criminal or fraudulent act by a client, unless disclosure is prohibited by Rule 1.6.

The comments following Rule 4.1 provide insight into the complex problems that a lawyer may confront in this arena, and the delicate balance that must be struck between fidelity to client and truthfulness to adversaries.

Misrepresentation

[1] A lawyer is required to be truthful when dealing with others on a client's behalf, but generally has no affirmative duty to inform an opposing party of relevant facts. A misrepresentation can occur if the lawyer incorporates or affirms a statement of another person that the lawyer knows is false. Misrepresentations can also occur by partially true but misleading statements or omissions that are the equivalent of affirmative false statements. . . .

Statements of Fact

[2] This Rule refers to statements of fact. Whether a particular statement should be regarded as one of fact can depend on the circumstances. Under generally accepted conventions in negotiation, certain types of statements ordinarily are not taken as statements of material fact. Estimates of price or value placed on the subject of a transaction and a party's intentions as to an acceptable settlement of a claim are ordinarily in this category, and so is the existence of an undisclosed principal except where nondisclosure of the principal would constitute fraud. Lawyers should be mindful of their obligations under applicable law to avoid criminal and tortious misrepresentation.

Crime or Fraud by Client

[3] Under Rule 1.2(d), a lawyer is prohibited from counseling or assisting a client in conduct that the lawyer knows is criminal or fraudulent. Paragraph (b) states a specific application of the principle set forth in Rule 1.2(d) and addresses the situation where a client's crime or fraud takes the form of a lie or misrepresentation. Ordinarily, a lawyer can avoid assisting a client's crime or fraud by withdrawing from the representation. Sometimes it may be necessary for the lawyer to give notice

of the fact of withdrawal and to disaffirm an opinion, document, affirmation or the like. In extreme cases, substantive law may require a lawyer to disclose information relating to the representation to avoid being deemed to have assisted the client's crime or fraud. If the lawyer can avoid assisting a client's crime or fraud only by disclosing this information, then under paragraph (b) the lawyer is required to do so, unless the disclosure is prohibited by Rule 1.6.

In dealings with opposing counsel or other third persons, lawyers are not permitted to make false statements, but they have no affirmative duty of disclosure under Rule 4.1 unless by withholding information the lawyer would be "assisting" a "criminal" or "fraudulent" act by a client. In that case, a lawyer is required to share the information unless revelation is not permitted under Rule 1.6. Like the other standards we have mentioned, this one raises more questions than it answers, especially because facts do not come with labels saying "true," "false," "material," or "fraudulent." Consider the following problem.

> **Exercise 13.4 Alimony and Child Support:** Maritza Karski was an extern in a domestic relations firm. Sam Guzman, her supervisor, invited Maritza to come to a meeting to negotiate a marital dissolution agreement for Catherine Carvino, a client of the firm. Maritza had been working on this case, calling the client to obtain various documents and information that Sam needed. The meeting was to be held at the law office of Travis Johnston, who was representing Alan Carvino, Catherine's soon-to-be-ex-husband.
>
> The case was simple enough. Catherine had stayed home for three years raising Jaden and Nicholas, the couple's two sons, and then had started working part-time in a daycare center. Alan worked as an air traffic controller, so most of the family income was from his earnings. The couple had separated after Alan confessed to Catherine that he had had a four-month relationship with a woman he met on the Internet.
>
> Catherine has accepted the inevitability of divorce, but she is anxious about her ability to manage as a single parent in the near term unless she receives substantial child support and alimony payments each month. Two weeks before the meeting, Maritza called Catherine to get a copy of one missing tax return. During their conversation, Catherine mentioned that her great-aunt Dana had just passed away after a long illness. Catherine said she would drop off a copy of the missing tax return that afternoon on her way to Dana's funeral. Catherine mentioned that Dana, who had no children of her own, had promised to leave her 24-acre estate to Catherine.

"This could make all the difference in our lives," Catherine said. "There's a four-bedroom house, and a barn, and a pond. The boys would be so happy there."

"Are you sure she's leaving the estate to you?" Maritza asked.

"I haven't actually read the will," said Catherine, "but Aunt Dana and I have talked many times about this. We had one conversation about it three days before she passed away. I promised to take good care of the house and to try to keep it in the family."

"I'm sorry for your loss, but that's really good news about the estate," said Maritza. "When you get a copy of Dana's will, perhaps Sam can look it over for you."

"Yes, that would be great," said Catherine. "I'll ask the executor for a copy."

Maritza meant to tell Sam about what Catherine had said, but Sam was in court the afternoon that she talked with Catherine, and it slipped her mind. Maritza's spring break started the next day, and she spent eight wonderful days at the beach. The next time Maritza saw Sam was the week after spring break, when they met in the elevator on the way to the settlement meeting. Alan and Travis, Alan's lawyer, also were on the elevator, so there was no chance to talk.

During the meeting, Catherine sat between Sam and Maritza on one side of the table. Alan and Travis sat on the other side. After it was agreed that Catherine would have primary custody of the children, Sam and Travis reviewed the financial statement listing the earnings, assets and debts of both parties, and began to discuss how much child support and alimony Alan would pay each month.

Maritza sat in the meeting looking at her own copies of the documents. She noticed that there was nothing on Catherine's financial statement about her great-aunt Dana's house. Then Travis asked Sam and Catherine:

"Do you anticipate any changes in Catherine's financial situation that would change this picture in any way?"

Sam looked at his client for an answer. Catherine said "Not unless I win the lottery."

If Sam knew about the bequest, what would be his ethical obligations in this situation? Does his ignorance excuse him from any possible duty of disclosure? What does Maritza need to do?

Communication

Lawyers owe duties of candor and professional courtesy to other lawyers and to unrepresented persons with whom they deal. As with other ethical duties, a lawyer may not ask an employee to do something that the lawyer may not do herself. Many legal externs interview witnesses, deliver papers, make phone calls, and do other delegated tasks that involve dealing with opposing counsel, witnesses, and others, so externs need to be familiar with these boundaries.

Communication With Represented Persons

> ■ *Rule 4.2. Communication with Person Represented by Counsel*

In representing a client, a lawyer shall not communicate about the subject of the representation with a person the lawyer knows to be represented by another lawyer in the matter, unless the lawyer has the consent of the other lawyer or is authorized to do so by law or a court order.

This rule means that a lawyer or someone working for the lawyer may not call or visit an adverse party in a case or someone else who is represented in the matter by another lawyer unless the other lawyer has given permission for the contact. Even an informal conversation with a represented adverse party could lead to disciplinary action or to disqualification of the lawyer whose employee (or extern) had the prohibited contact. If you are uncertain about whether the person you are contacting is represented, the first question to ask when you contact that person is, "Do you have a lawyer?" If the answer is yes, simply get the name and number of the lawyer and consult with your supervisor about next steps.

This rule seems simple enough, but there are some wrinkles. If the opposing party is a government agency, the rule may not apply, because citizens have constitutional and legal rights to communicate with government officials. If the opposing party is an organization that is represented by counsel, a lawyer (or a legal extern) may communicate directly with some employees of the organization but not others. Comment 7 after Rule 4.2 provides the following in part:

> In the case of a represented organization, this Rule prohibits communications with a constituent of the organization who supervises, directs or regularly consults with the organization's lawyer concerning the matter or has authority to obligate the organization with respect to the matter or whose act or omission in connection with

the matter may be imputed to the organization for purposes of civil or criminal liability. Consent of the organization's lawyer is not required for communication with a former constituent. If a constituent of the organization is represented in the matter by his or her own counsel, the consent by that counsel to a communication will be sufficient for purposes of this rule.

If you are asked to interview employees of an adverse party that is an institution, first study your jurisdiction's version of Rule 4.2 and its comments, and then consult with your supervisor about which employees you may interview.

Communication With Unrepresented Persons

If the opposing party in a case is not represented, a lawyer may communicate directly with that person. In this situation, however, a lawyer must take care not to mislead the other person or to give legal advice to the other person.

> ■ *Rule 4.3. Dealing with Unrepresented Person*

In dealing on behalf of a client with a person who is not represented by counsel, a lawyer shall not state or imply that the lawyer is disinterested. When the lawyer knows or reasonably should know that the unrepresented person misunderstands the lawyer's role in the matter, the lawyer shall make reasonable efforts to correct the misunderstanding. The lawyer shall not give legal advice to an unrepresented person, other than the advice to secure counsel, if the lawyer knows or reasonably should know that the interests of such a person are or have a reasonable possibility of being in conflict with the interests of the client.

These constraints are intended to prevent lawyers from taking advantage of others whose understanding of law and the legal system may be limited. A lawyer who misleads an unrepresented person also may be found to have violated Rule 8.4(c), which prohibits all "dishonesty, fraud, deceit or misrepresentation."

Exercise 13.5 A Fender Bender: Julie Maynard is a legal extern at the state Department of Consumer Affairs (DCA). She assists with investigations of complaints of unfair and deceptive trade practices by local merchants. The agency has recently received several complaints about the Mitch Dawson's Auto Body Shop. State law requires all merchants who perform car repairs to give customers itemized written estimates of the cost of repairs before doing any work. The law also prohibits charging customers more than the amount stated on the estimate. Mitch Dawson apparently tends to provide no estimate or only a "ball-park" oral estimate before doing work on a car. Leo Gonzales is Julie's supervisor at DCA. He's preparing to file suit against Dawson. One morning, Julie's car gets rear-ended on the way in to the office. The back fender is crumpled. Julie is late to work and comes in frazzled, explaining apologetically about the accident.

"It wasn't my fault," Julie tells Leo, "but I had to stay until the police had completed their report."

Leo's eyes twinkle. "Tell you what," he says, "Why don't you take your car in to Mitch Dawson. Put this tape recorder in your jacket pocket, and turn it on before you get there. Just act like a normal customer. Tell him you want him to fix your fender and ask how much it will cost. Regardless of whether he gives you an estimate, leave your car for him to repair. If he follows the law, no problem, you get your car fixed. If not, you can be a plaintiff in the case and be my star witness. If we win, you may get a refund of the cost of the repair and possibly additional damages. Okay?"

How does Julie need to respond to Leo's request? Are there any ethical or legal problems with this plan? If so, is there a way that Julie could undertake this investigation without violating the rules?

Litigation Ethics From a Judicial Perspective

Many law student externs work in judges' chambers or for courts. They may encounter some of the litigation ethics issues addressed above and other issues as well. The American Bar Association has produced a Model Code of Judicial Conduct, which, like the model rules for lawyers, is reviewed by the state supreme courts and often adopted, with or without modifications, as an ethics code that governs the conduct of state court judges in the relevant state. The United States Judicial Conference adopted a Code of Conduct for Federal Judges. All federal judges except those serving on the U.S. Supreme Court are bound to comply with that code. The U.S. Supreme Court has not adopted a code of ethics.

Judicial externs should review the code of judicial conduct that applies to the judges for whom they are working. As employees of the judge, externs must not engage in conduct that would violate the code if done by a judge. Below are some examples of issues that could arise. See Chapter 19 on Judicial Externships.

Ex Parte Communications

A judge may not discuss a pending matter ex parte with a lawyer working on the matter. The Code of Conduct for United States Judges lays out this boundary as follows:

Canon 3: A Judge Should Perform the Duties of the Office Fairly, Impartially and Diligently

(A) Adjudicative Responsibilities.

    (4) A judge should accord to every person who has a legal interest in a proceeding, and that person's lawyer, the full right to be heard according to law. Except as set out below, a judge should not initiate, permit, or consider ex parte communications or consider other communications concerning a pending or impending matter that are made outside the presence of the parties or their lawyers. If a judge receives an unauthorized ex parte communication bearing on the substance of a matter, the judge should promptly notify the parties of the subject matter of the communication and allow the parties an opportunity to respond, if requested. A judge may: . . .

        (b) when circumstances require it, permit ex parte communication for scheduling, administrative, or emergency purposes, but only if the ex parte communication does not address substantive matters and the judge reasonably believes that no party will gain a procedural, substantive, or tactical advantage as a result of the ex parte communication; . . .

As an employee of a judge, a judicial extern also must observe this restriction, so she may not discuss the matter with a law student working for one of the lawyers. While not likely, it is possible that a law student working for a lawyer on a matter and law student working for the judge hearing the matter might be friends or might be students in the same externship seminar. It is important for issues like this to be identified early, because a classroom conversation about a case that might otherwise be proper could violate the prohibition on ex parte communications with judges. Because this issue might arise in a social setting as easily as in a classroom, each judicial extern must be aware of the prohibition on ex parte communications and must exercise care not to violate the rules.

Seeking Expert Guidance

A law student might be assigned to write a memo or to draft an opinion for a judge. A question that arises for some judicial externs is whether they may obtain guidance or advice on questions about the assignment from a law professor, a reference librarian at the law school, or from a parent or other relative who is familiar with the area of law. Most law students have no prior experience of drafting judicial opinions, want to do their best, and fear that they will miss something important. It would be tempting to consult an advisor without telling the judge. This would be a bad idea. Canon 3 (A)(4)(c) of the Code of Conduct of United States Judges provides that a judge may

> obtain the written advice of a disinterested expert on the law, but only after giving advance notice to the parties of the person to be consulted and the subject matter of the advice and affording the parties reasonable opportunity to object and respond to the notice and to the advice received.

Because a judge cannot consult a law professor friend or a lawyer not involved in the case without notifying the parties in advance and providing a process for objection, a law student extern in a judge's chambers also may not seek outside advice without following these procedures.

Any discussion of cases pending before a judge outside of chambers is potentially problematic. Although some topics might be unobjectionable, a law student extern would be well-advised to avoid discussion of pending matters in general and consult with the judge before engaging in any external discussion of a particular matter. If, for example, a judicial extern needs to make a presentation in class about some aspect of the externship, the extern should seek the judge's approval before including any topics that would touch on the substance of a pending matter.

There are many topics about a student's experience in a judicial externship that do not raise this level of sensitivity. For example, a student might discuss the way the work is organized in the chambers, the dynamics of any events that take place in open court, or his or her interaction with the judge or with other staff in the chambers. Discussion of pending matters, however, should be handled with extreme care.

Conclusion

In this chapter, we have examined only a few of the ethical rules that constrain the conduct of lawyers in litigation. There are many other relevant rules and an enormous variety of situations that might present ethical quandaries for legal externs. For example, what if you are preparing documents to respond to a discovery request and your supervisor instructs you not to produce a particular document that you believe is covered by the request? What if you believe that client or a lawyer has altered a document that must be produced?

This and the preceding chapters on legal ethics aim to provide you with some practice in attending to your own moral radar. As an extern and as a lawyer, you need to exercise independent ethical judgment, even when you work with experienced lawyers who have high standards of professional conduct. As a law student, it is important that you become familiar with the ethics rules and the other law that governs lawyers. Also, you also need to hone your ethical sensitivity—your ability to recognize ethical dilemmas.

Your placement can provide rich opportunities to notice and think about ethical issues. You might encounter some issues that you do not want to ask your supervisor about. Some may seem trivial; others might raise questions about the conduct of your supervisor or another lawyer in the office. It is worthwhile to notice and evaluate the questions that occur to you even if you do not raise them at work.

Here is a simple protocol for increasing your ability to recognize and evaluate ethical dilemmas: Pay attention whenever you see or do something that makes you feel a bit uneasy. Once you notice a question, do a little research. Is there an ethics rule or some other law that addresses the question? Discuss the question with your externship teacher or with a friend or family member—if you can do so without revealing client confidences. Exploring the questions about ethical issues that you encounter in early practice experiences will give you the skills you need to address larger issues in the future.

ENDNOTES

1   The bracketed language in Rule 3.8 and in comment 1 below is included in the Model Rules of Professional Conduct and in the rules adopted by a number of states, but has not been adopted by the state of Delaware. *See Rules of Delaware State Courts*, Del. St. Cts., http://courts.delaware.gov/Rules/?DLRPCwithComments_Oct2007.pdf (last visited February 7, 2015).

CHAPTER 14

Learning About Lawyering

ALEXANDER SCHERR

T his chapter talks about what lawyers do. Your externship offers the chance to work alongside lawyers, to watch what they do, to assess how they think, and to gauge their effectiveness in helping their clients. From this experience, you can draw conclusions about legal work: its challenges and intricacies, and its extraordinary effect on the lives of the people and causes for whom lawyers work. You can start to develop a sense of your preferences among the many ways of practicing law and to formulate standards of practice for your own work.

Getting a complete picture of the lawyering at your placement can present some challenges. You may only do certain kinds of tasks, in only one part of your office, on only certain parts of cases. Your schedule may keep you from observing important parts of what your office does. The kinds of cases or other matters your office handles may take longer than a semester to resolve. You may not get to see key events or be included in critical meetings. Much like the blind men who tried to describe an elephant by touching a leg, an ear, or a trunk, you may see only a part of the lawyering around you, limiting your perspective on how lawyers solve problems and plan for the future.[1]

This chapter helps you by painting an overall picture of what lawyers do and how they do it. In Chapter 2, you can find advice about how to plan for your professional development, in part by creating a list of your opportunities to watch how lawyers work at your placement.[2] Yet, you may not be aware of all there is to see. This chapter seeks to fill some of the gaps in what you know about lawyering and to develop a more complete picture of lawyering.

The chapter starts with a review of some of the most well-known descriptions of what lawyers do. It then turns to two key features of effective lawyering: the exercise of good judgment; and the process of legal problem solving, from first contact to closure of a legal matter. The chapter describes helpful practice habits as well as some of the key challenges of legal decision making, including incomplete knowledge, uncertainty, bias, and doubt. After a review of different types of law practices, the chapter ends with an audit exercise that helps you to identify and assess the complex dimensions of lawyering at your placement.

What Lawyers Do: Perspectives

The experience of law practice is complex and multi-faceted; it calls upon a wide range of abilities, including intellectual, emotional, and moral capacities. So it should not surprise you that efforts to describe what lawyers do lead to diverse descriptions. This section reviews some of the most recent and well-known efforts to paint such a picture. As you will see, while they overlap, these images vary both in detail and in the questions they set out to answer. The descriptions can vary depending on different goals for the writer: to allocate training of lawyers between law schools and the practicing bar; to reform legal education; to identify good candidates for effective practice; or to test whether a candidate should get the credentials to practice.

> **Exercise 14.1** Before reading this section, jot down your own tentative impression of what lawyers do. Consider all the sources that may have formed this impression including what you have seen yourself and heard from others: news reports, fiction and film, popular culture. Once you have formulated an impression, hold onto it as you read the following sub-sections. Keep track of any new ideas you encounter. Start to relate them to what you might encounter at your placement.

Who Should Train Young Lawyers: The MacCrate Report

In 1992, a section of the American Bar Association issued a report on the ways in which law schools and the practicing bar might share the common enterprise of training young lawyers for the practice of law.[3] The MacCrate Report called for a re-examination of the ways in which law schools trained lawyers and for a continued commitment to what it called "the growth of the skills curriculum." As part of this call, this report sought to create "an all-inclusive overview of the profession today," as well as an "in-depth study of the full range of skills and values that are necessary for the practice of law."[4]

The MacCrate Report enumerates and concentrates on these necessary skills and values for two different reasons: first, as a set of learning goals for students in law schools; and second, as a way of prompting institutional and systemic reforms in legal education and in the training of newly admitted lawyers. The Report disclaims success at making a definitive statement. Rather, it stresses the importance of articulating such a picture both to young lawyers and to those who teach them. While it acknowledges the importance of specialization, the Report suggests that competent representation requires some abilities all lawyers need in order to be effective:

> [C]ompetent representation of a client still requires a well-trained generalist—one who has a broad range of knowledge of legal institutions and who is proficient at a number of diverse tasks. This is so because any problem presented by a client ... may be amenable to a variety of types of solutions of differing degrees of efficacy; a lawyer cannot competently represent or advise the client or other entity unless he or she has the breadth of knowledge and skill necessary to perceive, evaluate, and begin to pursue each of the options.[5]

The Report describes lawyering as the exercise of ten core skills and the pursuit of four core values. The skills include both analytical and other capacities. Analytical capacities include problem solving and legal analysis and reasoning. Other skills include legal research, fact investigation, communication, counseling, and negotiation. Related capacities include the capacity to advise about dispute resolution and the administrative skill to organize and manage a law office, as well as the capacity to recognize and resolve ethical dilemmas. The four values include practicing competently, striving to promote justice, enhancing the capacity of legal institutions to promote justice, and continuing to pursue professional self-development.[6]

The Report does not rank or sequence the elements of what lawyers do. It provides no checklist for how to choose courses in law school, how to handle a case, or how to manage your career. At the same time, these competencies have many complex interactions; performance in one area influences and is influenced by performance in others.

Notably, "problem solving" constitutes the first of the ten core skills and the Report assigns it special importance. Describing it as foundational, the Report notes that this skill includes diagnosing the problem, generating and evaluating options for solution, formulating a plan, implementing that plan, and keeping the plan open to new facts and ideas. In this sense, "problem solving" draws together all of the other things lawyers do, with a view to accomplishing the client's goals. See Appendix I for the full list of skills and values.

Exercise 14.2 Consider the list of skills identified above as well as in Appendix I. How has your experience in law school helped you to develop and strengthen each of these skills? How will your placement this semester continue that development? Your law school or your placement might develop several of these skills at the same time. If so, try to tease out which experiences seem to do so most successfully.

Reforming Legal Education: The Carnegie Report

Published in 2007, the Carnegie Report[7] takes a distinctly different approach to its recommendations about legal education. Instead of focusing on specific skills or competencies, this Report articulates three broad concerns that structure its recommendations for reform: legal analysis, practical skills, and professional identity. These aspects of lawyering experience interact and support each other:

> The two kinds of legal knowledge—the theoretical and the practical—are complementary. Each must have a respected place in legal education. Further, each sort of knowledge, with its own characteristic setting and ways of teaching, can be made to advance when it is understood in relation to its complement, so that neither remains what it would be if it continued to develop in isolation. This process of mutual development will progress best when it is directed by a focus on the professional formation of law students . . . . In short, we propose an integration of student learning of theoretical and practical legal knowledge and professional identity.[8]

The Carnegie Report proposes that law schools offer students three different kinds of apprenticeships: one intellectual and cognitive, a second focused on expert practice, and a third focused on identity and purpose. In formulating these apprenticeships, the Report creates a lens through which to identify the strengths and deficiencies of legal education. For more detail on the Report's three apprenticeships, see Appendix I.

The three apprenticeships also offer a compelling picture of lawyering itself. Lawyers integrate cognitive knowledge and practice-based expertise, all the while acting with an understanding of their role and identity as professionals. Cognitive knowledge includes the capacity to find and analyze law and legal doctrine as well as formal legal process. Practice expertise includes the ability to make use of law and legal process in the service of practical outcomes through a range of different competencies. Finally, lawyers integrate formal knowledge and practice-based knowledge into actions consistent with the lawyer's own values as a professional and as a human being. See Chapter 24 on Professional Identity and Formation.

> **Exercise 14.3** Every law school course, whether clinical or not, has the potential to help you integrate your knowledge of the law, your practical expertise, and your professional identity. Consider which past courses have had the most powerful impact on you and the reasons they influenced or affected you. Now consider whether and how your placement this semester could have the same impact. In doing so, identify any experiences you can seek out at your placement that will help you to integrate the three "apprenticeships" identified in the Carnegie Report.

Assessing Applicants to Law School: Lawyering Effectiveness Factors

In 2008, Marjorie Shultz and Sheldon Zedeck issued a report that sought to help law school admissions offices predict more reliably which applicants would both perform well in law school and become effective lawyers. Their study sought to expand on the use of standardized testing, such as the LSAT, as a predictor of first year performance. These tests "have value as predictors, but they do not attempt to account for all the factors that contribute to law school grades or to broader performance in law school, and even less to success in lawyering."[9] The study sought to describe "what lawyers view as factors important to effective lawyering" and to create valid measures of "what lawyers see as more or less effective lawyer behavior to form measures of professional effectiveness."[10]

This list of "26 Effectiveness Factors" appears in Appendix I. The study groups the factors into eight broad categories: intellectual and cognitive, research and information gathering, communication, planning and organization, conflict resolution, client and business relationships, working with others, and character.[11] Several of these factors are identical to skills addressed in the MacCrate report; for example, both highlight fact investigation and legal research. These factors also overlap with aspects of lawyering stressed in the Carnegie Report, such as the importance of practical judgment, community involvement, and service.

The Shultz and Zedeck study also goes beyond the categories in the earlier reports. While MacCrate included organizing and managing law practice as core skills, Shultz and Zedeck add factors related to business development including networking and developing relationships within the legal profession. The study also highlights what the authors informally refer to as factors of "character": passion and engagement, diligence, integrity and honesty, stress management, and self-development. These factors overlap with many of those discussed in the Carnegie Report as elements of "professional identity." Indeed, they suggest that effective lawyering includes both professional and personal traits that form part of our identity as individuals.

> **Exercise 14.4** What factors do you think make for an effective lawyer? List your top five to ten factors, making sure to include factors relating to knowledge or skill and those relating to character and personality, as highlighted by Shultz and Zedeck. What traits do you possess that meet your own picture? What traits would you like to acquire? How will your placement help you to do so?

Testing for Admission to Practice: Skills and Abilities of Newly Licensed Lawyers

In 2011–2012, the National Conference of Bar Examiners (the "NCBE") commissioned a study to determine the areas of knowledge and the skills and abilities most widely recognized as necessary for a newly-licensed lawyer.[12] The NCBE creates many of the tests bar applicants take during the bar examination, including the Multistate Bar Examination, the Multistate Professional Responsibility Test, the Multistate Essay Examination, and the Multistate Performance Test. The NCBE commissioned the study to describe the knowledge and abilities commonly seen as important for new lawyers in an effort to assess and develop new approaches to testing applicants to the bar.

A listing of the skills and abilities assessed in the NCBE study appears in Appendix I ranked by the degree of importance assigned to each item on the list by survey respondents.[13] The five "skills/abilities" with the highest scores for importance to a newly-licensed lawyer include written communication, paying attention to detail, listening, oral communication, and professionalism. By contrast, the five viewed as least important, at least on this list, include non-electronic researching, jury selection, legal citation, trial skills, and document review for attorney-client privilege. The comparison suggests that skills that cut across a wide range of practice areas are likely to be more widely applicable to a young lawyer.

Many items on this list involve abilities that would be difficult, if not impossible, to test in a traditional bar examination format. Consider, for example, how you might test professionalism for a new law graduate. What aspects of professionalism might you test? See Chapter 9 on Professionalism. What standard would you use and how would you compare responses across the tens of thousands of applicants that sit for the bar each year? Some aspects of admission to the bar go beyond what a written examination can test. These qualities of mind, spirit, and character become part of the other entrance process, related to finding a job. See Chapter 26 on Externships and Career Planning. As a thought exercise, you might reflect on how to test characteristics such as "professionalism" or "integrity." What role might letters of reference, or performance in a clinical course, or personal interviews play in such a process?

> **Exercise 14.5** Consider the different tests that you face in becoming a lawyer. You have already passed many of them: success on the LSAT, admission to law school, and maintaining more than the minimum GPA. This section has discussed at least one more, passing the bar exam, in each of its many forms. But others exist, including finding a job and establishing a successful and sustainable practice. Consider the skills and abilities that you bring to passing these latter challenges. How does your placement help you with the bar exam and also with the other challenges you will face in your first few years of practice? See Chapter 24 on Professional Identity and Formation and Chapter 25 on Work & Well-being.

Judgment and Lawyering Process

As noted earlier, how you describe lawyering depends on your reasons for describing it. The previous section illustrates how descriptions can vary when one seeks to reform legal education, to allocate the training of lawyers between law schools and the bar, to identify good candidates for effective practice, or to test whether a candidate should be given the credentials to practice.

This section presents an alternate perspective, one designed to help you understand and make the most of your experience at your placement. It suggests that all lawyers share two distinctive capacities: the exercise of problem solving judgment and the handling of client matters through a regularized process of problem solving. It begins with a discussion of the importance of practical judgment in legal decision making. It ends with a general description of a lawyering process, that is, the series of steps and competencies through which lawyers work on cases.

As an initial matter, the term "problem solving" suggests that lawyers work only in situations involving conflict or other difficulty. In this chapter, however, problem solving also includes the work that lawyers do in creating deals and reducing the risks of future problems. The MacCrate Report make this point as follows:

The term "problem" is conceived as including the entire range of situations in which a lawyer's assistance is sought in avoiding or resolving difficulties, realizing opportunities, or accomplishing objectives—situations as diverse as those in which a dispute has arisen between the client and another individual or entity; those in which a client may need to define legal rights or relationships in a contract, lease, will, or other instrument; and those in which a government agency may wish to promulgate or amend a rule.[14]

In short, lawyers respond to requests for help both to resolve disputes and to accomplish future goals.

Lawyers, Decisions, and Judgment

Consider the following question: if plumbers work with pipe, and carpenters with wood, with what do lawyers work? Reasonable answers to this question might include words, or people, or laws, or values, or money. A more general answer suggests that lawyers work with decisions. More specifically, lawyers work with clients and with the decisions that clients bring to them. Lawyers help to assess, create, and implement choices between alternate stories from disputing parties, between alternate agreements, and between different ways to structure behavior in the future. Early on in your externship, it is useful to think about the impact your work has on decision making at your placement and to consider how all aspects of the practice work together to resolve conflicts or create new rules or relationships for the future.

Lawyers do not hold a monopoly on helping people with decisions; the helping professions generally advise people struggling with important choices. Indeed, your placement may rely on these other professionals as part of its practice, including doctors, accountants, psychologists, business executives, social workers, and the like. Yet lawyers do have a monopoly on decisions directly affected by the law and situations that require access to legal process, such as litigation. Lawyers assess how the law affects particular decisions and how legal processes can advance particular goals. Lawyers mediate the influences of the law on client decision making.

Most decisions respond to a variety of influences, not just the law. Lawyers need to become as adept in working with these influences as they are in analyzing the law. These influences include many realities, in several dimensions:

- the situation's history and momentum;

- the emotional and moral realities in the situation for all participants;

- the web of relationships from which the situation grows;

· the relative power of the participants;

· the magnitude and intensity of the stakes; and

· the limitations on solutions, such as money, time, and other realities.

Legal decision making asks lawyers to integrate the law into situations shaped by all of these influences and more. You may notice how much more real legal issues feel at your placement. That happens because of the immediacy and complexity of the human context in which legal problems occur.

> **Exercise 14.6 Seeing Context:** Select a project on which you are working or which you have observed. Do a standard law school assessment: identify the legal issues and ask how they apply to the facts as you understand them.
>
> Then step back and ask other questions: Who are the parties? What is their relationship? What else do you know about the history? What do you know about the parties' interests? What kind of power do they have to pursue those concerns? What needs will your legal work satisfy? What resources can each party bring to bear?
>
> Now bring the legal issue back into focus: How do the issues of the project you selected relate to the contexts you have identified? The legal issues should now appear as threads in a complex web of influences, with a strong, and perhaps even decisive, influence on the outcome.

Decisions made by lawyers and their clients become the law that governs the outcomes. As Karl Llewellyn says in his classic book for new law students, THE BRAMBLE BUSH, " . . . [J]udges or sheriffs or clerks or jailers or lawyers . . . are officials of the law. What these officials do about disputes is . . . the law itself."[15] In effect, what lawyers do about their cases becomes the law itself, even if only for a particular dispute or transaction.

As an extern, you are helping your supervisors make law. This law is often transient and local, may bind no one other than the client, and may have limited impact even there. The practice habits and analytical assumptions of lawyers, however, become the templates for future handling of the same or similar problems. More generally, the practice habits of lawyers help to structure the norms of both disputes and deals, norms that shape both routine and unusual client actions and affect how specific, local concerns evolve into common law, statutes, and regulations. Your placement positions you perfectly to observe how the norms at your placement embody what the law is and influence what it may become.

Decision making requires the capacity to choose among several available courses of action, commonly referred to as "judgment." Judgment is the ability to make small and large choices and is a fundamental life skill we exercise daily. Despite its universality, however, identifying and discussing good legal judgment can be difficult. Law school education can obscure the central nature of decision making by fractionalizing lawyering behaviors. The curriculum often has separate classes that teach intellectual competencies, such as doctrinal knowledge, legal analysis, or legal research; or performance competencies, such as trial advocacy, negotiation, or legal drafting. These courses typically leave discussions of judgment, especially overall judgment about case handling, to active experience in law practice, including your experience in a clinic or externship.

Part of the challenge lies in deciding what makes for "good" judgment. You can easily recall both the good and the bad decisions you have made. Even if you listed and assessed all of them, it still would be hard to define criteria for good or bad judgment that apply to every situation or even to specific situations. Good judgment is local and problem specific; it affects people with diverse goals and values and tries to balance varying risks and opportunities. Good legal judgment requires more than good legal analysis. A lawyer has to account both for legal rules and processes and for the non-legal influences that affect the decision. Because it weighs both legal rules and non-legal realities, decision making by lawyers is deeply pragmatic.

Some believe you cannot learn good judgment; like talent or cool, you have it or you do not. And in reality, the consistency with which some people make good (or bad) decisions supports the idea that judgment grows from innate abilities. Importantly, though, you can strengthen your capacity for practical judgment through practice and reflection. You will most likely not acquire it in a day, a semester, or even a year; instead, you will develop it over time, through incremental growth as you work on real cases. Practical judgment requires you to understand a decision in different dimensions, including the conceptual framework of the law, and also the human realities from which the decision emerges and which the decision will affect. Practical judgment matters the most when exercised over time and in the real world, on real problems, and for real clients.

You may not understand all of the reasons why your supervising attorneys make certain decisions. Nonetheless, you can learn a lot by watching how they choose to proceed, asking them their reasons, and evaluating their answers against your own sense of what to do. Many young lawyers do not participate in or even get to see the decisions their supervisors make with clients. Instead, especially in practices that have large teams of lawyers, the lawyer with primary responsibility to the client assigns the parts of a decision-making process to other lawyers to complete. These tasks contribute to the ultimate resolution, but it can be hard for a young lawyer to understand how they do.

> **Exercise 14.7** Your placement will often bring you into direct contact with the lawyer and client whose judgments will influence the outcome of the case. Make sure to take advantage of this contact. Choose a case on which you work and make sure to make time to ask your supervisor about the judgment calls and decision making that the case requires. Make a habit of asking these questions on your own, and occasionally check your answers with your supervisor. As you do, reflect, both then and later, about what you have heard. Do you agree with your supervisor's approach? If so, be specific about how and the reasons you agree. If not, think through the specific reasons for your disagreement. Consider writing a portion of a journal on these thoughts, always consistent with maintaining the confidentiality of your placement's work.

Your reputation as a lawyer will rest in large part on your ability to make and to implement good decisions, consistently and over time. To learn how to exercise judgment reliably, you will want to avoid repeated mistakes and build on your successes. You will benefit from considering the full dimensions of each decision, including both the legal and the other influences on the outcome.

To do this effectively will require you to develop the capacity for reflection. The practice of reflection helps you learn the most from your externship. It is also a crucial professional competency, affecting your ability to make wise decisions and to exercise good judgment. Use your journals to describe what has happened at your placement and also to assess who made the underlying decisions and their reasons for making them. In doing this analysis, you will start to develop your own judgment toward the day you become responsible to your own clients. See Chapter 8 on Reflection and Writing Journals for more on how reflection improves judgment.

Practical Judgment and the Lawyering Process

Exercising legal judgment occurs in real time, in the real world, and in active relationship to other people, tasks, and deadlines. This section talks about lawyering as a process, that is, a series of behaviors through which lawyers encounter, make, and implement their decisions. This description offers you a roadmap of the core competencies of lawyering.

Legal problem solving has a work flow similar to other problem solving. It includes identifying the problem and assessing its dimensions, formulating alternatives, choosing among them, and implementing choices through planned action. This work flow is goal oriented and moves generally from initial contact to final resolution. This process generally moves forward, but does not always move in one direction. Lawyers often move back and forth between assessment, decision making, and action as they move toward their clients' goals.

Remember, you may work on only a narrow portion of the overall task. For example, researching the law, organizing documents, or drafting a single clause in an agreement are discrete activities that contribute to the outcome, yet form only part of the overall case handling. In many cases, you will only witness discrete events: a single hearing in a judicial placement, or one deposition in a litigation placement, or the closing in a transactions placement. These tasks and events represent separate stages in the overall handling of the matter by your office.

The rest of this section gives you a roadmap of the most common phases of legal problem solving. It can help you to understand how your specific assignments fit into the overall flow of problem solving. It also can help you to identify other opportunities for work or observation that can round out your understanding of the lawyering process at your placement.

Assessment

Good lawyering depends on accurate assessment of cases. A lawyer's appraisal shapes the client's choices and the lawyer's actions. Appraisal and reappraisal occur throughout a lawyer's work. The lawyer must respond to new information, new theories, and new pressures from other parties.

Thus, acquiring good habits of case appraisal represents a key part of your abilities as a lawyer. Your placement should give you many chances to observe and evaluate different methods of preparing and assessing cases. Keep an eye out for how your placement acquires its cases, how it develops the relevant facts and law, and how it assesses the likely outcomes of its work.

First Contact: All lawyering starts with an initial encounter, which might take the form of a phone call, a client interview, a police referral, or the assignment of a file by a docketing clerk. First impressions matter. During this encounter, the lawyer develops an initial theory of the case and charts the early steps of case development. These first impressions and the choices they prompt influence what the lawyer does next and how the lawyer understands and addresses the problem itself. Given the importance of first impressions, the lawyer faces several risks: focusing too early on a single aspect of the problem, failing to notice key issues, or misunderstanding the goals or interests of the client or the parties. Whatever the source of first contact, lawyers should take pains to keep an open mind and to consider carefully all of the information available. For more on first contact with clients and the issues that may arise in the attorney-client relationship see Chapter 15 on Client Relationships.

Factual and Legal Development: Your office also must develop the factual information and legal concepts that are necessary to predict outcomes, identify risks, and make plans. As an extern, you are likely to help develop the facts and the legal principles of a problem by reviewing papers or interviewing witnesses or through legal research and writing. These two abilities interact: you will research the law based on assumptions about the facts, and you will reconsider what you know about the facts based on what you discover in the law. If your supervisor has incomplete facts, you may be asked to assess how different scenarios might lead to different outcomes. Similarly, you may need to interview witnesses and review documents in support of a particular legal claim or to see how many legal claims a given set of facts might support. In effect, investigation and research converge, each informing and shaping the other.

Merit Assessment: The task of merit assessment is where the lawyer integrates facts and law to understand how the law affects the problem. For example, litigators must predict the likely outcome of litigation in order to assist client decision making, plan for trial, and prepare for negotiations. Similarly, transactional lawyers must determine the extent to which the law will regulate or even permit a proposed deal. In either case, the lawyer must integrate an appropriately thorough legal analysis into a reasonably thorough version of the facts, so as to appraise the likelihood that legal rules will permit the client's desired result. This assessment directly affects the office's handling of a case. Even as an extern, you may be asked for your recommendation on what to do in light of the known facts and law.

As important as the legal assessment is, however, it forms only a part of legal problem solving. The lawyer still must integrate that assessment with other practical realities. For example, a litigator must assess the likelihood of success in court and also the client's tolerance for risk, need for a remedy, and aversion to trial. Similarly, a lawyer helping to form a business must determine what business forms are available, and also help the client assess how those forms help or hinder the client's ability to achieve personal and financial goals. Finally, judges often engage in pragmatic considerations, balancing the correct legal result with the practical demands of docket management and the longer term interest in achieving a durable solution to the dispute.

The lawyer's assessment task thus weaves purely legal assessments together with other practical dimensions to see the problem in depth and generate effective solutions. At your placement, keep track of what happens to the legal analyses you perform. How do your assigning attorneys use them? What effect do they have on decisions in the overall cases? What other factors seem to influence how decisions take shape and strategies develop? Answering questions like these will deepen your grasp of lawyering at your placement.

Decision Making

It pays to distinguish between a final decision and the decisions that lead to it. While all lawyering seeks a final decision (a verdict, a binding agreement, a judicial opinion), finality emerges from a series of smaller, connected decisions shaped by the lawyer's appraisal and handling of the case. Moreover, legal decision making occurs from a particular point of view: both advocates and planners seek to advance particular goals and interests. This section talks about two tasks: the development of choices and strategies, and the process of deciding itself.

Preparing for a decision means identifying choices and developing strategies to accomplish each choice. The identification of choices starts early, during the assessment phase. While gathering information and analyzing the law, the lawyer will gain a better sense of the possible outcomes the problem allows. At the same time, the lawyer will start to identify what it will take to achieve those outcomes and the collection of actions, events, or strategies that may accomplish each outcome. In so doing, the lawyer must be both creative, able to imagine the goals and means relevant to the problem at hand, and also realistic, able to assess how plausible each outcome and strategy is within the restrictions of time, energy, and resources. This ability to assess legal and practical realities and to create a reliable picture of available choices and strategies lies at the heart of "thinking like a lawyer."

Consider these illustrations:

- In a litigation placement, a tenant has asked the lawyer for help with an eviction notice. After investigating and researching potential defenses, the lawyer concludes the client has plausible but not airtight affirmative defenses based on the landlord's failure to maintain the property, which if lost at trial might form the basis for a successful appeal. The client's fundamental options include staying in the apartment with or without necessary repairs or moving either now or in the future. Strategies include litigation through trial to appeal; litigating, but seeking a settlement that allows the client either the ability to stay or the time to move; or vacating the premises without litigation. The lawyer faces the task of advising the client on which of these best meets the client's goals and interests. If your placement also charges the client a fee, the cost of pursuing litigation also becomes a significant factor.

- In a transactional placement, a community group wants to encourage local economic development. After interviewing the group's participants and researching relevant possibilities, the lawyer concludes that the group should consider adopting one of several different business structures, including an informal association, a nonprofit corporation, or even continuing as an unstructured volunteer effort. Strategies include continuing without further legal organization or adopting a formal legal structure, with subsidiary choices of for-profit or nonprofit status. The lawyer faces the task of helping the client assess which option best meets the group's collection of goals and interests.

- In a judicial placement, a judge has been assigned a complex tort lawsuit involving multiple plaintiffs and a large corporate defendant. Upon reviewing the pleadings and pending motions, the judge and the judge's clerk conclude that the issues of causation and damages might be triable separately and that causation involves contested facts that require expert testimony. The judge will have choices about bifurcating the trial, the admissibility of expert testimony, and the use of special masters. The judge can develop these choices in many ways: waiting to respond to motions from the parties or using pretrial conferences to encourage the parties to reach agreement on what to do. The judge faces the task of working with the parties and attorneys on a trial process that leads to an accurate and final resolution of the relevant claims.

When you are assigned a case at your placement, take the time to ask how your assignment relates to the ultimate outcome of that case. When you observe a hearing or a negotiation, try to discern how each lawyer's actions express and advance particular goals. The more you understand the choices and strategies underlying the work you do or see, the more you can learn about how lawyers identify and pursue the solutions they achieve.

We have left until now the question of how to decide among choices and strategies. Legal problem solving does not stop with thorough assessment and careful construction of strategy. Choices must be made about which goal to pursue and in which way. The process through which this decision occurs is traditionally called counseling and, in the most traditional sense, it involves a conversation between a lawyer and a client. In the direct representation model, a lawyer presents her assessment of the case, identifies options and associated strategies, and evaluates how those options will accommodate the client's various goals and concerns. The client chooses what to do, and the lawyer proceeds to implement the client's choice.

While this direct representation model is still in place for many lawyers, it is possible that you will never see it at your placement. First, your particular placement may assign you to tasks that do not involve clients. If this is true, consider asking to sit in on a counseling session as an observer. Second, your placement may not have a "client," at least in the traditional sense. Consider a prosecutor's office, a federal enforcement agency, corporate counsel, or a county attorney. Each of these practices works with distinct interests and concerns, though none has a single individual as the "client." At best, a particular individual has representative authority to make decisions. In some cases, such as for a prosecutor, the decision maker may be the attorney herself. Finally, the traditional model breaks down completely when applied to judging. Judges are subject to a range of different influences, including the parties to a case, appellate courts, and the legal system itself, but do not have a client. See Chapter 15 on Client Relationships.

Try to determine early in your placement exactly who the "client" is and what your placement's governing concerns are. In asking the question, consider not just which individual or group appears to have final say over cases, but also what goals or interests your office seeks to pursue. When representing an individual, a lawyer pursues that client's goals. When representing an agency, a lawyer makes decisions under an overarching statutory mandate to enforce certain laws and policies. Prosecutors must make their case decisions in the interests of the public, a moving target that incorporates legal, pragmatic, and political influences. Finally, as already noted, judicial decision making occurs under a range of influences, from the competing claims of the parties, to the judge's pragmatic sense of durable outcomes, to the risk of reversal on appeal.

The process by which decisions are made may match the direct representation model, yet other processes exist as well. For example, in agencies, the process may involve internal office hierarchy or stated office priorities. An assistant prosecutor may have to seek approval from the elected prosecutor to pursue a controversial case. Decision making may involve multiple people or groups of people. For example, a consumer fraud lawyer may have to seek approval from an agency panel to pursue a new class of commercial offenders. As you explore this decision-making process, consider the relative role and influence of each person in the process. As you do, pay particular attention to the lawyer's role. By gathering the facts and articulating legal theories, the lawyers exert a distinct influence on the decision, through both their assessments and the options they develop for various decisions.

Action

We have become accustomed to thinking of lawyers as litigators, typically in the criminal justice system, focused on the demands of advocacy. This image severely understates the variety of ways lawyers work. From politics to private transactions, from litigation to arbitration to mediation, from judging to legislating to deal-making, lawyers as problem solvers occupy a diverse field of action. Lawyers focus their practices in particular subject areas (e.g., criminal law, commercial contracts, estate planning), around particular skill sets (e.g., brief writing, case management, interviewing), and in particular venues (e.g., the courtroom, the legislature, a regulatory agency). Indeed, larger firms usually divide their practice into groups focusing on particular kinds of legal action, even within the same subject area; for example a commercial contracts group would be separated from a commercial litigation group. This chapter covers some of the distinctions between types of law practices a bit later. This section focuses on the core activities of lawyering and on how they relate to the other phases of the lawyering process.

Three kinds of legal work form the basic structure of lawyering: advocacy, planning, and negotiation.

- **Advocates** take on the task of persuading a decision maker to rule for the advocate's client. Advocates typically work on disputes arising from past events and use formal procedures to force or to resist a particular outcome to those disputes. Advocacy includes litigation, as well as, increasingly, arbitration, administrative hearings, and similar processes. Advocacy is fundamentally adversarial in nature: the advocate acts in opposition to other advocates. Final decision making rests with a neutral actor—judge, jury, hearing officer, or arbitrator.

- **Planners** take on the task of structuring future behavior, relying on the parties' consent as binding authority. A planner's work anticipates and assesses future risks and opportunities, usually from a perspective that stresses the durability of her plan against future change. These practices cover many kinds of planning: for individuals, as in estate planning; for two parties, as with many contracts and real estate transactions; for multiple parties and groups, as with business formation or construction contracts; and for whole communities, as in zoning ordinances or state-wide legislation. The heart of planning lies in the anticipation and management of risk. The planner seeks to create a transaction that satisfies the client's goals for the foreseeable future. Decision-making authority rests with the parties rather than with neutral non-parties. The lawyer will not know the success or failure of their work for some time. The deal becomes final when the parties have completed performance or, as with business structures or legislation, as long as the structure or statute remains in place.

- **Negotiators** take on the task of reaching a solution by consent. Advocates use negotiation to expedite the resolution of their disputes and to settle claims. Planners rely on negotiation to achieve binding consent to a longer-term transaction. Like advocates, negotiators engage in persuasion; unlike advocates, negotiators also must be open to persuasion if a settlement is to be reached. Like planners, negotiators seek a result through agreement. These negotiations also include discussions between lawyer and client, as they try to work out a path to meet the client's goals through negotiation.

One difference between advocacy and planning practices emerges from the written work each requires. Advocacy practices require skill at persuasive writing, presenting a position to move a decision-maker to favorable action. By contrast, planners must draft legal documents that will elicit the consent of all parties and serve as the private constitution for future behavior. Planners take pains to use precise language that will minimize the risk of disputes that arise out of ambiguity. Litigators are like novelists, telling stories about the past so as to move their audiences to act for their client. By contrast, planners are like playwrights, creating scripts other actors will perform. The measure of a planner's success is the extent to which those actors stick to the script, minimizing improvisation.

QUESTIONS TO CONSIDER

Do advocacy, planning, and negotiation fully describe the range of activities in which lawyers engage? For example, consider the role lawyers play in passing legislation. Legislative processes include negotiation and planning, and lobbyists often look and act like advocates for the interests they represent. Yet the mechanics of group voting and the politics of mutual influence arguably create a wholly different kind of action, both for lawyer-legislators and for lobbyists.

As another example, consider a "compliance lawyer." This kind of lawyer reviews the activities of a business or institution to determine whether they comply with existing law, to note areas of non-compliance, and to draw the client's attention to the need for reform. This kind of lawyering sets the stage for planning and may include negotiation between the lawyer and the regulated business. Here, however, the lawyer has a distinctive role, one that includes a potential threat of reporting non-compliance to outsiders.

As a final example, consider a judge. We do not think of judges as negotiators because they have the authority to make decisions to which the parties must typically defer. But watch a settlement or case conference and track the conversation between the judge and the lawyers; you may find yourself surprised at how much it looks like negotiation. We do not think of judges as planners because they work to resolve disputes. But watch a settlement conference or a sentencing hearing; you may find the judge actively engaged in working out how this decision will affect the parties long into the future. Finally, we do not think of judges as advocates because they have no "clients" and must remain neutral. But listen carefully as judges write their explanations for a given decision; you may conclude that the judge is advocating for the fairness and legitimacy of a particular ruling, to persuade the parties to accept the outcome and to avoid the risk of long-term conflict.

You likely will find your supervisors engaged in some measure of all three activities: advocacy, planning, and negotiating. Litigators and planners use negotiation as a central part of their practice. If possible, try to observe those negotiations and ask yourself the reasons the attorneys chose to negotiate then, on those issues, and with what goal. Less obviously, both advocates and planners usually acquire some capacity for the other's skill set. Litigators must decide what remedy will satisfy their client's goals in the dispute; these choices affect the parties' lives long after the dispute. Similarly, planners regularly assess whether a future dispute will arise from the proposed plan. Indeed, the written memorialization of a deal often includes a dispute resolution clause that structures how future disputes will be handled. You can track this overlap at your placement. For each case you work on and each event you observe, try to sort out the long-term consequences of advocacy or the disputes that might arise out of a planned transaction.

This overview of the phases of the lawyering process can deepen your grasp on your placement's approach to problem solving. Remember that neither the process nor its component skills or competencies are goals in themselves, no matter how much time you spend in mastering them. Rather, they are the means through which lawyers exercise practical judgment to address the underlying problem. The craft and challenge of lawyering focuses on the lawyer's ability to manage the relevant process to exercise good judgment to reach a satisfactory outcome.

This section describes practical judgment and the process of lawyering primarily in terms of an individual lawyer dealing with a particular case or situation. The description here assumes all lawyers tailor their advice and their strategies to the goals and circumstances of their clients, producing a highly individualized product. However, this book also offers a different picture of lawyering, one that focuses less on individually customized solutions and more on the commoditization of lawyering. Commoditized legal solutions can meet the needs both of those who cannot afford lawyers and of those individuals and businesses that deal in large-scale, relatively routine transactions. The image of a wise counselor who helps clients tailor decisions to particular goals and interests has enormous appeal. But it may no longer reflect the economic and technological realities you will encounter upon graduation. See Chapter 27 on the Future of the Legal Profession, which describes this commodification of law practice and discusses several different realities driving the change.

The Experience of Legal Decision Making

The previous section describes legal decision making as an idealized practice: the exercise of judgment using a well-established process of problem solving. The living reality of lawyering, however, includes challenges that temper this aspirational model. These challenges include the lack of information, the prevalence of uncertainty, the pervasiveness of bias, the specter of regret, and the imperative of good practice habits. This section addresses these realities in turn, encouraging you to consider how these play out for you and your supervisors over the course of your externship.

Incomplete Information

Throughout law school, you work with complete sets of facts: the hypotheticals of Socratic dialogue, the fact patterns of an issue-spotting exam, the stories of in-class simulations, the files created for mock trial or moot court. This information may have complexity, include gaps you have to fill, and allow for multiple interpretations. Yet in every case, you can safely assume you have all the information you need. Indeed, in some cases, you are specifically instructed not to go beyond the facts as given.

None of this is true in the real world of lawyering. You will never have perfectly complete information. You frequently will find that, despite your best efforts, you do not even know enough to reach a settled conclusion about the past or a reliable understanding of the present. This incompleteness happens for good reasons. Documents go missing. People forget or reorganize their memories. Stories conflict, with no way to resolve the conflict. You distrust certain sources or discover that even reliable sources offer inconsistent information.

The reality of incomplete information has a powerful impact on legal problem solving. At a minimum, it means you must infer what you need to know from whatever reliable information you have. In some cases, the inferences will be reasonably direct; in others, you may find that what you know supports several different conclusions. This leads to a second reality: the need to work in the alternative and formulate decision-trees along the lines of "if this is true, then we need to do one thing; and if not, we need to consider doing something else."

In addition, information changes over time, requiring you to keep your mind open to new inferences and new alternatives. The task of re-analyzing inference conclusions as your data changes over time reflects a well-established practice in the social sciences, including law.[16] As a practical example, litigators frequently revise their settlement positions during trial depending on the performance of a witness or the outcome of a ruling on evidence. Similarly, negotiators in the merger of two businesses may add or revise clauses in the closing documents to reflect changes in each business's financial and market position.

QUESTIONS TO CONSIDER

At your placement, keep track of the information you and your supervisors use to formulate recommendations and reach conclusions. Do you or your supervisors keep your minds open to new information? How committed do you become to certain conclusions in the face of contrary or inconsistent evidence? Try to understand those situations in which your supervisors make decisions even though they acknowledge they lack complete information. Should the lawyer have waited? Or is the demand to move toward resolution and closure so strong the lawyer and client decide to act even knowing their information is incomplete?

Uncertainty

A related problem in legal decision making has to do with the ambiguity and uncertainty of the information you have. In the strictest sense, the problem of uncertainty reflects a variation on the problem of incomplete information: in the absence of conclusive data, the lawyer has to deal with the reality that what is known can lead to two or more inferences that in turn lead to distinctly different decisions. Ambiguity and uncertainty can arise both with facts and law. For example, despite detailed investigation, you may still not know enough to assess the reliability of commitments made by another party to a negotiation. Similarly, after a relatively thorough job of legal research, in which you find what you consider to be all of the relevant sources in your jurisdiction, you may still not be able to determine exactly how a particular rule might apply to your client's question. For more on coping with ambiguous results in research, see Chapter 17 on Writing for Practice.

The problem of uncertainty is universal in our lives; it affects decisions both large and small. The study of "decision making under conditions of uncertainty" constitutes a major focus of cognitive psychology. In a highly useful and entertaining book, THINKING FAST AND SLOW, Daniel Kahneman describes how human beings make decisions in the face of uncertainty and inadequate information.[17] He suggests that people work with two minds: "System 1" that makes rapid decisions based on easily accessible memories and inferences; and "System 2" that edits the conclusions of System 1 and undoes them if they conflict with a more reliable rule of logic or decision making. See Chapter 6 on Navigating Cultural Difference.

Routine actions and decisions are often controlled through System 1 without conscious thought. To make sure of these decisions and to consider and reflect on them, requires more mental effort. This phenomenon does not mean that System 2 is always correct; a conclusion is only as good as the data or rule or inference that produces it. It does mean that we do not always think and reflect in depth about judgments and decisions. Making the effort to reflect more carefully may not produce a better result; however, if you do, the odds are good you will notice and consider dimensions you had not considered before.

> **Exercise 14.8** Try out the following problems (answers and explanations in the endnotes):
>
> - If it takes five machines five minutes to make five widgets, how long does it take 100 machines to make 100 widgets?[18]

- Imagine a single, outspoken woman named Linda who has a graduate degree in philosophy. As a student, Linda was deeply committed to combating discrimination and social injustice. Is it more likely that Linda is 1) a bank teller, or 2) a bank teller who is also active in the feminist movement?[19]

These exercises rely on a particular kind of logic, one rooted in the estimation of probabilities and the quantification of outcomes, a logic frequently called "rational decision making." The exercises focus on calculating quantifiable outcomes, such as how long it takes a machine to produce a widget or on assessments of probability, such as whether a person is more likely to be part of a larger or a smaller group. The decisions lawyers face in practice include these kinds of assessments. Yet they also incorporate other forms of assessment, including the influence of emotion, the dynamics of power, or the presence of strongly-held values.

The cognitive science of decision making helps to illustrate important aspects of legal problem solving, discussed in the next several paragraphs. For now, think back to situations at your placement in which you were asked to make a recommendation without knowing enough or a situation in which your supervisor acted without all of the available information. Assess these situations based on your current knowledge. Did the supervisor make a bad choice? Will intuitive decision making always lead to bad decisions? Kahneman states, "The focus on error does not denigrate human intelligence, any more than the attention to diseases in medical texts denies good health. Most of us are healthy most of the time, and most of our judgments and actions are appropriate most of the time."[20] This reality suggests that the need for a more reflective process of judgment may depend in part on what is at stake.

Bias

This book discusses bias in several different chapters. In Chapter 6, you can learn about bias as it relates to personal identity and to differences in cultural backgrounds. In Chapter 7, you can learn about how you might encounter bias in law practice and the in legal system and about what you can do when you encounter it. The descriptions of bias in these chapters have powerful implications for legal decision making, affecting virtually every interaction between lawyers, clients, and other people in the legal process. See Chapter 6 on Navigating Cultural Difference and Chapter 7 on Bias in the Legal Profession.

This section discusses bias in a different frame of reference, one provided by cognitive psychology. Cognitive bias refers to a pattern of judgment in which the decision maker reaches a conclusion about people or events through an illogical thought process. Cognitive bias often results from taking mental short-cuts called heuristics, which permit you to draw conclusions quickly without working out all of the reasoning that might support your conclusion. For example, in Exercise 14.8 above, if you answered that Linda was a feminist bank teller, you used a "representativeness heuristic": the description of a "feminist bank teller" seemed more representative of how Linda was described in the question.[21]

A large number of cognitive biases have been identified and studied by cognitive scientists.[22] Consider some familiar examples:

- **availability cascade:** "A self-reinforcing process in which a collective belief gains more and more plausibility through its increasing repetition in public discourse (or 'repeat something long enough and it will become true.')"

- **hindsight bias**: "Sometimes called the 'I-knew-it-all-along' effect, the tendency to see past events as being predictable at the time those events happened."

- **planning fallacy**: "The tendency to underestimate task-completion times."[23]

These biases may look familiar, either from observation of others or from self-knowledge. Cognitive biases reflect patterns of thought you likely have encountered already and have come to see either as flaws in judgment or as useful ways of coping with decisions involving uncertainty or inadequate information.

Many of these biases can occur in some of the most common tasks of lawyering. For example, the following biases can play a noticeable role in negotiation:

- **anchoring bias**: the tendency to rely too heavily on a single fact or reality in making a decision. Anchoring bias shows up in the tendency of negotiators to focus their discussions on the first proposal, such as first suggestion of a dollar value for a settlement.

- **reactive devaluation**: the tendency to discount a proposal solely because your opponent made it.

- **zero-sum heuristic**: the tendency to assume a "zero-sum" situation; that is, to assume that any gain by an adversary will come at your expense, and vice-versa. Many negotiations do have zero-sum elements; yet many also have opportunities for each party to gain without loss to the other. The zero-sum heuristic might keep a negotiator from noticing opportunities to build additional agreements.

These biases affect the lawyer's own decision making; it is just as plausible that lawyers might use others' biases to produce a favorable outcome. Consider the rhyme-as-reason effect: "Rhyming statements are perceived as more truthful. A famous example [was] used in the O.J Simpson trial with the defense's use of the phrase 'If the gloves don't fit, then you must acquit.'"[24]

Cognitive science stresses that these biases represent a natural part of decision making. They can grow from many of the problems discussed elsewhere in this chapter: inadequate information, uncertain outcomes, time pressure. Moreover, these biases can often lead to useful, even "correct" outcomes. For example, reactive devaluation springs from common sense: you should think critically of proposals made by those who do not have your or your client's interests at heart. Awareness of the influence of these biases can help you improve your intuitive decision making in important situations so your conclusions and proposals rest on judgments that are less reactive and more reflective and well-considered.

Regret, Doubt, and Lack of Control Over Outcomes

Experienced litigators often say if you stop being nervous when you step into a courtroom, you should stop going to court. We can say the same about any of the decisive events in lawyering, including negotiations, the closing of a business merger, or counseling sessions with clients. The statement expresses one of lawyering's fundamental realities: no lawyer can control outcomes and rather must learn to work with the uncertainties that arise when other people's decisions and actions influence the result.

The lack of control over outcomes, while pervasive, is also variable. Skilled lawyers, with expertise in particular laws and particular processes, often can reduce the possible outcomes to an acceptable range. Indeed, some part of every practice includes cases with virtually certain outcomes: a simple will, a well-financed sale of real estate, an uncontested traffic ticket. At the same time, every lawyer's docket includes cases and problems that are too close to call. These problems involve unstable contingencies that ask lawyer and client to choose and re-choose, often between unattractive alternatives, with no certainty the client's goals will be met.

For this reason, the experience of doubt and regret are central to legal decision making. Doubt refers to the feeling you might have as you try to achieve the best possible result in a case, knowing you cannot control the outcome. Regret can be understood as doubt after-the-fact, the feeling a chosen strategy may not have worked as well as an approach not taken. Both of these feelings can arise in the "too-close-to-call" cases. If powerful enough, they can drive you to make or revoke decisions repeatedly, in ways that may prove counterproductive to your client's interests and even your own well-being. Even in less difficult cases, you may find yourself living with a nagging sense you could have done better by prompting a better verdict, negotiating for more money, or leaving the client more satisfied with the result.

> **Exercise 14.9** Pick a time at your placement when you were asked to recommend a course of action. This assignment can occur in small ways, such as a statement about how the law resolves a particular question, and in larger ones, such as a recommendation to your supervising judge about how she should decide a motion, or to a supervising attorney about how to advise a client. Think to back to the process you used to formulate your recommendations: What doubts did you have and how did you resolve them? How did your supervisor react to your recommendation? What other perspectives did your supervisor bring to the question?
>
> Now consider your recommendation after the fact. Do you see any reason to regret your choice? Think specifically about the alternatives you rejected. If you are confident about your choice, what helped you become confident? Consider the following: the depth and thoroughness of your preparation, feedback from your supervisor, reactions from your client, and the extent to which your recommendation achieved the relevant goals. Each of these factors affects what you learn from the choices you made and how you make use of that learning in the future.

Doubt and regret can make the experience of lawyering feel harder; yet they have enormous positive value. During the decision-making process, your doubts can prompt you to move from unconsidered decisions to more reflective ones and can motivate you to a more well-considered process of preparation, assessment, and action. After decision making, the presence of regret can motivate you to a careful and critical assessment of your work, strengthening your ability to learn from experience and to retain what you learn.

You can use your experience at your placement to develop your ability to work effectively in the presence of doubts and regrets. This ability can become a central aspect of the satisfaction you take in legal problem solving. Finding ways to work through doubts and to achieve results that survive post hoc evaluation can become one of the most satisfying and sustaining aspects of your work as a lawyer. Finally, lawyers who work with clients face the additional task of working with the doubts and regrets clients experience. Learning how to work with clients' anxiety during the process of lawyering and to help clients understand and cope with regrets can improve a lawyer's collaboration with clients and offer better chances they will accept the outcome.

Habits of Practice

The experience of decision making as a professional includes the power of habit and structured activity. Acquiring a professional identity involves developing a host of new capacities: intellectual analysis, interpersonal ability, ethical awareness, and a reorientation towards service to others. Figuring out how to sustain good practice habits represents an early and sometimes unfamiliar challenge, one that has long-term effects on the quality of your work.

This section will identify a few of the most important habits, but cannot cover in depth all of the different practice habits you might need. As a general matter, most accounts of lawyering stress the importance of effective organizational ability in lawyering, including the MacCrate Report,[25] the Shultz & Zedeck study,[26] and the NCBE study.[27] Careful organization and effective handling of routines can have a significant impact on the quality of your decision making. See Chapter 27 on the Future of the Legal Profession, which discusses the development of technological solutions to many of the routine and not-so-routine aspects of law practice.

The following paragraphs present a non-exclusive list of some of the most important practice habits you can acquire:

- **Documenting decisions and actions**: Most lawyers develop a practice of documenting important thoughts or conclusions about their work as well as noting the facts and content of all contacts relating to a case. This practice includes storing documentation in an easily retrievable location such as a physical file or a case management system. Developing the habit of careful documentation can present a challenge for young attorneys, who may not yet have a sense of the consequences that might flow in its absence. Good documentation has at least three purposes. First, it protects the firm against malpractice, making sure records of key advice, research, or communications can be verified. Second, it improves the quality of decision making, by reducing reliance on a busy attorney's memory, by preserving an early impression that may vary from later impressions on the same point, and by making sure the file has a contemporaneous record of activity. Third, it fosters effective collaboration within practice teams, by making sure all team members have access to earlier activity on the case.

· **Time-keeping and time awareness**: Many externship courses place students in practices in which time-keeping does not occur because clients are not billed, e.g., judicial placements, private nonprofit placements, and governmental agencies. At the same time, most externship courses require students to keep time records to verify completion of their work and to encourage the habit of effective time management. Whether you keep time for your placement or for your course, take advantage of the opportunity to develop your awareness of the time you spend on various tasks. A habit of time awareness can help you assess how long common tasks will take and allow you to allocate your time more effectively to key parts of the decision-making process. Often seen as a necessary evil for law practices that bill clients, time-keeping habits and strong time awareness can help you function more efficiently and devote more of your time to those tasks that need your best energy.

· **Using forms and templates critically**: Law practices thrive on the use of standardized documents and templates for routine activities. Indeed, the ready availability of computerized forms represents a major feature of ongoing changes to the legal profession. See Chapter 27 on the Future of the Legal Profession. You will find such forms and templates at your placement and may confront the choice whether to use the form unedited or to draft from scratch. You will most likely take a third course: using the form as a starting point for a solution that is customized to the situation. This process can include boilerplate text in a draft decision for a judge, standard allegations on jurisdiction in a pleading, or a previously-drafted merger clause in a contract.

Recognize that the use of forms and templates has both benefits and risks. Forms and templates allow you and your practice to save time and to deliver your work at a pre-approved level of quality. At the same time, use of a form developed for one situation may introduce assumptions and approaches that do not apply to another, unless the form is used critically and revised as appropriate to that situation. In some cases, both lawyers and clients may be willing to accept a certain degree of imprecision in a form in exchange for savings in transaction costs. In others, the use of a form may cut against the client's desire for an argument or a document tailored specifically to their concerns.[28] See Chapter 23 on Transactional Practices for more on the use of forms in planning work.

Law Practices

By now in your law school career, you will have noticed the wide variety of work for graduates of law school. To list all these jobs would take more space than we have. It is ambitious even to map out the major distinctions in the type of problems on which lawyers work. Having said that, we think it helps to have a point of comparison between your placement and what lawyers do in other types of practices. In reading what follows, consider where your placement's practice fits and how your placement's problem solving matches or contrasts with the problem solving of other lawyers.

We already have introduced one major distinction between types of law practice: the distinction between transactional and dispute-resolving practices. While this is a major distinction, other important distinctions in practice type also exist. Chapter 15 on Client Relationships discusses these in the context of the different types of clients lawyers can represent. Some important distinctions include the following:

- criminal justice practices and civil law practices;

- practices focused on commercial activity and those focused on personal concerns;

- governmental practices and private practices;

- public interest practices and private practices; and

- practices where lawyers represent specific clients, such as individuals, businesses, or agencies, and practices that focus on consulting or policy-making.

Most law practices fit into one or more of the categories identified above. As you consider where your placement fits, remember that these practice types often overlap. You can find civil law practices that combine many of the features of different types of lawyering. Large private firms, governments, and large corporate legal departments often seek to cover all of these areas, even though individual lawyers within those practices are specialized. A civil poverty law practice may have lawyers working on litigation, administrative hearings, health care planning, will drafting, policy advocacy, community education, and testimony before legislative bodies.

These distinctions focus on the lawyer's role, the type of client, and the subject matter or nature of the problem. Practices also differ in the way legal work is organized and managed:

- **Billing/non-billing practices**: In billing practices, lawyers charge clients a fee for services, based on an hourly rate, a flat rate, by service, or as a percentage of the recovery. Billing lawyers must justify fees to clients and face the market pressure of competing with other lawyers. By contrast, many lawyers work in practices in which no fee is charged. For example, public defenders and criminal prosecutors or nonprofit poverty lawyers and government attorneys usually do not bill for their services. Ask yourself what impact these arrangements have on how your supervisors handle their cases.

· **Fee-paid/salaried practices**: In fee-paid practices, especially in smaller firms, the lawyers' income relates directly to the fees they collect. The lawyers take the risk their work will produce sufficient fees and sufficiently reliable payment from clients to cover their costs and also provide a reasonable return. Both solo firms and large firms face the same pressures. By contrast, salaried practices buffer lawyers from this risk to a greater or lesser extent. Government lawyers, private nonprofit lawyers, and corporate counsel all provide examples of salaried practice. Salaried lawyers may still face funding challenges or have to justify costs. Corporate counsel may face demands from management to justify salaries; management of a nonprofit organization may spend more time seeking grants and gifts than on law practice; government lawyers may have to fight for their department's share of the agency's budget. Consider how your placement's practice is funded, how your supervisors are paid, and how these arrangements affect their legal problem solving.

· **Practice structure**: Solo practitioners provide the simplest organizational model. Decision-making authority over cases, financial risks, and ethical responsibility all rest in the individual lawyer. Partnership practices diversify these risks and responsibilities. The partners must determine how to decide on acceptance of cases, distribute gains and losses, and absorb the practice's costs. Hierarchical practices cover a broad range of legal work. Government lawyers working in a civil service model, public interest lawyers working in private nonprofit corporations, and associates in a commercial law firms often are organized hierarchically, which can be a stricter or looser hierarchy. Lawyers in one practice may have strict oversight from management, seeking formal approval of major and minor case decisions, while lawyers in other practices may enjoy autonomy in case decisions. You can learn a lot at your placement by tracking the autonomy supervisors have in handling their cases and their accountability to others in the office.

· **Case volume and selectivity**: The ability to control the volume of one's caseload represents a key determinant of the work life of a lawyer. The number of cases flowing through the practice affects each lawyer's individual caseload, as well as the demands of managing the overall practice and the resources required to sustain it. The decision about what cases to take affects the size of individual caseloads, the scope and direction of the substantive work, and in many practices the scope of the financial rewards. Some practices, such as a public defender's office, have little power to select, while others maintain strict control over their caseload and refuse to accept cases that would stretch them beyond their resources. Most practices fall in between these extremes, routinely accepting cases for some portion of their practices and exercising discretion over the rest. At your placement, pay close attention to how cases are selected, including the difference between an initial screening and the decision to invest substantial amounts of legal work in a case. See Chapter 20 on Criminal Justice Practices for a discussion of the ethical issues associated with excessive caseloads.

· **Specialization/generalization**: Many if not most lawyers specialize in particular legal issues, types of lawyering, and even on processes or skills. Specialization has distinct advantages. It makes it more likely that a lawyer can develop appropriate strategies more efficiently with less time needed to get up to speed. Specialization also can offer the marketing advantage of exposure to a concentrated pool of clients. How does the organization of your placement capitalize on the advantages of specialization? A public defender's office may encourage its lawyers to specialize in certain types of cases (felonies, misdemeanors, or delinquency), in certain types of offenses (violence against persons, drugs, gangs, or embezzlement), or particular courts (juvenile) and judges. At your placement, consider whether and how lawyers specialize and sub-specialize and the effect specialization choices have on your placement's ability to manage its practice.

All of these distinctions in practice type, focus, organization, and compensation can overload you as you try to determine which type of practice will offer you a rewarding and sustainable career. Your experience at your placement provides you with insight into how each of these dynamics might affect you. Do you like working in a larger or a smaller group? Do you prefer hierarchical structure or a more collaborative approach? Do you embrace or reject the demands of time-keeping? Do you favor the entrepreneurship of billing practices or the relative security of salaried practices? Answering these and other questions can help you make the most of your placement as part of your job search. See Chapter 26 on Externships and Career Development.

Bringing It Together: A Lawyering Audit

This chapter has discussed three main aspects of lawyering: the exercise of legal judgment, the nature of lawyering process, and various types of law practices. This section weaves these threads together into an "audit" of the lawyering at your placement, a series of questions that focus the early parts of this chapter on your placement. To illustrate differences in context, each question discusses three practice types: one that directly represents individuals; a government enforcement agency; and a judge's chambers. (Judicial clerks also might try to apply the questions below to the practices of attorneys that appear before their judge.)

General Questions

- What type of legal problems does your placement handle? For the nonprofit, identify both the overall goals of the practice and the more specific case acceptance criteria. For the agency, identify the statutory mandate, as well current policy about which cases to pursue within that mandate. For the judge, consider the court's subject matter jurisdiction and ask how many of each type of case the court handles during your placement.

- What client groups or interests does your placement represent? For the nonprofit, list the specific client demographics or problem types accepted. Agencies have the public and the public interest as their client, but they also might have a specified segment of the population (e.g., individuals with disabilities) to protect. Judges do not represent clients in the traditional sense, although you might assess your judge's sense of accountability. What obligations does the judge feel to the parties? their attorneys? the docket? the appellate courts? See Chapter 15 on Client Relationships for a discussion of a judge's different constituencies.

- What role does a lawyer at your placement play? For example, judges act as decision makers, and also as administrators, office supervisors, and even time managers for the lawyers on each case. Agency attorneys frequently assume specialized roles; some are primarily litigators, while others write regulations or develop policy. Nonprofit attorneys may be litigators, planners, or negotiators. Try to assess where on the continuum between generalization and specialization a given attorney falls.

- What size caseload do attorneys at your office carry? Assess the number of cases and also the rate of turnover, the average time elapsed between opening and closing, and the number of tasks involved for each case. From this information, consider what role time pressure plays in case handling. How does the attorney assure adequate attention to each issue within the overall time demand of the practice?

- What organization does your office have? Judicial chambers usually work hierarchically, with the judge at the apex, but you might examine the working relationships among the judge and the law clerks, between judges within the forum, or between the judge and the clerk's office. Government agencies are often hierarchical, with a regional chief overseeing a local office within a national or state-wide agency; yet many agencies give more autonomy to regional offices and to individual attorneys within offices. Try to map the lines of authority within your office. The intensity of oversight and management varies considerably within nonprofits. Your office may make many decisions in staff meetings in a more or less collaborative format.

Assessment Questions

- How do cases start at your office? Nonprofits often handle intake in stages, with phone calls going to an initial screener and live contact reserved for a later interview with an attorney. Some agencies may select cases from among citizen complaints, while others may seek out particular types of behavior to target. Judicial chambers will have highly regularized intake, with filed cases assigned to individual judges through a routine case assignment mechanism.

- Who investigates facts at your placement? Both agencies and nonprofits may have a separate pool of investigators or paralegals who investigate claims, though lawyers may handle this task as well. How does the office divide up case investigation responsibilities: are lawyers integrated from the start or do they review summaries prepared by others? Of course, judges do not normally investigate cases, but judges generally help parties sort out contested from uncontested facts through case conferences or rulings on evidentiary motions, so as to assure a focused and efficient trial. In all cases, ask yourself the impact that investigation and factual development have on the ultimate handling of the underlying problems.

- Who does the legal research and analysis? Most offices allocate the task of legal research and analysis to lawyers. For agency and nonprofit practices, this task usually goes to the attorney assigned the case, but that attorney may delegate some or all of the task to law clerks (including you) and also may bring especially thorny questions to other attorneys or to a staff meeting for fuller discussion.

In theory, judges wait for the attorneys to present legal arguments, then assess and select between those arguments; in practice, however, judges often do substantial research in preparation for cases and may discuss legal issues with the attorneys both informally in conferences and formally in hearings as they develop their opinions.

- Who assesses the merit of cases in your office? In both nonprofits and agencies, merit assessment will often occur in two phases. An individual attorney (or investigator, or even extern) will assess a legal problem as worthy of pursuit. Then, that assessment will receive one or more layers of review and approval before the office formally accepts the case. For judges, the rules of procedure typically give distinctive powers of "merit assessment." Motions for dismissal, summary judgment, and directed verdicts permit judges to make a decision as a matter of law where the known facts do not justify a hearing before a jury.

- How does case acceptance occur at your placement? Both agencies and nonprofits will have some way to decide which cases to pursue and which to reject. Some may be screened out at the point of initial contact, while others might require further development before the office makes a decision to accept or reject. Try to find out what happens to rejected cases. Does the office offer some form of opinion, quick advice, or referral? Judges, of course, usually cannot refuse cases placed on their docket but may recuse themselves in some cases.

Decision-Making Questions

- What options and strategies does your placement typically consider? Each legal problem is unique and, in theory, the choices available for handling one problem will not suit any other. In reality, however, law practices typically consider a standard range of choices in deciding how to proceed on their legal problems. A nonprofit focused on helping clients get public benefits typically might consider negotiating with a case worker, filing for administrative review, or advising the client to abandon the claim. An agency enforcing a particular law might choose to refuse a particular claim, send a warning letter, file an individual case, or pursue a class of offenders. Try to identify what choices the office routinely considers, recognizing the range of choices will vary from problem to problem.

- In theory, judges respond to options for decision presented to them by the parties and only rule on motions initiated by the parties. In practice, however, many judges act more assertively to prod parties toward particular ways to resolve a case, through conferences, motions, pre-trial memos, and the like. Moreover, judges often face decisions that are very similar from case to case. Does the judge maintain a databank of language that can be used and reused in these cases? If so, what effect does this practice have on the judge's thinking about the underlying problem?

· Who serves as the primarily responsible attorney? Most law practices designate a particular attorney as lead counsel on a given case to make and implement decisions in consultation with the client. Consider who has this role at your placement. Both agencies and nonprofits will assign single attorneys to cases, but also may assign teams of attorneys, especially on larger deals and disputes. Judges usually retain ultimate case handling responsibility for cases on their docket, but may delegate some portion of the responsibility for a disposition to magistrates or special masters. When and how does the judge use these devices? And what role do you and other law clerks play?

· How does your placement manage client relationships? This question makes the most sense for the lawyer who represents individual clients; such a lawyer has several different models of client relationship to adopt. In the absence of an identified client, neither judges nor agency attorneys face the same set of choices. For more on how different kinds of practices manage clients and other sources of accountability, see Chapter 15.

· When and how does decision making on cases occur at your placement? This question is not as easy as it looks. Remember the discussion of decision making over time. While in some law practices decisions occur as a single event, in many if not most, decisions occur over time in response to new events and new information. A litigator may file pleadings and conduct discovery only to reconsider her approach in response to a disclosure, a judicial ruling, or a settlement offer. A transactional lawyer may formulate an initial proposal for a transaction, only to adjust its parameters in response to new events and the shifting interests of the various participants. A judge may hear argument pre-trial, but reserve final decision on a particular motion until trial itself. Try to get a sense of the patterns of decision making over the whole course of legal problem solving. What effect do early decisions have on later ones? What seem to be the key points of decision? How does your office prepare for and handle those moments?

Action Questions

· Which legal processes does your placement routinely use and for what purposes? By definition, litigation and other advocacy practices use the courts, administrative agencies, and private arbitrators to resolve disputes. In addition, the purposes of advocacy may vary: a nonprofit lawyer may use litigation either to achieve a remedy for an individual client or to establish a precedent helping a group of clients. An agency may file suit to rectify a single harm or deter a group of potential offenders. If your placement handles litigation, try to understand both the short- and long-term goals of the litigation.

By contrast, in transactional practices, the legal process often depends on routine practices of that type of deal to structure its activities. For example, an agency responsible for guaranteeing loans for the construction of housing projects may have a many-layered process for reviewing and approving potential deals. A municipal attorney may face a series of committees and boards in drafting and implementing a zoning ordinance. Whenever possible, try to get a sense of the nature of the processes that structure your placement's activity and assess how the process serves the underlying goals of the parties to the deal.

· How does your placement assure strategic action in its handling of cases? All lawyering benefits from careful planning and thoughtful implementation of decisions, but the pressure of deadlines, limited resources, and active caseloads often forces attorneys to react rather than act. Consider how your attorneys and your practice assure that case handling remains tied to client goals and overall strategy. This array of strategies can include effective practice habits, restrictions on new intake, and the reallocation of resources in times of high-demand. For example, a judge facing the demands of a capital murder trial may need to negotiate with other judges to handle the other parts of her caseload.

· What role does negotiation play in your placement's problem solving? Consider how much time your supervisors spend in negotiation, on what kinds of issues, for what purpose, and at what point. For example, a private nonprofit lawyer may suggest an early resolution of an eviction notice that satisfies the client's goals, rather than pursuing a legally questionable defense. An agency attorney may seek an early agreement with a less serious offender in an enforcement action in an effort to obtain information vital to pursuing other offenders. Judges may use their scheduling authority to push the attorneys on the case to focus on settlement in an effort to reduce the court's overall docket and free up judicial time for other trials. Attorneys and offices use negotiation in different ways and for different purposes. Try to track both the content and the style of negotiations you observe at your placement.

 · How does your office define success? In theory, this question seems easy: for all lawyers, success means the accomplishment of the goals identified at the start of the process with a minimum of transaction costs. And for many lawyers, success also means the client is satisfied with the outcome of the case. Even so, defining success offers you a rich field for reflection. For example, in a private nonprofit practice, limitations on client resources may make full achievement of a client's goals impossible. Consider how lawyers work with their clients in these cases to achieve some degree of closure for the client who faces nothing but bad choices. Similarly, an agency attorney may face a variety of different measures of success that apply to its work: successfully deterring a particular behavior, obtaining public exposure of a particular fraud, or satisfying a quota for a particular case type. Judges also may have differing metrics: one judge may focus on a low reversal rate, another on efficient management of the docket, and a third on a resolution that keeps parties from returning to court. Ask your supervisors how they define satisfactory handling of cases and listen carefully for the assumptions and values on which they base their answers.

Conclusion: "Good Lawyering"

One of the most valuable takeaways from your placement involves answering the question: what makes for "good lawyering"? Your experience at your placement will give you many opportunities to reflect on this question. The practice audit in the preceding sections assumes two initial answers: good lawyering successfully achieves the goals identified at the start of the lawyer's work, and good lawyering achieves those goals with a minimum investment of time and resources. These answers apply to most lawyering.

You can find other answers from observing lawyering carefully at your placements. With luck, you will see nothing but the best lawyering: cogent and persuasive argument; clear, well-written briefs; unambiguous contracts, wills, and other documents; careful, well-balanced judicial opinions. In practice, however, you likely will encounter a lot of bad lawyering. Each exposure to bad lawyering offers a learning opportunity. Ask yourself why you react as you do; what do you think makes the lawyer's performance subpar. Consult with your supervisor and ask his opinion. In your reflection, consider what led the lawyer to act in that way and what you would have done differently if you had handled the case. This kind of reflection is a vital step in developing your own standards of quality.

Additionally, try to assess how your placement as a whole assures the quality of its work. The task of assuring a consistent quality of practice under intense case pressure and time demands constitutes one of the most difficult tasks of law practice management. A key part of this task focuses on the avoidance of ethical violations and legal malpractice: consistent documentation of case handling in files, effective use of calendars and other deadline management systems, and clear accounting for time and client contact.

Avoiding ethical complaints and malpractice actions is necessary, but not sufficient. Your office will have systems in place that assure the best possible practices consistent with available resources. Common approaches include careful screening, hiring, and training of new attorneys, mentoring of younger attorneys, regular performance reviews, reporting and critical assessments of caseloads, rigorously applied case selection processes, and other similar devices. Frequently, quality control relies on office culture, a combination of mutual expectation, respect, and pride in the work that can reinforce more mechanical devices. In assessing your experience, leave room to assess how well your office accomplishes quality control.

Finally, recognize that the concept of "good lawyering" is inherently ambiguous. While it may refer to the skillful achievement of goals at minimum cost, it also includes active participation in a community of lawyers that seeks to improve the legal system and spread respect for the law and access to justice as broadly as possible. See Chapter 9 on Professionalism. "Good lawyering" may also refer to work that pursues the lawyer's own deeply held values, in ways that can improve society, strengthen client autonomy, and combat injustice. See Chapter 24 on Professional Identity and Formation. A practice that turns on strongly held values may also foster and sustain the lawyer's satisfaction and well-being, yet another definition of "good lawyering." See Chapter 25 on Work & Well-being.

These opportunities and uncertainties are yours to resolve, through the choices you make about how to practice and to what end. Your experience this semester will let you take steps to improve your judgment and to begin to master the lawyering process. And yet, these are only first steps toward choices that define you as a lawyer, a public actor, and a human being. The exercise of judgment and the handling of the lawyering process on behalf of others offer deep challenges and rich satisfactions. At the same time, practical judgment and the lawyering process also determine the shape of the law as it applies to clients and causes.

FURTHER RESOURCES

A.B.A. Sec. of Legal Educ. & Admissions to the Bar, Legal Education and Professional Development—An Educational Continuum, Report of the Task Force on Law Schools and the Profession: Narrowing the Gap (1992).

Robert M. Bastress & Joseph D. Harbaugh, Interviewing, Counseling And Negotiating (1990).

Gary Bellow & Bea Moulton, The Lawyering Process: Materials for Clinical Instruction in Advocacy (1978).

David A. Binder, Paul Bergman, Paul R. Tremblay, & Ian Weinstein, Lawyers As Counselors: A Client-Centered Approach (3d ed. 2011).

John S. Bradway, How To Practice Law Effectively (1958).

Robert F. Cochran, Jr., John M. DiPippa & Martha M. Peters, The Counselor-At-Law: A Collaborative Approach To Client Interviewing And Counseling (2d ed. 2001).

Daniel Kahneman, Thinking Fast And Slow (2011).

Stefan H. Krieger & Richard K. Neuman, Jr., Essential Lawyering Skills (4th ed. 2011).

William M. Sullivan, et al., Educating Lawyers: Preparation for the Profession of Law (2007).

ENDNOTES

1   See *Blind Men and an Elephant*, Wikipedia,, https://en.wikipedia.org/wiki/Blind_men_and_an_elephant (last visited July 17, 2015).

2   *See* Chapter 2 on Charting your Path to Success—Professional Development Planning.

3   A.B.A. Sec. of Legal Educ. & Admissions to the Bar, Legal Education and Professional Development—An Educational Continuum, Report of the Task Force on Law Schools and the Profession: Narrowing the Gap 3 (1992) (The "MacCrate Report").

4   *Id.* at 6–7.

5   *Id.* at 124.

6   *Id.* at 135–141. For a full list of these skills and values, *See* Appendix A.

7   William M. Sullivan, *et al.*, Educating Lawyers: Preparation for the Profession of Law (2007). The book "is one of a series of reports on professional education issued by The Carnegie Foundation for the Advancement of Teaching." *Id.* at 15.

8   *Id.* at 13.

9   Marjorie M. Shultz & Sheldon Zedeck, *Predicting Lawyer Effectiveness: A New Assessment for Use in Law School Admission Decisions*, CELS 2009 4th Annual Conference on Empirical Legal Studies Paper 18 (July 31, 2009), http://ssrn.com/abstract=1442118.

10   *Id.* at 15 (emphasis in original.) To do this, Shultz and Zedeck conducted hundreds of interviews with individuals and groups, including lawyers, law faculty, law students, judges, and clients. They asked questions about what any of these people would find important in hiring a lawyer, teaching law students or becoming a lawyer. "In a rolling process we gradually selected, added to, subtracted from, defined and redefined *Id*entified factors, seeking rough consensus through successive discussions with lawyers in many field, settings, and career stages. We distilled a list of 26 Effectiveness Factors important in the eyes of these varied constituencies to being an effective lawyer." *Id.* at 25.

11   *Id.* 26–27.

12   Steven S. Nettles & James Hellrung, A *Study of the Newly Licensed Lawyer* (July 2012), http://ncbex.org/pdfviewer/?file=%2Fdmsdocument%2F56, linked at http://ncbex.org/publications/ncbe-job-analysis/ (last visited July 20, 2015). The NCBE study developed a list of knowledge domains and common skills and abilities for newly licensed lawyers, then reviewed feedback to surveys on these factors from 1,669 response.

13   *Id.* at 313. Note that the NCBE study did not include several "skills/abilities" because the survey results indicated that they were not sufficiently significant.

14   The MacCrate Report, *supra*, note 3, at 141 note 1.

15   *See* Karl Llewellyn, The Bramble Bush 3 (1930).

16   *See Bayesian Inference*, Wikipedia, https://en.wikipedia.org/wiki/Bayesian_inference (last visited July 22, 2015): "Bayesian inference is a method of statistical inference . . . used to update the probability for a hypothesis as evidence is acquired . . . Bayesian inference has found application in a wide range of activities, including science, engineering, philosophy, medicine, and law."

17   Daniel Kahneman, Thinking Fast And Slow (2011).

18   *See Cognitive Obstacles: Why Distractions Can Improve Creativity and Problem solving*, Why We Reason (Nov. 14, 2011) http://whywereason.com/tag/shane-frederick/ (describing an experiment conducted by M.I.T. professor Shane Frederick.) Most people follow the intuitive logic that says "5 makes 5 in 5" and give 100 minutes as the answer. But the correct answer is 5 minutes, a result you might achieve by slowing down and reasoning more carefully: "if 5 machines each make a widget in 5 minutes, than each machine makes a widget in five minutes. So 100 machines would each take 5 minutes to make a widget."

19   Thinking Fast And Slow, *supra* note 20, at 156–165. *See also Conjunction Bias*, Wikipedia, *https://*en.wikipedia.org/wiki/Conjunction_fallacy (last visited on July 22, 2015) ("The conjunction fallacy is a formal fallacy that occurs when it is assumed that specific conditions are more probable than a single general one.") Most people will answer that Linda is a feminist bank teller. But that does not answer the question of what is more probable. It is more likely that Linda is a member of the larger group of all tellers (feminist or not) than that she is a member of the smaller group of feminist bank tellers. Again, you might achieve this result by slowing down and reasoning about which group is the larger. If it's any comfort, according to Kahneman, 85% of students at the Stanford Graduate School of Business, who presumably had extensive training in probability theory, also chose incorrectly. *See also* Stephen J. Gould, "The Streak of Streaks", The N.Y. Rev. of Books (1988) ("I am particularly fond of [the Linda problem] because I know that the [conjoint] statement is least probable, yet a little homunculus in my head continues to jump up and down, shouting at me—'but she can't just be a bank teller; read the description.'").

20   *Id.* at 4.

21   *Cognitive Bias*, Wikipedia, https://en.wikipedia.org/wiki/Cognitive_bias (last visited on July 23, 2015).

22   *List of Cognitive Biases*, Wikipedia, https://en.wikipedia.org/wiki/List_of_cognitive_biases (last visited July 22, 2015) (summarizing a list of over 175 distinct forms of cognitive bias, including those referred to in the text.) This list groups different biases into categories: decision making, belief, and behavioral biases; social biases; and memory error or biases.

23   *Id.*

24   *Id.*

25   The MacCrate Report, *supra* note 3, at 199–203 (Identifying "organization and management of legal work" as a fundamental lawyering skill).

26   Shultz and Zedeck, *supra* NOTE 9 (including "organizing and managing one's own work" and "organizing and managing others (staff/colleagues)" as one of the lawyering effectiveness factors).

27   Nettles & Hellrung, *supra* note 15, at 313 (listing "using office technologies" and "organizational skills" as two of the top eleven most significant skills and abilities for young lawyers).

28   Chapter 27 discusses the tension between customized, "bespoke" solutions and the creation of new forms of law practice based on commoditized solutions.

Client Relationships

ALEXANDER SCHERR

L awyering is responsible work, which means in part having responsibility **for** outcomes and in part having responsibility **to** someone or something else. This chapter talks about the "responsible to" part: the people, issues, causes, or institutions to which lawyers owe both practical and ethical responsibilities.

In the simplest sense, addressing this topic means talking about clients and about lawyers' relationships to clients. You already may have a sense of this relationship. Popular media routinely identify lawyers with their clients, both in the real world and in fiction. Many of the most well-known ethical duties arise from a concern for this relationship, including confidentiality, avoiding conflicts, communication, competence, and avoiding commingling funds. Your law school likely has courses that help you to work with clients, including clinical courses and classes that teach about interviewing, counseling, and other interactions.

This chapter explores the diversity in client relationships. It starts by discussing several kinds of clients, including a few that can fairly be described as prototypes. It then highlights the kinds of work that lawyers do with clients and discusses the dynamics of decisionmaking between lawyer and client. Next, it assesses some of the most common challenges that emerge from the lawyer-client relationship. Finally, the chapter revisits the notion of responsibility and prompts you to consider how your preferences about client relationships can influence the course of your career.

First, we ask "who is the client?"

Identifying the Client

To answer the question, "who is the client?" a short exercise or two can help.

> **Exercise 15.1** Take out a sheet of paper or open a blank computer file and jot down a few phrases answering the question, "Who are the clients at your placement?"

For example, say you are working in a criminal defense office. Your answer to this question should be an easy one in most cases: you represent individuals charged with crimes.

The answer may not be as clear for other placements. For example, you may work in a municipal attorney's office, a prosecutor's office, or a federal agency. Or you may work in a judge's chambers or in the office of a lawyer-legislator where the question "Who are the clients?" may seem nonsensical. Even in these cases, try to answer the original question about the "client" and consider other questions as well: "To whom are the attorneys at my placement accountable? For whom (or for what) are they responsible?"

For more information on client relationships, see Chapters 20, 21, and 22 on Criminal Justice, Public Interest, and Public Service Practices.

How you respond to Exercise 1 will depend in part on your externship course. Some law schools offer courses in which students work in several kinds of placements. Others offer only subject or practice-specific placements: judicial chambers, government agencies, prosecutorial offices, or civil legal services practices. Consider the following exercises:

Exercise 15.2 If your externship seminar class is with students in many types of placements, list the kinds of placements at which other students work. Then seek out one or two students who work at placements different from yours and ask them who their placement represents or alternately, to whom their attorneys are accountable or responsible? Make a note of their answers and consider the differences from your placement.

Exercise 15.3 Go to your law school's website and look for the descriptions of each of your law school's clinics and externships. As you review them, ask yourself about the kinds of clients with whom each clinic works. Are they individuals, businesses, agencies, organizations, governments, or someone else entirely? Try to imagine what it would be like to work with these kinds of clients.

Answering the "who is the client?" question provides essential context for the topics discussed throughout this chapter. As you read on, come back to this question and ask how each topic below relates to what you have observed at your placement. The topics discussed here also will help you start to consider longer-term questions: What kind of clients do you want to represent? What kind of relationship do you want to have with those clients?

Individuals as Clients

The most familiar type of client is the individual, and the simplest type of relationship is the one-lawyer-one-person relationship. Many ethical rules seem grounded in the assumption that lawyers represent individuals, and there are separate rules for more specialized types of clients, such as businesses or the public. In addition, many texts that teach about client relationships focus on individuals, and many law school courses stress the one-to-one nature of client interactions. In fact, it may well be that the "client contact" offered by your school's clinical courses primarily involves representation of individuals.

Some lawyers focus mainly on issues that affect individuals. For example, a criminal defense lawyer handles urgent questions involving an individual client's personal freedom. Similarly, "personal" practices might include employment discrimination, certain tort or contracts cases, and some advocacy for individual consumers. Many lawyers find this work on behalf of individual clients compelling because it can have a direct impact on an individual's life, often on matters of vital importance. Working with individual clients also gives the lawyer the opportunity to forge a stronger and more personal relationship with the client than is often the case when, for instance, the client is a business entity. See Chapter 20 on Criminal Justice Lawyering.

Other lawyers may find this kind of "personal" practice less appealing for a variety of reasons, including its emotional intensity, the weight of responsibility, or what may be limited financial rewards. Many lawyers prefer to work for businesses or other institutions. Even there, however, the lawyers still deal with individual people who serve as representatives or agents of the business or institution. To be sure, in such practices, the client remains the organization and the chance for harmful effects on individuals may seem to be secondary. These areas of practice nevertheless have important relational dimensions, including the challenges and rewards of dealing with people facing important and sometimes stressful situations.

Exercise 15.4 If you can, retrieve the essay you wrote for your application to law school. In that essay, many students talk about their goals for becoming a lawyer and the kinds of service they want to provide. If you did, consider the kinds of clients that you had in mind. What kind of impact did you say you wanted to have as a lawyer? Try to visualize the people or the groups or the individuals you wanted to serve. How does your current placement compare with those goals? Has your intended client group changed since you came to law school? See Chapter 2 on Professional Development Planning.

Businesses and Organizations as Clients

Many law school graduates start out their careers representing businesses and not individuals. Data from the National Association of Law Placement (NALP) indicates that, for the graduating class of 2013, 18.4% of graduates took jobs in the "business" category, while 51.1% of graduates found jobs in "private practice."[1] Of the graduates in private practice, 31.6% took positions in firms with more than 100 lawyers and 20.7% took positions in firms with more than 500 lawyers. It may be reasonable to assume that a substantial percentage of those graduates are representing business or commercial interests in one way or another.[2]

Representing a business client creates distinctive dynamics for the lawyer. The lawyer must be adept at discerning and pursuing the goals of a group of people engaged in a common endeavor. This role requires understanding more than just the business's legal structure and legal issues. It may also require the lawyer to grasp the organization and internal politics of the client, to become familiar with the client's business activities, to appraise the client's financial realities, and to assess business interests within the complex web of commercial realities. These in turn create unique ethical and practice issues. See Chapter 23 on Transactional Lawyering Practices.

Representing Groups and Communities

The representation of businesses falls within a larger category of client work: the representation of groups engaged in a common endeavor. In the case of businesses, lawyers have an identified legal entity to work with, one the law recognizes for the most part as an "individual." In many cases, however, lawyers represent groups of individuals that lack formal organization. These groups eventually may become formalized, by turning into nonprofit corporations, unincorporated associations, or other kinds of entities with a clearly defined structure and set of roles. In such cases, the lawyer's role often focuses on helping the group to create a formal structure and, once created, on representing the organization in much the same way a business lawyer might represent a business.

In other cases, lawyers represent communities, including groups of people living in the same geographic area or with common interests and characteristics. This form of practice has become known as "community lawyering." A common understanding of community lawyering is that it reflects "a social justice lawyering practice that places commitment to something called 'community' . . . at its core." [3] In this case, the lawyer's relationship to a group takes on a specific meaning. This kind of practice may involve traditional lawyering activities, including individual representation, planning and development of businesses, and representation in front of administrative or legislative bodies. At the same time, an important feature of these kinds of practices relates to the lawyer's conception of his or her work: that clients exist in a community of people who share a common social and political experience and that legal services and advocacy advance both individual and group injustices arising from that experience. [4]

Group and community lawyering thus can differ from the lawyer's work for an individual client in several ways. First, a lawyer representing a group may play a role in organizing and shaping the group decision-making process. Second, a lawyer representing a group may play a more prominent role in discussing and strategizing group goals. Finally, lawyers representing groups may bring their own goals and values to the representation in ways that create unique and often challenging tensions between lawyer and client. For more on this kind of lawyering, see Chapter 21 on Public Interest Lawyering.

The Government as a Client

Government clients cover an enormous range of jurisdictions and encompass a broad diversity of types of work. Lawyers represent small towns and counties, state and federal executives, agencies at all levels, legislatures, judiciaries, and many other entities. The range of legal work for governments is similarly diverse: litigation, legislative advocacy and legislative drafting, rule-making, compliance monitoring, investigation and intervention into community crises, prosecution of crimes, negotiating treaties, negotiating contracts for routine operations, and much more. Working for the government represented 11.5% of the jobs acquired by the class of 2013. [5]

The diversity of government lawyers' client relationships matches the diversity of practices and jurisdictions. In some cases, the government lawyer's role is nearly identical to that of in-house counsel: advising a municipality or an agency, risk prevention, monitoring legal changes to see if they affect a government client, and making decisions about handling or outsourcing potential litigation for or against that client. See Chapter 23 on

Transactional Practices. In others, the government lawyer negotiates deals essentially as a transactional attorney, from the most routine of government business transactions to treaties between states and nations. In still others, the government lawyer serves as a policy advisor and even a policy maker, such as when an agency lawyer helps to formulate regulations under a statutory mandate.

Government lawyers face some unique challenges, including distinctive lines of accountability. They are often responsible to identified individuals within the various branches of government and must conform their advice and advocacy to the interests of that agency.[6] They frequently have a responsibility for implementing some form of legislative mandate, such as when attorneys for the Environmental Protection Agency pursue particular kinds of environmental violations. They also may have responsibilities to groups within the government, such as the role legislative counsel plays in drafting proposed laws for legislative committees.

Finally, government lawyers have responsibility to the public as a whole, in addition to any identified agency staff to whom they may report. Criminal prosecutors provide the clearest example. They are directly accountable to the "state," an accountability reinforced by the electoral process. See Chapter 20 on Criminal Justice Lawyering.

Having the public as a client raises distinct practical and ethical questions. Because the public often does not speak with one voice or have one set of interests, who decides which interests to pursue in a given case? What ethical challenges arise when the lawyer's view of the public's interest conflicts with the view defined by agency staff? For more information about these and similar questions, see Chapter 22 on Public Service Lawyering.

Policy Lawyering and Representing Causes

Some lawyers do not represent individuals at all and instead pursue changes in policy or advocate for social justice on a broader level. In one version of this practice, lawyers work in private nonprofit organizations and take a particular position on matters of public concern. The American Civil Liberties Union offers one archetypal example. It is a nonprofit entity that employs lawyers and other advocates "to defend and preserve the individual rights and liberties guaranteed by the Constitution and laws of the United States."[7]

Another example involves a consulting law practice. For example, consider a nonprofit firm that has expertise in "smart growth" and sustainable development and offers consulting services on land use regulation to municipalities or counties. In this kind of practice, "customers" consult the firm for advice about law and regulatory policy. Indeed, the "customer" knows that the lawyer pursues a particular agenda and hires the lawyer for advice on how to pursue that agenda. The lawyer advocates for the "customer" to make particular kinds of changes in policy and does not have the same ethical duties of a more traditional attorney-client relationship

"Cause lawyering" offers a variation of this kind of practice, or at least an alternate name for it. Cause lawyers dedicate their practice to using the law to promote social change. Cause lawyers may seek to change legal rules, but they do so in order to create social or political change, using the law as a tool for pursuing that goal. Consider, as an example, the role played by the N.A.A.C.P. in the decades leading up to *Brown vs. Board of Education*. In that case, the organization's lawyers used specific legal processes to produce changes in social relations that went far beyond the legal parameters of the particular dispute. Many cause-oriented lawyers also view themselves as doing community lawyering, discussed earlier.

For all of these lawyers, the cause or the policy provides the point of reference for making both tactical and strategic decisions. The cause or policy also serves as a strong motivator for the lawyers. Lawyers may take on individual or organizational clients as necessary to present legal cases. Where they do, they owe the same ethical responsibilities to those clients as any other lawyer. Usually, these clients share the goals of the lawyer who represents them. On occasion, however, similar to the discussion earlier about community lawyering, a tension can arise between the interests of an individual client and the interests of the lawyer in the case. See Chapter 21 on Public Interest Lawyering.

Judges and Accountability

At first blush, it seems absurd and vaguely unethical to suggest that judges have clients. When it comes to litigants, judges must act impartially and fairly, without bias or prejudice.[8] Further, judges cannot let personal values or political beliefs influence their role or their decision making as a judge.[9] To suggest that judges have clients seems to undercut the very function of a judge in our system of public dispute resolution.

And yet judges act within strongly stated limits of accountability. Instead of asking who a judge's client might be, it may make more sense to ask to whom or to what is a judge accountable.

One common answer holds judges accountable to the law, that is to applying the law fairly and accurately within the confines of a case. On a practical level, most judges are accountable to appellate courts through a formalized process of judicial review. An overlapping set of obligations arises from judges' obligation to manage their dockets, an obligation often reinforced by explicitly stated accountability to a court administrator or chief judge. At some point, virtually all judges respond to the processes of politics, whether through election or confirmation. Finally, both the rules of judicial ethics and common practice reinforce the obligations of the judge to the parties in the case, including practical obligations of competence and efficiency.

Judges thus face multiple influences both in individual decisions and in an overall docket. How judges accommodate these influences goes a long way toward defining a given judge's style and effectiveness in role. When you observe a judge in court, consider how all of these influences affect the judge's decision making. If you work for a judge, observe how the judge accounts for all of these varied constituencies in the way chambers are organized. For more on judges and judging, see Chapter 19 on Judicial Externships.

The previous sections survey some of the most common types of client relationships. They do not cover all of the possibilities; rather they illustrate some of the likely influences that can arise in the lawyer-client relationship. These examples at a minimum should suggest something about the complexity of the client relationship. Even where an identified client exists, lawyers often have other influences that interact and sometimes conflict with the client's interests. In "clientless" practices, lawyers still remain accountable to a wide range of complex influences.

> **Exercise 15.5** Return to your answer to Exercise 15.1. Given the preceding sections, reconsider the range of realities that influence the relationship between lawyers and clients at your placement or between lawyers and the complex web of interests to which they hold themselves accountable. If you can, make a note to yourself to revisit these questions over the course of the semester. What other influences do you see over time? How do the lawyers at your placement balance these influences?

QUESTIONS TO CONSIDER

Learning about Clients at "Clientless" Practices: If you work at a practice without an identified person, business, or institution as a client, you may be wondering, "What can I learn about clients at all?" Consider at least two answers. First, go back to the preceding exercises and make sure that your placement really lacks a client. For example, you may learn that a government lawyer may well have an identified individual or body to whom the lawyer must report.

Second, even though your placement may lack an identified client, odds are good that your attorneys will work with or oppose lawyers who do. For example, most judges work in litigation with lawyers who represent clients. Observe how lawyers work with their clients in and outside the courtroom. Do they consult with and defer to their clients? Or do they treat them with indifference? How well does the lawyer relay the client's goals and interests in court and in negotiations?

Working With Clients

Lawyers have contact with clients in a host of ways. This section describes some of the most common interactions lawyers have with clients, including interviewing, counseling and decision making, and writing to clients. It also discusses the challenges of understanding clients, especially where the lawyer and the client do not share common life experiences or cultural assumptions.

> **Exercise 15.6** Take a short inventory of the client interactions you observe at your placement. As you read through this section, keep track of the occasions on which your placement's lawyers interact with their clients. If you work in a "clientless" practice, consider how the interactions discussed here (first contact, case development, decision making, negotiation, and advocacy) occur in your practice and how lawyers structure the role of a client in their work. Finally, if you work in a court, note your opportunities to watch lawyers working with their clients, both during litigation and in the hallways.

First Contact and Interviewing

Lawyers start cases in many ways. For lawyers working with identified individuals, the most common method is an initial client interview. Other possibilities include reading a file, receiving an oral assignment from another lawyer, reviewing the results of a police investigation, or deciding to pursue a case or an issue on your own initiative. The dynamics of case handling will change depending on whether it starts with an interview. At your placement, consider how the presence or absence of an initial contact with an individual affects the way the lawyers proceed with the case.

The start of a client relationship requires both ethical and pragmatic alertness. All law practices should have in place a process for comparing a potential client to their list of past clients and opponents to avoid conflicts of interest. Lawyers must assess their competence to handle a given client's concern and make an appropriate referral if they do not have the requisite expertise. In addition, most lawyers will need to make the practical decision whether or not to accept the case, even if the case has legal merit. And, of course, the lawyer will make an assessment of whether what the client wants to do is legal.

More pragmatically, a lawyer will have to decide whether the financial benefit to the lawyer will justify the investment of the lawyer's time, a fact especially relevant in contingency fee cases. In other billing arrangements, the lawyer will want to assess whether the client can afford to pay for the outcome, even if the lawyer expects it to be successful. Prevailing standards of ethics place the lawyer under no obligation to take a client, even if it makes financial sense to do so for both lawyer and client. Lawyers are free to decline cases for a variety of reasons. The rules of ethics exhort each lawyer to take a fair share of unpopular cases; and general law and ethics rules prevent lawyers from discriminating in case selection on the basis of age, race, disability, and other protected status. For more on merit assessment and case acceptance, see Chapter 14 on Learning about Lawyering.

All of these assessments start with the initial client interview. Given the stakes, this interview has several goals and presents distinct challenges. The lawyer usually wants to form a trusting relationship with the client. At the same time, the lawyer wants to assess the client's information with enough skepticism to determine its reliability and the need of for further investigation.

Assuming that no conflicts exist and that the lawyer feels competent to handle the case, the client may have quite specific, even urgent questions requiring immediate answers and may want a preliminary assessment from the lawyer about these concerns. Lawyer and client also set the pattern for their working relationship, including who will do what and the nature of their future contact. Finally, in virtually all interviews, the lawyer and client discuss the terms of the legal contract between them, often including review and signing of a written retainer agreement.

Accomplishing all of these goals involves a set of skills that requires a great deal of observation, practice, and reflection to learn effectively, especially in light of the ethical and pragmatic considerations highlighted above. Much has been written about client interviewing, and there are a number of excellent texts that can help you understand

and develop these skills.[10] As you interview clients yourself or observe others doing so, consider the following challenges:

Style of questioning: Pay close attention to how to ask the client questions and especially the impact various styles of questioning may have on the information obtained during the interview. Many interviewing courses encourage the use of open-ended questions early in an interview to permit clients room to tell their stories in their own way without shaping by the lawyer. Typically, it is suggested that the interviewer reserve more pointed, closed-ended questions for pinning down details and filling in specific gaps. Some suggest a combination of the two approaches, leading into a topic with open-ended questions, shifting into "yes or no" questions to focus on the details of that topic, then shifting back out to open-ended questions to move on in the overall story. As you engage in and observe interviews, keep track of the styles used by lawyers. If you ask the questions, keep track of how various approaches produce differing results with a range of clients.

Structure of the interview: It also can be valuable to monitor an interview's structure, that is, the sequence of topics and phases used by the lawyer to lead the client through the interview. Again, assuming that a conflict check already has occurred, some standard parts of a client interview include the following:

- Introductions and ice-breakers;

- Explanation of the legal service offered by the lawyer;

- Client storytelling, prompted by open-ended questions;

- Lawyer review of the client's story, using both open and closed-ended questions;

- Lawyer's summary of the client's questions and concerns;

- Initial discussion of possible outcomes along with an estimate of the cost of pursuing those solutions;

- Retainer agreement;

- Next steps and task planning.

This particular sequence of phases offers a workable approach to interviewing clients. At the same time, no interview will ever happen in the same way. You may find interviews that rearrange or even omit these phases as well. If you are relatively new to client interviewing, it can help to have a sequence in mind. You certainly will have the opportunity to observe many approaches in the interviews you observe.

Balancing trust-building with fact assessment: It makes sense for lawyers to build trust with their clients. Doing so can foster a more productive relationship, in which lawyer and client cooperate in the task at hand and in which the client feels more comfortable disclosing difficult or embarrassing information. At the same time, it also makes sense for the lawyer to test the reliability of the information that the client offers. Even clients intent on reliable reporting can leave things out, especially when under stress, and some clients may have reasons not to disclose. A lawyer must balance carefully the skepticism necessary for careful inquiry with the need to gain the client's trust.

These challenges and practices cover only a few of the realities that you will encounter in interviewing or observing interviews. The more you observe and do, the more you will come to appreciate how each client may require a separate approach. You also will start the process of determining the style and structure that best suits you.

Counseling Clients

The counseling relationship forms the heart of most lawyer-client relationships. "Counseling" refers to the tasks of giving advice to and eliciting decisions from the client. It is tempting to describe counseling as a singular event: a conversation in which the lawyer reviews options and evaluates choices, the lawyer and client discuss all of the ramifications, and the client reaches a decision, freeing the lawyer to implement that choice. You may witness and even participate in such conversations at your placement.

More typically, however, counseling occurs over time, in response to evolving circumstances and deadlines. A lawyer and client may make an initial choice early in their work together, revisit that choice as they learn more about facts and law, modify the choice after interactions with other parties or courts, and revise or even reverse choices as the stakes and the costs of their work become clearer. A lawyer and client also revisit their earlier estimates about the cost of the lawyering process, continually weighing the ongoing costs against their changing estimates of success. In short, counseling usually occurs in a series of smaller conversations spread over time and alters in response to new events and new knowledge.

Like all aspects of lawyering, counseling benefits from careful and thorough preparation. Lawyers must have a sufficient grasp on the facts of the client's situation to offer advice rooted in the real situation. This level of knowledge requires the lawyer to verify the information provided by the client from sources outside the relationship. Lawyers also must have a sufficiently detailed and accurate understanding of the law so the client can assess the potential outcomes of a dispute or the range of options permitted by a transaction. Additionally, lawyers must learn how to help the client identify choices that meet client goals, develop strategies to accomplish those goals, and evaluate how alternative approaches may meet client interests. For more on the counseling aspect of lawyering, see Chapter 14 on Learning About Lawyering.

Counseling clients also has special ethical dimensions, which overlap with the following:

- **Strategy and tactics:** The rules of ethics allocate responsibility for decisions about strategy and tactics. Clients determine the goals of the representation and make final decisions about any binding agreements. Lawyers may make most tactical decisions about the means through which to accomplish those goals, although they must consult with the client about these means. A grey area exists between these two categories of decision making. The lawyer has the implied authority to take those steps that fall within the overall authority given by the client; yet the lawyer must consider which tactical choices sufficiently impact the client's overall goals so as to require client's consent.[11]

- **Independent judgment and delivering unwelcome news:** The rules of ethics generally require the lawyer to exercise independent professional judgment. This requirement includes counseling that is free from conflicts of interest, bias, or prejudice. It also means that the lawyer must be prepared to deliver advice that the client might find unwelcome.[12]

- **Addressing non-legal as well as legal matters:** Legal problem solving usually mixes specific legal advice with other considerations, including the effects on other relationships, financial consequences, and even moral or ethical concerns. A lawyer must at least provide competent advice on the legal dimensions of the problem. To the extent that a full appreciation of the client's choices includes discussion of these other dimensions, a lawyer may properly discuss them with the client.[13]

At the center of all of these considerations lie important concerns about the power dynamics between lawyers and clients. Lawyers can have a significant impact on client decision making, in part because of the knowledge, experience, and professional status that they bring to the relationship. At the same time, clients retain ultimate authority over decision making and can exercise practical control in several ways. The shifting dynamics of shared decision making have given rise to several models for lawyer-client relationships:

- **Client-centered:** In a client-centered relationship, the lawyer focuses on and seeks to encourage the client's decision-making authority. The lawyer prepares and reviews choices and strategies with the client. The lawyer may evaluate alternative options and focus those evaluations on how those options might or might not meet the client's goals. A lawyer who uses this approach would normally not recommend a specific option, either explicitly or by implicit structuring of the choices and rather would seek to give the client information to make an informed choice. The client-centered model is rooted in respect for the client's autonomy as well as concerns for the strength of the lawyer's potential influence over the client.

- **Lawyer-centered (or "traditional"):** In a lawyer-centered relationship, the lawyer focuses on delivering his or her legal expertise to the client and on providing the client with the lawyer's own sense of the best choice among those available. The lawyer still prepares and reviews choices and strategies and assesses how options do or do not meet client goals. A lawyer who uses this model goes further and provides his or her own recommendation about which choice is the best, given the client's goals. This model is rooted in deference to the lawyer's experience and expertise and in the notion that many clients may prefer to rely on the lawyer's evaluation in the face of complex, unfamiliar legal concerns.

- **Collaborative (or "negotiated"):** In a collaborative relationship, both lawyer and client exert control over the process of decision making. The lawyer still prepares in the same way, yet engages the client in an active discussion about how each option might accomplish the client's goals. In this model, lawyers often will offer their opinions and evaluations and will elicit the same from the client, as part of a process in which both lawyer and client shape the ultimate decision. This model ideally represents a blending of the other two approaches. In practice, it also reflects the reality that, in most cases, neither lawyer nor client is completely passive or completely dominant in the relationship.

A lawyer rarely follows any of these models all of the time, although lawyers may have stylistic preferences for a particular approach. The lawyer's choice of approach can and does vary from client to client and may depend at least in part on the context of the relationship. At the very least, these models can help you structure what you see and how you are trained at your placement.

Exercise 15.7 A lawyer regularly represents low-income clients in immigration court in removal cases. The lawyer often appears before a particular judge who has a habit of requiring clients to disclose health information that in other circumstances would remain confidential. The lawyer believes this requirement to be illegal and knows that to challenge the practice would require repeated refusals. Yet the lawyer also knows that any client who complies with the judge's request has a much higher likelihood of a favorable ruling. Despite this understanding, the lawyer makes it a practice to refuse the judge's request for her clients.

The lawyer will need to talk with the client in this situation every time the issue arises. How would you present the issue? What model of lawyer-client decision making would be more useful in this situation? Does the proper approach depend on other factors, including the particular personalities and backgrounds of a given client?

Exercise 15.8 Review the various type of "clients" described early in this chapter: individuals, business organizations, groups, governments, policies and causes, and the various constituencies and influences for judges. How might these varying client relationships affect the dynamics between lawyer and client? For example, do poverty lawyers representing tenants in urgent eviction cases face one dynamic while commercial litigators seeking to maintain long-term relationships with high-volume clients face another? Does it matter that in one case the client may have no other option for legal help than this lawyer, while in the other case the client can readily move the legal work to another lawyer? How might this difference affect the lawyer's choice of approach to clients in each group?

Communicating With Clients

All lawyers face the challenge of communicating with clients about the law. Law school can develop habits of speech that assume that all conversation occurs between trained professionals. This practice has several advantages. The use of technical legal words and of familiar rhetorical devices to express legal analysis can be less time-consuming and more precise than using overly general terms. Indeed, the difficulty and discipline of first-year classes arises in part from learning how to use these terms and devices accurately and to master the art of speaking with other lawyers and judges effectively and efficiently.

Using insider language runs serious risks when communicating with clients. Clients may simply not understand the words that you use and tune out where you want them to pay attention. Clients also may hear technical words that also have non-technical meaning and mistake what you say for something you do not intend. Even a client who understands the language may have a hard time grasping the flow of your logic. Missing a step or two along the way may reduce the client's ability to understand how you reach your conclusion, potentially reducing the client's willingness to take your advice or even make a choice at all.

Reliance on formal legal vocabulary and rhetoric also affects the lawyer-client relationship. It assumes that communication is a form of exchange, where the lawyer's job is to deliver information, education, and evaluation while the client conveys reactions, questions, and decisions back to the lawyer. Consider instead a model in which lawyer and client engage in a dialogue that creates a new understanding, one that goes beyond the information that lawyer and client already have. In this model, communication is the pathway along which lawyer and client build an effective working relationship. See Chapter 5 on Effective Communication and Professional Relationships. To clothe your part of that relationship in professional language and to veil your advice in unfamiliar rhetoric can reduce severely the potential for your effective work together.

To avoid these risks, consider alternatives. Avoid complex sentences with multiple dependent clauses and embedded asides. Use short declarative sentences. Faced with the choice of a lawyer's versus a lay-person's word, ask whether the client needs to know the technical term for a particular reason. If so, state explicitly that you are using technical language and explain both what it means and the reasons the client needs be familiar with it. If not, use the word or phrase a lay-person likely would use. Finally, most legal concepts rely on knowledge and concepts that lawyers share and about which clients may have no clue. If so, back up and explain the assumption first.

For example, consider a married client who owns his house for life and whose sons will take ownership when he dies. Tension has arisen between the father and his sons. He wants to know whether he can give the property to his wife and whether she can claim ownership after he dies. You might decide to explain things to your client like this:

> The quitclaim deed which transferred the property to you and your sons gave you a life estate in the residence and designated your sons as holders of the remainder interest. You cannot alienate the property in any way that would survive you. After you pass on, your sons' remainder interests ripen into fee simple ownership by operation of law. Your wife would become a tenant at will, subject to summary ejectment in your sons' sole discretion.

This explanation is accurate, has relevant content, and is fairly complete. It might reassure another lawyer that you have a grasp on the legal concepts involved in the advice. But the odds are good that your client will grasp little to none of what you say. Consider instead the following explanation:

> The deed that gave you the property also gave you what the law calls a "life estate." That means that you have the right to own the property and to live in it, but only as long as you are alive. The deed also gave your sons the right to take ownership after you pass on. This happens automatically. They do not have to go to court or file another deed. Because you only own the property while you are alive, you cannot give your wife anything that would last after you die. Once you die, your wife will have no legal interest in the property. Your sons could ask a court to move her out whenever they choose.

This second explanation is a little longer and has the same conceptual complexity. It may even add a little content to the first explanation. At the same time, it uses only one piece of legalese, the term "life estate," which is explained. Otherwise, it sticks with relatively short sentences and makes legal concepts and processes concrete and specific. Odds are good that the client will understand this information more readily and can turn more easily to working out practical solutions with you.

You sometimes hear this second approach referred to as "dumbing it down," a disparaging phrase that assumes that clients will never be able to understand lawyers. This assumption is inaccurate. The second approach does not eliminate any important part of the advice and includes all of the content of the first approach. Instead, it offers advice that is exactly as complex as it needs to be, respects the client's ability to understand his own situation, and helps the client to understand, accept, and transform the advice into productive problem solving.

> **Exercise 15.9** As you work at your placement, take advantage of the chance to observe lawyers with their clients. These observations may occur within your own office, in interactions with lawyers outside your office, or in work you observe lawyers doing in a courtroom. How do they convey what they have to say? What kind of language do they use, and how do they structure the content of what they have to say?
>
> You may not be able to hear what the lawyer or the client says. If so, observe their manner and body language. Does the lawyer maintain eye contact or pause to ask the client a question? Does the lawyer talk in extended bursts with little response from the client? Does the client seem engaged in what the lawyer says?

> **Exercise 15.10** You may have the opportunity to attend court or to observe a negotiation or the closing of a deal. Compare how the lawyers talk with each other and how they speak to the clients in these situations. Are these conversations similar? If not, how?
>
> In a courtroom, take the opportunity to observe bench trials or hearings and to compare them to jury trials. Compare how lawyers convey their messages to judges as opposed to lay juries?
>
> In a negotiation setting, watch the flow of discussion between lawyers and clients. Who talks with whom? How do the lawyers speak when talking with each other outside the client's presence?

Challenges in Working With Clients

As you master the fundamentals of working with clients, you may well find that your relationships proceed relatively smoothly from initial contact through final resolution. However, the relationship can often present distinct challenges. This section discusses some of the challenges lawyers often encounter with clients.

Client Truthfulness

Lawyers rely on their clients for their first knowledge of the situation. As a result, the client's story has an enormous impact on the lawyer's understanding of the issues. As noted earlier, a lawyer is well advised to confirm the key details of the client's story through outside investigation.

It is equally critical that the lawyer make an assessment of the client's reliability as a reporter. First, if the lawyer determines that the client has not provided reliable information, it can affect the lawyer's attitude and relationship with the client and can influence the approach the lawyer takes to interviewing, follow-up, and counseling. Second, the client's reliability affects how the lawyer might structure her approach to resolving the issue, especially where the possibility exists for ongoing relationships between the client and other people. Third, the client may be called upon to speak in a public setting during the representation, as a witness in a trial or as a participant in a negotiation.[14]

The client may relate facts inaccurately for several reasons and not just an intention to deceive. Clients may not have observed the events they describe fully and may have filled in the gaps with inferences and guesses. The client's memory may have failed, in whole or in part, under the pressure of time or a natural tendency to reorganize memory around current goals and motivations. The client may have difficulty telling the story in a way that the lawyer can understand, a factor that can reflect as much on the lawyer as on the client.

Finally, the client may intend to deceive the lawyer, providing information that the client knows to be false. There are several reasons why this may occur, in addition to an intention to deceive. The client may want to give the lawyer as positive a version as possible, may be deeply reluctant to expose a potential vulnerability, may be trying to protect someone else, or may consider the statement peripheral.[15] For these clients, the lawyer can use both corroboration from outside sources and reassurance about confidentiality as a way to encourage a more accurate flow of information.

Many lawyers pride themselves on having the ability to detect lies and inaccuracies from clients. Some claim to do so through sharp observation of behavior, looking for tells as if they were playing poker: the tug of an ear, a weak handshake, a break in eye contact. Others lay claim to a more intuitive capacity, an ability often couched in physical terms: "the hair on my neck stood up." A more reliable approach for most lawyers requires listening carefully to the whole story, noting internal inconsistencies, and comparing the story to other information known to be accurate. In short, reliable assessments of credibility more commonly depend on careful factual analysis than on some innate inner lie detector.

Lawyers often face a particular risk in detecting inaccuracies from their clients when lawyer and client come from distinct cultural backgrounds. It is common for all of us to assess the plausibility of the stories we hear by comparing them to the way we think the world usually works. "That would never happen that way," we might think; or "That just doesn't add up." In doing this analysis, the lawyer is not comparing the story to specific, verifiable information but rather to a more general sense of how the lawyer views the world. The risk is obvious: the client may have told a story about events through a lens on the world or a culture the lawyer has never encountered. In this sense, cultural difference can pose a major problem for the lawyer's ability to assess accuracy. For more on the impact of cultural difference on lawyering, see Chapter 6 on Navigating Cultural Difference.

Exercise 15.11 You may or may not have the chance to meet with clients and make your own determinations about their credibility. That said, very likely you will have the chance to watch lawyers assess credibility. These opportunities include placements that serve clients and also "clientless" practices that make assessments about the credibility of witnesses and even opposing counsel. It also includes judges in bench trials and in non-jury hearings, who sit as finders of fact and routinely assess witness credibility. Make a list of the occasions at your placement in which lawyers or judges assess the credibility of clients or witnesses.

Then choose one of these sessions and plan to attend and observe. As you do, keep track of your own belief in the stories that you hear. Do you find the speaker to be credible? What tools are you using in making that decision? If you can, check in with the lawyers or judges that you observed and ask them what they thought. You might also ask how they reached that decision and how they assess credibility more generally.

Disagreeing With Clients

Earlier, this section discussed the dynamic of lawyers and clients working together to reach decisions. That section assumed they would agree on what to do; yet agreement does not always occur. What happens when lawyers and clients disagree over decisions about the representation?

The lawyer may want to adopt a particular set of tactics for handling the client's concerns, only to find after consulting with the client that the client wants the lawyer to do something else. The lawyer may have concluded that one course of action represents the best way to accomplish the client's goals, only to find that the client disagrees on how to weigh those goals and move forward. The lawyer may have recommended immediate action to address a specific risk, only to find that the client delays or even declines to act at all.

When working with clients, caution and a concern for malpractice liability suggest that lawyers address any disagreement clearly and in writing, stating their advice and including a clear description of the risks of the course of action the client has chosen to pursue. In some cases, the lawyer's concern may run more deeply. For example, the client may want to follow a path the lawyer believes would constitute a crime or a fraud,[16] or a path the lawyer thinks would harm the client's own interests irretrievably. In such cases, although the lawyer needs to work with the client to resolve the disagreement if the disagreement touches a fundamental point, the rules of ethics usually permit the lawyer to withdraw.[17] And, of course, the client can always fire the lawyer.

Disagreements also arise in clientless practices. In a firm that engages in policy advocacy, such as a private nonprofit public interest firm, disputes can arise within the organization about both the goals and means of representation. It is possible that the disagreement would become an organizational as well as an ethical issue, requiring resolution by an executive director or even a board of directors. A government attorney also may be asked to take a public position in a highly political case that conflicts with the attorney's own strongly held views on that issue. For more on decision making in public interest and public service practices, see Chapter 21 on Public Interest Practices and Chapter 22 on Public Service Practices.

Even judges face the prospect of disagreement, although as noted earlier, these disagreements may occur both with individuals and with other constituencies or institutions. Except for the highest appellate courts, all judges face the risk of reversal, a reality that understandably affects a judge's approach to particular legal issues. Judges also face the risk of disagreement from political institutions, whether through impeachment or election results.[18] Finally, judges and arbitrators at all levels sit in panels and must find a way to manage disagreement within the decision-making group. These disagreements lead to negotiations that fascinate outsiders about the formulation of majority and dissenting opinions.

Exercise 15.12 As you work at your placement, keep alert to situations in which a lawyer or a judge encounters disagreement or dissent with a client, a policy, a reviewing court, or an electorate. When it occurs, consider writing about it in your journal, keeping in mind that you should protect confidential and private information. See Chapter 8 on Reflection and Writing Journals. Try to specify the main point of the disagreement and to describe the interests on all sides of the dispute. What is at stake in the disagreement? Is it purely local and tactical, or does it go to the heart of the lawyer's or judge's role? If the latter, what options do the lawyer or judge have?

Exercise 15.13 A lawyer encounters a client who wants to pursue a path that the lawyer considers ill-advised. In the lawyer's judgment, the disagreement does not justify withdrawal. The lawyer decides to go forward but must find ways to remain assertive on the client's behalf despite doubts and strongly held beliefs that the representation may harm the client. What are the risks of the lawyer's decision to go forward both in the short and the long term?

> **Exercise 15.14** A judge encounters a high-profile decision in which strongly-stated public opinion favors a particular outcome. With your help, the judge determines that the weight of authority calls for some other decision. The judge could in good faith reach the result favored by public opinion if the judge uses an analysis that would almost certainly result in reversal. The judge faces a non-partisan reelection campaign within the next two years and already expects opposition. What path would you suggest the judge follow? How would you balance the judge's accountability to the appellate courts, the parties in the case, and the preferences expressed by public opinion?

Mental Capacity

Lawyers sometimes develop serious concerns about a client's capacity to make decisions. As an initial matter, it makes sense to draw a sharp line between doubts over the client's credibility or disagreement with a client's decisions and a conclusion that client has a diminished capacity to make decisions. The conviction that your client is lying or the belief that a decision is ill advised does not, standing alone, justify a conclusion that client in unable to make decisions.

However, lawyers do encounter situations in which they come to believe that the client is affected by some kind of mental condition that affects the client's decision-making capacity. Several factors might lead a lawyer to this conclusion:

- The client seems unable to understand the legal situation, the lawyer's advice, or the consequences of the various options.

- The client seems unable to reason about the choices at hand. This might become apparent if the client's expressed thoughts jump around without apparent connection or if the client's speech shows leaps of logic from one point to another point where there is no apparent connection.

- The client seems unable to communicate a decision about choices. A client may remain persistently silent in the face of repeated efforts by the lawyer or may speak in a way that, despite good faith efforts and accommodations, the lawyer simply cannot understand.

If this situation happens, the rules of ethics provide guidance though not a checklist about how the lawyer needs to handle the situation. As a general matter, the rules require lawyers, as far as reasonably possible, to "maintain a conventional relationship" with a client with diminished capacity and to treat the client with the same dignity and respect they would give to any other client. A lawyer ought to make a concerted effort to determine whether a client can understand, reason about, and communicate choices. If so, the lawyer needs to give those choices weight and accept the client's guidance. In some cases, the lawyer may seek outside assistance in the form of services or the appointment of a guardian or guardian ad litem. The rules give permission to do so, but only where the client faces severe harm and only if the lawyer concludes that the client cannot communicate or cannot reason about his or her choices.[19]

Representing clients with mental disabilities poses serious challenges and offers compelling opportunities for insight and understanding. Challenges include extra time needed for communication, a somewhat higher risk of misunderstanding and disagreement between lawyer and client, and a persistent, pervasive bias against those with mental illness in a legal system focused on reasoned decision making. The requirements of the Americans with Disabilities Act affect some of these challenges, such as the use of technology to improve access and communication.

At the same time, clients in this situation often have astute insights into their situations and into you, which they may have no hesitation in sharing. Finding effective ways to communicate and work together can strengthen a lawyer's capacity for patience, compassion, and self-awareness. Finally, as would be true with any client facing an intractable problem, clients in this situation can inspire you with their humor, uniqueness, and ability to survive and thrive despite or even because of their life circumstances.

> **Exercise 15.15** The legal system generally values and depends heavily on the capacity for reasoned decisions. Perhaps because of this expectation, many lawyers find working with a person with a disabling mental condition particularly difficult. You may not encounter such a person during your time at your placement. If you do, talk to your supervising lawyer or judge about the experience. Listen to how they describe the individual and also their work with the individual. Consider whether you would have the same reactions and whether you would want to emulate or change how the lawyer or judge chose to work with that individual.

Personal Boundaries With Clients

A lawyer faces important decisions about the nature of the interpersonal connection with the lawyer's client. Is the relationship similar to a friendship? Or is it more appropriate to draw a sharp line between personal connection and professional role? How should lawyers draw boundaries in their work with clients?

> **Exercise 15.16** Consider the following choices by lawyers:
>
> 1. A homeless client works with a lawyer on a claim for public benefits. During one winter meeting, the client tells the lawyer that he has no place to sleep that night, he has not eaten in two days, and has no coat. Without being asked, the lawyer drives the client to a restaurant and buys a meal, takes the client to a thrift store and buys a coat, and calls in a favor with a local shelter to get the client a bed for the night.
>
> 2. A young lawyer has just started work with a small firm in a mid-sized city. The lawyer joins the Junior League, becomes active in the organization's activities, and makes friends with people in the local chapter's leadership. These efforts bring in extra business for her real estate practice. She then invites clients to her home for meals, arranges outings on the weekends, and swaps child-care responsibilities in emergencies.
>
> 3. A lawyer works for a client in a sharply-contested divorce. The legal issues include disputes over custody, the timing of visitation, and division of the couple's main asset, their house. In discussing proposals for custody, the lawyer tells the client about similar questions in his divorce and describes the options the lawyer considered at the time.
>
> In each of these situations, some would approve while others would disapprove of what each lawyer did. What do you think? What explanations can you offer for the choices that each lawyer made? What risks do you see in the lawyers' choices? Do you give the same answers in each situation? What your reasons?
>
> If you think that one or more of these lawyers crossed some sort of line, try to describe where you would draw that line. Be specific about what you would or would not change.

Lawyers always work with clients on issues that are important enough to require professional help. This reality means that lawyers often work with clients in crisis or in situations in which the client shares personal information. Legal work is often hard work, meaning that lawyers and clients develop a relationship focused on difficult decisions, challenging negotiations, or intense advocacy. Creating and maintaining strong personal connections with clients can be useful professionally, both in accomplishing the goals of a particular case and in ensuring that a client comes to the lawyer again for future business.

Very few rules exist for determining whether and how a lawyer should set boundaries between the professional and the personal aspects of a client relationship. Some ethical rules affect these choices. A lawyer must exercise independent judgment, avoid conflicts of interest, and be prepared to advise against poor decisions and even withdraw if the client goes beyond what the lawyer ethically can accept. Most lawyers also charge clients and may face disputes over the amount and reasonableness of fees.

At least one definition of "professionalism" stresses the need to keep "professional boundaries" between lawyer and client. This view sees boundaries as essential to the task of effective, even-handed representation:

> Professional boundaries define effective and appropriate interaction between an attorney and the client. Boundaries exist to protect both parties. No conscientious professional sets out to violate the standards of professional relationships with clients. However, violations can happen, even to those that are dedicated, moral and highly responsible in the overall conduct of their practice. As you know, failure to set healthy boundaries with clients can lead to [ethical] violations on the topics of fees, communication, and other ethical responsibilities.[20]

The quoted article identifies several ways to maintain appropriate boundaries, including "increase structure," "maintain consistency," "manage expectations," and "set limits."[21]

Yet, lawyers can still establish a more personal connection to clients and maintain professional boundaries. A more personal relationship with clients is professionally appropriate and can promote a more trusting exchange of information and decisions. It also allows the lawyer more insight into the client's context and situation and improves the depth and range of the knowledge that the lawyer brings to the representation. This view does not require the lawyer to disclose personal information, to give the client's gifts or exchange favors, or to discuss the lawyer's own personal choices. That said, the lawyer who seeks to understand the client in greater depth and on a more personal level may face tensions about how much of the lawyer's own life and views should become a part of their conversations with clients.[22]

Consider how these tensions play out at your placement. If you work at a placement that serves individual clients, you may notice several approaches among the lawyers you observe. You also might consider that the way a lawyer sets limits in relating to clients may connect to how the lawyer sets limits between commitments to work and to other parts of the lawyer's life, including family, community, and personal well-being. See Chapter 25 on Work and Well-being.

Clients and Your Career

You will find that the kinds of clients with whom you work and the relationships you have with them has a huge impact on your choice of career. Whether deciding on a first job or moving to another job, many lawyers choose a practice because it offers the chance to help particular people in a particular way and to have a particular relationship with them. Revisit Exercise 15.15. While the questions in that exercise focus on boundary concerns, each of the stories describes a specific kind of service in which the lawyer forms a characteristic kind of relationship with a client.

The first part of this chapter identifies many of the types of clients you might consider. Lawyers develop strong preferences between them. Some lawyers prefer working with individuals on deeply personal concerns. Others prefer working on larger issues that affect groups of people. In some cases, lawyers prefer working with clients who desperately need legal assistance to survive or to stay out of jail. Others prefer working for clients who want to create something new: a business, a building, or a plan for personal health care. And still others prefer working with clients who do not engender a strong personal or emotional investment by the lawyer.

The end of your externship offers an ideal time to reflect on how your experience has influenced your future choices about clients and relationships with clients.

> **Exercise 15.17** Once again, consider the people, organizations, and institutions affected by your placement's work. Before you leave your placement, make a connection with one of your lawyers or judges in down time or over coffee or a meal. Ask them what they like and dislike about their clients or constituencies and the reasons they chose to serve them. Did they choose this practice because of the work or for some other reasons?
>
> After this conversation and on your own, compare the answers you receive to what you have observed throughout the semester. What kinds of connections and relationships did you observe lawyers making with clients? How did your judge relate to parties, attorneys, other judges, even (at a distance) with appellate courts or the electorate? Make sure to include both work-related contact and contact outside the regular practice, including social interactions and activities in the community.

> When you have sketched out what you can, ask yourself, would I want to work with these people in this web of relationships? What would be the advantages and disadvantages? Do I like the way I have seen lawyers or judges work with those they help? What would I prefer?

This chapter began with the proposition that lawyering is responsible work, meaning in part having responsibility **to** someone or something else. Clinics and externships give you the chance, and sometimes your first chance, to feel what it is like for your actions and decisions to have an effect on someone other than yourself. At the heart of every client relationship lies a powerful moral experience, the assumption of responsibility for helping other people with choices that can affect them long into the future.

> **Exercise 15.18** At the end of your placement, think back to the occasions in which you realized that someone relied on your work to make a real decision. The work product might be a brief your supervisors used in court. It might be a piece of advice you suddenly realized your client would accept. It might be a draft order a judge issued with her signature. In each case, you might have found yourself saying: "Really? I'm just a law student. How can my work have this impact?"
>
> Ask yourself how that responsibility felt to you. Did it feel heavy or light? Daunting or exciting? All of these and more? Imagine how it might feel to encounter this day in and day out, for many years. Recognize that some legal problems might weigh more heavily on a lawyer than other problems. In addition, one lawyer might get great satisfaction from working with a set of client concerns that another lawyer might find overwhelming. What have you learned about the kinds of client responsibilities you want in your career?

Over the course of your career, you will make important choices about who to serve, how to relate to them, and how to find satisfaction in your work for them. These choices are central to your professional identity, including how you see yourself and how others see you. For more on the formation of professional identity, see Chapter 24 on Professional Identity and Formation. Finally, the choices that you make about your responsibilities have a profound impact on your well-being and your satisfaction with your work. See Chapter 25 on Work & Well-being. Your placement can help you assess whom you will represent and how that choice will affect the shape of your career of service.

ENDNOTES

1 *See* National Association of Law Placement, Class of 2013 National Summary Report (July 2014), http://www.nalp.org/uploads/NatlSummaryChartClassof2013.pdf.

2 *Id.* By contrast, 42% of graduates took positions in firms with between two and ten lawyers, while another 4.8% went into solo practice. A significant percentage of these lawyers would represent businesses.

3 Juliet Brodie, *Little Cases on the Middle Ground: Teaching Social Justice Lawyering in Neighborhood-Based Community Lawyering Clinics*, 15 Clin. L. Rev. 333, 339 (2009).

4 *Id.* at 344.

5 *Id.*

6 Geoffrey P. Miller, *Government Lawyers' Ethics in a System of Checks and Balances*, 54 U. Chi. L. Rev. 1293, 1298 (1987) ("[Q]uestions of intrabranch conflicts can be subtle and complex, but in principle their answer is easy: the attorney's duties run to the officer who has the power of decision over the issue.").

7 Am. Civ. Liberties Union, https://www.aclu.org.

8 Model Rules of Judicial Conduct r. 2.1, 2.2 (2011).

9 *Id.* at r. 2.4.

10 *See* David Binder, Paul Bergman, Paul Tremblay & Ian Weinstein, Lawyers as Counselors: A Client-Centered Approach (3rd ed. 2011); Stefan Krieger & Richard Neumann, Essential Lawyering Skills (4th ed. 2011); Robert F. Cochran Jr. & Martha Peters, The Counselor-at-Law: A Collaborative Approach to Client Interviewing and Counseling (3rd ed. 2014).

11 *See* Model Rules of Prof'l Conduct r. 1.2(a) & cmt. (ABA, 1983).

12 *See* Model Rules of Prof'l Conduct r. 2.1 & cmt. (ABA, 1983).

13 *Id.* at cmts. 2–4.

14 A lawyer has special ethical duties if the lawyer knows that the client intends to give false information in courtroom testimony. *See* Model Rules of Prof'l Conduc R. 3.3 & cmt. (ABA, 1983).

15 For more on different kinds and motivations for lying, *see* Sissela Bok, Lying: Moral Choice in Public and Private Life (1979) (containing separate chapters on white lies, excuses, justifications, lies in a crisis, lying to liars, lying to enemies, lies protecting peers and clients, lies for the public good, and other behaviors).

16 *See* Model Rules of Prof'l Conduc r. 1.2(d) (ABA, 1983).

17 *Id.* at r. 1.2, cmt. 2 (1983).

18 For an overview of the means by which judges are selected and reviewed in the different states, *see Judicial Selection in the States: Georgia*, Nat'l Ctr. for St. Cts., http://www.judicialselection.us/judicial_selection/index.cfm?state=GA.

19 *See* Model Rules of Prof'l Conduct r. 1.14, cmt. 1 & 5 (ABA, 1983).

20 *Are You Setting Boundaries with Your Clients?*, Wash. St. B. Ass'n, http://www.wsba.org/Resources-and-Services/Lawyers-Assistance-Program/Self-Care/Boundaries (last visited June 9, 2015). The article goes on to describe "signs that you may be at Risk of Violating Boundaries," "Possible Consequences of Boundary Violations," and "Setting Boundaries."

21 *Id.*

22 *See* Jane Aiken & Stephen Wizner, *Law as Social Work*, 11 Wash. U. J.L. & Pol'y 63, 76 (2003) ("The lawyer as social worker spends a good deal of time with the client, and also in the community to gain insight into the context in which problems may arise. She establishes a trusting relationship with her clients by being reliable, following problems through completion, being a good listener, and being committed to client empowerment. She is attentive to the many constituencies within the community that work toward that community's goals.").

Collaboration and Teamwork

JANET WEINSTEIN & LINDA MORTON

I n 2014, General Motors, once on the rebound with its largest profits and strongest industry-wide sales since the recession, was accused of over 60 deaths due to faulty ignition switches in its small cars. In May 2014, the National Highway Traffic Safety Administration (NHTSA) fined GM 35 million dollars–the maximum allowed–after a report finding systemic problems throughout the organization, including delayed reporting of the deadly ignition switch problem. CEO Mary Barra summarily dismissed fifteen employees, including top-level legal counsel. As of June, 2014, the company had paid at least 1.7 billion dollars in recall costs for the prior year.

What went wrong? Why did it take GM over ten years to resolve a problem, known to its employees, that was causing fatalities? Barra referred to a lack of leadership and extensive compartmentalization within the company, which discouraged information sharing. "[N]obody took responsibility," said Barra. The CEO described a facet of the corporate culture, called the "GM nod," as the moment when "everyone nods in agreement to a proposed plan of action, but then leaves the room and does nothing."[1]

The GM story is a cautionary tale about what can happen when collaboration fails. The remainder of this chapter will help ensure the collaborations in your own practice are successful.

> **Exercise 16.1** You are being interviewed for your first attorney job. The interviewer asks you to describe your strengths and weaknesses working on a team. What would your response be? Complete the self-assessment in Appendix 16.1.

Collaboration requires (1) individuals working together (2) toward a shared objective (3) for which they are accountable. Although some may consider "teams" to be more formalized collaborations, for purposes of this chapter, we use the terms collaboration and teamwork interchangeably. The more conscious the process of collaboration is and the more dedicated the participants are to the group's success, the more effective the results will be.

Why Collaboration is Essential in Today's Law Practice

Collaboration is important for lawyers if
they wish to avoid becoming irrelevant.[2]

—ABA JOURNAL, June 2014

Employers, such as the one in this video (*What Employers Want*: https://www.youtube.com/watch?v=Rjxqbv3pS90), have indicated through their preferences in hiring that teamwork is a critical lawyering skill. The ULTIMATE LAW GUIDE lists "Teamwork" first among 15 skills, other than academic credentials, required to be a lawyer.[3] A 2008 study by Berkeley law professor Marjorie Shultz with partner Sheldon Zedeck listed "Working with Others" as an "Umbrella Category" that includes some of the main factors that can be used in measuring professional effectiveness. See Appendix I.3 for more on the Shultz and Zedeck study. It is not surprising then that employers are looking for good team players.[4]

Although traditionally the legal profession has been associated with independent, autonomous, and competitive work, all lawyers must collaborate to thrive in today's legal and economic environment. Knowledge of and comfort with collaborative work, sometimes referred to as "collaborative intelligence," results in more effective client outcomes.

As law firms develop new clients, they continue to search for the best ways to retain their client base. One of these best practices is "knowledge management" or the ability to fully leverage a firm's resources including documents, attorney experience, and technology, to offer the highest quality and most efficient services to a client. Collaboration, a key element to knowledge management, is paramount to both profitability and superior service.

Collaboration is not always in person. New tools that support virtual teamwork and collaboration are making the practice of law more efficient. Online professional networking platforms for lawyers, such as Legal OnRamp, assist firms and businesses in their collaborative efforts. With its staff of more than 50 recent law graduates, Legal OnRamp offers businesses efficient, cost-effective processes for managing large-scale work by collecting and sharing information virtually through a collaborative software program. For example, a team of Legal OnRamp attorneys can assure compliance in thousands of bank contracts far more quickly and cheaply through the process of massive online legal analysis (MOLA).

The outcome of a team with collaborative intelligence is superior to the sum of its individual members' attributes. In addition to improved results and efficiency, collaboration adds to the enjoyment of work by offering a shared sense of accomplishment. The teamwork process also enhances individuals' self-awareness, career satisfaction, and relations with others. Partners who collaborate create a more harmonious environment.

How Lawyers Collaborate

By bringing together professions with different bases of expertise, a collaborative approach to serving clients has the potential to develop more innovative outcomes that are customized to the specific needs of the client, thereby increasing satisfaction and repeat business. Moreover, as individuals in a firm bring together their distinct expertise and knowledge to form innovative solutions, they may create entirely new types of service that can attract new clients.[5]

– Heidi K. Gardner, Assistant Professor, Harvard Business School, referring to necessary strategies for today's law firms.

Teamwork takes shape in a wide swath of practice areas, including arbitration and judicial panels, prosecution teams, litigation teams, regulatory compliance teams, transaction teams, judges' chambers, and multidisciplinary teams.

Teamwork can involve a variety of individuals and entities, including law firms, businesses, courts, agencies, judges, administrative groups, clients, professionals from other disciplines, and non-legal entities that service clients, such as hospitals or schools. Even solo practitioners find themselves collaborating to help each other, as the comments from this judge describe. *The Role of Teamwork in Today's Law Practice*: https://www.youtube.com/watch?v=2TlnqEBTTJY.

The attributes of collaboration are becoming more essential as tomorrow's law practice expands into such areas as project management, unbundled legal services, outsourcing, multi-sourcing, and Collaborative Law practice.

Multidisciplinary teamwork adds an additional challenge, as professionals from different disciplines need additional skills and characteristics to work effectively across discipline cultures. For example, the Collaborative Law movement came into existence largely because professionals recognized the need for communication among the various disciplines working for clients in the family law system. In family law cases, it is not unusual for attorneys, therapists, and financial planners to work with one or both of the parties. A lack of communication among these professionals can lead to ineffective services and poor outcomes. In Collaborative Law practice, the lawyers are hired to help the parties reach a settlement and work closely as a team with professionals from other disciplines and the parties to this end. The Collaborative Law movement has spread to other areas of practice.[6]

Multidisciplinary teamwork is growing at a rapid pace. The employment market is looking for creative individuals who can work in interdisciplinary teams to resolve larger societal issues such as income inequality, access to affordable healthcare, climate change, sustainable development, and immigration. To hear from a current practitioner as to the value of teamwork in the non-profit sector, take a look at the following video, *The Value of Teamwork in the Non-profit Sector*: https://www.youtube.com/watch?v=79ztf5_XT0I.

Here are two examples that demonstrate the problem-solving strengths of multidisciplinary teams:

- The Street Vendor project of Candy Chang and Sean Basinski, in collaboration with the Center for Urban Pedagogy, highlights how a thoughtful partnership among lawyers, designers, education specialists, and other professionals can help to deliver effective, empowering messages about rights as well as legal duties to a group that otherwise would be legally vulnerable and largely disenfranchised. The project uses easy-to-follow graphics, supplemented by text written in languages used by the street vendors themselves so that they can understand and comply with applicable regulations, stand up for their rights, and grow their businesses while respecting the law and its institutions. http://welcometocup.org/ http://candychang.com/street-vendor-guide/

- Corporate Counsel at the Wikimedia Foundation spent much time fielding questions from the public and other businesses about their use or display of various Wikimedia trademarks. To help these potential users and save attorney time, the Foundation wanted to develop a simple web page that could guide potential licensees.

A Finland-based Ph.D. student in Information Design worked with Wikimedia and others to convene two "Legal Design Jams"—one at Stanford University and one in San Francisco—that brought together law students and faculty, graphic design students, and practicing attorneys to consider how the details of Wikimedia trademark licensing policies could be presented visually. The law students knew almost nothing about graphic design principles, and the design students knew little about trademark licensing. Nonetheless, they worked together successfully in a brainstorming atmosphere to construct an easily-navigated Webpage that answers many inquiries simply and directs more complex questions to additional information links. http://commons.wikimedia.org/wiki/Commons:Village_pump/Copyright.

> **Exercise 16.2** You have been assigned to your firm's litigation team that will be representing a large class of tenants in an action against the owners and property management companies for failing to provide safe and habitable rental dwellings. The tenants have complained of asbestos, lead paint, absence of lighting in stairwells and halls, and fire escapes in disrepair. These conditions have caused a variety of physical injuries and poor health conditions. What types of collaboration would be necessary to succeed in this endeavor? Who should be involved? What online tools might you use? Be as specific as you can.

Despite lawyers' claims that teamwork is vital in 21st century law practice, and the fact that most employers list "teamwork" as a skill of high importance, the reality is that not every team is successful; often the experience is trying, if not arduous. Sometimes, as in the GM situation opening the chapter, the problem begins with the failure to acknowledge the presence of a team or a lack of leadership. Instead, employees approach the project in a disconnected or even competitive manner. When individuals assigned to projects that require teamwork fail to work collaboratively, tension is sure to follow. Ultimately, the work, the client, the lawyers, and all involved with the team suffer economically and psychologically.

> **Exercise 16.3** Consider at least two collaborations you have observed or been involved in at your placement. Was the collaboration process ever discussed? If so,

describe the discussions. Were these collaborations effective? Why do you think the collaborations were effective or ineffective? If you are in a placement where collaboration does not seem to take place or be valued, how do you see that affecting the workplace?

Why Collaborative Efforts Fail

Starting from our youngest years in grade school, teamwork is constantly emphasized, but often poorly taught. Nearly all of us have had at least one unpleasant experience working with others. For some, it may have been a school project, for others, a work assignment. Even when the "team" is supposed to be doing something for fun, such as a team sport or a video game, some groups fail while others thrive. As you read through the next couple of pages, consider the problem at GM described at the opening of this chapter.

Teamwork involves both individual and group dynamics. This means the personal attributes of the individual members impact the group. You know people with whom you would be happy to work–perhaps you trust their knowledge, skills, and work ethic. In addition, you know that working with them will be a pleasant experience, most likely because they have adequate EQ or CQ (emotional or collaborative intelligence). On the other hand, you know people with whom you would not choose to work. Perhaps you have had a prior experience with a person who did not meet your standards or had other work habits that bothered you. As a result, there was a loss of trust, and likely an unsuccessful end product.

> **Exercise 16.4** Think of a collaborative experience you have had in your life that did not turn out the way you had hoped. Were there particular personality traits of group members that affected the group's work? You might find it helpful to use this example as a point of reference as you continue with this chapter.

At least in your first professional jobs, you may not have any choice about who your teammates will be. Moreover, the senior partner or supervisor likely will not be interested in your opinion about the deficits of one or more of your team members. If you encounter a difficult team dynamic, it may be helpful to understand the individual characteristics that are not conducive to collaborative work. Additionally, you may be able to address some of these difficult dynamics when a "challenging conversation" is required, as described below. Characteristics not conducive to teamwork include

- poor communicator (includes poor listening skills),

- self-centered,

- domineering,

- careless,

- not self-aware, and

- defensive.

Beyond the issue of problematic individual characteristics, including our own at times, there are skills required for group work that are not required when working as an individual. In law school, there traditionally has been a heavy value on individual work and competition; this emphasis can conflict with the skills and attitudes necessary for successful teamwork.

A group is more than just a collection of individuals; a group has its own dynamic. In part, the dynamic comes from the characteristics of the individuals. In addition, there is a separate mechanism that drives the group. Some teamwork problems stem from individual issues that become multiplied in the group context and affect the group's ability to perform. For example, when individual team members are not committed to the group or the group's goals, the team as a whole suffers. In addition, if individuals are unclear as to their roles on the team, problems may ensue.

Issues about team leadership frequently arise in teamwork. Group members may not see the need for team leadership or may compete for leadership roles. Some experts maintain that a group requires a leader to achieve good results. The leader does not necessarily have to be formally selected; often, one member of the group steps into that role, and the other members are comfortable with that arrangement.[7] Sometimes a group member attempts to take a leadership role or dominates without other members' acquiescence, resulting in accusations of bossiness, resistance to direction, gossip, and back-biting, overall bad feelings, and a poor outcome for the group's work.

A team may not recognize the importance of setting clear goals. When conflict takes place, there is little or no structure to keep the team focused on its objectives. Members may not be aware of the stages of teamwork beyond goal setting; as a result, often they will try to avoid conflict, as opposed to using disagreements as opportunities to move the team forward.

Groups need time for people to get to know each other, learn how to communicate with each other successfully, and trust each other. Teams often fail to discuss a process for resolving conflict. Without a process for airing issues and amicably working through them, the team may dissolve or suffer through the work toward an undesirable end.

Addressing issues like leadership, process, participation, trust, and communication often requires challenging conversations. Those conversations are uncomfortable even when all members are committed to the group and its goals. When that commitment is lacking, very few people are willing to open themselves to that discomfort.

The good news is that many of these issues can be prevented or remedied with a basic understanding of the stages of the teamwork process and the tools necessary to repair damage to the collaborative effort. Ultimately, here are the qualities you are looking for in your team:

1. communication skills–including listening; expressing oneself clearly with appropriate tone, eye contact, and body language; offering and receiving effective feedback;

2. shared commitment to collaborative goals–often cemented by a team charter;

3. clearly defined roles—including effective leadership;

4. mutual trust;

5. self-awareness; and

6. other individual attributes, including honesty, positive motivation, understanding other disciplines, empathy, curiosity, and creativity.

Critical Stages of the Teamwork Process

Basic teamwork theory postulates that all groups go through a number of stages in their work. Awareness of these stages helps team members approach difficulties in their process as a natural outcome of teamwork and as opportunities to enhance their outcomes. The five-stage model we present below most closely conforms to the teamwork process that has succeeded for our students in their legal work. Each stage offers guidelines for effective collaboration.

Forming

In this first stage, team members introduce themselves and begin to build the team foundation. Group members are generally cordial and cooperative. To build a strong foundation, your team should engage in meaningful introductions in which members of the team share information about their prior group experience, their experience with this type of project, the skills and knowledge they bring to this project, and concerns they might have. Your team also should discuss its objectives and a plan for accomplishing them, how the team will work and communicate, and methods for dealing with conflict. It is best to include these understandings in a written agreement or team charter, such as the one in Appendix 16.2.

> **Exercise 16.5** Watch *Stage 1: Forming* at https://www.youtube.com/watch?v=PF59v6Of1-s. What kind of foundation is this team creating? What is missing from their discussion?

Norming

In the norming stage, the team settles into its work and progresses toward its objectives. Your team members should be clear on their individual roles, such as leadership, editing, calendaring meetings, etc. After some time, however, tensions among your teammates can arise for a number of reasons, including individual characteristics that may be annoying to some members, or group dynamics such as hesitancy to disagree. Think back to the GM story at the beginning of this chapter in which the "GM nod" significantly harmed an internationally recognized company. If your team is not prepared to deal with these tensions effectively, it will progress to the storming stage. On the other hand, if your team has created a charter that addresses the issues underlying the tensions, it might be able to slide through or even avoid this next stage.

For example, if the issue of delayed responses to emails arises on your team, you should be able to examine your team charter and agree on a new provision that clarifies deadlines for responding to emails. An issue such as timely email responses often can inspire additional provisions to the charter. Your team might consider a more specific timeline for edits to a draft report or other team tasks. Or your team might reconsider its communication methods for urgent items, such as resorting to text messages or cell phone calls when emails remain unanswered.

> **Exercise 16.6** Watch *Stage 2: Norming* at https://www.youtube.com/watch?v=7-RN7AK_6VM. What tensions do you observe?

Storming

Storming is the stage of conflict and its aftermath. Members of your team may become angry or threaten to leave the team; some may avoid the conflict altogether by doing the work themselves or withdrawing. While this stage may be uncomfortable, it offers an opportunity for learning to deal with communication and for recommitting–often with greater strength of purpose—to your team's vision. Research shows that many, if not most, successful teams pass through the storming stage. The next section offers tools for your team to use when things go wrong.

> **Exercise 16.7** Watch *Stage 3: Storming* at https://www.youtube.com/watch?v=By1iNhnfuBM. Does any of this look familiar? In retrospect, what could the team have done in the earlier stages to avoid this conflict? If you were the designated leader of the team, what might you have done to resolve the situation?

Reforming

To move on from the storming stage, have your team discuss what happened and come up with a plan to resolve the future conflicts and problems with an open conversation and egos put aside. Without this phase, your team may disband—not usually a good result for the team members or the client. The section below discusses how to have this discussion. For example, your team might revisit its charter and decide to impose on itself more structure, change its objectives, or be clearer about what roles various members should be playing. If your team has been operating without a charter, it may decide one is needed. Further ideas are offered in Chapter 5 on Effective Communication and Professional Relationships.

Performing

Once the team has settled back into its work, usually with greater commitment, it can reach its objectives or "perform." When your team reaches this stage, the members will realize their contributions have produced an outcome stronger than any outcome they would have achieved on their own. It is a gratifying, often celebratory time when all of the struggle becomes meaningful. Most importantly, the client is served by having had the benefit of an effective team working on the project.

What to Do When Things Go Wrong

*Conflict is the sound made by
the cracks in the system.*

– Kenneth Cloke, Director of the Center for Dispute Resolution

Conflicts within teams are inevitable. The form they take and how they are resolved can make or break a team. If team members can use conflicts as indicators of where the system needs attention, as opposed to opportunities to "fix" individual members, the team has a better chance of reaching its goals. Paying attention to the cracks when they occur can unify a team, improving both the outcome and the team experience.

Recall the team in the Storming phase in Exercise 7, and consider how the following strategies might have helped the team:

Think of this conflict as normal and predictable.

Remember that all successful teams pass through this stage at some point. Acknowledge-even welcome—it as an opportunity to reconsider and perhaps reframe the team's objectives, structure, and leadership. Take a deep breath and then come up with a strategy for moving forward.

Create, review, or recreate a team charter.

As discussed above, many teams create some form of written agreement or charter, outlining key aspects of the collaboration such as goals, communication processes, work distribution, leadership, deadlines, and methods to resolve conflict. Initial conflict could be an indication that such a charter is needed. If the team already has one, the members should review and perhaps revise or supplement it to resolve the conflict.

For example, the team may realize it needs to choose a team leader or perhaps create a structure in which the leadership is shared. The charter might need to be more explicit on the duties of the leader. Focusing on a document, rather than an individual, usually will help the team both address and deescalate the problem in a peaceful manner.

Offer feedback and encourage discussion.

Sometimes, it is the person. In the past, we have all been recipients of negative feedback. To be an effective team member, and in particular, team leader, one must be able to give feedback in ways that move the team forward.

For example, a team member consistently turns in poor work. The other members who are picking up the slack are increasingly discontented. Here are some strategies we use in approaching these challenging conversations:

Think it through first.

- Take a breath. What are you feeling?

- What is the recipient of your communication likely to be experiencing?

- What is the essence of what you want or need to communicate?

- How can you say it in a way that reflects your awareness of your own contribution to the problem you are experiencing?

- How can you say it so that it can be heard without making the person defensive or angry?

- Is it possible to acknowledge something positive about the person and/or situation?

- Is there some way to find a connection between you and the other person, perhaps identifying a common interest?

When you are ready to speak to the individual.

- Acknowledge the positive aspects of the person's behavior while making sure it does not come across as patronizing or condescending.

  "You did a great job getting folks to meet with us about the problem."

- Acknowledge your own contribution to the problem.

  "As you know, I get really worried about meeting deadlines."

- State what happened. Pause. If necessary, ask the individual to explain.

> *"Your past few assignments have been late. Is something going on we don't know about?"*

- Check with the other person to be sure that you have understood his/her response, again, being conscious of your tone and word choice.

> *"Ok, so if I understand correctly . . . ."*

- Acknowledge common interests. Look to the future.

> *"We both want to do well on this project. What can we do so we're both comfortable with the process?"*

- Summarize the agreement, adding to it what you will contribute.

> *"Ok, so we've agreed that in the future we will . . . ."*

The main idea to remember in such discussions is to avoid direct criticism and blame. Instead, listen, speak respectfully, acknowledge your role in the situation, look for common goals such as your shared interest in the project's success, work out issues together, and focus on the future. You can find more suggestions for handling these discussions in Chapter 5 on Effective Communication and Professional Relationships. You can also review an example of how this looks at the following link, *Collaborative Dialogue* https://www.youtube.com/watch?v=lFgNy_fAvn8.

Ask for feedback, and take it well.

On rare occasions, we are the culprits. If you sense discomfort on a team, consider opening up a conversation in which you ask for feedback. Whether you initiate the conversation, or your team members do, when the feedback is negative, here are some suggested responses:

- Acknowledge the feedback specifically. You do not have to agree with it.

- Thank the person offering the feedback, if you can in that moment.

- Suggest the group meet again to discuss ways of moving forward. This gap in time will give you time to think about the feedback you just received.

It may be that your team members have misjudged your work efforts. If so, acknowledge their efforts to communicate the problem to you and, without sounding defensive or patronizing, offer them the information they need in order to make a more complete judgment.

Call in the experts.

If the conflict has escalated to the degree that the team cannot move forward, consider asking for outside help from those trained to resolve such conflicts. Individuals trained in such fields as mediation, facilitation, dispute resolution, and dispute systems design can often resurrect team efforts that are floundering.

Abandon ship.

Finally, keep in mind that not every team assembled can do the work, no matter how much effort is applied. There may not be time to accomplish the objectives. Team members may not have the requisite motivation or skills. Goals may become moot or obsolete.

Awareness of the team's functions and dysfunctions is key. If it is in fact time to abandon ship, a closing discussion of what, if anything, the team did accomplish, what went wrong, and why, can improve members' understanding of teamwork, and perhaps improve chances of success in the individuals' next team experiences.

It is our failure to become our perceived ideal that ultimately defines us and makes us unique. It's not easy but if you accept your misfortune and handle it right your perceived failure can become a catalyst for profound reinvention.

– Conan O'Brien, Dartmouth Graduation Speech, 2011

Exercise 16.8 Watch and critique the conversation at Collaborative Dialogue 2: https://www.youtube.com/watch?v=HogmhLqXmII. Do you foresee additional problems down the road?

Ensuring Success in Collaboration—For the Team and for Yourself

The skills of working collaboratively come more naturally to some than to others, yet, everyone who is motivated and has an open attitude can learn them. Awareness of how to form your team to gain maximum performance and how to address difficulties when they arise will give your team a strong advantage. As you build your knowledge, skills, and attributes of teamwork, your enjoyment of collaborative projects will increase, and your outcomes will be both more efficient and more effective for your clients. Your efforts will reward you with a more satisfying career in 21st century law practice.

> **Exercise 16.9** Reconsider the question from Exercise 1. You are being interviewed for your first attorney job. The interviewer asks you to describe your strengths and weaknesses working on a team. What would your response be? How is your response now different from what it was before you read the chapter?

FURTHER RESOURCES

Books

Eileen Scallen, Sophie Sparrow, & Cliff Zimmerman, Working Together in Law: Teamwork and Small Group Skills for Legal Professionals (2014).

Susan A. Wheelan, Group Processes: A Developmental Perspective (2d ed. 2005).

Susan A. Wheelan, Creating Effective Teams (1999).

Team-Based Learning: A Transformative Use of Small Groups in College Teaching (L. Michaelsen, A. Knight, & L. Fink eds., 2004).

Team-Based Learning: Small-Group Learning's Next Big Step (L. Michaelsen, M. Sweet, & D. Parmelee eds., 2008).

Websites

Team-Based Learning Collaborative, www.teambasedlearning.org.

Team Builders Plus, www.Teambuildinginc.com.

Videos

See Summary: https://www.youtube.com/watch?v=hLWB7RAw43I for a compilation of statements about teamwork by our guests on earlier videos within this chapter.

ENDNOTES

1　Ben Klayman, *GM Top Executives Spared in Internal Report on Safety Failure.* REUTERS (June 5, 2014), http://www.reuters.com/article/2014/06/06/us-gm-recall-idUSKBN0EG1KI20140606.

2　VICTOR LI, LEXTHINK.1 TACKLES HOW COLLABORATION MAY HELP FIRMS STAY RELEVANT DURING FLUX, ABA Journal (June 1, 2014), http://www.abajournal.com/magazine/article/lexthink.1_tackles_how_collaboration_may_help_firms_stay_relevant_during.

3　*What Skills Are Required To Become A Lawyer?*, ULTIMATE LAW GUIDE, http://www.ultimatelawguide.com/careers/articles/what-skills-are-required-to-become-a-lawyer.html (last visited Jan. 23, 2015).

4　Marjorie Shultz & Sheldon Zedeck, *Predicting Lawyer Effectiveness: Broadening the Basis for Law School Admission Decisions*, 36 L. & SOC. INQUIRY 620 (2011). *See* Table 5 at 644, Table 6 at 645, and Table 8 at 653. *See also* Appendix 1.3.

5　Heidi K. Gardner, *Effective Teamwork and Collaboration,* in MANAGING TALENT FOR SUCCESS: TALENT DEVELOPMENT IN LAW FIRMS, 145, (R. Normand-Hochman, ed. 2013).

6　INT'L ACAD. OF COLLABORATIVE PROFESSIONALS, https://www.collaborativepractice.com/ (last visited Jan. 23, 2015).

7　In its hiring, Google looks for "emergent leadership," defined as the ability to step in when leadership is needed, and then to step back and stop leading when one's leadership is no longer necessary. According to the Senior Vice-President of People Operations of Google, this quality of emergent leadership is second only to general cognitive ability in its hiring priorities. Thomas L. Friedman, *How to Get a Job at Google*, N.Y. TIMES (Feb. 22, 2014), http://www.nytimes.com/2014/02/23/opinion/sunday/friedman-how-to-get-a-job-at-google.html.

SELF-ASSESSMENT

1. Describe your background, interests, and expertise.

    What are your strengths and weaknesses?

    What do you bring to the team?

2. Which aspects of your project interest you the most?

    What interests you the least about your project?

3. What are some positive experiences you have instead of you've had working on teams?

    What made these experiences positive?

    What do you think will be positive about this team experience?

4. What are some negative experiences you have had working on teams?

    What did you learn from those experiences?

    What are your concerns, if any, about this team experience?

5. What are your expectations for your team?

    What are your goals for your team?

    What are your goals for yourself?

    What skills and knowledge do you hope to improve during the teamwork process?

6. What is most important to you regarding your team's and individual's work ethic?

7. What role do you see yourself fulfilling for your team?

    What other roles are important to ensure a successful team?

    Should your team choose a team leader? What would that person's duties be?

8. What kind of rules or guidelines should there be for team processes, including

    – team meetings?

    – communication?

    – conflict resolution?

    Specifically, how will your team raise and deal with any conflicts that arise?

APPENDIX 16.2

TEAM CHARTER

- Our team goals are

- Our expectations of each other are

- Our team roles will be

- Our process for communicating with each other will be

- Our process for creating our reports will be

- We will make decisions by

- We will prevent conflicts by

- We will resolve conflicts by

Team Signatures: Date:

CHAPTER 17

Writing for Practice

KENDALL L. KEREW

Introduction

E xternships provide a unique opportunity to sharpen research and writing skills. At this point in your law school career, undoubtedly you have been exposed to the basics of legal research and writing. In some cases, you are coming to your externship with experience in an advanced course or some legal work experience that has given you a good foundation for the type of research and writing assignments you will face in your externship.

Whatever your experience, legal research and writing takes practice. Texts, blogs, and continuing legal education seminars focused on enhancing legal research and writing skills abound. Likewise, lawyers face a constant stream of new research tools and ways to navigate those tools. Even experienced lawyers struggle with, aim to improve, and rarely feel they fully master this necessary set of skills. That is not to say lawyers do not consider themselves skilled at research and writing. Most of them do. But practicing lawyers constantly must work to sharpen their research and writing skills, because how lawyers use these skills can change outcomes for clients and define a lawyer's professional reputation.

This chapter does not aim to "re-teach" you legal research and writing. You already received the essentials in your first year of law school: the foundations of how to navigate research sources, the elements of written legal analysis, and the mechanics of writing. Instead, this chapter will give you tools to navigate the differences between legal writing in law school and writing for practice. To improve your legal research and writing skills, you need to be able to do two things: (1) embrace the opportunity to learn new and different ways of writing from practicing lawyers and (2) recognize and manage the differences between the research and writing you have done in law school and that which you do in your externship.

Opportunities for Development of Research and Writing Skills

An externship provides a unique opportunity to develop a number of legal research and writing skills. Because an externship is a class, you will have the opportunity to identify personal learning objectives in the context of an active learning environment. See Chapter 2 Charting Your Path to Success—Professional Development Planning for further discussion on setting learning goals.

When identifying learning objectives related to research and writing, take some time to consider the skills and abilities identified by practicing lawyers in the National Conference of Bar Examiners (NCBE) Job Analysis. See Appendix I.4 for more on the NCBE study. Although initially you may narrow your focus to the skills and abilities directly related to the mechanics of research and writing (i.e., written communication, critical reading and comprehension, fact gathering and evaluation, issue spotting, synthesizing facts and law, legal reasoning, and electronic researching), you also may want to consider the underlying skills and abilities needed for successfully completing research and writing assignments (i.e., paying attention to details, listening, knowing when to go back and ask questions, working within established time constraints, decisiveness, judgment, diligence, and awareness of personal and professional limitations).

It also may be helpful to consider previous feedback you have received in legal research and writing courses or past work experiences. What have you done well and what have you been told you need to improve? Being deliberate about your learning objectives will help your supervisors tailor your research and writing assignments and give you focused feedback.

How Writing for Practice Is Different

Research and writing in practice and in law school, while drawing on the same foundational skills, differ in significant ways. If you have prior work experience, especially in the legal field, you may be familiar with these differences. To do your best and learn the most from your externship, you will want to be mindful of the ways writing for practice is different and adjust your approach and work habits accordingly.

The research and writing you do will matter. Unlike the insulated, carefully considered hypotheticals you encounter in many of your courses, the work in your externship involves real legal problems that affect real people. Your work may help clients advance a position in a lawsuit, impact the structure of a transaction, or become the body of a court order. The impact of your work on others can be the most daunting, challenging, and exciting part of the work you do in your externship. Your supervisor will expect and rely on the thoroughness and quality of your research and writing.

The research and writing you do will involve new time pressures. You will have to complete assignments in enough time for others to use them. You will have to determine when to stop researching and begin writing to meet an assignment deadline. You likely will have to manage multiple assignments and multiple deadlines while also figuring out how to fit in unexpected assignments. You may have to turn your work around quickly. In doing so, you will face the challenge of sacrificing thoroughness for speed, sometimes at your supervisor's request. As a result, you will need to determine how to prioritize your work and maximize efficiency.

The research and writing you do may differ as to form, purpose, and audience. Regardless of your level of legal writing experience, you are likely to encounter research and writing assignments different from those you have seen in law school. You may be expected to use forms (e.g., bankruptcy, IRS, civil rules forms, pattern jury instructions) or templates developed by attorneys at your externship site that leave little room for creativity. You will likely encounter persuasive and analytical work, and you also may have to write quick summaries, policy proposals, contracts, client letters, and the like. And you may have to write for non-lawyer audiences: clients, staff, administrators, the public, and others.

Navigating Research and Writing Assignments

Before you begin your first research or writing assignment, consider your approach to research and writing generally. Are you a planner, or do you tend to dive right in and figure things out along the way? While your general approach to research and writing may be less methodical than others, consider taking the time to develop a strategy for approaching research and writing assignments. Doing so will help you to organize your work, enhance your efficiency, and improve the overall quality of your work product. This section outlines a strategy for approaching new and different research and writing assignments in a time-pressured environment.

Understanding the Assignment

The first and most important step in executing any assignment is to know what your supervisor wants. Even if you are familiar with the area of law or a particular form of writing, a clear understanding of the assignment can maximize your efficiency and lead to the most useful work product for your supervisor. In most instances, your supervisor will already be familiar with the area of law, type of case, or case facts. Some supervisors will clearly communicate exactly what they want and will provide you with examples. Others will be less clear and may not give you much guidance on how to complete the assignment. This section focuses on three important aspects to understanding an assignment: identifying the assigned task, confirming your understanding, and communicating about the assignment along the way. See Chapter 3 Learning from Supervision for further discussion on clarifying assignments.

■ *Identify the Assigned Task*

Depending on your supervisor's time and preference, you will be assigned tasks either orally, in writing, or some combination of the two. If your supervisor assigns you a task orally, listen carefully without interrupting. Take notes. Taking notes will help you remember the assignment, and also will assist you in identifying questions and gaps of information. Likewise, if your supervisor assigns you a task in writing, review the assignment carefully and identify questions and gaps in information. Ask clarifying questions and secure any missing information. Will you need to research, write, or do both?

For research assignments, try to identify the precise legal question or questions that need to be answered. Ensure that you have an idea of the best place to start by making sure you have identified the relevant body of law, any helpful secondary sources, any known primary sources (case, statute, regulation, etc.), the legally significant facts, any related legal issues, any necessary assumptions about the facts or law, and whether there is a "research bank" or other collection of research on similar or related topics.

For writing assignments, ensure you know the format and structure of the expected work product. Will you be writing an email, letter, memo, brief, pleading, etc.? To the extent possible, find examples of the writing you have been asked to do. Also, determine if you will be expected to use a form or template. If so, make sure you know if you will be expected to use the form or template "as is" or make modifications to it.

Importantly, for both research and writing assignments, be sure you understand the context, which includes the assignment deadline, how the assignment fits into a broader strategy regarding a particular case or matter, any work upon which the assignment relies, how your work will be used, the intended audience, the procedural posture, the location of the case file, and any documents or records that would be helpful to your understanding of the assignment.

■ *Confirm Your Understanding*

Even if you think the assignment is clear, confirm your understanding of the assigned task. If you receive the assignment orally, confirm your understanding at the time you receive the assignment by engaging in active listening, a form of communication in which you ask questions and restate what you have heard to confirm that both parties are on the same page. Then, write down the assignment and send it to your supervisor so you both have a reminder of what was said. If you receive the assignment in writing, consider summarizing the assignment in your own words, especially if the assignment is long or complicated, and share the summary with your supervisor to ensure you have a correct understanding. See Chapter 3 Learning from Supervision and Chapter 5 Effective Communication and Professional Relationships for more information about this and related topics.

■ *Communicate Your Work on the Assignment*

Keep in contact with your supervisor as you work. Doing so has many advantages. It allows you to convey your progress and to get updates on deadlines. It can give you the chance to make short oral reports, which in turn assure both you and your supervisor you are on the right track. It also allows your supervisor to fine tune the assignment while you are working on it.

Communicating with your supervisor as you work on an assignment also will allow you to clarify the assignment and communicate sources of confusion and uncertainty. Especially in situations where you have been given a broad assignment, you may have to do some initial work and then follow up with your supervisor to narrow the inquiry. After beginning an assignment, you may feel unsure about what you are supposed to be doing. It can help to revisit the assignment with your supervisor. Ask necessary follow-up questions and restate your understanding of the assignment. See Chapter 3 on Supervision for further discussion of learning from feedback.

Be alert for some common mistakes when communicating about assignments:

· Not asking questions for fear of looking incompetent. Remember it is better to communicate while you are working on the assignment than to turn it in only to find out it is not what your supervisor wanted.

· Asking questions to which you can fairly easily find the answers on your own. Think about your questions and consider whether a little research could help you find the answers. Your supervisor will appreciate being asked only those questions that truly stump you. If you are confused and ask questions, you will almost inevitably be asked what you did to try find the answer yourself.

- Failing to organize your questions before meeting with your supervisor. Before you approach your supervisor, sit down and write out your questions. Organizing clarifies the questions both for you and your supervisor and shortens the time both of you will spend on them.

If you have questions, consider trying to meet with your supervisor in person so you have the opportunity to explain your points of confusion and gain further understanding during the course of the conversation. When meeting, remember to engage in active listening.

Finally, keep in mind that communicating about an assignment may include having to present your findings orally. Not every assignment will result in written discussions of the law, even if that was the intent of the initial assignment. You will need to be able to deliver an organized oral presentation and be prepared to answer follow up questions, communicate objectives, and describe your research/conclusion. See Chapter 18 Making Presentations for guidance on making oral presentations.

Developing and Implementing a Research Strategy

Some assignments may be quick and to the point, while others may involve significant research. Whatever the length of the task, you may be tempted to dive right into a legal research project. The work you do will be more efficient and organized, however, if you devise a research strategy before you begin. This section focuses on three steps to devising a successful research strategy: orient yourself, determine your starting point, and follow through.

■ Orient Yourself

Revisit the assignment. Be sure you have a good understanding of the legal question or questions you have been asked to research. Before you begin researching, identify the legal issue(s), a relevant secondary source (e.g., a treatise, practitioner handbook, legal encyclopedia, ALR), any identified primary sources (e.g., a statute, case, regulation, rule), the proper jurisdiction, the type of proceeding (i.e., civil, criminal, or administrative) or transaction (e.g., contract, deed, business plan), the facts pertinent to the legal question, and how your research will be used.

If you do not have a good handle on what you have been asked to research, go back to your supervisor and ask follow-up questions. Remember, your supervisor is looking for both efficient and effective research. If you do not have a good sense of what you are researching, you likely will waste valuable time while becoming frustrated and confused. Before checking with your supervisor, try to resolve your confusion by revisiting the legal questions posed, the jurisdiction, the type and hierarchy of authority in that jurisdiction, and the pertinent facts.

If you do not have a good grasp of the pertinent facts, review the case file or follow up with your supervisor. In considering the facts, think about how you will be able to expand the range of search terms you might use when researching.[1] For example, suppose one of the legally significant facts informing the legal question is that one of the parties drove a truck. If you limit your search to the word "truck" without considering ways to expand the word, you may not find the most applicable law. To expand the search, you need to expand the word both horizontally and vertically.[2]

Horizontal expansion uses synonyms:

· Truck–Pick-up–Tractor Trailer

Vertical expansion uses broader and narrower words:

· Car–Truck–Automobile–Machine

Consider using the Legal Research Worksheet (found at Appendix A to this chapter) to ensure that you keep your research organized and focused.

Determine Your Starting Point

If your research assignment involves more than one issue, determine the issue you will research first. Always begin with foundational or dispositive questions. If you are unfamiliar with the area of law you have been asked to research, consult a secondary source to orient yourself. One of the best places to start may be the research guides created by your law librarians. If you take the time to gain a general understanding of the legal context at the outset, your research will be more effective and efficient.

If you already are familiar with an area of law and you have a citation to a primary source, start there. If you do not have a citation to a primary source, a secondary source is a good place to start. Once you have selected your source, consider a terms and connectors or descriptive word search. In devising this kind of a search, keep in mind that you will need to expand and contract the language you use. Avoid the temptation to use terms and connectors or descriptive word search as a starting point. This approach may lead you to search aimlessly, which will adversely impact your efficiency.

Be judicious in the use of computer-based research. As you know, most electronic legal research platforms are not free. The research you do as a practitioner will flow to your clients, and your externship is a good place to get a sense of that cost. Also, keep in mind that some lawyers still use the books and may expect you to do the same.

Follow Through

As you conduct your research, keep a research log. Be sure to update the log after every search and at the end of each research session. That way, you will not waste valuable time re-orienting yourself with where you are in the research process. In addition, a research log will allow your supervisor to assess your research skills and see the path you took. If you feel lost or unproductive, the research log will help you have a follow-up conversation with your supervisor and quickly identify the sources and search terms used. For this reason, you may want to consider giving your research log to your supervisor at the conclusion of the assignment.

Your research log should include each source you used, the search terms you used when researching in that source, the number of relevant results you found, each additional source you looked at, and how you revised or modified your search. Some electronic legal research platforms allow you to track your research as you go. Take the time to learn about and take advantage of that function.

> **Ethical Considerations for Research:** Be sure you are aware of any limits on the use of commercial electronic legal research tools (e.g., Lexis, Westlaw, Bloomberg Law). Check with both your externship teacher and your supervising attorney regarding any limitations on the use of your school account for research assignments conducted on behalf of the externship site.
>
> - If you seek help with legal research from someone outside your externship placement, be sure to protect confidential and private information.
> - A research log can assist in a later malpractice or ethical review by confirming you reviewed and considered particular sources during the handling of a case.
>
> See Chapter 11 Ethical Issues in Externships: Confidentiality for further reading.

Research Challenges

You can expect challenging research assignments in your externship. The challenge may come from having had few opportunities to practice your legal research skills, researching in an unfamiliar area of law, or the nature of the research question itself. The most common challenges you may face are knowing when to stop researching, dealing with too many results, and handling unclear or conflicting answers.

■ *When to Stop Researching*

You may struggle with the feeling you are spending too much time researching. While it is important to be thorough and conscientious when conducting research, it is equally important to know when to stop. If you think you might be at a stopping point, review your research. What authorities have you found? Do you have primary authority directly on point? Does the same primary authority continue to pop up despite the modifications you are making to your search? Are you getting consistent references to authority you have already found? If the answer is yes, stop researching. Report your findings to your supervisor or, if the research is linked to a writing assignment, construct an outline and begin writing.

■ *Too Many Results*

You may run into the problem of finding too much "relevant" authority. If after extensive searching, you uncover an endless quantity of authority that seems to be on the right track but is not exactly on point, consider revisiting the research assignment and your research strategy. It is possible that you need to state more precisely the legal question posed. If you are unclear about how to narrow the question after a review of the assignment, make an appointment to meet with your supervisor and take your research log with you. You may need additional information or input from your supervisor to help you to narrow the research question.

■ *Unclear Answers or Conflicting Answers*

Not all legal research questions have clear answers. The "right" answer may be that the law is conflicting or unclear. It may be there is nothing on point. Coming up empty can be frustrating to be sure. Keep in mind that sometimes finding nothing directly on point is just what your supervisor needs to know.

If the authority you find does not directly answer the question posed or the authority is in conflict, stop researching. Consult your research log and outline your results.

How does the authority fit together? What are the points of conflict? How might you be able to predict an outcome using the authority you found? Once you have outlined the authority, check in with your supervisor to report your findings. It may be that your supervisor wants to modify the question or has an idea of how to approach the related writing assignment based on your research results. This may be the time your supervisor wants you to shift focus and get creative by making analogies to other areas of law or by considering relevant policy implications.

Tackling the Writing Assignment

The total quality of a piece of writing equals the sum of its parts. This section focuses on the structure of a well-written document using recognized clear writing principles. Clear writing is important to any piece of legal writing no matter the form. Whether you are writing a memo to your supervisor, a document to be filed with the court, or a letter to a client, you will need your writing to communicate the intended message effectively and efficiently

Orient Yourself

While you may be tempted to start writing as soon as possible, doing so may cause you to retrace your steps and detract from efficiency. Before beginning to write, consider revisiting the goals of the writing assignment. Who is the audience? Is the writing meant to be objective or persuasive? How will it be used?

Be sure you understand the format your supervisor expects you to use. You will have learned a particular way to format legal writing in your law school courses, but that format may not match what your supervisor wants. Ask for examples of the format your supervisor expects. Consider any limits the format may impose on how you report your research results.

Try to get an example of your supervisor's writing style. Pay attention to your supervisor's word choice, use of verbs, and sentence structure. Your supervisor may expect you to write with this same style. To the extent you choose not to meld your style with your supervisor's, be thoughtful and deliberate about the reasons you departing from your supervisor's style. Often, you can learn from your supervisor's style, which will help to improve your own.

If you have a good grasp of the purpose, format, and style of the writing assignment, your writing process will be that much more successful. That said, it is important to give yourself enough time to devote to the writing process. Begin writing with enough time to allow yourself the chance to close gaps in analysis, conduct additional research if needed, focus on clear writing techniques, and proofread.

Use Clear Writing Techniques

All legal writing, especially when addressing complex concepts, must be clear and precise. Because your intended audience (be it a judge, lawyer, client, or the general public) likely will be both busy and unfamiliar with the underlying facts, law, or both, you will need to provide the necessary information without requiring the reader to work for it. As you write, remind yourself that the reader will need to get to the point quickly and easily. After all, if a concept or argument is too difficult to understand, the reader may not be convinced of your position or have the necessary information to make an important decision.

Careful attention to clear writing techniques will help you to achieve your intended purpose. While clear writing is not always easy, it is necessary to effective communication. Numerous legal writing scholars and practitioners have provided pointers, tips, and strategies to help law students and practicing lawyers learn and practice clear writing techniques. A list of additional resources is provided at the end of this chapter as Further Resources. With this collective wisdom, it is safe to say that clear writing requires attention to the overall organization of a document, and also paragraph structure, sentence structure, and word choice.

■ *Overall Organization*

The first step to achieving a strong piece of legal writing, whatever its form, is using straightforward organization. Because you still may be learning how best to organize your legal analysis, this task may be the most challenging. Just as with legal research, if you need to address more than one issue, organize the issues in a logical fashion and deal with any dispositive issues first. If you need to address several related issues, make sure you organize them in a way that avoids repetition. Communicate your organization at the outset using an introductory roadmap. Use sub-headings to signal the reader regarding your overall structure and what to expect next, especially for longer assignments. If it is a particularly lengthy assignment, consider providing a summary introduction.

■ *Paragraph Structure*

Once you have determined the overall organization, focus on the structure of each paragraph. Clearly sequenced paragraphs will increase the accessibility and impact of your analysis. By structuring paragraphs as a concrete series of steps, your writing will be more easily followed and understood by the reader.

To achieve a logical progression between paragraphs, use transition words to connect paragraphs. Give special consideration to transition words when you are setting forth a list, adding to a previous point, highlighting a similarity or difference, or leading up to a logical conclusion.

Within paragraphs, you can achieve a logical progression by beginning each paragraph with a topic sentence (the conclusion supported by the rest of the paragraph) to convey the main point the paragraph will address. In addition, use transitions to demonstrate the logical connections between sentences. Most sentences link information. Start with the known information and add the new information at the end of the sentence to facilitate the logic of your analysis.

> **Example:** The plaintiff suffered a **permanent injury**. This **permanent injury** will require continued **medical services**. These **medical services** include periodic evaluations, testing, and continued treatment.

■ *Sentence Structure and Word Choice*

After you have focused on paragraph structure, focus your attention on writing concise sentences. Try not to get caught up in extraneous matter, especially facts. Limit sentences to one thought wherever possible. Use proper grammar and punctuation. Be deliberate about the words you choose, especially if they have legal meaning. Use plain, concrete, familiar words. Eliminate redundancies. Use active voice.

Examples:

- **Original**: As a commercial truck driver, the plaintiff testified that, on occasion, he has assisted other truck drivers along his routes and has been the recipient of help or assistance from other truck drivers.

- **Clear Writing Edit**: As a commercial truck driver, the plaintiff assisted and received assistance from other truck drivers.

- **Original**: The testimony of the plaintiff shows that, subsequent to the accident, he was transported to the emergency room of a local hospital by ambulance. The plaintiff was discharged from the hospital after securing and receiving initial medical treatment relative to his injuries.

- **Clear Writing Edit**: After the accident, an ambulance took the plaintiff to the local hospital's emergency room, which provided initial medical treatment and discharged him.

Ethical Considerations for Writing

- If you need to work on a writing assignment outside of the office, be sure to comply with office policy regarding removal of case files/documents and use of your personal computer. Some externship placements prohibit off-site work.

- Never misstate the law. Know the difference between persuasion and misrepresentation.

- Maintain your credibility and that of your supervisor. You must address the weak points as well as the strong points.

- Provide complete and accurate citations to authority.

See Chapter 10 Ethical Issues in Externships: An Introduction and Chapter 11 on Confidentiality for further information.

Proofread All Written Work

Always turn in your best work. Even if your supervisor asks for a rough draft, make sure it is a polished work product. Eliminate preventable errors. Proofread and edit everything you write. The necessity of proofreading applies as much to emails as to lengthy writing assignments. Double-check case citations and quotations. Re-examine your tone. Is it suited for the intended purpose and audience?

Correct grammatical errors and eliminate typos. Be particularly mindful of typos that will not be picked up by spell check. For example, the misplaced "trail" when you meant "trial," "please" when you meant "pleas," "plead" when you meant "pled," and the most embarrassing of them all, "pubic" when you meant "public." Review headings consisting of words in all capital letters because spell check will not pick up on those misspellings either.

Because it is often hard to catch your own errors, when you produce a multi-page product try to budget your time so you can set your writing aside and review it with a fresh eye. Consider creating or using a writing checklist to guide your editing process. In some instances, you may want to ask another extern or attorney at your externship site to read your work before giving it to your supervisor.

Special Considerations

- *For Emails*

You likely will use email to communicate with your supervisors and, possibly, with clients. Even if you regularly send business email, the following are important reminders:

State important information at the outset. Use the subject line to identify quickly the nature of the email—the reason(s) you are sending the email and the subject to which it relates.

- Communicate the needed action or answer to a question in the first sentence. If you are asking multiple questions or providing multiple answers, separate them into numbered paragraphs.

- Be mindful of the reader's attention span. Often people retrieve email while multi-tasking and may not give it the same level of attention they give to other writing. Plan for the reader to skim the email. Keep it short.

- Reread and edit your email before you hit "send." Review the email for errors in spelling, punctuation, and grammar. Check the email for tone, which can sound very different than it would in a letter or personal conversation.

- Avoid abbreviations, emoticons, and overuse of capitalization and exclamation points.

- Do not put in an email what you would not say to someone in person or what you do not want to be held accountable for in the future.

Consider the differences between Email A and Email B below. What are the problems with each email? How could you improve them? See Chapter 9 Professionalism for further information.

Email A:

To: Supervisor

Subject: Your question

Hey there!

Just wanted to let you know that I researched that question you asked. It seems like there may not be a clear answer. I think we should meet to discuss my findings and determine where to go from here.

Btw, I loved that joke u told at lunch. Lol.

Email B:

To: Supervisor

Subject: State v. Smith – Research for Motion to Exclude Evidence

Joe,

I wanted to give you an update on my research. I haven't been able to find a case that clearly supports our argument. For your reference, attached is my research log reflecting the research terms and resources I used.

Do you have any additional search terms or resources you would like me to use? If you would prefer to talk in person, I will be in the office today until 5 and tomorrow from 12–5.

Thank you,

E. Extern

Ethical Considerations for Email

- Do not use business email for personal use.

- Double-check the "to" line to make sure it matches your intended recipient before hitting the "send" button. Simply because an email is labeled as confidential and/or an attorney-client privileged communication does not mean it will be treated as such. If the email contains privileged information, never forward the email to someone who is not part of the attorney-client relationship.

- Beware of the "reply all" function.

- Do not use your personal email account to send email to clients or to email work product.

See Chapter 10 on Ethical Issues in Externships and Chapter 11 on Confidentiality for further information.

■ *For Writing to Non-Lawyers*

Perhaps the most challenging legal writing you will do is that intended for non-lawyers (e.g., a newsletter, blog post, policy statement, etc.). While on its face this type of writing may seem easy, it likely will provide some of the best opportunities to improve your writing skills. The purpose and intended audience probably will be straightforward. What will be harder is communicating a legal term or premise in easily understandable prose. As important as clear writing is to legal writing generally, it will be even more crucial when writing for a non-legal audience. Remember to lead with the most important information. Keep concepts simple. Use plain language. And be as careful, if not more, with word choice. For more on writing to clients see Chapter 15 on Client Relationships.

■ *Challenges of Writing*

As you undoubtedly have experienced, sometimes writing does not come easily. Writing can be especially challenging when you face an assignment that feels entirely unfamiliar either because it involves a new area of law or requires you to write in a different form. Because your supervisor will evaluate you based on how and what you write and what you write will have an impact on real people and real legal issues, you may find yourself paralyzed in pursuit of perfection.

The pressures of turning out good quality work product can lead to a lack of self-confidence, fear of making mistakes, procrastination, and writer's block. If you experience these thoughts and feelings, take a step back from writing. Ask yourself if there is another reason for what you are experiencing. Are you unclear about the assignment? Are you unsure of your research results? If the answer is yes, identify the area of uncertainty and talk to your supervisor. If the answer is no, take an affirmative step toward the end goal. Organize your research. Create an outline. Start writing what is easiest. Put words on paper without worrying about how it sounds. Then edit your work.

At the other end of the spectrum, you may feel like the writing you are being asked to do is not challenging, which can lead to frustration. You may be instructed to use stock or borrowed language from previous briefs or forms. In that instance, take a step back and ask yourself: What is the purpose of the assignment? Is there a need to use the same language or a particular form from a strategic or procedural standpoint? Identifying the purpose and goal of the assignment may alleviate your concerns. To the extent you are still uncomfortable, seek out your externship teacher for advice.

■ *Learning from Feedback*

The easiest way to facilitate feedback on your writing is to ask for the feedback when you turn in the assignment. If you struggled with a particular aspect of the assignment or you want to improve a specific writing skill, include that information in your request for feedback. Consider keeping a running list of questions or decision points you came across in writing and use those points in feedback meetings. Sometimes students can help their supervisors give more useful feedback by asking better questions. Some include a cover page with specific questions to facilitate the feedback process for supervisors.

Many students do not want to bother their supervisors and ask for feedback, or they do not want to point out where they struggled because they do not want their supervisors to think poorly of them. Do not fall into this trap. Keep in mind that your externship is a class. You are expected to learn. While it might be difficult to highlight points of difficulty, it will help your supervisor focus on what you want to learn and need to improve.

Even if you ask for feedback in advance, supervisors may give feedback in different forms. It may be through oral discussion, written comments, both oral discussion and written comments, or comparison of what you turned in and what was ultimately filed. When you see the final product, compare and contrast what you did to the final product so you can learn from the revisions made. When possible, make the edits yourself.

You also may have the opportunity to learn from feedback you give others. Another extern, or even your supervisor, may ask you for feedback on a particular piece of writing. Consider the components of good feedback and take that opportunity to practice the approach you want to take when giving feedback to others. See Chapter 3 Learning from Supervision for more information about this topic.

■ *Developing a Writing Sample*

One learning objective you may wish to satisfy through your externship is the development of a usable, "real life" writing sample. To the extent it is one of your goals, be sure to talk with your supervisor about this possibility at the beginning of your externship. The writing sample needs to be short (not more than 5–7 pages) and demonstrate your ability to put legal analysis into writing. It also needs to be your own work with limited supervisor edits.

> **Ethical Considerations for Writing Samples:** Before you use a piece of writing from your externship, discuss the way you plan to redact the document and be sure your supervisor does not have any concerns with confidentiality.
>
> If your work used a form or externship site's template, consider whether the writing sample is truly representative of your work.
>
> See Chapter 11 on Confidentiality for further information.

Conclusion

Legal research and writing takes time, patience, and persistence. Learning and improving these skills can be difficult. Do not give up or settle for mediocrity. Take this opportunity to hone what will be some of your most powerful lawyering tools. And never forget that what you research and what you write can and will make a difference in someone's life.

FURTHER RESOURCES

Books

Anne Enquist & Laurel Currie Oates, Just Writing (4th ed. 2013).

Bryan A. Garner, The Redbook: A Manual on Legal Style (3d ed. 2013).

Austen L. Parrish & Dennis T. Yokoyama, Effective Lawyering: A Checklist Approach to Legal Writing & Oral Argument (2d ed. 2012).

William Strunk, Jr. & E.B. White, The Elements of Style (4th ed. 1999).

Richard C. Wydick, Plain English for Lawyers (5th ed. 2005).

Articles

Megan E. Boyd & Adam Lamparello, *Legal Writing for the "Real World": A Practical Guide to Success*, 46 J. Marshall L. Rev. 487 (2013).

Blogs and Websites

Grammar Girl, http://www.quickanddirtytips.com/grammar-girl.

Research Guides, Ga. St. L. Libr., http://libguides.law.gsu.edu/.

Lady (Legal) Writer, http://ladylegalwriter.blogspot.com/.

Law Prose, http://www.lawprose.org/blog.

Legal Writing Pro, http://www.legalwritingpro.com/articles/.

The (New) Legal Writer, http://raymondpward.typepad.com/newlegalwriter/.

WordRake, http://www.wordrake.com/writing-tips/.

iPhone Application

iWriteLegal, https://itunes.apple.com/us/app/iwritelegal/id561864315?mt=8.

ENDNOTES

1　Amy E. Sloan, Basic Legal Research: Tools and Strategies 30 (5th ed. 2012)("You can increase the breadth of the list by identifying synonyms and terms related to the initial search terms, and you can increase the depth by expressing the concepts in your search terms both more abstractly and more concretely.").

2　*Id.* at 30–31.

APPENDIX 17.1

Legal Research Worksheet

Created by Austin Martin Williams
Coordinator of Research Instructional Services
Georgia State University College of Law Library

Client & Case Number:

Date Received:

Assigned By:

Date Due:

Time & Cost Restraints:

End Product: [ ] *Opinion Letter*   [ ] *Memo*   [ ] *Brief*   [ ] *Other*

Background Facts: *What are the legally significant facts?*

Issue Statement: *What are you trying to find? What is the legal issue? What are the general rules of law you need to find and the basic concepts that define the issue?*

[Legal issue should be only 1 or 2 sentences.]

Jurisdiction *(State, Federal, etc.):*

Key Terms: *Terms that are most related to your issue. Exclude terms that are so common that they would return results not related to the issue. Consider synonyms and antonyms for your terms. Also consider broader or narrower related terms.*

Source Selection: *At this point, one should decide what sources to consult. Secondary sources are a great place to start if one is unfamiliar with a particular are of law or if one does not have any citations to primary sources. On the other hand, primary sources may be a good place to start if one already has a citation. Shepardizing/Key Citing a case or using an annotated code can provide one with more sources on a topic.*

Secondary Sources: *Treatises, Legal Encyclopedias, ALR, Law Reviews & Journals*

Creating Terms and Connectors Search Form:

Variations in Key Terms:	Use Connectors to specify relationship between terms:	
! (obey! = obey, obeys, obeyed, obeying)	w/s (same sentence)	and
* (r*n = run, ran)	w/p (same paragraph)	or
	w/# (within # words)	

Terms:

	and, w/p, w/s, w/___	
	and, w/p, w/s, w/___	
	and, w/p, w/s, w/___	

Database(s):

Relevant Cases, Statutes, Regulations, Topics and Key Numbers:

Making Presentations

LEAH WORTHAM

Most law students make at least one moot-court appellate argument while in law school. Many take simulation courses involving trial and motion practice skills, and a number do real-world clinical work that entails some litigation-based legal advocacy. These experiences enhance students' proficiency in legal analysis, thought, and expression, and also provide training in litigation skills. In their careers, however, many lawyers rarely if ever make an appellate argument, argue a motion, or appear at a trial, while virtually all make presentations to others with a goal of getting some kind of desired outcome.

For example, lawyers make presentations that include the following:

· briefing a supervisor on the results of research and a recommended course of action;

· educating colleagues about an area of expertise e.g., scientific, statistical analysis, accounting, or technology, in connection with a legal matter in their practice;

· briefing a government agency decision-maker on a course of action involving a lawyer's substantive legal or policy expertise;

· teaching a colleague or supervisee a skill that will help them to be more effective and efficient;

· chairing a meeting in which people with disparate points of view need to make a decision;

· training a client's employees on how to comply with the many laws and legal pitfalls for which the employer might be liable;

- educating groups of people about their legal rights and obligations, when they might need legal help, and what they can do for themselves (sometimes called legal literacy, community education, or street law);

- lobbying government officials to make a change, take an action, or not to do so;

- arguing for funding in a variety of contexts, e.g., for an increase in a governmental unit's budget (or avoidance of a cut), foundation funding for a non-profit, a contribution from a private donor;

- convincing members of the public about the wisdom of a course of action a government entity is taking or the reasonableness of something your private client is doing;

- pitching a potential client about services the lawyer's firm might provide.

This chapter operates on two tracks. First, it speaks to those of you who are enrolled in externship classes that assign students to do presentations. Second, in providing resources for making your class presentations as effective as possible, it helps you develop approaches that will be useful for presentations you are likely to make in your future careers.

Presentations allow class members to benefit from the backgrounds, experiences, and insights of other law students. An individual can have a limited number of field experiences in law school; presentations open a window into other opportunities in legal work. You probably are generally aware of what might be of interest and use to your classmates, and presentations allow the focus of the course to be tailored to the interests of students in that particular class.

Presentations allow you to set your own goals and be self-directed. You can choose a topic of interest, practice a method in which you would like to become more proficient, and use the presentation as well as the field experience to enhance your learning goals. You can move out of the traditional active-teacher/passive-student model with you, the student, taking on the teacher role and the faculty member offering collegial suggestions.

Chapter 3 focuses on giving and receiving feedback. Your teacher may ask you to give feedback on other students' presentations as a way to practice the principles in that chapter. Law school does not generally focus on non-litigation skills, but they likely will be important in your future career. In addition to the substantive enhancement to the learning in the externship course, creating, organizing, and making a presentation, receiving feedback, and observing other students' presentations will build your capacity for effective future presentation-giving.

Getting Started

Assignment Guidance

First, review the guidance your externship teacher provides on presentations and ask questions if anything is unclear. That guidance might include these parameters:

- how much time you will have and whether there are any guidelines on how the time should be used;

- whether and how far in advance you should meet with your teacher and how you need to prepare for that meeting;

- what technology is available, when and how to reserve anything that might not be built into your classroom, and whether there are law school resources (staff, materials, videos) to train you on using such resources;

- whether you can assign homework to other students and deadlines for distribution of assignments and materials;

- what guidelines your teacher has given you on topics or methods to be used;

- whether presentations must be done individually or can or must be done in teams;

- what expectations your teacher has for the depth of the presentation, e.g., whether outside research on the topic is expected;

- what goals your teacher has asked you to pursue in the presentation.

Intentionality About Presentation Objectives

This book stresses conscious choice and intentionality. The first question for any presentation needs to be, "What is it I want to accomplish with the participants in this presentation?" It can be useful to make the general goals more concrete: "What do I want my audience to be able to do and/or be motivated to do as a result of the presentation?" You are in the role of teacher. For a teacher, the ultimate measure of a class is not what is **taught** but what is **learned.** Probably most presentations will involve at least a degree of "teaching" for which you will be helped by formulating the learning objectives you have for your "learners."

It can be tempting to say, "my goal is to complete this requirement for the extern-ship course to be sure I get credit." Planning and executing presentations that leave participants changed in at least some small way—a new understanding or appreciation, some skill-building, a motivation to do something—will complete the assignment and do so in an excellent manner that has benefitted your classmates.

As you read through the topic examples in the next section, think about the different audience outcomes the presenter wants to elicit. If your presentation involves circulating a piece of writing for critique, you presumably want to generate a dialogue on what effective writing is for that type of piece. You also might have a secondary teaching objective of stimulating discussion on how a supervisor can be most effective in giving critique.

Some presentations ask class members to assume a role other than law students in an externship class. The chapter offers examples below. For such situations, think of two levels of objectives: 1) what you would want "real people" in the roles students are playing to be able or be motivated to do and 2) in what ways you want participation in the simulation to benefit your classmates. For example, if you choose making a presentation on client development or applying for funding, you would be asking the audience to play the role of prospective clients or funders. You are not expecting your classmates to hire or fund you, although they can give opinions on whether a real audience would have been persuaded by your presentation and how it could have been strengthened. This topic could lead to a group discussion on what makes such a presentation effective and be useful to class members regarding their own future careers.

If you choose to simulate the briefing of a supervisor on research you have done, the class again could be in role. You would ask class members to put themselves in the shoes of busy attorneys and give feedback on whether the presenter was clear, adequately concise, and gave sufficient information. You also might take on the role of a lawyer briefing a non-lawyer client or manager about law relevant to a decision to be made. This approach challenges your audience to think how understandable and effective the presentation would be to someone without legal training and with concerns different from the lawyer's.

Choose a Topic of Significant Interest to You

Review your initial learning agenda or goals statement for the externship. Is there a topic that could further one of the goals you listed?

Suppose you are externing at a prosecutor's office and one of your goals is "Explore a possible career path in criminal prosecution." You might prepare a presentation on career paths in prosecution covering such topics as desirable credentials in securing a position, useful law school preparation, and common career paths after the entry-level job. Researching this topic would push you to look at literature such as bar journals and give you a reason to talk with lawyers about these questions.

Suppose one of your goals was "Learning about practice management in solo practice." You might envision a presentation on the top ten things to consider when going out on your own. To prepare, you could review articles on this topic in bar journals and legal newspapers and interview some solo practitioners. Chapter 27 on the Future of the Legal Profession and Legal Services Market discusses many ways this kind of law practice is changing. Many of the changes are enabled by technology. The chapter suggests a number of resources, including websites and blogs, with tips in this regard.

In presentation planning meetings, students sometimes say, "I don't know if this topic would be interesting for other students." If the topic is interesting and important to you, it is useful to think about how it could be **made** interesting to others. Advice about effective presentations usually includes the importance of authenticity—projecting your own interest and passion about the subject. If you do not think this is an important topic, you likely will not convince your audience it is.

· **Consider several alternative topics before settling on one**

Make notes on several possibilities. Start sufficiently in advance of the deadline for choosing a topic so ideas can percolate.

· **Assess your audience**

You know a great deal about law students at this point, and you likely have even more familiarity with the people in this particular class. Think about their starting point for your topic—what they already know, what background they will need, what hooks are most likely to get them interested. If your presentation will put them in role, think also about what the interests, needs, and wants of the people the students will be playing would be. Clients often criticize lawyers for insufficient empathy for, and understanding of, the client's concerns, situation, and desires. Consider the framework of concerns, situation, and desires for the roles students will take in your presentation. If a presentation simulates a non-profit organization's pitch to a funder, look at some websites giving criteria for that funder or type of funder. What do they say about why they fund projects and what information they need? Always try to put yourself in your audience's shoes looking for the overlap of your objectives and theirs.

· **Consider selecting a topic that will allow you to practice an unfamiliar skill.**

You could plan a simulation, lead a discussion, or develop some diagrams or other visual aids to illustrate your ideas. If you are interested in learning more about technology, you could explore what equipment and resources your law school has available. Can someone assist you with the editing of a video recording regarding your presentation or help you learn how to use presentation software more effectively?

· **If you work on your presentation in teams, practice your collaboration skills.**

Look at Chapter 16 for its suggestions on what makes collaboration and teamwork effective.

· **Link the goals for your externship, the fieldwork, and the presentation.**

Think about topics related to your fieldwork. Use this as a chance to enhance the learning from your externship and share some benefits with other students.

· **Think about the power of stories, your central theme, and the presentation's structure.**

Most presentation guidance reminds us that people are "wired for stories," and effective presentations often include or are organized around a compelling story that illustrates the central theme. After thinking about your objectives, consider how they can be reduced to a simple overall theme and a cohesive structure in which all parts will contribute to the theme.

· **Consider confidentiality and privacy concerns.**

While you are urged to link the presentation to your fieldwork, be mindful of confidentiality considerations. You, of course, must be careful not to disclose client confidences. Merely deleting client names often is not enough for adequate protection. Consider also office confidences regarding the people with whom you work. You may want to take an idea from something at work and change the personalities and details enough so it is not recounted as what happened at your externship. Concerns about an externship that would be appropriate to discuss with your externship teacher might require adaptation before a presentation to the full class. Questions in this regard should be worked out with your teacher. See also Chapter 11 on Confidentiality.

Possible Topics

The following is a list drawing on recollections from a number of externship teachers on presentations from their classes that were particularly interesting and effective. Your teacher may have class guidelines for presentations that would exclude some of these topics, and you doubtless will be able to think of other possibilities. This list is presented to supplement your creativity rather than a menu from which you should make a choice. Additional topic possibilities can be generated from exercises in other chapters of this book.

- Identify a significant problem that can arise in the work place. Plan a presentation on how it could be addressed and resolved. For example, a presentation might focus on what steps to take if one has a colleague with a substance abuse problem, a supervisor engaging in sexual harassment, an office director exercising poor management skills, or an attorney struggling with an ethical issue. For further resources on these topics, see Chapter 10 regarding both substance abuse and sexual harassment, Chapter 7 on options in responding to bias and harassment, Chapter 3 on supervision and its relationship to management skills, and Chapters 9–13 generally on professionalism and ethical issues. Chapter 5 on effective communication discusses approaches to difficult conversations.

  For a topic like these, you might get the class started with an illustrative incident or situation presented in a scripted video, a scripted live role-play, or a written description. A number of other chapters include scenarios that could be starting points for a presentation. If you wish to use an exercise in the book as a starting point for a presentation, ask your teacher to share the notes in the Teacher's Manual, which the author prepared about the exercise so you can see what the author had in mind with the exercise.

  Consider how to use the methods mentioned in the last paragraph for presenting on the externship/supervisor relationship, such as a supervisor who is always too busy to talk or does not give useful feedback.

- Interview some lawyers or other employees in your office about a topic of interest and report the results to the class. A student externing at the General Counsel's office of a government agency made an excellent presentation based on interviews with lawyers there about whether they ever had to do things or take positions on issues that differed from their personal political or moral views and how they handled it. See also Chapter 22 on public service lawyering, which discusses this issue and includes some interesting problems. You might talk with employees of your judge's chambers and some of your neighboring chambers about common mistakes made by novice litigators. See Chapter 19 for other possible ideas about judicial externships. You could interview lawyers in your office about their career decisions, job satisfaction, or concerns about balancing personal life and professional life. See Chapter 25 on Work and Well-being. You also might interview lawyers on the criteria for making partner in a law firm or comparable advancement in another type of work place. Some research would turn up bar journal and legal press articles on all the previous topics to help shape the questions to ask and give a basis for comparison with the answers.

· In the same spirit, create a practice biography of an attorney in your office. Develop a list of questions for the attorney as preparation, then interview the attorney about these and other questions that occur to you. Consider videotaping the interview and presenting excerpts from the video as part of your presentation.

· Your placement may be dealing with an interesting or a high-profile legal problem, where much of its work appears on the public record. For example, your judge may by trying an interesting case; you may have observed an oral argument on an important appeal; or you may be helping to advocate for adoption of a particular piece of legislation. Develop a presentation that tells your classmates about the case and highlights the distinctive challenges for you and the lawyers in handling the case. If you do this type of presentation, make sure to check with your placement about confidentiality concerns that may persist even though the case is in the public record.

· Develop a presentation related to the funding of the type of organization in which you are externing or wish to work in the future.

· Invent a law firm or other legal services organization and market its services. Law firms sometimes refer to presentations to prospective clients as "beauty contests." Plan the agenda for such a presentation, which might be in the form of a lunch with a prospective client or a written advertising piece. Ask your classmates to critique your effectiveness and consider the propriety of your approach in light of bar ethics rules. Two students who externed at a recording industry trade association simulated a presentation for agents to explain how the recording artists they represented would benefit from the association's service that would collect royalties gathered by a central fund and return the royalties to them. This required explaining provisions of the copyright law and offering a quick and persuasive explanation why the artists would be better off using the association's services rather than trying to collect the royalties on their own.

· Write a draft grant proposal or fund-raising letter for a public interest group or legal services organization. For a grant proposal, gather criteria from government or foundation funding sources on how such proposals are evaluated and ask your classmates to evaluate your draft against the criteria. This exercise might lead to a discussion of funding sources and strategies for a particular type of organization.

· Choose a "new law" venture of the type described in Chapter 27 on the future of law practice. From company websites and articles in the press, prepare a pitch to a venture capital firm as to why this start-up is a good investment.

· Circulate copies of a piece of writing you have done for your externship. Ask the class to edit and critique it. This exercise could be used to discuss standards against which this type of writing should be judged. See Chapter 17 on Writing for Practice. Be sure the writing sample does not include any confidential information. Regardless, make sure you get specific approval from the field supervisor to use it in the class.

· Reenact a situation in which you gave an oral briefing to a supervisor on research results or create a scenario in which research you did would be presented in this fashion. Have your classmates critique whether the presentation was clear, easy to follow, contained an appropriate amount of detail, and would have given the supervisor sufficient information to take the next steps. Discussion then could follow on questions like how a presentation might vary based on the supervisor's knowledge and personality and how to seek clarification from a supervisor on what the supervisor wants in the research and the report. See Chapter 3 on supervision and Chapter 17 on writing, both of which give suggestions on how to get adequate direction on assignments.

· Use your observations and interviews to gather material on a topic to present to the class and elicit discussion from class members on how their organizations compare on various dimensions such as the following:

  – **Mission:** What is the purpose or mission of the legal organization where you are doing your externship? What is it trying to accomplish? Who decides the mission? Do the people who work there have a shared vision and sense of purpose? What characteristics of the organization make the work go better or worse? What, if any, lawmaking function is performed by the institution, and how does that occur?

- **Opportunity to balance personal and professional life:** What policies are in place to assist employees in balancing personal life and professional life? Are employees availing themselves of them? If not, why not? What changes in workplace policy, structure, or culture might be useful to employees?

- **Planning:** How is a project planned in your externship? Who does the planning, and how is it done? What is the role of collaboration?

- **Diversity:** Share observations about the impact of sex, race, age, political beliefs, or other differences on the working relationships of the people in the externship with one another or with you.

- **Development of lawyering skills or ethical decision making:** Reenact part of a hearing or a deposition, using a transcript if available, as a take-off point for a discussion on lawyering skills or an ethical issue.

- **Career planning:** Discuss the impact your externship is having on your career goals or on how you plan to carry them out and spark comparisons with the experiences of your classmates.

· Create a simulation that would place all or some of the students in the class in a situation in which you participated, observed, or you could imagine occurring. For example, put the class members in a role as lawyers in a firm or public interest organization and ask them to make a decision of the type that could arise in such an organization. This might relate to strategy on a particular case or to a policy, business, or ethical decision facing the entity. Chapter 21 on public interest placements includes a number of scenarios in this regard. A former student, working for a high-technology company, assigned each class member a company management position, e.g., sales, risk management, engineering, with instructions about the concerns a person with that type of job would have. He then assumed the role of in-house counsel briefing the company's top management about changes in export control laws with a goal of securing their cooperation in compliance. The presenting student had to consider how much information about the new law was sufficient, how to make it intelligible to this sophisticated but not legally-trained group, and how to motivate managers to be interested in compliance.

- Was there a situation in your externship in which you had to teach yourself something new, e.g., use of particular software, a scientific topic, background on an area of law in which you had not taken a course? Consider a presentation on how you went about this on-the-job learning. What worked well and what did not? What other ways might you have gone about it? Classmates might suggest other options for self-directed learning, and the class members might consider how they would differ among themselves on effective ways to learn new things.

- What is your previous academic training or work experience? If you studied business management, give your classmates a quick course in some management theory and discuss its application in your various externships. If you studied communication, give some examples of effective and ineffective communication you have noted in the externship and link it to material from your earlier studies. Someone with a grounding in math or science may have noted an instance in the externship in which use of statistics or a scientific concept was a problem for the lawyers. Recreate the situation and fill in what people needed to know. A student with a previous career in social work might talk about lessons lawyers in the current externship could take from that discipline. A student working at the Justice Department section that prosecutes violations of child pornography laws gave a memorable presentation on secondary-post-traumatic-stress disorder. She gave a quick literature review and reported on interviews with lawyers in her division about strategies they used to cope with the distressing nature of their work.

- Is there a novel, short story, movie, or television show that stimulated your thinking about the externship or lawyering generally? Show your classmates an excerpt and share reactions. An excerpt from a law review article also could be a takeoff point for discussion of its relevance or irrelevance to your externship experience.

- Some of you may be in a class that involves on-line synchronous or asynchronous classroom segment joining students in different locations. This structure may provide an opportunity to practice managing a webinar or other software used for such virtual meetings. As you read the following section on Structuring the Class, consider how the methods might change for on-line participants rather than people in the same room.

Planning Your Presentation

Too often, students spend the bulk of their time on the content of a presentation and too little time on how to present it. An important part of the presentation assignment is to push your thinking on what captures and holds people's attention and will achieve the desired behavioral outcomes with audience members.

Do not wait until you have finished your background research or interviews before you start to rough out the presentation. At the start, write down some initial ideas on how your presentation might be structured. Keep refining these notes as your research progresses. Thinking through the steps of what you will present and how you will present it exposes holes and gaps in what you need to know and plan.

Sources for Background Research

Readings: Computerized research tools offer a quick way to check most topics in the law review literature, legal press articles (e.g., NATIONAL LAW JOURNAL, AMERICAN LAWYER, LEGAL TIMES), bar journal articles (e.g., state bar journals, national bar associations and their section publications), and popular press. Chapter 27 on the future of the legal profession lists a number of blogs regarding developments in the legal profession, legal services market, and law practice management, and there are likely to be blogs related to almost any topic of interest. Your presentation may take off from something in literature or from a nonfiction book on a controversial topic. The topic you contemplate may involve some additional research in cases or statutes.

Things to view: Today, of course, a wealth of video resources are "out there" on the internet. Many of you will have made your own videos for pleasure or past course assignments. Check also what resources may be available from your law school library. Some schools will have a library of mass-market films or television shows on topics related to legal practice.

Observation: Chapter 4 concerns learning from observation. Could you undertake a structured observation related to your topic? Do you have past observations that are relevant to your topic?

Interviews: A number of the topic examples suggest interviewing lawyers in your externship or elsewhere. The interviewee's responses can be compared to ideas found in your background reading. Interviewing co-workers for a presentation can provide an opportunity for more personal contact with them, which may be useful if networking was one of your goals.

Structuring the Class

Lecture

When there is a need to present something, we often instinctively think of lecturing. Lectures offer some advantages. A lecture can provide material not available in writing and a synthesis of diverse sources. Some listeners prefer to receive information orally. A dynamic lecturer can add visual and other physical cues to focus attention. A lecturer can observe the audience, ask and answer questions, and otherwise adapt to visual cues about what interests the listeners and how they are grasping the material. The credentials, position, and personal presence of the lecturer may enhance the lecturer's credibility and the interest of the audience in the lecture.

Lecturing, however, has its pitfalls and cannot be presumed to be the best method. As a listener, have you ever thought: "Why couldn't the speaker just give me the material to read so I don't have to sit here?" Adults can read at an average speed of 700 to 800 words per minute. Average oral communication is 100 to 125 words per minute, with a rapid speaker only reaching 150 to 175. Thus, it takes an hour to say something that probably could be read in ten to fifteen minutes.

Lecturing allows listeners to be passive, and their thoughts easily can wander. The lecturer can get some visual cues, but this may not provide reliable information on whether the listeners are learning, being informed, being persuaded, or whatever other objective the lecturer may have. Lecturing puts the burden on the speaker to perform without challenging the listener to think about what he may want to learn or need to know.

A lecture may be a useful component of your presentation—for setting up the class exercise, introducing a discussion, reporting interview results, or synthesizing some theory from another discipline to be applied. Given the comparison to the relative efficiency of reading, consider whether any of these purposes might better be served by written material.

Consider the following alternatives (and complements) to lecture:

Simulations and Role Plays

A number of the topic examples suggest putting class members in role. People often gain insights and reach different conclusions about a topic when they confront what they would do and how they would react in a situation.

You may plan a large single role play in which everyone in the class participates: for example, where all the class takes on the role of the supervisor being briefed. You might script a situation and ask small groups of students to take the roles involved, such as having all students form pairs as a supervisor and supervisee to act out a situation. For such a role play, you may want to script instructions for each role on differing things they know, assumptions they have about proper behavior, and personal characteristics they are to exhibit.

You might script a role play and have it recorded or performed live for the class. It can be useful to freeze frame a video or a live role play by stopping the action and interspersing discussion.

Video Recordings

The previous paragraph suggested use of a video recording of a role play. The background research section suggests additional sources of filmed material that might be useful in a presentation. If you are going to show a video recording, you may want to let participants know in advance of seeing the video what you will ask them to do with it afterward. For example, you might direct the participants to watch for certain types of behavior, to pay particular attention to body language, or to think about what they would have done if they were the student in the role play. Unless you plan to freeze the frame frequently, it may be useful to direct viewers to take notes consistent with the purposes for which you are asking them to view the video recording.

Discussion

Discussion usually will be more fruitful if people have a common example or experience as a starting point—a case study, a video, a role play, or a reading. Think about effective and tactful ways to involve the whole class in the discussion and avoid monopolization by one or two students. Watch the professors in your classes for a few days. What techniques do they use in this regard?

Brainstorming can be an effective technique for getting a discussion started. Record responses to a question on a board or flip chart. As leader, you might ask follow-up questions to clarify a comment or make affirming comments like "interesting;" however, in the original idea-gathering stage, try to avoid discussion or argument about the ideas being put up as well as evaluative comments that could constrain the free flow of ideas. This technique is meant to stimulate creativity by urging people to think broadly and not self-censor initial ideas. Brainstorming can free people to offer a number of possible points of view without a need to "own" the ideas offered as necessarily their own or good ones. Putting ideas on the board can encourage more honest and free-wheeling discussion because disagreement is directed to the board rather than toward the person who offered it. Flip charts allow one to tear off the initial page and mount it on a wall while then grouping ideas or homing in on particular points for further discussion. Asking each person in turn for an idea can assure that shyer participants also are part of the discussion.

Once brainstorming is complete and you move to a discussion phase, watch the group dynamics. Are people submerging disagreements that would stimulate discussion? Was a student's interesting point passed over by the group such that you want to restate it? "A moment ago, Carmen suggested XXXXX. What do you think about that?"

You could assign particular points of view to class members and ask them to reflect these perspectives in the discussion. It may be easier for people to represent another's viewpoint than their own.

Consider letting people create pairs or small groups for some preliminary discussion before opening the floor to the full class. This gives everyone a chance to verbalize their thoughts. Some people are more confident about sharing their thoughts with the class if they have a chance first to refine their ideas in a smaller group. Each group can be asked for a report on a question. This process can give a more accurate sense of the views of the full group than hearing from only a few volunteers.

Much of good communication is asking good questions. Anticipate the way discussion might go and prepare a list of possible follow-up questions in advance. Listen carefully to the discussion to consider when inserting a new question would move things along.

Try to become more comfortable with silence. Ask a question and force yourself to wait for an answer. Silence is powerful. Eventually someone will break it—and it is better for it to be someone other than the discussion leader. At the same time, watch faces and see if silence has come from lack of understanding the question that could be helped by rephrasing.

Listen carefully to responses. Ask follow-up questions to probe more deeply if it seems more commentary or explanation would stimulate the thoughts of others. If one student has commented about how something works in the placement in which the student is externing, ask another student whose placement might raise similar issues if things there are the same or different.

Leading a discussion is an active role—framing provocative questions, listening carefully to responses, managing silence. Too much talking by the discussion leader becomes a lecture rather than a discussion.

Self-Tests and Games

A quick written or oral self-test of the audience can shift the audience from, "What are you going to teach me?" to "What do I need to learn?" The device requires some engagement from the audience and moves them from a passive role to a more active one. A self-test about the audience's current knowledge, attitudes, or past experiences also gives the presenter a baseline to gauge what it will take to achieve the presenter's goals with regard to increasing the audience's knowledge or changing attitudes.

A contest or competition can be motivating. Two students' joint presentation sought to interest classmates in the relevance of public international law to day-to-day domestic law practice and their lives. Class members divided into teams and competed on knowledge of some public international law concepts, which were presented as they arose in situations in current events.

Some effective presentations have used various board game or quiz show formats to engage participants actively in the substance.

Check with your school's technology services or with the library about various ways to poll students during class and display the results in real time. This approach allows you to frame questions that prompt different points of view, display the different views on screen, and encourage conversation about the results in class.

Guests

You might bring an expert to talk about the topic or react to a presentation. Many supervising attorneys are pleased to be asked to come to the law school and meet with a seminar group. You may know other lawyers who would be good resources on your topic. Your externship teacher may have suggestions. Alumni and other lawyers also often enjoy opportunities to interact with students in the externship class. But bringing a guest speaker does not get you "off the hook." You must plan carefully what you want the person to do, adequately prepare the speaker, monitor the time so that it is used effectively, and be prepared to shift the discussion diplomatically if it goes off track.

TED Talks

According to the TED website, "TED began in 1984 as a conference where Technology, Entertainment and Design converged, and today covers almost all topics from science to business to global issues . . . . Our mission: Spread Ideas." Many if not most of you are familiar with the TED talk format of a presentation of 18 minutes with many considerably less. In 2006, TED started posting videos of talks on the TED website, YouTube, and iTunes. The TED blog reports that talks were viewed two million times in the first year, growing to 200 million at the end of 2009. By November 2012, the talks reached their one billionth view. TED also spawned TEDx where local entities can organize conferences with talks in the TED format.

The Further Resources section includes a useful short article by Chris Anderson, TED curator, on what makes TED talks effective and the best ones so compelling, as well as suggestions on how to prepare. You might consider giving a presentation in TED talk format, though, as Anderson's article describes, they typically are carefully scripted and memorized and take a lot of time to prepare and practice. Even if you do not go "all the way" to a TED format, Anderson's article offers useful insights applicable to a range of kinds of presentations.

Logistics and Rehearsal

Consider how much **time** you have for the presentation. Decide how long to spend on each part. Class presentations often go more slowly than you might expect. Time a trial run. Plan for contingencies if the presentation goes more slowly or more quickly.

Consider the **physical layout** of the room where the presentation will be conducted. Where will you position yourself within the room so all students can see you and you will not have your back to any audience members? If you will divide students into groups or involve them in some exercise, how will that be accommodated in the space?

As previously mentioned, if this is an on-line seminar, consider all the ways the various factors change for that type of interaction.

Eye contact with the audience is important to establish rapport and maintain attention. Looking at your audience also will allow you to read the audience's reaction and respond to them. If you will be using something visual, where will you stand so the audience can all see the screen or the board and allow you to maintain eye contact?

People vary in their preferences for oral, visual, and kinesthetic learning. Kinesthetic learning refers to someone being involved in physical activity, e.g., students themselves being involved in a simulation. Consider whether it is possible to incorporate elements of each. Consider some kind of **visual reinforcement** of points being made orally or whether there is some **experience** they might have or **things they might do** as part of the presentation.

Consider whether you want to use **presentation software** and, if so, what would be effective for your presentation's purposes. The Abela book in Further Resources discusses the difference in a "ballroom style" presentation where a number of slides with interesting visuals may be appropriate versus a "conference room style" where a few carefully designed slides distributed on paper may be more effective in persuading a small group of people to take a recommended action. PowerPoint probably is the most often used presentation tool and too often not used very well, e.g., too many boring, difficult-to-follow slides with way too much text. You may have seen Prezi, a more visual and less linear tool. Mind-mapping software can allow you to add ideas from your audience during the presentation. If you are using **presentation tools**, consider the ratio of text to visual images, whether the size and color of the text or images will be readable throughout the room, and whether what is on the screen will be visually appealing. Rehearse with a partner so you can get feedback on whether the pace and coordination of your speaking with the presentation tool allows the audience to comprehend the points you want to make. If you are using text, listeners may become bored if the speaker merely reads everything on every slide. Slides can be helpful to emphasize key points or to display data the speaker will discuss. On the other hand, it is difficult to read a quotation while a speaker is talking. If a quote is important, it is helpful for the speaker to read it and allow the audience to focus on it for a moment. Think about whether audience members might want hard copies of some or all of your slides.

Consider information that will be too complicated to follow if explained orally, e.g., a case study for discussion, simulation instructions. Prepare **written materials** in advance and think about whether it would be easier for audience members to have their own copies rather than reading from a slide or board.

Be conscious of the **intelligibility** of your voice: pitch, volume, speed, projection, diction, articulation, and grammar. Ask your practice partner to comment on **how easily you are understood.** Be conscious of **mannerisms**. Do you fiddle with your hair or repeat certain phrases, e.g., "if memory serves" or "like" in a way that is distracting or annoying?

Some people will remember a presentation better if they are able to refer to some **written or visual take-away.** A summary of important points, a document copy used in an exercise, or some discussion questions can help secure the substance of the presentation in people's memory.

If you will be **distributing written materials**, think carefully about when and how to pass them out. If there are several pieces, generally it is best to collate and distribute them at the outset or have them waiting for students at their places. It can be distracting when multiple handouts come around separately. Time is wasted on assuring everyone in the audience has the right materials and understands which one the group is working with at a given time. If there is a piece people should look at later, you can ask them to put it aside. Photocopying multiple handouts on different colored paper can make it easier for people to keep track of what they are supposed to work with at a particular time, i.e., "Please look at the problem on the yellow sheet of paper."

Review your presentation for **unity**, selecting only that content which is necessary; **coherence**, connecting and relating each part to each other; and **emphasis**, giving the correct degree of **prominence** to each part.

Rehearse what you plan and try to have at least one run-through with someone observing. As previously mentioned, a practice partner can provide you with feedback on intelligibility of your voice, distracting mannerisms, and effectiveness of visual aids. Practice also will free you from notes to maintain eye contact, expose gaps in logic or clarity to be filled in, and allow you to explore with your test audience whether your goals for the presentation were met. Be sure you have **rehearsed use of any technology** in the room where the presentation will be and with the equipment that will be used. Have a **back-up plan** for what you will do if technology fails.

Enjoy yourself. Elsewhere this book stresses the value of a growth versus fixed mindset approach to life. You will learn both from what goes well in your presentation and from what does not go well. Your presentations are an opportunity to share your gifts and experiences with your fellow students.

FURTHER RESOURCES

Books

ANDREW V. ABELA, THE PRESENTATION: A STORY ABOUT COMMUNICATING SUCCESSFULLY WITH VERY FEW SLIDES (2010). A short book about adapting presentation style to the type and objectives of the presentation.

CHIP HEATH & DAN HEATH, MADE TO STICK: WHY SOME IDEAS SURVIVE AND OTHERS DIE (2008). The authors synthesize considerable social science research on what makes ideas have "staying power" so people remember and are persuaded by them.

BRIAN K. JOHNSON & MARSHA HUNTER, THE ARTICULATE ATTORNEY: PUBLIC SPEAKING FOR LAWYERS (2d ed. 2013). This book focuses on specific things one can practice regarding use of the body, brain, and voice for more effective speaking and reducing jitters.

DANIEL H. PINK, TO SELL IS HUMAN: THE SURPRISING TRUTH ABOUT MOTIVATING OTHERS (2012). Another quite readable book applying social science research on what is effective in persuading people, along with the insight that most of us today spend a lot of our time trying to convince someone else to do something.

Article

Chris Anderson, *How to Give a Killer Presentation*, HARV. BUS. REV. (June 2013), at 121, https://hbr.org/2013/06/how-to-give-a-killer-presentation. TED Curator Chris Anderson gives a number of useful suggestions based on his observation of many TED talks, which are applicable to other kinds of presentations as well.

Website

PRESENTATION ZEN, www.presentationzen.com.

Judicial Externships

MARIANA HOGAN & MICHAEL H. ROFFER

> *Law Clerks are not merely the judge's errand runners. They are sounding boards for tentative opinions and legal researchers who seek the authorities that affect decision. Clerks are privy to the judge's thoughts in a way that neither parties to the lawsuit nor his most intimate family members may be.*
>
> —Judge Alvin B. Rubin,
> *Hall v. Small Business Administration*, 695 F.2d 175, 179 (5th Cir. 1983)

Introduction

J udicial externs are in the courthouse. They have access to the judge's chambers. They enter the well, and perhaps even sit behind the bench, of a courtroom. Short of donning robes, externs are as close as possible to seeing the court system from the judge's perspective. The opportunity to be a participant-observer of the judicial process is something few lawyers experience in their careers in the law.

While externs will learn a great deal by doing the research and writing the judge and law clerks assign, the opportunity to learn from observing cases in the courts may be even more valuable. With attentiveness, exposure to courtroom advocacy can help develop advocacy skills. Observation of the judge and the other players at the courthouse is a learning bonanza. To realize the potential of these opportunities for observational learning at the courthouse, Chapter 4 on Observation and Chapter 8 on Reflection and Writing Journals will be especially helpful.

As with any externship, the greatest benefits from the judicial externship will come from reflecting on the big picture. To capitalize on access to the courts, it is important to look beyond individual cases and assignments. The materials in the second part of this chapter provide a brief description of how various judges and courts fit into our judicial system and offer a framework for analyzing the work of a particular judge and the relationship between the courts and society. Reflecting on the wider implications of the experience at the courts will make you a better lawyer.

Preparing for the Judicial Externship

Other sections of this book provide information on learning from supervision, developing skills, and addressing ethical issues. This chapter begins by supplementing those materials with information that is unique to judicial externships, including sections on special ethical concerns for judicial externs, the cast of characters at the courthouse, and the research and writing assignments that most frequently arise in judicial externships.

Ethics for Judicial Externs

Significant ethical responsibilities accompany the extraordinary opportunities of a judicial externship. For the purposes of understanding and negotiating the ethical constraints on a judicial extern, you should regard yourself as a law clerk employed by the judge for whom you extern. Federal court law clerks are guided by the Code of Conduct for Judicial Employees (1996), including Advisory Opinions issued by the Judicial Conference Committee on Codes of Conduct, in particular, Advisory Opinion No. 111, Interns, Externs and Other Volunteer Employees; the Ethics Reform Act of 1989 and Judicial Conference regulations promulgated under the Act; and any local court rules or guidelines of the clerk's own judge. The Federal Judicial Center publishes and makes available online *Maintaining the Public Trust: Ethics for Federal Judicial Law Clerks* (4th ed. 2013), which provides an overview of law clerks' ethical obligations and identifies various sources for additional information. State courts have comparable sources for resolving ethical questions. Before beginning work in chambers, externs must familiarize themselves with the guidelines applicable in their jurisdiction and any other sources identified by faculty supervisors or chambers personnel.

In all jurisdictions, three of the most significant ethical issues externs are likely to face are confidentiality, conflicts of interest, and decision making on the record.

Chapters 10–13 on Ethical Issues in Externships provide a more extensive treatment of ethics issues for all types of externs.

Confidentiality: What Goes on in Chambers Stays in Chambers

Perhaps no other single ethical issue is as important as understanding the need for and the extent of preserving the confidentiality of the work of chambers. The relationship between the judge and the judge's clerk is many faceted—at times teacher-student, at other times colleague-colleague. The relationship often is a close and confidential one. This is necessary for many reasons, not the least of which is the need for the judge to feel free to explore with the clerk the judge's most personal thoughts about matters for decision. If the judge is not confident she can share questions, soul searching, and preliminary ideas leading up to a publicly-declared decision, the judge may keep these thoughts internalized, and the decision-making process, made possible only through a free-ranging exploration of ideas, is seriously impaired.

In addition, telling tales out of chambers runs the risk of harming the reputation of the judge and undermining public confidence in the judiciary. All rigorous decision-making processes tend to be messy, and judicial decision making is no exception. The judge initially may consider factors that ultimately are discarded as irrelevant, inappropriate, or without sufficient merit, and a snapshot view of that process could easily be misinterpreted and turned against the judge and the courts.

Social media adds a wrinkle to the issue of confidentiality and raises other related ethical issues. All court employees, including externs, must be particularly careful with their social media activities given the permanence, access, and searchability of all posts. In addition to being vigilant about protecting confidential material and refraining from commenting on pending matters, court employees also must be aware of additional dangers such as postings that detract from the dignity of the court or suggest special access to the court or favoritism. Courts are taking steps to address the ethics and privacy issues posed by social media. Many state courts and federal district courts have adopted standards that balance the ethics and security goals with the privacy interests of their employees.

> The National Center for State Courts maintains on its website the Social Media and the Courts Network, compiling information and guidance on courts' usage of social media and its impact on courts, ranging from judicial ethics issues to jury issues to human resources issues.

Confidentiality does not mean you cannot discuss your externship experience in seminar meetings, with your faculty supervisor, or in journals, but it does mean that you must be careful when you do so. You may discuss anything that happened in open court and anything that is part of the public record. That may sound simple, but it can be tricky for you to distinguish between what you observed in open court and what you may be privy to because of your special access to the judge and chambers. Be particularly careful when discussing pending matters. For instance, you would not want to inadvertently suggest which way the judge is leaning. When in doubt about a potential disclosure or comment, remember that discretion is a highly valued trait in the legal profession. It is important for lawyers and prospective lawyers to demonstrate that they can be trusted to maintain secrets and confidences.

Conflicts of Interest

Externs need to be vigilant to actual and potential conflicts of interest between their past, current, and future work as an employee, extern, or volunteer, or simply as someone with knowledge of people or facts, and the work of the court to which they are assigned. The goal is to avoid any appearance of impropriety. Therefore, any suspicion that there may be a conflict of interest with respect to a matter on which an extern has been assigned to work, or on which he or she may be assigned to work, requires informing the judge immediately. In most cases the actual or potential conflict of interest can be avoided by reassigning work to another extern or to the judge's clerk and ensuring that the conflicted extern has no further involvement in or access to the matter.

The most common sources of conflicts of interest include work an extern may have done in the past on a case that is now before the judge for whom he or she is externing, matters in chambers that involve a law firm to which the extern has applied for employment or wishes to apply for employment in the future, and matters about which the extern has personal knowledge of the facts, parties, or attorneys.

Decision Making on the Record

A law clerk is constrained by the factual record developed by the parties and is not permitted to conduct any investigation to more fully develop the factual record, except as to facts of which the court may take judicial notice. Therefore, an extern may not visit the scene in order to gather information on which the judge might base a decision in the case or otherwise communicate facts to the judge not developed by counsel but known to the extern because of familiarity with the events or locations of the case or obtained through factual research the extern has conducted. Rather, externs are to research the law to be applied to the issues and facts in the case as presented by the parties. Thorough research includes checking the authorities cited by the lawyers to determine the relevance and the accuracy of the citations and independent research to determine whether the lawyers have overlooked controlling precedent or authority that may be helpful even if not controlling.

The Courthouse Players

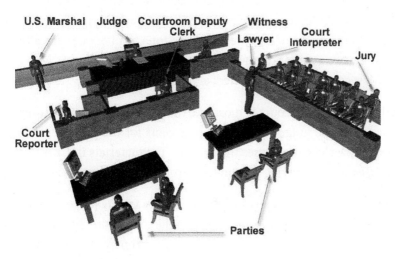

Source: Federal Judicial Center

Who Does What in the Courtroom

Although it is natural to focus energy and attention on the judge, lawyers also interact with other personnel in the courthouse. This section reviews the players in the courthouse, focusing on the ways that they support the judge and interact with lawyers and litigants.

The cast of characters may differ depending on the level of the court, appellate or trial, and the jurisdiction, federal, state, local, or administrative. Even where the roles are similar, titles may vary from jurisdiction to jurisdiction. Because there is more commonality among the federal courts, the descriptions here will focus on the federal courts, but the players in a state trial or appellate court system are similar and should be recognizable to externs working in those courts. Under current Judicial Conference policy, courts of appeals judges can hire up to five people as law clerks or judicial assistants; district judges can employ up to three people; bankruptcy and magistrate judges up to two people. The judge decides how to allocate these positions to best accomplish the work of chambers.

The judge's chambers is typically staffed with one or more law clerks and a judicial assistant. The judge's **Judicial Assistant** helps administer chambers operations and often acts as the gatekeeper for the judge and clerks.

The **Law Clerks** do legal research and writing for the judge and perform other tasks as directed including, especially in chambers with fewer employees, many of the tasks performed by the Judicial Assistant, courtroom deputy, and bailiff. Beyond research and writing, one extern observed, "The clerks are there to debate, to discuss, and to challenge." In most chambers, law clerks are appointed for a term of one year, although some are employed for two years and others may be permanent employees with no set termination date. Most courts have one law clerk although some will have more than one.

The judicial extern's role at court is most like that of the law clerk. Most judicial externs collaborate with the judge's law clerk on projects for the judge and in some chambers the judge's law clerk supervises the externs. The materials in Chapter 16 on Collaboration and Teamwork provide guidance on working collaboratively.

In addition to the law clerk or clerks working directly for the judge in chambers, there may be other clerks available to all of the judges in the courthouse. In federal district courts with a heavy docket of filings from prisoners, the court may appoint **Pro Se Law Clerks** to review cases filed by prisoners and other unrepresented parties. The pro se clerks assist the court by screening the complaints and petitions for substance, analyzing their merits, and preparing recommendations and orders for judicial action. Pro se clerks usually are long-term employees of the court. At the appellate level, the federal circuit courts employ staff attorneys. Although the tasks assigned to staff attorneys vary from circuit to circuit, generally they include reviewing correspondence from pro se litigants to determine the legal sufficiency of the correspondence as an appeal or request for writ of mandamus; reviewing appeals and applications for habeas corpus involving collateral attacks on state or federal criminal convictions; preparing memoranda of law and recommending disposition of the issues raised by motions; and assisting in case management and settlement procedures.

> **Exercise 19.1** A 2011 Survey of Clerks of Court and Chief Judges in the U.S. District Courts revealed that a top concern among both groups is the impact of pro se litigation on court staff. Special training for designated court staff and referral of pro se matters to specialized clerks and magistrate judges were among the procedures the clerks and judges respectively found most helpful. What are the implications of these procedures? Do they improve the process for pro se litigants whose cases are reviewed by staff with special training and expertise, or do they create a separate track for this class of litigants to minimize their impact on judicial resources? Does this approach signal a view or result in a perception that pro se cases are less important?
>
> Consider the pro se litigants who have appeared at your placement. What procedures does your court have in place for dealing with them? Do you see any differences in the way that your judge handles proceedings involving pro se litigants? What challenges does the presence of an unrepresented party create for your judge?

Judges also have staff to support their work in the courtroom. Most judges have a **Courtroom Deputy** or "minute law clerk" or "case manager." The deputy is an employee of the clerk of court's office, although the deputy serves the judge to whom assigned. In trial courts, nearly all courtroom deputies record the minutes of the court and assist the judge with scheduling trials, hearings, and argument on motions. The deputy's duties may include administering oaths to jurors, witnesses, and interpreters; maintaining custody of trial exhibits; maintaining the court's docket; serving as liaison between the judge's chambers and the clerk of court's office; and other duties as assigned by the judge. The courtroom deputy handles the judge's calendar and case records, so lawyers rely on courtroom deputies to help locate files and documents and for information on the status of cases and scheduling. Courtroom deputies can be good sources regarding the judge's courtroom practices and preferences.

Many judges also have a **Bailiff** or **Crier** who attends sessions of court and announces openings of court, recesses, and adjournments. The bailiff maintains order in the courtroom under the direction of the judge and is responsible for conducting the jury to and from the jury room. Except in a few courts where recording devices are in use, when the court is in session there is a **Court Reporter** or stenographer present who creates the official record of all court proceedings that are required to be recorded and prepares a written transcript when requested by the court or the parties. Attorneys and court personnel contact the court reporter when they need to make reference to the record of a court proceeding.

In federal courts, courthouse security is provided by the **United States Marshals** Service, sometimes in conjunction with private contract court security officers. The U.S. Marshals also move prisoners; supervise the department's Witness Security Program; apprehend federal fugitives; and execute writs, process, and orders issued by the court. In many places, the marshal or marshal's deputy is in complete charge of the jury. The marshals know when a defendant or witness who is in custody will be produced in the courtroom, and they can help to locate prisoners.

From time to time other players will appear in the courtroom, often to assist the judge by providing information necessary to the judge's work. Each federal district court has a **Probation Office** whose officers conduct pre-sentence investigations and prepare pre-sentence reports on convicted defendants; supervise probationers and persons on supervised release; oversee payment of fines and restitution by convicted defendants; and conduct investigations, evaluations, and reports to the Parole Commission when parole is being considered for an offender or when an offender allegedly violates parole. Some courts may have a separate **Pretrial Services Office** whose officers assist the judge in making bail determinations on criminal cases and supervising defendants who are released pending trial. Finally, anytime a non-English-speaking party or witness appears in court, an **interpreter** attends to provide translation.

In certain cases, judges require specialized assistance. Under Federal Rule of Evidence 706 the judge may appoint a **Court-Appointed Expert** witness to help the court and jury understand complex matters outside the common understanding of the court and lay jurors, including helping to understand the often conflicting testimony of the parties' own experts. Federal Rule of Civil Procedure 53 authorizes any district judge before whom an action is pending to appoint a **Special Master** as an impartial expert designated to hear or consider evidence or to make an examination with respect to some issue in a pending action and to make a report to the court.

There are two groups of attorneys who appear regularly in the federal courts: **United States Attorneys** and **Public Defenders**. In all cases in which the United States is a party, a representative of the Department of Justice is the attorney for the government, usually the U.S. Attorney or an Assistant U.S. Attorney for the district in which the case is pending. The counterparts in state courts are local prosecutors and attorneys from the state attorney general's office. The Criminal Justice Act of 1964 (18 U.S.C. § 3006A) requires each federal district court to have a plan to ensure that federal defendants are not deprived of legal representation because they cannot afford it. This need may be met by assigning cases to private attorneys or, in districts where at least 200 appointments are made annually, by establishing a public defender organization.

State and local governments may have comparable systems in place. A more detailed discussion of these issues appears in Chapter 21 on Criminal Justice Law Placements.

Moving from the courtroom to the remainder of the courthouse, there are two significant resources that attorneys use: the Clerk's Office and the library. The **Clerk of Court** in a federal district court serves as the chief operating officer of the court, implementing the court's policies and reporting to the chief district judge. The clerk's responsibilities include maintaining the records management system to safeguard the official records of the court, accepting pleadings and other papers required to be filed with the clerk, issuing subpoenas, and managing the jury selection process. Each chief clerk is assisted by one or more deputy clerks and clerical assistants. Depending on the size of the jurisdiction, deputy clerks and assistants may have specialized duties. The clerk's office establishes the procedures for filing cases, serving documents, obtaining court orders, and finding court records.

Most externs find their way to the library in the courthouse. The **Librarian** is a source for resources and techniques to help deliver a more efficient and reliable product to the judge. Attorneys who understand the resources that are available to the judges and their law clerks can tailor their advocacy accordingly.

Judicial externs are likely to come into contact with most if not all of the persons described above, but there are others employed in the courthouse, some less visible but nevertheless serving important functions, with whom there may be interaction. All interactions with members of the courthouse community present valuable opportunities to gain knowledge that will inform practice as an attorney. One extern shared the following insight on courthouse interactions:

> *I have always had a policy of getting to know those individuals in a work environment whose tasks seem more removed from mine both as a showing of respect for their work, and as an investment in general good will.*
>
> —Student Journal

Research and Writing for Judges

> *This matters. Unlike the briefs I wrote for first-year legal writing class or other legal analyses that I've made in school or on other issues, which involved imaginary parties or hypotheticals, this was a real person whose life I was affecting.*
>
> —Student Journal

The primary players at the courthouse are the judges, and just as the supporting cast described above work to assist the judge, much of an extern's experience and learning will revolve around helping the judge. In almost all courts, judicial externs will do some research and writing. This section identifies some of the idiosyncratic writing products that judicial externs may be asked to prepare and provides some general advice about research and writing in judicial chambers. Additional assistance on further developing research and writing skills is provided in Chapter 17 on Writing for Practice. In addition, a number of helpful resources appear at the end of this Chapter under Further Resources.

Opinions are of varying complexity and length. "Full-dress" opinions are those that require structured discussion of the facts, legal principles, and governing authorities. **Memorandum opinions** are used where the decision does not require a comprehensive, structured explanation but still needs some discussion of the rationale. They are generally brief and informal and may or may not be published. **Per curiam opinions** issued in the name of the court as a whole and identifying no single judicial author, generally are included in this category. **Summary orders** simply state the disposition of an issue or the case, sometimes with a brief statement of findings and conclusions, but often with little or no explanation. Summary orders usually are not published.

Orders are many and varied in complexity and form, from an Order of Judgment disposing of a case after a jury verdict to an order granting an unopposed request for an extension of time. Some orders of judgment may be as detailed as a full-dress opinion, such as where a complex matter was tried to the court sitting without a jury. Other orders are so routine in nature they are prepared by the office of the clerk of court rather than in chambers. In some jurisdictions, the parties prepare proposed or draft orders and the judge just signs them.

A **voting memorandum** presents the view of a judge on a panel to the other members of the panel. It is usually more succinct than the related bench memorandum and typically will reflect the view of the case that was developed at oral argument.

A **bench memorandum** typically is a brief document prepared to orient the judge to the facts of the case, the arguments of the parties, and the applicable law. It may be prepared by the parties or by the clerks. In a trial court, it may be as short as a page or two in length and include the facts as presented by the parties, the applicable law, an analysis, and a conclusion or recommendation to the judge. In an appellate court, the bench memorandum typically is longer, as it must deal with all issues raised by the parties' arguments. For the appeals court judge, the memorandum is most often a summary of the briefs of the parties, together with an analysis of the validity of the respective positions of the parties, and an identification of issues that require further inquiry at oral argument.

A **single-issue memorandum** is a research memorandum that deals with a single issue that arises during trial, often as a result of inadequate preparation by counsel, an unexpected development during trial, or the judge's wish to pursue an aspect of the case not fully developed by the attorneys.

Some trial court judges may ask clerks or externs to draft case summaries of recent appellate court opinions to keep the judge apprised of current developments without the judge having to read the entire opinion.

Rarely will the clerk or extern be asked to prepare routine correspondence for the judge's signature. On occasion, however, the task may fall to the clerk or, less likely, an extern. The judge will always sign such correspondence because the clerks and externs should not have any contact with the parties or their attorneys unless directed to communicate with them by the judge.

General Advice—Research

Regardless of the nature of the written product externs are asked to prepare, it is likely that some research will be necessary to gather the facts and law required to prepare the document. Chapter 17 on Writing for Practice contains additional material to help externs become more proficient at research; Chapter 3 on Learning from Supervision contains material on working with supervisors on written assignments. One word of caution—although a number of courts have begun citing to Wikipedia, at least with respect to facts deemed incontestable, the practice is far from universal. Externs should be guided by the preferences of their respective judges.

Clarify the Assignment

Whether the assignment is simple or complex, a clear understanding of the research and writing tasks involved is essential to doing an effective and efficient job. Asking for answers to fundamental questions after receiving the assignment but before leaving the clerk's or the judge's office to begin organizing the task often can save hours of fruitless work and dead ends. At a minimum it is important to have answers to these questions: In what format should the project appear when turned in? Where the format is unfamiliar, are there any examples to review? What is the deadline for the project? Are there any sources or resources to use or be aware of in working on the project?

Organize the Project

Upon receiving the assignment, establish a work schedule and a work plan. Usually the first step is to collect all of the materials needed to commence researching the project. For example, when drafting an order granting or denying a motion, be sure to collect all of the papers filed by the parties in support of or in opposition to the motion as well as any notes created by the judge that reflect the judge's thinking on the outcome.

Check for Conflicts

As soon as possible after receiving an assignment, an extern should familiarize himself or herself with the parties involved in the matter and determine whether there is an actual or potential conflict of interest because of a relationship to the matter or one or more of the parties. For example, the physician whose expert opinion's admissibility is in dispute may be an aunt or next door neighbor or former employer. Externs should discuss the potential conflict with the clerk or the judge and resolve the question of conflict of interest before proceeding any further.

Do Background Research

Unless you already have a citation to a primary source, the best place to begin almost any research project is usually in a secondary source, such as specialized treatises and texts, legal encyclopedias, law review articles, loose-leaf services, and ALR annotations. Do not hesitate to ask the law clerk, the judge, or a reference librarian for suggestions. After the judge and judge's clerk, the most important and helpful person may be a good reference librarian, either at the court's library or your law school library.

Keep a Research Log

A research log or journal, especially for long-term, complex research tasks, can be invaluable, providing a detailed trail of your research through all of the materials consulted. A well-maintained research log helps avoid duplication of efforts, especially if there is a time lapse between research sessions. It can also be very useful to someone else—such as the law clerk or another extern—should it be necessary to pass off the assignment. Finally, a research log can form the basis for a discussion of any problems encountered in the course of research. There is no single best format or style of log but a simple form would identify each resource consulted, describe the search path used within the resource, record the relevant results of the use of the resource, and describe any limitations or problems with the resource.

General Advice—Writing

■ *Know the Audience*

When turning from the research task to the writing task, it is important to be clear about the format for the document and its intended audience. A bench memorandum is for the judge's eyes alone but should be in a familiar format so that the judge easily can find the information needed. An order disposing of a routine motion is addressed to the lawyers for the parties and, to a lesser extent, the parties themselves. The language used should reflect this audience. Opinions are written primarily for the litigants and their lawyers, but opinions also serve to guide the future action of others: lawyers, lower courts (appellate opinions), agencies, and the general public. The broader the intended audience, the more important the appropriate tone, language, and detail of fact and analysis become.

■ *Keep It Simple*

Written work should always be clear, concise, and logical. To ensure that everything pertinent is included in the draft, it is helpful to prepare a sentence or topical outline before beginning to write. In general, less is almost always preferable to more: fewer words are better than more words; shorter words are better than longer words; shorter sentences are better than longer sentences. The use of abstract or obscure words and phrases, flowery language, or complex literary devices may interfere with the reader's ability to understand the point. Leave flourishes to the judge.

■ *Adopt the Judge's Preferences*

Not all judges have the same philosophy or approach to writing. Some prefer to write their own opinions while others look to their clerks to provide drafts that they then edit—some lightly, some heavily. Some will expect their clerks and externs to draft memoranda that the judge will work with to craft his or her own final document. Learn the judge's personal style preferences and use them. For example, the judge may prefer to write "plaintiff and defendant" or "the plaintiff and the defendant" or to substitute the name of a party (Smith) or a descriptive term (tenant) for plaintiff and defendant.

Know which style manual to use. Not all courts or judges use THE BLUEBOOK and the citation style should conform to that which the judge uses.

■ *Proof and Edit the "Draft"*

All players in the game depend on and use other people's writing when producing their own. I relied on the parties' legal writing to draft my memorandum and my judge used mine to draft her opinion.

—Student Journal

The draft should be an extern's "final" product. Even though the clerk or the judge may ask for a draft memorandum, only best efforts should be provided to them. For all but the most basic documents, a second draft will likely be required after receiving input and edits from the clerk, the judge, or both. Nonetheless, every document should reflect an extern's best effort at preparing a final product. This means employing the proper document format, ensuring that references are appropriate and accurate, and thoroughly proofreading the document to catch all spelling and grammatical errors as well as typos. Using a computer's spell check function is necessary, but never sufficient. For many of us, it is much more effective to proofread from printed pages than from a computer's display. If it is possible to do so without violating the rules of confidentiality, it can be helpful to ask a colleague for an additional proofread before submitting the document.

■ *Check in With the Clerk or Judge*

Throughout the research and writing process, do not hesitate to ask the clerk or the judge for further guidance on the assignment, help in doing research, or suggestions in writing. Be mindful, however, of their limited time: consult additional resources on your own first; ask multiple questions at one time rather than posing each question as it arises; learn the times of day when interruptions are least disruptive and approach the clerk or judge with questions at those times unless the question requires urgent attention.

Context for Analyzing Your Judicial Externship Experience

There are many ways law students might improve their research and writing ability during law school, but where, other than a judicial externship, could they observe a judge at work? Understanding the work of the judge and the implications of the judge's approach to his or her work potentially has a huge payback that transcends all other gains externs may make during a semester at the court. Using time in the courthouse to observe and analyze the judicial process and its implications in real cases is bound to improve advocacy skills. Analyzing the judicial externship experience in the broader context of the judicial system also will give working with an individual judge, in a single courtroom, in just one courthouse, in a specific jurisdiction, more universal meaning and value.

The Work of a Judge

> *As a lawyer, you don't get a choice which side to argue, but you have to see both of them and figure out ways to dismiss the opposition. As a judge, on the other hand, you do get that choice and there lies the problem because people's lives depend on you being right, not simply on you out-arguing your opponent. It must be extremely difficult to turn off the "argumentative" side and be able to function as a neutral party.*
>
> —Student Journal

What are the elements of the judge's work? Typically, we picture judges hearing legal arguments, reading briefs, and researching and analyzing the law all in order to render a well-reasoned written decision. Certainly, opinion writing is central to the judge's role, but the work of a judge, particularly a trial judge, includes making a variety of decisions beyond the published written opinions that are so familiar to law students. In addition to rendering written and oral decisions on a range of issues, judges engage in increasing amounts of what has been called "case management"—all of the other work that goes into managing and resolving a large docket of cases.

The Judge's Role as Decision Maker

> *I cannot imagine the level of self-control and dedication it takes to make decisions strictly based on legal principles. We are taught in law school that the rule is most important and that our arguments always need to be supported by legal principles; however, there is always so much emotion and passion that gets intertwined into those arguments. The judge is faced with aggressive and passionate litigators who make it extremely difficult to ignore those emotions, and I am always amazed at a judge's ability to make sound legal decisions amidst all that chaos.*
>
> —Student Journal

When we think of what a judge does, decision making is likely the first thing that comes to mind. In fact, the verb form of the word "judge" is synonymous with the words "decide" and "determine." The essence of the judicial role is deciding things; yet, the process by which judges make decisions is difficult to discern. Justice Benjamin Cardozo noted that even judges have difficulty describing how they make decisions:

> The work of deciding cases goes on every day in hundreds of courts throughout the land. Any judge, one might suppose, would find it easy to describe the process which he had followed a thousand times and more. Nothing could be farther from the truth.

> —Benjamin N. Cardozo, THE NATURE OF THE JUDICIAL PROCESS 9 (1921).

So how can we start to determine how judges make decisions? Cardozo attempted to further the inquiry:

> What is it that I do when I decide a case? To what sources of information do I appeal for guidance? In what proportions do I permit them to contribute to the result? In what proportions ought they to contribute? If a precedent is applicable, when do I refuse to follow it? If no precedent is applicable, how do I reach the rule that will make a precedent for the future? If I am seeking logical consistency, the symmetry of the legal structure, how far shall I seek it? At what point shall the quest be halted by some discrepant custom, by some consideration of the social welfare, by my own or the common standards of justice and morals? Into that strange compound which is brewed daily in the caldron of the courts, all these ingredients enter in varying proportions. Id. at 10.

Understanding the way a particular judge brews the "strange compound" to make a decision is a skill that good advocates cultivate. Externs can use their time at the court and interactions with the judge to begin to develop that talent.

Judges are confronted with different types of decisions. It is possible to categorize them in any number of ways, including by type: findings of fact, statutory interpretations, and application of standards or rules. Some judges distinguish between decisions based on their level of difficulty. Cardozo describes three types of cases:

> Of the cases that come before the court in which I sit, a majority, I think, could not, with semblance of reason, be decided in any way but one. The law and its application alike are plain. . . . In another and considerable percentage, the rule of law is certain, and the application alone doubtful. A complicated record must be dissected, the narratives of witnesses, more or less incoherent and unintelligible, must be analyzed, to determine whether a given situation comes within one district or another upon the chart of rights and wrongs . . . . Finally there remains a percentage, not large indeed, and yet not so small as to be negligible, where a

decision one way or the other, will count for the future, will advance or retard, sometimes much, sometimes little, the development of the law. Id. at 164–65.

Does your experience at the court confirm Justice Cardozo's assessment that the majority of cases present only one possible result? How do judges decide that small number of very meaningful cases that move the law? Cardozo suggests that a judge must

balance all his ingredients, his philosophy, his logic, his analogies, his history, his customs, his sense of right, and all the rest, and adding a little here and taking out a little there, must determine, as wisely as he can, which weight shall tip the scales. Id. at 162.

Writing almost 100 years after Cardozo, Judge Richard Posner, who sits on the United States Court of Appeals for the Seventh Circuit, rejects what he terms "formalist approaches to law," which he says "are premised on a belief that all legal issues can be resolved by logic, text, or precedent, without a judge's personality, values, ideological leanings, background and culture, or real-world experience playing any role." Richard A. Posner, REFLECTIONS ON JUDGING 1 (2013). Is this contemporary approach consistent with Cardozo's?

> **Exercise 19.2** Take a difficult issue in one of the cases before the judge with whom you are externing and analyze the judge's decision making on that issue. What "ingredients" did the judge consider? Of those, were some more meaningful to the judge than others? How, if at all, did the judge reveal her inclinations to the lawyers? How effective were the lawyers' arguments, written and oral, in recognizing those "ingredients" and their relative importance to the judge?

At her 2009 Senate confirmation hearing, Judge, now Justice Sonia Sotomayor explained her judicial philosophy as "Simple: fidelity to the law. The task of a judge is not to make the law—it is to apply the law." *Confirmation Hearing on the Nomination of Hon. Sonia Sotomayor to be an Associate Justice of the Supreme Court of the United States Before the S. Comm. on the Judiciary*, 111th Cong. 59 (2009) (statement of Hon. Sonia Sotomayor). Compare that statement with another from Judge Posner:

Judges tend not to be candid about how they decide cases. They like to say they just apply the law—given to them, not created by them—to the facts. They say this to deflect criticism and hostility on the part of losing parties and others who will be displeased with the result, and to reassure the other branches of government that they are not competing with them—that they are not legislating and thus not encroaching on legislators' prerogatives, or usurping executive-branch powers. Posner, supra at 106.

If judges are "just saying" they are applying the law, what is it they are actually doing?

Justices Cardozo and Sotomayor and Judge Posner were reflecting on the judge's decision-making process at the appellate level. Many externs are placed in trial courts. Trial judges are called upon to do more fact finding than appellate judges. In one classic text on judging at the trial level, Jerome Frank distinguishes fact finding from other types of judicial decision making. He refers to facts as guesses and notes that the judge, in finding facts, is subjectively judging the testimony of witnesses. Jerome Frank, COURTS ON TRIAL 22 (1950). Frank suggests that the trial judge's ability to find the facts plays a determinative role in many cases all the way through appeal. Does that shed a different light on the importance of the trial judge's findings of fact?

> **Exercise 19.3** Do you always agree with your judge's assessment of witnesses' credibility and her determination of the facts of the case? Pay particular attention to the testimony of a witness at a hearing where the judge will be making findings of fact. Develop your own findings of fact based on the testimony of the witness. Compare it to the facts as found by the judge. If your findings of fact are different, analyze the application of the law to the facts as you found them. Is your result different from the judge's? Why?

Finally, to what extent do judges bring their personal beliefs into the decision-making process? Even Cardozo, a judge renowned for his legal reasoning, recognized that "the likes and the dislikes, the predilections and the prejudices, the complex of instincts and emotions and habits and convictions, which make the man" influence judges' decisions. Cardozo, op. cit. at 167. Most judges try to resist the temptation to substitute personal preferences for principles. Is it realistic to expect that judges can make purely principled decisions? Judge Frank seemed to think it was not possible: "[the trial judge's] decisional process, like the artistic process, involves feelings that words cannot ensnare." Frank, op. cit. at 173. If that is the case, what does that teach you about how lawyers should approach legal arguments?

Does personal experience play a role in judicial decision making along with law and ideology? A recent study of 2,500 votes by 224 federal appeals court judges found that judges with at least one daughter were more likely to find in favor of women's rights. What does this finding mean for judicial selection and the importance of diversity on the bench? How does it affect public confidence in the judiciary? Adam Liptak, *Another Factor Said to Sway Judges to Rule for Women's Rights: A Daughter*, N.Y. TIMES, June 16, 2014, at A14.

The Judge's Role as Case Manager

My experience externing has allowed me to witness first-hand how matters are "moved along" and the attempts to balance the interests of justice against the time constraints imposed by enormous caseloads.

—Student Journal

The sheer volume of cases requiring decision has the potential to overwhelm the judiciary. Courts struggle to reduce, or at least control, persistent backlogs. How can the courts, which seem to be swimming against the tide, hold their ground and offer judges the opportunity to make reasoned, not rushed, decisions?

Exercise 19.4 Analyze the caseload your judge is handling. How many cases are on the judge's docket? How old is the oldest case? If your judge holds regular "calendar days," how many cases does she typically have on the calendar in a single day? How long, on average, does she spend on each case? How many cases does she close each month? Compare this to the number of new cases added to her docket each month. How many of those are newly-filed cases and how many are cases being transferred from another docket?

The past several decades have seen an increased focus on judicial case management. Some have argued that aggressive judicial case management techniques have contributed significantly to managing effectively the increasing number of case filings. Not everyone credits case management with improving the pace, much less the quality, of justice. One federal judge, criticizing legislation aimed at moving civil cases through the federal courts more expeditiously, summed up the challenges:

There is little consideration of quality control, as such, but the judge, wearing two hats—quality control and assembly line monitor—knows that both aspects of the case are her concern. Moving the case along without concern for the substance of what is happening is not only a useless act, but it just doesn't work. Images of *I Love Lucy* with Lucy on the assembly line in the candy factory come to mind.

—Judge Marjorie O. Rendell, *What is the Role of the Judge in Our Litigious Society?*, 40 VILL. L. REV. 1115, 1126 (1995).

What does the judge's role as case manager entail? Case management takes many forms—some more substantive than others and even the ostensibly routine ministerial procedures can have a significant impact on the outcome of a case. Judicial involvement in discovery, scheduling, and settlement are all types of judicial management. Even mundane matters like the frequency of and length of time between adjournments leading up to the trial are management issues. Some judges like to call the attorneys and parties into court frequently while others prefer to let the cases proceed largely outside the courthouse and only calendar the most significant case markers like the pre-trial conference and the trial itself. Whom does the judge want to see in court at each of these adjournments? Some judges require an attorney or party with settlement authority to appear each time the case is on the calendar, while others routinely excuse the parties in civil matters requiring only the lawyers be present.

Court systems and individual judges also have different approaches to the flow of cases. Does the judge routinely grant extensions of deadlines and adjournments on the consent of the parties, or is he largely unyielding? Some of the more aggressive means of judicial management include setting hard and fast trial dates and restricting discovery. Courts routinely using more aggressive management methods have earned names like the "rocket docket" or are termed "fast track" courts. Even judges whose courts have not earned such monikers sometimes resort to those tactics to move a particular case forward or at the request of one of the parties.

Effective litigators research the management policies of the judges and courts in which they appear, and they think about whether there are ways to use the policies to their clients' advantage in litigation. They use their understanding of case management techniques to inform strategy decisions at every stage of a case, beginning with the decisions of what kind of case to bring and where to file it.

As an extern, be alert to the management techniques in use in your court. Pay particular attention to when and how the judge becomes involved in cases and who initiates the judge's involvement, the judge or the parties. Think about whether any of the methods of case management your judge uses potentially have a disparate effect on different kinds of litigants or attorneys. For example, short and unrelenting discovery deadlines are likely to benefit the party with greater resources to devote to the case. Do the lawyers try to exploit the case management techniques, and, if so, how does the judge react?

> **Exercise 19.5** Many judges have their own rules and procedures that they provide to attorneys and litigants at the beginning of each case. Find out if your judge has individual pre-trial practices. If so, how does she convey them to attorneys and litigants? Go to www.uscourts.gov and follow the links to your local federal district court's website. If you work in a state court, go to the comparable website for that court. Explore it, paying particular attention to the information individual judges have posted. You are likely to find a variety of individual practices that the judges expect attorneys appearing before them to follow. Print out one example and compare it to your judge's practices.

The Judge's Role in Settlement

It's not always clear whether the judge is suggesting settlement because he or she thinks it is in the best interest of the parties, or whether he or she is suggesting it because it is in the best interest of the court. Settlement is easy. It saves time and money.

—Student Journal

Settlement before trial has become an essential case management tool available to judges. Judges make choices regarding the role they will play in the process. There are a wide range of views on the appropriate role of the judge in facilitating settlement. One prominent critic of settlements contends that the judge's role is not "to secure the peace, but to explicate and give force to the values embodied in authoritative texts such as the Constitution and statutes: to interpret those values and to bring reality into accord with them. This duty is not discharged when the parties settle." Owen M. Fiss, *Against Settlement*, 93 YALE L.J. 1073, 1085 (1984). Proponents of settlement see benefits when judges use the settlement process selectively to craft quality solutions, not simply to clear the docket. Each judge has her own viewpoint about the role she should play in the settlement process ranging from those who disdain involvement to those who aggressively pursue settlement.

The judges who eschew a role in the settlement process do so for a variety of reasons. Some judges believe that any urge to settle should come from the parties rather than being imposed upon them, but the pressure of heavy dockets makes it increasingly difficult for the judiciary to sustain a hands-off policy. Participation in the settlement process arguably calls into question the judge's impartiality. It may be difficult for a judge who has actively participated in settlement negotiations to preside impartially over later proceedings if the settlement talks fail. Without empirical research it is difficult to assess the effects of judicial involvement in settlement, but lawyers surveyed in several jurisdictions express concern about the impartiality and effectiveness of settlement negotiations conducted by the trial judge. The majority of those surveyed express strong preference for negotiations conducted by staff mediators noting their ability to devote ample time to the discussion and their specialized communication skills. Roselle L. Wissler, *Judicial Settlement Conferences and Staff Mediation Empirical Research Findings*, Dispute Resolution Magazine, Summer 2011 at 19. Other solutions to the impartiality concern include assigning cases that do not settle to a different judge for trial or having the trial judge's law clerk oversee settlement discussions. Do these solutions resolve the problem?

Among the judges who view encouraging settlement as part of their role, there are a range of techniques and styles. Some judges actively analyze the merits of the case, suggest an appropriate figure, or formulate proposals not contemplated by the lawyers. Other judges encourage compromise without endorsing a number or assessing the strength or weakness of the respective cases. Judges may require attorneys and their clients to attend the settlement conference. Some judges even bypass the attorneys and advocate settlement directly to the litigants. Another technique favored by some judges is meeting with each attorney separately to discuss settlement. Do you see any potential problems with these meetings? Other judges use more indirect means of encouraging settlement such as setting a quick or unmovable trial date or alluding to the weakness of a key motion made by the attorney for a recalcitrant litigant. Attorneys who anticipate and understand how the judge is likely to encourage settlement can use the judge's participation to their clients' advantage. For example, an attorney who recognizes that a particular judge is likely to encourage settlement by moving the case to trial quickly will be certain to prepare for trial early so that the judge's technique will not impose undue pressure to settle. An attorney who knows that the judge is prone to argue settlement directly to the parties by noting the weakness or strength of a pending motion will take pains to impress upon the judge the relative strength of any motion he has pending during a settlement conference.

A wide range of techniques for encouraging settlement are acceptable up to and including sanctions, but there are limits. The law "does not sanction efforts by trial judges to effect settlements through coercion." *Kothe v. Smith*, 771 F.2d 667, 669 (2d Cir. 1985). In *Kothe*, the U.S. District Judge had threatened to impose sanctions on the party rejecting his recommended settlement if a comparable settlement was reached after the trial started. The parties settled the case one day into the trial, and the judge imposed the sanction on one of the defendants. The appellate court vacated the sanction as coercive. Sanctions are more likely to be upheld where they are applied for failure to send an attorney or party with settlement authority to the court appearance. See *G. Heileman Brewing Co. v. Joseph Oat Corp.*, 871 F.2d 648, 654 (7th Cir. 1989) (en banc); *Official Airline Guides, Inc. v. Goss*, 6 F.3d 1385, 1396 (9th Cir. 1993).

Exercise 19.6 Think about the settlements you have seen during your externship. What role has the judge or her clerk played? What techniques does the judge or clerk use? Are any of the techniques arguably coercive?

Analyze a particular settlement you have seen. Do you think the settlement was "fair" to both sides? Was justice served by settlement? Do the parties seem satisfied? Have you ever seen the judge voice concern over the fairness of a settlement? Describe the circumstances.

Plan how you would approach a settlement conference with your judge or her clerk if you represented a plaintiff in a case.

One extern reported that a plaintiff's attorney told her:

The trial judge will always tell you your case is terrible. They will tell you to settle and take whatever you are offered. They will tell you what your case is worth and do everything they can to shake your confidence about going to trial. Don't listen to them.

How does this advice square with your observations?

Watch the settlement conference in the movie THE VERDICT or read Judge Saxe's fictionalized depiction of a settlement negotiation in a medical malpractice case. David B. Saxe, *Anatomy of a Settlement*, 79 A.B.A. J. 52 (1993). Compare and contrast actual settlement conferences at the court.

The Judge's Role at Trial

For that small percentage of cases that do not settle, there will be a trial. For judges, presiding over trials is a complex, and sometimes frustrating, function. In a frequently quoted passage, the United States Court of Appeals for the Second Circuit adopted the trial judge's view that he "need not sit like a 'bump on a log' throughout the trial." *United States v. Pisani*, 773 F.2d 397, 403 (2d Cir. 1985). Yet, in the adversary system, the attorneys have the more apparently active role in trying a case. Francis Bacon warned, "Patience and gravity of hearing is an essential part of justice; and an over speaking judge is no well-tuned cymbal." What is the judge's role during a trial, and what are the limits of judicial intervention?

In a jury trial, the judge typically structures the selection of the jury, instructs the jury on the law, controls the flow of the trial, and admits the evidence. In a non-jury trial, the judge also evaluates the credibility of witnesses and assesses the evidence to "find the facts." The judge is expected to produce a just, speedy, and economical trial. It sounds straightforward, and many judges make it look easy, but presiding over a trial while maintaining impartiality is a difficult task.

Think about the number and variety of decisions the judge must make during the course of a trial. The pace of trial often requires instantaneous rulings from the bench on legal and evidentiary issues. Throughout the trial, not just during the charge, the judge instructs the jury on the law. Knowing many areas of the law is only one part of the decision-making process. Frequently, the judge has to make a factual determination before making a legal ruling so that, even in a jury trial, the judge acts as a fact finder. The decision-making process is complicated. To determine the facts, the trial judge must evaluate witnesses:

> He must do his best to ascertain their motives, their biases, their dominating passions and interests, for only so can he judge of the accuracy of their narrations. He must also shrewdly observe the stratagems of the opposing lawyers, perceive their efforts to sway him by appeals to his predilections. He must cannily penetrate through the surface of their remarks to their real purposes and motives. He has an official obligation to become prejudiced in that sense. Impartiality is not gullibility. Disinterestedness does not mean child-like innocence. If the judge did not form judgments of the actors in those court-house dramas called trials, be could never render decisions. Frank, op. cit. at 414–15.

Even before the trial begins, the judge can make rulings that have a dramatic impact on the case. One of the more controversial steps judges may take in exercising control over the trial process is to set hard and fast time limits for the presentation of evidence at trial, sometimes enforcing the limits with a stopwatch. Judges who have set limits cite the benefits to counsel of editing their presentation to the jury. Critics express concern about the fairness to the party with the higher burden. See Debra Cassens Weiss, *Federal Judge to Time Lawyers in 9/11 Trial 'Like a Speed Chess Match,'* A.B.A. J. Law News Now (April 28, 2011, 8:24 AM), http://www.abajournal.com/news/article/federal_judge_to_time_lawyers_in_9-11_trial_like_a_speed_chess_match/ (last visited Aug. 5, 2014).

Judges also may determine the structure of the trial, for example bifurcating the presentation of evidence on liability and damages.

Jonathan Harr's book, A Civil Action, chronicling the litigation of a mass tort case in a federal district court, vividly describes the impact of the judge's decision on the structure of that trial.

The procedural rules leave the judge broad discretion in controlling the conduct of trials within her courtroom. The judge is charged with establishing trial procedures effective for determining the truth, avoid wasting time, and protect witnesses from harassment and undue embarrassment (see Fed. R. Evid. 611). That is no small task, and potentially contradictory. (Fed. R. Evid. 611). In addition to making decisions regarding the structure of the trial, for example, whether it is by judge or jury, when it will begin, and whether it is consolidated with another related matter, (see Fed. R. Civ. P. 39, 40, 42), judges also control the flow of the trial by determining the structure and length of the voir dire, the order and number of witnesses, and the length of witness examinations and attorney argument (see Fed. R. Civ. P. 47; Fed. R. Evid. 611).

Trial judges may even call witnesses and may question witnesses whether called by the court or by a party, for example, under Fed. R. Evid. 614. Judges also have inherent power to control the conduct of attorneys, parties, witnesses, and jurors during trial. In addition, the judge controls seemingly mundane matters such as where attorneys may stand when questioning a witness, how evidence and exhibits will be handled, when and how matters will be discussed outside the presence of the jury, and how objections may be made. All of these elements of the conduct of the trial may affect the outcome, particularly if an attorney has not anticipated them when planning trial strategy. During your externship be attentive to the varying abilities of counsel to exploit, or at least cope with, the judge's direction of the trial.

> **Exercise 19.7** Some judges provide trial attorneys with a list of trial conduct rules they expect the attorneys to follow. Think about what sorts of trial procedures your judge employs and how she communicates them to attorneys. Consider how the judge's control and structure of a trial you have observed affected the lawyering or the outcome of the trial.

Judges must perform all these trial functions impartially. What constitutes impermissible partiality? Jerome Frank sums up the quandary "[T]here can be no fair trial before a judge lacking in impartiality and disinterestedness. If, however, 'bias' and 'partiality' be defined to mean the total absence of preconceptions in the mind of the judge, then no one has ever had a fair trial and no one ever will." Frank, op. cit. at 413. Whatever opinions the trial judge holds, she must be careful not to signal to the jury bias toward any party. Judges who call or question witnesses, comment on witnesses or testimony, or repeatedly rebuke counsel in front of the jury, sometimes find their behavior the subject of appellate review. The bar is high for overturning a verdict based on the judge's intervention at trial. The party asserting the claim of improper bias by the judge must show not only that the judge in fact displayed bias to the jury but also that serious prejudice resulted from the showing of bias. Appellate courts look at the totality of the trial and assess the quantitative and qualitative nature of the judge's questioning as well as the witness to whom the questions were directed and the presence or absence of curative instructions. Reversal is only warranted in extreme circumstances where the judicial intervention was substantial and prejudiced the outcome. Reversals are more likely when the judge questions a defendant in a criminal case joining the prosecutor as a "tag team," as one court described. See *United States v. Filani*, 74 F.3d 378 (2d Cir. 1996). Appellate courts often refuse to reverse based on regrettable comments towards counsel or witnesses, noting the trial judge's duty to manage trials to eliminate confusion and prevent them from becoming needlessly protracted and costly. In other words, only the most egregious intervention by the trial judge is likely to result in reversal.

> One extern remarked that the judge "*adjusts his level of involvement depending on the parties before him and their resources—taking more or less control over the litigation as needs dictate. But he is just leveling the playing field to ensure that un- or under-represented parties receive the protections and advantages to which they are entitled under the law. While he cannot correct for the circumstances that brought a party into his courtroom, he can and does at least make sure that they receive a*

fair day in court." Have you noticed whether your judge alters her involvement when pro se litigants appear before her?

In classic texts on the role of the trial judge, two experienced judges urged restraint by the trial judge. Bernard Botein suggested that a trial judge should remain aloof emotionally from the trial, keeping only a finger on its pulse to ensure healthy progress. TRIAL JUDGE 125 (1952). Is this a realistic approach? In the televised O.J. Simpson murder trial, the presiding judge was criticized for his laid-back demeanor that gave substantial leeway to trial counsel and arguably prolonged the trial. Marvin Frankel raised another concern. He noted that judges, by virtue of their role, have limited knowledge of the cases that come before them. Intervening from a position of ignorance they risk clumsily interfering with each side's trial strategy. Marvin E. Frankel, *The Search For Truth: An Umpireal View*, 123 U. PA. L. REV. 1031, 1042 (1975).

> **Exercise 19.8** Do you think the judge's manner or participation at a trial you have watched has hurt or helped one side? Did the attorneys do anything to provoke the judge? Could they do anything to blunt the impact of the judge's behavior on the jury? Did the judge's behavior differ depending on whether or not the jury was present? If the judge's participation arguably helped one side, did the attorneys for that side capitalize on the judge's favor? Is it appropriate to take advantage of a conflict between the judge and your adversary?

Selection and Evaluation of Judges

After reviewing all of the elements of the judge's role and the myriad ways judges control and shape the judicial process, you can see why savvy lawyers like to know about the judges before whom they appear. The judge's background and experience prior to donning the black robes may inform a lawyer's advocacy. Similarly, the judge's experience, route to the bench, and term of office provide externs with important context for evaluating and analyzing their experiences at the court.

Qualifications

Consult the materials compiled by the "Judicial Selection in the States Project" on the American Judicature Society website at www.ajs.org for a summary of judicial qualifications in your state.

The federal constitution and the constitutions and statutes of each state set out the qualifications for judges. Typically, these qualifications are sparse. Not all jurisdictions require the judges in all levels of their courts to be licensed lawyers. Several minimalist states simply require their judges to be "learned in the law." In those states that do require their judges to be licensed attorneys, not all require a minimum number of years of legal experience. The range in those that require experience is from four to thirteen years. Many states impose residency requirements ranging from requiring the judge to be a resident at the time she takes the bench to five years in the jurisdiction. There is also no uniformity in age requirements. Thirty is the most common minimum age in jurisdictions where there is an age provision. The federal courts and some state courts do not have mandatory retirement, and in those states that do, the retirement age ranges from seventy to seventy-five years of age. The legal requirements are noticeably silent on what qualities effective judges should have.

What are the qualities that we ought to look for in candidates for judicial office? Alexander Hamilton, writing in *The Federalist* No. 78, sets a high standard:

> [T]here can be but few men in the society who will have sufficient skill in the laws to qualify them for the stations of judges. And making the proper deductions for the ordinary depravity of human nature, the number must be still smaller of those who unite the requisite integrity with the requisite knowledge.

Francis Bacon said, "Judges ought to be more learned than witty, more reverent than plausible and more advised than confident. Above all things, integrity is their portion and proper virtue." How does this seventeenth century standard hold up today?

In 2000, the ABA issued standards for judicial selection and retention setting out five criteria for judicial selection: experience, integrity, professional competence, judicial temperament, and service to the law and contribution to the effective administration of justice. The ABA standards recommend a minimum of ten years admission to the bar, and its definition of professional competence includes "intellectual capacity, professional and personal judgment, writing and analytical ability, knowledge of the law and breadth of professional experience." Judicial temperament includes, "a commitment to equal justice under law, freedom from bias, ability to decide issues according to law, courtesy and civility, open-mindedness and compassion." The service criteria encompasses "a commitment to improving the availability of providing justice to all those within the jurisdiction." These last two standards arguably recognize the need for diversity on the bench, racial and gender diversity as well as diversity of practice experience. *Standards on State Judicial Selection: Report of the Commission on State Judicial Selection Standards,* A.B.A. STANDING COMMITTEE ON JUDICIAL INDEPENDENCE (July 2000). Traditionally, fewer judges have ascended to the bench from solo or small practices, from civil rights work, or from the defense bar. Justice Sotomayor, a proponent of diversity on the bench, argues that public confidence in the judiciary will increase if the public sees more judges from their own background. Tony Mauro, *Sotomayor Says Lack of Diversity is 'Huge Danger' for Judiciary*, THE BLT: THE BLOG OF LEGALTIMES, (Nov. 20, 2013, 10:28 AM), http://legaltimes.typepad.com/blt/2013/11/sotomayor-says-lack-of-diversity-is-huge-danger-for-judiciary.html (last visited Aug. 5, 2014).

There are also many qualities that the standard does not mention, and it does not address the varying needs of different jurisdictions and judicial assignments. The volume of cases judges handle suggests that decisiveness, organization, and management skills might be critical to the role. The advent of more specialized courts also raises the question of whether judges sitting in those courts should have specialized experience to match. (The subject of specialized and problem-solving courts is addressed later in this chapter.) While specialized knowledge has obvious benefits, there are risks to having judges hear a steady diet of similar claims and issues. Fresh perspectives can be valuable. Judge Posner suggests that the use of specialized, expert judges was "the dream of the Progressive movement and led to a proliferation of administrative agencies, many of them specialized courts in effect (such as the Federal Trade Commission and the National Labor Relations Board) . . . ," which he labels "a flop," with the principal exception of the Bankruptcy Court and the partial exception of the Tax Court. He concludes "specialized courts just don't 'work' in the federal system." Posner, op cit. at 94. What are some reasons for Judge Posner's conclusion?

> **Exercise 19.9** Create a list of the qualities you think are most important in our judiciary. Compare your list to the ABA standards. How would you rank the ABA standards in order of importance? Would the nature of the court where the judge is

to preside (trial, appellate, or administrative) or the types of cases she is to hear (for example: criminal, family, or civil) affect your list or rankings?

Research the background and experience of the judge with whom you work as an extern. Do your own analysis of the qualities and qualifications that suited your judge to judicial service. Redo the analysis using the ABA qualifications. Compare the two.

Selection

The judicial selection process can be controversial. The crux of the controversy is the tension between ensuring judicial independence and maintaining judicial accountability. Reduced to the simplest terms, judges are either elected, in partisan or non-partisan contests, or appointed, but there are countless variations on both processes, and all seem to have imperfections. Frequent elections maximize accountability while lifetime appointment enhances independence. The myriad methods of judicial selection in effect throughout the country are all attempts to balance these competing interests.

Exercise 19.10 How did the judge you work with get on the bench, and how long will she serve? Answering these questions may be complicated by the fact that in some states and counties, and even within some courthouses, there are multiple routes to the bench, each with different terms of office. What are the implications of the selection process that put your judge on the bench?

- *Elections*

Popular election of judges takes many forms. The first distinction is whether the judicial elections are partisan or non-partisan. Non-partisan elections attempt to insulate the electoral process from politics by having the judge run without party affiliation. In partisan elections, the process for nominating judicial candidates varies and may involve nomination by a county political leader or through a party convention. Political nomination processes open the door to allegations that spots on the ballot are bestowed as political favors.

For an engaging description of one jurisdiction's nominating process, see *Lopez Torres v. New York State Board of Elections*, 411 F. Supp.2d 212 (E.D.N.Y.), aff'd,

462 F.3d 161 (2d Cir. 2006), rev'd, 552 U.S. 196 (2008). In that case, a candidate for a judgeship in New York State challenged the political process for selecting candidates for the New York State Supreme Court bench. The district court ruled for the challenging candidate in a lengthy decision chronicling the overtly political process. The Supreme Court reversed the district court 9–0, ruling that the First Amendment gives broad protection to political parties regarding how they select and endorse judicial candidates. *New York State Board of Elections v. Lopez Torres*, 552 U.S. 196 (2008).

- *Campaign Finance and Free Speech*

Whether the elections are dubbed partisan or non-partisan, judges running for office have to face the issue of campaigning. Given the role of judges as fair and impartial interpreters of the law, judicial campaigns are potentially unseemly. The problems posed by the need to finance political campaigns generally are seen as more critical in judicial elections because the most likely contributors to judicial campaigns are the lawyers and potential litigants in the jurisdiction where the judge is seeking election. Restrictions on contributions, however, may limit judicial candidates to the wealthy, jeopardizing the goal of a diverse bench of the most qualified candidates. Mandatory disclosure of campaign contributors and publicly-financed judicial campaigns are two frequently proposed solutions that ameliorate but do not completely resolve this problem.

In order to preserve the impartiality of the judiciary and the public's confidence in the impartiality of their judges, most states have prevented judges and judicial candidates from expressing their views on disputed legal or political issues. The various ethical provisions prohibiting judges from announcing their views were designed to insulate judicial candidates from feeling bound by statements they might otherwise make during the course of a campaign, but the provisions also deny voters some meaningful information upon which to base their votes. The Supreme Court's 5–4 decision in *Republican Party of Minnesota v. White*, 536 U.S. 765 (2002), and a subsequent related decision by the Eighth Circuit Court of Appeals, freed judicial candidates in Minnesota from some of these ethical restrictions on free speech grounds.

In the wake of these decisions, states are grappling with the limits on judicial campaign speech. Critics of the *White* decisions fear that politicizing judicial elections will detract from the independence and integrity of the courts and harm public perception, while proponents of the outcome note that elections in which judges are free to campaign promote accountability of judicial candidates and informed choice by voters. Litigants are not without recourse if their adversary has made recent and significant contributions to the judge's election. In a 5–4 decision the Supreme Court required the recusal of a judge who had benefited from millions of dollars of campaign contributions from one party on the ground that the risk of potential bias violated the Due Process Clause. *Caperton v. A.T. Massey Coal Co.*, 556 U.S. 868 (2009). In addition, a number of states have enacted court rules limiting the ability of judges to hear cases in which any of the attorneys or parties made donations above a set level. William Glaberson, *New York Takes Step on Money in Judicial Elections*, N.Y. TIMES, Feb. 13, 2011, at A1.

> **Exercise 19.11** If the judge with whom you extern is elected, research her campaign to see what statements she made while campaigning. Did they give an indication of the way she would decide any types of cases or issues? Is her behavior on the bench consistent with her campaign statements? If you were appearing as an attorney before your judge, do you think knowledge of those statements would be helpful to your preparation?

The designation "popular election" may be a misnomer when applied to judicial elections. Many judicial elections are not contested, and, even in contested elections, voter turnout is typically low. One commentator estimates that typically 80 percent of the electorate does not vote in judicial elections and cannot even identify the candidates for judicial office. Charles Gardner Geyh, *Why Judicial Elections Stink*, 64 OHIO ST. L.J. 43, 54 (2003). This suggests that most voters know little about their choices in judicial contests, which makes it likely that name recognition and information provided by the ballot, such as affiliation with a political party, play a large role in judicial voting.

More than 100 years ago, Roscoe Pound asserted that judicial elections had "almost destroyed the traditional respect for the bench." Roscoe Pound, *The Causes of Popular Dissatisfaction with the Administration of Justice*, 29 REP. A.B.A. 395 (1906), reprinted in 35 F.R.D. 273 (1964). The passage of time indicates that the situation was not that dire, but the controversy continues. Do you think the democratic value and judicial accountability attributed to judicial elections outweigh the potential detriment?

■ Appointment

The hallmark of an appointment process is that the executive—the President, Governor, Mayor, or County Executive—has the authority to make appointments to the bench. There are variations on how each executive informs his selections. Some processes, including the system for appointments to the federal courts, involve confirmation of appointees by the legislative branch. Judicial appointment may take the judicial candidate off the campaign trail, but it is difficult to claim that the appointment process is not political. The controversies over federal judicial appointments have been continuous, often culminating with Democrats and Republicans in the Senate squaring off over appointees. Appointment processes in states and localities frequently involve their own brands of local politics.

Much of the controversy surrounding judicial appointments stems from how the executive chooses appointees. Appointment by a single person is susceptible to accusations of cronyism. Executives who seek input only from their own staff or other leaders in their own party may appear to be doling out political favors. There is also the fear that, once appointed, the judge will feel he owes allegiance to the person or party who appointed him.

The least controversial appointment processes involve bi-partisan or multi-partisan screening panels that include a diverse group of lawyers and non-lawyers selected by a wide variety of politicians, bar leaders, law school deans, and citizen groups. The panel reviews candidates' qualifications and makes recommendations to the executive. The executive appoints judges from among the candidates recommended by the panel. This sort of process is touted as a "merit selection" process. The first merit selection system was adopted in 1940 by Missouri voters in response to the notorious machine politics of Democratic Party boss Tom Pendergast. In one variation, sometime after appointment, usually a year, the judge faces the electorate in what is called a retention election. Most often, the judge runs unopposed, and the retention election acts as a sort of referendum on her performance by the electorate.

The merit selection system with a retention election combines the best features of merit appointment with the accountability of elections, but even this system has flaws. Judges who have made unpopular decisions prior to the retention election have been subject to ruthless ouster campaigns, and studies have shown that absent noisy campaigns, retention elections are subject to voter apathy. Malia Reddick, *Merit Selection: A Review of the Social Scientific Literature*, 106 DICK. L. REV. 729 (2002).

■ *Does Independence Trump Accountability?*

Which system offers the best hope of promoting public trust and confidence in the judicial system while at the same time putting a diverse group of the most qualified judges on the bench and ensuring their independence and impartiality? Elections appear to offer accountability but at a cost to independence and the appearance of impartiality.

Moreover, the accountability provided by elections is arguably illusory given the apathy of voters and the dearth of information available to them on the candidates. Appointment by a single executive also compromises independence and impartiality unless the executive relies on a diverse, non-partisan screening committee committed to seeking out the most qualified candidates. Ultimately, the best test of a judicial selection system is the quality of the judges selected.

The debate about the relative benefits of merit selection versus election has not proven easy to resolve. Beginning in the 1980s, a series of studies conducted by academics, bar associations, and even the Chamber of Commerce, have attempted to compare the quality of judges elevated to the bench under each system analyzing legal experience, diversity, ideology, work product, and ethics. Each of these categories poses research challenges, and the results are varied and mixed. The difficulty begins with determining what makes a "quality" judge. Even the benefits to diversity on the bench under each system have proven difficult to gauge. While studies have found that appointive systems are more effective in creating a diverse bench than electoral systems, some scholars have noted a "threshold effect," arguing that appointive systems are only more effective at initially diversifying a non-diverse court, and that they subsequently fail to maintain that result. Rachel Paine Caufield, *What Makes Merit Selection Different?*, 15 ROGER WILLIAMS U. L. REV. 765 (2010).

Evaluation of Judges

It isn't until one closely observes, perhaps even shadows a judge over a period of time that one can get a true feel for a judge's temperament and the way in which she approaches a variety of cases, including trials and settlement conferences.

—Student Journal

The move to develop evaluation systems for the judiciary is relatively recent. Concerns about judicial independence and the difficulty of evaluating the complex and specialized work of a judge make implementing an evaluation system a delicate process. Since 1987, several organizations, including the National Center for State Courts, the Judicial Conference of the United States, and the American Bar Association, have recommended or issued guidelines for the evaluation of judicial performance. The result has been the development of court-sponsored evaluation plans in many jurisdictions. Local bar associations also have stepped in to evaluate judges, particularly where the courts do not sponsor an evaluation plan. The overarching purpose of judicial evaluation is to improve the quality of the judiciary, but the plans can have more specific purposes. Judicial evaluations can have public purposes, such as to enhance public confidence in the judiciary or to provide information to those responsible for continuing judges in office. Within the court system they can have administrative purposes such as informing judicial assignments and determining where training and education would be beneficial to the judges, and, individual judges can use them for self-improvement.

Courts and bar associations implementing an evaluation system confront a daunting task. In 2005, the ABA adopted Black Letter Guidelines for the Evaluation of Judicial Performance, which include three guiding principles: evaluations must be confidential; they must be based on actual observation of the judge; and the sampling and selection of respondents, information collected, and the methods of collecting and analyzing must comport with accepted scientific standards. Anonymous evaluations may encourage forthright responses, but does anonymity risk unfair comments? To avoid results tainted by rumor or heavy media coverage of a few notorious cases, it makes sense to survey only those with firsthand knowledge of the judge's performance. That includes the attorneys who have appeared before the judge, litigants, witnesses, jurors, and court personnel who have seen the judge in action. Do non-lawyers possess sufficient understanding of the judge's role to meaningfully evaluate judicial performance? Can litigants fairly evaluate the judge who heard their case?

Threshold questions on methodology include determination of who should conduct the evaluation, whom they should survey, and what information they should seek. Generally, it is agreed that obtaining balanced information requires assembling a diverse group of stakeholders to design and implement the process. No single interest group should control the evaluation process. There are a number of criteria on which a judge might be evaluated. The choices made about which criteria to include in an evaluation may reveal the priorities of the group doing the evaluation. There are also questions about how to structure the evaluation. The ABA recommends asking for behavior-based information. Are some criteria more or less susceptible to evaluation on behavior-based grounds? The ABA makes no recommendations as to the relative weight various criteria should be given. Are all criteria of equal importance? The challenges are formidable.

Exercise 19.12 There are countless evaluation forms in use throughout the country. Start by looking at the Judicial Performance Resources on the ABA site www.aba.org. Look at the differences among the forms designed for attorneys, jurors, court staff, and the judge him or herself. Do they accurately capture the differences in perspective each group brings to the process? Are there criteria that are not included in the ABA Guidelines? How would you rank the importance of the various criteria that are included? The Quality Judges Initiative of the Institute for the Advancement of the American Legal System (IAALS) at the University of Denver has information on the judicial evaluation plans that have been implemented in many states. Check to see if and how the judges in your jurisdiction are evaluated and to whom and how the results are disseminated. http://iaals.du.edu/initiatives/quality-judges-initiative/implementation/judicial-performance-evaluation. If your jurisdiction has an evaluation form, complete it using your courtroom observations of the judge with whom you work. Review your completed evaluation. Do you think it conveys an accurate assessment of the judge? How would you improve the evaluation form? Do you think the judge could or would benefit from seeing the evaluation? If there is no evaluation form available in your jurisdiction, choose an evaluation form from another jurisdiction or use the sample Trial Attorney Evaluation of Judge form on the ABA site and reproduced in Appendix 19.1.

Two recent studies raise questions about the ability of non-lawyers to fairly evaluate judges. A 2011 study conducted by Simon and Scurich showed that lay evaluations of judicial decisions and judges were "highly contingent on the decision outcomes. Participants gave favorable evaluations of the judges and their decisions when they agreed with the judges' outcomes, but reported negative evaluations when they disagreed with them." Recognizing that the public gets much of its information about judicial decisions from the media, the authors conducted a follow-up survey to determine the extent to which lay people's judgments of judicial decisions are influenced by expert commentators. They found "that the experts' commentaries do not alter participants' evaluations of the courts' decisions." Dan Simon & Nicholas Scurich, *The Effect of Legal Expert Commentary on Lay Judgments of Judicial Decision Making*, 10 J. EMPIRICAL LEGAL STUD. 797 (2013). What implications do these findings have for judicial selection and oversight? Courts are making significant efforts to influence public perceptions of the courts. What do these findings suggest about their potential for success?

Issues surrounding judicial evaluations are also discussed below under Judges, Courts, and the Public.

Judicial Oversight

Elections and evaluations are not the only ways to hold judges accountable. The trial courts and the intermediate level appellate courts are accountable for their legal reasoning through appellate review. Frequent reversals may motivate a judge to decide cases differently. Appellate courts do not necessarily limit their review of judges' conduct to the merits of decisions being appealed. In late 2013, the Second Circuit Court of Appeals removed District Judge Shira Scheindlin from a controversial case that had been tried before her and ordered the case reassigned to another judge. The court's sua sponte ruling was predicated on its conclusion that Judge Scheindlin had, among other things, compromised "the appearance of impartiality" through the "improper application of the Court's 'related case rule,' . . . and by a series of media interviews and public statements purporting to respond publicly to criticism of the District Court." *In re Reassignment of Cases*, 736 F.3d 118 (2d Cir. 2013).

Even the highest appellate courts in each jurisdiction may be reversed by the legislature in some cases. If a judicial decision is unpopular, the legislature may "correct" the law through new legislation.

Judicial conduct commissions oversee other forms of judicial behavior. Under the Judicial Improvement Act of 2002 (28 U.S.C. §§ 335–364), anyone may file a written complaint against a federal judge whom they believe has engaged in "conduct prejudicial to the effective and expeditious administration of the business of the courts" or "is unable to discharge all duties of office by reason of mental or physical disability." The states have comparable oversight systems to investigate allegations of judicial misconduct, although there is variation in the composition of the oversight body, the investigatory process, whether and to what extent the proceedings are confidential, and the appeals processes.

> The American Judicature Society website has a wealth of information on judicial oversight with links to specific information for each state. www.ajs.org.

There are other less formal methods of "oversight" that also aid in ensuring judges remain accountable. A host of services, in print and online, collect and disseminate evaluative information about judges. Beyond basic biographical background, some of these sources offer generalized insights about individual judges' practices and tendencies through anonymous comments from members of the bar who practice before them. (See Further Resources at the end of this chapter.) Some popular web sites, including The Robing Room which describes itself as "where judges are judged" go further offering numerical ratings on federal and state judges based on lawyer-submitted data.

> Judge Alex Kozinski of the United States Court of Appeals for the Ninth Circuit suggests that one important constraint on judicial decision making is an internal one:

the judge's own self-respect. Kosinski posits that because "[j]udges have to look in the mirror at least once a day" and "have to like what they see," they are likely to hew to the correct decisional line. Do you think this form of self-oversight works? Does it obviate the need for other forms of oversight?

Academics, too, are playing a role in providing oversight, offering empirical analyses of judicial opinions that purport to yield objective measures of judicial performance. See Robert Anderson IV, *Distinguishing Judges: An Empirical Ranking of Judicial Quality in the United States Courts of Appeals*, 76 Mo. L. Rev. 315 (2011) (ranking judges based on positive and negative citations to their judicial opinions).

Empirical analysis also plays a role in some commercial tools (e.g., WestlawNext Attorneys & Judges Profiler and Lexis Advance Litigation Profile Suite) offered to litigators that structure judicial profiles of individual judges based on the judge's historical docket, offering aggregated information on cases by practice areas, types of motions filed and the average time to decide various motions, awards by resolution, and appellate record.

One frequent complaint about our judicial system is its lack of efficiency, including judges' productivity. A court system's administrative office may monitor productivity by recording and publishing statistics on caseloads, such as the number of cases each judge resolves, the average number of days before each judge renders a decision on a motion, the number of cases pending on each judge's docket, the average age of the cases on the judge's docket, and the like. Court administrators may react to an individual judge's statistics by reassigning the judge to a different court or altering the number or types of cases the judge is assigned.

Exercise 19.13 Does the court where you are externing keep case statistics? Who keeps the statistics? Do individual judges keep them? Are the statistics available to the public? Are the statistics conveyed to the judge? Think about the impact the statistics have on the judge.

Finally, citizen groups, bar associations, and the media use a variety of methods to hold judges accountable. Citizen groups sometimes send court watchers to monitor what is happening in the courts. Bar associations may survey their memberships and produce reports on judges in the jurisdiction. The media report on cases of note and instances of egregious judicial conduct. In some jurisdictions the media is not limited to sending reporters to the courthouse; cameras bring televised proceedings into viewers' homes.

Cameras in the courtrooms offer another possible avenue for judicial oversight, although cameras are not permitted in all jurisdictions. If they are, their use is likely to vary from judge to judge and, perhaps, even case to case. Despite decades of experience with cameras in the courts, there is no consensus on whether the behavior of judges, lawyers, and witnesses improves under the camera's watchful eye. There is some concern that conduct deteriorates because participants "play to" the cameras. Other concerns include whether cameras in the courtroom discourage knowledgeable witnesses from coming forward and whether televising court proceedings enhances public understanding of the courts or, because of the sensational trials that attract public attention, contributes to skewed notions of the judicial process.

> The Radio Television Digital News Association, http://rtdna.org, offers a state-by-state guide to cameras and electronic coverage in state court courtrooms (current as of summer 2012). The federal judiciary has completed the first three years of a four-year pilot program to evaluate the effect of cameras in the courtroom. Fourteen federal trial courts are participating in the pilot program. See www.uscourts.gov.

While much of the media coverage of the judiciary furthers the goals of public access to the courts and judicial accountability, some forms of public criticism of judges threaten judicial independence. It is difficult to defend ad hominem attacks on judges as productive, but where is the line between harsh, but permissible, criticism and personal attack? When a judge is subject to unfair or inaccurate criticism, what is the proper response, and who should respond? Judicial ethics rules in many jurisdictions strictly limit the judiciary's response to criticism of judges' decisions. Should judges who anticipate a public reaction to a decision take greater pains to explain their reasoning when they rule? What role should the bar associations play in defining the limits of permissible criticism and responding to improper criticism of judges and the judiciary? Whether good or bad, sensational or mundane, media coverage of the judiciary is not just a form of oversight. It also contributes to public opinions of the judicial system.

> **Exercise 19.14** One extern reported the following: "[F]rom reading the news stories [about the judge] I had preconceived notions about him. However, after working with him I realized that these stories were published from one point of view and the

> Judge was in fact a very nice, respectful, and approachable judge . . . . I remind
> myself that what I hear or see through second-hand accounts or media portrayal is
> not necessarily what is reality."
>
> If there is media coverage of a case with which you are familiar through your
> externship, read or watch the coverage with a critical eye. Write a journal entry
> analyzing the accuracy of the coverage and the effect, if any, of the media scrutiny on
> the judge, lawyers, witnesses, and parties. What effect do you think media coverage
> might have on public opinion of judges and our judicial system?

Judges, Courts, and the Public

Judges may appear to be put on a pedestal—we refer to them as "Your Honor," we don't interrupt them, and we rise when they enter and exit. However, when important decisions are being made involving people's lives—whether it be their liberty money or property—society benefits from the appearance and practicality of someone "put on a pedestal," who is well-respected, independent, and not subject to outside influence.

—Student Journal

Another of the benefits of a judicial externship is the opportunity to reflect on the role of judges and courts in society and the public perception of that role. Judicial externs become insiders in a major cultural and political institution that much of the public sees only through the filters of media coverage or pop culture, as litigants represented by lawyers or as jurors fulfilling specific functions. Clients impose their expectations of the judiciary and the courts on their attorneys, and those expectations can inform their positions on how their cases should be handled. Litigators argue their clients' cases to jurors who bring to that role certain expectations of the court system. Their reactions to the evidence and arguments are colored by their image of the system. But these are instrumental reasons to think about public perceptions of the judicial system. The more critical reason why public perception of the courts is of consequence was well put by Justice Felix Frankfurter: "The Court's authority—possessed of neither the purse nor the sword—ultimately rests on sustained public confidence in its moral sanction." *Baker v. Carr*, 369 U.S. 186, 267 (1962) (Frankfurter, J., dissenting).

Recognition of the importance of the public's perception of justice led the American Bar Association Judicial Division Lawyers Conference to host "Perception of Justice" events across the country between 2008 and 2012. Through town hall meetings, small group sessions, and panel discussions members of the judiciary, lawyers, and community members shared perceptions and suggestions on how to improve perceptions of justice. The most frequent discussion topics included procedural justice and user experience in the courts; the impact of public outreach and education; and the impact of race, ethnicity, religion, gender, and sexual orientation. Jurisdictions continue to host these events. Has your jurisdiction held a Perception of Justice event? If so, what was the outcome? Were changes made?

Exercise 19.15 Take the opportunity at the beginning of your placement in chambers to assess your own image of the courts in your community. What do you know about the particular judge for whom you will be externing? Start by completing the short survey found in Appendix 19.2. Compare your responses to the responses of members of the general public about their perceptions of the courts in their communities, which are contained in David B. Rottman, et al., Nat'l Ctr. for State Courts, *Perceptions of the Courts in Your Community: The Influence of Experience, Race and Ethnicity, Final Report* (2003), https://www.ncjrs.gov/pdffiles1/nij/grants/201302.pdf.

At the end of your placement, come back to the survey and take it again. Reflect on any changes in your responses now that you have become an insider in the court system and a member of your individual judge's inner circle. If there are differences in your responses, do they raise any concerns about the ability of the public to fairly and accurately evaluate judges and the judicial system?

What is the Public Perception of Courts and Judges?

Since 1977 most of what is known about the public perception of courts and judges is through public opinion surveys that have been conducted over the years on both the state and national levels. A 2003 report by the National Center for State Courts reviewed many of the previous state and national surveys and reported findings from those surveys and concluded that there was an "apparent lack of significant change in public opinion about courts" over the years covered by the surveys. The authors of the Report note that "[t]he core public image of state and local courts is a stereotype—one that seems to change little over time or differ from state to state or locality to locality." The stereotyped images have both negative and positive facets.

The positive images include the perception that "judges are honest and fair in making case decisions, that they are well trained, that the jury system works, and that judges and court personnel treat members of the public with courtesy and respect."

The negative images center on perceptions of limited access to the courts due to cost and complexity, delays in the processing of cases, unfairness in the treatment of racial and ethnic minorities, leniency toward criminals, and a lack of concern about the problems of ordinary people. Specific concerns include a perception of leniency in sentencing in criminal matters and favoritism toward the corporate sector and the wealthy in the civil justice system. There also is strong evidence of public concern that political considerations, especially related to campaign fundraising, exert an undue influence on the judiciary.

The authors of the 2003 Report noted that "distinctive views of the courts are associated with race and ethnic groups. African-Americans tend to have distinctly lower evaluations than do whites of the performance, trustworthiness, and fairness of courts. Latinos emerge as generally holding the most positive assessments of the state courts, but present a mixed picture in terms of specifics. . . . " A national survey conducted by Pew Research Group a decade after the 2003 Report shows views of the courts continue to be divided on racial lines and reveals a parallel urban/rural divide as well. Forty percent more of the black respondents than white respondents believed that blacks are treated less fairly by the courts than whites, and 17% more of the urban participants than the rural respondents shared that view. Eileen Patten, *The Black-White and Urban-Rural Divides In Perceptions of Racial Fairness*, PEW RESEARCH CENTER FACTTANK (Aug. 28, 2013), http://www.pewresearch.org/fact-tank/2013/08/28/the-black-white-and-urban-rural-divides-in-perceptions-of-racial-fairness/. What are the potential consequences of having any group feeling they are receiving disparate treatment by the courts?

> **Exercise 19.16** Differing perceptions of the courts along racial, ethnic, or gender lines within our society raise concerns about the fairness of the courts to different segments of society. Bias or the perception of bias in the courts runs counter to the core values of our judicial system. Over the last several decades most state and federal courts have studied the issue of fairness to diverse segments of society and issued reports. Do you see any evidence of bias in your court? Look at any reports on bias in the courts issued in your jurisdiction. The *National Center for State Courts Gender*

and Racial Fairness Resource Guide has a wealth of information with data and links to many of the state reports on their website http://www.ncsc.org. The federal circuits also have done reports, many of which are available through the Circuit Executive at the court. Pull the most recent reports from your jurisdiction and compare your own observations with the results presented in the reports.

How are Public Perceptions of Judges and Courts Formed?

How do people form their perceptions of their local courts? Several studies have attempted to answer that question. A 1999 national survey by the National Center for State Courts interviewed 1,826 randomly-selected Americans. Approximately 53% of the respondents indicated some personal involvement in the courts, with almost one-half of personal experience taking the form of jury service. About half (48.7%) of the respondents felt they knew "some" about the courts, but only 14.1% felt they knew "a lot."

The sources identified by the respondents as regularly providing information to them about the courts were as follows: some personal involvement with the courts (53%), electronic sources (59%), and print sources (50%). Interestingly, TV dramas and comedies were identified by 25.6% of the respondents as regularly providing information about the courts, and TV reality shows (for example, *Judge Judy* or *The People's Court*) regularly provided 18.3% of the respondents with information about the courts.

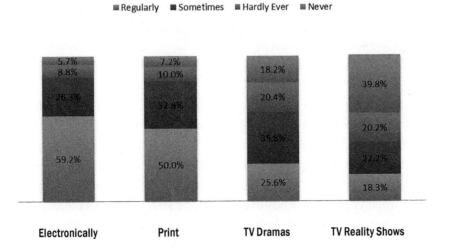

Where do you most frequently get information about the courts?

■ Regularly   ■ Sometimes   ■ Hardly Ever   ■ Never

The survey analyzed in the 2003 Report only asked for sources of information that contributed to an overall impression of how courts in the community worked from respondents who indicated that they or a member of their household had any personal involvement in the courts in the preceding 12 months. Seventy-one percent rated their experience in court as a very important source of information. Further down the list was TV news (23%), newspapers (27%), and TV reality programs (8%). Generally, the three identified racial and ethnic groups, African-Americans, Latinos, and whites, reported similar patterns of information sources. African-Americans, however, were most likely to cite personal experiences in court (77%) compared to whites (70.4%) and Latinos (55%), and Latinos were more likely to cite TV reality shows (21%) than African-Americans (15%), and whites (3%) as important sources of information about the courts.

Overall, the data suggest roughly 50% of Americans have had some personal experience with the courts that is used to inform their images of the judiciary and judges, but even those with personal experience also report relying on TV news and newspapers for a significant amount of information about the courts. The other 50% of the population necessarily relies on media sources, such as sensational news stories and TV dramas, for much of its information about the courts. Recognizing the sources of public perceptions of the courts, astute litigators follow media and pop culture coverage of the courts and adapt their presentation style, evidence selection and jury arguments to meet and address juror beliefs and expectations. Have you seen the judge or lawyers either explicitly or implicitly attempt to address juror perceptions of the court system?

> Compare your perceptions of the court in which you are externing with those of the general public as reflected in these data. What similarities and differences emerge? Can you think of any suggestions for your judge or the administrators of the court system in which you are working they can undertake to improve the public's perception of them?

By learning about public perceptions of the courts and how they are formed the judiciary can take steps ensure that all segments of society have confidence in the fairness of the judicial system. David B. Rottman, the author of studies on public perceptions of the court, emphasizes the importance of procedural fairness: "In fifteen years writing and researching about public opinion on the courts, I have found no more powerful predictor of whether people are positive or negative about the courts than perceptions of procedural fairness." David B. Rottman, *How to Enhance Public Perceptions of the*

Courts and Increase Community Collaboration, COURT EXPRESS (Nat'l Ass'n for Court Mgmt.), Fall 2013, at 3.

Procedural fairness has four basic components: respect, neutrality, participation, and trustworthiness. These aspects of procedural fairness apply to every interaction at the courthouse, not just proceedings before the judge. Be alert to issues of procedural fairness at the court. How are witnesses, litigants, jurors, and observers treated in all parts of the courthouse? Once litigants are before the judge, how much time does the judge take to explain matters to them? Are litigants offered ample opportunity to be heard? Does the judge effectively convey genuine concern for the litigants? What about jurors and witnesses? How does the judge interact with them? How does Rottman's view about the significance of procedural fairness square with the Simon and Scurich findings about public judgment about judicial decisions described in earlier in this chapter under Evaluation of Judges?

Exercise 19.17

The judge is at all times respectful, affable, and courteous to the jury. In many ways he exhibits all the traits of a good host attending to the comfort of his guests . . . .

—Student Journal

Jury service is one of the most frequent ways that members of the public interact with the courts. If you have an opportunity to watch a jury trial, try to put yourself in the shoes of the jurors. How have they experienced the court system? How do you think their experience has affected their view of our judicial system? How did the judge interact with them? Can you identify some ways the judge could limit any frustration jurors seemed to experience during your observation?

For fascinating first-person accounts of jury service by former jurors, read D. Graham Burnett, A TRIAL BY JURY (2001) and William Finnegan, *Doubt,* THE NEW YORKER, Jan. 31, 1994, at 48.

Courts Adapting to Change

The static nature of public perception of the courts may be a manifestation of the public's belief the courts do not change. There is value to stability and predictability in a judicial system, but constancy does not preclude modernization to improve delivery of services. Courts across the country are constantly innovating. Sensitivity to public perceptions prompts improvements to the court system. The procedural fairness movement, community courts, and outreach and education programs are just a few of the innovations in response to public opinion. Breakthroughs in technology, changing demographics, and new studies and findings by social scientists also inspire court innovations. Courts are alert to changing demographics so they can both anticipate and respond to new demands. The growth of the elderly population, the "silver tsunami," and the number of veterans returning from service abroad have prompted courts to look for ways to better serve these groups' legal needs. Social science also prompts change. One example is the increased use of Evidence Based Decision Making (EBDM), a movement widely used in medicine in which research tracking past outcomes informs decision making. EBDM has gained increased traction in a number of jurisdictions, particularly in criminal and juvenile courts.

One of the most significant issues the courts face is access to justice. In 1994 Washington formed the first statewide Access to Justice Commission and in the two decades since 33 states have followed suit. The Commissions typically include representatives from the courts, members of the bar, legal services providers, law school faculty, and community leaders. Technology has provided some of the most promising tools for increasing access to justice. In 2011, a Tech Summit brought together representatives from the National Center for State Courts, the Legal Services Corporation, the American Bar Association, the United States Department of Justice Access to Justice Initiative, the National Legal Aid and Defenders Association, the New York State Courts, and the Self-Represented Litigation Network to work on using technology to improve access to justice.

Technology

Technology has been a boon to court clerks and lawyers craving paperless litigation. E-filing, the filing and storage of court documents in an electronic format rather than on paper, has many benefits. E-filing offers obvious savings on paper, copying, postage, couriers, storage space, and staff time. Electronic documents also are easily accessible and searchable. E-filing is mandated in all federal courts and is in use in an increasing number of state court systems.

Electronic filing presents special challenges to pro se litigants, but it also has tremendous potential. The federal courts are exploring systems that would lead pro se filers through the creation of pleadings and "document assembly programs" are already in use in some jurisdictions. The Do-It-Yourself Forms Project in New York, providing tenants with forms through the Internet or at terminals in the courthouse, is an example of a document assembly program. A number of states have partnered with organizations like Pro Bono Net to provide pro se litigants with these computerized forms that use prompts to help non-lawyers draft pleadings and papers. See Chapter 27 for further discussion of use of technology to enhance access to justice.

> Courts are experimenting with other ways to use technology to serve different constituencies. Nevada has an Appellate Court App with access to documents, court calendars, court rules, and decisions. The civil courts in the District of Columbia launched a live-chat feature where during business hours the public can get information about the status of cases, court procedures, availability of forms and filing processes. The federal courts have introduced an online eJuror system, and jurors in New Jersey can opt to use an online system and receive notifications by email or text message. Juror attendance is taken by scanning each juror's assigned barcode. The defendants in federal cases now provide information to probation and pre-trial services officers electronically at kiosks, by phone, or over the Internet through the new Electronic Records System (ERS). Many states are using Video Remote Interpretation (VRI) to provide language interpretation and use of a cloud-based service is under investigation. Does your court use technology in innovative ways?

Advances in technology have also dramatically changed communications. New avenues of communication flow both in and out of the courthouse. Our networked society allows for instantaneous and worldwide information sharing. These developments present challenges and opportunities for the courts. Traditional media outlets are no longer the only source of information. Websites as well as user-generated content on social media sites like Facebook, Twitter, and blogs give the courts and everyone else an opportunity to be heard and unprecedented and immediate access to information. To what extent are the courts tapping into such sources to inform and educate the public and to give greater access to justice?

Court websites vary widely. Some are relatively static, offering little fresh information. Others include published opinions, calendars, and judicial profiles. The most innovative websites have begun to realize the public relations potential of the Internet by posting information in a more user-friendly format. A number of states post case summaries, court news, and some even include a court blog. North Dakota's court calendar includes case summaries and links to court documents.

> **Exercise 19.18** Take a look at your court's website. What kind of online presence do the court and judge have? What information is available for the court's constituencies: lawyers, litigants, witnesses, jurors, the general public? To what extent is the court using its website to educate the general public? What, if any, resources are available? Is the site multimedia? Is the site interactive? If not, can you imagine ways it could be interactive; video it might include? What information does the site have about your judge? Is there information you would recommend adding?

The accessibility of electronic court records gives new meaning to the notion of public access to the courts. To examine traditional court papers, an individual would have to travel to the court and request the one physical set of court records on a matter from the court clerk. Electronic records can be available online to anyone with Internet access. The wider access to electronic records and the ability to search electronic records with a keystroke raise confidentiality and privacy concerns for lawyers and courts. Identity theft, corporate espionage, and unfair competition are some of the potential misuses of information in court files. Courts are grappling with ways to strike a balance between the privacy concerns presented by Internet access and the fundamental right of public access to the courts.

> **Exercise 19.19** Look at the court file for one of the cases before the judge. Is there information in the file that you would characterize as "private"? What makes the information "private"? Could the information be used to embarrass or harm someone, for an illegal purpose such as insider trading, or for a commercial purpose? Weigh the privacy concerns you have identified against the three fundamental values of public access to court records: monitoring the court system to promote fairness and honesty, protecting public health and welfare, and allowing the media to report on matters of public interest and concern.

How are the courts coping with issues such as increased scrutiny, misinformation about their decisions and proceedings, and the ready availability of information to jurors? The challenges social media presents to the jury system are telling. Courts across the country have seen various types of juror misconduct related to Internet use. For example, jurors have consulted Wikipedia for definitions of legal terms, done Internet research on scientific evidence, attempted to "friend" witnesses, and "googled" the parties to the litigation. The federal courts and many states have responded by adding language to their jury instructions explicitly admonishing jurors not to consult various Internet-based sources. Other steps either taken or contemplated by courts include polling the jurors after the verdict, displaying warning posters in jury rooms, providing Internet training for prospective jurors, and enacting specific punishment for violations.

In late 2009, the Judicial Conference Committee on Court Administration and Case Management in the federal courts drafted Proposed Model Jury Instructions on The Use of Electronic Technology to Conduct Research on or Communicate about a Case. Here is an excerpt of an instruction the judge can give at the beginning of the trial:

You may not communicate with anyone about the case on your cell phone, through email, Blackberry, iPhone, text messaging, or on Twitter, through any blog or website, through any internet chat room, or by way of any other social networking websites, including Facebook, My Space, LinkedIn, and YouTube.

Exercise 19.20 Technology is a good litmus test for innovation. One student intern previously reported: "I see very little evidence of technology in the courtroom." To what extent have you found technology in use in the courtroom, courthouse, and the clerk's office? Is Internet access available in the courthouse to lawyers, to members of the public? What are the implications of your findings?

Courtroom Technology

The potential for use of new technology in the courtroom to present and argue cases is vast, but courtroom technology has been slow to spread. In 1993, the National Center for State Courts and William & Mary Law School unveiled Courtroom 21, a courtroom designed to experiment with the use of technology to improve the legal system. Since then, a number of jurisdictions have opened showcase high-tech courtrooms with innovations such as real-time court reporting facilities; real-time streaming video to other locations; interactive whiteboards; touch-screen monitors in the witness box; integrated electronic podiums and benches; personal computer docking stations at counsel tables, the witness box, and on the bench; equipment and monitors for presentation of electronic evidence; and wireless Internet access points. Some courts also have technology available to bring into courtrooms on request. The cost of outfitting and, in many instances, retrofitting courtrooms has been an impediment to rapid deployment of new technology, but these obstacles have diminished with improved wireless capabilities and the availability of lower cost equipment.

> Jurors who participated in a 2010 D.C. Superior Court survey on the Use of Technology in the Courtroom overwhelmingly favored the use of technology and reported that it improved their ability to serve as jurors. Hon. Herbert B. Dixon, Jr., *The Evolution of a High-Technology Courtroom*, FUTURE TRENDS IN STATE COURTS 2011, at 28 (Aug. 5, 2014) http://www.ncsc.org/~/media/Microsites/Files/Future%20Trends/Author%20PDFs/Dixon.ashx.
>
> During your externship has technology been used in the courtroom? Did it enhance the presentation of evidence to the judge or jury?

Cost concerns aside, technology in the courtroom presents questions about reliability, access, and training, as well as presentation issues. For example, is it preferable to have one large central monitor or separate ones for individual jurors? Litigators prefer to have a central screen that encourages eye contact with the presenter. Who should have control over the images and sound projected in the courtroom? Typically the judge or court clerk plays this "traffic cop" role rather than the attorneys litigating the case. When mistakes happen, as they inevitably will, how should judges respond? Many courts install a "kill switch" to allow the judge to rapidly turn off screens and sound. These are just a few of the additional decisions courtroom technology present for judges, but as technology becomes more pervasive, courts are adapting.

Specialization

Our society is increasingly complex resulting in more specialization in the profession. Professor Richard Susskind, who writes and speaks frequently on the future of the legal profession, predicts increased specialization among lawyers—through what he describes as "multi-sourcing"—as a matter of professional survival. Richard Susskind, TOMORROW'S LAWYERS (2013). How does greater specialization affect the courts? Should they follow suit? Many states have specialized courts at the trial level, but state appellate courts continue to hear all kinds of cases. In the federal courts, both trial and appellate judges hear a mixed docket, although federal district court judges who have reached a certain age may opt out of hearing certain kinds of cases. Administrative tribunals are specialized. What has motivated the creation of specialized courts? What are the pros and cons of specialized courts?

Some trial level state courts are specialized courts. The specializations can be as a result of a statute that establishes the jurisdiction of the court or they may be by administrative assignment of the chief judge or other court administrator. Some jurisdictions have statutorily established courts to handle certain types of cases—for example criminal, housing or family courts.

> **Exercise 19.21** Take a look at the statutorily-established specialty courts in your jurisdiction. What kinds of cases do they hear? Who are the typical litigants? One commentator has dubbed many of these courts "poor people's courts." Russell Engler, *Connecting Self-Representation to Civil Gideon: What Existing Data Reveal About When Counsel is Most Needed*, 37 FORDHAM URB. L.J. 37, 39 (2010). Is that a fair description in your jurisdiction? What are the implications of creating "poor people's courts"?

Within a court of general jurisdiction, the court administrators may designate judges to hear either criminal or civil cases rather than a mix of both. One recent trend has been to assign business cases or complex commercial matters to particular courts for resolution. Court administrators also can assign judges to hear only certain stages of the litigation—for instance judges may hear only the pre-trial aspects of the case, or cases may be referred to them only for the actual trial. Administrative assignments can allow the court administration to play to individual judge's experience and strengths and offer judges more targeted training. However, there is the potential for court administrators to use assignments politically or for politicians or bar groups to pressure administrators to move judges who have made unpopular decisions.

Problem-Solving and Community Courts

One form of specialization that has taken hold in the state courts is the creation of problem-solving courts. The movement to address societal problems that were bringing repeat offenders into the criminal justice system began in the late 1980s and early 1990s with experimental programs in several jurisdictions. The most typical problem-solving courts handle criminal cases and fall into four categories: community courts, domestic violence or DV courts, drug courts, and mental health courts. The hallmark of these problem-solving courts is they attempt to resolve the criminal case while also addressing an underlying or related social or psychological problem. Courts continue to experiment with the problem-solving approach. Recent innovations include veterans courts aimed at addressing the issues that bring returning veterans into the court system, reentry courts for recently released prisoners, landlord and tenant courts focused on addressing homelessness, and specialized courts for human trafficking cases.

The first problem-solving courts were drug courts, and they continue to be the most prevalent. Beginning in Miami in the late 1980s, the drug courts spread across the county targeting the huge number of non-violent offenders with substance abuse problems. Drug courts vary in their approach, but their goal is to stop legal and clinical recidivism by referring offenders to drug treatment services. These courts use different means of diverting cases, offering pre-plea supervision and treatment, or various forms of post-plea supervision. Mental health courts have similar goals and approaches, and with a 2006 Bureau of Justice Statistics report estimating that more than half of all prison and jail inmates had a mental health problem, the need for services is undeniable. The domestic violence courts are probably the most controversial of the problem-solving courts. With stated goals of victim safety and batterer accountability, DV courts have been criticized by public defenders as "victim's courts," and some argue that because of their goals, they are not technically problem-solving courts.

Community courts attempt to address quality-of-life issues in a particular neighborhood. The first community court, the Midtown Community Court, opened in 1993 in the Times Square area of New York City. It targeted low level crimes that had plagued the area such as prostitution, graffiti, vandalism, and shoplifting. Rather than dispensing the short jail sentences that had been typical in those cases, the court combined community service sentences with social service programs. In the last two decades, dozens of jurisdictions have created community courts.

> The Center for Court Innovation website has a full list of community courts, www.courtinnovation.org.

In 2000, the Conference of Chief Justices and Conference of State Court Administrators adopted a resolution in support of problem-solving courts and efforts to integrate their principles and methods into court operations generally to improve processes and outcomes. Some of the challenges to greater integration of the problem-solving methods include resource allocation, training, and the extent to which standardization may detract from the flexibility these courts have employed. Cost is certainly a concern. As one extern noted, "Problem-solving courts require enormous support structure, which requires substantial funding." During the experimental phase, many of these specialty courts were subsidized, which meant they were not drawing significant resources from the rest of the court system in their jurisdictions. The support services associated with problem-solving courts are only one part of the added expense. With greater specialization the courts lose economies of scale.

Money aside, problem-solving courts are not without controversy. Some defense attorneys question the inquisitorial nature of proceedings in problem-solving courts, arguing the process starts with a presumption of guilt. Other critics, while recognizing the generally good intentions of the judges in these courts, express concern about judges imposing their values on people from different backgrounds. The tendency of the courts to continue defendants under their supervision over long periods of time also raises concerns. Mental health and drug treatment professionals have raised concerns in their arenas about the compulsory nature of the treatment available in those courts. Even where a defendant's participation is voluntary, experts express concern about whether individuals in these specialized courts really understand they have a choice. Judges in the problem-solving courts have specialized support services available to them, but participants in these courts often describe the judge as adding cheerleader, social worker, and therapist to his or her role, raising the question of whether these additional roles add to or detract from the judge's effectiveness.

The advent and proliferation of problem-solving courts raises more general questions about what role the courts and judges should play in addressing social problems. Courts continue to innovate and study the results of these experiments, but the jury is out on whether or not problem-solving courts are making an appreciable difference toward improved outcomes in the areas they target. Community and problem-solving courts are prime candidates for Evidence Based Decision Making (EBDM). Empirical research on outcomes is a promising tool for courts and judges in their efforts to address social problems and achieve just and lasting results.

Conclusion

Initially, I viewed my externship as a list of requirements to fulfill. Complete the hours, check. Write a journal, check. Impress my Judge, check. I started this journey with the list of tasks I needed to accomplish to satisfy other people. The first week was interesting, but I was wondering if the hype of an externship was about a break from academic pressure. I welcomed that, but I had set my expectations prematurely.

—Student Journal

As the student author of the journal quoted above learned, there is so much more to a judicial externship than fulfilling course requirements and impressing the judge. Use this overview of the courtroom as classroom as a starting point for exploration of the court system. A semester in the courthouse is an opportunity to evaluate the judicial system and consider systemic improvements. The courts are also a rich resource for learning about lawyering and improving a variety of skills. Embrace the boundless opportunities for personal growth. Research, writing, and legal analysis are only a few of the skills a judicial externship can develop. Working with the judge, law clerks, and court personnel can improve interpersonal skills and offer opportunities for collaboration. Observing lawyers at trial and in other court proceedings can develop advocacy skills. And for some externs the opportunity to experience the judicial system may even solidify career goals:

> *Observing a trial . . . I wanted to tell the lawyer to just let me do it. That was a moment that shook me a little. I no longer felt like an apprentice or an outsider. I wanted to do this. The courtroom pews felt like a bench and I wanted the coach to put me in.*
>
> —Student Journal

The opportunities for learning are unlimited. *Carpe diem.*

FURTHER RESOURCES

General Materials

Law Clerk Handbook: A Handbook for Law Clerks to Federal Judges (Sylvan A. Sobel, Fed. Jud. Ctr. ed., 2d ed. 2007).

Calvert G. Chipcase, Federal District Court Law Clerk Handbook (2007).

David J. Richman, *How to Be a Great Law Clerk*, Litig., 16 (Summer 2009).

Judge D. Brock Hornby, Working Effectively with Your Judge: An Outline for Remarks (Federal Judicial Center 2008).

Victor E. Flango & Thomas M. Clarke, Reimagining Courts: A Design for the Twenty-First Century (2014).

Ethics for Judicial Externs

Maintaining the Public Trust: Ethics for Federal Judicial Law Clerks (Federal Judicial Center, 4th ed. 2013), http://www.fjc.gov/public/pdf.nsf/lookup/Maintaining-Public-Trust-4D-FJC-Public-2013.pdf/$file/Maintaining-Public-Trust-4D-FJC-Public-2013.pdf.

National Center for State Courts, *Ethics Resource Guide*, http://www.ncsc.org/
Topics/Judicial-Officers/Ethics/Resource-Guide.aspx.

Code of Conduct for Judicial Employees, U.S. Courts, http://www.uscourts.gov/
rulesandpolicies/codesofconduct/codeconductjudicialemployees.aspx.

James J. Alfini, Steven Lubet & Jeffrey M. Shaman, Judicial Conduct and Ethics
(4th ed. 2007).

Research and Writing for Judges

Jennifer Sheppard, *The "Write" Way: A Judicial Clerk's Guide to Writing for the Court*,
38 U. Balt. L. Rev. 73 (2008).

Judicial Writing Manual: A Pocket Guide for Judges (Fed. Judicial Cetr., 2d ed.
2013).

Ruth C. Vance, *Judicial Opinion Writing: An Annotated Bibliography*, 17 J. of the Leg.
Writing Inst. 197 (2011).

Michael G. Walsh, *Learning to Write as Judges are Taught to Write* (Part 1) 59 No. 4
Prac. Law. 5 (Aug. 2013).

Michael G. Walsh, *Learning to Write as Judges are Taught to Write* (Part 2) 59 No. 5
Prac. Law. 5 (Oct. 2013).

The Judge's Role as Decision Maker

Corey Rayburn Yung, *A Typology of Judging Styles*, 107 Nw. U. L. Rev. 1757 (2013).

Benjamin Cardozo, The Nature of the Judicial Process (1921).

Richard A. Posner, Reflections on Judging (2013).

Frederic Block, Disrobed: An Inside Look at the Life and Work of a Federal
Trial Judge (2012).

Judges on Judging: Views from the Bench (David M. O'Brien, ed., 4th ed. 2013).

The Judge's Role as Case Manager

Tobias Barrington Wolff, *Managerial Judging and Substantive Law*, 90 WASH. U. L. Rev. 1027 (2013).

NATIONAL CENTER FOR STATE COURTS, COURTOOLS, http://www.courtools.org/).

Civil Litigation Management Manual, Fed. Judicial Ctr., 2d ed. 2010, http://www.uscourts. gov/FederalCourts/PublicationsAndReports/CivilLitigationManagementManual.aspx).

JUDGE BARBARA J. ROTHSTEIN, CHAMBERS AND CASE MANAGEMENT (Fed. Judicial Ctr., 2009).

ROBERT C. LaFOUNTAIN ET AL., EXAMINING THE WORK OF STATE COURTS: AN OVERVIEW OF 2012 STATE TRIAL COURT CASELOADS, NAT'L CTR. FOR ST. CTS. (2014), http://www. courtstatistics.org/~/media/Microsites/Files/CSP/NCSC_EWSC_WEB_NOV_25_14. ashx.

The Judge's Role in Settlement

Roselle L. Wissler, *Judicial Settlement Conferences and Staff Mediation: Empirical Research Findings*, DISP. RESOL. MAG. 18 (Summer 2011).

Peter Robinson, *Opening Pandora's Box: An Empirical Exploration of Judicial Settlement Ethics and Techniques*, 27 OHIO ST. J. ON DISP. RESOL. 53 (2012).

Official Airline Guides, Inc. v. Goss, 6 F.3d 1385 (9th Cir. 1993).

Donna Stienstra, *ADR in the Federal District Courts: An Initial Report* (Fed. Judicial Ctr. 2011).

Selection and Evaluation of Judges

NATIONAL CENTER FOR STATE COURTS, *Judicial Selection and Retention Resource Guide*, http://www.ncsc.org/topics/judicial-officers/judicial-selection-and-retention/ resource-guide.aspx.

NEW YORK CITY BAR ASSOCIATION, *Judicial Selection Methods in the State of New York: A Guide to Understanding and Getting Involved in the Selection Process*, http://www2.nycbar.org/pdf/report/uploads/20072672-GuidetoJudicialSelection- MethodsinNewYork.pdf.

American Bar Association Coalition for Justice, *Judicial Selection: The Process of Choosing Judges*, http://www.americanbar.org/content/dam/aba/migrated/JusticeCenter/Justice/PublicDocuments/judicial_selection_roadmap.authcheckdam.pdf.

U.S. Chamber Institute for Legal Reform, *Promoting "Merit" in Merit Selection, A Best Practices Guide to Commission-Based Judicial Selection*, http://ilr.iwssites.com/uploads/sites/1/meritselectionbooklet.pdf (2009).

Bert Brandenburg & Roy A. Schotland, *Justice in Peril: The Endangered Balance Between Impartial Courts and Judicial Election Campaigns*, 21 Geo. J. Legal Ethics 1229 (2008).

New York State Bar Association, Judicial Section, *Judicial Diversity in New York State: A Work in Progress* (Sept. 14, 2014), http://www.nysba.org/judicialdiversity report/.

Oversight and Review

Elizabeth Smith & Mark Thompson, New York Judge Reviews and Court Directory (2013).

Almanac of the Federal Judiciary (Aspen Publishers ed., 2013).

Robert Anderson IV, *Distinguishing Judges: An Empirical Ranking of Judicial Quality in the United States Courts of Appeals*, 76 Mo. L. Rev. 315 (2011).

Jordan M. Singer, *Gossiping About Judges*, 42 Fla. St. U. L. Rev. 427 (2014).

American Bar Association Judicial Division, *Judicial Performance Resources,* http://www.americanbar.org/groups/judicial/conferences/lawyers_conference/resources/judicial_performance_resources.html.

American Bar Association, *Black Letter Guidelines for the Evaluation of Judicial Performance* (February 2005), http://www.americanbar.org/content/dam/aba/publications/judicial_division/jpec_final.authcheckdam.pdf.

Jordan M. Singer, *Attorney Surveys of Judicial Performance: Impressionistic, Imperfect, Indispensable*, Judicature 20 (July/Aug. 2014).

Judges, Courts, and the Public

National Consortium on Racial and Ethnic Fairness in the Courts, Research & Resources, http://www.national-consortium.org/Research-and-Resources.aspx.

Mark Soler, *Reducing Racial and Ethnic Disparities in the Juvenile Justice System, In* National Center for State Courts, Trends in State Courts: 2014, 27 (Carol R. Flango, Deborah W. Smith, Nora E. Sydow, Charles F. Campbell, & Neal B. Kauder, eds., 2014), http://www.ncsc.org/~/media/Microsites/Files/Future%20Trends%20 2014/2014%20NCSC%20Trends%20Report.ashx.

Judge Steve Leben, *The Procedural-Fairness Movement Comes of Age, in* National Center for State Courts, Trends in State Courts: 2014, 59 (Carol R. Flango, Deborah W. Smith, Nora E. Sydow, Charles F. Campbell, & Neal B. Kauder, eds., 2014), http://www.ncsc.org/~/media/Microsites/Files/Future%20Trends%202014/2014%20 NCSC%20Trends%20Report.ashx.

National Center for State Courts, *Public Trust and Confidence Resource Guide*, http://www.ncsc.org/topics/court-community/public-trust-and-confidence/resource-guide.aspx.

Technology

Administrative Office of the U.S. Courts, *Long Range Plan for Information Technology in the Federal Judiciary* (Fiscal Year 2014 Update, September 2013), http://www.uscourts.gov/uscourts/FederalCourts/Publications/2014-IT-long-range-plan.pdf.

Mary-Rose Papandrea, *Moving Beyond Cameras in the Courtroom: Technology, the Media, and the Supreme Court*, 2012 BYU L. Rev. 1901.

National Center for State Courts, *Technology in the Courts Resource* Guide, http://www.ncsc.org/Topics/Technology/Technology-in-the-Courts/Resource-Guide.aspx.

Rochelle Klempner, *The Case for Court-Based Document Assembly Programs: A Review of the New York State Court System's "DIY" Forms*, 41 Fordham Urb. L.J. 1189 (2014).

Judge Herbert B. Dixon Jr., *PowerPoint Jury Instructions*, Judges' J. 37 (Winter 2011).

James J. Sandman & Glenn Rawdon, *Technology Solutions to Increased Self-Representation, in* National Center for State Courts, Trends in State Courts: 2014, 55 (Carol R. Flango, Deborah W. Smith, Nora E. Sydow, Charles F. Campbell, & Neal B. Kauder, eds., 2014), http://www.ncsc.org/~/media/Microsites/Files/Future%20Trends%20 2014/2014%20NCSC%20Trends%20Report.ashx.

RICHARD SUSSKIND, TOMORROW'S LAWYERS: AN INTRODUCTION TO YOUR FUTURE (2013).

Social Media

Meghan Dunn, *Jurors' Use of Social Media During Trials and Deliberations, A Report to the Judicial Conference Committee on Court Administration and Case Management* (Fed. Judicial Ctr., 2011).

Judge Antoinette Plogstedt, *E-Jurors: A View from the Bench*, 61 CLEV. ST. L. REV. 597 (2013).

Judge Amy J. St. Eve, Judge Charles P. Burns, & Michael A. Zuckerman, *More From the #Jury Box: The Latest on Juries and Social Media*, 12 DUKE L. & TECH. REV. 64 (2014).

NATIONAL CENTER FOR STATE COURTS, *Social Media and the Courts Network*, http://www.ncsc.org/Topics/Media/Social-Media-and-the-Courts/Social-Media/ Home.aspx.

John G. Browning, *Why Can't We Be Friends? Judges' Use of Social Media*, 68 U. MIAMI L. REV. 487 (2014).

Specialized Courts

Jennifer Koshan, *Investigating Integrated Domestic Violence Courts: Lessons from New York*, 51 OSGOODE HALL L.J. 989 (2014).

Judge Joyce Cram, *Elder Court: Enhancing Access to Justice for Seniors*, in NATIONAL CENTER FOR STATE COURTS, TRENDS IN STATE COURTS: 2014, 77 (Carol R. Flango, Deborah W. Smith, Nora E. Sydow, Charles F. Campbell, & Neal B. Kauder, eds., 2014), http://www.ncsc.org/~/media/Microsites/Files/Future%20Trends%202014/2014%20 NCSC%20Trends%20Report.ashx.

Daniel M. Fetsco, *Reentry Courts: An Emerging Use of Judicial Resources in the Struggle to Reduce the Recidivism of Released Offenders*, 13 WYO. L. REV. 591 (2013).

APPENDIX 19.1

Judicial Performance Evaluation Program

Trial Attorney Evaluation of Judge_____

In an effort to improve the quality of the judiciary and justice system the above-named judge's performance on the bench is being evaluated. A critical component of this effort is to obtain the thoughtful, considered input from individuals who have appeared before the judge. As part of this process, attorneys who appeared before the judge during past twelve months are being asked to complete a brief questionnaire.

Court records indicate that you appeared before the judge during this time period. As you have had the opportunity to personally observe the judge on the bench, you are in a position to provide meaningful, reliable information to this evaluation by completing the attached questionnaire as completely and forthrightly as possible.

The survey should take 5 to 10 minutes to complete. Your responses will remain totally confidential and will be attributed to you in no manner. Neither your name nor any other identifying information will be asked and should not be provided on the questionnaire. Any potentially personally identifying information will remain confidential and responses will be reported only in summary form and aggregated with the other attorneys that complete the survey.

For each of the statements on pages 2 and 3, mark the box that best represents your own perspective on the topic, based solely on your experience appearing before the above named judge. On pages 4 and 5 you will be asked to provide demographic and other background information that will help put the survey results into context. On the final page of the questionnaire is space for you to provide any comments or additional information on the judge's performance or the evaluation materials and procedures.

Thank you for your participation and effort in this important endeavor[1].

Trial Attorney Evaluation of Judge _____

Please rate the judge's performance, <u>based on your own personal experience</u>, using the following scale:

A Excellent   **B Very Good**   **C Acceptable**   **D Poor**   **F Unacceptable**

Please answer **Don't Know/Does Not Apply ("DK/DNA")** for any items in which you lack sufficient information from your own observation to fairly and accurately rate the judge's performance or items which do not apply to your interactions with the judge.

---

1   Source: American Bar Association, Judicial Division, Trial Attorney Evaluation of a Judge, http://www.americanbar. org/content/dam/aba/migrated/jd/lawyersconf/performanceresource/survey/trial_court_attorney.pdf,

	A	B	C	D	F	DK/DNA

Section 1   Legal Ability

	A	B	C	D	F	DK/DNA
a. Legal reasoning ability. (1.1)	□	□	□	□	□	□
b. Knowledge of substantive law. (1.2)	□	□	□	□	□	□
c. Knowledge of rules of procedure and evidence. (1.3)	□	□	□	□	□	□
d. Keeps current on developments in substantive law and rules of procedure and evidence. (1.4)	□	□	□	□	□	□

Section 2   Integrity and Impartiality

	A	B	C	D	F	DK/DNA
a. Avoids impropriety and the appearance of impropriety. (2.1)	□	□	□	□	□	□
b. Treats all people with dignity and respect (2.2)	□	□	□	□	□	□
c. Willingness to make difficult or unpopular decisions. (2.7)	□	□	□	□	□	□
d. Acts fairly by giving people individual consideration. (2.4)	□	□	□	□	□	□
e. Considers both sides of an argument before rendering a decision. (2.5)	□	□	□	□	□	□
f. Presents a neutral presence on the bench. (2.1)	□	□	□	□	□	□
g. Refrains from inappropriate *ex parte* communication. (2.1)	□	□	□	□	□	□
h. Bases decisions on the law and facts without regard to the identity of the parties or counsel. (2.6)	□	□	□	□	□	□
i. Keeps an open mind and considering all relevant issues in making decisions (2.5, 2.6)	□	□	□	□	□	□
j. Acts without favor or disfavor toward anyone, including but not limited to favor or disfavor based upon race, sex, religion, national origin, disability, age, sexual orientation, or socioeconomic status. (2.3)	□	□	□	□	□	□

IF YOU ANSWERED A, B, C, OR DK TO QUESTION J ABOVE, PLEASE **SKIP** TO SECTION 3

k.   If you believe the Judge acts with favor or disfavor to anyone based upon personal characteristics such as those listed above, please list the characteristic(s) giving rise to your belief. (2.3)   _____

_____

	A	B	C	D	F	DK/DNA

Section 3 Communication

	A	B	C	D	F	DK/DNA
a. Uses clear and logical oral communication while in court. (3.1)	□	□	□	□	□	□
b. Uses plain English and understandable language when speaking to prospective or seated jurors, litigants, and witnesses. (3.1)	□	□	□	□	□	□
c. Prepares clear and logical written decisions and orders. (3.2)	□	□	□	□	□	□

Section 4 Professionalism and Temperament

	A	B	C	D	F	DK/DNA
a. Acts in a dignified manner. (4.1)	□	□	□	□	□	□
b. Treats people with courtesy. (4.2)	□	□	□	□	□	□
c. Is attentive to proceedings. (4.1)	□	□	□	□	□	□
c. Acts with patience and self-control. (4.3)	□	□	□	□	□	□
d. When working with *pro se* litigants and litigation does so fairly and effectively. (4.4)	□	□	□	□	□	□
f. Has appropriate levels of empathy with the parties involved in proceeding. (4.1, 4.2, 4.3)	□	□	□	□	□	□
g. Promotes public understanding of and confidence in the courts. (4.6)	□	□	□	□	□	□

		A	B	C	D	F	DK/DNA

Section 5 Administrative Capacity

		A	B	C	D	F	DK/DNA
a.	Is punctual for court. (5.1)	□	□	□	□	□	□
b.	Is prepared for court. (5.1)	□	□	□	□	□	□
c.	Maintains control over the courtroom. (5.2)	□	□	□	□	□	□
d.	Appropriately enforces court rules, orders, and deadlines. (5.3)	□	□	□	□	□	□
e.	Makes decisions and rulings in a prompt, timely manner. (5.4)	□	□	□	□	□	□
f.	Manages the court's calendar efficiently. (5.5)	□	□	□	□	□	□
g.	Uses settlement conferences and alternative dispute resolution mechanisms as appropriate. (5.6)	□	□	□	□	□	□
h.	Demonstrates appropriate innovation in the use of technology to improve the administration of justice. (5.7)	□	□	□	□	□	□
i.	Fosters a productive work environment with other judges and court staff. (5.8)	□	□	□	□	□	□
j.	Acts to ensure that disabilities and linguistic and cultural differences do not limit access to the justice system. (5.10)	□	□	□	□	□	□

Section 6 Background and Demographic Information

a. How long have you been a practicing attorney?

☐ Less than 1 year

☐ 1–2 Years

☐ 3–5 Years

☐ 6–10 Years

☐ 11–20 Years

☐ More than 20 years

b. Which of the following areas of law best describe your practice (select up to 2 items)

☐ Civil Tort—Defense

☐ Civil Tort—Plaintiff

☐ Criminal—Defense Attorney

☐ Criminal—Prosecution

☐ Commercial & General Civil

☐ Juvenile Offender or Dependency

☐ Domestic Relations/Family Law

☐ Estate/Probate

☐ Government Practice

☐ Other (Please Specify)

c. Which of the following best describes your work setting?

☐ Prosecuting Attorney's Office

☐ Attorney General's Office

☐ Public Defender/Department Of Assigned Counsel

☐ Legal Aid

☐ In House Corporate Counsel

☐ Private Practice

☐ Other (Please Specify)

d. How many attorneys are employed by your firm?

☐ Sole Practioner

☐ 2–5 Attorneys

☐ 6–10 Attorneys

☐ 11–20 Attorneys

☐ Greater than 20 Attorneys

e. What best describes your racial background? (Please check all that apply)

☐ Caucasian/White

☐ African American/Black

☐ Asian/Pacific Islander

☐ Native American

☐ Other (Please Specify)

f. Are you Hispanic/Latino?

h   How many times have you appeared in Judge's court over the past year?

☐ Never

☐ Once

☐ 2–3 times

☐ 4–10 times

☐ More than 10 times

Comments:

Please provide any additional comments, clarifications, or details related to either the items raised in this questionnaire or the judge's performance on the bench in the space below. You may use the back of this page or add additional pages if needed.

Thank you very much for your time and effort.

Perceptions of the Courts Survey

Adapted from David B. Rottman, et al., Perceptions of the Courts in Your Community: The Influence of Experience, Race and Ethnicity (Final Report) (National Center for State Courts 2003), https://www.ncjrs.gov/pdffiles1/nij/grants/201302.pdf

1. On a scale from 1 to 5, with 1 being least favorable and 5 being most favorable, how would you rate how you feel in general about the courts in your community? If you feel neutral, use 3.

2. How often do you think people receive fair outcomes when they deal with the courts? Would you say:

   (1) always, (2) usually, (3) sometimes, (4) seldom, (5) never, or (6) don't know?

3. How often do you think the courts use fair procedures in handling cases?

   Would you say:

   (1) always, (2) usually, (3) sometimes, (4) seldom, (5) never, or (6) don't know?

4. For each of the following statements about courts in your community, indicate how strongly you agree or disagree with each. Would you say you strongly agree, somewhat agree, somewhat disagree, strongly disagree, or don't know?

   a. The courts are concerned with people's rights.

      (1) strongly agree, (2) somewhat agree, (3) somewhat disagree,
      (4) strongly disagree, (5) don't know.

   b. The courts treat people with dignity and respect.

      (1) strongly agree, (2) somewhat agree, (3) somewhat disagree,
      (4) strongly disagree, (5) don't know.

   c. The courts treat people politely.

      (1) strongly agree, (2) somewhat agree, (3) somewhat disagree,
      (4) strongly disagree, (5) don't know.

   d. The courts make decisions based on the facts.

(1) strongly agree, (2) somewhat agree, (3) somewhat disagree, (4) strongly disagree, (5) don't know.

e. The judges are honest in their case decisions.

(1) strongly agree, (2) somewhat agree, (3) somewhat disagree, (4) strongly disagree, (5) don't know.

f. Courts take the needs of people into account.

(1) strongly agree, (2) somewhat agree, (3) somewhat disagree, (4) strongly disagree, (5) don't know.

g. Courts listen carefully to what people have to say.

(1) strongly agree, (2) somewhat agree, (3) somewhat disagree, (4) strongly disagree, (5) don't know.

h. Courts are sensitive to the concerns of the average citizen.

(1) strongly agree, (2) somewhat agree, (3) somewhat disagree, (4) strongly disagree, (5) don't know.

i. Court cases are resolved in a timely manner.

(1) strongly agree, (2) somewhat agree, (3) somewhat disagree, (4) strongly disagree, (5) don't know.

5. Some people say that the courts treat everyone equally, while others say that the courts treat certain people differently than others. How often are each of the following groups of people treated worse than others by the courts? Are they always, often, sometimes, rarely, or never treated worse than others?

a. An African-American?

(1) always, (2) often, (3) sometimes, (4) rarely, (5) never, (6) don't know.

b. A Latino or Hispanic?

(1) always, (2) often, (3) sometimes, (4) rarely, (5) never, (6) don't know.

c. A Non-English speaker?

(1) always, (2) often, (3) sometimes, (4) rarely, (5) never, (6) don't know.

d. Someone with a low income?

(1) always, (2) often, (3) sometimes, (4) rarely, (5) never, (6) don't know.

6. How important are the following sources of information to your overall impression of how the courts in your community work? Are they very important, somewhat important, or not at all important?

a. Your prior experience in court?

(1) very important, (2) somewhat important,
(3) not at all important, (4) don't know.

b. Court experiences by a member of your household?

(1) very important, (2) somewhat important,
(3) not at all important, (4) don't know.

c. Court experiences of a close relative?

(1) very important, (2) somewhat important,
(3) not at all important, (4) don't know.

d. Court experiences of a friend?

(1) very important, (2) somewhat important,
(3) not at all important, (4) don't know.

e. Court experiences of someone you work or go to school with?

(1) very important, (2) somewhat important,
(3) not at all important, (4) don't know.

f. Your past or current educational experiences?

(1) very important, (2) somewhat important,
(3) not at all important, (4) don't know.

g. What you see on television news?

(1) very important, (2) somewhat important,
(3) not at all important, (4) don't know.

h. What you read about court cases in newspapers?

(1) very important, (2) somewhat important,
(3) not at all important, (4) don't know.

i. What happens during television programs such as Judge Judy or Judge Joe?

(1) very important, (2) somewhat important,
(3) not at all important, (4) don't know.

The previous questions asked your perception, in general, of the courts in your community. Now consider your preliminary perceptions and understanding of the court and judge for whom you will extern. Identify at least five significant roles that your judge performs as part of his or her official duties:

1. _____

2. _____

3. _____

4. _____

5. _____

How would you rate the competence and judicial temperament of the judge for whom you will extern? Use a scale of 1 to 5 with 1 being the lowest and 5 the highest rating; use 3 if you feel neutral.

1. Does the judge possess a general working knowledge of the substantive law in the fields that are likely to come before the judge?

2. Does the judge possess a good working knowledge of the procedural and evidentiary law of the jurisdiction?

3. Are the judge's decisions well reasoned and well thought out?

4. Does the judge ask relevant, perceptive questions about matters before him or her?

5. Does the judge issue timely rulings and judgments?

6. Does the judge generally start trials on the first day they are scheduled to start?

7. Is the judge consistently courteous in his or her dealings with others, including counsel, litigants, jurors and staff?

How would you rate the integrity of the judge for whom you will extern? How would you rate the competence of the judge for whom you will extern? Use a scale of 1 to 5 with 1 being the lowest and 5 the highest rating; use 3 if you feel neutral.

1. Does the judge decide cases on the facts and law, without consideration of public appeal?

2. Does the judge recuse himself or herself whenever his or her impartiality might reasonably be questioned?

From what primary sources do you draw your information for your ratings on competence and integrity?

1. _____

2. _____

3. _____

4. _____

5. _____

CHAPTER 20

Criminal Justice Law Placements

RUSSELL GABRIEL & HANS P. SINHA

C riminal law practice is an intensely personal and rewarding practice. It involves violations of social norms and standards, accusation, judgment, and the infliction of punishment on real people, at times in response to injury to equally real people. Criminal conduct—especially violent crime, and also other kinds of highly destructive behavior—leaves victims forever harmed and changed. At the same time, regardless of the measure of injury to anyone else criminal defendants and their families undergo intense upheaval from the time of arrest onward. Finally, as if the above is not enough, criminal law is also unique in that it is the only time and place in civilian society that we legally sanction the killing of fellow human beings.

Your participation in a criminal externship, whether you are working on behalf of the prosecution or defense, has the potential to introduce you to criminal justice practice and to transform you. It provides you with a unique opportunity to learn about the law, society, and yourself. The goal of this chapter is to help you maximize this opportunity.

The chapter starts with an overview of criminal justice externships. It discusses different kinds of criminal justice practice and describes the most common players in criminal work: the defendant, the victim, and the judge. It helps you to assess different opportunities, develops your abilities as a lawyer, and highlights some of the unique ethical challenges of criminal justice work. It then discusses criminal justice in a broader social context, including both race and poverty. Each section also dives deeper into topics that have particular resonance: starting a case, being client-centered, developing case theory, and coping with high caseloads.

> The existence of capital punishment highlights the intersection of our criminal justice system and personal morality. For example, do you think a pro-death penalty belief should be a litmus test for a position as a prosecutor or opposition to the death penalty for a position as a public defender? Can you personally be against the death penalty yet prosecute death cases, or conversely, be in favor of the death penalty

yet defend against such cases as a public defender? The death penalty may be the starkest example of the confluence of personal morality and public policy. However, is there a sliding scale in this context? What if you substituted "war on drugs" for "death penalty" in the above sentences? Would your answer(s) be the same?

Externships in the Criminal Justice System

Good criminal law practitioners develop an extraordinary range of capacities:

- The practice is both adversarial and transactional. The U.S. Supreme Court has acknowledged the criminal justice system today is largely a system of pleas. Most pleas are negotiated agreements between the prosecution and the defense.

- The cases are fact driven. Both sides must thoroughly investigate and develop relevant evidence. Factual investigation requires knowledge of investigative technique and all manner of forensic knowledge.

- The practice demands knowledge of statutes and cases defining crimes and defenses, procedural and evidentiary rules, sentencing laws and practices, probation rules, rehabilitation and treatment options, and alternative courts.

- The practice requires understanding how outcomes may be affected by culture, and how culture varies with language, location, education, occupation, immigration, poverty, housing, age, gender, race, and religion—to name a few. Perhaps more than any other area of the law, criminal law practice demands an understanding of the human condition.

- The practice of criminal law puts all of this knowledge to work. Prosecutors work on investigations, direct the drafting of arrest and search warrants, and initiate formal charges. They meet with, counsel, and provide support to victims and victims' families, and they interview witnesses and prepare cases for motion hearings and trials. Defense attorneys counsel and provide support to clients and clients' families, lead investigations, draft pre-trial motions and briefs, and provide a check on the prosecution. Attorneys on both sides handle bond, committal, and pre-trial hearings; conduct judge and jury trials; negotiate and litigate sentencing; and deal with post-trial hearings, appeals, and habeas proceedings.

You will encounter core lawyering skills at all stages of the process. Lawyers negotiate pleas within days of arrest and within minutes of a jury verdict. Litigation skill is applied as much to initial case evaluation and subsequent plea negotiation as to trial advocacy. Lawyers must constantly read human nature in dealing with victims, clients, witnesses, police, judges and jurors, and throughout must maintain ethical and professional standards. How you approach your criminal justice externship depends on you. It is important that you assert ownership over the experience. The first step is to identify your goals and the opportunities available to you. See Chapter 2 on Professional Development Planning. Some goals focus on the nuts and bolts—how to write, file, and argue a motion; pick and choose a jury; or do a direct and cross examination of a witness. Other goals focus on the fundamental fairness and morality of the criminal law system. Even routine practice decisions implicate larger issues of individual and community dignity, poverty, race, equality, fairness, and efficiency, to name a few. The question of justice hovers, always.

Your externship lets you observe the criminal justice system—feel it, think about it, participate in it, and understand it from the ground up. This chapter explores some of the possibilities and includes examples of learning goals drawn from this exceedingly varied menu. These are general themes, waiting for your specific externship experiences to fill in the content.

Criminal Justice: Courts and Cases

Jurisdictions and Practice Areas

Criminal law practice varies from place to place, depending on many variables. It varies with the type of court—state or federal; felony, misdemeanor, or juvenile. It varies among regions of the country, states, counties, and even municipalities. It varies with the jurisdiction's character as urban, suburban, or rural; the jurisdiction's racial and ethnic composition; its wealth and its poverty; its crime rate; the emphasis placed on types of cases by law enforcement or the larger community. Each jurisdiction's practicing bar has its own culture. Judges perpetuate habits of practice and cultural norms within their courthouses. So keep in mind that your externship will provide an example, but not a model. This subsection discusses some differences based on different courts' subject matter jurisdiction.

Misdemeanor courts have the highest volume of cases, receive the least scrutiny, and affect the greatest number of Americans. These courts typically handle traffic cases, misdemeanor drug cases, public intoxication, shoplifting, and minor assaults and batteries including some domestic violence cases. Prosecutors and public defenders assigned to these courts handle hundreds of cases monthly, if not daily. Sentencing is most often probation with various conditions attached—fines, community service, substance abuse treatment, or drunk driving school, for example. Confinement, if any, is measured in days or months rather than years and is typically served in city or county jails rather than in prison.

Courts of general jurisdiction handle misdemeanors as well as the full range of felonies from thefts to capital murder cases where the death penalty is sought. Some jurisdictions have specialized criminal courts that handle only criminal matters, while others have courts that handle both civil and criminal cases. While the volume of cases tends to be somewhat less in the felony-level state courts compared to misdemeanor courts, these courts also suffer under excessive caseloads. The chief prosecuting attorney in these courts may either be elected or appointed. The State Attorneys General may also prosecute in these courts. Sentences run longer in these courts, with convicted defendants serving time in prison.

Juvenile courts deal with cases involving defendants under the age of 18 and also may deal with cases involving child protective services. The system recognizes that children present different issues than adults and sometimes require different rules. These differences include different sentencing guidelines as well as different procedural rules. Children charged with crimes retain basic constitutional rights, such as the right to proof beyond a reasonable doubt and the right to counsel, but some public defenders also work in child protection cases, where the procedural rules may be different. The most significant difference between adult and juvenile courts lies in the goals of sentencing: the juvenile system focuses on education, treatment, and rehabilitation in the "best interests of the child;" the adult system focuses more on punishment and the protection of society.

Federal district and magistrate courts have original jurisdiction over felonies and misdemeanors under federal criminal law. United States Attorneys appointed by the President and affirmed by the Senate, together with their staff attorneys, act as the prosecutors in each federal district. Federal caseloads tend to be more manageable compared to those in state courts. This occurs in part because of the limitation to federal crimes and in part because of Department of Justice policies. Federal prosecutors also may exercise more discretion to focus their caseloads on particular issues than their state counterparts, so different federal districts may focus on quite different kinds of criminal activity.

Federal prosecutors use several well-established principles in deciding how to exercise discretion. See, e.g. Principles of Federal Prosecution, United States Attorney Manual, 9–27, available at http://www.justice.gov/usam/usam-9-27000-principles-federal-prosecution#9-27.001. At the same time, the Department of Justice also adheres to the "Petite Policy," from *Petite v. United States*, 361 U.S. 529 (1960), formally known as the "Dual and Successive Prosecution Policy." In general, this policy sets a self-imposed restriction that federal prosecutors will not prosecute federal cases based the same facts or transactions as a previous state prosecution, absent a compelling reason. The Emmett Till Unsolved Civil Rights Crime Act of 2008 offers a great example of both policies. The Act authorizes both the Department of Justice and the FBI to work with state authorities to coordinate the investigation and prosecution of Civil Rights Era homicides that occurred on or before December 31, 1969.

Starting a Case

Pick up and read any case file. It does not matter whether you are an extern at a prosecutor's or a public defender's office. As you read, ask yourself how the case began.

From Arrest to the Prosecutor's Office

Criminal cases typically start with an actual or perceived violation of a criminal statute. There is no case, however, until a specific individual is accused, and normally a case is not transferred from law enforcement to the prosecuting attorney unless the accused is "caught." Many crimes never make it into the system because no one was ever arrested. The file that you pick up most likely began with an arrest. In some jurisdictions and in some kinds of cases, prosecutors work hand-in-hand with the police from the outset. In others, prosecutors maintain a hands-off approach to the police work until the post-arrest investigation is fully completed. Keep alert to how this typically works in your jurisdiction.

Screening and Charging

Once the prosecutor receives a case, she must decide whether to start a prosecution and, if so, what charges to bring: the screening and charging stage. "Screening" refers to decisions about whether to bring charges, while "charging" refers to decisions about what charges to bring. Typically, screening and charging decisions take place at the same time. This phase is when the prosecutor's discretion, and thus her power, is at its greatest. Both screening and charging start with the prosecutor and occur in her office, although both screening and charging can be influenced by other role players, including grand juries and occasionally defendants or defense lawyers.

The screening decision is supposed to be based on the totality of circumstances. Considerations include the nature of the offense, the strength of the evidence, victim input, and the accused's criminal background and dangerousness to society. Resource allocations and docket management considerations may also come into play. Each prosecutor's office has its own standards and policies to guide screening and charging. In most cases, the prosecutor focuses most closely on what charges can be proven beyond a reasonable doubt considering the admissible evidence.[1]

Asking whether the case can be proved beyond a reasonable doubt represents a higher standard than that required by the rules of ethics. Model Rule 3.8(a) states that a prosecutor shall refrain from prosecuting a charge that the prosecutor knows is not supported by probable cause. If you extern in a prosecutor's office, try to ascertain whether the office uses a probable cause or reasonable doubt standard.

The process for screening and charging varies among jurisdictions. Some require prosecutors to start cases through grand jury indictments, while others require bills of information or accusations, and still others require a combination of both. A "bill of information" denotes a form listing the defendant and the associated charges, signed by a prosecutor and filed with the court. In many states, a prosecutor must start all felony prosecutions through a grand jury process, while others permit a bill of information for non-capital felonies carrying less than life or death sentences. In the latter case, the prosecutor may have the discretion to choose to present non-capital cases to the grand jury as well.

The extent of involvement by a defense attorney in the screening and charging process varies with the jurisdiction of the court and the resources available for criminal defense. Although *Gideon v. Wainwright* held that an indigent defendant is entitled to representation of counsel,[2] the funds available for criminal defense representation vary wildly among jurisdictions. In turn, the quality of indigent defense representation ranges from superficially processing cases and facilitating pleas to thorough, aggressive, effective, and ethical representation.

Criminal defense externs neither make screening or charging decisions nor observe prosecutors making them. However, you and your supervising attorneys will likely have the chance to challenge a faulty charging document. A wide range of potential challenges exist: failing to state the elements necessary to charge a given offense, failing properly to follow grand jury process, failing to state sufficient facts to support the charge. As a criminal defense extern, consider what went into the prosecutor's decision to charge as a way to learn, anticipate, and plan for the prosecution's actions. A good defense must understand the offense and vice versa.

A public defender extern, however, will see the impact of screening and charging decisions on the defendant. Consider a client sitting in jail. It may be the client's first time in the system; the client may have a family and a job; the client may have a good fourth amendment defense; and the client may in fact be innocent. The client may not be able to post bail. The prosecutor may have done a cursory probable cause review before charging the client. This client faces a choice: to sit in jail for months awaiting a chance to clear himself or plead guilty to get out on probation. Seen in this light, the impact of a prosecutor's screening and charging policy quickly becomes apparent.

In the words of Attorney General, Associate Supreme Court Justice and Chief Nuremberg Prosecutor Robert H. Jackson, the prosecutor "has more control over life, liberty, and reputation than any other person in America."[3] This is true for all aspects of a prosecutor's job and is especially true with regard to the screening and charging power. The prosecutor's discretion over charging amounts to unreviewable power. As a prosecutor extern you will have the unique opportunity to see this power exercised, and as a public defender extern you will have the opportunity to see the effects of how this power is wielded.

The Grand Jury

When required, the grand jury serves as the mechanism for issuing indictments and as a secondary screening device that incorporates members of the community in the charging process. It is secondary in this sense: cases go to a grand jury only after the prosecutor decides sufficient evidence exists to warrant a prosecution. Even where a jurisdiction requires that charges be brought through grand jury indictment not all cases reach this point.

When cases are brought to the grand jury, however, it is likely that the eventual indictment will mirror the charges the prosecutor sought. The overwhelming frequency with which grand juries return the charges sought by the prosecutor has led to criticism of the process and skepticism of whether the purported independence of the grand jury truly exists. It is telling that author Tom Wolfe, in his book THE BONFIRE OF THE

VANITIES, picked up on the colloquial saying that a prosecutor can have a grand jury indict a ham sandwich should she so desire.

Control over the grand jury process cuts both ways. Just as a prosecutor can persuade a grand jury to issue an indictment of her choice, she also can persuade the grand jury not to issue an indictment: a **no true bill**. Grand juries also can **pretermit** charges, which means that the grand jury neither finds probable cause nor no probable cause. Finally, a prosecutor also can choose to present evidence even-handedly, letting the grand jury make a truly independent decision about charging.

Grand jury process occurs in secret, enabling the grand jury to make decisions in a neutral and fair fashion. At the same time, that secrecy, together with the prosecutor's exclusive access, can also lead to abuse allowing a prosecutor to avoid prosecuting a high profile case or to decline charging whole categories of cases, even where probable cause to charge exists. In such cases, secrecy acts to shield the prosecutor from criticism, shifting blame to the grand jury. This secrecy can lead to public questioning of a grand jury decision even where the prosecution acts in good faith and in compliance with the highest standards.

Both prosecution and defense externs have a chance to learn from grand jury process. Learn the nuts and bolts of the process, while also remaining alert to the possibility that the mechanics you learn may not necessarily be the best or the correct way. Whatever access you have to the grand jury process, critique what you observe. Sometimes it falls to the unbiased eyes of an extern to challenge practices that might otherwise go unchallenged. Use your discretion in choosing whether to raise criticisms with your supervising attorneys, though be sure to raise them in your classroom and in your reflective writing.

Criminal Justice: The Players—The People

Many students bring with them preconceived notions about defendants and victims. Students also can bring preconceptions about judges. This section prompts you to challenge those stereotypes. If you do not challenge them, you risk adopting habitual practices that allow you to treat victims, defendants, witnesses or others unfairly, or habits that allow you to accept a system that does so.

The Defendant/Client

The defendant is the one most obviously "labeled" by the system. Not surprisingly, two different frames of mind about defendants permeate the criminal justice system: the demonized defendant; and the humanized defendant. This subsection addresses each in turn.

Demonizing the Defendant

As an initial matter, consider whom the prosecution represents: "State," "Commonwealth," "People," or "United States." Whatever the label, the prosecution may seek to inflict punishment, and in some cases execution, on a human being who, together with his or her friends and family, are part of the People whom the prosecution represent. Awareness of that reality can lead to reaffirming a prosecutor's duty to treat each defendant with fairness and dignity and respecting each defendant's legal rights.

Contrast this perspective with tactics that you may observe during your externship, whether in a prosecution or a defense office. For example, you could observe a trial in which a prosecutor uses the term "scumbag" or "sleazebag" to describe the defendant in her closing arguments. Or you could attend a trial involving allegations of truly heinous conduct in which a prosecutor may deliver gut-wrenching closing arguments demonizing the defendant as less than human. Both cases may result in convictions. You will likely walk out of that courtroom knowing in your gut that the conviction resulted at least partly from the emotions unleashed by the prosecutor.

In these cases the prosecutor has crossed a line by demonizing the defendant. The prosecution's central task does not entail demonizing the defendant but rather presenting admissible evidence supporting proof of the elements of the crime.

The use of derogatory terms inside a courtroom demonstrates a systemic failure on the part of all the stakeholders—the prosecutor's office, the defense bar, and the judiciary—to maintain a fair, ethical and professional criminal justice system. Misuse of emotion lowers the reasonable doubt standard for the jury; indeed, the more awful the facts and the more derogatory the language, the lower the standard that juries will use to convict. As a prosecutor you want the verdict of guilty to rest on the evidence, not on the manipulation of emotion.

Labeling also can skew a view of the evidence and legitimize outcomes that we otherwise would consider illegitimate. This can happen to both defense and prosecution. But the prosecutor's tremendous discretionary power greatly amplifies the impact of stereotyping. The resulting abuse tends to manifest itself more powerfully on the prosecution side.

For the prosecution extern, we encourage you not to let any labels, whether innocuous ones such as "defendant" or judgmental ones such as "criminal," permit you to forget the prosecutor's duty to ensure a fair system of justice. Prosecutors must ensure that every defendant is treated fairly, professionally, and with dignity before, during, and after every proceeding, even those that result in conviction.

A prosecutor who presents her case in a professional manner does not in any way act less zealously for her side whether termed the people, the commonwealth, the state, or the federal government. In the long run, a prosecutor who acts ethically and professionally will carry the day. If she screened and charged correctly, the defendant is guilty of the charged crime and deserves punishment. Because of the prosecutor's unique dual role as an advocate and a minister of justice, this hard fight also must be fair.

Humanizing the Defendant

- *Defense Externs and Clients*

A public defender extern has an incredible resource that is not available to a prosecution extern—clients. Understanding the individuality of clients is one of the most important learning experiences you can have. Meet as many clients as possible. Make opportunities for in-depth conversations with clients. Your client is a person with unique experience, capabilities, personality, goals, and worth. You never know who the client will be until you have talked with him or her.

- *Be Alert to Judgments About Your Client—Including Your Own*

Judgment upon judgment lies at the heart of the criminal law system. With the decision to arrest, law enforcement has judged the person. A host of subsequent judgments follow in lock-step behind the arrest. Jailors, judges, prosecutors, the media, friends and family of the accused, sometimes even the accused, make judgments based on the simple fact that an accusation has been made, well before the case is concluded. It is not surprising that clients may expect that their lawyers also have judged them, and clients may well be right.

We are in an era of mass incarceration. The U.S. imprisons more people per capita than any other country in the world. It arrests and convicts men and women, but the system is overwhelmingly used against men. It arrests and convicts people of all races, but it is overwhelmingly used against persons of color, and particularly against African-American men. The fact that we have slipped into an era of mass incarceration is evidence of how unmoored the system has become from awareness of its impact on individuals, families, and communities. This in itself should cause us to question the system's habitual practices and habitual culture. Humanizing criminal defendants, maintaining their autonomy, dignity, and individuality runs counter to the mass incarceration trend. It must be harder to do than it sounds. During your externship, you might ask the questions, "Why is that so difficult?" "Who has the power, and who has the privilege, and what are they doing with it?" "What might I do were I in their shoes?"

For most of us, it takes work and practice to be non-judgmental. See Chapter 5 on Effective Communication and Professional Relationships. After all, being a lawyer requires assessing and making judgments about the case, the evidence, and the law. Engaging in a more neutral assessment about whether the evidence will show that a client did a particular deed is different than assessing the worth of the client as a person. Clients are especially sensitive to this latter form of judgment. Others already have judged the client to be unworthy; moreover, this judgment often is the gateway to denying the client fundamental dignity and autonomy. A defense lawyer can push back against this kind of judgmental posture, first, by refusing to participate in it herself.

Examine the beliefs you develop as a result of the allegations against your client. Remember, they are allegations and nothing more. The defense attorney owes no deference to the police report or the prosecuting attorney's accusation or the grand jury's indictment. You cannot ignore the allegations, just as you cannot ignore the facts, the evidence, or the law, in order to evaluate the persuasiveness of the government's case. Assessing the other side's position, however, does not mean accepting that position as true.

You can further counteract this pressure to judge the client by seeking to understand the context of the client's life: the client's community, the client's history, the client in jail, and the client in court.

▪ *The Client's Community*

Understanding your client's community helps you to understand your client. Try to meet the client's family, partner, friends, and anyone else who knows the client. This helps to build your legal case and expands your frame of reference. Investigate the strengths and weaknesses of the client's support network—know those persons who might be an asset at a bond hearing, in plea negotiations, at trial, at sentencing, as emotional support for the client, and in other ways. Reach out to people who know your client—call them, meet them in person at their home, place of work, on the sidewalk, in the car, at the coffee shop, or at the park. In doing so, you develop valuable investigative skills and learn to individualize the client.

▪ *The Client in Jail*

If the client is in jail, go there to talk to him or her, and to see, hear, smell, and feel how it is. When the steel door closes behind you, you will not have the same feeling as a newly-arrested person may have, but you will appreciate the client's circumstance much more than you would with a telephone call, a video conference, or a letter. Go to jail as often as you can. It builds rapport. It tells your client you care. And the jail is part of your classroom: like the court, your office, or the scene of an incident.

▪ *The Client in the Court Process*

In many cases, the length of your externship will not allow you to follow one client from arrest through the end of trial. Still, go to court and watch your client, shackled and in an orange jumpsuit, beltless and baggy, standing before the judge, or sitting at the defense table during a pretrial hearing. Watch a jail calendar, where dozens of people are sent to jail or to prison. Imagine what it feels like to be one of a long list of inmates, "men in shackles, moving throughout the courtroom," as one student's journal put it. Watch every type of proceeding. Watch the defendants with private counsel and those with appointed counsel and those with public defenders. Assess how this system may reduce the client's dignity. Doing so helps you prepare to advocate for that dignity yourself.

▪ *Participant vs. Spectator*

Finally, in coming to know your client, consider whether your reactions might differ if you did not know the client. Here is how two students described the value of just getting to know clients:

To be honest, I was a little concerned about working at a public defender office. I had never been involved in criminal law in any way. I had never been arrested. I had never been to jail. None of my friends or family had ever been to jail. Walking in the jail for the first time and conducting my first interviews was a very scary time for me. I did not know what to expect. I thought most of our clients were bad people who do bad things. I could not have been more wrong. I have grown so much over the last eighteen months because of the clinic. I walk away from this experience as a better person and as a better lawyer.

—Student Journal

This year, I have had the pleasure of working at the Public Defender's office. I have seen a slew of clients who are not morally corrupt, horrible degenerates. Instead, I see mistakes. I see someone trying to get their life back, but who was with the wrong crowd. I see someone who shoplifted to pay for her children's food. I see someone who tried to get to work the next morning after a night of drinking, thinking he was okay. I see a couple who got in an argument that got too heated. I also don't kid myself that all clients are simple mistakes. I know there are people that intentionally break the law. Repeatedly. But I also realize a lot of charges are the product of bad circumstance. Several client interviews have ended with truly remorseful defendants, crying, explaining they'll never get in trouble again.

—Student Journal

Now compare those views of clients with a spectator's view, also by law students:

I arrived at the court room before the inmates, and my heart just dropped when I saw them herded in like cattle and shackled up from wrists to feet. It was particularly sad, because after sitting there a good portion of the day I learned that the crimes they were accused of were not serious or even violent. Yet, they were shackled at the wrists, waist, and feet.

—Student Journal

Not only does the county give the defendants rags that it tries to pass off as clothes, but they are chained around the feet, waist, and ankles. Further, all of this is before they have been adjudicated guilty. It begins as early as the bond hearing, where the standard is simply probable cause. They march these PEOPLE into the courtrooms and sit them before someone whose job is to judge them. That is inherently demeaning and condescending. I guess that is the nature of the criminal justice system, but there is no regard for the dignity of these individuals.

—Student Journal

The Victim

Victims and their families often comment that the criminal justice process centers on the defendant. As frustrating as it is to victims and often to prosecutors, our system focuses on the defendant. We have chosen a system of **public** prosecution on behalf of the **state** against the **defendant**. The word "victim" does not appear in that sentence. This subsection compares the role of the victim and the defendant, describes the role of victim advocates, discusses how prosecutors work with victims, and assesses the extent to which victims do or do not direct prosecutions.

Victims are not parties in criminal cases, and they are not clients of the prosecuting attorney. Though victims have come a long way since the birth of the Victims' Rights Movement four decades ago and have gained deserved respect by the criminal justice system, victims remain witnesses, not parties. The victim cannot bring a prosecution through a private attorney, sit at the prosecution table, question witnesses, including the defendant, during trial, or be a party to appellate proceedings. Interestingly, victims have these rights in some countries, particularly those operating under a civil law system. The fact that victims are not parties and therefore cannot control the course of a criminal prosecution may seem unjust to externs who have the opportunity and privilege to work with them. However, criminal law violations are prosecuted as offenses against the state. Case captions and court documents read the "state," the "people," or other terms **versus** the defendant. This may be easiest to understand in "victimless" crimes such as a drug cases, but it is equally true where there is an identifiable human victim. As a result, the role of the victim stands in stark contrast to the role of the defendant.

As a prosecution extern, you often will have the chance to work with, prepare, and counsel victims. This exposure can show you an important motivator for many prosecutors: working with and achieving restoration and justice for victims. This commitment to victims' restoration and justice includes victims across the spectrum of harm. Those who have been injured to extents unimaginable and those whose harm is minor—all deserve justice. The bond that you establish with some victims may form the most compelling experiences of your placement.

Prosecution offices are supported in this task by a victim coordinator. This role has developed to avoid past practice in which police and prosecutors had no training in working with victims and were as likely to impede victim's recovery as to foster that recovery. For instance, prosecutors might change over the duration of a case and successively ask victims to retell, and thereby relive, the traumatic events at the heart of the case. Today, prosecution offices place much greater focus on the victim's welfare by instituting practices that ensure victims remain informed and treated with dignity and respect, and by instituting "vertical prosecution" so the same prosecutor remains with a case from beginning to end.

Despite this support, the final responsibility for working with the victim in the context of the criminal case rests with the prosecutor. The prosecutor must know what the victim knows, how the victim will present such information, and how the victim will act and react in the courtroom. The prosecutor must ensure that victims are comfortable with testifying, prepare them for direct and cross-examination, and try to assure that the experience of testifying does no further harm.

The depth and extent of the interaction needed to accomplish these goals depend in large part upon the type of case. A theft of an automobile case, for example, simply demands that the victim take the stand and testify that (1) she owns the car and (2) she did not give the defendant permission to break her driver side window, stick a screwdriver in the ignition, and drive off with her car. The inconvenience caused to the victim from theft of the car is great, at least for some victims, although the loss may not cause severe or lasting emotional trauma.

By contrast, a prosecutor would engage in dramatically different preparation with a victim or victim's family of a shooting, a rape, or a homicide. Being shot or raped or having a child murdered creates a significant likelihood of severe trauma. In addition, the defense to such cases generally will require more of the victim. A car theft victim generally cannot expect much in the way of cross-examination. A rape victim likely will encounter extensive cross-examination.

Observe how prosecutors at your placement handle this aspect of their job. Where do they interview victims? How often do they do so? How early and how in close in time to the court appearance? You will find that different prosecutors have different answers to these questions.

Experienced prosecutors often go well beyond an occasional office interview, at least with compelling victims who have suffered severe injury. Some prosecutors may prefer an office setting and some the home of the victim. Many will want to meet the victim at the scene of the crime and go over the testimony there if circumstances warrant. Similarly, for certain victims—child victims in particular—a dry run of the anticipated questions may take place in the actual courtroom a week or so before the trial.

In all of this work with victims, the prosecutor must exercise great caution. By definition, victims have experienced injury when they come to you. They can be extremely vulnerable and open to suggestion. They also may develop an unhealthy hero worship of you, their prosecutor. These realities can affect the reliability of their testimony and also the quality of their experience of the justice system.

Recognize that what you tell victims may not be what they hear. As such, it is crucial that you keep your relationship with victims professional and do not cross the line into friendship. You are **the** prosecutor, not **their** prosecutor. You must ensure that when you instruct them to tell the truth, they understand that instruction and do not misread you. A professional relationship allows you to fulfill your duties as a minister of justice more easily and readily.

Recognize also that, as the representative of the state, your interests may vary from and may even be opposed to those of the victim. Indeed, your interests may conflict with other players in the criminal justice system. A police detective whom you trust may become a defendant in a brutality case. A judge on a case in which you appear may later become a defendant in a corruption case. The victim into whose case you put your sweat and heart may later testify under oath—falsely—that you told her to lie on the stand.

A final and fundamental question asks whether and to what extent victims should be involved in or even direct a prosecution. Most jurisdictions have "victims' rights" statutes, with which you should become familiar. These statutes do not create "rights;" the victim has no remedy if her wishes are not followed. Moreover, all of these statutes include language that says, in effect, that the "victim does not direct the prosecution." In other words, the prosecutor, not the victim, has the decision-making responsibility from the inception to the conclusion of a case.

With this in mind, observe what weight your office gives to the victim's wishes about the case. Ask how much victims are involved in deciding whether and how the case should be charged, whether a plea bargain should be offered, and what sentence should be recommended or imposed? Assess whether the prosecutors give different weight to different kinds of victims. The seriousness of a crime or the amount of injury will likely make a difference. You might also consider whether a victim's social status, wealth, education, race, or gender affects prosecutors' deference to the victim's wishes.

How a prosecutor and a prosecution office relate to victims reflects a policy question that falls squarely within the prosecutor's discretion. To give the victim real and enforceable rights would shift power from the prosecution to the victim. More fundamentally, it would transform the system of justice from one driven by **public** prosecutorial goals to one driven by **private** goals. You may have a hard time imagining such a system. Greater victim involvement and victim rights, however, are the norm in many nations. Just because we do things one way does not mean it is the **only** way to do things.

The Judge

Judges are important decision makers and, to be an effective advocate, it is useful to try to understand them. Your externship will provide the opportunity to observe judicial conduct directly. Often judges will greet externs with open arms; this openness is not always their attitude with lawyers. Make the most of your externship opportunity to observe and also to meet and talk with different judges.

Unlike the lawyer immersed in advocacy, another advantage of your role as extern is that you can step back and try to take an objective view of the judge and the proceedings. In court, observe everything the judge does. How does she treat lawyers, civilians, defendants, witnesses, and victims? Does she favor some lawyers over others: a familiar over an unfamiliar lawyer; a prosecutor over a defense lawyer; an older over a younger lawyer? Does the lawyer's race or gender seem to matter? What about the race or gender of the defendants, the police, witnesses, or victims? Does the judge demand respect in the sense of ritual deference, or does her conduct and comportment elicit respect? Does she model respect for others in her treatment of them? What effect does this modeling have on the atmosphere in her courtroom and the fairness of the proceedings themselves?

Do not discount your impressions because you are a student. Trust your instincts about a well-run courtroom and reflect on them later. The situations where lawyers fail to challenge criminal "justice" practices that should be changed usually occur with regard to judges and their behaviors. Here more than elsewhere, fresh eyes can see through the mantra—"that's the way we've always done it"—and reflect critically about the need for change.

Earlier we addressed the important critique that the criminal law system plays a role in creating and perpetuating disparities of race and poverty. We encourage you to observe the existing system closely with this critique in mind. A system that perpetuates disparity, even injustice, must also perpetuate itself. It must legitimize its decisions. What mechanisms does this system use to legitimize itself?

Judges are likely the most powerful actors in the criminal law world. You might consider, then, what mechanisms are employed to legitimize the judiciary. Are judges treated like regular people, or are they privileged? Does that privilege insulate them from critique? Does it serve the ends of justice or does it perpetuate the status quo? Consider for an instance what role law schools play in privileging the judiciary. Are judicial opinions granted superior status to statutory and administrative rules? Is the analysis of judicial thinking privileged over the analysis of courtroom strategy or the analysis of client counseling? Law schools see judicial clerkships as prizes for academic achievement, and the hierarchy of the courts is used to rank the importance and value of the clerkship. In a system where maintaining the dignity and autonomy of every party is the goal, does it undermine that goal to place the judge above others in the system? As you observe judges conduct business and attorneys advocate before judges, consider whether there is a conflict between the attorney's desire to please the court and the attorney's duty to advocate for her client.

In addition to these general observations, we encourage you to consider strategies for addressing two additional issues about judges: judicial bias and non-judicial temperament.

■ *Judicial Bias*

On your own and by talking with attorneys in your placement, you may well be able to determine quickly if a particular judge favors the prosecution or the defense. Talk with students and attorneys in the opposing office; you may find that they have a completely opposite impression of the judge than you do.

If possible, identify a judge who all parties agree is fair and neutral and compare that judge to one that many consider biased. How does the bias manifest itself? Are the judges' backgrounds relevant? Were they former prosecutors, criminal defense attorneys, or civil lawyers? Were they appointed or elected? We do not suggest that you challenge or try to reform a particular judge. Rather, we suggest that judicial ethics, like attorney ethics, be part of the running conversation you have in your own mind and with others. See Chapter 7 on Bias in the Legal System.

■ *(Non-) Judicial Temperament*

Another recurring issue is how to practice before a judge who lacks what is generally known as a judicial temperament, meaning a calm, even-keeled manner. Again, as with bias, talk with the attorneys in your office. They usually can identify particular judges as abusive, rude, a "screamer," moody and unpredictable, or tyrannical. Observe how various attorneys who appear before these judges handle the relevant character traits. Plan how you will act when you appear before the same or a similarly difficult judge. Keep in mind that your efforts are not about you as much as they are in the service of your client. You are working in a process that has many levels. You will want to modulate your personal feelings and reactions based upon what is best for your client or your side.

"Client-Centeredness"

Earlier in this chapter we spoke about the discipline of remaining non-judgmental toward your client. This practice forms part of a broader notion about how lawyers relate to clients, known as "client-centered representation" or "client-centered lawyering."

Lawyer-centered lawyering is an occupational hazard of the legal profession. This is legal representation where the attorney-client relationship seems centered on the lawyer, rather than the client.[4] The lawyer makes the decisions, gives the orders, controls the situation and controls the client.[5] It is the lawyer's training, judgment, prestige, and perhaps arrogance that define the case, not the client's situation and not the client. The "best interests" of the client may prevail, although the lawyer determines those "best interests." The client as an individual with dignity and autonomy tends to be ignored. For more on models of lawyer-client decision making, see Chapter 15 on Client Relationships.

Lawyer-centered lawyering poses a special risk in indigent criminal defense work, where caseloads are high and the judiciary pressures attorneys for both sides to move cases quickly. Faced with those circumstances, the lawyer-centered defense lawyer will readily negotiate pleas and advise clients to accept them without taking the time or making the effort to understand the client's perspective, needs, or goals. The idea of "client-centeredness" directly responds to this self-centered, ethically compromised model of the lawyer.[6] The term recognizes the power imbalance in the lawyer-client relationship, which can shift the center of focus away from the client. This is all the more true where clients are indigent criminal defendants, an especially powerless group.

The perception of lawyers as powerful derives from several sources. For instance, a lawyer has specialized knowledge of the law. A lawyer understands legal processes and the local decision makers and knows how to get things done within the local legal culture. A lawyer may have influence and prestige as a member of a "learned" profession. A lawyer may have a degree of affluence, especially in comparison to the indigent client. In theory, a lawyer might use the power derived from knowledge, experience, affluence, and relationships with other players in the system to benefit the client. Seen in this light, non-lawyers perceive lawyers as powerful authority figures and may hire them for this very reason. Of course, lawyers may perceive themselves this way too. The net result, however, does not empower clients; it empowers lawyers. It does so in a way that can be counter-productive to the client's autonomy, dignity, and, often, best interests.

In addition to the power imbalance within the attorney-client relationship, other forces make client-centered lawyering difficult. Judicial preferences, scheduling conflicts, the lawyer's personal needs and wants, and—especially in the case of public defenders—the pressure of excessive caseloads all shift the lawyer's focus away from the client.

Excessive caseloads affect the entire criminal law system, and they particularly make it difficult for public defenders to cultivate meaningful relationships with their clients. Clients deserve time and attention, which takes a personal effort by the defense attorney, in addition to the time required to perform factual and legal investigation, and otherwise be an effective advocate. Like judges and prosecutors, in many instances defense lawyers also feel a pressure to move cases, manage their caseloads, and get an early resolution for the client. For public defenders with excessive caseloads, however, performing the proper duties of an attorney for every client in every case can be nearly impossible. The institutional pressure to engage in "docket-centered lawyering" or "judge-centered lawyering" or even "legal-profession-centered lawyering" is tremendous.[7]

Client-centered lawyering acknowledges these pressures and reminds you that you render your service to the individual client, not to the judge, not to the prosecutor, not to the public, and not to yourself. A client-centered lawyer seeks to engage the client fully in decision-making and engage all of the legal actors fully in acknowledging the value of the defendant's autonomy and dignity.

This client-centered approach is consistent with the lawyer's ethical responsibilities and with effective advocacy. The Rules of Professional Conduct speak of the duties of advocacy and client loyalty that attach to the attorney-client relationship. Effective practice requires defense lawyers to paint a compelling picture of their clients, so that the decision maker **wants** to find in the clients' favor. Centering advocacy around a client's individuality thus has intrinsic value to the client and also has a functional impact on the case. Being client-centered also distinguishes your case from the mass of cases and your client from the mass of defendants.[8]

We mentioned at the outset that the practice of being non-judgmental is related to client-centered representation. It is related because being non-judgmental is essential to establishing trust and rapport in the attorney-client relationship. The better the relationship, the better the attorney is able to understand the client's uniqueness and portray that uniqueness to others—prosecutors, judges, and juries. Ultimately, the defense lawyer's ability not to judge the client is critical to enabling the legal system to make a proper judgment about the client. Commitment to client-centered lawyering is a value, rooted in the American legal system's respect for every individual's autonomy and dignity. Far more than a choice of style or of personal morality, it helps guarantee effective advocacy, compliance with professional ethics, and compliance with the constitutional right to counsel.

Observe and reflect on the way the lawyers at your placement relate to their clients. What values do you think underlie the way they treat clients? Do the pressures under which they operate allow them to practice consistently with these values?

> **Exercise 20.1** Many jurisdictions have established standards for defense lawyers. Many derive from the national models, such as the ABA Performance Standards for the Defense Function. With this in mind:
>
> 1. Find out whether there are specific standards that apply to your jurisdiction. Then assess the common practice in your placement office based on these standards. For instance, the ABA standards cover initial interviews and investigations. You might pick a few specific standards to compare and contrast with your jurisdiction's actual practice.
>
> 2. Does the office have caseload standards? Are they enforced? What are the caseloads in your office per attorney per year? Think about how you might best find the answers to these questions. Keep in mind that not all offices are open to this inquiry, and be sensitive to the fact that you are only a guest. At the same time, these are questions that most offices address to one degree of another, so they may be accustomed to the question.
>
> 3. What sort of training do the attorneys attend? Are there particular values that are articulated within the office? How are they reinforced?

▪ *Client-Centeredness and the Prosecutor*

As a practice and a value, client-centeredness presents a question more for the defense extern than the prosecution extern. Between prosecution and defense counsel, only the latter truly has a client in the client-centered context. As discussed above, a prosecutor has as a client the "public" on whose behalf she brings cases. Sometimes those cases will have human victims; regardless, however, the prosecutor brings the case in the name of the state, the people, the commonwealth, or the government.

A prosecutor thus does not generally have a conflict between being lawyer centered and being client centered. The prosecutor fully directs the prosecution. The prosecutor may consult the victim for input at various times and may inform the victim about their decisions and reasons. However, even when the goals of a victim and of society do not coincide, the prosecutor decides how to resolve the conflict. This authority extends both to tactics, such as who testifies at trial, and to strategy, such as whether to offer or accept a plea.

Even so, a prosecutor may face some pressures similar to those encountered by a public defender. Caseload pressures may cause the prosecutor to move cases without full investigation and preparation to clear dockets. An individual prosecutor may experience a conflict between his personal desire to spend more time on the cases of certain victims with whom he has developed a strong connection and his office's desire to move cases quickly. The proper resolution of these conflicts will likely involve conversations and even advocacy among prosecutors, including supervisors, but not between the prosecutor and victims.

This stands in stark contrast with the duty of the public defender; if her office pressures her to move cases for the sake of docket management as opposed to the choice of the individual client, the public defender must refuse. Her ultimate allegiance lies with her client and **only** her client, not her office.

Developing Lawyering Skills in Criminal Justice

Opportunities to Learn about Lawyering

You will have many chances to develop your knowledge and talents in a criminal justice placement and will encounter several ethical questions along the way. We cannot cover all of them. The following examples may help you develop learning strategies, regardless of the particular assignments or the demands of a particular case.

■ *Legal Research/Motion Drafting*

Because of caseload pressures, attorneys in both public defender offices and prosecution offices tend to focus on what the law **is**, not what the law **might be.** Your supervising attorney may need a complete brief on an issue and may ask you for in-depth research. More likely, when your supervisor asks for research, she will want a quick answer. She may know that the law is settled, and she needs only a reminder on a specific point. Make sure to clarify the depth and scope of the research assignment and the form of the work product. Doing so at the outset will go a long way toward meeting your supervisor's expectations. See Chapter 3 on Learning from Supervision on assignment clarification and Chapter 17 on Writing for Practice.

Legal research can pose ethical issues. The duties of diligence and competence, not to mention your responsibility to your client, require that research be thorough and accurate. For the defense lawyer, failures in research can have disastrous consequences for the client, may constitute ineffective assistance of counsel, and can even lead to malpractice claims. Lawyers for both sides can be subject to bar discipline. Your supervisor also owes a duty of candor to the court to disclose favorable and unfavorable law. Thorough research makes sure that you and your supervisor will comply with that duty.

Note how state criminal practice and federal criminal practice are often stereotyped, with federal practice sometimes being portrayed as higher quality and more intellectually driven. Consider the role such generalized assumptions play in, for example, (1) constructing and perpetuating the very difference they describe, (2) undermining the intellectual achievement of state judges and state criminal law practitioners, (3) undermining the intellectual accomplishment that underlies lawyering skills other than legal analysis, and (4) inculcating a sense of hierarchy about lawyers, judges, and law. Consider the role of law schools in maintaining this hierarchy. This is the sort of critical thinking we hope you will do with all of your learning—look beneath the surface at the assumptions and implications of practice, procedure, habit, and language, and understand not just the explicit conversation, but also the implicit messages, and investigate them.

■ *Witness Preparation*

Witness interviewing for the purpose of investigation and witness preparation for the purpose of testimony are separate-yet-related activities. Although you can read about handling witnesses, you will need to **watch** and **do** interviews with witnesses to become proficient. Defense attorneys do more witness interviews in the context of investigation than prosecutors because defense attorneys do not have law enforcement agencies and crime labs at their disposal in the way prosecutors do. Prosecuting attorneys do more witness preparation (which includes some interviewing) because prosecutors have the burden of proof and must present witness testimony in every case. So while defense attorneys may interview witnesses more often than prosecutors during their investigations, prosecutors likely prepare witnesses to testify more than defense attorneys. Both require skill.

We suggest that you make the most of your chance to interview/investigate or prepare witnesses. When asked to interview a witness or a victim, plan for your interview. First, study the case so you know the other witnesses, the evidence, the theory of the prosecution and the theory of the defense. Then outline the substance of what you think your interview should cover. Consider how this witness' testimony fits in the overall case presentation. Will the witness establish an element of the crime, buttress someone else's testimony, lay the foundation for an evidentiary issue, cast doubt on previous testimony or your opponent's theory, elicit sympathy for your position? How you handle your witness preparation will affect the witness's testimony, which in turn can have an enormous impact on the outcome of the trial.

Once you finalize a plan for the interview, see if you can discuss it with your supervisor. If he does the interview, speak with him afterward to ask about his reasoning for approaching the interview the way he did. If possible, observe the witness's actual testimony in court. Assess the value of the pre-trial witness preparation against how effectively your supervisor presents and handles the witness in court, how the witness testifies, and how the witness handles cross-examination. Finally, make sure to "debrief" yourself in your journal entries, reflecting on all of these aspects. Doing so will ensure that your next witness preparation will improve over your last.

■ Discovery

Both prosecution and defense externs will work on discovery: the formal exchange of information before trial. Discovery rules define the minimum level of information that your office must provide to the opposing party before trial. Read these rules. Familiarize yourself with the prosecutions' constitutional obligation to provide to the defense exculpatory or impeaching information under the *Brady v. Maryland* line of cases, and with your jurisdiction's version of Model Rule of Professional Conduct 3.8(d).[9] We strongly recommend that you read these rules even if you are told "this is how we do things here."

Because it is routine, the exchange of discovery materials tends to become rote and mechanical. Prosecution externs will likely be told "this is what we provide" and then be sent out to provide only that. Public defender externs may be charged with reviewing the discovery that has been provided and simply cataloging the information. We encourage you not to get caught in the routine. Instead, develop the habit of questioning what is provided, how it is provided, and when. For example, it is policy in some prosecution offices to provide "open file" discovery, which means that a prosecutor will turn over the entire file to the defense. If your prosecutors provide less than "open file" discovery, ask for the reasons. If they have an "open file" discovery policy, how is an "open file" defined? In both cases the prosecutor may choose to give less than all of the information in her possession to the defense. How is this approach justified? From the defense point of view, should not the defense have all of the witness statements available to the government, not just the statements of witnesses who will testify at trial? From a prosecutor's point of view, while it is true that the less the defense knows, the easier it is to convict, is a conviction fair if it is based on incomplete pre-trial disclosure?

Contesting the scope of the prosecution's disclosure can put the defense in a bind. How can you litigate a failure to disclose when you do not know what has been withheld? The defense can be faced with a conundrum: "I want what I don't have, but I can't tell you why I want it because I don't know what it is"—an argument worthy of Alice in Wonderland.

A prosecutor may have legitimate reasons to withhold discovery material. For instance, there may be a substantial risk that the pre-trial disclosure of information could lead to harm to certain victims and witnesses. The prosecutor must make an initial determination. As a matter of fairness, the prosecutor needs to notify the defense that information otherwise discoverable has been withheld, so that the matter may be submitted to a judge for a final decision. Even if a judge orders the disclosure, the prosecutor can choose not to comply if she concludes that danger to a witness or to an ongoing investigation is too great. In such a case, the prosecution can choose simply to dismiss the case.

> **Exercise 20.2** Consider the following questions: What does your state's version of ABA Model Rule 3.8(d) specify in terms of timeliness, i.e., when exculpatory material must be turned over by the prosecution to the defense so that non-disclosure does not rise to unethical conduct?
>
> - Does the rule distinguish between exculpatory material and impeaching material?
>
> - What if the exculpatory material covered by Rule 3.8(d) is not covered by your jurisdiction's regular discovery rules?
>
> - Can the prosecutor intentionally withhold exculpatory material from an initial disclosure and provide it later in the proceeding?
>
> - Finally, may a prosecutor participate in a guilty plea without providing the exculpatory material to the defense?

Full disclosure seems central to our adversarial system, where advocates on both sides seek justice based on a shared pool of information. But this sharing does not always occur, especially if the prosecution claims a proprietary interest in exculpatory material. As stated in the comments to North Dakota's version of Rule 3.8, "[d]iscovery of [exculpatory material] by the prosecutor confers no property right in the same upon the prosecutor; rather, in the interest of seeing that the truth is ascertained and all proceedings justly determined, the defense should be accorded ready access to any such information."[10] Might North Dakota be onto something? European nations seem to think so: there, all evidence collected by the state goes into a court dossier available for all to use, whether prosecution, defense, or court.

■ *Courtroom Experience*

Appearing in court, especially on contested issues, offers one of the most meaningful learning experiences in a criminal law externship. Although court is the place where trials occur, we also can describe it as a theater, where present-time actors re-enact past-time events. Of course, trials produce real outcomes, a hugely important difference from theater.

Trials often have multiple story lines, plots, and subplots. Even motions hearings and other non-trial proceedings usually involve layers of multiple and conflicting goals. Each proceeding has a formal goal—to set bond, to admit or suppress evidence, to challenge an indictment. Each proceeding will also have informal goals—goals that are distinct from the formal purpose. Consider a bond hearing. The prosecution seeks to offer sufficient evidence to convince the judge to deny bond, as well as to set the bond high enough to insure the defendant will return to court. The defense likely wants bond set low enough so that the defendant can post it and secure release. Both sides may also have additional motives. The prosecution may want to begin influencing how the judge views the defendant throughout the proceedings. By contrast, the defense may use the bond hearing as early discovery of the state's case or to question prosecution witnesses under oath, creating a record with which to impeach the witness at trial.

Similarly, in preliminary hearings, a court determines whether there is sufficient probable cause to allow the prosecution to go forward. The prosecution wants to put on as few witnesses as necessary to convince the judge. The defense wants to question prosecution witnesses and also to orchestrate the facts and the law for eventual trial. Observing these hearings offers a tremendous introduction to multiple strategies that may be in play during specific criminal proceedings.

Whether prosecution or defense, try to get into court as often as you can. You will likely find that the prosecutor does more direct examinations while the defense has more opportunities to cross-examine witnesses. Conducting a compelling direct examination is vitally important. And yet, delivering an effective cross-examination is, in many ways, the epitome of courtroom performance. Some argue that public defenders have the best opportunity to hone that skill. See if you can identify the differences between masterfully and effectively cross-examining a scared, nineteen-year-old defendant as opposed to a thirty-year veteran homicide detective.

Developing Case Theory

Developing case theory can be a core learning experience in a criminal law externship. This section describes what "case theory" is, discusses how to develop it, and highlights its distinctive features for both defense and prosecution attorneys.

In litigation, the outcome turns on the description of past events. Accordingly, an effective advocate must develop a coherent narrative of those events, one that is legally viable, factually supportable, and emotionally compelling. We use the term "case theory" to refer to this coherent narrative. Case theory is not a theme or a catchphrase; rather it is a story that explains the evidence in a way that is consistent with the facts and the law, and is persuasive to the decision maker.

Lawyers start to develop case theory from the moment they start work on a case, although the initial theory should remain fluid and open to change as the lawyer investigates the facts and appreciates the relationship between those facts and the law. Case theory does not trump facts, nor is a story brought forth from the imagination. Facts support and shape theory, as do the legal elements in the case and the overall persuasiveness of the story. Case theory responds to the facts in evidence, to the law, and to their combined impact on the decision maker.

The prosecutor has the burden of proof "beyond a reasonable doubt," so you might think that only the prosecutor needs a theory of the case. You might think that the defense needs only to poke holes in the government's case and argue "reasonable doubt." This may work in some cases, with some juries. However, experienced defense lawyers know that they create reasonable doubt more effectively by presenting a positive alternative to the government's story of what happened. That positive alternative is the defense theory of the case. Presenting a strong case theory gives jurors a reason to doubt the prosecution's story on the merits, not just as a technical matter. Jurors want to believe they are doing the right thing. They more easily equate the "right thing" with innocence if they have an alternative narrative that leads to the belief that the government has erred. While foundational, reasonable doubt alone has limited persuasive value. It needs case theory to resonate with the jury.

Moreover, the fact that few criminal cases actually go to trial does not make case theory irrelevant. Though most criminal cases are resolved through a plea bargain or are dismissed, having a compelling case theory is instrumental to plea bargaining and to sentencing advocacy. Indeed, opposing counsel can be as much the target audience for a theory of the case as a judge or a jury. Similarly, assessing the strengths and weaknesses of the opposing side's theory helps the lawyer to appreciate what the opposing attorney will accept during negotiation. Observe how your office develops case theory. Talk to your supervising attorneys about how they develop case theory, recognizing that they may use different terms for the concept. See if you can participate in group discussions about how to present a case, both formal and informal. While lawyering requires case theory, some lawyers and some offices emphasize it more than others. You will be able to discern what emphasis your office or supervising attorney gives to case theory development by speaking with them. The point is not to judge what they do, but to find out what they do and to participate in it if possible.

■ *Brainstorming Case Theory*

Developing case theory has some distinct phases a lawyer can use when working a case. This approach entails a structured sequence of questions: explaining the known facts; identifying new and unknown facts for investigation; researching and assessing the law; and constructing case theory. This sequence works best if you allow your ideas to flow freely and without judgment, so as to encourage creativity and thoroughness. Eventually you will narrow the theories after you have explored a wide range of possibilities.

We encourage you to see this as a disciplined practice, in which non-judgmental and creative exploration can lead you to rethink a case to make your representation more effective. This practice has value for both defense attorneys and prosecutors. For example, many wrongful convictions occur when law enforcement narrows the focus to a single suspect too early in the process, jumping to conclusions and ignoring evidence that points to the real perpetrator.

Actual cases of wrongful convictions and the investigations and trials that led to them are numerous. An excellent catalogue of actual innocence cases is included in the website of The Innocence Project at Cardozo School of Law at Yeshiva University in New York City, http://www.innocenceproject.org/. Among other things, Cardozo's Innocence Project operates as a clinical program for Cardozo law students.

■ *Assess the Known Facts*

In this step, the lawyer or student handling the case presents the facts as she knows them. You should do this without reference to the law; focus instead on the factual events, free of the required elements. Keeping the law out of it poses difficulties for law students and lawyers, who are trained to keep the law in it. Letting the facts come through unfiltered by the law has real benefits in terms of understanding the power of facts, identifying missing information, or developing different versions of events.

What is the difference between a factual conclusion and a legal conclusion? "She acted in self-defense" is a legal conclusion. "She stabbed him" is a factual statement. "She stabbed him because she was afraid for her life" is also a factual statement, even if it might lead to a legal conclusion. Appreciating the difference between facts and law is important for the development of case theory, and for understanding how facts, rather than law, are used to create a narrative.

■ *Develop Additional Information*

In this step, the lawyer asks questions about what she knows and starts to evaluate the value of known facts to the case. Flesh out all of the facts: good facts, bad facts, neutral facts, and questions about facts. Do not censor your questions; there are no "stupid questions." The questions that you do not ask may be exactly the questions that will trouble a jury or a judge or your adversary.

It can be especially helpful to work this step in a group, either informally or in a staff meeting. One lawyer may not find a line of questioning to be important, while another may think the opposite. Bring a non-judgmental mindset to this discussion; doing so can reveal lines of factual inquiry that you might have dismissed. Assume that the person with the initial story does not necessarily know all of the facts.

Group brainstorming this discussion has value because a group includes people with different life experiences. People interpret facts differently, want answers to different questions, and respond differently to the same story. For example, one person may find a police officer's manner intrusive and insulting, while another person sees it as an appropriate exercise of authority.

As another example, people read different intentions into a defendant's flight from a police officer. The killing of a young, unarmed African-American man by a police officer in Ferguson, Missouri, in 2014, and the leaving of the young man's body on public display for hours after the shooting provides a tragic example. Different people read very different meanings into this incident. As theories of what happened and why develop, even subconsciously, seeking and respecting differences in opinion helps you keep open valuable lines of inquiry.

As you question the facts that you know, make sure to consider the **emotional theory** of the case. Here, focus on what features of the case might move people to find in favor of one side or the other. What about the circumstances leading to the charges would make people want to find for the client? What is it about the client, no matter how attenuated from the charges, that might compel people to find in his favor? Is that evidence admissible? Is there something about the government's witnesses that might make the client look sympathetic?

Acknowledging the emotional component of any factual presentation is part of the objective assessment of the facts. Injecting emotion where it does not exist raises ethical concerns. However, the presence of honest emotion is a fact and an emotional theory of the case is a component of a well-constructed factual theory. Judgment is a function of heart and mind working together, and lawyers understand that legal decision-making can have an emotional component. In this sense, judgment has much in common with all other decision-making.

■ *Identifying Legal Theory*

In this step, try out different legal theories with as little self-censorship as possible. From the defense point of view, consider all available legal theories as useful, from the failure of the prosecution to prove an element of the offense to the availability of an affirmative defense. Unlike factual development where you consciously omit the law, here facts need to be considered with the law from the outset. Moreover, you will find it useful to consider not only your own legal theories, but those of your opponent, at a minimum to see whether you can contest the legal sufficiency of their case.

In this phase, it is also useful to explore theories about evidence, meaning the information likely to be admitted at trial. See how every piece of evidence fits or does not fit a theory of the case. Does it help the prosecution prove an element of an offense? Does it help the defense prove an element of an affirmative defense? Does it disprove the prosecution's theory? The defense theory? Does it undercut the credibility of a witness? The theory of the case needs to accommodate and respond to all of the evidence to be introduced by either side.

■ *Stating a Case Theory*

Considering the facts, the emotional impact, and the law puts you in a good position to create a case theory. Working through this process allows you to create a narrative that accommodates all the facts, favorable and unfavorable, facts beyond change and facts open to interpretation. You can develop a narrative that is consistent with a theory of innocence or a theory of guilt.

Your office may use the method described above. If it does, try to participate actively both on your own and in-group discussions. If it does not, you can still use this method on your own, whether developing your own cases or assessing others. Use these ideas or methods in working with your supervisors, especially if they welcome your initiative. Organize a brainstorming session with fellow students in the office. Our fundamental point is that effective attorneys construct case theory.

Case Theory in the Prosecutor Setting

Prosecutors also must develop case theory. However, the prosecutor faces unique realities in how cases come to her office and how she can develop them, which temper her ability to develop theory in some ways and, in others, make the process even more crucial.

A prosecutor's case theory is both linked to and limited by what she can charge and prove. In many cases the prosecutor may believe that the accused has acted in a certain way but lacks enough admissible evidence to prove it beyond a reasonable doubt. In such cases, she should decline to prosecute. In other cases, the prosecutor will have sufficient admissible evidence to support her theory and bring charges. Once she does, absent new evidence, she is bound exclusively to this initial theory.

Given this set of limitations, the prosecutor has to develop her theory after in-depth investigation yet before she brings charges. The prosecutor has a duty to bring only those charges that she **knows** she can support with admissible evidence.

Consider a scenario where the facts and admissible evidence support two alternate and mutually exclusive theories. In this situation the prosecutor cannot proceed under one theory and then, after acquittal or a hung jury, try the second theory in the retrial. Similarly, there are serious due process concerns that limit the circumstances in which a prosecutor can proceed under one theory of the case against one defendant and then proceed under a conflicting theory of the case in a separate trial against a second defendant. This practice often leads to public outrage and rebukes from appellate courts. In some cases, this dilemma will mean that the prosecution cannot proceed and that some defendants may go unpunished for their conduct, an undesirable but necessary result of the values underlying the rules.

Prosecutors routinely develop case theories and continuously need to question the known facts, the unknown facts, the emotional impact, and the legal elements of their cases. But the prosecutor is more constrained by the facts than the defense. While the defense may not present a theory they know to be false, they may question and challenge the state's case, including presenting alternate theories even when those may not be supported by the facts. The prosecutor may not.

The key consideration is what the prosecutor "knows" to be true. In most cases, a prosecutor does not objectively know what happened; she only knows what the facts tell her happened. What a prosecutor **knows** rests in turn on the facts given to her by law enforcement. The danger exists that the prosecutor's initial interpretation of these facts becomes cemented in her mind as the **truth**. The prosecutor must take care to avoid accepting law enforcement's theory without question. This acceptance can happen even in the face of other more plausible theories of the case, including those leading to lesser offenses or even actual innocence. The prosecutor must at all times engage in rigorous process of case theory development, especially the process of developing additional information.

Ethical Dimensions of Criminal Justice Practice

The rules of ethics define boundaries and aspirations both for what happens in and outside of the courtroom; think carefully about what you observe in both contexts. In open court, while ethical concerns abound, the lawyer's conduct can be more easily observed and assessed. Out of court, it is likely that only the lawyer will know if an ethical shortcut was taken, so out of court practice requires that lawyers be especially watchful for ethical dilemmas. Recognizing ethical issues requires both knowledge and trust in your own instincts. In many cases, you will "know it when you see it"—or feel it in your gut—in the sense that your intuition will send the alarm that you are close to an ethical boundary. Trust this intuition as a starting point; there is likely to be a reason for your discomfort. But do not assume either that you will intuitively recognize all ethical lapses or that your own gut feelings are consistent with what the rules might require. Some issues are complicated, others are specialized, and others can creep into established practice so slowly that you are not aware of them. Once you recognize an issue, dealing with it can require more than good intuition and disciplined analysis. It also may require the courage to challenge practices that an attorney or an office has accepted without question.

A criminal law practice is fraught with ethical concerns; this chapter cannot hope to cover them all. For some common issues, see Chapters 9 to 13 on Professionalism and ethical issues in externships. In the meantime, consider the following two situations as typical of some special concerns in criminal justice practices.

First, say a witness initially expresses uncertainty about her identification of the defendant. After the interview with your supervising attorney in a prosecution office, the witness walks out 100% certain of her identification. You have cause for concern, but you need to know more. Your supervisor may be very adept at interviewing witnesses; after a careful and restrained interview, the witness remembers the incident with more certainty. But what if your supervising attorney told the witness two other witnesses also selected the accused, or as part of the interview process, shared the defendant's long criminal history? Or, what if the change occurred after the witness reviewed her grand jury testimony or other grand jury witnesses' testimony? Answers to these questions may give you cause for concern. Make sure that you distinguish carefully between concern for the witness' reliability and concern about an ethical lapse by the attorney.

Take another example. An alleged victim in a domestic violence case walks into a public defender's office and announces she wants to drop charges against your client. You could draft an affidavit for the witness to sign and thank her, or you could question the witness more thoroughly and try to determine whether she is being coerced to take this position. Do you have an obligation to do the latter? Recognize that the prosecution makes the decision to drop the case, not the victim. Both good practice and the obligation of zealous advocacy may require that you question the witness to determine whether she is credible and genuine in her resolve to end the prosecution.

Domestic violence cases are difficult for both prosecution and defense. As a defender, you may encounter a domestic violence victim who comes to your office to drop charges. Some will do so under their own volition; others will be acting under duress or coercion. As a prosecutor, you may also have to grapple with victims who want to drop charges. Does your supervising attorney accede to the victim's wishes or continue with the prosecution, compelling the victim to testify at the expense of the victim's autonomy and dignity? In either case, observe how your supervisor handles the situation and ask him why she chose the path she did. These kinds of problems illustrate the seriousness and difficulty of domestic violence cases and the need for additional reading and training if you want to work in this area.

In both scenarios, there may or may or may not be clear right and wrong answers. At this stage of your learning experience, it is useful to focus on how to recognize potential issues and how to articulate the ethical rules that apply. Discuss them with both your supervisor and your externship teacher. You may receive conflicting answers, though the effort will sharpen your ability to handle ethical issues in the future.

Judges also can play a role in identifying and handling ethical lapses by attorneys who appear before them. For example, a court may have ruled that a prosecutor failed to turn over exculpatory material, in violation of *Brady*. Observe the trial judge's actions towards the prosecutor who erred. Does she take any action and if so, what? For another example, consider "meet 'em and plead 'em" representation, when a public defender meets a client for the first time in the courtroom and pleads him guilty after a five-minute conversation. The plea bargain may be a good one, in the sense that the same result would have occurred after more thorough legal work by the lawyer. But the situation is fraught with ethical challenges. Consider the judge's role in this practice and whether that role might impede the judge from inquiring into the ethics of the attorney.

Excessive Caseloads

Earlier we discussed the impact of excessive caseload on the defense lawyer's relationship with her client. Here, we discuss the effects of caseloads on standards of practice for both prosecution and defense.[11]

Excessive caseloads implicate the most fundamental Rules of Professional Conduct, including the duties of diligence and competence and the duty to communicate with the client. The conflict of interest rules come into play, as do the rules on supervising and subordinate attorneys.[12] Public defender offices typically represent all of the indigent criminal defendants in their jurisdiction. Unlike private lawyers, they do not have the option of rejecting a case. Many jurisdictions have adopted the ABA standard of 150 felony cases per year per attorney, including cases that plead out. But felony caseloads two, three, or four times that number are common. The situation is often the same or worse in misdemeanor and juvenile courts.[13]

■ *Excessive Caseloads as Conflicts of Interest*

Typically, public defender offices do not handle cases where there is a conflict of interest between clients.[14] Many lawyers, however, do not conceptualize excessive caseloads as causing a conflict of interest, though they clearly do. Excessive caseloads limit the time an attorney can devote to any one client. The time it takes to represent existing clients can leave no time to represent new clients; nonetheless, the attorney continues to receive new clients. Representation of the new clients suffers because of the attorney's work for the large number of existing clients.

An attorney with fifty clients on an arraignment calendar might well decide that she cannot speak to any of them before arraignment. Instead, she might rely on speaking with them briefly in court. At that time a client may quite rationally decide to accept a plea agreement, especially one that allows release of the client that day with a sentence of probation or credit for time served. The plea will be entered; the sentence imposed; and the case will be closed.

Consider the work that the attorney did not do:

- Investigate the factual basis for the charges;

- Review the reliability of the state's evidence;

- Assess the admissibility of evidence;

- Identify valid constitutional issues that might affect the outcome;

- Review mitigating facts related to the charged event or to the defendant;

- Investigate how collateral consequences might change the client's decisions or the prosecutor's position on sentencing; and

- Counsel the client in regard to all of the above.

The lawyer might have given advice that produced the same result as would have happened after doing all this work. But in the meet 'em and plead 'em situation the advice itself is speculation—at best, an educated guess. Regardless of the reasons, the client's decision will not have been reached after advisement from a well-prepared attorney.[15] This is not ethical legal representation. Would anyone hire a private lawyer to do this little?

Consider an example of the impact thorough investigation can have on the case.

A public defender asked an externship student to help with a probation revocation hearing scheduled for the following day. The client was in jail without bond and was alleged to have violated his probation by failing to report to his probation officer and pay required monthly installments on his fine. The probation officer and the prosecutor were seeking revocation of the client's probation and that he serve the remaining two months of his sentence in jail.

During an interview at the jail, the client told the student that he had a medical condition. Believing that the condition might help the client, and with the client's permission, the student went to the man's apartment to retrieve medical records. The records from a Veteran's Administration hospital included the fact that the client was a U.S. Army veteran who received two bronze stars for heroic action on the battlefield during two tours of duty in Vietnam. The client never mentioned it, nor had he been asked.

The student realized the profoundly persuasive impact of this military service, even though it was decades past. The student gave copies of this record to the prosecuting attorney and the probation officer. Both agreed not to revoke the defendant's probation and recommended that the defendant be released from further probation altogether. The judge agreed with this position, largely due to the client's military service. The client was released from jail, his probation was terminated, and he was released from the obligation to pay the fine.

While this scenario, a true story, raises serious questions about the criminal law system, for present purposes it illustrates the importance of fact investigation. The adversarial system relies on both parties to develop facts and arguments and to present them persuasively.[16] In this case, without a meeting with the client, the defense would not have known about the client's military service and would not have had the record available as evidence. The availability of a student extern was serendipitous; assigning this student to the case was random. Without this rudimentary investigation, the adversarial system would fail to function, and the attorney would violate the duties of competence, diligence, and communication. Had the case gone badly, this would likely have been the result of the attorney's excessive caseload—the attorney's work on some clients' cases prevented her from fulfilling her ethical duties to other clients.

■ *Excessive Caseloads and the Defense Attorney*

Working in a public defender office gives you the opportunity to observe and experience how the office approaches the issue of excessive caseloads. You can consider how caseloads affect public defenders' practice as well as their lives. How do public defenders stay client-centered, survive, and thrive in their practice and avoid burnout? For example, how do caseloads affect plea bargaining, the single most common resolution for criminal cases? Are the attorneys able to avoid taking shortcuts that imperil effective representation?

Workload can affect defense attorneys themselves. Except for verdicts of not guilty and cases that are dismissed, the end of a case for the attorney signals the beginning of punishment for the client. The length and type of punishment varies immensely with the offense, but all punishment, just or otherwise, involves the intentional infliction of suffering. Defense attorneys watch their clients accept punishment week after week and year after year, a reality that takes its toll. Attorneys may feel they shoulder some of the responsibility for that suffering.

This serial enactment of punishment, exacerbated by excessive caseloads, can have profound effects on attorneys. To survive, attorneys may put psychological distance between themselves and their clients, using labels and stereotypes to create that distance. Attorneys can also dial back the intensity of their advocacy. You might ask how public defenders stay on top of their game after repeatedly witnessing the punitive hammer of the state pounding their clients. How do they prevent themselves from being worn down by the system?

You can sort out these questions by talking with your supervisors and helping with their cases. You may need to buy them a cup of coffee and catch them when they have the time and willingness to reflect. See if you can talk to many lawyers, older and younger, including those handling juvenile cases, misdemeanor cases, and serious felony cases. You also can read what some lawyers have written on the subject.[17] Be alert to the fact that public defenders, like anyone else, may be sensitive to the implied criticisms. See Chapter 25 on Work & Well-being for general strategies that can help with self-care in the face of these challenges.

> What is the duty of a prosecutor who observes that a defense attorney is ineffective because of excessive caseload? Can or should the prosecutor take advantage, or does the prosecutor have a duty to ensure the defendant has effective representation? What would you do if you were the prosecutor in the infamous Sleeping Attorney case from the Fifth Circuit? For background, read *Burdine v. Johnson*, 262 F.3rd 363 (5th Cir. 2001).

▪ *Excessive Caseloads and the Prosecutor*

Excessive caseloads pose different questions for prosecutors. Unlike the public defender and the judge, a prosecutor serves as the gatekeeper for the number of cases coming into the system. Through the screening and charging power, the prosecutor can influence the ebb and flow of crimes accepted for prosecution. In a real sense, the prosecution sets caseloads for themselves and for all the participants in the criminal justice system.

The prosecutor also can affect the time spent on such cases once they enter the system. A prosecutor who devotes time to investigating cases at the screening and charging stage can ensure that she brings only provable cases for prosecution. When this screening happens at the inception of the case, other participants, including defense attorneys and judges, have to expend less effort in those cases.

Excessive caseloads can have a powerful effect on this screening function. They will lead to more unsuccessful prosecutions. They will increase the length of time cases stay on the docket, thereby increasing caseload for the entire system. They can affect the prosecutor's ability to act as a minister of justice and to ensure fairness.

It may seem that prosecutors simply cannot use their screening power to lessen caseloads. But, prosecutors have several means to screen in a way that lowers caseloads. For example, prosecutors can shift resources to the charging and screening stage, weeding out a larger percentage of arrests from becoming prosecutions. Too many prosecutors let police arrests and investigations dictate what prosecutions to bring. Under such a system, a majority of cases tend to be over-charged, in terms of the severity (vertical over-charging) and number of charges (horizontal over-charging). This over-charging shifts the serious assessment of cases until formal charges are brought and public defenders are appointed. In effect, initial case assessment is shifted to defense attorneys, who, with their investigation and plea suggestions, cause the prosecutor to revisit his case assessment, often resulting in a reduction in the types and the number of charges. A process called **hard charging** offers a workable alternative. Under this approach, the prosecutor intensively investigates all cases the police bring, not just major crimes such as rapes and homicides. The prosecutor brings only the **appropriate** charges, based upon what the prosecutor can prove successfully beyond a reasonable doubt. In theory, prosecutors who institute hard-charging as a policy also adopt a no-plea bargain policy; because the cases are appropriately charged at the outset, the defendants' only options should be to plead guilty as charged or go to trial. This approach can mean that a much higher percentage of arrests will never reach the formal prosecution stage, decreasing the subsequent caseload for prosecutors as well as for judges and defense lawyers. Hard charging occurs to some extent on the federal level and can be successfully implemented on the state level.[18]

As a matter of policy, a prosecution office can decide not to prosecute certain types of cases. In doing so, the prosecutor uses her executive branch discretion to act as a de facto legislative power. The fact the legislature criminalizes certain conduct does not impose on the executive branch the obligation to prosecute every instance of such conduct. The prosecutor has the power and the duty to use government resources wisely and effectively, so prosecutorial discretion includes the power to say no even to provable cases. Excessive caseloads provide an additional reason for a prosecutor to decline cases. For example, on both resource and policy grounds a prosecution office might decline low level drug offenses or divert them to a fine-only status offense.

Public opinion also can have an impact on prosecutorial decision-making. The more serious the crime, the less leeway the prosecutor has to decline to prosecute without push-back from her constituency—for the simple reason that the electorate pays more attention to the serious cases. While this may reflect the political accountability of the democratic process, it can also create tension between the attorney's obligation to act independently and in good faith, and the political realities of maintaining public support for re-election.

Criminal Justice in Context

How we handle criminal justice affects more than the individuals caught up in the system; it impacts and shapes our society. The United States today has a higher incarceration rate per 100,000 people than any other country, a rate that is more than five times that of most other countries. Moreover, this rate of incarceration perpetually demonstrates a dramatic racial disparity. More African-Americans have been under sentence in the current era of mass incarceration than were subjected to American slavery.

But statistics do not paint the picture nearly as well as will your experience as an extern working in the criminal law system. You can see criminal defendants and get to know them, their families, and their friends. You can witness the impact that a single criminal prosecution has on the individual and the community. For students placed in public defender programs, exposure to this human story, one person at a time, frames a compelling picture. Similarly, for students placed in prosecutor offices, juxtaposing a single drug prosecution with the knowledge of the overall effect drug prosecutions have on our society may well lead to soul searching.

The system has many other effects on our society, based on gender, age, mental capacity, and similar realities. This section focuses on only two: the effects based on poverty; and the effects based on race.

Poverty

The vast majority of criminal defendants are poor. Eighty percent of defendants are indigent and must depend on the government to provide the assistance of counsel. Governments—local, state, and federal—do so with reluctance, if they do it at all. Both prosecution and defense externs have a chance to understand the role of poverty in the criminal law system. This understanding certainly includes the structure of indigent defense administration. It also includes other effects, direct and collateral, on the lives of defendants and victims.

Crime as a whole places a much heavier toll upon the poorer sectors of society than upon the wealthier parts. Consider a single mother and sole family breadwinner faced with the theft of her car. The costs of that theft ripple outwards to loss of transportation, loss of a job, and possible eviction from housing. Also, simply coming to court or going to the prosecution office can cost days of work. Just as the criminal justice system overall disproportionately affects poorer defendants, the criminal conduct of defendants has a disproportionate effect on poorer victims.

Poverty is shorthand for a life where the balance between opportunities for success and opportunities for failure weighs heavily toward failure. As Stephen Wexler put it:

> Poor people do not lead settled lives into which the law seldom intrudes; they are constantly involved with law in its most intrusive forms. . . . Poverty creates an abrasive interface with society; poor people are always bumping into sharp legal things. The law school model of personal legal problems, of solving them and returning the client to the smooth and orderly world in television advertisements, doesn't apply to poor people.[19]

What follows are some suggestions about how to learn about the sharp edges of the criminal justice system as it affects the poor.

■ Observe Court

Go to court on a busy arraignment day. Most state courts schedule fifty to one hundred arraignments or pleas on the same day. Pay particular attention to defendants who have no bond set at all or who do not have the assets to post bond. Watch the differences in the treatment of defendants who were released on bond and those who are still incarcerated. You may find that those with assets receive different treatment than those without.

■ Understand the Appointment Process

How do indigent defendants request counsel? How soon do they first see their lawyers—not a paralegal or an investigator or a student extern, but a lawyer? You may have to talk to several people to get answers. If you are a public defender extern, ask some criminal defendants as well, when you can do so in conjunction with your externship. How do defendants describe the representation they receive from the public defender office? In an era of consumer research, there is startlingly little research on indigent defense representation that asks for the opinions of the consumer—indigent defendants.

■ *How Much Does It Cost to Be a Criminal Defendant?*

Consider the following list:

· paying a bonding company

· paying for health care in jail

· paying for items at the jail commissary

· paying fees to apply for indigent defense

· paying probation supervision fees

· paying fines and fees attached to fines

· paying for phone calls from the jail

· missing work to go to court.

Assess the amount of these various charges and make sure to ask who profits from them—i.e., where does the money go? For instance, inmates in jail often pay exorbitant phone rates. Who profits from the contracts with the telephone service provider? You will not find information about the flow of money collected in any one place; you will have to investigate the system to find the answers. Watch sentencings where fines and fees are imposed. Talk to lawyers, defendants, probation officers, and judges. Talk to jailers. Talk to probation officers about these costs, and if you are a public defender extern, talk to your clients and to clients' family members, provided this line of inquiry is approved by your supervising attorney.

Often defendants simply cannot pay for these things and their inability to pay results in returning to jail or staying in jail until the case is resolved. As part of your work in a defense externship, you may interview a client to determine financial eligibility. This interview is a good place to develop insight into defendants' financial stability or fragility.

■ *Investigate the Collateral Consequences of Conviction*

The effect of a criminal conviction extends far beyond the actual sentence. It can affect employability, driver's licenses, and eligibility for food stamps, public housing, and federal student loans. It can harm chances for admission to post-secondary education, and can harm eligibility for a professional or trade license, military enlistment, permanent immigration status, and even continued residence in the United States. The law imposes some of these consequences, but many reflect decisions by private individuals and corporations. These can affect how you counsel a client about the impact of a conviction. You need to know the law and also to understand actual practices, especially where decisions are left to the discretion of private actors or local officials.

> *One of the toughest things I have had to come to terms with this semester is that the amount of money one has really affects one's success and treatment in the criminal justice system. Although I have done criminal defense work for the past two years, working with clients in the clinic exposed me to a different segment of society—the impoverished, the homeless, and the underprivileged. At the private defense firm where I worked, clients paid absurd amounts of money to retain a defense attorney and were almost always able to post bond when bail was set. Working at the public defender office through the defense clinic, far too often I have seen bail set for clients at an amount too high for the client to afford, thus forcing the client to remain in jail. At countless jail calls, clients would be locked up for violating the terms of their probation, which many times involved the clients failing to pay their supervision fees or fines. Frequently, clients would have their probation revoked and be released from jail on the condition that they pay a certain fine before release. I was shocked the first time I helped a client who needed to call someone to pay probation 70 dollars before he could be released from jail. I figured that would be easy and the client would be released that day. Unfortunately, I was wrong. For a lot of people 70 dollars would not seem impossible to scrounge up in order to get out of JAIL; however, for a lot of our clients it is.*

> —Student Journal

Recognizing Race in the Criminal Law Externship

The issue of race pervades the criminal law system in the United States. Racial disparity is reflected in every stage of the process. The rate of stops, of frisks, searches, arrests, pre-trial detention, filing of formal charges, and sentencing consistently reflect racial disparity. The criminal justice system brands brown- and black-skinned people, mostly younger men, with convictions at a much higher rate than it does white people. Author Michelle Alexander titles this "The New Jim Crow," placing the racial disparity in an American tradition of racial discrimination dating back to the beginning of the country and arguing that over time racism merely takes different forms as law, culture, and practice evolve.[20]

We strongly recommend that you consider race if you want to look closely and critically at the criminal law in operation. You have a great opportunity to view the system's racial disparity close up through your externship. It is important to think deeply about race, and to appreciate that racial issues in the United States encompass different races, languages, cultures, histories, and regions of the country, and that the experience of race is both individual and collective. Further, recognize that, while racial disparity is undeniable, economic disparity is equally stark. The intersection of race and poverty is at the center of the map drawn by criminal law.

Make no mistake: you will encounter significant barriers. First, 21st century law is race-neutral on its face and its language is color-blind, even where its impact is not. This use of legal language stripped of references to race creates a dilemma. You can sit through an entire day of courtroom proceedings where nearly all of the defendants are persons of color. And yet, often you will hear not a single word that refers to race. Prosecutors can proceed without reference to race; defense lawyers can represent defendants without reference to race; judges can convict and sentence without reference to race. You face the challenge of finding a voice and a forum for talking about race within the formal legal system.

Second, the quest for race neutrality has left many people uncomfortable talking about race. As a result many people, and white people especially, stay away from the conversation. By not talking about race, we lack practice in speaking about it. This failure to create a dialogue about race contributes to a failure to think deeply about racial issues. Too often, when you inquire of regular actors—lawyers, judges, probation officers, police, and even defendants—you will find that they are inept at the conversation and stressed and uncomfortable in the attempt. This is especially true where the participants are not all the same race; cross-racial conversation is often the hardest and most avoided. You will face the challenge of getting comfortable with the conversation, or getting comfortable with being uncomfortable, and helping others do the same.

Third, you will face the challenge of developing empathy and understanding for persons of different racial experiences than yourself. We emphasize racial experiences because you cannot make assumptions about a person's experience based on racial appearance alone. This challenge reaches well beyond race to any number of possible variables—gender, language, age, religion, ethnicity, immigration history, to name a few. Here the challenge is presented by what might be called the intersection between race and individuality, the intersection of race with the sum total of a person's experiences. For more on cross-cultural understanding, see Chapter 6 on Navigating Cultural Difference and Chapter 7 on Bias in the Legal System.

Fourth, you face the challenges associated with discretionary decision making in the criminal law system. By definition, law does not control discretionary decisions tightly. It only regulates them on distant margins. These discretionary decisions include those by judges on the record with clear-cut findings of fact and conclusions of law. Many such decisions occur when they are hard to observe and assess: the assignment of law enforcement resources to certain neighborhoods, the individual police officer's decision to stop one car and not the next, the decision to arrest rather than to warn, the prosecutor's screening and charging decisions, a judge's decision to believe certain witnesses and doubt others during a motion to suppress, a judge's decision to set bond, the selection of jurors and the exercise of peremptory strikes, the framing of conduct as threatening or as reasonable self-defense, the approach to cross-examining a witness, the judge's decision to sentence to prison or probation, and many others.

Race-based decision making operates throughout this system of discretionary judgments. Discretionary decisions involve both conscious and unconscious influences. Typically, the fact that it is discretionary means that no explanation for a particular decision need be given. The decision maker does not have to articulate a rationale, publicly or privately. The aggregate sum of these decisions tells a racial story—a story about which the individual decisions are silent. Piercing this silence is the fourth challenge.

Talking about race is a lawyering skill: across races and classes, over time, with agility and empathy, in depth, and with an appreciation for its power to influence others. We encourage you to make this skill a specific focus and learning goal. If you do, you will end up well ahead of where you started. The criminal law system is a major player in the historical and ongoing racial narrative. Learning to navigate that narrative is essential lawyering.

Conclusion

Working in a criminal justice externship allows you to deal with people and with the things people do to one another on a fundamental and visceral level. You will seldom find a boring case. Even the most repetitive, plain, and simple case can prove fascinating when you peel away its many layers, not just in that one case but as a marker for the systemic effect of the law in our society. Make the most of your immersion—learn how this system breathes, operates, and functions. As you do, make sure to question, challenge and reflect upon what you have observed and done. If you think critically and with an open mind, you will not just have learned **how to** act in this system. You will have opened a window into **why** the system functions as it does. Both are important. You may want to focus more on the **how to** part. But it is the **why** part that will remain with you throughout your life.

ENDNOTES

1   For some guidance in terms of the prosecutor's role in charging, *see* ABA PROSECUTION STANDARDS 3-3.4 (Decision to Charge) and 3-3.9 (Discretion in the Charging Decision), as well as the NAT'L DIST. ATTORNEYS ASS'N'S NAT'L PROSECUTION STANDARDS 42.3 (Factors to Consider) and 42.4 (Factors Not to Consider). ABA STANDARDS FOR CRIMINAL JUSTICE: PROSECUTION AND DEFENSE FUNCTION (3d ed., 1993).

2   Gideon v. Wainwright, 373 U.S. 375 (1963). Gideon and its progeny hold that indigent defendants cannot be convicted and sentenced to confinement, probation, or even a suspended confinement sentence unless they are provided with constitutionally effective counsel and necessary expenses for investigation and expert assistance.

3   Attorney General Jackson uttered these famous words in a speech to federal prosecutors on April 1, 1940. *See,* Robert H. Jackson, *The Federal Prosecutor*, 24 AM. JUD. SOC'Y 18 (1940).

4   *See, e.g.*, Katherine Kruse, *Engaged Client-Centered Representation and the Moral Foundations of the Lawyer-Client Relationship*, 39 HOFSTRA L. REV. 577, 579 (2011).

5   Or, in the words of Richard Gere playing a famed defense lawyer in Gregory Hoblit's PRIMAL FEAR (Paramount Pictures 1996): "I am your attorney, which means I'm your mother, your father, your best friend and your priest."

6   DAVID BINDER, PAUL BERGMAN, PAUL TREMBLAY, AND IAN WEINSTEIN; LAWYERS AS COUNSELORS: A CLIENT-CENTERED APPROACH (3d ed., 2012).

7   *See* ABA COMM. ON ETHICS & PROF'L RESPONSIBILITY, FORMAL OPINION 06-441 (2006) ("Ethical Obligations of Lawyers who Represent Indigent Criminal Defendants When Excessive Caseloads Interfere with Competent and Diligent Representation").

8   A leader in the training of public defenders is the non-profit organization, "Gideon's Promise," which provides training and support to public defenders, particularly in the southern United States but increasingly across the country. Founded by Jon Rapping, Gideon's Promise is a leader in promoting the concept of client-centered lawyering in the specific context of public defender offices. See GIDEON'S PROMISE, http://gideonspromise.org/ (last visited Aug. 3, 2015).

9   You must know your jurisdiction's discovery rules, the Brady line of case—Brady v. Maryland, 373 U.S. 83 (1963), Giglio v. *United States*, 405 U.S. 150 (1972), United States v. Agurs, 472 U.S. 97 (1976), United States v. Bagley, 473 U.S. 667 (1985); Kyles v. Whitley, 514 U.S. 419 (1995)—and your jurisdiction's version of Rule 3.8(d) of the Rules of Professional Conduct.

10   N.D. RULES OF PROF'L CONDUCT, r. 3.8, cmt. 1 (2006).

11   A good starting point for reading is ABA COMM. ON ETHICS & PROF'L RESPONSIBILITY, FORMAL OPINION 06-441 (2006) ("The Ethical Obligations of Lawyers who Represent Indigent Criminal Defendants when Excessive Caseloads Interfere with Competent and Diligent Representation").

12   *See* MODEL RULES OF PROF'L CONDUCT r. 1.1 (Competence), r. 1.3 (Diligence), r. 1.4 (Communication), r. 1.7 (Conflicts of Interest), r. 5.1 (Responsibilities of Partners, Managers and Supervisory Lawyers), r. 5.2 (Responsibilities of Subordinate Lawyers).

13   *See, e.g.*, NAT'L. RIGHT TO COUNSEL COMM., JUSTICE DENIED: AMERICA'S CONTINUING NEGLECT OF OUR CONSTITUTIONAL RIGHT TO COUNSEL, 67–70 (2009), http://www.constitutionproject.org/documents/justice-denied-america-s-continuing-neglect -of-our-constitutional-right-to-counsel/.

14   MODEL RULES OF PROF'L CONDUCT r. 1.10 defines imputed conflicts. Essentially, all of the attorneys in a single law firm are prohibited from representing a party who has a conflicting interest with the client of a different lawyer in the same law firm. Most jurisdictions across the country consider public defender offices to be "law firms" for purposes of this rule. The classic example is the representation of one co-defendant who testifies for the prosecution against another co-defendant. This is a clear conflict: what benefits one client will injure the other.

15   There is a growing body of literature addressing this issue. *See, e.g.*, AMY BACH, ORDINARY INJUSTICE: HOW AMERICA HOLDS COURT (2010). There is also litigation that attempts to address excessive caseload issues. *See, e.g.*, Public Defender, Eleventh Judicial District of Florida, et al., v. State of Florida, 115 So.3d 261 (Fla. Sup. Ct., 2013).

16   *See* Missouri v. Frye, 132 S. Ct. 1399 (2012) & Lafler v. Cooper, 132 S. Ct. 1376 (2012), both holding that the 6th Amendment right to effective assistance of counsel extends to cases that result in guilty pleas.

17   *See, e.g.*, Jon Rapping, *Directing the Winds of Change: Using Organizational Culture to Reform Indigent Defense*, 9 LOYOLA J. PUB. INT. L. 177 (2008); Charles Ogletree, *Beyond Justifications: Seeking Motivations to Sustain Public Defenders*, 106 HARV. L. REV. 1239 (1993); Barbara Babcock, *Defending the Guilty*, 32 CLEV. ST. L. REV. 175 (1983).

18   *See, e.g.*, Ronald Wright & Marc Miller, *The Screening/Bargaining Tradeoff*, 55 STAN. L. REV. 29 (2002).

19   Stephen Wexler, *Practicing Law for Poor People*, 79 YALE L. REV. 1049 (1970). Wexler's article has been described as "[o]ne of the canonical pieces in the cause-lawyering literature." David Luban, *The Moral Complexity of Cause Lawyers within the State*, 81 FORDHAM L. REV. 705, 710 (2012).

20   MICHELLE ALEXANDER, THE NEW JIM CROW: MASS INCARCERATION IN THE AGE OF COLORBLINDNESS (2010).

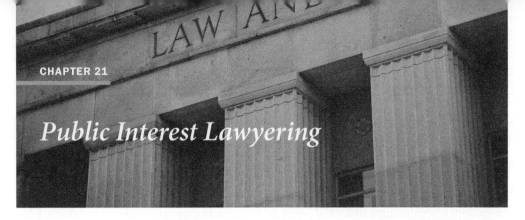

Public Interest Lawyering

SUSAN B. SCHECHTER & JEFFREY R. BAKER

Today's public interest lawyers . . . have moved us a little closer to the ideal of equal justice for all.[1]

–Thurgood Marshall, U.S. Supreme Court Justice and Founder, Executive Director, and Public Interest Lawyer for the NAACP Legal Defense and Educational Fund from 1940–1961

Introduction

Many law students come to law school because they want to help others through the law. Some students define this work as "public interest," indicating their desire to do meaningful work that will help promote access to justice for individuals, communities, or causes. Whatever your reason for pursuing a public interest placement, you can expect to be exposed to the varied ways public interest lawyers approach their practices, including developing your lawyering skills, addressing professionalism issues, and exploring your career options as you work with clients, appear in court, advocate for a cause, or draft policies and legislation that advance the public interest.

A public interest placement is an ideal way to explore either a public interest career or help you make informed decisions about the type of lawyer you want to be. Your placement may be your first glimpse into the world of public interest lawyering. A public interest placement will challenge your assumptions, motivate you in whatever path you may pursue, and allow you to serve the public good along the way. Your placement can help you explore public interest law in a safe and supportive environment while you assess the practical realities of day-to-day practice in the public interest.

This chapter will start by providing an overview of public interest careers and the need for public interest lawyers. Then, it will discuss public interest lawyering from the perspective of the client and how public interest lawyers approach their practices. The chapter will end with a brief discussion of life as a public interest lawyer.

Many government lawyers and private practitioners engage in public interest lawyering. For purposes of this chapter, the discussion will be limited to non-profit or tax-exempt organizations that exist solely to advance their public interest missions. For more discussion on related practices, see Chapter 22 on Public Service Lawyering, as well as Chapter 19 on Judicial Externships, Chapter 20 on Criminal Justice Lawyering and Chapter 23 on Transactional Lawyering.

QUESTIONS TO CONSIDER

· As you start your placement, what do you think it means to be a public interest lawyer? Make a list of those attributes that seem most important and save the list. Refer back to it as the semester progresses. Would you remove anything, change anything, or add anything?

· Listen to how the lawyers at your placement describe the work they do and the goals they have for their work. Keep asking yourself whether their goals match the actual impact of their work. Start to think through the ways in which your placement is serving the public.

Career Paths and Preparation

According to the National Association for Law Placement (NALP), a 20-year review of employer types indicated that the percentage of graduating law students starting public interest jobs increased from 2.3% in 1993 to 7.2% in 2012.[2] With all the media coverage about a shrinking job market and the decline in law school admissions, this growth is an interesting phenomenon. One explanation might be that students are coming to law school with a more directed public interest focus. A second might be students' ability to take advantage of loan repayment programs or other types of fellowship programs that enable them to pursue these career options. A third possibility is that students are being more creative and effective in finding or creating public interest positions.

Another explanation may be that law schools now provide more resources for students wanting to pursue public interest work, often through public interest career advisors or offices. Funding opportunities to support pro bono work have expanded, including summer and graduate fellowship programs both within law schools and in law practice. Incubator programs at some schools support and prepare students to start their own public interest practices while they help to address unmet legal needs in their communities.[3]

There is a myth that there are too many lawyers. In reality, there are not too many lawyers. The problem is a mismatch in the distribution of lawyers. There are plenty of clients in need of legal services and too few resources to serve those clients and needs. To illustrate the point, there is only one legal aid attorney for every 6,415 persons below 125% of the federal poverty line, as compared to one attorney for every 469 people above that income level.[4]

The profession is struggling to seek ways to match the countless clients in need of legal services and the many law graduates eager for public interest jobs. If you plan to pursue public interest law as a career, use the resources available to you in law school, including the networking you can do at your placement, to help find the clients with whom you want to work. See Chapter 26 on Externships and Career Planning for more ideas.

Even if you do not pursue a public interest career path, know that your pro bono work will still meet critical needs. Consider also the discussion in Chapter 27 on the Future of the Legal Profession and Legal Services Delivery regarding innovations to enhance access to legal services.

Your field placement will allow you to explore a possible career that can inspire you, strengthen your skills, and expose you to important ethical and professionalism issues. It will allow you to explore a work environment and examine issues of balance between personal and professional life. See Chapter 25 on Work and Well-being for a deeper discussion of these issues. In addition, you will work with public interest practitioners who can model how to build a public interest career or engage in meaningful pro bono work. Finally, the lawyering you do in your public interest placement will be invaluable to you no matter what career path you pursue.

QUESTIONS TO CONSIDER

· If you know that you want to be a public interest lawyer, what led you to that choice? What prior experience do you bring to your field placement? What do you see at your placement that confirms your career choice? What concerns you?

· What motivates you and connects you to public interest work generally and any particular subject matter interest within the field?

· If you are unsure about a career in public interest, what makes you curious about the work? What aspects of the actual work interest or appeal to you? At your placement, what do you see that draws you in, and what pushes you away?

Defining Public Interest Law

Lawyers have practiced public interest law for a long time, though it was not until the beginning of the 20th century that public interest law came into being as a concept in the form of legal aid societies. Legal aid societies were charitable institutions organized to serve people in need including immigrants, women, and children. In the 1960s, public interest law evolved into a practice area.[5]

At its foundation, public interest law practice provides a vehicle to amplify underrepresented voices and communities. As Nan Aron, the founder of the Alliance for Justice stated, "Philosophically, public interest law rests on the assumption that many significant segments of society are not adequately represented in the courts, Congress, or the administrative agencies because they are either too poor or too diffuse to obtain legal representation in the marketplace."[6] To this day, it is important to note, there is no clear agreement or consensus about what it means to practice law in the public interest.

Initially, legal services organizations existed mainly to provide individual representation on a wide variety of matters. Over time, the work of public interest lawyers has expanded beyond individual representation to include class actions, community organizing, policy analysis, and legislative or administrative advocacy. Lawyers have found it necessary to get more creative and go beyond traditional practice methods to promote their clients' needs. Throughout, the focus remains on using the legal system to address social and economic injustices.

Your work at a public interest placement will prompt you to explore issues central to a democratic society: social justice, access to justice, equity and inclusion, and restorative justice. This exposure happens while you are doing important legal work.

> ## QUESTIONS TO CONSIDER
>
> · How do you define public interest law? What does it mean to you? Is there value in reaching an agreement about what public interest law is and is not?
>
> · What part of the public interest does your office represent? How does your office discuss or evaluate its work to gain a broader perspective? How does your office understand its history and its current mission?
>
> · How does your organization interact with the larger public interest community, both legal and non-legal organizations? Does your placement work in collaboration with other organizations? How does that happen, and what does it look like?

The Work of Public Interest Lawyers

While there are many ways to learn from your public interest placement, this section focuses on three topics that can serve as a lens through which you may view your learning: professional responsibility including the critical questions of who is the client, what is your relationship to the client, and how you represent that client. This section begins with a discussion of key ethical and professionalism questions and then turns to a discussion of clients, lawyering skills, and professional identity.

Professional Responsibility

The exercises in this section raise some of the more prevalent and vexing topics of confidentiality, conflicts of interest, and competence that you will encounter in your work.[7] As you work through them, consider how you and your supervising attorney would react. Identify the ethical issues, evaluate your options, and imagine how you would respond to the client.

> **Exercise 21.1** You are an extern in a legal aid office with a thriving family law practice, and a local domestic violence shelter refers many of your clients. The legal aid office and the shelter have a long and productive relationship and often work with common clients. You are working with a client to obtain a civil protection order against her abusive spouse, which normally includes a non-contact order. In the

course of your representation, you learn from the client that she has continued to have contact with her spouse primarily about the location of their child. The client has told her spouse that she has the child with her in the shelter but not where the shelter is located.

A licensed social worker from the shelter calls to ask you about the client. She is concerned the client is considering returning to her spouse. The social worker suspects the client has been in contact with her spouse in violation of shelter rules. She asks whether you know anything that can help her prepare for the next counseling meeting. What should you tell the counselor?

Exercise 21.2 You are working for a public interest law organization that specializes in impact litigation to effect policy change in education, housing, and health care. For years, your organization has been seeking a plaintiff willing to challenge a city's public housing policy many believe is racially discriminatory. Several potential clients decided they did not want to be involved in litigation, but recently a family agreed to sue the city. For months, the suit has proceeded through several contentious and expensive phases, but on the eve of several depositions of city officials, the city's attorneys write to your organization to make a very generous settlement offer. The city has offered enough money for the clients to move out of the housing project and buy their own comfortable home in return for dropping the suit and signing a stringent confidentiality agreement.

Your organization knows it is unlikely to find another plaintiff soon or easily to challenge the city's policies, and you believe that other families will suffer under the discriminatory policies. You also know the settlement offer would be a huge financial relief to your client. How will you address the settlement offer with your client?

Exercise 21.3 You are working for a local legal aid program that offers regularly scheduled single-day clinics with volunteer lawyers around the city. Each week, your program recruits volunteer lawyers to spend a day at a clinic with the incentive that they satisfy the bar's pro bono requirement. Usually the work is advice-and-counsel or limited to discrete legal tasks like wills, powers-of-attorneys, or benefit applications, and you provide very short training on these topics to the volunteers immediately before each clinic. Clients who make an appointment for the clinic sign a limited-representation agreement to acknowledge they are waiving conflicts of interests and are not forming an attorney-client relationship that will extend beyond the day in the clinic.

At the current clinic at a community center in a poor neighborhood, most of the volunteers are associates in a big law firm's appellate practice area. Most of the clients are seniors who want wills, powers-of-attorney, or advanced health-care directives. As the clients gather for their appointments after your training, you hear one volunteer say to another, "I have never drafted a will in my life. I barely remember the class in school." The other volunteer laughs and replies, "I know. I don't think they'll know the difference, though. Besides, we must be better than nothing, right?" How could you engage the volunteers about their statements and ideas about the work?

The exercises above illustrate several different ethical challenges that occur in public interest practices. In considering your responses, you will necessarily consider the applicable rules of ethics. These rules vary from state to state. For a further discussion of ethical issues, see Chapter 10 on Ethical Issues in Externships: An Introduction; Chapter 11 on Ethical Issues in Externships: Confidentiality; Chapter 12 on Ethical Issues in Externships: Conflicts of Interest; and Chapter 13 on Ethical Issues in Externships: Duties to Tribunals and Third Parties. In addition to their more specific ethical requirements, almost all of the rules call for lawyers to help provide legal services to those in need, ensure equal access to support, and enhance our system of justice under the rule of law.[8] These principles reflect some of the core aspirations of our system of self-regulation.

The Client

As your public interest placement strives to fulfill unmet legal needs, think carefully about identifying the client and the lawyer's responsibility to the client. Typically, your placement will represent one or more of these three types of clients: individuals; organizations, communities or groups; and causes. This section explores some of the predominant lawyering skills and professional identity issues that arise with each type of client.[9] See Chapter 15 on Client Relationships for more discussion of working with clients and Chapter 24 on Professional Identity and Formation for more discussion of professional identity.

■ *Individuals*

Most public interest law organizations serve the needs of individual clients. There are different models for individual representation. For example, client-centered lawyering focuses efforts around the client's goals and treats the client as an effective collaborator.[10] By contrast, a more traditional or lawyer-centered model puts the lawyer at the center of decision-making, not just about tactics but also often strategy.

Both models can create dilemmas in the public interest setting when potential clients ask for help to "save" them or "solve" bad situations or when a client insists on representation toward goals or interests with which the lawyer disagrees.

QUESTIONS TO CONSIDER

- Lawyers and students who see the same problem case after case sometimes ask whether they can do something differently. It can seem like there should be a better or more efficient way to help individuals than one at a time. How might lawyers who do this work for a long period of time handle this dilemma?

- For many clients coming into your organization, there may not be a legal answer to their problem. The client may need other resources, including other service providers to address the problem fully. As you are working with clients, what are the limits of your role in advising and assisting them?

- Other clients face more than one legal problem and have limited resources to deal with them. These situations raise difficult choices for the client. Counseling clients in such situations poses special challenges. Do you push the client toward one way of resolving these conflicts? Provide them with a range of choices but leave the choice to them? What if you recommend a solution, but the client wants to pursue a direction you believe will not get them what they want?

Public interest practices that do individual client work often have large caseloads and face difficulties in figuring out when to turn clients away. The size of the caseload and the frequent limitations on client resources can create concerns about self-care for some lawyers and can affect the long-term sustainability of the practice for others.[11]

Exercise 21.4 You are meeting with a client and her son at your legal services agency and as you are interviewing them you see them eyeing the day-old coffee cake sitting on a nearby counter. When you ask if they are okay, they inform you they have not eaten in a day or two. What do you do?

Exercise 21.5 You are doing intake at a non-profit organization, and you have been instructed that all the lawyers have full caseloads and cannot manage one more case. A needy client comes in with a compelling case. What do you do? As you think this through, consider checking the following information about your placement: the size of the caseloads for individual lawyers, considering that the demands may vary with the type of case; the written statement of intake criteria at your placement; the process by which an office makes decisions on individual cases as well as decisions to shut down new intake.

■ *Organizations, Communities and Other Group Clients*

In many instances, public interest lawyers represent organizations or community groups in pursuing their issues and concerns. Public interest lawyers must be cognizant of the fact that groups are made up of individuals who may or may not share the same interests or goals.[12] This type of representation can create complex issues of client identification, loyalty, and confidentiality. A public interest lawyer must be cautious when identifying and navigating potentially competing or conflicting relationships.

If your public interest placement represents groups, observe how the lawyers discern their role in representing the organization or individuals within the organization. In addition, the lawyer must work to identify who has the authority to speak for the organization and guide the lawyer's work. In group representation, the lawyer must determine whether her role is as an advisor or advocate. Determining the lawyer's role is critical for ethical and other reasons.

QUESTIONS TO CONSIDER

· Assume your organization represents groups. Consider who makes decisions, legal and otherwise, for the group: is it the lawyers or the group's designated leaders? Who makes the decisions about legal strategy? In the relationship, is the lawyer authorized to make strategic and tactical decisions without the client's approval or ratification? Are the lawyers there for advice and counsel alone or as full stakeholders in the work of the organization?

· What is your role as the law student working with your lawyer and the organization? Is it merely to shadow the lawyer? Can you also advise the members of the group about the law? Can you go beyond counseling to advocate for them with others?

· How do the lawyers in your organization deal with the dilemma when a group wants to pursue a course with which the lawyer or organization does not agree? Is there a process set up to deal with such disagreements?

Exercise 21.6 The organization with which you are doing your field placement represents a community group opposed to the building of a large chain department store in their neighborhood. You attend a community meeting with your supervising attorney and find out not all the members of the community group are opposed to the store. How does your organization proceed?

Exercise 21.7 Your public interest law office represents a community group but does not represent individuals in that group. A member of the group asks for help with a personal legal problem. How do your lawyers respond to the individual group member? How does their response involve or affect the lawyers' professional responsibility to the community group?

Questions involving conflicting interests within a group arise frequently in group-oriented practices, as do questions about doing individual work for group members. If your office works with groups, explore with your supervising attorney what procedures they use to resolve these questions. Does the lawyer's role change when trying to build consensus within a group?

■ *Causes*

A "cause" lawyer is dedicated to the practice of law for the promotion of social change, or sometimes resisting change. In either case, the cause or issue is paramount to the individual client's or group's needs. Cause lawyering can raise especially interesting questions about the role of the lawyer in relationship to the client and the legal profession.

Other terms used to describe cause lawyering are "social justice" lawyering or "rebellious" lawyering.[13] Professor Thomas Hilbink divides cause lawyering into three types: proceduralist, elite/vanguard, and grassroots. Using this rubric allows you to think through the role of the lawyer and the lawyer's work with cases and clients. The three types differ in their views of the legal system, cause, and relationship between the lawyer and the client. The relationship between cause lawyers and client autonomy is contingent on the approach the lawyers take and their understanding with the clients.[14] Keep in mind that many public interest practitioners may not be familiar with this framework and how and where their work fits in, and they may not feel the need to define in which category their "cause lawyering" fits.

Hilbink describes the three types of cause lawyering in this way:

1. A proceduralist lawyer views law and politics as distinct and separate; considers the legal system to be fair, just, and a stabilizing force; and has an individualistic understanding of social ills. To a proceduralist, the cause is delineated by professional ideals and led by the profession. The proceduralist emphasizes procedural justice, and her goal is client representation. She views the client as an individual who comes first, and the lawyer as servant maintains a neutral perspective.[15]

2. The elite/vanguard cause lawyer views law as the best form of politics that can render substantive justice. The elite/vanguard lawyer views the cause as delineated by legal ideals; led by lawyers, with the legal outcome as the goal; putting an emphasis on substantive legal justice. The elite/vanguard views the lawyer as the leader in the lawyer-client relationship, with the general public or an overarching principle as the client. The cause comes first, and the lawyer finds clients who seek to pursue the same cause.[16]

3. The grassroots cause lawyer views law as another type of politics and the legal system as often corrupt, unjust, or oppressive. The grassroots lawyer views the cause as being led by clients as part of a movement with an emphasis on substantive social justice, delineated by political ideals with political success as the goal. To a grassroots cause lawyer, the cause and client fight come first,

with the lawyer as a participant or supporting player. Grassroots lawyers view their cause as empowering clients and communities; representation enhances autonomy because it is organized around identifying and advancing client goals.[17]

The definition of cause lawyering includes both those who seek to promote change and those who seek to resist it. The history of cause lawyering is filled with examples of cause lawyers at all ends of a particular spectrum of values. Modern day debates over abortion, gay marriage, and civil liberties include active legal work by groups of lawyers on all sides.

QUESTIONS TO CONSIDER

· What kind of cause lawyering are you seeing at your field placement? Is it effective? What role does the lawyer play? Is it always clear what type of cause lawyering you are witnessing?

· How do the lawyers with whom you work navigate the potential for conflicts among the clients and the cause, the strategy and tactics, and the role they play in the process? Have you seen any such conflicts? How were they handled?

· What concerns are likely to arise when a lawyer or public interest law organization takes on a cause or has a political agenda? Consider not only ethical concerns but also practical ones, including disagreements over strategy, limitations on resources, and tensions with other related organizations.

· Does cause lawyering only cover those who work for the economically and socially oppressed or for social change? How might understanding that your opponents are motivated by a strong commitment to their ideology and personal values help you in your work?

Exercise 21.8 Your placement works to decriminalize drug use. The directors on the organization's board come from a wide range of political perspectives on this issue. Some board members agree all drugs should be decriminalized, while others support partial decriminalization, and still others think people charged with drug crimes should face charges but have a broader array of sentences, including treatment. How does your organization handle these differences? What is the lawyer's role in navigating these differences?

Exercise 21.9 You are working for an environmental law organization working on climate change. You find out one of your major funders is a solar company, and you have concerns the organization may not be working solely in the public interest as they may have a conflict or at least may not have clearly disclosed where their funding comes from. Some of the lawyers in your organization do not think it matters where the funding comes from as long as they work to promote renewable sources of energy. What issues does this situation raise?

In your field placement, you may find your organization works with all three kinds of clients—individuals, groups, and causes. Being aware of the differences and similarities and how they operate will deepen your experience and provide you with perspective about how public interest lawyers approach their practices. Being aware of the differences also will ensure that you provide ethical and competent service to all three.

The Way Public Interest Lawyers Practice

In representing the different types of clients, public interest lawyers have a wide range of approaches to help their clients meet their goals. In your field placement, you are likely to see a combination of five general types of practice: direct service, impact litigation, community lawyering, policy advocacy, and law reform.

Direct Service

In the practice of public interest law, legal services or legal aid programs typically provide direct service in the form of civil representation for free or at a reduced cost to low-income clients. Much of a legal services lawyer's work involves working with individual clients when a client's rights and needs are threatened or harmed. While litigation is a common form of direct service, client direct services also include counseling, document preparation, non-legal problem solving, and other types of advocacy.

Exercise 21.10 A homeless client comes in and meets with you for the designated half-hour your legal services has slotted for individual meetings. However, after the half-hour, it is clear the client still has more legal and non-legal issues she wants to share with you. You sense she is lonely and has not had anyone to talk with in a long time. How do you respond to this client's need for additional time and possibly non-legal support?

Exercise 21.11 A client comes to your legal services office with a concern that does not rise to the level of a legal issue, but you believe can be resolved with a quick telephone call, or perhaps a follow up letter. You believe you can help the client much more effectively and efficiently than the client can do on his own. What do you do? What potential problems can arise from the telephone call on behalf of the client? When should you help the client and when should the client help himself?

Impact Litigation

Impact litigation refers to public interest lawsuits designed to advance social change as "part of a conscious, strategic effort to change the law and address social issues that affect a wide range of people."[18] Versions of impact litigation include lawyers using test cases, often as class actions, to establish new rights or legal principles, defending the validity of a law or set of laws designed to further social reform, attacking an unjust law, or coordinating litigation with an organization to advance a specific objective.[19] Public interest lawyers also participate in a limited, but growing, role as amicus curiae in cases brought by other parties.[20]

Exercise 21.12 You are working at an environmental organization that has occasional legal team meetings to decide whether to take on specific impact litigation cases. You are asked to do some preliminary research on an issue about climate change. Even though the case is viable and your supervisor is eager to file, you find that reasons exist why this might not be the right time to file a lawsuit. However, you believe very strongly in the case and think the issue matters more than the perceived strategic timing. You are invited to the team meeting and asked to present your findings. How do you present the legal findings and other concerns? Do you meet with your supervising attorney before the meeting? How do you handle any disagreement with her at the meeting? How will you react if the team overrides your opinion and decides to wait?

Exercise 21.13 You are an extern at an organization that is working on an impact case in a coalition with other local and national organizations. In your research you find case law that is not friendly to your position. Your organization is preparing to present the findings to the coalition. They have asked you to draft the memo and present the findings to the group. What do you need to know about the meeting and its participants, and how do you prepare for it? What are your likely goals for the meeting? How will you present the contrary law in a constructive way?

Exercise 21.14 You are working to evaluate a consumer protection case to challenge the predatory lending practices of a pay-day-loan company based on a number of complaints your organization has received. You identify a client with a meritorious claim that could be an effective vehicle for real change in the industry. In interviewing the client; however, you discover the client's history of prior criminal convictions, dysfunctional relationships, and poor job performance. These factors are not relevant to the claim against the pay-day-loan company, but you expect they will be known to the defendant and may weaken the lawsuit. How should you counsel a client with a colorable, strong claim but who has bad personal facts?

Community Lawyering

Community lawyering centers on building and sustaining relationships with clients and their communities. It incorporates a respect for clients that empowers them and assists them in the larger economic, political, and social contexts of their lives beyond their immediate legal problems.[21] The role of lawyers in this model requires a political and strategic approach in working with clients.[22]

Community lawyering involves formal or informal collaborations with client communities and community groups to identify and address client community issues. Community lawyering follows the client-centered model by enlisting the community members in active problem solving, enabling the members to make decisions, and considering legal and non-legal impacts of problems.[23] An important goal of this collaborative approach is to encourage communities to gain control of the forces that affect their lives. Community lawyering also promotes economic and social justice and fosters broad systemic change rather than individual dispute resolution.[24] The substance of this lawyering approach is primarily the representation of groups rather than individuals, and it calls for lawyering which joins, rather than leads, the persons represented.[25]

> **Exercise 21.15** You accompany your supervising attorney to a community meeting and at the meeting you find your attorney is less than respectful to the community leaders. What do you do? How do you respond to a community member who complains to you about your supervisor and asks for your direct opinion?

> **Exercise 21.16** You work with a family law non-profit organization that handles adoptions. The non-profit wants to organize and collaborate more with the community from which it receives most of its individual clients. They have asked you to help them develop a community-oriented strategy to promote adoption, recruit new families, and build collaborations with other agencies. Where and how do you start on this request?
>
> Assume the organization also wants to strengthen its partnership with your law school community both to recruit students to help now and expand programs in the future. How do you advise the organization to reach out to students? And what role could students serve in the work? How could the student role be sustained after you graduate?

Policy Advocacy

Policy advocacy in achieving social goals is an important and growing approach to public interest law. It can include non-legal and legal solutions. Lawyers often play an important role in influencing federal, state, and local administrative agencies' promulgation of regulations or in advising their clients about relevant regulations and policies.

Policy advocacy can be effective to advance policies that promote justice or advance the lawyers' or clients' causes. While policy advocacy may entail working to advance legislation or regulations, it can also work at the local, state, and national level to raise awareness of issues and propose solutions that do not necessarily require legislative advocacy or reform.

> **Exercise 21.17** Members of a low-income community are frustrated by the lack of access to funds to buy their own homes. They come to your non-profit housing organization for assistance. Your director decides this matter would be better handled by advocating for a change in government mortgage lending policies instead of individual litigation. He asks you to research the relevant laws, policies, and agencies that have the power to make the changes these clients are seeking. You have an idea how to do the legal research, but not how to get a sense of the big picture and where change might be possible. How do you educate yourself about the world of affordable housing and how your clients might be able to buy their own homes? What kinds of resources, information, and insight do you need to handle this assignment?

> **Exercise 21.18** You are working at a legal services organization that helps people recently coming out of prison reenter their communities and find resources for housing, employment, etc. You believe if these clients can get access to resources they are less likely to reenter the criminal justice system. You have read about some decriminalization laws for nonfelonies and for clean-slate laws that help people leave their criminal records behind them. While you are eager to help the individual clients, you think working on some policy changes might help more clients in the long run. As a law student, what is your role in proposing policy advocacy at your placement? How do you assess the effectiveness of a policy-based solution? In answering these questions, what alternatives might you consider to promote your cause and its strategies?

Legislative/Law Reform

Legislative/law reform is advocacy through a formal legislative process. This work may involve lobbying or drafting statutory language for new bills or amendments to existing laws, drafting memoranda, arguing for or against legislation that could affect the interests of constituent groups, and performing background research for policy analyses that support or oppose arguments for specific legislation.[26] Additionally, regulatory advocates can pursue similar strategies by participating in rule-making procedures before agencies on important issues.

Exercise 21.19 Your non-profit organization, which works with people with disabilities, has been asked to draft legislation providing tax and other incentives to employers who hire people with disabilities. You have been asked to help draft the legislation. Where do you start to plan your proposed legislation or amendments? Where will you go with questions about the drafting? What will your final draft include?

Exercise 21.20 You work at a legal services non-profit, and you have recently learned a very harmful bill is making its way through the state legislature. You know it will negatively impact your organization's clients. How can you find out more about the substance and legislative history of the bill? How do you find out what the rules and restrictions are regarding whether you may get involved in the advocacy at the state legislative level? Is your role different at the local or federal level? What is your role and what can you do?

Integrated Approaches

The above-mentioned approaches are the most common strategies for addressing public interest clients and issues. However, there are other types of public interest lawyering that can expand public interest advocacy, such as the following: transactional practice, particularly in the field of community economic development; media and public educational strategies designed to build public support related to other initiatives; and mediation, consensus, and collaborative approaches, especially in the area of family law.

Public interest law is not practiced in a vacuum. Public interest legal organizations likely will use more than one strategy to achieve their clients' and their own goals. By working in collaboration with other public interest legal and non-legal organizations and others entities and individuals, lawyers can pool their limited resources and be more effective. See Chapter 16 on Collaboration and Teamwork for further discussion. By adopting strategies that range from direct service to general education, and everything in between, public interest advocates can begin to address access, fairness, and justice issues in our society.

The Life of a Public Interest Lawyer

In your placement, you will have the opportunity to observe public interest practitioners. Public interest lawyering has many benefits including doing work you believe in that helps others; gaining autonomy and greater case responsibility early in your career; integrating life and work on issues that you consider personal and important; and engaging in ground-breaking work that can contribute to making the world a better place. The work can bring many challenges too, including the potential for burnout, financial constraints, the frustration of losing, and routinized practice.

Your placement will expose you to lawyers who have taken on the role of public interest attorneys, and you should talk with them about their career paths and practice decisions.

QUESTIONS TO CONSIDER

- At your field placement, do the lawyers see themselves as public interest lawyers? What does that mean to them? What does that mean to you?

- Given often heavy caseloads, how do the lawyers at your placement structure their jobs in a sustainable way, and how do they sustain themselves?

- What is the path the lawyers at your placement have taken to get there and where do they see themselves going in 5, 10, 15 years?

- If your field placement has affirmed your decision to pursue a public interest career, what are your next steps? Where will you go for mentoring and other types of support?

- If your field placement has made you realize you want to pursue a different career path, how will you maintain your commitment to pro bono work, which is the responsibility of every lawyer?[27]

Conclusion: Some Final Reflections

In your public interest placement, you will enjoy the dual benefits of learning while you are in a dynamic practice and doing good for individuals and the community. Lawyers have a historic and formal obligation to provide service to the people most in need, promote access to justice, and ensure that the promises of legal representation are available to all.

Whether your placement confirms your calling to public interest work or shows you another path, your lessons from public interest work can inform every kind of practice you will encounter in your career. Public interest lawyers engage in the practice of law through advocacy, evaluation, negotiation, advice and counsel, policy, and law reform: activities in which lawyers in any kind of practice engage. This work creates great good but also imposes significant pressures on lawyers and their clients and can generate complex ethical challenges that push the traditional boundaries of lawyers' professional roles. It requires expertise, creativity, discipline, and passion. It also requires hope and humility, realism and vision, strategic imagination, and tactical toughness.

While in law school, you can get mired in court holdings and precedents. Through your public interest placement, you can see the great potential of a law degree in the service of justice in the world and the power of a career as a full-time public interest attorney or a committed pro bono attorney. It is helpful to remember the privilege of a law degree carries great responsibilities and obligations to communities and people without access to justice. The road to justice is a long and winding one, and it depends on ethical and dedicated lawyers with vision, humanity, and balance. Public interest placements can be a powerful way to start on this road.

FINAL QUESTIONS TO CONSIDER

In your organization, do you think the public interest is served? Could it be served better? Is lack of resources—staff, money, and space—a problem?

Do you agree it is in the public interest for all people to have access to justice? If so, what opportunities and challenges do you see facing the legal profession in terms of access to justice and ensuring that unmet legal needs are addressed in our society? If not, do you see other reasons for assisting a person who might otherwise lack access to a lawyer or to the courts?

Is it reasonable to expect the legal profession to take on issues of access, justice, and inclusion? What is the role of lawyers in addressing some of the very big societal concerns facing our world today? Should the responsibility of addressing those issues rest largely on public interest lawyers, or should it rest somewhere else?

Is law enough? Can we and should we rely on our legal system to solve so many problems that individuals and communities are facing today?

To quote Bryan Stevenson, Founder and Executive Director of the Equal Justice Initiative in Montgomery, Alabama, Professor of Law at New York University School of Law, and Public Interest Lawyer: "Finally, I've come to believe that the true measure of our commitment to justice, the character of our society, our commitment to the rule of law, fairness, and equality cannot be measured by how we treat the rich, the powerful, the privileged, and the respected among us. The true measure of our character is how we treat the poor, the disfavored, the accused, the incarcerated, and the condemned."[28]

FURTHER RESOURCES

Michelle Alexander, The New Jim Crow: Mass Incarceration in the Age of Colorblindness (2010).

Equal Justice Works: Helping Lawyers Help Community, http://www.equaljusticeworks.org/.

The Politics of Law: A Progressive Critique (David Kairys ed., 3d ed. 1998).

National Legal Aid and Defender Association (NLADA), http://www.nlada-100years.org/.

PSJD: Your Pathway to Public Service Legal Careers (A NALP Initiative), https://www.psjd.org/.

William P. Quigley, *Letter to a Law Student Interested In Social Justice*, 1 DePaul J. Soc. Just. 7 (2007).

ENDNOTES

1   Thurgood Marshall, *Forward to Ford Foundation, in* Am. Bar Ass'n Special Comm. on Pub. Interest Practice, Public Interest Law: Five Years Later 6–7 (1976).

2   Nat'l Ass'n for Law Placement (NALP), Jobs & JDs: Employment and Salaries of New Law Graduates, Class of 2012 9, 15 (2013).

3   Reinventing the Practice of Law: Emerging Models to Enhance Affordable Legal Services (Luz Herrera, ed., 2014).

4   Legal Services Corporation, Documenting the Justice Gap in America: The Current Unmet Civil Legal Needs of Low-Income Americans 20 (2009).

5   *See* Alan K. Chen & Scott L. Cummings, Public Interest Lawyering: A Contemporary Perspective (2013).

6   Nan Aron, Liberty and Justice for All: Public Interest Law in the 1980s and Beyond 3 (1989).

7   *See* Alexis Anderson, Arlene Kanter & Cindy R. Slane, *Ethics in Externships: Confidentiality, Conflicts, and Competence Issues in the Field and in the Classroom*, 10 Clin. L. Rev. 473 (2004).

8   ABA Model R. Of Prof'l Conduct R. 1-5 (2014 ed.) [hereinafter ABA Model Rule(s)].

9   Marjorie M. Shultz & Sheldon Zedeck, *Predicting Lawyer Effectiveness: Broadening the Basis for Law School Admission Decisions*, 36 Law & Soc. Inquiry 620, 630 (2011).

10   Stefan H. Kriefer & Richard K. Neumann, Jr., Essential Lawyering Skills: Interviewing, Counseling, Negotiation and Persuasive Face Analysis 16 (2d ed. 2003) (citing David A. Binder, Paul B. Bergman & Susan M. Price, Lawyers as Counselors: A Client-Centered Approach (1991)).

11   Brittany Stringfellow Otey, *Buffering Burnout: Preparing the Online Generation for the Occupational Hazards of the Legal Profession*, 24 S. Cal. Interdisc. L.J. 147 (2014).

12   Stephen Ellmann, *Client-Centeredness Multiplied: Individual Autonomy and Collective Mobilization in Public Interest Lawyers' Representation of Groups*, 78 Va. L. Rev. 1103, 1106 (1992).

13   Carrie Menkel-Meadow, *The Causes of Cause Lawyering: Toward an Understanding of the Motivation and Commitment of Social Justice Lawyers*, in Cause Lawyering: Political Commitments and Professional Responsibilities 33 (Austin Sarat et al. eds., 1998).

14   Thomas M. Hilbink, *You Know the Type: Categories of Cause Lawyering*, 29 Law & Soc. Inquiry 657, 663 (2004).

15   *Id.* at 664–673.

16   *Id.* at 664, 673–681.

17   *Id.* at 664, 681–690.

18   Chen, *supra* note 5, at 209.

19   *See id.*

20   *Id.* at 212.

21   Karen Tokarz, Nancy L. Cook, Susan Brooks & Brenda Bratton Blom, *Conversations on "Community Lawyering": The Newest (Oldest) Wave in Clinical Legal Education*, 28 Wash. U. L.J. & Pol'y 359, 364–365 (2008).

22   Charles Elsesser, *Community Lawyering—The Role of Lawyers in the Social Justice Movement*, 14 Loy. J. Pub. Int. L. 375 (2013).

23   Tokarz, *supra* note 21.

24   *See id.*

25   William P. Quigley, *Reflections of Community Organizers: Lawyering for Empowerment of Community Organizations*, 21 Ohio N.U. L. Rev. 455, 456 (1994).

26   Chen & Cummings, *supra* note 5, at 259.

27   ABA Model Rule 6.1; *see* Am. Bar Ass'n, Ctr. for Prof'l Responsibility, *supra* n. 9, at 139–142.

28   Bryan Stevenson, Just Mercy: A Story of Justice and Redemption 18 (2014).

Public Service Lawyering

JEFFREY R. BAKER & SUSAN B. SCHECHTER

Introduction

S tudents working in public service placements can start their work with a range of stereotypes and preconceptions. They may believe that government lawyers are the ultimate bureaucrats, agents of a dominant power structure, or place-holding functionaries serving out time under the protection of the civil service. They may worry the practice is boring, unrewarding, and second-best to lucrative private practices.

These stereotypes may characterize some lawyers and some practices, but actual experience paints a much richer picture. Public service lawyers do all of the following and more:

- litigate high profile cases,

- advocate for crucial legislative reform,

- formulate rules that shape major sectors of the economy,

- oversee free and fair elections,

- intervene in heated political conflicts,

- investigate and bear witness to unjust practices,

- help local governments respond to neighborhood needs, or

- negotiate major international agreements.

These lawyers face complex issues of significant public concern. They work in practices in which many attorneys have passionate commitments to the office's mission. Government lawyering embodies a mixture of politics, ideology, bureaucracy—at its best and worst—as well as the opportunity for balance between work and other life commitments.

National, state, and local governments employed about 8% of all practicing lawyers in 2013.[1] For the class of 2012, just over 12% of jobs for graduates were in government law practice.[2] This work occurs across the spectrum of branches and agencies at every level of government.[3] These practices of public service lawyers vary widely. Lawyers may give advice and counsel to chief executives or negotiate contracts with local vendors. They may enforce regulations or litigate constitutional questions. They may evaluate regulatory compliance or draft legislation, and they may engage in many other forms of practice.

Distinct from other forms of practice, government lawyers' clients are the governments or the agencies for whom they work. Those agencies and their lawyers bear responsibility to their larger governments and ultimately to the citizens whom they serve. They are bound by the rules of professional conduct and also by the rules that regulate their employment as civil servants working for the state.[4]

These dynamics shape the practice of government lawyers as they navigate the law and legal processes, the vicissitudes of politics, the stewardship of public resources, and the obligations of public trust.[5] When working with lawyers in public service, law students can accelerate the synthesis of doctrinal knowledge, technique, and professionalism.

This chapter first addresses the work of public service lawyers, their clients, and constituents. Next, it examines the organization of their practices and the challenges that public service lawyers face in their work. Then, the chapter addresses how students can learn from the practice of public service lawyers in varied roles: giving advice to government officials and employees; assuring compliance with laws and regulations; representing the government as a plaintiff or defendant in civil litigation; promulgating rules and regulations; engaging in policy advocacy; and participating in the legislative process. Throughout the chapter, students will encounter questions to consider and exercises as a way to think through how government lawyers approach their work.

This chapter focuses on lawyers in government service but does not address prosecutors or public defenders. For detailed discussion on externships in criminal justice practice, see Chapter 20.

The Work of Public Service Lawyers

Lawyers who work for the government must employ the same spectrum of knowledge and skills as lawyers in any practice. Their legal work can vary as widely as lawyers in private practice. They may give advice and counsel, advocate, represent, and guide transactions. They may work in compliance, conflict resolution, litigation, policy analysis, lawmaking, and adjudication. They may practice in small offices to represent local governments or in massive bureaucracies serving the nation.

Lawyers' roles will differ depending on their clients and constituency, although their obligations as lawyers, public citizens, and officers of the court remain similar to the role of lawyers in other practices. At the same time, dynamics unique to public service complicate ethical questions and situations for government lawyers. Client identification can be complex as a lawyer discerns whether loyalty lies with the agency, political appointees, the state, or the public. Freedom of information rules, public disclosures, political pressures, competing authorities, and client loyalty can force hard decisions about a lawyer's duties and roles.

Identifying the Objectives and Expectations of Supervising Attorneys for the Externship

In a public service externship, students can satisfy distinctive pedagogical and professional goals. First, the student can observe the scope of a government lawyer's practice, shaped by different realities than private practice. Second, the student can encounter a particular bureaucratic and political context in a government law office. Third, the student often encounters unique professional and ethical obligations imposed on government lawyers by the rules of professional responsibility and also by the Constitution, laws, rules, and regulations governing their work as state actors. Fourth, as in any placement, the student will have the chance to be useful to the practice and to experience the impact of excellent work for their clients.

To make the most of this experience, externship students need to discern the expectations of the office early in their placement. Externs should be open to instruction and orientation and ask questions to ensure they have clear and precise understanding of their roles and work in the office. If students do not feel well oriented or prepared for their work, they need to seek guidance from supervising attorneys and staff to ensure clarity before guessing or making avoidable mistakes. See Chapter 2 on setting goals and Chapter 3 on Learning from Supervision.

QUESTIONS TO CONSIDER

What are your expectations from working in a governmental practice? What questions do you expect to ask and answer about working as a public servant? How will you make sure you achieve your goals in the practice? For example, if you want to experience client contact, how will you meet and learn about agency decisions makers and other staff?

Consider other legal work you have done before this semester. How do you think your role this semester in government practice might differ from your past experience? How do you think your experience in public service differs from your counterparts in other placements? How can you test these expectations in your field placement this semester?

Clients and Constituents

Identifying clients, constituents, and jurisdictional power may be one of the most challenging questions for a student in a governmental placement. Determining the answer may be as easy as asking the supervising attorney, yet understanding the relationships can be an important learning opportunity for the student. Knowing when, how, and with whom a lawyer creates an attorney-client relationship is essential to any area of practice.[6] The entity to which the government lawyer's professional duties extend most likely is the agency or political division for which the lawyer works, though the problems can be complex.

In government law offices, attorneys generally function as in-house counsel for the agency for which they work; however, the agency itself may answer to multiple, perhaps competing, constituencies or branches of government. For example, a lawyer working for the United States Department of Agriculture (USDA) owes professional duties to the agency. At the USDA, the lawyer may work to ensure the agency complies with federal laws and regulations that govern it. The lawyer may draft proposed regulations on behalf of the agency that affect farmers in the field. The lawyer may draft responses to Freedom of Information Act (FOIA) requests. The lawyer may work to enforce existing regulations on companies and products within its regulatory jurisdiction. The lawyer may litigate to defend lawsuits against the USDA by citizens or corporations contesting its application of law to their industries. In all of these situations, determining the attorney's loyalty may not be straightforward. See Chapter 15 on Client Relationships for more on the constituencies of public service lawyers.

The lawyer also may be required to submit information, prepare disclosures, or draft testimony for legislators, executives, and other agencies. In such cases, lawyers must consider whether their primary duties flow to the agency or the government of which it is a part. The lawyer must consider whether the client is the USDA, the Secretary of Agriculture, or the President of the United States. Determining the client is critical to navigating hard questions of strategy and ethics.

> **Exercise 22.1** To explore the challenges of client identification, answer the following questions as if you were the extern in the situations:
>
> You have begun work at a field placement for a state's transportation department. Your supervisor assigns you to research whether the city, county, or state has responsibility for installing and maintaining guardrails on a stretch of road where several accidents have occurred. Litigation is pending against all three entities. You are to prepare a memo addressing the responsibilities and potential liability of each entity and present it to the state Secretary of Transportation in a ten-minute meeting scheduled in three days. Before your meeting, a senior staffer from the Office of the Governor emails you and asks to see a copy of your memo when you have completed it.
>
> 1. What are the interests of the various offices and agencies in this matter?
>
> 2. Who is your client? How might different answers to that question affect your approach to the underlying problem?
>
> 3. How will you determine who your client is?
>
> 4. How will you respond to the staffer who wrote to you?
>
> 5. How will you present information that might not favor the state government?

> **Exercise 22.2** In your memo you conclude the state, through the Department of Transportation, is responsible and liable for maintaining the guardrails on the problematic stretch of road, not the co-defendant county and city. You are very confident in your conclusion, and your supervisor agrees with you. In your meeting with the Secretary, she accepts your recommendation but instructs your supervisor to continue to deny liability and advance the position the city had primary responsibility. She also instructs your supervisor to refuse any settlement offer that would imply the Department of Transportation could be liable for the guardrails.

1. How should your supervisor respond to the Secretary? How would you respond to the Secretary?

2. What questions would you ask your field supervisor?

3. Do you or your field supervisor owe any duty to the Governor who appointed the Secretary of Transportation?

4. If you or your supervisor believes the Secretary's position will be harmful to citizens and city officials, how would you or the lawyer respond? Is a duty owed to anyone other than the Secretary?

Exercise 22.3 Pick a case or project at your government placement and learn as much as you can about it. Which agency or which part of an agency serves as the client? Who are the stakeholders in the situation, including other parts of the agency, opponents, and other individuals, groups, or institutions affected by the case? To whom does the attorney responsible for the case report? How do decisions about the case get made as far as you know? Are you aware of any tension between the attorney's responsibility to the agency and the attorney's accountability to the public at large?

The Organization of Public Service Law Practices

Law offices in government agencies can vary widely in their organization and protocols. From small municipalities to the national government, lawyers may find diversity in the forms of practice, the degree of autonomy in their decision making, the scope of their authority, the opportunity for creativity, and the roles they play. Some lawyers may have near complete independence to pursue the role of their offices. Others may have to work within highly regimented bureaucracies with strict protocols.[7]

Lawyers may have discretion to determine the merit of a case and design litigation strategy, or lawyers may have virtually no options regarding the cases to which they are assigned. Some government practices may demand constant, critical interaction with the public and constituents, and some practices may be insulated and isolated within an agency. In some contexts, lawyers may be involved in tedious, detailed, exhaustive factual investigations with voluminous data. In other contexts, government lawyers may be engaged in sweeping theoretical debates about strategy, policy, and justice.

Understanding the power, authority and scope of practice for a law office in a government agency is critical to an extern's experience in the field placement. It is helpful for students to learn the process by which work comes to the office and how the lawyers choose or prioritize cases or matters. In order to deliver the most useful work, the extern will want to understand to whom the office is accountable and over whom it has authority or influence.

QUESTIONS TO CONSIDER

To ensure a good understanding of the context of your work, consider these questions:

1. What is your agency's formal responsibility and jurisdiction within the government? From what law does your agency derive its authority and mission?

2. What official is responsible for your agency and the matters the lawyers handle in the office? Who directs and decides what the work of your agency and office will be?

3. To what other officials or agencies is your office accountable, and over what other agencies or officials does your office have power?

4. Is your agency's responsibility to change policy, implement policy, defend a policy, or enforce policy?

5. Who may be your formal adversaries in your work? Who may be its informal rivals?

6. To what extent do political dynamics affect the work of your agency or office?

Challenges and Pressures in Public Service Practice

At least three dynamics significantly affect the practice of government lawyers: duty to the public, the influence of politics, and the necessity of collaboration with other agencies.

■ *Duty to the Public*

In a government "of the people, by the people, for the people," a lawyer in service to that government feels a calling to serve the people well by promoting good, just governance. When faced with a moral dilemma, a lawyer may feel dissonance between the action of the government—which the lawyer represents—and the effects of that action on the public. In such a moment, the lawyer must consider morality, ethics, politics, and law, and the lawyer must navigate the internal conflict of interest created by the moral conflict.[8] The lawyer must consider the legal and procedural means to register objection or to counsel a different course. In extreme cases, the lawyer must decide when the course of action needs to be resignation or civil disobedience.

Note that the next three exercises describe situations new attorneys might encounter early in their career in a government office. Make sure to ask how similar issues would be handled in your placement, especially if you have a hand in resolving them. See Chapters 10–13 for a general review of ethical issues as they may arise in externships.

Exercise 22.4 You are in your first year as an attorney in the Office of White House Counsel for the President of the United States. During an election year, several people are arrested for hacking into the secure servers of the opposing political party to steal proprietary information about campaign strategy and opposition research. A Congressional investigation commences and serves subpoenas duces tecum to the White House seeking documentation and audio files that may implicate the President in a conspiracy to steal the other party's information. In the course of preparing a response, you learn such documentation and audio files exist, and the President authorized the intrusion.

You are convinced there is no privilege or other theory that will prevent their disclosure to Congress. The senior counsel, however, instructs you to assert executive privilege and to prepare a statement denying the President's involvement.

- Assuming the President is your client, how do you respond to your supervisor's instructions?

- Do you comply with the instructions, despite your own professional and personal judgment?

- Do you refuse and accept the professional consequences?

- Do you resign? If you resign, do you resign without comment, or do you report your reasons to an authority or tribunal?

- Do you disclose the materials to Congress or to the press? If so, do you disclose them as the President's lawyer, or do you leak them surreptitiously?

- What consequences or ramifications do you expect if you disclose the documents as a lawyer or as an act of civil disobedience?

- Is this situation different from a conflict in private practice because it involves the President?

■ *The Influence of Politics*

Elected officials bear ultimate responsibility for governance at all levels. Politics are an essential part of their election to office. Government lawyers may be political appointees, such as the U.S. Attorney General or United States Attorneys, or they may be career civil service lawyers who work for those appointed lawyers. Appointed lawyers are more susceptible to the vicissitudes of electoral politics for their job security, and politics can affect the practice and positions of career lawyers as well. The potential for conflicts between a lawyer's own political convictions and those of the elected official for whom the lawyer works is ever present, especially when power changes hands during and after an election. The lawyer in public service must consider closely how to navigate this conflict personally and professionally in order to ensure ethical loyalty to the client and adherence to the law.

Exercise 22.5 You are a deputy attorney general in a state Attorney General's office. The Attorney General is elected by statewide election. Since you started working, the legislature passed a law strictly limiting drilling for natural gas near incorporated cities in the state. You strongly oppose the law because you believe the government should encourage the careful development of natural resources. The Attorney General who hired you also opposed the law and declared she would not defend the law if it were challenged in court. In a recent election, a new Attorney General took office who has not expressed an opinion about the law but who believes the Attorney General must defend all of the state's laws as a matter of public duty. When a suit is filed, the Attorney General assigns you to the team of lawyers responsible for defending the law in federal court.

- Do your personal politics create a conflict of interest that will require you to withdraw or to ask for a new assignment?

- How may your political objections interfere with your advocacy for the state?

- Would you discuss your political position with the Attorney General? If so, how? If not, why not? How might your response differ as an extern versus an attorney in the office? Why might your role make a difference?

- Do you have the ability financially, politically, or in other ways to support your view on this issue? Can you work to oppose the law outside of the office? Do you think you might feel strongly enough about an issue to quit a job?

▪ *Collaboration with Other Agencies*

Lawyers in one agency often collaborate with lawyers and officials in other agencies in the course of practice. While collaboration will be necessary and can help achieve better outcomes and more just policies, communicating with counterpart lawyers can raise issues of politics and privilege. These dynamics go to the fundamental question of client identification, especially when the agencies serve the same sovereign and are under the authority of a common elected chief executive. Interagency rivalry can present lawyers with compelling ethical questions and professional dilemmas.

Exercise 22.6 You work in the General Counsel's office for the municipal Parks and Recreation Department in a major metropolitan city.[9] Your department is responsible for the administration and maintenance of 40 city parks, 20 after-school programs, 20 senior centers, and 10 recreational sports leagues. You work with three other lawyers on issues that vary from contract negotiations to employment policies, to liability waivers, and even First Amendment litigation. The Mayor is the chief executive for the city, and the Director of Parks and Recreation is an official appointed by the Mayor. Your office reports directly to the Director.

Three months ago, you received a report of a child who was injured while playing in a city park. The child was playing in a grassy patch with his parents when he ran after a ball onto a sidewalk where he collided with a police officer on a bicycle. The police officer was on regular patrol duty for the city police department when she struck the child and crashed his bike. The accident occurred during twilight after the sun had set. The parents have obtained counsel who has written to the Parks and Recreation Department and to the City Police Department demanding compensation for the child's past and future medical expenses. The parents claim the park had insufficient lighting on the sidewalk and increased lighting would have prevented the accident, and also accuse the police officer of operating her bike negligently.

- Parks and Recreation is part of the same municipal government as the City Police Department. Does that relationship automatically mean they share the same interests and concerns? What challenges will affect their cooperation? If their interests conflict, who resolves the conflict, and what role might a municipal attorney play?

- Will you collaborate and cooperate with the City Police Department as you evaluate the claim or prepare for litigation? What information do you need to know to inform your decision?

- What benefits might come from cooperation with the City Police Department? What risks might come from cooperation?

- What advice would you give to the Mayor if you believed that the police officer was completely at fault?

Learning from the Practice of Lawyers in Public Service

Lawyers in public service may have occasion to work in nearly every role available in the profession: representative, advisor, advocate, evaluator, and neutral.[10] As externs work on difficult substantive issues, complex procedural conflicts, litigation, negotiation, or policy matters, they have an opportunity develop every aspect of their professional capacity. In such a rich context, students in public service placements can accelerate their learning for practice and their formation as professionals through the great variety of practice settings in public service.

As discussed here, in public service students may work with attorneys to give advice and counsel to client agencies and officials to ensure compliance with the law. Students may engage in civil litigation to defend the government or to enforce laws in dispute. Students may navigate complex regulations and administrative regimes, and students may join the work of drafting new laws and crafting public policy.

Advice, Counsel, and Compliance

Students may be part of the process of advice and counsel to their clients or principals. This may be advice about the state of the law when the agency is facing a decision. Externs may assist in evaluating the risk of liability as the agency contemplates a course of action or assist in assessing an official's compliance with the statutes and regulations that authorize the office. In some practices, externs may help the agency prepare for transactions in which the agency is a party.

Students may receive assignments to support or write memoranda, opinion letters, or briefing notes to provide advice and counsel to a client agency or political unit. This work will transfer to lawyering in virtually any practice in the students' career because the progressive process of advice and counsel generally follows a logical path.

Consider the sequence of activities in handling a case in a government law office:

- developing a thorough, detailed knowledge of the client and the client's business;

- acquiring a clear understanding of the client's goals and the questions at issue for the client;

- formulating an accurate list of the questions to which the client wants answers;

- conducting appropriate legal research to inform the legal analysis;

- relating legal analysis to the client's goals, the material facts, and other factors;

- generating conclusions, opinions, and ideas, including specific proposals and choices;

- communicating advice about legal options to supervisors and often to clients, and helping clients assess the advantages and risks of possible outcomes.

This list lays out a model sequence students and lawyers alike will use with clients throughout their law practices. Often, time and other limitations may cause a student or lawyer to truncate, rush, and compress this progression. Paying attention to this sequence and practicing it repeatedly in unpressured situations can lead you to use it effectively under stress and guard against mistakes and bad outcomes. See Chapter 14 for more on Learning about Lawyering.

Exercise 22.7 Your field placement is with the City Attorney of a major metropolis and state capital. Your supervisor has asked you to research the law and draft an opinion letter to the Mayor regarding new federal regulations. The new regulations require every unit of government that receives federal funds to adopt policies concerning non-discrimination on the basis of sexual orientation in city hiring and contracts. The city employs tens of thousands of people and contracts with companies that employ more than one hundred thousand people. Your assignment is to begin research on the regulations' requirements and current policies that will be affected by them and then draft a legal opinion to the mayor about the current state of compliance.

- What courses in law school have you taken to help prepare you for this assignment?

- This is a big project and may seem intimidating. What do you see as the challenges of this project?

- Generally, what questions will you need to ask and answer to provide a sound opinion to the Mayor?

- Consider other kinds of legal work you may have done. Have you encountered similar assignments there?

Civil Litigation

In a governmental placement, externs may work with lawyers on civil litigation, either defending the government from a civil suit or asserting a claim against a private party or even another government. Subject to sovereign immunity and tort claims acts, the government or its agency can sue or be sued in civil courts. As in all civil litigation, government lawyers will be responsible for pre-trial litigation that includes case evaluation, pleadings, discovery, motion practice, and dispositive motions. This practice may include trial and appellate practice, including similar pressures and expenses as civil litigation between private parties.

Students working in civil litigation for the government will experience the lawyers' roles as advocate, evaluator, and negotiator. In doing so, externs can explore the virtues of civility, diligence, communication, and preparation necessary for successful outcomes in every context of litigation. See Chapter 5 on Effective Communication and Professional Relationships and Chapter 9 on Professionalism for specific guidance on these topics.

Civil suits in governmental practice follow a similar progression to civil suits in private practice, from small claims to major impact litigation:

- After meeting and understanding a client, the lawyer must evaluate the merits of a potential cause of action, either to sue a defendant or to defend against a plaintiff.

- In the pleadings stage, with complaints and answers in all their derivations, the attorneys set out the parameters and landscape of the suit, thus defining the boundaries of the suit.

· The parties engage in investigation and discovery to learn about opponents, substantiate claims and defenses, and accelerate the resolution of the suit.

· The parties also engage in motion practice to defend their clients and maneuver strategically in advance of trial.

· Throughout, the parties engage in formal and informal negotiation that often results in agreement or settlement.

· Without a settlement, the case proceeds to the final stages, whether summary judgment or trial.

While rules of civil procedure govern the phases of civil suits in courts, note that many government lawyers also litigate extensively in administrative forums, where the procedural rules may be substantially different and less familiar.

Exercise 22.8 You are assigned to assist with document production in discovery in a Section 1983 civil rights lawsuit in which your agency, the county attorney's office, is defending against a claim of gender discrimination in an employment context. The plaintiff has sent you requests for production, including payroll records for hundreds of other employees during the time of the plaintiff's employment. Your assignment is to redact identifying information from copies of employment records for a certain class of county employee.

- Which rules govern your assignment?

- If you find a document that is damaging to the county's defense no one else will likely see, how will you respond? What rules and other considerations govern your response and your next steps as an extern?

- What other courses in law school are relevant to this assignment?

- How might this assignment transfer to your future in law practice?

Regulation and Administrative Law

Government law practice likely will require close attention to regulatory and administrative law, either to draft new regulations or to ensure compliance with current regulations. Lawyers may be responsible for translating statutory law into administrative procedures with an eye toward real-world application. Lawyers also may be responsible for counseling their own agency or its constituents on compliance with complex, shifting regulations. This work requires attention to fine details and disciplined, intricate research.

The work of regulatory compliance will intersect with the work of advice and counsel described in the previous sections. Every government or its agency will have a constitutional provision or statute that creates and empowers it. By the authority of those statutes, the agency almost always will have regulations that guide and limit its work. In addition to the regulations that govern the agency, doing its work will require understanding and adherence to the regulations that govern its business. Ensuring compliance requires constant attention to interpret and apply regulations to the work of the agency. For example, a city attorney's office must ensure compliance with the regulations that govern the municipality within state law, and the city attorney often must guide the city to enforce regulations against businesses operating within its boundaries.

The work of distilling statutory law into workable regulations is a task more common for, but not unique to, government lawyers, and it requires lawyering attributes common to many types of practice. To draft practical and fair regulations first requires an expert sense of the foundational law and its policy. Good regulations are thorough, clear, equitable, concise, and accurately articulate the purpose of the law they implement. This requires creativity to imagine how a law can work fairly in practical contexts, while conforming to constitutional principles of due process and equal protection. Students will be able to translate these experiences to other areas of private practice when drafting bylaws, policies, and procedures for institutional clients in business, charity, education, healthcare, and other fields.

> **Exercise 22.9** Your field placement is with a public university's general counsel's office. Last year, the law school's student body adopted a new honor code. The honor code includes provisions for adjudicating allegations of cheating, but it does not include procedures for implementing the policies. Your assignment is to generate a set of procedures to implement these provisions of the honor code: "Trials must be conducted before a jury composed of impartial law students. All aspects of the trial must be confidential, including jury selection, the trial proceedings, and the verdict."
>
> - How would you go about gathering information and researching law to help you design an impartial process?
>
> - Which legal principles you have studied inform your work on this assignment? Which courses?
>
> - What are the risks of designing and writing a procedure that does not fairly implement the policy of the new honor code?

Note that many of the activities described in the last exercise will occur in other non-governmental practices, prominently including corporate and in-house counsel practices. See Chapter 23 on Transactional Lawyering.

Legislation, Policy Advocacy, Policy Making and Implementation

Policy advocacy and the legislative process stand at the intersection of law practice and politics. Lawmaking requires a comprehensive understanding of constitutional principles, skill to translate a policy idea into the language of a statute, expertise in legislative processes, ability to articulate complex ideas quickly and concisely, nuanced appreciation of political dynamics, and patience with often intentionally inefficient systems of deliberation.

The work of legislation and policy advocacy tests the lawyer's roles of advocate, negotiator, and representative. The work also requires attendance to the lawyer's role as a public citizen committed to improvement of the law, access to the legal system, and the administration of justice.[11] In pursuit of a particular policy, the lawyer must navigate constitutional and legislative processes, political strategy, and attention to constituents and stakeholders.

Effective lawmaking and reform requires sophisticated knowledge of the law as it is and critical examination of what the law might be. Diligent research and preparation will help the lawyer to anticipate challenges and obstacles and will foster the creativity to anticipate the consequences of reform. The lawyer needs skill in precise communication to persuade voters and legislators, and good writing to draft effective and constitutional bills. Understanding power and influence is as essential to a lawyer as nuanced expertise in the law. Lawyers are operatives of the rule of law. Shaping and making law will draw on a lawyer's skills and instincts as dealmaker, theorist, policy shaper, writer, advocate, and critic.

> **Exercise 22.10** In your externship with the City Attorney's office, your supervisor asks you to draft a policy with language for an ordinance to address day laborers in the city limits. The City Council has asked for guidance on creating a humane policy that will address increasing instances of day laborers congregating in certain parking lots to secure jobs with area contractors or homeowners. The city council does not want to ban day labor and does not believe it could, but it wants to ensure compliance with traffic, property, and employment rules and to promote worker safety and fair wages. It also wants to maintain the market for such work because of its net benefit

to the local economy. Some community members are lobbying to ban the practice outright and discourage these workers from working in the city. Others support the workers and are lobbying to resist any regulation other than rules that would protect the workers' safety.

- What social, economic, or community information do you need to consider to design a workable, just policy?

- How might you anticipate political pressure on the city council members from their constituents so the policy has a good chance of passing?

Conclusion

Students in public service externships will encounter law practice that is complex and critical, diverse and sophisticated, and demanding and rewarding. Government lawyers bear all the ethical burdens of the profession in addition to the obligations of public trust. Through this practice, students can increase knowledge, develop wisdom, hone skills, and apply their training to the problems of governance, law making, and law enforcement. With disciplined reflection, externships in public service can accelerate a student's preparation for the practice of law in any context and deepen the student's understanding of the role of lawyers in society.

FURTHER RESOURCES

NANCY W. HUNT, LAWYERING IN THE NATION'S CAPITAL (forthcoming 2016).

GOVERNMENT LAWYERS: THE FEDERAL LEGAL BUREAUCRACY AND PRESIDENTIAL POLITICS (Cornell W. Clayton ed., 1995).

THE PUBLIC LAWYER (the journal of the ABA Government and Public Sector Lawyers Division).

THE URBAN LAWYER (the journal of the ABA Section of Local Government).

Careers in Federal Government, PUB. SERV. JOB DIRECTORY, http://www.psjd.org/Careers_in_Federal_Government.

Federal Legal Employment Opportunities Guide 2014–15, PUB. SERV. JOB DIRECTORY, https://www.psjd.org/getResourceFile.cfm?ID=75.

ENDNOTES

1   *Lawyer Demographics Table*, Am. B. Ass'n. (2014), http://www.americanbar.org/content/dam/aba/administrative/market_research/lawyer-demographics-tables-2014.pdf (not including public defenders or lawyers in the judiciary). *See* also Am. Bar. Found., *The Lawyer Statistical Report* (2005).

2   Nat'l Ass'n for Law Placement, Jobs & JDs: Employment and Salaries of New Law Grads, Class of 2012 32 (2013) (including prosecutors but not public defenders among areas of public service practice).

3   *See e.g.*, 5 U.S.C. §101 (2012) (Executive Departments).

4   *See* 28 U.S.C. §530B (2012) (stating that attorneys for the federal government are bound by the rules of professional conduct in the states where they practice). *See generally*, Model Rules of Prof'l Conduct (Am.Bar.Ass'n 2015) [hereinafter Model Rules]; Model Rules r. 1.11.

5   *See generally* Government Lawyers: The Federal Legal Bureaucracy and Presidential Politics (Cornell W. Clayton ed., 1995).

6   *See, e.g.*, Model Rules r.1.11–1.18.

7   *See, e.g.*, 5 U.S.C. §§2101–2109 (2012) (statutory authority generally governing federal employees).

8   Model Rules r. 1.7, 1.8.

9   For a pop culture version of the problems faced by a municipal agency, see *Parks and Recreation* (NBC television broadcast 2009–2015).

10   Model Rules pmbl. & scope.

11   Model Rules pmbl.

Transactional Lawyering

ANN VESSELS, STACEY BOWERS, & MARK POPIELARSKI

Introduction to Transactional Law Practice

It is estimated that over 50% of all law practiced is transactional in nature.[1] Lawyers in a transactional practice create value for their clients. Transactional lawyers do deals, e.g., create business entities and write contracts for the sale of property or products. The transaction or the client represented by the lawyer must be worth more as a result of the lawyer's participation, or the lawyer will lose the work.

The first part of this Chapter describes transactional law practice generally, i.e., practice settings, substantive areas of law typically included in a transactional law practice, the kinds of projects in which transactional lawyers engage, and the basic competencies lawyers need for a successful transactional practice. The second part describes some tools of transactional practice to provide context for your externship and help you integrate quickly into the organization where you are externing. Next, the chapter focuses on the in-house transactional lawyer—the role of in-house counsel as lawyer and business partner, the critical skills for the in-house lawyer, and the ethical issues unique to in-house practice. The final section discusses transactional law in the private firm setting.

Transactional Law Practice Settings

Lawyers practice transactional law primarily in two settings: private law firms and business organizations. Transactional practice in private firms exists in three primary settings:

- large firms that typically have one or more transactional practice groups;

- small boutique firms dedicated to a specific substantive area of practice, such as intellectual property; and

- small general practice firms in which the lawyers represent "whoever walks in the door."

In the in-house setting, lawyers work for a business entity—a nonprofit, for-profit, or governmental organization. Lawyers do similar kinds of transactional work in each of these organizations. For example, the lawyer may draft an employment agreement, an agreement to purchase products or services, or a real estate lease in any of these organizations.

Substantive Law in Transactional Law Practices

Transactional law encompasses many substantive areas of law. Some of the most common areas include intellectual property, business entities, mergers and acquisitions, nonprofit law, banking and finance, real property, real estate, bankruptcy, commercial law, tax, and contracts.

Some transactional practices are even more specialized. For example, a natural resources practice deals with laws about oil and gas, mining, and renewable energy. An environmental law practice might include water law, public lands, or wildlife law. Some practice areas combine transactional law and litigation. For example, lawyers in an employment law practice may write employment contracts or policies, or work in the area of employee benefits. Lawyers may also litigate a company's non-competition policy or an employment contract. In a firm that specializes in construction law, some lawyers might negotiate and write contracts, while other lawyers litigate contract disputes.

The kind of substantive law you work with at your externship depends in large part on how the firm or entity organizes the work. In many firms and organizations, practice areas focus distinctly on transactions or litigation. Generally, there is more specialization in the larger firms or organizations. If you work in-house, there is a good chance you will do transactional work, though you may also manage litigation with outside counsel.

Transactional Law Projects

Transactional practice is both forward looking—creating entities and other things that generate value—and preventive—creating policies and ensuring compliance with regulations. The following is a list of the some of the types of projects you might work on during your externship. It is a sample of the work transactional lawyers do rather than a comprehensive list.

- Negotiating and Drafting:

  - Negotiating and writing a contract for the purchase or sale of a business entity;

  - Negotiating and writing a contract for the purchase or sale of real property;

  - Negotiating a real property or equipment lease;

  - Drafting or reviewing contracts;

  - Drafting or commenting on proposed regulations;

  - Drafting employment law policies or manuals.Advising and Due Diligence:

  - Providing compliance advice;

  - Providing tax advice, e.g., information about how to prepare tax forms such as the 990 for a non profit organization or the 10K for a public organization;

  - Advising about employment law issues;

  - Advising management or the board of directors about corporate governance or other business issues;

  - Advising a home owner's association about covenants or creating the covenants;

  - Creating a crisis management plan or assisting during a crisis, e.g., an oil spill or terrorist attack.

- Working on Administrative Law Issues:

  - Preparing a response to a charge of employment discrimination;

  - Assisting an employee with a worker's compensation claim;

  - Defending an unemployment claim or an employment discrimination claim;

  - Investigating an alleged incident, e.g., sexual harassment or the allegedly fraudulent actions of the officers of an entity.

- Planning and Reorganizing Businesses:

  - Creating entities;

  - Helping entities merge;

- Helping entities dissolve, e.g., bankruptcy, dissolution after merger;

- Helping entities obtain permits or licenses;

- Protecting a client's intellectual property.

Basic Competencies for Transactional Lawyers

Your transactional law externship is a great place to work on the following five competencies that are important for new transactional lawyers, whether they work in a large specialized practice, a small general practice firm, or in-house.

1. **Understanding business associations and structures and drafting documents related to business associations**: This includes understanding the different types of business entities, how to create them, and how to advise a client about the best entity for their business. To do this work well, lawyers need to have a basic knowledge of financial statements. See Appendix 23.1 to this Chapter for a primer on reading and understanding accounting and financial statements.

2. **Investigating facts:** This competency is critical to any legal practice, and it has particular relevance for the junior deal lawyer. Most junior deal lawyers perform due diligence reviews. These reviews include an extensive investigation of an organization as part of a potential merger or acquisition. The matters investigated during a due diligence process include all of the obligations and liabilities of the company: debts, leases, lawsuits, product warranties, customer agreements, employment contracts, as well as company holdings such as real and intellectual property. Deal lawyers also investigate employee issues and gather the facts necessary to write or negotiate contracts or advise management on particular issues, among other things. A common form of investigation requires reading financial statements.

3. **Researching the law**: As in any externship, you will probably do research. Excellent resources, focused specifically on legal research in transactional law, are a tremendous help to you during your externship. Take a look at the primer on transactional law research included in Appendix 23.2.

4. **Drafting and negotiating contracts:** Deal lawyers write contracts. Writing contracts is different than other types of writing. A contract must "describe with precision the substance of the meeting of two minds, in language that will be interpreted by each subsequent reader in exactly the same way."[2] Attention to detail is critical. Participating in contract negotiations is a great way to experience the breadth of contract drafting. Ask your supervising attorney if

you can take part in a contract negotiation during your externship. Drafting and negotiating contracts is an iterative process—drafting and negotiating the contract build on each other until the contract is executed.

5. **Understanding the ethical implications of transactional practice:** Ethical issues and professionalism are key aspects of any type of law practice. The Rules of Professional Conduct are a start, yet, particularly in the in-house setting, issues often arise in a different context than many students and lawyers typically see. For example, the in-house lawyer represents the entity, rather than one individual or group of individuals. But an entity acts through its people. If the president of the company to whom the lawyer reports acts in a way that may harm the company, can or should the lawyer talk with or assist the president in any way? Or, should the lawyer work with someone else on the issue—perhaps another senior manager, or the board, or outside counsel?

While the Rules of Professional Conduct apply to in-house lawyers, there is only one rule specific to in-house counsel, Rule 1.13, and it is a particularly tricky rule. Rule 1.13 and other ethical issues for the in-house practitioner are discussed later in the chapter.

Providing Context for Your Externship—Jumpstarting the Experience

We expect a lot from externs. To have a successful experience, students must do in a short period of time what often takes months for employees. To do a good job, you need to understand the organization in which you are working, become familiar with its processes and procedures, and meet people—lots of people. If you extern in-house or in a private firm, the items in the following list suggest ways you can deepen your understanding of your placement:

Research the Organization. If you are externing in-house, research the organization before you begin your externship. If you understand the business, you can provide excellent legal advice and add value from the first day of your externship.

If you are externing in a private firm, ask for a list of clients early in your externship to help you develop a basic understanding of the firm's clients. As you work on each case, be sure to do basic research about the client. This will help you effectively integrate the legal and business aspects of any issue that arises.

Review the Organizational Chart. All companies and most firms have "Organizational (or Org) Charts." These charts tell you who reports to whom. This information helps you understand the role of the legal department and your supervising attorney. Take a look at some of the following items on a typical Org chart:

- **To whom does the General Counsel (GC) report?** Some GC's report to the CEO or the Board of Directors, while others report to the Chief Financial Officer (CFO) or a different member of Senior Management.

- **To whom does your supervising attorney report?** If you are externing in-house, your supervising attorney may be the GC or another lawyer in the legal department. Understanding to whom the GC and your supervising attorney report will help you understand your audience.

  If you are in a firm, your supervising attorney may be the partner who chairs a transactional practice group or another lawyer in the firm.

- **What are the functions of the Legal Department?** Many functions in an organization have legal components, but may not be strictly legal, e.g., compliance and risk management. You may have an interest in working on issues that are outside of the Legal Department, and knowing which department works on those issues gives you the opportunity to seek the work you want to do.

- **Who are the members of the Senior Management Team?** If you extern in-house, your "client" is the organization, which consists of different units or departments. Thus, the leader of each team will typically be your client.

- **Meet people in the organization.** As in any externship, meeting people early in your externship helps you integrate into the organization. When people know you and the kind of work that interests you, they are more likely to consider you for that kind of work. Good judgment is important in determining who to meet. Consider meeting paralegals and administrators along with attorneys. Paralegals and administrators generally know the processes and procedures well and can help you throughout your externship. Ask your supervising attorney to suggest people to meet during your first or second week, and then add to the list as appropriate. If you are externing in-house, consider meeting people in other departments who may be your clients. In a law firm, meeting other lawyers—litigation attorneys, as well as transactional attorneys working in a variety of substantive areas—helps you understand the firm's work. With this information, you can ask for specific work of interest to you during the semester.

How you meet people depends on several factors including your style and comfort level in talking with other people, the organizational culture, and how much time you have. You may want to drop by an office briefly to introduce yourself and express your enthusiasm about externing for the organization. Or, you could invite someone to coffee or lunch. At a minimum, consider telling the people you meet your name, that you are a legal extern, and that you are excited to work in their organization and eager to work with them. If, like many people, you are a bit shy or nervous about introducing yourself, prepare a short introduction. Being prepared generally makes people less nervous. When meeting people, try to remember their names and then greet them by name next time you see them.

Exercise 23.1 After reviewing the Org Chart for your placement, ask your supervising attorney the questions listed above. Discuss whether it makes a difference if the GC reports to someone other than the CEO. For example, if the GC reports to the Chief Financial Officer, what happens if a legal issue involves that CFO? Does this create a conflict? How does the GC deal with this? These questions provide a springboard for you to learn many things about your placement.

Exercise 23.2 Create a chart to keep track of people you meet at your externship and people you want to meet. Focus on their names, their area of specialty, and any projects on which they are working. It is also helpful to keep track of something personal they mention, such as names of their children or particular interests. This shows your interest in them and is a great way to keep information for networking purposes after you leave your externship. Your chart might look like this:

Name	Specialty	Projects	Personal	Date Introduced	Follow Up
Sue Smith	Real Estate	Purchase of new plant	2 young children	Sept 5	Ask to help with the contract for the plant purchase
Joe Davidson	Employment Law	Rewriting employee manual	JD from Denver Law	Try to meet by Sept 14	See if I can help with employee manual

- **Find out the Substantive Areas of Law on which the Department or Firm Focuses**. Externing in a transactional practice often provides the opportunity to work in a variety of substantive areas. Understanding the different kinds of substantive work the company or firm does allows you to ask for the work you want to do in order to accomplish your goals for your externship.

As you gain an understanding of the organization or firm by doing the things listed above, start drafting your goals for the externship. See Chapter 2 on Charting Your Path to Success—Professional Development Planning. There are so many opportunities in a transactional law externship, and drafting your goals in the first week or two of your externship helps ensure you accomplish your goals. Appendix 23.3 is a draft Learning Agenda for a transactional externship. This draft provides a compilation of different projects transactional externs typically do. Consider which projects you want to do this semester. As you work at your externship and continue to learn about the work attorneys do there, add new projects to your Learning Agenda or Professional Development Plan. It is a dynamic document that you can change as the semester progresses and you gain familiarity with the work of the organization and transactional law.

Practicing Transactional Law In-House

The General Counsel

The General Counsel is the chief legal officer of the organization. This role is complex and requires skills far beyond simply being a good lawyer. The General Counsel must lead a legal department, which requires managing resources in a complex environment, serving as chief counsel to the CEO and the Board of Directors on a variety of legal and non-legal issues, and helping shape the strategy of the organization.[3] The General Counsel today is an important business partner.

The Role of In-house Counsel v. Outside Counsel

- **The Client—Singular yet Multifaceted:** In-house counsel have only one client and the in-house lawyer is economically dependent on that client. Having only one client allows the in-house lawyer to know the client and its business very well. This intimate knowledge creates value by helping the lawyer find creative solutions the outside lawyer might not consider. The client is also multifaceted, comprised of employees, executives, shareholders, and board members. This complexity can create ethical challenges for the lawyer as the organization's interests may conflict with some of its constituents.[4]

- **The Multiple Roles of In-House Counsel:** Many in-house lawyers, and particularly the General Counsel, fill more than one role in the organization. In addition to serving as the attorney for the organization, counsel may have non-legal responsibilities for a particular business unit or operational division of the organization. For example, counsel may be responsible for Human Resources, Compliance, or Risk Management. The multiplicity of roles requires skills beyond basic lawyering skills, such as management and leadership skills.[5]

- **The Legal and Business Advisor:** Outside counsel typically have a tactical role—they solve particular problems.[6] In contrast, the in-house lawyer, and particularly the general counsel, is fully integrated into the business activity of the organization. She is part of a management team—either the senior management team or a mid-level team. In this capacity, in-house counsel has access to institutional knowledge and information and the ability to influence action—both proactively and reactively.[7]

In-house legal departments are sometimes described as either "Departments of Yes" or "Departments of No." In a Department of Yes, lawyers try to find solutions to the issues the client brings instead of simply dismissing ideas. Rather than saying the client cannot do something, lawyers provide alternative means to solve the client's issues and ensure the legality of the organization's actions. Departments of Yes are more proactive than Departments of No. The client feels comfortable seeking advice before an issue arises. If the legal department is a Department of No, clients may act first and hope negative legal implications do not arise as a result of their actions.

> **Exercise 23.3** Determine if your legal department is a Department of Yes or No. During your externship, pay close attention to the kinds of issues lawyers work on and when they receive work. Does the client seek advice **before** there is a legal issue? If so, what kinds of advice do the lawyers give? Do the lawyers try to find a creative solution to the issue, even if there are legal challenges? If the client seeks advice **after** there is a legal issue, is the issue one that could have been resolved if the legal department had been asked about the issue at an earlier stage? What might be the reasons the legal department was not asked about the issue earlier?

Critical Skills for In-House Counsel

To be effective in her strategic role, the in-house lawyer must "earn a seat at the table," i.e., earn the respect of others in the organization. This status requires the lawyer to employ many non-legal skills. These skills are important for all successful lawyers, and yet they have special significance for in-house lawyers who work and collaborate daily with non-lawyer clients.

■ *Business Acumen—Understanding the Business*

Business acumen is at the heart of everything the in-house lawyer does. This starts with understanding how the business makes money. What is the business environment of the organization? Who are its competitors? Customers? To understand the business, it is critical to understand how to read financial statements. See Appendix 23.1.

Once you have a basic understanding of the business, it is important to understand technical aspects of how the company operates—how it actually produces a product or serves its customers. This is very important when drafting and negotiating contracts. A good way to learn about the business is to take a field trip: to a plant where the products are made, to a call center, or perhaps the "home" office if you work in a satellite office. For example, if you extern for a gold mining company, take a trip to the gold mine, observe the work, and talk with the employees on location about their work. Ask your supervising attorney about such opportunities early in your externship. Your supervisor may make weekly trips to the field and may not realize you would be interested in such a trip.

Understanding the organization's strategy helps the lawyer align the legal objectives with the organization's business objectives. An understanding of the strategic mission of the organization helps the lawyer problem solve and create a "Department of Yes." Most organizations have a strategic plan. Ask your supervising attorney for a copy of the plan, and spend some time reviewing it early in your externship. Senior management often discusses key aspects of the business in weekly meetings. The general counsel or other senior lawyer usually participates in these meetings. Ask if you may observe, present, or otherwise participate in one or more of these meetings during your externship. In these meetings you can quickly gain an understanding of the complexity of the organization, its key issues and strategies, and the role of the general counsel and other lawyers

■ *Judgment*

When considering someone for the position of general counsel, good judgment is key. It requires the sophistication to evaluate and weigh different factors and options and understand their impact on a particular course of action. Experience is a critical factor in gaining this skill, and your externship is an excellent place to develop insight into and practice judgment. Watch how lawyers display judgment—both good and bad. Review the business and legal factors they considered in making their recommendation or decision, whom they consulted within and outside the organization, and what factual and legal research they relied on. See Chapter 14 on Learning about Lawyering for a more detailed discussion of judgment.

■ *Communication*

In-house lawyers need strong communication skills. Effective communication starts with speaking in "plain English," not legalese. Most in-house clients are not lawyers, and while they certainly are bright, they are not trained in the law. It is important to speak in the language they understand. Strip out unnecessary and confusing legal language in written and verbal communication. Justice Sonya Sotomayor spoke to students at the University of Denver Sturm College of Law. Her excellent communication skills are demonstrated in this video, available at: http://www.c-spanvideo.org/program/295200-1 Pay close attention to the language she uses, how she relates to her audience, and the use of storytelling in making her points. See Chapter 5 on Effective Communication and Professional Relationships, Chapter 15 on Client Relationships, and Chapter 17 on Writing for Practice.

■ *Collaboration*

In-house lawyers frequently work in teams, and collaboration also depends on good communication. A recent empirical study about collaboration showed the importance of face-to-face communication, even in this age of electronic media.[8] In your externship, consider when it is best to communicate via text, email, phone, or face-to-face. How you choose to collaborate and communicate can have a significant impact on the outcome. Other dimensions of collaboration are discussed in Chapter 16 on Collaboration and Teamwork.

■ *Interpersonal Skills and Emotional Intelligence*

Interpersonal skills include many of the points mentioned above related to communication and collaboration. Emotional Intelligence (EQ) is a core interpersonal skill, worth highlighting separately as it is not often discussed in law school. See Chapter 5 on Effective Communication for more on EQ. EQ consists of a group of skills that help individuals maximize their own and others' performance.[9] These skills include:

- Self-Awareness: Knowing one's own strengths, weaknesses, drives, values, and impact on others;[10]

- Self-Regulation: Controlling and redirecting disruptive impulses and moods;[11]

- Motivation: Relishing achievement for its own sake;[12]

- Empathy: Understanding other people's emotional makeup;[13]

- Social skill: Building rapport with others to move them in desired directions.[14]

Interpersonal skills generally can be improved, and EQ typically evolves as one matures. You can focus on improving your emotional intelligence during your externship by observing the people in your organization with high EQ. These are the "go-to" people—the people others trust and with whom they want to work. Watch how these go-to people build relationships and work with others.

> **Exercise 23.4** Read "Emotional Intelligence, Developing Strong 'People Skills'" http://www.mindtools.com/pages/article/newCDV_59.htm. Implement at least three of the strategies suggested in the section of the article titled "How to Improve Your Emotional Intelligence." The suggested strategies include observing how you react to and interact with others, doing a self-evaluation that includes examining your strengths and weaknesses and how you react to stressful situations, and practicing humility. Observe how your emotional intelligence develops during your externship.

■ *Problem Solving*

All lawyers problem solve, and having an effective process helps produce an excellent result. It helps to have a routine process for solving problems. One standard model of legal problem solving includes the following steps: identifying and framing the problem itself; finding and analyzing the law and facts related to the problem; formulating potential solutions; evaluating potential solutions; framing client choices; and developing a plan of action. For more on problem solving and lawyering process, see Chapter 14 on Learning about Lawyering.

Key Ethical Issues for In-House Lawyers

The in-house lawyer has only one client. She is an employee of that client, working side by side with other employees, often in a preventive rather than remedial role. The lawyer is also a business partner and trusted advisor. This unique position in the client entity creates pressure on the in-house lawyer to be all things to all people—pressure that can lead to ethical conflicts.[15] Here, we consider a few ways in which the in-house lawyer's unique position can affect ethical considerations:

Objectivity and Independence: If the lawyer takes a position contrary to her client, she can be fired. Thus, in-house lawyers must be able to deliver sound advice and also remain objective. The in-house lawyer is not a hired gun, a simple mouthpiece of senior management. As an employee, she must live with the results of accommodating a client who does something foolish.[16]

In the Enron scandal, outside counsel allegedly informed inside counsel about questionable practices of management.[17] Enron hid billions of dollars of debt from failed projects and ultimately filed for bankruptcy, resulting in tremendous losses for its shareholders, employees, and other involved companies. An investigation by the New York City Bar concluded that the in-house lawyers were in a position to question management's conduct and inform the Board of Directors, but never did.[18] Imagine how the result might have been different if the lawyers had acted independently and objectively in the face of such actions by the senior management.

One Client, but Who?: The in-house lawyer represents the entity and has an obligation to serve its best interests.[19] But what is the entity? Is it individual employees, managers, departments, or directors? As an entity can only act through its representatives, the attorney works with these people in representing the entity. Indeed, one definition of the in-house counsel's client might be "any of the company's representatives with whom she works and who have the capacity to be an agent of the organization, but only for so long as they are pursuing the best interests of the entity."[20]

> **Exercise 23.5** Consider the following situation: The CEO of the company is allegedly acting inappropriately toward women in the organization. Following an investigation of the CEO's actions, the in-house lawyer concludes that the company could face a charge of sexual harassment, though she feels uncertain about some of the allegations. If the lawyer confronts the CEO, perhaps the conduct will then stop. But, how will the lawyer know for sure? And, will the CEO fire her for raising the issue? Should the lawyer report the conduct to the Board of Directors? Who is her client?

Define the Client's Best Interest, and Then Advise: In client-centered lawyering, the client decides what is in its best interests, and the lawyer provides the legal advice. See Chapter 15 on Client Relationships. How does this relationship work as a practical matter when the lawyer is both a trusted business partner and the legal advisor? Should the lawyer's legal and business judgment "replace, complement, or be barred from influencing" management's judgment?[21] Is the lawyer's assessment of the business opportunity better informed than that of management? And what about the lawyer's moral judgment? Should the lawyer adopt the moral judgment of her business partners? Or should the lawyer insert her own moral judgment into the legal advice she gives?

According to the Rules of Professional Conduct, the lawyer advises the client. She does not replace her judgment with that of the client. When we consider the corporate scandals of the past several years, however, such as WorldCom, Lehman Brothers, and Enron [22] commentators admonish corporate lawyers for not being the "gate keepers," for not replacing their judgment with that of their client.[23] This critique puts the in-house lawyer in a very difficult position. When the lawyer makes a business judgment, courts may treat the in-house lawyer as the client, rather than the client's lawyer. One of the results of such attribution, as we will see below, can be a waiver of the attorney-client privilege.

There Are No Legal Problems, Just Business Problems: In-house counsel must balance the business acumen that makes her so valuable with the company's legal needs. There is no such thing as a legal problem, rather there are business problems with legal implications.[24] In-house counsel do not represent their clients at arm's length; they are not disinterested parties. Rather, they have "skin in the game" in ways outside counsel do not. This investment is part of the value of in-house counsel—the deep institutional knowledge they bring to any issue. They do not simply advise their clients; they responsibly deliver "compliant behaviors and great business results."[25] This tension creates some of the most challenging ethical issues.

While the in-house lawyer must abide by all of the Rules of Professional Responsibility, two rules create particular challenges for the in-house lawyer: Rule 1.6, Confidentiality and the related evidentiary attorney-client privilege, and Rule 1.13, Organization as Client, sometimes referred to as the duty to "report up the corporate ladder." See Chapter 11 on Ethical Issues in Externships: Confidentiality.

■ *The Attorney-Client Privilege*

The basic elements of the attorney-client privilege are as follows:

- A client;

- A lawyer;

- A communication

  – between the client and lawyer,

  – made in confidence,

  – for the purpose of securing legal advice.

The following paragraphs flesh these elements out in more detail.

The Client: Who is the client and who speaks for the client? Must the client be a representative of management? Or, can any or any employee who has information about a particular issue be a client? Each jurisdiction is different, and it is important to understand how courts apply the law in your jurisdiction. The following three tests, or a combination of them, often determine if the attorney-client privilege applies:

- Control Group—This test, one of the first created by federal courts, limits the privilege to those in a position either "to control or take a substantial part in controlling the action that the corporation might take in response to the legal action."[26]

- Subject Matter—The control group test excludes lower level employees with significant factual information essential to legal advice. Thus, the courts developed a "subject matter" test that extends the privilege to communications with lower level employees related to the subject matter of the representation.

- Upjohn—In *Upjohn Co. v. US*, 449 U.S. 383 (1981), the Supreme Court developed a more flexible standard, stating the court should consider the following factors in determining if the privilege applies:

  – Were the communications made by employees to in-house counsel to secure legal advice?

  – Were the employees cooperating with counsel at the direction of corporate superiors?

  – Did the communications concern matters within the scope of the employees' employment?

  – Was the information available from higher-level management?

The *Upjohn* test provides a flexible standard but is applied inconsistently. Some courts forgive the failure to meet one or more elements and other courts reject the privilege in nearly identical circumstances.[27]

The Attorney: Because the privilege only applies to communications made by or to a lawyer, the organization needs to establish that a lawyer who has both legal and non-legal responsibilities acted in her capacity as a lawyer at the time of the communication. This requirement can create a challenge, as the lawyer often provides business and legal advice in the same communication. In one case, a lawyer gave advice about whether to honor a line of credit. The court held that because there was no legal analysis and the communications were predominantly commercial in nature, the privilege did not apply.[28]

The Communication: Only communications made by or to a lawyer for the purpose of obtaining or giving legal advice on behalf of the organization are privileged. The privilege does not attach simply because the communication was written by a lawyer. For example, it does not apply if the lawyer writes an email suggesting a particular business strategy for a negotiation.

In Confidence: Only communications the client reasonably believes to be confidential qualify for the privilege. If the client thinks she is talking to a business advisor rather than a lawyer, the privilege does not apply. The lawyer must make it clear to the client that the communication is confidential and is about a legal matter. If too many employees have access to a communication, the court may find a waiver of the attorney-client privilege. One of the factors courts consider is whether only those employees with a "need to know" received the communication.

■ *The Duty to Report Up (and Out)*

Rule 1.13 is the only rule that applies specifically to in-house counsel. The rule is ambiguous, difficult to apply, and requires the lawyer to make many judgment calls. The first part of the rule is often referred to as the duty to report up. Rule 1.13 mandates an in-house lawyer to refer a matter to a higher authority, and, "if warranted," to the "highest authority" in the organization, if it is "in the best interests of the organization" and "likely to result in substantial injury" to the organization.

To understand how the rule works, do the following exercise.

Exercise 23.6 The General Counsel (GC) reports to the CEO and is a member of the Board of Directors. The GC learns the accounting department is engaging in questionable accounting practices that she believes are fraudulent. The CEO is involved in the accounting practices. The Board members, who are not part of management, are unaware of the practices. You report to the GC and she asks you what she should do. Prepare your recommendation and come to class prepared to discuss your recommendation. You might want to consider the following in making your recommendation:

- The GC thinks the practices are fraudulent, but is not certain.
- The CEO is the GC's boss.
- How does the GC know if the actions are "likely" to result in "substantial injury" to the organization?
- What is "substantial injury?"
- The GC must proceed as is "reasonably necessary" in the "best interests of the organization." What is "reasonably necessary?" Who defines "best interests?"

After researching Rule 1.13, you advise the GC to report the apparent fraudulent activity to the Board of Directors. The GC does so, but the Board fails to remedy the accounting practices. The company is a public company. The GC is unsure of the extent of the possible injury. The GC wants your advice about what she should do next. Rule 1.13 tells you that if the "highest authority", in this case the Board of Directors, refuses to act, and the lawyer "reasonably" believes the violation is "reasonably certain to result in substantial injury" to the organization, the lawyer **may** reveal such information to authorities outside of the organization such as the U.S. Securities and Exchange Commission (SEC) or the Attorney General, even if it violates the confidentiality requirements of Rule 1.6. This practice is referred to as "reporting out."

Exercise 23.7 Prepare a recommendation for the action you believe the GC should take after the Board fails to act. Come to class prepared to discuss and support your recommendation. In making your recommendation, you may want to consider the following:

- What should the GC consider in being "reasonably certain" the violation will result in "substantial injury?"
- What is "substantial injury"?
- Does it matter if the Board is acting in good faith?

Consider the very difficult situation Rule 1.13 creates for the lawyer who is also an employee of the organization and a trusted advisor to the management and the directors. The lawyer's role is not to replace her business judgment with that of her client. The comment to Rule 1.13 makes this role clear, stating that the lawyer must ordinarily accept decisions of the organization, even if their "utility or prudence is doubtful." But, the comment also makes clear that the lawyer must take action when she knows the organization is likely to be substantially injured by an action that violates a legal obligation of the organization.

Rule 1.13 highlights a major difference between in-house and outside counsel. If outside counsel reports such misconduct, she may lose the client. Because she likely has multiple clients, she will not lose her job and her colleagues.

Practicing Transactional Law in a Private Firm

Much of this chapter discusses practicing transactional law in the in-house setting because of the uniqueness of that setting. If you are externing in a private firm, the work you do will be determined by your client. In some instances the organization will not have in-house counsel, and thus, the private firm lawyer will function as general counsel to the client. In this case many of the topics discussed above will also be applicable to the outside counsel. The outside counsel can be a very intimate partner in the work of the client, giving both business and legal advice. In other instances, when the organization has in-house counsel, the role of the private firm lawyer will usually be very discrete. The lawyer will work on a specific project, such as assisting with a piece of litigation, creating policies like an employee manual or a compliance project, or protecting the intellectual property of the organization.

Regardless of whether your Supervising Attorney functions as the general counsel for an organization or works on discrete projects, the following attributes are important to the relationship between the attorney and her client.

Relationship with In-House Counsel

Outside counsel are usually hired because they are experts in what they are asked to do, or because the in-house counsel does not have the time to devote to the project. Regardless of the reason, the relationship between in-house counsel and the outside lawyer is critically important. The in-house counsel manages the work of outside counsel. She determines how much time and money can be spent on a project, whether other lawyers in the firm can work on the project, if certain issues the outside counsel wants to investigate are warranted, etc. Trust is a key aspect of this relationship.

Gaining the Trust of In-House Counsel

Legal departments are expense centers, not revenue generators. Thus, in-house counsel must create value for the organization. The most successful outside counsel also understand this distinction and find ways to provide value during the representation. They have a deep understanding of their client's business, and both the client and the in-house lawyer consider them their partner.

Conclusion

It is difficult to define transactional lawyering and the skills necessary to excel as a deal lawyer. This role includes many facets. The deal lawyer—whether in-house or outside counsel must create value for the client. Transactional lawyers are an amalgam of business and legal advisors. They have a breadth of substantive legal knowledge and basic lawyering skills. They also have a deep understanding of their client's business—the technical and financial aspects as well as the business strategy and management vision for the future. They are creative problem solvers and excellent communicators with high levels of emotional intelligence; and they know how to collaborate. Your externship is a great place to observe transactional lawyering in practice and begin to develop the core skills of successful transactional lawyers.

ENDNOTES

1   Lisa Penland, *Hypothetical Lawyer: Warrior, Wiseman, or Hybrid?* 6 Appalachian J. L. 73, n 2 (2006) (noting the common assertion that at least half, and perhaps more than half, of practicing lawyers are not litigators).

2   Charles M. Fox, Working With Contracts: What Law School Doesn't Teach You, 273, n.38, (PLI 2002).

3   Association Of Corporate Counsel, *Skills For The 21St Century General Counsel* (2013) (prepared jointly by the Center for the Study of the Legal profession, Georgetown Law and the Association of Corporate Counsel).

4   Omari Simmons & James Dinnage, *Innkeepers: A Unifying Theory of the In House Counsel Role*, 14 Seton Hall. L. Rev. 77, 111–112 (2011).

5   *Id.*

6   The role of outside counsel is different if the outside counsel serves, in essence, as the General Counsel. In this situation, there are few, if any, in-house lawyers in the organization.

7   Simmons & Dinnage, *supra* note 4, at 113.

8   Alex Pentland, *The New Science of Building Great Teams*, Harv. Bus. Rev. (April 2012).

9   Daniel Goleman, *What Makes a Leader*, Harv. Bus. Rev. (June 1996).

10   *Id.*

11   *Id.*

12   *Id.*

13   *Id.*

14   *Id.*

15   Susan Hackett, *Corporate Counsel and the Evolution of Practical, Ethical Navigation: An Overview of the Changing Dynamics of Professional Responsibility in In-House Practice*, 25 GEO. J. LEGAL ETHICS 317 (2012).

16   *Id.* at 319.

17   Enron Corporation was a large energy company that employed about 20,000 employees. It claimed revenues of over $100 billion dollars annually and was once named by Fortune magazine as one of the United States' most innovative companies. But its financial success was the result of an accounting fraud. It is a well-known example of corporate fraud and greed and was a factor in the promulgation of the enhanced financial regulations for corporations known as the Sarbanes-Oxley Act of 2002. It filed for bankruptcy in 2001, and several executives were convicted of securities fraud, insider trading, and other things, and sentenced to prison terms.

18   Task Force On The Lawyer's Role In Corporate Governance, ASS'N OF THE BAR OF THE CITY OF N.Y., REPORT (November 2006).

19   MODEL RULES OF PROF'L CONDUCT, r. 1.13 (2011).

20   Hackett, *supra* note 15, at 320.

21   *Id.* at 322.

22   In 2002, WorldCom, one of the largest telecommunications' companies in U.S. history, also fell prey to fraudulent accounting practices that resulted in its assets and revenues being grossly overstated. Several of its executives were convicted of securities fraud, conspiracy and filing false documents. Lehman Bros was involved in the subprime mortgage crisis of 2007–2008. Lehman Bros borrowed large amounts of money to fund its investing, much of which was invested in housing-related assets. It was one of the many victims of the housing downturn that led to the recession that began in 2008. In all of these cases, employees and investors lost significant amounts of money.

23   *Id.*

24   Hackett, *supra* note 15, at 325.

25   *Id.* at 326.

26   JOHN K. VILLA, 1 CORPORATE COUNSEL GUIDELINES, CH. 1 SUMMARY SECTIONS 1:2–1:3 (2011).

27   *Id.*

28   MSF Holdings, Ltd. v. Fiduciary Trust Co., Int'l, 03 Civ. 1818, 2005 U.S. Dist. LEXIS 34171 (S.D.N.Y. Dec. 7, 2005).

Accounting and Financial Statement Basics

Introduction

Open almost any textbook that professes to teach accounting, and in particular accounting for lawyers, and it will inevitably state that "accounting is the language of business." In order to understand the corporate clients you will represent as a transactional lawyer, you must have a basic comprehension of how their businesses function and operate. You should know the assets your client owns, as well as its liabilities. You should grasp how your client makes money or revenue and what expenses it incurs to create those revenues.

According to a recent article about the types of skills transactional lawyers should possess, it was noted that a young transactional lawyer "should be knowledgeable in basic entity finance, including an understanding of financial statements."[1] Additionally, a 2011 survey of law firm training and development professionals indicated that 75% of the respondents "strongly agreed" or "agreed" that entry-level transactional lawyers should have the ability to undertake financial analysis.[2] To comprehend the financial aspects of a deal, you must be able to read and decipher the financial statements of the businesses involved. The way to gain financial statement aptitude is to learn the basics of accounting.

This primer on basic accounting knowledge and the different types of financial statements is not a substitute for more thorough training. It is a starting point designed to introduce you to most of the major concepts.

Accounting Overview

Accounting is the system of tracking and recording the assets, liabilities, revenues, and expenses of a business. A business's accounting records and financial statements can answer many questions including: (1) is it financially healthy? (2) does it have enough cash on hand to pay its bills? (3) is it growing or declining? and (4) do its revenues exceed its expenses?

Whether small or large, a business should be tracking its day-to-day operations by keeping an accurate record of its financial transactions. These transactions are accumulated for a period of time and used to prepare and present the financial condition of a company through its financial statements. While a small business may prepare only limited financial statements on a yearly basis, a large business usually prepares extensive financial statements on both a quarterly and yearly basis.

The accounting profession uses a set of rules and procedures to prepare financial statements called generally accepted accounting principles or GAAP. GAAP provides a set of authoritative standards, guidelines, and commonly accepted practices for recording and reporting financial information. While a large publicly traded company is required to prepare its financial statements in accordance with GAAP, there is no such requirement that a privately owned company do so, unless mandated by an investor, lender, or other third party. Many companies and their accountants, however, choose to follow GAAP in preparing their financial statements because it provides a familiar set of standards and guidelines to follow. Financial statements prepared in accordance with GAAP follow established guidelines, a practice which results in standardized financial disclosure that is consistent from year to year.

Depending on the type, size, and situation of a company, it may rely on internal accountants to prepare its financial statements or engage the services of an outside accountant or accounting firm. In addition, many companies retain public accounting firms to audit their financial statements and issue an opinion as to whether or not the financial statements fairly and accurately present the company's business operations and financial position.

Financial Statement Overview

Financial statements are formalized records of a business's activities. There are three main financial statements that a company may prepare: the balance sheet, income statement, and statement of cash flows. Some companies also prepare a statement of changes in stockholders' equity. In certain situations, the financial statements are accompanied by footnotes that offer additional details about the company and the preparation of its financial statements, as well as further explanation regarding the numeric disclosures. The financial statements can be used to assess and analyze a business and its financial condition in a variety of ways. The next two sections discuss in detail the most frequently encountered financial statements, the balance sheet and income statement, and the final two sections briefly discuss the statement of cash flows and statement of changes in stockholders' equity.

■ *Balance Sheet*

The balance sheet is a summary of what the company owns, what the company owes, and the amount that remains for the shareholders. This information is reflected on the balance sheet at a certain point in time such as month-end, quarter-end, or year-end. The company discloses what it owns as assets and what it owes as liabilities. The difference between what it owns (the assets) and what it owes (the liabilities) is the amount that makes up the equity account or stockholders' equity. This leads to the fundamental accounting equation, which states:

$$\text{Assets} = \text{Liabilities} + \text{Equity}$$

No matter the type of company, small or large, assets must always equal the sum of liabilities and equity.

Assets are those tangible and intangible items a company owns. Tangible items include cash, accounts receivable, inventory, and equipment. Intangible items include patents, copyrights, and goodwill.[3] Assets are generally classified as either current or long-term. Current assets are those items than can be converted into cash within 12 months, while long-term assets are those that cannot be so quickly converted. When examining a balance sheet, the current assets will be listed in order of liquidity, meaning cash will always be listed first. Long-term assets are those that are meant to be held by the business for the long-term. Long-term assets may be classified as property; plant; equipment (PP&E), also known as fixed assets; or as other assets which include those items that do not readily fit into the previous categories such as land, building, or equipment.

Liabilities represent what the company owes to other businesses or people and include items such as accounts payable, income taxes payable, and long-term debt. Like assets, liabilities are generally classified as either current or long-term. Current liabilities are those the company is obligated to pay within 12 months, while long-term liabilities are those that are not due within 12 months.

Equity represents the amount that remains once the company's liabilities are deducted from its assets. This is often referred to as the net worth or book value of the company and reflects the shareholders' value or ownership interest. There are three main components of the equity section on the balance sheet: capital stock, additional paid-in capital (APIC), and retained earnings or accumulated deficit. The capital stock and APIC accounts reflect the investments of shareholders in the business, whether initial or additional investments. The retained earnings account reflects the undistributed profit the company has made over time. If the company is in a situation where it has a negative balance in the retained earnings account, meaning it has incurred losses over time, it instead is called an accumulated deficit.

The following is a classified balance sheet for a fictitious business, XYZ Company, as of its December 31 year-end:

XYZ Company Balance Sheet
December 31

ASSETS		LIABILITIES & STOCKHOLDER'S EQUITY	
Current Assets		*Current Liabilities*	
Cash	500,000	Accounts Payable	400,000
Accounts Receivable	350,000	Income Taxes Payable	75,000
Inventory	150,000	*Long-Term Liabilities*	
Property, Plant, & Equipment		Long-Term Debt	625,000
Building	150,000	**Total Liabilities**	**$1,100,000**
Equipment	125,000		
Other Assets		*Stockholder's Equity*	
Patent	25,000	Capital Stock	10,000
Total Assets	**$1,300,000**	Additional Paid-In Capital	90,000
		Retained Earnings	100,000
		Total Stockholder's Equity	**$200,000**
		Total Liabilities & Stockholder's Equity	**$1,300,000**

The cash, accounts receivable, and inventory are current assets of the company as they can generally be converted into cash quickly or within 12 months. The building and equipment are long-term or fixed assets and represent items the company intends to hold on to for some time. The patent falls in the other assets category, as it does not fit within the current assets or PP&E category.

The accounts payable and income taxes are current liabilities as these obligations are due within 12 months. The long-term debt represents a long-term liability, as it is due more than 12 months out. The capital stock and additional paid-in capital represent the shareholders' investments in the company and the retained earnings account reflects the accumulated earnings the company has made over the course of its operations.

Balance Sheet Exercises

Exercise 23.1: For purposes of this exercise, assume that XYZ Company operates in a state that utilizes the balance sheet insolvency test regarding dividend distributions. This test permits a company to issue a dividend to its shareholders, but only up to the amount that assets exceed liabilities less any preferred stock guaranteed dividend payment, meaning a payment that the company is obligated to make to its preferred stockholders before it is entitled to make a distribution to its common stockholders.

1. Using the balance sheet above, how much money could XYZ Company distribute to its shareholders as a dividend payment?

2. Using the balance sheet above, how would your answer to question #1 change if XYZ Company increased its long-term debt by $100,000, by $200,000, or by $300,000?

3. Using the balance sheet above, how would your answer to question #1 change if XYZ Company had a guaranteed preferred stock dividend payment of $150,000, or of $175,000?

Income Statement

The income statement summarizes a company's revenues, sometimes referred to as sales, and expenses. It reflects this information for a particular period of time such as for the entire quarter or year, and shows whether the company has made a net profit or loss for the period.

A company reflects its revenues, or the amount of money it has earned, on the first line of the income statement. Revenues result from the sale of goods, such as selling a bicycle or a book, or the sale or completion of a service, such as the fee for reviewing a contract for a client or the fee for auditing a company's financial statements.

Next, the company reflects its expenses for that period of time. Expenses are outflows by the company to operate its business. Expenses include items such as the cost of goods sold, wages and salaries, rent and utilities for the building where the company operates, and interest on an outstanding loan.

The difference between the revenues a company makes and all of the expenses it incurs is the company's net profit or net loss for that period of time. As you will recall from the balance sheet discussion, the net profit or loss is reflected in the stockholders' equity section in the retained earnings or accumulated deficit account.

An income statement can be simple, showing only revenues and all expenses combined to reach net profit or loss. Alternatively, an income statement can be more complex, showing revenues and breaking the company's expenses into various components or steps, such as those that are directly associated with revenues and those that are not directly associated with revenues but instead are general operating costs of the business.

When a company chooses to use a multi-step approach for expenses, the first expense reflected on the income statement is the direct expense incurred to produce the goods sold or the costs to provide the services rendered. In the case of goods, this expense is called the "cost of goods sold" (COGS); and in the case of services, this expense is called the "cost of services" or "cost of sales" (COS). The COGS expenses include such items as raw materials to make the products, cost of the labor to produce the products, and manufacturing overhead. COS direct expenses include such items as the salary or fee of the professional who rendered the service and other costs incurred to deliver the service such as direct legal research database costs. The difference between the revenues and COGS or COS is the company's gross profit. The gross profit indicates how efficiently the company uses its labor and supplies to produce its goods or provide its services.

After calculating its gross profit, the company then deducts its operating expenses and other expenses to reach its net income or net loss. Operating expenses are those costs that are not directly associated with producing goods or services but rather are associated with operating or running the business generally. These expenses include items like selling, general, and administrative expenses (SG&A); the cost of research and development; and depreciation expenses. Examples of SG&A costs are front office staff and executives' salaries, advertising costs, rent and utility costs for the corporate offices, and legal and accounting fees. Other expenses, meaning those that are not directly related to producing goods or services or operating expenses, include such items as interest expenses and income taxes.

The company's gross profit less its operating and other expenses results is its net income or loss for that period. The net income or loss is often referred to as the bottom line and indicates the overall profitability of the company.

The following is a multi-step income statement for a fictitious business, XYZ Company, for the fiscal year ended December 31:

XYZ Company Income Statement
For the Period Ended December 31

Revenues	$750,000
Cost of Goods Sold	<u>400,000</u>
Gross Profit	350,000
Operating Expenses:	
Selling, general, and administrative	175,000
Research and development	50,000
Depreciation	<u>25,000</u>
Operating Income	100,000
Interest Expense	<u>45,000</u>
Income before income taxes	55,000
Income Tax Expense	<u>20,000</u>
Net Income	$35,000

As is always the case, revenues are reflected as the first line item of the income statement. In this scenario, XYZ Company produces some type of goods, so it has a COGS expense it deducts from its revenues to determine its gross profit. The operating expenses, which include SG&A, research and development, and depreciation, are deducted from the gross profit to determine XYZ Company's operating income. Operating income reflects the profits the company earned from its operations. Next, XYZ subtracts other expenses of interest and income tax to reach the bottom line or, in this case, its net income.

Income Statement Exercises

Exercise 23.2 How would you classify each of the expenses listed below using these three categories: direct expense (COGS or COS), operating expense, or other expense?

1. Salaries paid to the management team who run the business
2. Raw materials to create the products a company sells

3. Income taxes due to the state and federal government

4. Wages paid to employees who make the products a company sells

5. Costs to create a new product the company wants to sell

6. Depreciation associated with the machinery a company uses to make its products

7. Costs of the marketing materials a company uses to sells its products or services

8. Interest costs associated with paying a company's long-term loan

9. Salary paid to the accountant who works on a company's client accounts

10. Rent to lease the space where a company operates

Exercise 23.3 Using the information in the table below, indicate this company's revenues, gross profit, operating expenses, operating income, and net income or loss.

SG&A	200,000
Interest Expense	10,000
Sales	575,000
Depreciation	45,000
Income Taxes	25,000
COGS	300,000

Statement of Cash Flows

The underling purpose of the statement of cash flows is to show how cash is flowing in and out of the business. This financial statement reconciles the net income shown on the income statement with the changes in the cash balance of the company from one period to the next. Similar to the income statement, the statement of cash flows reflects information over a certain period of time and generally for the fiscal year. There are three main categories included on the statement of cash flows: cash from or used in operating activities, investing activities, and financing activities. After all of the changes in these activities are recorded, the company will know how its cash balance changed from the beginning to the end of the period, meaning did cash increase or decrease. The company will also be able to determine where it is expending or generating its cash. The statement of cash flows ultimately reflects a company's movement of cash in and out of the business and indicates where the company is spending its money and where it is generating its money.

Statement of Changes in Stockholders' Equity

The statement of changes in stockholders' equity reflects the changes in the shareholders' equity accounts of the business over a period of time, generally for the fiscal year. Typical changes reflected on this statement include increases from net income or decreases from net losses, increases in capital due to additional issuances of stock, decreases due to dividend payments, other gains and losses, and increases or decreases from the effects of changes in accounting policies or prior period corrections. The statement of changes in stockholders' equity identifies in detail all of those things that caused the equity accounts to change over the accounting period.

APPENDIX ENDNOTES

1   Lisa Penland, *What a Transactional Lawyer Needs to Know: Identifying and Implementing Competencies for Transactional Lawyers*, 5 J. Assn Legal Writing Directors 118 (2008).

2   Carl J. Circo, *Teaching Transactional Skills in Partnership with the Bar*, 9 Berkeley Bus. L. J. 187 (2012).

3   Goodwill is an intangible asset that results from the acquisition of one company by another company for more than its book value or net worth. Examples of what constitute goodwill include the acquired company's: well-known name or brand; strong employee morale or relationships, and strong customer base.

APPENDIX 23.2

Legal Research—A Critical Skill for Transactional Practice

A fundamental reality of legal education is that law school classes only provide limited exposure to the important core lawyering skill of legal research. Considering the limited treatment it receives in school, you may be surprised to discover how many assignments law student employees and new attorneys receive which require significant legal research. While in law school, you may want to take practice-oriented and advanced legal research classes which will expose you to many different tools of the trade and help you develop more sophisticated research skills. One of the best ways to learn effective research skills is through hands-on practice dealing with real-world clients. Externships provide an excellent opportunity to gain this experience.

Researching for Transactional Practice

A critical lesson when it comes to legal research is the importance of developing and implementing an effective legal research strategy. While in law school, it is difficult to develop a full appreciation for the costs associated with being a practicing attorney. Subscription databases can be expensive and employers prefer to hire attorneys who effectively manage their time and use of these resources so as to avoid incurring unnecessary expenses which will be billed to the client or absorbed by the employer. Taking just a few minutes to plan before you begin research can mitigate these financial considerations in addition to saving you a lot of headache and frustration.

Any research strategy should begin with a thorough review of any facts provided. If you need additional information to tackle the project, ask follow-up questions of your externship supervisor or solicit more information from your client/employer. For example, you may wish to ask what kind of potential transactions, whether one type or multiple options, are being considered. Choice of jurisdiction also is an important consideration because the choice of law incorporated into the agreement may be different from your home jurisdiction. You may wish to ascertain what documents you need to draft. Multiple legal documents may be required for a transaction. Finally, consider asking your supervisor where to find some useful legal research tools such as subject-specific treatises and transactional practice tools.

Keep in mind that as your research progresses, you may encounter additional factual and legal issues which escaped your initial review. The legally significant facts and issues you identify can provide a good starting point to ascertain potentially relevant areas of law and search terms. It is important to cultivate a mindset which recognizes that legal research is an iterative process which may require you to modify or expand your original search criteria. Throughout this process, you should utilize a research log in order to keep track of the resources you have consulted and search terms employed in order to avoid needless duplication of effort. For further suggestions on developing a research plan, see Chapter 17 on Writing for Practice.

Online Platforms and Print Resources

A common observation among law librarians when they assist students with research projects is that students tend to conduct their research exclusively using the main search bar on one of the two major subscription platforms—Lexis and Westlaw. While these platforms can supply a wealth of content and searching them has become easier than ever, this approach can be problematic.

Neither platform provides fully comprehensive access to legal information. As a result of ownership rights or licensing agreements, many important works are exclusive to one online research platform. If you limit yourself to either Lexis or Westlaw, your search may be incomplete because an extremely helpful publication may be located on a different platform than the one you are using. Learning where different resources are located comes from experience. Since effective legal research requires developing a familiarity with the online platform's underlying content, overreliance on the main search bar while in law school may hinder the development of your legal research proficiency.

Some researchers fail to expand their research beyond Lexis and/or Westlaw—likely because of the significant attention each platform receives in law school. However, law schools and legal employers may also subscribe to a host of different online research platforms with their own exclusive content such as Bloomberg Law, CCH IntelliConnect, RIA Checkpoint, Loislaw, and HeinOnline.

Additionally, while many resources now are available through one of the many different legal research platforms, there are many useful publications which, for a variety of reasons, still must be used in print. Overlooking different online research platforms or print materials may complicate your research process, resulting in increased delay and frustration or the omission of important potential issues from your analysis.

Secondary Sources and Practice-Oriented Publications

Secondary sources and practice-oriented materials can be invaluable tools when conducting legal research—especially if you are unfamiliar with the subject material. These resources, which can include analytical texts such as treatises and drafting guides, can help you identify additional legal issues, increase your understanding of the law, and improve the quality of the transactional documents you draft. These publications focus on specific areas of law and/or jurisdictions. Some resources may provide comprehensive analysis on an entire subject area, such as Nimmer on Copyright; focus on a narrower legal topic, such as Sarbanes-Oxley implementation; or address specific legal scenarios, such as launching a start-up company. Practitioners view certain publications, such as Nimmer on Copyright, as preeminent works because of their high quality and reliability. A simple internet search of academic law library websites for a treatise finder resource will help you to identify these secondary sources and their online availability, if any.

Transactional-Focused Tools

One of the main responsibilities for a transactional attorney is drafting different kinds of agreements or other relevant documents. Many commercial vendors offer online and print products designed to assist lawyers in creating quality legal documents. Attorneys use these drafting guides for two main purposes: to reduce time and effort—no need to "reinvent the wheel"—and to keep track of the potential legal considerations implicated when drafting a document, which helps reduce the risk of accidentally omitting important legal considerations.

Lexis and Westlaw each maintain a transactional-focused legal research platform which should be available through your regular law school subscription: Lexis Practice Advisor and Practical Law respectively. Each platform provides access to useful transactional law information, but the main resources of each platform are the analytical tools and drafting aids. When we refer to "drafting aids," there are three major types of resources: checklists, template documents, and template clauses.

Drafting aids are valuable because they serve as a starting point to help attorneys identify legal issues and draft transactional documents. Checklists provide a collection of legal considerations which should be reviewed when dealing with a particular transaction-type or document. They can help a transactional attorney identify, organize, and keep track of the important legal issues which need to be addressed. Template documents and clauses are sample agreements, or individual clauses related to an agreement, which will provide you with a starting point for drafting the agreement. In all likelihood, the sample will require modification to fit your client's particular situation.

While these drafting guides are helpful when writing a document, exercise caution when using guides. Checklists may contain a lot of useful information, but they may not be comprehensive or may not reflect subsequent changes to the law. Template documents and clauses also may be outdated, poorly worded, or omit some relevant legal considerations.

A practical consideration when using these template documents and clauses, or when receiving "form" agreements from opposing parties, is that these documents are just starting points and not the way that a particular document necessarily is required to be drafted. In fact, templates and "form documents" provided by opposing counsel, may contain language which is unfavorable to your client. If this proves to be the case, check to see if you can locate templates which contain more favorable language. If you are unable to locate a more favorable template, it may be necessary to modify the less favorable document to make the agreement more acceptable to your client.

Beyond these template documents and clauses, which are published by legal vendors, the Securities and Exchange Commission (SEC)'s EDGAR database provides access to real-world examples of executed transactional documents and agreements. These real-world examples are filed by publicly-traded companies as part of their mandatory disclosure requirements. When a company is required to submit a regulatory disclosure form such as the 10-K or 8-K discussed under Company Research below, the company may include one of these agreements as an attachment called an "Exhibit." While these documents can be searched and accessed through the SEC's free online portal, these documents and specific clauses can be more easily researched through robust subscription platforms such as Bloomberg Law.

Company Research

While legal research plays an important role in conducting transactional work, you will encounter various situations which require you to perform non-legal research. One common type of research transactional attorneys may encounter involves gathering intelligence about another business' activities. There are many reasons why your client/employer may want this information, such as a contemplated merger, acquisition, or a major contract with a supplier or distributor. In these cases, you may be helping your client ascertain the other company's financial health, their business entanglements, and/or their litigation exposure in order to inform the client's benefits-risk analysis and subsequent legal discussions.

When it comes to conducting this type of business research, there are three major categories of company for which there are special research considerations. These three major company types are publicly-traded companies, privately-held companies, and nonprofit organizations.

As discussed in the financial statements section, publicly-traded companies are required to make certain mandatory disclosures to the SEC through various forms and their attached exhibits. Filings submitted from 1996 forward can be accessed electronically through the EDGAR platform. In addition to the free EDGAR service, these filings can be researched through subscription databases which tend to offer more robust search options. When attempting to locate regulatory disclosures made through EDGAR, it is best to use a unique identifier associated with the company to avoid research complications that can occur if there is confusion between similarly named businesses or a company conducts business under a different name than the one under which it is registered. These unique identifiers can include the Central Index Key (CIK) which is a numerical code assigned by the SEC to each individual company or the company's ticker symbol under which it is listed on one of the stock exchanges—such as the New York Stock Exchange (NYSE)—or the Over-The-Counter Market (OTC)—for example NASDAQ. In addition to EDGAR, recent major filings made by the company such as its 10-K annual financial disclosure, typically is located on the organization's investor relations page.

Unlike publicly-traded companies, researching privately-held entities can pose a greater challenge because they are not subject to the same mandatory disclosure requirements. As a practical matter, it is important to temper your expectations about the type, quantity, and quality of information you may be able to locate. You may be able to access business information about these companies from other sources through subscription legal research platforms such as Bloomberg Law and business-oriented research tools such as Hoover's Online and Thomson One. In some instances, privately-held companies may be required to make certain disclosures to the SEC such as when a business permits all employees to purchase stock in the employer's company or when institutions are member- or customer-owned businesses.

Even if the business entity is not required to make mandatory disclosures to the SEC, it may be required to submit publicly-accessible information to other federal or state regulatory agencies, such as the mandatory reporting disclosures made by financial institutions like banks and credit unions. A public records search can uncover valuable information such as details about real property owned by the company. Also, useful information may have been disclosed in court docket filings where the company you are researching was engaged in litigation. Legal, business, and/or mainstream news publications may report about business details not otherwise available to the public. If needed, a company research report can be commissioned from a commercial provider, but the costs may vary.

The difficulty level for researching a nonprofit company falls somewhere in between publicly-traded and privately-held entities. Depending on the nonprofit's mission and objectives, these organizations may choose to voluntarily disclose financial and other pertinent information through their websites. Certain charitable organizations, to maintain their tax-exempt status, may be required to make mandatory disclosures to the IRS using the agency's Form 990. The online resource Guidestar provides free access, with registration, to these IRS disclosures. As is the case with privately-held companies, and publicly-traded ones as well, public records, litigation documents, and news articles can be mined for potentially valuable information concerning the nonprofit organization.

APPENDIX 23.3

Learning Agenda

University of Denver

Sturm College of Law

A signed pdf copy must be uploaded to TWEN on or before the due date specified in the Course Requirements.

Student:

Office:

Supervising Attorney:

You will use this plan in developing the Learning Agenda for your externship, in conjunction with your Supervising Attorney. Use this plan to make note of specific areas in which you would like to improve during your externship, and the activities you will try to do to improve in that area. This form is due within the first two weeks of your externship.

While the questions on this form address the student's learning goals, the Legal Externship Program at Denver Law recognizes and believes that a Legal Externship is an experience that should benefit the host organization just as it benefits the student extern. In determining what assignments to give to law students, Supervising Attorneys should, of course, prioritize the organization's goals and needs along with the student's learning objectives.

1. What areas of substantive law will you focus on during this externship?

    ☐ Employment law

    ☐ Health Law

    ☐ Employee benefits: ERISA, COBRA, HIPAA

    ☐ Securities

    ☐ Environmental law: CERCLA, NEPA

    ☐ Foreign Corrupt Practices Act

    ☐ International Law

    ☐ Ethics and Compliance

- ☐ Real Estate
- ☐ Intellectual Property
- ☐ Administrative Law
- ☐ Understand legal issues as related to business issues that frequently arise in industry

2. What activities or projects in this externship placement could help strengthen your legal research skills?

- ☐ Research re motions, briefs, discovery
- ☐ Research re policy issues
- ☐ Research re employee manual

3. What activities or projects in this externship placement could help strengthen your oral communication skills?

- ☐ Improve ability to ask relevant questions to clarify assignments and communicate findings effectively
- ☐ Participate in conference calls with clients and management, understand better legal communication within the business context
- ☐ Observe and participate in client and management meetings
- ☐ Create a presentation and present to management a topic of interest, e.g. contract review system
- ☐ Present results of legal research orally in one-on-one and group settings; field questions

4. What activities or projects in this externship placement could help strengthen your written communication skills?

- ☐ Draft letters and memos—internal clients, third party affiliates, vendors, etc.
- ☐ Draft/edit/review contracts (e.g. sales, purchases, non-compete, non-disclosure, employment, etc.)
- ☐ Prepare motions, briefs, discovery, etc.
- ☐ Prepare policy summaries, draft policies
- ☐ Have a writing sample at the end of the externship
- ☐ Draft employment policy and/or handbook
- ☐ Draft compliance program

5. What activities or projects in this externship placement could help strengthen your fact investigation skills?

   ☐ Participate in internal company investigations and apply facts to law to make recommendation to internal client

   ☐ Apply both internal company fact investigation and external fact investigation to law, business policy, etc. in solving a complex legal/business problem

   ☐ Become familiar with research methods outside of Westlaw/Lexis that in-house counsel find helpful and efficient

6. What activities or projects in this externship placement could provide you with an opportunity to interact with clients?

   ☐ Attend meetings with internal client, participate in client interviewing and counseling sessions

   ☐ Understand structure of organization, and work with as many different departments as possible

7. What activities or projects in this externship placement could help strengthen your understanding of how to manage a legal practice of this type?

   ☐ Understand cost benefit of using in-house versus outside counsel

   ☐ Understand pros and cons of using contract lawyers, from both the perspective of the company and the contract lawyer

   ☐ Exercise time management with respect to school and work at externship: Learn at least two new time management tools

   ☐ Prioritize tasks: Ask attorneys how they would like me to prioritize tasks if I don't know

   ☐ Understand legal issues that commonly arise in my company/industry and implement effective and efficient ways to deal with them

8. What activities or projects in this externship placement could help strengthen your sense of professional identity? "Professional identity" includes understanding and respecting the Rules of Professional Conduct, demonstrating awareness of conflicts and obligations beyond those of the Rules of Professional Conduct, developing a sense of self as a professional, and dealing with stress in productive way.

☐ Meet with at least 3 attorneys in office and discuss work/life balance; how they obtained their positions, satisfaction/dissatisfaction with their positions and the practice of law, etc.

☐ Continue to develop sense of self as professional

☐ Define myself as professional employee and an individual

☐ Understand how personal values impact work/life balance

☐ Understand culture of office and assimilate into that culture, while preserving my own identity

9. If this legal organization is covered by Colorado's Student Practice Act,[1] and you are eligible to practice under the Act, what activities or projects in this externship setting could provide you with opportunities to appear in court?

10. What skills, apart from the ones mentioned above, are essential in order to excel in this practice area? What activities or projects in this externship placement could help you learn these skills?

☐ Regularly reflect on meetings, client contact, different lawyering styles, legal vs. business decisions, professionalism, etc.

Signature of Supervising Attorney (required)   Date

Signature of student   Date

ENDNOTES

1   For information on the Student Practice Act, please see Rule 226.5, or refer to the Student Practice Act section of the LEGAL EXTERNSHIP HANDBOOK, http://www.law.du.edu/index.php/legal-externship-program/legal-externship-handbook. Students must have completed 60 credit hours in order to be eligible to practice under the Act.

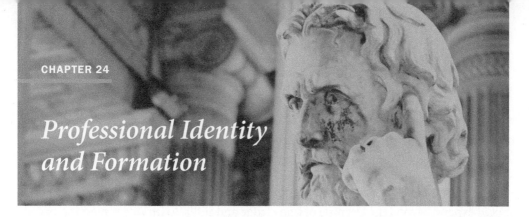

Professional Identity and Formation

DAISY HURST FLOYD & TIMOTHY W. FLOYD

*"I wish my identity weren't
so wrapped up with who I am."*

Introduction

Much of your legal education has been devoted to learning substantive law and to learning how to analyze legal materials—that prototypical but elusive skill of "thinking like a lawyer." You probably also have taken courses in which you have learned lawyering skills such as interviewing, negotiation, drafting, and trial advocacy. And as you already have recognized, one of the most important ways to learn lawyering skills is to take a "real world" experiential education course such as an externship.

Yet, there is more going on in your legal education than learning valuable knowledge and skills. You are in the midst of a transformational experience. As you go through law school, you are taking on a new professional identity as you move from being a non-lawyer toward becoming a lawyer. You are learning about the law, acquiring the distinctive skills and habits of being a lawyer, and developing an understanding of the many ethical obligations that guide a professional's actions. You are developing new ways of thinking, talking, writing, and interacting with others.

In recent years, law schools have begun to recognize that the goals of legal education should expand beyond the learning of knowledge and skills, to include something called "professional formation," sometimes also referred to as "formation of professional identity."[1] This educational goal of professional formation recognizes that legal education is a transformative process that happens whether or not you are conscious of it. Your goal should be to make the transformative process a conscious one: to pay attention to your transformation and make deliberate choices in shaping that process so it helps you become a competent, ethical, and fulfilled attorney.

Making deliberate choices about the professional formation that occurs in law school will help you in three ways: First, it will allow you to practice with excellence by integrating essential knowledge, skills, and values you are gaining in law school. During moments of professional practice, lawyers must call on multiple capacities in an instant, and integration of professional knowledge, skills, and values will allow you to be effective at that task.

Second, proper formation is essential to ensuring you will act ethically in your role as a professional. Acting ethically requires more than knowledge of the legal rules; it is at least as much about having certain kinds of personal characteristics as it is about what you know. In the midst of the pressures of practice, characteristics such as self-awareness, courage, resilience, emotional intelligence, and judgment are crucial. The process of professional formation will help you develop the characteristics that define the kind of lawyer you want to be.

Third, this formative process is essential to your well-being as a lawyer. Proper and healthy formation of professional identity allows lawyers to live lives that are personally and professionally satisfying. Studies show that lawyers who are professionally excellent and who practice with the highest ethical standards are also the lawyers who experience the most internal satisfaction from their careers.

This chapter will define what is meant by professional formation and offer suggestions for ways in which an externship can support your healthy professional formation.

How to Develop your Professional Identity

There are many ways you can use your legal education to support your own professional formation. Participating in one or more externships during law school can be crucial to that end. An externship is an ideal opportunity to focus on your own emerging professional identity and pay attention to the transformative aspect of your education. Importantly, externships allow you both to observe lawyers in action and to practice some lawyering tasks yourself, thereby providing a chance to develop professional and personal habits that will help you become an effective and ethical lawyer and live a life of satisfaction and fulfillment in the law.

Becoming an effective, ethical, and fulfilled lawyer is a complex undertaking that will not happen overnight. And it will not happen automatically. Instead, studies have shown that professional formation is developmental, meaning that it will happen over time. Moreover, unless you are intentional about this process, you will not develop the characteristics that will allow you to be the kind of lawyer you want to be.

Your goal should be to develop habits of action that will support your work as a lawyer. In the midst of practice, there may not be time for extensive deliberation or thorough investigation. Good lawyers are able to act effectively in the moment because they have developed habits of effective and ethical practice. The time to begin acquiring those habits is while you are a law student. Many people assume that law school is for learning substantive law and legal analysis and other skills and you begin and build your practice habits only after graduation. While you will be developing habits then, you do not need to wait to acquire habits of practice; you can use your time as a law student to acquire good habits. Legal education provides you a support system for trying out different habits and learning what does and does not work well.

An externship supports your development of good professional habits through observation, practice, and reflection. You will observe lawyers in action and engage in some lawyering tasks under the supervision of a lawyer. Just as importantly, the externship provides you opportunities to reflect upon what you have observed or experienced so you are constantly improving your newly-acquired lawyering skills. Research shows people do not improve over time just because they gain experience. Rather, they improve only if they reflect upon their experiences and then use that reflection to improve the next time they do something. A repeated cycle of reflection and improved action allows you to develop the right kinds of habits. But, reflection is not only about how to improve actions that did not go well. Reflection is also important when things go well so you know how to repeat successful actions. This cycle of reflection and successful action will benefit your professional development whether you are reflecting upon your own actions or someone else's actions. See Chapter 8 on Reflection and Journal Writing.

The externship course is specifically designed to allow you to observe others, practice your developing lawyering skills, and reflect upon what you have seen or done. It also provides you with support for these tasks in the form of your supervising attorney, your externship teacher, and your classmates. Externship courses expect that supervisors take on externs because they want to help with the students' development. When you are engaging in lawyering tasks, you always have the safety net of a supervising attorney who wants to help you do your best and continue to improve. Your externship teacher is assigning readings and exercises designed to help you work on skills of reflection. And, your fellow students in externships are going through similar experiences and are a good resource for reflecting on your collective experiences.

Developing Habits That Integrate Multiple Lawyering Capacities

So, what kinds of habits can you be developing during law school and later? It is helpful to think about habits that support integration of everything you are learning about being a good lawyer. Law school is typically organized so you learn about different skills or knowledge in discrete courses. Nevertheless, there are many competencies and capacities needed by good lawyers, and acquiring those competencies requires you to integrate all you are learning. It is helpful to think of three types of integration that support the excellent, ethical, and fulfilling practice of law:

- First, excellence in practice requires the integration of professional knowledge, skills, and values and the ability to access multiple capacities at once in the midst of conditions of inherent uncertainty.

- Second, ethical practice requires that you internalize the rules and values of the profession and also develop traits to support ethical action such as courage, vision, and wisdom.

- Third, fulfillment in practice requires that you integrate personal and professional values and avoid rigidly separating yourself into personal and professional roles.

Supporting Excellent Practice: Integration of Knowledge, Skills, and Values

First, a good lawyer integrates knowledge, skills, and values. As a law student, you are integrating the lessons learned in the classroom with those learned through extracurricular activities and work experiences. And, all of those experiences integrate different kinds of lessons: some impart substantive knowledge, such as what negligence means; others help you develop particular skills, such as legal analysis or how to conduct a client interview; and yet others are about professional values, such as the fiduciary duty owed to a client or the requirement of attorney-client confidentiality. The best lawyers have fully integrated these three types of professional attributes: knowledge, skills, and values.

A successful and ethical lawyer will call upon multiple areas of knowledge, skills, and values every day. But, you do not call on them one at a time; successful lawyers are able to integrate and call upon these capacities as needed. For example, being knowledgeable about law and procedure, being a good listener, being skilled at legal analysis, being an effective communicator, and being honest are all important attributes of successful lawyers. You may need all of those attributes to help you form the right question in a deposition or make a compelling argument at the negotiating table. As a fully formed professional, therefore, you are calling on a capacity, a "professional identity," that allows you to integrate those attributes and turn them into effective action.

> **Exercise 24.1 "Role Model" Lawyer:** Choose one lawyer you particularly admire and describe that lawyer's characteristics or virtues you would like to emulate in your career. The lawyer you describe need not be perfect; no one is. Pick out a lawyer about whom there is at least one thing you especially admire. It may be a lawyer you know personally or have worked with or a lawyer you have only observed from a distance. It may even be a lawyer from history about whom you have read. It, however, should be a real lawyer and not one from fiction.
>
> Write at least two pages describing your lawyer and discussing why you chose that person. Be specific about why you admire this person, giving examples if possible. In particular, be specific about the characteristic or characteristics of that lawyer you admire and would like to emulate.

Supporting Ethical Practice: Integration of Professional Values

The principal skill taught in most law school courses is learning how to analyze rules and principles, including the particular ethical rules and standards that apply to lawyers. When crunch time comes, however, simply knowing the substantive and ethical rules and being skilled at analysis will not be enough. Knowing the right thing to do is difficult enough, but actually doing the right thing is even more difficult, and of course it is doing the right thing that is essential.

The psychologist James Rest has described four distinct yet interactive components to moral action: moral sensitivity, moral motivation, moral reasoning, and moral implementation. Without any one of the four, a person will find it difficult to act ethically. Good ethical reasoning is crucial, but ethical sensitivity, ethical motivation, and ethical implementation are also necessary conditions to ethical action. Law school classes focus heavily on developing your reasoning skills, but you rarely get a chance to put those skills into action. In an externship, however, you can observe others integrating ethical reasoning skills with the other conditions for ethical action, and you can begin to develop your own ability to integrate all four components.

Ethical **sensitivity** involves a deep awareness of various factors at play in any situation including recognizing ethical issues, which requires knowing the regulations, codes, and norms of the legal profession and when they apply; anticipating the reactions and feelings of others; considering alternative courses of action and possible consequences; and being able to see things from the perspectives of other individuals and groups, and from legal and institutional perspectives. Ethical **motivation** refers to the importance you give to ethical values in competition with other values. Values such as self interest in terms of income or wealth, protection of one's community or organization, or self-actualization may trump concern for doing what is right and mean that, even though one knows what the ethical action is, other values prevent acting ethically. Ethical **implementation** refers to whether the professional has sufficient toughness, ego strength, and courage to act ethically. Acting ethically is sometimes difficult; this component reminds us it can take courage and a clear vision of the kind of lawyer you want to be for you to actually implement an ethical decision.

As you participate in your externship, be aware of the difficult things lawyers do in their work. Take time to reflect upon whether the successful completion of a lawyering task has demonstrated ethical sensitivity, reasoning, motivation, and implementation.

For example, suppose you are placed in a prosecutor's office for your externship. You observe one of the senior lawyers in the office as the lawyer decides how to respond to a Brady motion seeking the disclosure of exculpatory information in a major felony prosecution. Imagine the prosecutor's files contain information that is arguably helpful to the defendant, but under the facts of this case, it is not entirely clear the law requires disclosure. The lawyer's supervisor, the elected District Attorney, would prefer not to disclose the information and has made an argument as to why the law does not require it.

The lawyer who is trying the case, however, has come to a different conclusion. She believes the law requires her to disclose the information that is helpful to the defendant and recognizes disclosure will likely jeopardize the successful prosecution of the case. She makes the difficult decision to disclose the information, and the case ends up being dismissed.

Think about what this lawyer did through the lens of the four components of ethical action. First, the lawyer recognized the Brady motion raised ethical issues, displaying ethical sensitivity and an awareness of the particular professional standards and rules that apply. She also used her ethical reasoning skills to reason through legal and ethical analysis and to conclude the information she ultimately disclosed was within the legal definition of what the Supreme Court has said is subject to a Brady motion. Additionally, by deciding to disclose the information, she displayed both ethical motivation and implementation: she valued acting ethically above her desire to have a successful prosecution and possible career advancement, and she displayed courage in contradicting her boss, never an easy thing to do. In this professional action, the attorney brought to the situation multiple capacities and demonstrated the four components of ethical action. See Chapter 21 on Criminal Justice Lawyering.

As you observe similar situations in your externship, you can begin to prepare for the kinds of difficult situations you will face as an attorney. Reflecting in this way upon an ethical decision you observe will help you understand the complexities of being a lawyer and develop your own habits of integrating the components of ethical action so you are prepared to be an ethical attorney. For further discussion of ethical issues that may arise in externships and in practice, see Chapters 10–13 on Ethical Issues in Externships.

Supporting Fulfilled Practice: Integration of the Personal and the Professional

A final type of integration that supports positive professional formation is the integration of the professional and the personal. Although you are acquiring new professional knowledge, skills, and values during your education, you do not lose the personal knowledge, skills, and values that helped define who you were before beginning law school. It is crucial that you see your responsibilities as a lawyer as integral to your identity as a person. In other words, professional identity and personal identity must be woven together.[2]

You arrived at law school as an adult, informed by your life experiences up to that point, including family and other relationships; physical, mental, and emotional experiences; and completion of high school and college. You have developed beliefs about a number of things, including a set of moral and ethical values that guide your conduct. It is tempting to believe that as a fully-formed ethical being, the values you have developed and relied upon so far will be all you need to guide you in living out your new life as a lawyer. However, while some of the values you will rely on in practice are things you knew before starting law school, others are things that are particular to being a lawyer and will have been developed during law school and afterward.

For example, before beginning law school, most people will understand that you should keep confidences when asked to do so. They will not know, however, about the definition of confidentiality that applies to a lawyer and that addresses a range of detailed topics: that the circle of confidentiality includes many people, such as the lawyer's secretary or paralegal; that the lawyer's duty of confidentiality begins at the moment a prospective client contacts the lawyer; and that exceptions to all these rules may exist.

The good news is that personal virtues and values do not need to be set aside as you develop your professional identity. For example, a personal value of treating others with respect is compatible with the lawyer's professional responsibility to negotiate with an adverse party. Your fiduciary obligation to your client requires you to try to achieve your client's goals, but it does not require you to treat adversaries with contempt or mislead them about a material fact.

The well-integrated lawyer can fulfill both personal and professional values at the same time. Atticus Finch is a hero to many, including lawyers, because he was the same person at home as he was in public.[3] But many express concern that lawyers lead divided lives—their professional roles require them to act in amoral or even immoral ways, acting in ways they would not act outside of their professional roles. That is a fundamental mistake. The separation of the professional role from the person of the lawyer is morally questionable; it is not convincing to tell yourself that "it's OK to act immorally because I'm just acting in my role as a lawyer." It is also psychologically destructive. None of us can separate our personal lives from our professional roles so easily, and the effort to do so can lead to distress.

As you integrate the personal and professional, it is helpful to be aware of whether the values guiding your conduct are based on intrinsic or extrinsic motivations. Intrinsic values and motivations are fulfilled when a person chooses an action she genuinely enjoys or which furthers a fundamental purpose. In contrast, extrinsic values and motivations drive a person to choose an action because of external rewards, such as money, grades, or honors; the avoidance of guilt or fear; or, to please or impress others. Research informs us that when intrinsic values are primary, people experience satisfaction and well-being. On the other hand, when extrinsic values are primary, they experience angst and distress.[4] To be sure, most people are motivated by both extrinsic and intrinsic values. Often, they are motivated by some combination of both. A similar combination of purposes guides most people in their professional work. Most work because they need to earn money, which represents an extrinsic motivation. But, those who can combine their need for money with doing something that fulfills a fundamental purpose or gives them enjoyment will be both happier and better at what they do. See Chapter 25 on Work and Well-being.

As you develop the habit of integrating your personal values and newly-acquired professional values, remind yourself about the reasons you came to law school and of the type of lawyer you want to be. The best and most fulfilled lawyers are doing work that both has value for others and brings them personal fulfillment. One without the other is very difficult to sustain. Therefore, reflecting on why you are on this path toward becoming a lawyer is crucial to integrating your personal and professional identity. In your other classes, you can get so caught up in the details and the discrete skills you are learning that it is hard to step back and reflect on these deeper issues. The externship course, however, asks you to do just that and provides you resources for doing so.

> **Exercise 24.2 Challenges to Well-being and Satisfaction in the Law:** Consider the following:
>
> - What challenges does law practice bring to one's satisfaction and well-being?
> - What challenges along these lines are experienced by the lawyers you have seen through your placement?
> - What tools are available for meeting those challenges—either those you are aware of or have observed?
>
> If you are comfortable doing so, you may want to ask these questions of the lawyers with whom you are working.

> **Exercise 24.3 Feeling Authentic and Alive:** In Transforming Practices: Finding Joy and Satisfaction in the Legal Life, by Steven Keeva, the author asks his readers: "when you are most yourself—that is, when you feel most authentic and alive—how does that affect the way you experience practicing law?"

Reflect on similar questions, but reframed:

Think about the times in your life when you have felt or you feel the most your-self—when you feel the most authentic and alive. Do these times occur when you are in a particular place, doing a particular thing, or with a particular person or people?

- What do these times tell you about who you are and what is important to you?

- Do you ever experience this feeling when you are doing something related to the law or being a law student?

- Do you think you can experience this feeling through being a lawyer, in whatever way you hope to put your education to work after graduation? Why or why not?

Summary: Using the Externship to Achieve Integration and Develop Good Professional Habits

An externship provides an unparalleled opportunity to build your individual skills of self-awareness and reflection. All of your experiences provide the opportunity not only to learn from the experience itself, but just as importantly, to learn from reflection upon the experience. As we have emphasized, effective ethical representation requires integration of multiple capacities and competencies. Reflection upon your experiences will allow you to recognize the interplay of these multiple capacities in your own professional practice.

Imagine, for example, that you are asked to do an intake interview with a client who is seeking to write a will. You have a basic knowledge of the law of wills, and you ask a series of questions aimed at getting the relevant facts for that purpose. You learn early in the interview that the client plans to leave nothing to her daughter and leave everything to her son. Assume you respond with obvious disagreement and ask in an incredulous tone if the client has really thought this through. At that point, the client becomes emotional and defensive and is reluctant to engage further with you.

If you want to maximize learning from this experience, after the interview is over you will take a few moments to reflect upon the experience and think about what went well and what did not go well. You might consider how you simultaneously drew upon knowledge, values, and skills, the first type of integration. How well did your substantive knowledge of the law of wills help you decide what questions to ask? Did you properly observe the professional value of client autonomy? Did you effectively use interviewing skills by using the right mix of open-ended and closed questions?

You also should realize, however, that effective use of knowledge and skills was not sufficient to provide quality representation of this client. The interpersonal dynamics, including the client's and your own emotional responses during the interview, played a crucial role in the meeting not going as well as you would have liked. When the client became emotional and defensive, and in response, you tried to justify your own question, the client became even more defensive. Upon reflection, you realize that nonjudgmental listening to the client about such an emotional topic may have done more to create trust and rapport. Once that relationship of trust is established, the client may be more likely to hear your concerns and questions about cutting out the daughter.

You also should consider how your own values may have affected your response to this client. Upon reflection, you may realize that you personally value even-handedness within families and you think the client is making a mistake in showing such partiality to one child over another. It is entirely appropriate for you as the legal counselor to engage with the client in a dialogue about treating children even-handedly. You must also recognize, however, that the client needs to be given the moral autonomy to exercise her own choice in this matter. If you wish the client to consider your views, you must be conscious of your own values, while also recognizing that the client's values may differ from yours.

Thinking about these questions raises both the second and third types of integration. Were the four components of ethical action relevant to this situation and, if so, did you display all of them? Did you properly balance your personal and professional values, or did your discomfort with the client's decision cause you to override her autonomy? Or was the difficulty not with the proper balancing of your personal and professional values, but rather with a failure of interviewing skills? Could you have approached this matter differently through better questioning to get the client to reconsider her decision?

The answers to these questions are not obvious. The important thing is that you ask them. If you engage in the kind of reflection described above, you will do a better job the next time you interview a client. You will appreciate the multiple dimensions and complexities of the task, and you will work consciously to integrate the multiple competencies and capacities needed for effective representation. In your next interview, you will try harder to engage in active, nonjudgmental listening before you jump to conclusions and offer advice. See Chapter 5 on Effective Communication and Professional Relationships. And you will recognize how your own values affect your reaction to the client's proposed course of action. For more on working with clients, see Chapter 15 on Client Relationships.

If, on the other hand, you do not reflect on the experience, you are likely to repeat your mistakes again and again and perhaps continue to blame these unreasonable clients—never realizing that the responsibility was in part your own.

Exercise 24.4 Rereading Your Law School Admission Essay: Review the essay you wrote for your law school admission application. Write about your reaction upon reading the statement, including reflecting on the following questions:

- As you read this statement from the perspective of having completed one or two years of law school, are you surprised by its content? Why or why not?

- Does the statement accurately reflect
  — Who you are today?
  — Your current goals with regard to law school?
  — Your current goals with regard to the practice of law or other post-law school experiences?

- As you remember writing the statement, reflect upon the ways in which law school has and has not changed you and describe those.

- What is the most powerful lesson you have learned about yourself during your time in law school?

Feel free to comment upon anything else that comes to mind when you read the statement.

Exercise 24.5 Imagining Your Future: Imagine your life about 15 years from now. In this life you are imagining, things have worked out very well for you; your work life and your professional life are as you would want them to be. We want you to imagine an ideal, but within the bounds of realism. (That is, do not assume you have won $100,000,000 in the lottery)

Describe your work: What kind of work are you doing? What do you find rewarding or fulfilling about that work? What kind of organization do you work in (e.g., corporation, government agency, law firm, solo practice, something non-law related)? Who are the people you work with? How closely do you work together with others? How much autonomy and flexibility do you have in your work? Where (geographically—city, town, region, country) do you work?

Describe your life other than your work: Where do you live (city, rural area, near the beach, etc.)? Who are the people you are closest to (family, friends, etc.)?

> How much time do you spend with the important people in your life? How do you spend your time when you are not working? Do you have any practices (such as exercise, spiritual disciplines, religious involvement, hobbies) that keep you grounded? What do you do for fun, and how much time do you spend on those activities?
>
> What concrete steps can you take to achieve this ideal?
>
> How do you expect to deal with the inevitable failures and losses that will arise in this journey?

Conclusion

Any time you have the opportunity to observe lawyers in action and to practice lawyering tasks yourself, you may learn things that will make you a better lawyer. The externship course provides you with more: in addition to being in a work environment, you will be able to reflect upon those experiences and discuss them with others. Most importantly, through those observations, experiences, and reflections, you can choose how you will use the externship to help you on the road to becoming an effective, ethical, and satisfied lawyer.

ENDNOTES

1   EDUCATING LAWYERS, a report of the Carnegie Foundation for Advancement of Teaching, is perhaps the most influential study of legal education in decades. WILLIAM SULLIVAN, ET AL., EDUCATING LAWYERS: PREPARATION FOR THE PROFESSION OF LAW (2007). The Carnegie Report uses the metaphor of "apprenticeships" to discuss legal education. There are three such apprenticeships: the intellectual or cognitive apprenticeship develops what a lawyer knows and how a lawyer thinks; the practical apprenticeship develops the skills that a lawyer must possess; and the normative apprenticeship develops the lawyer's professional identity and purpose. This third apprenticeship, the formation of ethical and committed professionals, includes both learning the rules of conduct for lawyers and, perhaps more importantly, inculcating the values and ideals of the profession. The Carnegie Report notes that law schools do an excellent job on the cognitive apprenticeship, and in recent decades they have improved markedly in the skills apprenticeship. The Report suggests, however, that law schools should do more to develop and integrate the formation of professional identity throughout the law school experience. For more on the Carnegie Report, *see* Appendix I.1.

2   Another way to think about the integration of personal and professional values is that doing so will help you develop authenticity as a lawyer. For a discussion of how one can use the experiences of law school to become an authentic lawyer, *see* Daisy H. Floyd, *The Authentic Lawyer: Merging the Professional and the Personal, in* ESSENTIAL TRAITS OF THE PROFESSIONAL LAWYER (2013).

3   HARPER LEE, TO KILL A MOCKINGBIRD (1960).

4   *See, e.g.*, Lawrence S. Krieger, *What Makes Lawyers Happy? Transcending the Anecdotes with Data from 6200 Lawyers*, 83 GEO. WASH. L. REV. 554 (2015).

Work & Well-being

MARJORIE A. SILVER

When work is a pleasure, life is a joy.
When work is a duty, life is slavery!

—Maxim Gorky

his chapter addresses a concern many law students, and indeed lawyers, share: whether it is possible to have a rewarding and fulfilling career as well as a happy personal life. The short answer is yes it is. But that does not mean it is easy. What follows are information and suggestions that can help you make choices to heighten your satisfaction with your work as well as the rest of your life.

After asking you to reflect on your values and goals, we explore the science of well-being: what we know empirically about what enhances and detracts from life satisfaction. This knowledge can assist you in making choices to maximize your contentment with your life. We then share some sobering information about the incidence of depression and other emotional disorders within our profession.

From there we move on to review findings from various studies of lawyers about professional satisfaction and personal happiness. We consider how different career choices and types of workplaces might affect your well-being.

Next we focus on structural changes to the workplace. Law firms traditionally have been behind the curve in adopting family-friendly work policies; happily that is changing. We consider how legal employers are rethinking the demands placed on lawyers and other personnel without sacrificing the quality, quantity, or satisfaction with the work legal professionals produce for their clients.

Finally, we loop back to you in the here and now. As you proceed through law school, how can you successfully deal with the stresses you already have faced and will continue to encounter? And how can you best use your externship to enhance your understanding of yourself and the legal profession to build toward a career that complements the life you envision?

Taking Inventory

Your externship, whatever your placement, creates an opportunity for you to reflect on your values and goals and examine whether your placement is representative of the kind of career that would enhance your overall well-being. This means considering the relationship between the work you are doing now, the work you hope to do in the future, and your feelings and thoughts about that work. Begin by completing the following exercises that take an inventory of some of the qualities that are most important to you as you consider your future career.

> **Exercise 25.1** What were your goals for law school when you started, and how have they changed at this point? Where would you like to see yourself three years after law school? What kind of practice do you hope to do? In what kind of environment, and with what kind of schedule?

What We Know About Well-being

This section introduces you to a variety of theories about well-being. By thinking about these theories and putting some of the suggested practices into your daily life, you may enhance your well-being now in school, in your externship, and in life in general. Equally, if not more importantly, you will be able to carry this knowledge into your life as a lawyer. As you have likely learned through personal experience, many lawyers are not happy with their career choices. There is no reason for you to be among them. Entering this profession with your eyes open, informed by neuroscience and social science literature, will maximize your chances of being among those for whom work is a joy!

Flourishing Through Positive Psychology: The Science of Human Thriving

Thanks in large part to Freud and his contemporaries, for many years the focus of psychology was on understanding and treating **dysfunctionality**. Psychotherapy and psychoanalysis were aimed primarily at treating anxiety, depression, and other forms of mental illness. Happily, great strides have been made in recent decades toward realizing the benefits of **positive psychology,** the use of science to aid people in achieving a more satisfying life.

One important research finding of positive psychology is that optimists tend to be happier than pessimists. They also live longer, have more friends, and enjoy more successful lives. Importantly, while most of us tend to be genetically inclined toward one or the other, optimism **can be learned.**

> In his excellent book, STRESS MANAGEMENT FOR LAWYERS: HOW TO INCREASE PERSONAL & PROFESSIONAL SATISFACTION IN THE LAW (3rd ed. 2007), the late psychologist Amiram Elwork shares a personal story, along with some advice:
>
> [O]ptimism was ingrained in me very early. I have vivid memories of my mother philosophizing about the selectivism of perception and advocating for how much healthier it is to create an inner reality that focuses on the positive. She did not argue that optimists are more accurate than pessimists—only that they are happier and therefore more successful. You must become your own parent and convince yourself that becoming an optimist will be very beneficial for you.[1]

Similarly, according to positive psychologist Martin Seligman, the pillars of a fulfilling life include positive emotion, engagement, positive relationships, meaning, and accomplishment, his acronym for which is PERMA.[2] In addition to an optimistic outlook, all of these elements contribute to well-being, and often they are pursued for their own sake and not merely to achieve some independent, instrumental goal.

> In at least one study, meaning, the M in PERMA, or a sense of purpose trumped all other well-being factors in determining human longevity, regardless of age.[3]

Empirical evidence has shown that well-being and happiness can be enhanced through simple exercises, many of which are described in Seligman's most recent book, FLOURISH (listed under Further Resources). Seligman's website, https://www.authentichappiness.sas.upenn.edu/, provides many interactive opportunities that allow you to join studies or engage in other activities designed to enhance optimism and PERMA.

For example, here is an exercise one of Seligman's graduate students developed:

Every night for the next week, set aside ten minutes before you go to sleep. **Write down three things that went well today and why they went well.** You may use a journal or your computer to write about the events, but it is important that you have a physical record of what you wrote. The three things need not be earthshaking in importance: "My husband picked up my favorite ice cream for dessert on the way home from work today." Or they could be more momentous: "My sister just gave birth to a healthy baby boy".

Next to each positive event, answer the question, "Why did this happen?" For example, if you wrote that your husband picked up ice cream, write "because my husband is really thoughtful sometimes" or "because I remembered to call him from work and asked him to stop by the grocery store." Or if you wrote, "My sister just gave birth to a healthy baby boy," you might pick as a cause, "God was looking out for her," or "she did everything right during her pregnancy."

By focusing on what goes well in our lives rather than on what goes wrong, we can retrain our brains to think positively. Sometimes, of course, we need to focus on what went wrong in order to learn from mistakes and avoid them in the future; however, always focusing on bad events is not helpful and often sets us up for anxiety and depression. Although this exercise may seem difficult at first, it gets easier, and if you stick with it for a week, experience demonstrates that you will likely be less depressed and happier. These effects will last for some time, even if you discontinue the practice.[4]

Czikszentmihalyi's Flow

His name may be difficult to pronounce (six-cent-mihaly),[5] but the concept associated with his name is one almost everyone has experienced at one time or another, when you are so caught up in an activity you lose all track of time. Whether it is through one's work, reading an engrossing novel, or playing a favorite sport, there are activities that so absorb us the rest of the world fades away, and the line of demarcation between us and that in which we are engaged seems to disappear. This is what psychologist Mihaly Czikszentmihalyi means by "flow;" it is the "engagement" element of Seligman's PERMA, and it is a state in which we feel most happy to be alive.

Exercise 25.2 Can you think of a time when you have experienced 'flow'? Write a journal entry about it.

Self-Determination Theory, Intrinsic v. Extrinsic Values, and Motivation

Self-Determination Theory (SDT), developed by Edward Deci and Richard Ryan, holds that the critical determinants of well-being include autonomy, competence, and relatedness. Not surprisingly, this theory shares several commonalities with PERMA. When we feel we do not have control of our lives because external forces dictate what we are able to do—be that external force an autocratic government or a controlling parent—our sense of self-worth diminishes with a consequential negative impact on our well-being. Similarly, when we are consumed with feelings of not being good enough—at our work or in our personal relationships—we suffer adverse repercussions. When we feel alone in the world, lacking in nurturing relationships, depression often sets in.

When we **do** feel that we have some control over our lives (autonomy), when we are able to achieve a satisfying level of competence at the tasks in which we are engaged, and when we feel connected to others, individually and as part of various communities, then we thrive. In this state, we present our authentic selves to the world, we are who we say we are, and we act in ways that comport with our core values. This is the essence of Self-Determination Theory.

> *The relationship between values and stress is very simple. When we do things that conform to our values we feel positive emotions (e.g., pride), and when we do not conform to our values we feel negative emotions (e.g., guilt).*[6]
>
> **—Amiram Elwork, STRESS MANAGEMENT FOR LAWYERS**

A good deal of empirical evidence has established a correlation between **intrinsic motivation** and enhanced well-being. Intrinsic motivation, according to Ryan and Deci, is **authentic**, either self-authored or endorsed and internalized. It is something undertaken for its own sake (self-authored) or embraced because of an appreciation of its value or importance (endorsed, internalized). An example would be studying hard because you love learning (self-authored). Or studying hard because you understand the connection between doing so and achieving your goal of becoming a lawyer (endorsed and internalized). **Extrinsic** motivation, on the other hand, is driven by a desire to achieve some other end: because you want to get a good grade, make law review, secure a job with a top firm, or impress your friends and family.[7] Most of us are driven by a combination of motives, some intrinsic, some extrinsic. Research shows the more people are motivated intrinsically, the more successful, persistent, and fulfilled they tend to be.[8]

Closely related to motivation are goals. And similarly, to the extent one is motivated largely by intrinsic goals (love of learning, desire to be of service to others, to forge strong interpersonal relationships, to seek justice), the pursuit of those goals, in contrast to the attainment of extrinsic aspirations (more money and possessions, more status, better grades), produces more life satisfaction.[9] Interestingly, extrinsic goals tend to be limited: there is generally a measurable and finite quantity, often resulting in competition among peers.[10] No such scarcity exists for intrinsic goals: my love of learning in no way subtracts from yours.

Relatedness

Relatedness, having meaningful and positive social relationships, has long been seen as essential to thriving.[11] Whether one finds these connections with a few close friends or family, through communities of common interests, or in the workplace, **all** human beings require such connections to thrive.[12] Without these connections, we wither. Supported by such connections, we are better able to navigate life's vicissitudes. Strong social connections enhance our ability to navigate difficult situations. The business world has begun to embrace the value of social connectivity to economic success. For example, many businesses sponsor service projects where, for a day, their employees work together to clean up local parks or paint community centers. Social connectivity is not only good for business, it provides crucial psychological benefits as well. Employees experience a sense of connectedness to each other as well as to the larger community.

> In her TED talk, positive psychologist and researcher Barbara Fredrickson, author of LOVE 2.0, claims that even micro-connections, little moments with complete strangers, actually strengthen our heart muscles.[13]

Growth Mindsets, Adaptability and Resilience

Another determinant of well-being is whether one has a "fixed" or "growth" mindset. People with a fixed mindset tend to see a failure such as a bad grade as due to their inherent inadequacy. Those with a growth mindset may feel unhappy or distressed, but they then regroup: "Okay, what went wrong, and how do I fix it going forward?"

There is a clear correlation between optimism and a growth mindset. Optimists tend to see setbacks as discrete in time and place, temporary and surmountable. Pessimists see them as pervasive, permanent and insurmountable.[14] Happily, studies show that, as with optimism, one can learn to move from a fixed to a growth mindset.[15]

Closely related to having a growth mindset is being resilient—the ability to bounce back from adverse events that all of us experience at one time or another. Lawyers score poorly overall on tests of resilience. Many tend to be thin-skinned, defensive, and do not rebound well psychologically from setbacks.[16] There is a difference between what happens in our lives and how we respond to what happens. There are things over which we have control, and others over which we do not. We cannot change the past, but we can learn from the past as we move into the future.

The good news is that resilience is much more learned than genetic, and law students and lawyers can enhance their resilience through simple repeated exercises.

> How well do you bounce back from setbacks? You might want to check out Drs. Karen Reivich and Andrew Shatté's program for enhancing resilience in THE RESILIENCE FACTOR (2002).

Mindfulness Meditation and Other Contemplative Practices

Perhaps one of the most ancient practices to enhance well-being dates back to the Buddha: meditation. Once a practice confined to contemplative practitioners in religious orders, mindfulness meditation and other contemplative methods are now used by millions in all walks of life. Their legitimacy as tools for enhancing the quality of one's life has been validated by numerous neurological studies of the brain. Meditation, once thought of as touchy-feely, is now backed by decades of hard evidence about its value in regulating emotions. The brain has extraordinary plasticity. These studies demonstrate that meditation and other contemplative practices such as yoga actually **change** the brain in ways that decrease depression and anxiety, improve our cognitive abilities and focus, and enhance our general sense of well-being. Ever-increasing numbers of lawyers and law students are discovering the benefits of mindfulness meditation and other contemplative practices in decreasing stress, improving concentration, and enhancing focus. Several law schools now offer credit-bearing courses in such practices; many more offer extra-curricular opportunities for meditation and yoga.

Healthy Habits

Commonplace as it may seem, what we eat, whether we exercise, and how well and long we sleep have a significant impact on our well-being. While the benefits for our physical health may seem obvious, what we eat affects the biochemistry of our brains, and good nutrition supports better cognitive functioning, as well as more positive moods.[17]

Research on students across the United States has shown that subjects who perform aerobic-type exercises generate twice as many brain cells as those individuals who do not exercise, and they perform better on national and international tests. In a German study, people learned vocabulary words 20% faster after exercising than before. Law students and lawyers benefit as well from any complex physical activities that increase the speed and quality of the neurons in our brain, which in turn increases cognitive and memory functions.[18] Moderate physical exercise also enhances well-being and decreases anxiety and depression.[19]

The importance of adequate sleep cannot be overstated. Studies demonstrate that inadequate sleep contributes to irritability, depression, slower response time, poor decision-making, troubled relationships, and poor performance at work and school, not to mention a deleterious impact on our short and long-term physical health.[20] Sleep enhances our ability to think and learn more efficiently. Although there is no universal agreement among researchers on the amount of sleep we need, whatever it is, not having that sleep affects our brain's ability to function, in ways often difficult to reverse. We need REM sleep to consolidate the "memories" we are accumulating during the day, and studies show that a loss of even two nights of sleep results in a 60% cognitive decline. Although an afternoon nap may be considered by many a waste of valuable time, a study of NASA pilots showed they performed 34% better with a 26-minute nap, while a 45-minute nap improved cognition for more than six hours.[21] While longer naps help boost memory and enhance creativity, short naps improve alertness.[22] Further, studies show that sleeping after learning something new improves the brain's ability to solidify that learning.

Taking breaks from work—even work we love—allows us to recharge our batteries and improve our vitality. Short breaks during the day, weekends or other days off, and periodic vacations allow us to return to our daily tasks with renewed vigor.[23] Studies show that vacations improve mental health, as well as correlate with enhanced cognition and stronger work performance.

Concluding Thoughts About the Science of Well-being

Being a lawyer requires some thinking negatively: anticipating what might go wrong, what our adversaries' best arguments might be, focusing on real and potential problems that may arise for our clients. Lawyers do not tend to spend a great deal of time focusing on the positive. Yet negative thinking can lead to depression, and as we next explore, lawyers suffer depression at far greater rates than those in other populations. By becoming more familiar with how our brains work and practicing techniques for enhancing our well-being, many resources for which can be found at the end of this chapter, lawyers and law students can prevent or reverse their unhealthy habits.[24]

When the ingredients needed for thriving are absent, the risk of serious emotional and psychological dysfunction unfortunately multiplies. Studies consistently have shown law students and lawyers are at greater risk for substance abuse and depression than the general population.[25] Since the first major economic downturn of the twenty-first century hit, Lawyer Assistance Programs (LAPS) have reported a dramatic increase in the number of lawyers presenting with mental health problems. Several sensational lawyer suicides have captured the attention of the media and have prompted bar associations and other organizations to ramp up programs to address these problems.

Studies of Washington state lawyers from the 1990's showed that 33% of respondents reported problems with alcohol, cocaine abuse, or depression, with 19% suffering from depression and 18% identifying as problem drinkers.[26] Only 2.27% of the general population showed depression symptoms at this level.[27] The rate of alcohol abuse for the general population is estimated to be only 7%.[28] Furthermore, chemical dependency and mental illness are estimated to be involved in 60% to 80% of disciplinary actions taken against lawyers.[29] Studies show that lawyers exhibit more depression than any other occupational group.[30]

Speaking personally, in recent years I have observed a noticeable uptick in the number of students—both men and women—confiding in me that they are suffering from major anxiety and depression. Many of them entered law school with a history of such problems, although some of those had had no difficulties academically or otherwise during their undergraduate years. As someone who has suffered several acute episodes of major clinical depression over the course of my adult life, I know that the risk of excessive stress causing a relapse is greater for those of us with such a history, and so I have learned to integrate strategies into my life to minimize that risk. These include meditation, yoga, and learning to limit what I take on to things that are important to me.

Law school, as you likely have learned from personal experience, ramps up the stress factors considerably beyond what most students have experienced previously. Thus, students who have had problems in the past are at greater risk of reoccurrences during law school, which presents new and intense sources of stress. However, even without a history prior to law school, problems may still arise during law school or in practice, especially given that major clinical problems often appear for the first time during early adulthood.[31]

Establishing the healthy habits discussed earlier and recognizing the sources of excessive stress may be your best defense against succumbing to incapacitating distress. Familiarizing yourself with the signs and symptoms of depression and substance abuse will enable you to seek help early, before major problems occur.

Signs and symptoms of depression include

- feelings of helplessness and hopelessness,
- loss of interest in daily activities,
- appetite or weight changes,
- sleep changes,
- anger or irritability,
- loss of energy,
- self-loathing, and
- reckless behavior.

Numerous resources are available to law students struggling with life issues such as excessive stress, anxiety, depression, addiction, and other mental illnesses. These include your local or state Lawyer Assistance Programs as well as your school's counseling services. Links to several of these resources, including how to find the LAP in your jurisdiction, can be found at the end of this chapter under Further Resources.

Lawyers and Career Satisfaction

Lawyer (and Law Student) Well-being

Recent years have seen a burgeoning number of studies concerning lawyers' satisfaction with their careers and levels of well-being. Despite much anecdotal evidence to the contrary, a substantial majority of those who respond to such studies report satisfaction with their chosen careers.[32]

After the JD Study of Lawyer's Careers, a leading study on legal careers published jointly by the American Bar Foundation and the NALP Foundation for Law Career Research and Education, has been tracking a nationally representative cohort of thousands of lawyers since they were admitted into the bar in the year 2000. The researchers have so far issued three reports examining topics such as career satisfaction, career patterns of women and minorities, and changes in practice fields and specialties. The findings of all three studies have consistently shown that approximately 76% of the participating lawyers were moderately to extremely satisfied with their decisions to become lawyers.

In a book we highly recommend to you, THE HAPPY LAWYER: MAKING A GOOD LIFE IN THE LAW, Nancy Levit and Douglas Linder report on data they compiled from numerous sources as well as interviews with over two hundred attorneys. In sum, they conclude that the five factors most closely tied to lawyers' happiness are (1) finding work that interests them, (2) aligning work with their values, (3) balancing their work with the rest of their lives, (4) deepening workplace relationships, and (5) savoring small pleasures.

Studies of law students show they begin their law studies with well-being equal to or surpassing that of the general college graduate population.[33] Within six months, however, many law students begin to show symptoms of dysfunction, including depression, anxiety, and substance abuse, well above those of the general population. These symptoms tend to last well into the third year and beyond. Much of the blame has been placed at the feet of legal education itself: the emphasis on grades; the zero-sum outcome of class rank (everyone expects/wants to be in the top 10% of their class, which means 90% will be disappointed); competition to make law review and find the "right" job. Also contributing is that traditionally, and still in many schools, there is little formative feedback in any given course and a student's grade depends almost entirely on one final evaluative final exam. So although most students enter law school with intrinsic motivations such as wanting to help people, seek justice, and improve social conditions, these intrinsic goals may well get crowded out by extrinsic factors, which can then lead to a variety of psychological ills.

Krieger and Sheldon, who conducted these studies, have found this pattern can be diminished by affirmative steps law schools as well as individual teachers and students can take. The more schools support students' autonomy, support them in gaining competence, and create opportunities for students to cooperate and not compete with one another, the more students thrive. Students can minimize chances their well-being will be affected negatively by their law school experience by recognizing the psychological hazards, focusing on the aspirations that brought them to law school originally, and remaining connected to their family and friends outside of law school.

The most recent study by Krieger and Sheldon, *What Makes Lawyers Happy: A Data-driven Prescription to Redefine Professional Success* sought to test their hypotheses about self-determination theory on practicing lawyers.[34] Members of four state bar associations representing geographically diverse regions of the country participated in the study, with responses from almost 8,000 attorneys. The data proved consistent with Krieger and Sheldon's earlier studies of law students regarding what determines well-being as well as the literature on the science of well-being discussed earlier. The study of lawyers, however, delved specifically into the relative factors contributing to life satisfaction. As the chart below demonstrates, the matters that tend to receive the most attention in law schools—grades, participation on law review, and money issues (law school debt and future salary)—showed zero to weak correlations with reported well-being among practicing attorneys. In comparison, well-being correlated very strongly with autonomy, relatedness, and competence—more than five times stronger than class rank and more than three times stronger than income or school debt. The correlation between internal motivation, intrinsic values, and reported well-being was also strong. The bottom line is that for most lawyers, happiness depends not on how much money they make or how much student debt they have, but rather on a sense that they are in charge of their lives, have rewarding relationships with others, and feel competent doing work that is meaningful.

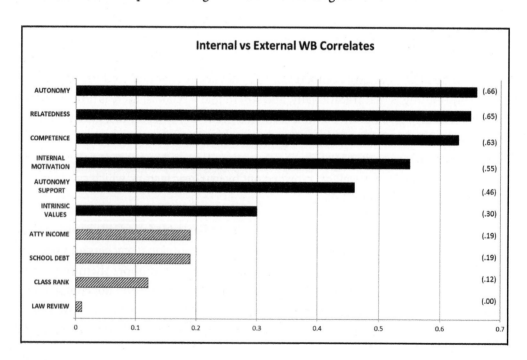

These studies, however, yield only statistical information. You are not a statistic. You likely will find some aspects of your externship work rewarding and intellectually stimulating while you may find other aspects stressful or uninteresting. We suggest you use your experience at your placement to sort out your priorities and goals and discern the kinds of practices in which you might thrive.

The Legal Workplace

One way to begin your self-reflective journey is to study and learn about the career and life satisfaction of those with whom you are working through informal observations and interviews. Ideally, it would be beneficial to have the opportunity to observe and participate in multiple legal settings; however, it would be next to impossible to observe or participate in all areas of law practice during your time at law school. Further, different settings within the same area of practice can vary widely in providing satisfaction depending on diverse factors such as how they are managed and who the people are with whom you work.

Given the wide range of work lawyers do, generalizations about what kind of work will comport with your career and life goals and enhance your well-being are challenging. Nevertheless, some observations may be helpful. For more about different kinds of clients, see Chapter 15 on Client Relationships; for more about differences in law practices, see Chapter 14 on Learning about Lawyering.

■ *Large Law Firms*

Some lawyers thrive in a large law firm environment and find the work exciting, intellectually interesting, and rewarding in helping business clients achieve their goals; in addition they appreciate the financial rewards. Indeed, for a long time, the emblematic brass ring for law students was a high-paying lifetime career at a large and prestigious law firm at which one would eventually become a partner. Lengthy careers at law firms and guaranteed partnership are no longer the prevailing reality and have not been for quite some time. Many associates join large firms with the expectations of staying only a few years, and firms themselves are volatile with lawyers at all levels often moving, practice groups splitting off, firms merging, and so on.

The new normal of job flexibility at large law firms offers advantages to many recent law graduates able to secure those positions. Large law firms often have resources for associate training programs and skills enhancements. They also often support young associates in doing extensive and meaningful pro bono work. On the other hand, many law graduates arrive at law firms only to find themselves doing less than glamorous, rather mundane legal tasks. Their assignments are dictated by senior associates or partners. As a result, they may well experience a lack of autonomy or relatedness, which, as previously discussed, are two important elements of well-being. In addition, because the clients that their firms represent tend to be large businesses, many associates report feeling their work lacks sufficient meaning.

At the same time, as described in Chapter 27 on the Future of the Legal Profession and Legal Services Delivery, corporate clients have been under increasing pressure to reduce legal costs, which is passed on to the firms that serve them. Clients are less willing to pay for work associates often found repetitive and boring, e.g., document review. Such clients also are often explicit about wanting to be billed only for time providing valuable service and are not willing to pay high fees for associate training. While this may mean the work for associates who have jobs will be more interesting, it also contributes to the contraction in law firm associate jobs.

For those working in large firms, associates still are expected to bill almost 50% more hours than what would have been expected fifty years ago when an ABA Lawyer's Handbook stated there were only about 1300 fee-earning hours in a year "unless the lawyer works overtime." Recent surveys of billing hour expectations show about 1900 hours to be the norm, with many firms expecting more and giving bonuses for exceeding the already considerable time that must be spent on firm work to reach those hour targets. And billable hours do not include the many hours spent on all the other work associates are expected to do for which clients cannot be charged. Judge Patrick Schiltz, in a powerful article, *On Being a Happy, Healthy, and Ethical Lawyer in an Unhappy, Unhealthy, and Unethical Profession*, warns students of the insidious temptation to cross the ethical line by exaggerating one's billable hours. Judge Schiltz also warns that the emphasis on material rewards and possessions creates a zero-sum game that no one can win.[35]

Some lawyers leave large firms and go on to do similar work as in-house counsel in new firms, for example, merging law with business process and technology analysis. Of course there are also thousands of law firms between the extremes of large and small firms, and the significance of the billable hour will vary among them, as will the firm's commitment to supporting their attorneys in finding some balance in their lives.

QUESTIONS TO CONSIDER

· Do you envision yourself working in a law firm?

· If so, what are you reasons for wanting to do so? Intellectually challenging work? Financial reward? Something else?

· What, if any, are your concerns?

■ *Solo and Small Firm Practice*

The risks and rewards of going into practice for oneself or with one or two other lawyers can be very different than working for a firm. In my own experience, my father was part of a small practice, and he worried constantly about his clients' problems and meeting overhead. Not all solo or small firm practitioners have this experience, and many feel comfortable, even exhilarated, by the challenge. Many attorneys who have chosen solo practice relish the autonomy it has provided them. A former student values the freedom he has to go watch his son's soccer game in the afternoon and return to the office afterwards. Thus, with regard to autonomy, an important contributor to well-being, a solo practice may have some unique advantages.

Autonomy may be constrained, however, by financial concerns.[36] To meet overhead and earn a living, you need clients, and that might mean taking on cases you would rather not for either philosophical, competence, or ethical reasons.[37] Many solos report working far harder than they did when employed by a law firm. My father's experience influenced me when I became a lawyer; I wanted to have a regular paycheck and benefits. Consider how you might respond to the special demands that face those who run small firms. How might you respond to the tradeoffs involved? Also see Chapter 27 on the Future of the Legal Profession for more on the ways technology and other factors are changing the nature of firm practice and delivery of service to clients.

■ *Government, Public Interest, Transactional Work, and In-House Counsel*

Studies consistently show that government lawyers and those doing public interest work report statistically greater levels of satisfaction than those working in the private sector.[38] The stresses tend to be less, and these lawyers generally have a sense that their work has more meaning. See Chapter 21 on Public Interest Practice and Chapter 22 on Public Service Practice.

The satisfactions and challenges of public service work also are relevant to how one might balance other responsibilities. For example, my career before I went into teaching was in a regional office of a federal government agency. At a time when I was a single mother with a young child, it afforded me regular hours, generally interesting work, and a salary and benefits that supported a comfortable, albeit not extravagant, lifestyle. The demands of government work differ greatly among agencies, but generally are not as all-consuming as either law firm or solo practice tends to be.[39] Consider whether you might find this special configuration of security and balance appealing.

Doing transactional work or serving as in-house counsel also may be more consistent with a balanced life than other legal careers. See Chapter 23 Transactional Lawyering. In-house attorneys, both those with more transactional practices as well as those who tend to litigate, generally have more flexibility in managing their time as compared to law firm lawyers.[40] Whether this holds true in any particular case, however, depends on the individual organizational culture.[41]

■ *The Integrative Law Movement*

Recent years have seen a growing interest in less adversarial, more healing ways to deliver legal services and resolve conflict. Known by many names, including Comprehensive Law, Holistic Law, Therapeutic Jurisprudence, Practicing Law as a Healing Profession, and most recently, Integrative Law, lawyers practicing this way strive to incorporate more humanistic, relational, and less adversarial approaches that endeavor to enhance the well-being of all stakeholders, including victims and offenders, clients and lawyers, judges and communities.

The Integrative Law Movement includes new models of "problem-solving" or "treatment" courts such as drug courts, mental health courts, domestic violence courts, veterans' courts, and community justice centers. The success of these programs relies on the skills of lawyers and other professionals trained to work in inter-disciplinary teams to address holistically the underlying problems that contribute to participants' entanglement with the justice system.

Restorative justice includes another set of integrative approaches. It has ancient origins, with roots in the conflict-resolution methods of aboriginal peoples around the world. In recent times, the number of restorative programs within schools, communities, and the criminal justice system has grown exponentially. In the mid-1990's, for example, David Lerman, an Assistant District Attorney in Milwaukee, dissatisfied with his role in the criminal justice system, created his office's Community Conferencing Program. The program gave victims a voice in what happened to offenders, and offenders an opportunity to understand the harm they had done to victims.[42] This restorative process enabled victims to heal and offenders to take responsibility for the harm they caused. Recidivism plummeted. An ever-increasing number of similar publically-sponsored restorative justice programs employ attorneys as facilitators, advocates, and administrators.

Restorative practices have applications beyond their use as alternatives to the traditional criminal justice system, such as in schools to address disciplinary matters. Other relatively new processes such as collaborative practices and certain forms of mediation tend to be more focused on the civil side. Collaborative divorce law was the brainchild of Minneapolis matrimonial attorney Stuart Webb, who was so demoralized by the harm done to families through divorce litigation that he was ready to quit the practice of law altogether. Instead, he created a model in which clients' counsel are part of a team approach assisting families in reorganizing upon divorce or separation, without resort to litigation. Now, there are thousands of lawyers around the country and around the world helping families reconstitute without the destruction of well-being and dissipation of finances caused by most divorce litigation. Similarly, transformative mediation, developed by Robert Baruch Bush and Joseph Folger, helps empower parties in conflict to gain mutual understanding and to discover their own paths for moving forward, whether or not resolution of the conflict results through that process.[43]

What some Integrative Lawyers have been doing:

- Carol Fisler is the director of Mental Health Court and Alternative to Detention Programs at the Center for Court Innovation, overseeing initiatives that address mental illness and courts and diversion programs for adolescents. She coordinated the planning and implementation of the Brooklyn Mental Health Court, the first specialized court for offenders with mental illness in New York.[44]

- Pamela Donison practices collaborative family law in Phoenix, Arizona. Her law firm's motto is "Legal issues don't have to break the bank or ruin your life."[45]

- In Oakland, California Janelle Orsi invented and practices "sharing law" an innovative and essential response to the numerous legal issues emerging in the sharing economy.[46] Her law office's motto is "Legal Services for a Sustainable, Equitable, and Sharing World."[47]

- Kim Wright, author, coach, teacher, and writer, has traveled around the country and the world over the past few years, connecting the profusion of lawyers who have discovered new ways to practice law consistent with their core values.

For further information about the Integrative Law Movement, check out Wright's book, Lawyers as Peacemakers: Practicing Holistic, Problem-solving Law (2010), as well as her website, www.cuttingedgelaw.com, which contains hundreds of videos with lawyers, judges and others involved in the transformation of both the practice of law and the administration of justice.

All these lawyers share a vision for what it means to be a lawyer and live in a just society that applies personal and professional values, and focuses on problem-solving, peace-making, and healing brokenness, while remaining client-centered. While perhaps these approaches are not for everyone, lawyers practicing in these new paradigms generally experience less stress and more of the indicia of well-being—autonomy, authenticity, relatedness, and meaningful work—than many lawyers in traditional practice. Through taking a holistic approach to client representation, these lawyers are able to increase their clients' well-being, as well as their own. Consider whether your own goals are consistent with those of Integrative Lawyers.

Defining Success: Balance or Integration?

You likely began law school with a desire **to be successful**. You hoped to do well in your studies and begin a successful career. But how do you define **success**? Some of you may define it in terms of landing a well-paid position with a large reputable law firm. Others, with whether you can find meaningful work that fights injustice, stems climate change, or improves opportunities for advancement among the disadvantaged in society. But what about success in your personal life? Is that any less important to you?

Studies show the cohorts known as Generation X and Millennials place more emphasis on their personal lives than had preceding generations.[48] While traditionally women have and still do place more emphasis on family and assume the burden of family responsibilities, men and women law students and lawyers alike are seeking balance or integration to a far greater extent than their predecessors.

Exercise 25.3 Define what professional and personal success mean to you. Your thoughts about values and goals should help guide your definition of success; for example, the relative importance of money, recognition, influence, providing help to others, relationships, family and so on.

Many of you likely have a fair degree of unease about what kind of work you will find after graduation. After all the time and effort you have invested in your education—and the debt you have likely accumulated—it is important that you find work that will pay the bills (we trust with a little left over) **and** work that you will enjoy—or at least do not dislike. You may have entered law school with a passion to do specific kinds of work or have developed such a passion since you started. Whether or not you are able to find such work in your first job out of law school, you want to develop a plan that will enable you to fulfill those dreams, work that comports with your core values, perhaps work you feel called to do, that is your vocation. Others of you may expect to find most of your happiness in your life outside of work. You may see work as a means to an end rather than a vocation. You may be content with work you do not dislike and feel sufficiently fulfilled through acquiring competence as a lawyer and finding satisfaction in work well done.

Regardless of whether you see work and the rest of your life as part of a continuum or not, your well-being, or lack thereof, in one sphere will certainly leak over into the other. Achieving balance, as opposed to integration, may be paramount in the early part of your career, while you are still figuring out the other central domains of your life: your social life, relationships, family, where you will live, etc. It may be less salient if and when your life outside of work has achieved some stability, especially if you have a passion for your work. Regardless, reflecting on how your well-being is now and will in the future be affected by the work you do should be important to you and a question to explore throughout your externship. See Chapter 8 on Reflection and Writing Journals.

Reimagining the Workplace

Law firms, albeit still lagging behind the business sector, are increasingly making part-time, flextime and other alternative work schedules available. Although not designed exclusively for women, studies consistently show women work part-time with far greater frequency than their male counterparts. As more men assume the roles of caregivers, however, the gap in these statistics is likely to narrow.

A twenty-year longitudinal study of the 1990 University of Virginia Law School graduating class, *Lawyers at Mid-Career* (LMC) noted pervasive gender differences in the personal and professional lives of its 260 respondents. Women were almost forty times more likely than men to interrupt or give up full-time employment (39% vs. 1%). The study revealed that 84.3% of respondents were working full-time. More specifically, the study showed that of all the respondents, 98.7% of men were working full-time compared to 61.1% of women. Over 80% of the respondents working part-time, all but one of which were women, stated they were doing so in order to care for children. There was a strong correlation between women working full-time and how many children they had: the more children, the more likely women were to work part-time.

In contrast to the LMC study that reported results of attorneys in the middle of their careers, the National Association for Law Placement (NALP) collects data annually from recent law school graduates. A 2011 report, *Longstanding Employment Patterns for Law School Graduates Interrupted*, showed since 1985 there has been a general decrease in full-time employment within the legal field for recent graduates. The average from 1985–1989 was approximately 83%. In the 1990's, the average rate dropped to about 73%. In 2010, that rate dropped to 68.4%. In contrast, the percentage of graduates obtaining part-time employment in the legal field increased from 2.6 % in 1985 to 10.7% in 2010. The rate of lawyers working part-time remained consistent through 2012, with 70% of those being women. These statistics likely reflect, in part, the economic decline which began around 2007. Many lawyers working part-time—men and woman—may not be doing so by choice.

NALP noted, however, the legal field is lagging behind other professional sectors in the use of part-time employment schedules. The report revealed that 13.1% of employees in all professional specialties were working part-time compared to a rate of 6.25% at major law firms. There has been a growing effort to raise awareness and encourage law firms to offer more flexible work schedules to promote a better work/life balance for all attorneys. Lawyers, especially those who have risen to the ranks of law firm partners, tend to be a conservative bunch, resistant to change. See Chapter 27 on the future of the legal profession for further discussion of this issue. Additionally, a stigma persists, often unconscious, for those who work part-time or have other atypical arrangements. Studies confirm, however, because lawyers on part-time schedules have additional time constraints, they tend to work more efficiently than their full-time counterparts.[49] Many younger lawyers—the cohort born since 1980—would be happy to trade higher salaries for more time away from work. A recent study by a legal recruiting firm showed that seven out of ten lawyers rated flextime and telecommuting as more important than additional monetary compensation.[50] As increasing numbers of legal employers learn that happier lawyers improve their bottom line without sacrificing service to clients, resistance to alternative work arrangements will be viewed, not as an accommodation to employees, but as good business. Furthermore, happier lawyers are more loyal, thus less likely to leave their places of employment.

Deborah Epstein Henry's consulting firm, Flex-time Lawyers, helps clients develop and sustain work environments more conducive to optimizing work/life balance. Her book, LAW AND REORDER: LEGAL INDUSTRY SOLUTIONS FOR RESTRUCTURE, RETENTION,

PROMOTION & WORK/LIFE BALANCE, explores issues affecting attorney well-being and offers practical advice for individual attorneys, as well as firms and other legal employers.[51] So, too, in their book, THE HAPPY LAWYER, Nancy Levit & Douglas Linder offer sound, empirically-backed advice for how law firms can make structural changes that will enhance their attorneys' professional satisfaction. In addition to part-time work, such restructuring includes flex-time, compressed work weeks, staggered work hours, telecommuting, and job-sharing.[52]

> Flex-time Lawyers.com contains abundant information about the benefits for promoting flexible work schedules, as well as current industry practices and emerging trends. Although geared towards women, the use of flexible or alternative schedules may be beneficial for men as well, especially as more and more men are assuming caregiver roles.
>
> These and similar developments likely will enable the possibility of greater work/life balance as you progress through your years at law school and eventually your job search. If this is important to you, be sure to inquire about the policies of the offices with which you interview.
>
> A terrific resource for assessing a firm's policies is the "Cheat Sheet" prepared by Flex-Time Lawyers in conjunction with the New York City Bar Association: http://www.nycbar.org/images/stories/diversity/thecheatsheet.pdf.

Keep in mind, the first law job you land may not have policies you view as ideal. Moreover, you probably will lack bargaining power at the outset of your career as to how your workplace is structured. However, one day you may well be in a position to transform your workplace and make it more conducive to optimizing work/life balance. It is never too early to be observing how it works—or does not work—in the various law practice settings you will experience while you are in law school as well as after you graduate, and what changes you think would benefit you, the profession and the clients it serves.

> **Exercise 25.4** Assume you are a management consultant who has been retained by your externship to improve efficiency and productivity. What recommendations would you make? For example, what aspects of the placement's work require physical presence at the work place? Could more work be done at home? Might this have an added benefit of improving worker satisfaction, and thus improving productivity?

Well-being and You in the Here-and-Now

This chapter has focused primarily on helping you evaluate how your future career is likely to affect your overall satisfaction with your life. We have shared what we know about well-being, as well as what we know about what causes unhappiness, dissatisfaction with one's life including more serious emotional distress and dysfunction. We have invited you to consider how the career choices you make may affect your well-being.

But we would be remiss if we did not recognize the real world stressors with which you are now dealing while you are still in law school. Many of you have incurred, and will continue to incur, substantial debt, and are worried about how you will repay it. As of this writing, the job market for lawyers is improving, but the profession is changing and what your immediate and long-term job prospects will be are uncertain for some of you. It may be difficult, if not impossible, to avoid worrying about grades and class rank, even though the empirical evidence discussed earlier demonstrates that once you are into your legal career their importance will diminish significantly. And you are likely currently juggling more responsibilities than you ever have before. Many of you have additional personal and family responsibilities which make this juggling act all the more challenging.

If you have student loans, and the vast majority of you do, it is critically important that you educate yourself about available loan repayment plans. Thanks to legislation Congress enacted in recent years, a variety of plans are available, including income-based repayment and loan-forgiveness plans. All of these are explained at https://studentaid.ed.gov/sa/repay-loans/understand/plans. In addition many schools have their own loan repayment programs. Be sure to discuss your particular circumstances with your school's loan officer.

We suggest you review the second part of this chapter, What We Know About Well-being, and if the stress is compromising your ability to perform at your potential, or to enjoy life, take advantage of some of the suggestions from the experts whose work is highlighted. This externship and this book should enable you to make better choices for your future, but be sure not to neglect the present in the process of doing so.

Do Not Settle!

Should you decide in your first job out of law school, your second, or at any point in your career that you made a mistake, do not be afraid to make major changes. The only true mistake is settling for being unhappy. According to Levit & Linder, 85% of lawyers change jobs at least once in their careers.[53] Many do so several times.

Your life is not something you figure out and then move on. Your goals may change, perhaps dramatically, as you grow older, have more experience from which to learn, and as your circumstances change. Assess and reassess what you want from your personal life and professional life. Revisit the first exercise in this chapter. Compare the results with how you are living your life. Probe what it will take to achieve the goals you seek. Consider the options when personal and professional goals seem to clash. Do not give up on the notion the legal profession can support a healthy balance in personal lives and professional lives for its members. You will be the generation in charge sooner than you think. Be ready.

FURTHER RESOURCES

Mihaly Czikszentmihalyi, Flow: The Psychology of Optimal Experience (1990).

Lawrence S. Krieger, with Kennon M. Sheldon, *What Makes Lawyers Happy? Transcending the Anecdotes with Data from 6200 Lawyers*, 83 Geo. Wash. L. Rev. 554 (2015).

Karen Reivich & Andrew Shatté, The Resilience Factor (2002).

Patrick J. Schiltz, *On Being a Happy, Healthy, and Ethical Member of an Unhappy, Unhealthy, and Unethical Profession*, 52 Vand. L. Rev. 871 (1999).

Martin E.P. Seligman, Flourish: A Visionary New Understanding of Happiness and Well-being (2013).

MENTAL HEALTH RESOURCES

Ronald C. Kessler, *et al., Age of Onset of Mental Disorders: A Review of Recent Literature*, 20 Current Opinions in Psychiatry 359 (July 2007), http://www.ncbi.nlm.nih.gov/pmc/articles/PMC1925038/.

Major Depressive Disorder, Internet Mental Health, http://www.mentalhealth.com/home/dx/majordepressive.html.

A.B.A. Comm'n. on Lawyer Assistance Programs, *Directory of Lawyer Assistance Programs*, http://www.americanbar.org/groups/lawyer_assistance/resources/lap_programs_by_state.html.

Dave Nee Foundation, http://www.daveneefoundation.com/.

Lawyers with Depression, http://www.lawyerswithdepression.com/.

MINDFULNESS RESOURCES

Anderson Cooper, *Mindfulness,* CBS News (Dec. 14, 2014), http://www.cbsnews.com/news/mindfulness-anderson-cooper-60-minutes/.

The Mindful Lawyer: Practicing Law with Presence, http://themindfullawyer.com/.

ENDNOTES

1   Amiram Elwork, Stress Management for Lawyers: How to Increase Personal & Professional Satisfaction in the Law 158-59 (3d ed. 2007).

2   Martin E.P. Seligman, Flourish: A Visionary New Understanding of Happiness and Well-being 16–20 (2013).

3   Patrick L. Hill & Nicholas A. Turiano, *Purpose in Life as a Predictor of Mortality across Adulthood*, 25 Psycho. Sci. 1482 (2014).

4   Seligman, *supra* note 2, at 33–34.

5   *See* Daniel Kahneman, Thinking Fast and Slow 40 (2011).

6   Elwork, *supra* note 1, at 169.

7   Richard M. Ryan & Edward L. Deci, *Self-Determination Theory and the Facilitation of Intrinsic Motivation, Social Development, and Well-Being*, 55 Am. Psych. 68, 71 (2000).

8   *Id.* at 69.

9   *Id.* at 75.

10   *See* Patrick J. Schiltz, *On Being a Happy, Healthy, and Ethical Member of an Unhappy, Unhealthy, and Unethical Profession*, 52 Vand. L. Rev. 871, 905 (1999).

11   *See e.g.,* Johnmarshall Reeve, Understanding Motivation and Emotion (5th ed. 2009).

12   Russell G. Pearce & Brendan M. Wilson, Ch. 4, Business Ethics in Handbook on the Economics of Reciprocity and Social Enterprise (Luigino Bruni & Stefano Zamagni, ed. 2013).

13   Barbara Frederickson, Love—A New Lens on the Science of Thriving, YouTube (Aug. 23, 2012), https://www.youtube.com/watch?v=ZxoPLtRnxZs.

14   *See* Corie Rosen Felder, *The Accidental Optimist*, 21 Va. J. Soc. Pol'y & L. 63 (2014).

15   Sarah J. Adams-Schoen, *Of Old Dogs and New Tricks—Can Law Schools Really Fix Students' Fixed Mindsets?*, 19 Legal Writing 3, 13 (2014).

16   Larry Richard, What Makes Lawyers Tick?, http://www.lawyerbrainblog.com/.

17 *See* Elwork, *supra*, note 1, at 75, citing WALTER WILLETT, M.D., EAT, DRINK, AND BE HEALTHY: THE HARVARD MEDICAL SCHOOL GUIDE TO HEALTHY EATING (2005).

18 Debra S. Austin, *Killing them Softly: Neuroscience Reveals How Brain Cells Die from Law School Stress and How Neural Self-Hacking can Optimize Cognitive Performance*, 59 LOY. L. REV. 791, 829–34 (2013).

19 *See* Kenneth R Fox, *The Influence of Physical Activity on Mental Well-Being*, 2 PUB. HEALTH NUTRITION 411–418 (1999).

20 *See* Wake Forest Baptist Med. Ctr., *Proper Sleep a Key Contributor to Health, Well-being.* SCI. DAILY (Jan. 22, 2014), http://www.sciencedaily.com/releases/2014/01/140122153606.htm; Dr. Dan Robotham et. al., *Sleep Matters: the Impact of Sleep on Health and Well-being*, MENTAL HEALTH FOUNDATION (2011), http://www.mentalhealth.org.uk/publications/sleep-report/.

21 Austin, *supra*, note 18, at 836–37.

22 *See* Jennifer Soong, *The Secret and Surprising Power of Naps*, WEBMD MAGAZINE, http://www.webmd.com/balance/features/the-secret-and-surprising-power-of-naps (last visited July 14, 2015).

23 Tony Schwartz, *More Vacation is the Secret Sauce*, HARVARD BUS. Rev. (Sep. 6, 2012), http://blogs.hbr.org/2012/09/more-vacation-is-the-secret-sa/.

24 *See* RICHARD DAVIDSON & SHARON BEGLEY, THE EMOTIONAL LIFE OF YOUR BRAIN (2012) (reviewing thirty years of brain research).

25 Katherine Bender, David Jaffe & Jerry Organ, *2014 Survey of Law Student Well-Being* (2014) (unpublished manuscript; on file with authors).

26 G. Andrew H. Benjamin et al., T*he Prevalence of Depression, Alcohol Abuse, and Cocaine Abuse Among United States Lawyers*, 13 INT'L. J.L. & PSYCHIATRY 233, 240–42 (1990). A new study, jointly conducted by the ABA and the Hazelden Betty Ford Foundation finds that lawyers continue to have serious problems with depression and alcohol abuse.

27 Connie J.A. Beck et al., *Lawyer Distress: Alcohol-Related Problems and Other Psychological Concerns Among a Sample of Practicing Lawyers*, 10 J.L. & HEALTH 1, 4 (1995–96).

28 *Alcohol Facts and Statistics*, NAT'L. INST. ON ALCOHOL ABUSE & ALCOHOLISM, http://www.niaaa.nih.gov/alcohol-health/overview-alcohol-consumption/alcohol-facts-and-statistics (last visited Aug. 3, 2015).

29 John Mixon & Robert P. Schuwerk, *The Personal Dimension of Professional Responsibility*, 58 LAW & CONTEMP. PROBS. 87, 96 (1995) (cited in Patrick J. Schiltz, *On Being a Happy, Healthy, and Ethical Member of an Unhappy, Unhealthy, and Unethical Profession*, 52 VANDERBILT L. REV. 871, n. 268 (1999)).

30 *See* William W. Eaton et al., *Occupations and the Prevalence of Major Depressive Disorder*, 32 J. OCCUPATIONAL MED. 1079 (1990).

31 See, *e.g.,* Ronald C. Kessler, et al., *Age of Onset of Mental Disorders: A Review of Recent Literature*, 20 CURRENT OPINIONS IN PSYCHIATRY 359 (July 2007), http://www.ncbi.nlm.nih.gov/pmc/articles/PMC1925038/; http://www.mentalhealth.com/home/dx/majordepressive.html.

32 Jerome M. Organ, *What Do We Know About the Satisfaction/Dissatisfaction of Lawyers: A Meta-Analysis of Research on Lawyer Satisfaction and Well-Being*, 8 U. ST. THOMAS L. J. 225 (2011).

33 Kennon M. Sheldon & Lawrence S. Krieger, *Does Legal Education have Undermining Effects on Law Students? Evaluating Changes in Motivation, Values, and Well-Being*, 22 BEHAV. SCI. LAW 261 (2004).

34 Lawrence S. Krieger, with Kennon M. Sheldon, Ph.D, *What Makes Lawyers Happy? Transcending the Anecdotes with Data from 6200 Lawyers*, 83 GEO. WASH. L. REV. 554 (2015).

35 Schiltz, *supra* note 10, at 894.

36 *See* NANCY LEVIT & DOUGLAS O. LINDER, THE HAPPY LAWYER: MAKING A GOOD LIFE IN THE LAW 227–28 (2010).

37 *See* Leslie Levin, *The Ethical Work of Solo and Small Firm Practitioners*, 41 HOUSTON L. REV. 309 (2004).

38   *See* Krieger, *supra* note 34, at 614-15, 627; Levit & Linder, *supra* note 36, at 231.

39   *See* Organ, *supra* note 32, at 265.

40   Joan C. Williams, Cynthia Thomas Calvert and Holly Cohen Cooper, *Better on Balance—The Corporate Counsel Work/Life Report—The Project for Attorney Retention Corporate Counsel Project Final Report*, 10 Wm. & Mary J. Women & L. 422, 448 (2003–2004).

41   N.Y. State Bar Assn' Special Comm. on Balanced Lives in the Law, Final Report 17 (Mar. 7 2008), available at http://www.nysba.org/WorkArea/DownloadAsset.aspx?id=26859 (last visited July 14, 2015).

42   *See* J. Kim Wright, Lawyers as Peacemakers: Practicing Holistic, Problem-Solving Law 42 (2010).

43   *See, e.g.* Heidi Burgess, Transformative Mediation, U. Colo. Conflict Res. Consortium (1997), http://www.colorado.edu/conflict/transform/tmall.htm. (last visited July 14, 2015).

44   Center for Court Innovation, Staff Listing, http://www.courtinnovation.org/staff (last visited July 14, 2015).

45   Donison Law Firm, http://www.donisonlaw.com/ (last visited July 14, 2015).

46   Janelle Orsi, Practicing Law in the Sharing Economy: Helping People Build Cooperatives, Social Enterprises, and Local Sustainable Economies (ABA Books 2012). Ms. Orsit's website is http://www.janelleorsi.com/.

47   Law Office of Janelle Orsi, http://www.janelleorsi.com/ (last visited July 15, 2015).

48   *See* Levit & Linder, *supra* note 36, at 165–66.

49   *Id.* at 182.

50   Andrew Strickler, *Flex Time Beats Cash in Legal Recruiting,* Law 360 (May 30, 2013, 6:13 p.m.), http://www.law360.com/articles/446009/flex-time-beats-cash-in-legal-recruiting-survey-finds.

51   Deborah Epstein Henry, Law And Reorder: Legal Industry Solutions For Restructure, Retention, Promotion & Work/Life Balance (2015). *See also* Deborah Henry Epstein, Finding Bliss (2015).

52   Levit & Linder, *supra* note 36, at ch. 6.

53   *Id.* at 225–26 (citing John Monahan & Jeffrey Swanson, *Lawyers at Mid-Career; A 20-Year Longitutinal Study of Job and Life Satisfaction,* 5 J. Empirical Legal Stud. 451, 451 (2009)).

CHAPTER 26

Externships and Career Development

AVIS L. SANDERS

The Role of Externships in Developing Career Plans

W ould you like to turn your externship into a full-time job? Do you want to continue working in the same field of law as your externship, or are you investigating different legal careers? Do you have the skills and knowledge you need in a competitive job market? How will you use this externship to move your career forward? The extent to which your externship experience has a positive effect on your career prospects may depend on how strategically you approach these types of questions.

Just as you set your GPS before heading off on a long trip, identifying your goals as you embark on your career can help you find your way to your destination. This chapter provides suggestions for leveraging your externship into a career:

- *Focus Your Career Goals*: Build a plan to pinpoint possible career paths.

- *Gather Information*: Identify and develop the skills, knowledge, and experiences necessary for competence and marketability.

- *Inventory your Skills, Close the Gap, and Leverage Your Externship*: Create your narrative for employers and carry that narrative through from resume to cover letter to interview.

- *Network and Use Social Media*: Learn to use tools to open doors to legal opportunities.

- *Reassess*: Adjust your plan to progress in your job search.

Developing a Strategy

Step One—Focus Your Career Goals

Your externship will serve as one of many building blocks in your professional narrative. There is rarely a straight-line trajectory leading from a placement to a "dream job." The experience, skills, knowledge, and connections you gain over the course of your professional life will qualify you for many different jobs. With each experience, you will find your goals will shift, your skills will grow, and your attitudes will change. Still, the more you reflect on your own career goals, even if they eventually shift, the more you can focus on your destination and move toward it.

In Chapter 2, Charting Your Path to Success—Professional Development Planning, you considered your overall goals for your career and for your externship. You can now return to your plan and narrow it further to help identify some specific jobs you may want to pursue and determine how your externship will move you toward these jobs.

Consider the following questions to narrow your career goals:

- What have you learned from your externship thus far about the areas of law that interest you? Are some areas of law now off the table? If you are not ready to begin narrowing your career goals, what skills can you build in your externship that will transfer to other practice areas?

- Does it matter to you who you represent? To what extent do your values need to align with those of your clients? See Chapter 24 on Professional Identity and Formation.

- In what setting would you like to work? A large firm? A small or medium-sized firm? A think tank? A public interest organization? State or federal government? In-house counsel? What have you learned about these venues? What conclusions do you draw from your experience in your placement regarding these choices? See Chapter 14 on Learning About Lawyering.Do you want to use your legal education to prepare for a job outside of conventional legal practice? Are you considering a career in business, politics, or community service? Are you interested in entrepreneurial ventures, perhaps joined with people with other types of training? As Chapter 27 discusses, the rapidly changing legal services market may mean your future could include careers not even envisioned today. See Chapter 27 on the Future of the Legal Profession.

- Are there jobs available in your fields of interest and in your preferred geographic area? Is there an industry that predominates in the local economy? How can you explore job markets in other areas of the country? Do you need to network and gain work experience in that geographic area to be competitive?

- What makes you happy? Studies show happy lawyers are those who experience "flow"—where time goes quickly because they are engaged in their work and they have a sense of autonomy and control over their work product.[1] What assignments provide you with this kind of satisfaction? See Chapter 25 on Work and Well-being.

Your placement offers an excellent "classroom" in which to observe the workplace as you consider all of these questions. Your first-hand experience may convince you to change direction. After you have come up with some possible career paths, turn your attention to what employers in these fields want to see in a job applicant, and develop a plan for how you can use your externship and other activities to develop those attributes.

Step Two—Gather Information: Identify What Employers in Your Field of Interest are Seeking in a Candidate

As you consider your career goals, you may also want to concentrate on understanding what different types of employers require or want from their new employees. This type of needs-based strategy can provide you with substantial guidance in determining the relevant legal experience you want to develop over the course of the semester. Focus your attention on learning what an employer in your field of interest will want to see on your resume.

Employers generally look for two main types of qualifications when hiring: (1) transferable skills such as writing, research, analysis, attention to detail, ability to communicate effectively, exercise judgment, solve problems, and collaborate; and (2) specific knowledge related to their practice.

■ *Transferable Skills*

There is an increasing movement toward preparing students who are able to practice immediately upon graduation. As discussed more fully in Chapters 2 and 14, there has been a great deal of conversation and scholarship around the question of the legal skills all lawyers should have when they graduate from law school, regardless of their specific area of practice. Reviewing the skills and "competencies" described in Chapters 2 and

14 and the longer lists in Appendix I provides an overview of the transferable skills employers seek.

In general, transferable skills, relevant to all legal practice, can be divided into a few general categories:

· Practice skills including legal research, writing, analysis, problem solving, capacity to exercise judgment, oral advocacy, case strategy, and identification of ethical issues;

· Interpersonal skills including listening, empathizing, getting along well with others, being responsive to criticism, curiosity and interest in the subject matter, and practical judgment;

· Professionalism skills including honesty, judgment regarding appropriate dress and demeanor, willingness to handle a range of tasks, punctuality, knowing when to ask for guidance, managing time, and the capacity to work autonomously and collaboratively. See Chapter 9 on Professionalism;

· Client development and law practice management skills including finding clients, networking, billing, and conducting legal research at a low cost.

■ *Subject-Specific Knowledge*

Beyond transferable lawyering skills, each practice area requires its own specialized skills and knowledge, and employers often seek candidates who can demonstrate this proficiency. For example, an energy conservation organization will seek applicants who are familiar both with environmental law in general and with regulations and procedures specific to energy law. Having a career focus, even if it changes over time, enables you to approach your externship experiences strategically and to ensure you develop the expertise employers seek.

The more knowledgeable you can become about specific areas of law in which you might want to practice, the more effectively you can use your externship to acquire skills, knowledge, and experience related to that work. Accomplishing all of these objectives successfully will help to make you more attractive as a candidate.

· Identify the specific types of knowledge and experience required for certain jobs. Find actual job postings in the field in which you are interested and read the job announcements and the job description. What skills do they require or prefer?

- Find attorneys working in that field (faculty, alumni, friends, attorneys at your externship, individuals you meet through your networking efforts, etc.) and ask them what they look for in job applicants. Your law school's alumni office may have suggestions. See Informational Interviews below.

- Review resources available online and through your law school, describing the specific skills and knowledge needed for common legal practice areas.

Based on the information you have collected, create a list of the skills, knowledge, attributes, and experience most important to employers in the practice areas that interest you.

Step Three—Inventory Your Skills

In Chapter 2, Exercise 2.3, you identified your current skills, but you may not have had a particular job in mind against which to evaluate these skills and determine whether you need to build your knowledge base. Consider the skills and knowledge, both transferable and specific, you already possess and those you are gaining in your externship. How do these compare to those employers seek? Are you getting the experience in your externship that will help you meet the needs of employers in specific legal practice areas?

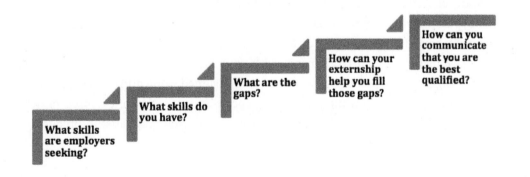

Step Four: Close the Gap

Once you identify the skills and knowledge you have and need to acquire for specific legal careers, you can work on closing the gap.

This goal can be accomplished through course work, extra-curricular activities such as attending lectures or events, working on law journals, joining professional organizations, and, of course, through work experience, such as your externship. You want to use all of these to build a narrative about yourself that includes having experience and expertise relevant to employers both generally and for specific jobs.

> **Exercise 26.1** Draft a detailed description of your externship as you would like to be able to describe it on your resume at the conclusion of your placement. This can serve as a roadmap for the skills you seek to acquire.

■ Seek Opportunities

Chapter 2 on Professional Development Planning, Chapter 3 on Learning from Supervision, and Chapter 4 on Observation suggest specific ways for you to use a proactive approach to gain the skills you have identified as essential career goals from your externship.

This exercise can raise a potentially difficult question. To what extent do you want to focus on your own goals as compared to your placement's work needs? On the one hand, you do not want to leave your externship without developing skills you think are most useful for you. On the other hand, you want to provide a beneficial service to the organization and make a good impression on your supervisor.

Many supervisors, once they are aware of your goals, are willing to mentor you, to make space for you to observe legal practice, and assign tasks that are primarily for your benefit. You will need to reflect on and weigh a number of factors in seeking certain experiences, including your relationship with your supervisor, your performance on previous assignments, the time sensitivity of your assigned work, and similar realities. There are ways to be useful while getting the experience you seek. For example, rather than simply asking to sit in on a deposition, ask whether you may assist in preparing for or taking notes during the deposition as well.

■ Take Risks

While it may seem safer to limit yourself to those areas in which you already excel, attorneys will recognize your willingness to challenge yourself and learn from mistakes.

■ Do Your Best

An assignment is not "done" until you consider whether anything else is needed.

■ *Learn From Feedback*

To learn from your assignments and recognize your strengths, it is necessary to receive feedback. For example, for written work, make sure to review any edits on assignments and offer to redraft them. Compare your work with the final document. See Chapter 3 on Learning from Supervision and Chapter 17 on Writing for Practice.

■ *Observe*

Watching attorneys engage with colleagues, opposing counsel, and clients is an invaluable way to learn the practice of law, particularly if your externship provides limited opportunities to develop transferable skills. Ask for opportunities to observe the attorneys working in your office. Your supervisors may be happy for you to listen to a phone call with opposing counsel, sit in on a negotiation, join a meeting of attorneys to discuss case strategy, etc. See Chapter 4 on Observation.

■ *Learn Interpersonal Skills*

Take advantage of your interpersonal relationships at your externship to hone your communication skills such as listening, empathizing with others, working with diverse clients, adapting to different supervision styles, etc. See Chapter 5 on Effective Communication and Professional Relationships and Chapter 6 on Navigating Cultural Differences.

■ *Become an Expert*

Learn the governing law, regulations, and administrative processes connected to the practice areas in which you will be seeking a job. To the extent possible, work on assignments that provide you with a breadth of experience in those fields. Take advantage of the attorneys in the office to gain first-hand industry knowledge. If you can communicate this kind of expertise during an interview, you will distinguish yourself from other candidates.

■ *Produce a Polished Writing Sample*

Externships, like seminars and independent study options, provide opportunities to draft subject-specific written work. Employers will be particularly interested in writing samples related to their field. See Chapter 17 on Writing for Practice.

*A student who can communicate that she
understands the background to the current issues
in corporate tax law, knows the key players, and
has a sense of how all the pieces fit together will far
outshine other applicants*

—Hiring Attorney, Tax Law Specialist

■ *Become an Insider*

All fields of law have ways in which industry information is shared, allowing lawyers to stay on top of important changes, issues, and debates in the law. Ask the attorneys in your externship where they get this type of industry information. Are there specific newsgroups, associations, or forums they recommend? Are there listservs you should join, blogs you should follow, or other social media you should use? These can open up networking opportunities, inform you of job openings, and help you become familiar with the lawyers in the field. Once you have identified resources and organizations, try to attend events and meetings and volunteer for tasks. Use this information during a job interview to show your knowledge of the field and to demonstrate you will be able to hit the ground running.

After you have completed these steps and maximized your qualifications for the jobs to which you might want to apply, you can turn your attention to how you will communicate your interests and experience to employers and use your externship to its full potential in your job search.

Leveraging Your Externship Into a Job

Communicating How Your Externship Has Prepared You for Your Next Job

You can increase the leverage of your externship by effectively communicating about your externship to employers through your resume, cover letter, and interviews.

To take full advantage of your externship to find a fulfilling career in a demanding job market, you will need to apply your lawyering skills to the application process. Good lawyers know how to build a narrative for their clients; they are able to tell an engaging story, focus on important facts, assess the audience, and address the audience's concerns. You need these same types of skills to leverage your externship into a full-time job.

Tip: Proofreading and avoiding typographical errors is absolutely necessary for all written submissions to prospective employers. These include resumes, cover letters, writing samples, thank you notes, and even informal emails. Given the number of candidates for most positions, many employers will use such errors as a simple way to narrow down the pool of applicants.

Exercise 26.2 Fill in the following chart by listing three specific assignments you have worked on in your externship, three new skills you acquired or significantly improved, three pieces of knowledge you gained, and three experiences you found most interesting or exciting.

Assignments Worked on	Skills Acquired and Improved	Knowledge Learned	Exciting/Interesting Experiences

▪ *Create Your Narrative*

A narrative is a story. It ties together diverse threads into one unifying theme. In order to use your externship to its full potential in your job search, craft a story that integrates the externship experience with other aspects of your life and education to convince employers you are the person most able to meet their needs. You will not present your narrative in a single document or presentation. Instead, your narrative will show up in all of your contacts with a prospective employer: your resume, cover letter, answers in interviews, even what you say about yourself in 30 seconds in an elevator. Having a narrative that accurately portrays your experience and fits with your goals and values will make all of these moving parts work together toward your goal of getting a job you want.

■ *Use Your Journal*

If you keep a journal, it can be a goldmine of material capturing the skills, knowledge, and experience you acquired in your externship, along with a reminder of how you felt and what you thought at the time you were engaged in these activities. All of this can be used in crafting your resume, cover letter, and preparing for your interview. See Chapter 8 on Reflection and Writing Journals for different ways to use your journal.

■ *Match Their Words*

Remember your destination. The more you know about the jobs for which you are applying, the more effectively you can tailor your resume and cover letter and prepare for your interview. If you are applying for a specific job, scour the job announcement for the specific language used to describe the experience sought. Wherever possible, include this language in your resume, cover letter, or in your interview.

■ *Be Prepared to Detour*

If your externship is unrelated to the job for which you are applying, or if things did not go as well as you would have hoped, you can focus on the transferable skills you learned and show enthusiasm for your work, even if you are not going to pursue the specific field further. You also can point to the decision-making process: "After spending a summer working on policy issues, I realize how important it is to me to work directly with clients . . . ." Note how this quote speaks positively about a desire to work with clients—always stress the positive and not the negative.

■ *Keep Privileged and Private Information Confidential*

Throughout the application process, you must balance your need to describe your work with your obligation to preserve the confidences of the client and the employer. Consider in advance how you will describe your externship experience without revealing these confidences. If you are unsure about how to describe a particular assignment, your supervisor likely can provide you with assistance. Avoid using the names of the parties in your application materials or in interviews. See Chapter 11 on Ethical Issues in Externships: Confidentiality.

Resumes

Your legal resume is likely to be different than those you have used in the past. Frame your experience, particularly your externship, in language that will convince a very specific audience you have the skills, experience, knowledge, and potential relevant to the legal job for which they are hiring. Your externship may be your most recent and, possibly, your only law-related job. The description you draft must be an effective advocacy piece. Make each word count.

■ *Focus on Writing, Research, and Analysis*

While cover letters and interviews are likely to be directed to a specific employer, your resume should focus on transferable skills, competencies that are important across the board to the practice of law. Most broadly, employers will want to know you can write, research, analyze, and are detail oriented. In addition, employers hiring for positions involving client contact will want to know you have a background that prepares you for direct services such as interviewing or counseling.

Consider the following examples:

· **Example One—Focus on transferable skills in the context of specific tasks.**

Anita externed for Environmental Solutions, Inc., an environmental advocacy organization. Much of her work involved lobbying efforts, but she also spent a considerable amount of time researching legislation and drafting summary memoranda regarding her research. Anita decided she was most interested in applying to a litigation firm involved in impact litigation rather than a policy or legislative advocacy firm.

OLD	NEW
Environmental Solutions, Washington, D.C.	**Environmental Solutions**, Washington, D.C.
Legal Extern, May 2015–August 2015	*Legal Extern,* May 2015–August 2015
Attended meetings of government officials. Assisted attorneys in lobbying for new regulations. Researched legal issues relating to environmental law.	Assisted in policy advocacy efforts on behalf of farmers seeking to strengthen laws related to the contamination of soil from acid rain. Researched and summarized regulations relating to revisions of the Clean Water Act. Attended meetings of organization leadership and high-ranking government officials and drafted meeting summaries distributed to all attendees. Researched and drafted policy statements used to educate state legislators and to advocate for increased funding for environmental studies of local water supply.

There are three important differences between the two resume entries. First, the old entry provided no explanation regarding the work of the organization. Second, it provided too few details about Anita's specific assignments. Third, it focused on her lobbying experience, which is not the substantive legal work that would matter to a litigation firm.

Many students generalize their externship experience so much it becomes impossible to determine the kind of work in which they were engaged. Do not assume lawyers will know anything about your placement, even if they work in the same field. Adding some specific information about the mission of the organization helps the reader understand the context of what you did in your externship.

Always include detailed information regarding writing assignments. Most attorneys spend the majority of their time writing and seek applicants with solid writing skills.

· **Example Two—Be specific.**

Robert worked on an employment discrimination case over the summer, assisting attorneys with preparing for discovery and trial. Compare the two resume entries.

OLD	NEW
Justice for All, Boulder, CO. *Legal Extern*, May 2015–August 2015 Assisted attorneys in preparing for trial. Drafted motions. Helped with discovery. Communicated with clients. Used Lexis and Westlaw to research case law. Created materials to be used at trial.	**Justice for All**, Boulder, CO. *Legal Extern*, May 2015–August 20125 Assisted attorneys with discovery and trial preparation for plaintiff-side employment discrimination claim filed in U.S. District Court for the District of Columbia. Interviewed witnesses. Drafted affidavits. Drafted interrogatories and requests for production of documents. Researched case law and drafted motions relating to admissibility of medical records. Prepared trial binders.

The first resume entry provides very little information to the reader regarding the actual scope of Robert's responsibilities. It might mean he provided administrative support with document production, cite checking, scheduling, or collating of documents. On the other hand, it might mean he researched legal issues relating to a specific area of law; drafted documents, such as interrogatories or production requests; and interviewed clients and potential witnesses to determine whether they should be deposed. It also says nothing about the kind of trial. Criminal? Civil? Personal injury? Contract dispute? What kinds of motions did he draft? He also includes unnecessary information such as familiarity with Lexis and Westlaw, which employers will assume.

The new entry provides examples of the specific legal tasks Robert performed and gives the reader context for understanding the type of work in which he was engaged. This is the type of law-related work experience in which prospective employers will be interested. In fact, additional details would not be inappropriate. Your externship is a legal job, and this is not the place to be stingy to try to save space.

· **Example Three—Avoid jargon and acronyms.**

Ellen was passionate about representing clients with disabilities, especially hidden or "invisible" disabilities. After working at her externship, she decided to broaden her job search to health law generally. Her resume contains a number of specialized references and acronyms likely to be unfamiliar to readers outside that field.

OLD	NEW
National Association for Disabled Persons (NADP) San Francisco, CA. *Legal Extern,* May 2015-August 2015 • Drafted contracts for the Tom Schooner Scholarship Fund scholarship to ensure compliance with Schedule H form 990, providing NADP with a framework for all future scholarships. • Organized thirty interns with disabilities in the Washington D.C. area, allowing them to take advantage of networking, advocacy, and employment opportunities. • Aided in negotiating a partnership agreement between NADP and the United States Corporate Network to cultivate the Disability Fairness List.	**National Association for Disabled Persons (NADP)** San Francisco, CA. *Legal Extern,* May 2015-August 2015 • Drafted scholarship contracts for students with disabilities to ensure compliance with relevant tax provisions, providing a framework for all future scholarships. • Reviewed and edited contracts with non-profit organization serving disabled community. • Aided in negotiating a partnership agreement with non-profit organization serving people with disabilities. Researched contract language to ensure limits on liability.

Students often write in shorthand easily understood by their externship placement colleagues but incomprehensible to anyone else. Many fields have their own language, which may be unfamiliar to lawyers in a different sub-specialty. If you do not use plain language, you may lose your reader. Review your resume for acronyms, jargon, and technical language. If the lawyers reviewing your resume do not understand the job description you have provided to them, you have wasted the space.

■ *Do Not Undersell or Oversell Yourself*

Many students have trouble taking credit for the valuable work they have done. Do not denigrate or underrate your experience. At the same time, avoid overstatement, puffery, or bragging. Focus on tasks for which you had major or sole responsibility. Remember you likely will be asked about these entries if you are interviewed, and your references also may be asked to comment. Be careful about stating that you "litigated" a case if you are not working under student practice rules; on the other hand, you do not need to say repeatedly you "assisted attorneys"—this is understood. You can ask your supervisor or another attorney with whom you work to look at your externship description for accuracy as well as any other suggestions they may have.

■ *Get Help*

Take advantage of your law school's Office of Career Services. If possible, meet with a counselor and follow up after you have re-drafted your resume in accordance with their suggestions. In addition, ask friends, professors, and attorneys with whom you are acquainted to review your resume. Be prepared to receive conflicting advice and select among the various suggestions you receive.

■ *Telling Your Story to Different Audiences*

You do not need a completely different resume for every application, but it is useful to create versions tailored to different types of jobs. Just as you learn to emphasize different aspects of a client's story to develop a case theory, look at your resume and consider how you might emphasize different aspects of your work and educational experience, depending on your long-term or immediate career goals. Your resume can take your various experiences, which may appear at first glance to be unrelated, and tie them together to create different narratives depending on the employer to whom you are applying.

■ *Weaving in Non-Legal Experience*

Employers do not expect law students to have years of legal experience. You can weave "non-legal" jobs into your narrative by considering the skills and knowledge you have gained that would transfer to legal practice. For example, an administrative assistant knows how to meet deadlines, pay attention to detail, organize documents, draft correspondence, etc. As described in Chapter 27, The Future of the Legal Profession, the legal marketplace has changed substantially in recent years, providing new challenges and new opportunities. Expertise related to technology, business, administration, and leadership may prepare you very well for jobs in this new economy.

Exercise 26.3 Toward the conclusion of the semester, review the draft description of your externship you wrote for your resume in Exercise 26.1. Redraft it to include your actual assignments, including those demonstrating both transferable skills, such as writing and research, and knowledge specific to the externship.

To determine whether a prospective employer would fully understand what skills and experience you acquired in your externship, ask a professor, mentor, career counselor, or classmate to review the description of your externship and tell you his or her understanding of what you accomplished. Is that person able to accurately identify the tasks you were assigned and the skills and knowledge you gained? Edit your description based on this feedback to improve clarity.

Cover Letters

A cover letter is not a recitation of what you have done; it is a guide to help the reader understand how your past work, life, and academic experiences have prepared you to be of service to the organization to which you are applying. While your resume may be more inclusive, your cover letter should focus on the particular job to which you are applying. The cover letter is not about you; it is about them. It should respond to the question in the interviewer's mind: What can this applicant do for me?

A well-drafted cover letter picks out selected details from the resume and weaves them together in a coherent whole. Like the resume, it is an advocacy piece. The more cover letters you draft, the more adept you will become at writing them. Generally, you should write a separate cover letter for each job application as you will want to tailor it to the specific employer. If you do draft general language to include in the cover letters that you would send to different employers in the same field, be sure each letter adequately explains your interest in that employer and highlights the relevance of your qualifications in light of that organization's needs. If you use a template for some of your language, be very careful to remove references to another organization.

Be sure your cover letter is free of typographical errors and mistakes in grammar, punctuation, and spelling. Your cover letter is your first writing sample. If it is not well written, it may be the only writing sample employers read. Do not rely on your own proofreading alone. Run spell and grammar check on your computer, but remember this will not find all errors. Ask someone else to do the final edits to ensure there are no mistakes.

■ *Know Your Externship*

Your externship is your most recent substantive legal experience. Your resume describes what you did in your externship. Your cover letter can focus on what you learned and what engaged you. Reflect on what you found meaningful and interesting. Explain how your placement prepared you for the position for which you are applying, either through the specific knowledge you acquired or the transferable skills you bring. Review your journals to remind yourself of the specific tasks you performed as well as some of the thoughts you had about your work to see if there were any tasks especially relevant to this particular employer.

■ *Know the Employer*

The most effective cover letters are those targeted to specific employers and tailored to address their interests.

> *I want to hear from applicants who have researched my firm and really want to work here. Everyone tells me that they are a "great fit" and that they have "honed their skills." I want them to talk about the cases we have won and why they want to work for us. I want them to tell me about the brief we submitted and how brilliant it was. I want a love letter.*
>
> **–Hiring Attorney, Boutique Litigation Firm**

Prior to drafting your cover letter, research the employer. Engage in "due diligence" to find out what their ideal candidate looks like. Talk to anyone you know who is familiar with the employer. Scrutinize the employer's website. What do they say about themselves? What kinds of cases or issues do they emphasize? Compare their website to similar employers. What is unique? On what do they pride themselves? What does their mission statement say about their values? Is there other information on the Internet? Are there articles about cases they have brought that have garnered publicity? If you really want to distinguish yourself, do a Lexis/Westlaw search. Read up on cases they have pursued or policies they have drafted and see whether you can weave some substantive mention of this into your cover letter. This information also will be very helpful in preparing for an interview.

Interviews

Your presentation during an interview is an opportunity for an employer to observe your communication skills, a vital legal competency. If you are enrolled in an externship seminar, take advantage of opportunities to practice discussing your externship. Some students find participating in mock interviews increases their comfort level and degree of preparation. Remember your demeanor will be an important consideration in an interview. You can prepare by following some of the suggestions below.

■ *Formal Interviews*

Know the employer: Just as you did before you drafted the cover letter, review the organization's website carefully and find out whatever other background information you can. An employer will expect you to demonstrate this knowledge during your interview. If you know the name of the person with whom you will be interviewing, make sure to investigate that person's background and work experience. Re-read the job announcement carefully to ensure you have tailored your narrative to the qualifications the employer seeks.

> *I regularly ask employers about the most common mistakes students make during the application process. The number one answer is that students are not properly prepared for the interview and need to research the employer more thoroughly.*

Collect stories: One aspect of being a reflective practitioner is the ability to find and articulate what is interesting and compelling in any situation. Throughout your externship, you should be thinking critically about what you have observed and accomplished. You can use this skill in the interview process to distinguish yourself from other applicants by speaking in an engaging and even passionate manner about your experience. Every day, you should collect stories about your work. These can be events that affected you, mattered to you, changed you, surprised you, challenged you, bothered you, amused you, and inspired you. You may have an opportunity to journal about these or discuss them in a classroom setting and, if you do, use this as a preview for how you might convey your enthusiasm and excitement during an interview. Your stories also will help you respond to some common interview questions.

Know your resume: Be prepared to answer questions about information you have presented in your resume, especially detailed questions about your externship. If your resume states you assisted an attorney in drafting a motion for summary judgment, be prepared to discuss the case and the type of work you did to the extent you may do so without revealing confidential information. To ensure you have an easy command of your accomplishments, review your externship journals in advance of the interview.

Know your goals: The time you spend discussing your goals in your externship seminar and in your reflective writing provide you with very helpful fodder for your job search as you consider how those goals relate to the job for which you are applying. Generally, employers will ask you questions about your goals outright, for example, "Where do you see yourself five years out of law school?" Most employers respond favorably to a student who presents herself as applying for a position after careful consideration of how the organization fits into her goals.

Reflect: During an interview you will likely be asked questions that require you to reflect on your externship and other aspects of your life rather than just describe your work. For example, "Describe an incident in which you needed to work in a team and tell me about the challenges you faced in doing that," or "In what ways did your stereotypes of clients change as a result of your work?" As you draft your journal entries over the course of the semester, you can develop your reflective skills, helping you prepare for such questions. If you are asked about subjects that did not arise in your externship, you will need to use these reflective skills quickly to find the common principles between the skills you have gained and those necessary for the job for which you are applying. See Chapter 8 on Reflection and Writing Journals.

Prepare questions: Almost every interview ends with the query, "Do you have any questions for us?" As you research the employer, consider what questions you will raise. This is one way to show the employer your interest in their organization and your preparation for the interview. In addition, during the interview, take note of any follow-up questions you might have.

Relax: One of the most important factors that determines whether or not someone is hired is whether the employer feels comfortable during the interview. If you find it difficult to relax, focus on the needs of the employer and how you might be able to assist with those needs, rather than on how you are presenting yourself.

> **Exercise 26.4** Resumes, cover letters, and interviews all develop your narrative in distinct ways. Select a prospective job to which you would actually apply and consider what skills, knowledge, and experiences from your externship you would highlight in each: your resume, your cover letter, and your interview? See Exercise 26.5.

Informal Interviews: Elevator Speeches, Table Talks, and Meeting Strangers

Your externship provides a ready-made topic of conversation, but you need to be prepared to take full advantage of the opportunities to have the conversation.

Elevator speeches: An "elevator speech" refers to a short conversation, in which you only have a few minutes to make a good impression (e.g., the time it takes to ride up an elevator). With an elevator speech, you are unlikely to know much about the person you are meeting; the emphasis has to be on your experience and your personality. If you have a chance to discuss your externship, you need to boil down your experience into just a few sentences and touch on one or two things that engaged you. Enthusiasm is key. You want to convey confidence, interest, listening skills, professionalism, and maturity as you speak briefly. If you have collected stories about your externship and reflected on your activities throughout the semester, you will be in a better position to engage quickly in an absorbing conversation about your work.

> **Exercise 26.5** You have been asked to accompany an attorney you have never met to an event taking place at the law school. The walk will last about five minutes. The attorney asks you about your externship. What do you want to cover in just a few minutes? Outline what you would emphasize during this brief conversation.

Table talk: Table talk refers to a brief discussion at a career fair or other career-oriented event. For this type of event you may have an opportunity to learn something about the employers before you chat with them. If there are some employers in whom you are particularly interested, investigate them with the same "due diligence" you would use if you had a formal interview. Make it clear you have chosen to speak to them specifically and you have a strong interest in their work. Think beforehand of the ways in which your externship experience has provided you with skills and knowledge relevant to the position you seek.

After the interview: Immediately following any meeting you have, write a few notes about the conversation so you can remember it later. If you get a business card, jot notes on the back to remind you when and where you met the person and a few things about the conversation. Use this information when you follow up with a note thanking the interviewer for her time and saying it was a pleasure meeting her.

> **Tip:** Whether you have interviewed for a position or had a chat with an employer at a job fair, always send a thank you note. Use this as an opportunity to reiterate your interest in the position. Include specific references to the conversation. Some employers will not consider applicants who have not followed up with a thank you note. Either an email or handwritten note will work.

Networking

Creating a Professional Network

Once you begin your placement, you are in a position to develop your network of attorneys, obtain valuable mentoring, and create the good impression you will use to parlay your work experience into a career.

Your placement provides a great opportunity to improve your networking skills by interacting with as many attorneys and other work colleagues as possible, including administrative staff and other externs. To the extent you find networking uncomfortable, think of it like any other legal skill that is part of your professional growth and can be improved with practice.

Do not limit yourself to meeting attorneys working directly in your fields of interest. Your career may unfold in many ways, so take any opportunity to create or enlarge the network of attorneys and others who can provide you with advice and assistance. You may find the connections you make lead directly to job opportunities—whether in your current field of interest or in other practice areas to which you never imagined you would be drawn. Many positions are not well advertised, and knowing attorneys in the field can improve your chances of finding out a position has become available. Also, many attorneys prefer hiring a known entity and will value a good word, even from someone who knows you only peripherally.

> **Tip:** Do not try to turn a networking conversation into a job application. Networking focuses on building professional relationships. Avoid asking someone if they have a job available; this type of direct overture creates an awkward situation that can bring the conversation to a halt.

Networking is not just about self-interest; good networking skills will benefit your clients and your employers once you become a lawyer. Think of networking as building a community, a network of mutually interdependent individuals who are available to help one another as the need arises. It is not a one-way street; those who help you also may need help in the future. Lawyers understand there is no way for them to succeed without this interconnectedness.

Creating a legal network can help you feel a part of a larger community and give meaning to your work. It can help you become a more effective attorney as you have access to information and assistance. It can build your social network to give you a fuller life outside of work, and, perhaps most importantly, it can make your work more enjoyable. Here are some of the ways you can incorporate networking into your externship experience:

■ *Be Pleasant and Stay in Touch*

Networking does not have to be complicated. It boils down to taking part in pleasant conversation, engaging with others, smiling, talking, listening, and showing interest in other people. It is also important to stay in touch with people in your network. Take contact information and follow up with email. Use social networking sites like LinkedIn or listservs in specific practice areas to communicate regularly.

■ *Help Others*

Think about what you can give, not just what you need. Become a "validator," someone who introduces people to each other in a professional context, in effect vouching for each one. You can take on this role even as an extern. For example, if you know of someone who you think would be a great extern for your placement, suggest this to both the student and the supervisor. Even if nothing comes of it, both the student and the supervisor will appreciate your efforts and remember you for it. A "validator" also acts a host, rather than a guest. A good host introduces guests to each other, finds areas of common ground between them, and helps those who are not as well-connected by including them in activities.

- *Join Professional Organizations*

Joining professional organizations in your field of interest provides access to the latest information and trends in the field, and offers opportunities to meet large numbers of attorneys who can be helpful in your job search. Many professional organizations welcome students, offer heavily discounted membership fees, and allow students to attend events free of charge. By attending these events, you will gain subject-matter expertise. Organization leaders and members will be pleased to see you and impressed you have made the effort to attend. In addition, professional organizations often provide students with opportunities to take on leadership roles and contribute to their publications.

> **Exercise 26.6** Create a list of your current professional network. Consider individuals you might go to for any sort of professional assistance, including former employers, friends, family, faculty, and people you know through school or professional organizations. Now, expand that list using contacts you have made at your externship; include supervisors, other attorneys, fellow externs, and staff with whom you have had professional contact.

The Informational Interview

This type of interview is used for strategic networking in which you meet with individuals who may not have a job available but have knowledge of the field or specific organizations that interest you. Externs are often in a phenomenal position to meet such attorneys, and you should seek out these opportunities to take full advantage of your placement. You do not need to ask specifically for an "informational interview." Instead, just explain that you are looking for information about the field and you understand this person is very knowledgeable. Do not be shy; everyone understands this is one of the ways law students learn about legal practice in general, as well as specific subject areas.

An informational interview can include finding out about a field of practice, strategies for personal advancement, or general information-gathering about legal careers. You may want to ask for such an interview with your supervisor, an attorney at your placement with whom you do not regularly work, or with anyone you meet you think would be amenable to such a conversation.

To learn more about practice areas, use the interview to ask about specific organizations—which ones might be hiring, which are the most respected in the field, and the major differences between them. Find out about job trends—whether there are some aspects of the practice area that are expanding and might be more likely to hire new attorneys.

Asking for strategic advice on your own career development is generally seen as a compliment, and attorneys are often happy to offer suggestions. Ask what qualifications are needed for competency and marketability: what courses you should take, what specific skills and knowledge you should develop, and what extra-curricular activities would be most helpful. You also can ask for advice on your resume and what aspects of your experience you should emphasize for this area of practice. Be prepared to discuss your own career aspirations and the personal considerations that have led you to legal practice or a particular field of interest.

Most attorneys like to talk about themselves and their practice and, as long as you do not seem disingenuous, will be happy to discuss their own career paths and provide you with career advice. You can ask about their work, how they made a career transition or practice change, and what led them to the field—topics that make it easy for them to talk. As with all such meetings, read up on the organization and the person with whom you are meeting in order to pose relevant questions. Share something about yourself and your externship. Be prepared with a number of specific questions, rather than just open-ended ones, and make sure to include the topics most important to you. Asking specific questions makes it easier for the person with whom you are meeting. At the conclusion of the interview, ask for suggestions for other contacts and ask whether you may use them as a referral. After the interview, reflect on what you learned, such as new information or new approaches you had not considered. As always, send a thank you note.

> **Exercise 26.7** **Research Practice Areas.** Identify three people in your field or area of interest and schedule interviews with them to learn about that practice area and job trends. Consider interviewing the following people:
>
> — Attorneys working in the field,
> — Law school alumni,
> — Law school faculty,
> — Career Services Office counselors.

Recommendations

Perhaps the most valuable form of networking available at your externship is to make a good impression and earn a strong letter of recommendation. A strong recommendation will move your resume to the top of the pile faster than anything else.

> *When I am hiring, I might get 500 resumes for one position. They all go into one pile. As I get calls and emails from friends and colleagues about the candidates, I pull those resumes and put them in a separate pile and these are likely to be the only people I will interview. After narrowing the pool down to five or so for call-backs, I follow up with the references who can speak to the applicants' work product and I base my decision in large part on the quality of the recommendation.*
>
> **—Hiring Attorney, Litigation Firm**

In addition to being able to call on people to recommend you, it is helpful to obtain a written letter of recommendation before you leave your placement, even if you have no pending job applications. By the time you need a recommendation, your supervisor may have worked with many other externs and no longer remember the details of the projects to which you were assigned and the quality of your work. Worse yet, your supervisor may leave the organization and be impossible to track down. There is no hard and fast rule as to when you should ask for a written recommendation. If you have a positive exit interview, that might be a good time. If your supervisor agrees to write a recommendation, offer to provide a list of your assignments and accomplishments from your externships. If you do, provide it by email so your supervisor has it in her files for future reference. Your externship journal is an excellent source for reminding you of the work you accomplished over the course of the semester.

There are many excellent resources that can provide substantial assistance with your networking efforts. Check with your law school's career development office.

Mentoring

To pursue a successful career, you will need to develop relationships with mentors—experienced attorneys willing to provide you with guidance and advice. Externships provide an excellent opportunity to build these mentoring relationships.

A mentor can

- Advise you on how to maneuver through the placement to get the most from your experience;

- Provide you with suggestions on how to make a good impression on other attorneys and provide background information on organizations and firms that work in the same practice area;

- Advise you on how you might break into the field;

- Review your resume;

- Provide suggestions on how to reframe your description of your experience to make it more appealing to attorneys in the field; and

- Discuss your career plans with you.

When looking for a mentor, consider attorneys who have established themselves in the workplace, and want to help you get the most out of your externship and help you succeed professionally. Choose a mentor who is willing to be honest, provide a realistic appraisal of your challenges, and help you to overcome them.

Note that your supervising attorney may not end up being your mentor. While many placements encourage supervising attorneys to act as mentors, not all supervising attorneys take on this role. The relationship you develop with your mentor will be personal, and, although this is a professional relationship, you will need to find someone with whom you are compatible. If you find your supervisor does not provide the guidance you hoped for, build other relationships that provide the mentoring you need.

Remember there is no formula for developing a mentoring relationship. Sometimes, it can occur by happenstance; other times it may develop through careful research and planning. You can expect to find many "mentors" serving different roles during the course of your career. You also may find your externship provides you with the expertise you need to "pay it forward" and mentor those who come behind you.

The Role of Social Media in Effective Networking

Once you start your externship, social media will become an important networking tool. It offers substantial benefits, as well as some potential pitfalls. If you use social media for networking, it is critical to stay aware of your online presence and monitor your digital footprint. On a regular basis, search for yourself online and check your privacy settings on all forms of social media you use. Be very selective about comments you make through any form of social media.

- *LinkedIn*

LinkedIn is a widely-used professional networking tool. You can and should add your externship to your LinkedIn profile soon after you start working. It allows you to find others and helps others find you and learn about your work experience. As you meet other externs, connect with them. You may want to wait to connect to attorney supervisors until after you have completed your externship, unless the requests come from them.

As with all social networking, think about its use proactively—how to use the site most effectively to increase the number of people with whom you are professionally connected. On a regular basis, add new contacts, keep your profile updated, and post a professional photograph of yourself. At the same time, think "defensively." Is there anything about your online presence that could concern employers? If you have edited your resume to emphasize certain jobs or experience, review your LinkedIn profile to see whether you need to make similar edits to the way you describe your background. If your LinkedIn profile does not match your resume, you will raise red flags for potential employers.

We always search social media sites to find out more about our job applicants. I am amazed at the number of people who make disparaging comments about their current jobs on these public sites. We figure if this is how they operate, the next time, they will post this sort of thing about us. We don't need to take that risk.

—Hiring Attorney, Public Defenders' Office

- *Facebook*

Facebook is a social network, rather than a professional network, and you are probably better off not "friending" anyone you with whom you do not already have a personal relationship. Keep in mind you never know who will see what is on your site and, regardless of your privacy settings and who you have already "friended," do not post anything you would not want your employer or a potential employer to see.

- *Twitter*

Twitter is as accessible to the public as Facebook, if not more so. Be aware of your privacy settings; anyone you follow has access to your tweets. This is public information, and, once public, it can never be private again. Make sure your username is professional and avoid controversial tweets.

- *Listservs and Blogs*

Many legal practice areas have listservs or blogs through which attorneys communicate. If you have a long-term interest in the field in which you are externing, ask attorneys with whom you work what professional social media sites they are on, what listservs and blogs they subscribe to, and how they follow current developments in the law. Comment judiciously. Commenting is a double-edged sword; it shows your interest in a specific field of law and topic, but it may be used against you if the topic becomes controversial.

- *Internet Surfing*

Avoid personal use of the Internet at your externship. If your supervisor sees you using social media or surfing the web while you are supposed to be working, you may never recover from the poor impression you have made. Strictly limit your use of the Internet to occasions when it is needed for the job.

Exercise 26.8 Search yourself on the Internet as if you were an employer looking for information. Use more than one search engine and search Facebook, Instagram, and Twitter. Did you find anything that you think would raise red flags for an employer?

Leaving Your Externship Happily

As your externship comes to its conclusion, consider several things you can do to ensure you are remembered favorably and receive good references from your supervisors. Remind your employer of your end date a few weeks in advance. Ask how you should focus your efforts before you leave.

Complete your assignments to the extent possible: Write a closing memorandum on each project left open at the end of your externship, including a summary of the work you completed and the location of all files. This will ensure your supervisor will not be frustrated, wondering where to find something you worked on, and your successor will not have to replicate your work. Provide your contact information and offer to be available to answer any questions.

Get names and contact information: Before you leave, get the contact information for the attorneys and staff with whom you worked. Keep a reminder of useful information, including the primary assignments on which you worked with each person. If you have reason to think someone with whom you worked might leave the organization, ask if there is another way to contact that person. Do not ask directly for home or other personal contact information. It may be offered, but you should not ask for it.

Schedule an exit interview: Throughout the semester, you should have been engaged in regular communication with your supervisor regarding the quality of your work, applying this feedback, and demonstrating growth and improvement. Still, you will want to ask for a final meeting to receive an honest appraisal of your work overall.

Generally, set the date when you still expect to be at the placement for at least another week or two, in case something comes up that can be corrected in your final days. Be prepared to ask specific questions. Communicate that you are receptive to constructive criticism. Ask about specific projects you worked on and how you might have improved. If you are interested in pursuing a career in the field, ask what additional skills it would be helpful for you to obtain. Try not be defensive about anything you are told. Thank your supervising attorney for the feedback, even if it is negative. See Chapter 3 on Learning from Supervision for more information about receiving feedback.

Make sure you tell your employer how much you learned from your externship and show enthusiasm for the experience. If the meeting goes well, it may be an opportunity to ask for a recommendation.

Stay in touch with your supervisor and with your colleagues: Start by sending a thank you note to your supervisors and other attorneys with whom you worked. If you developed friendly relationships, occasionally call or write to say hello, ask them how they are doing, and let them know what is going on with you. If you see a decision you think would help on a case or one that further develops the law in an area they work in, send it to them. Consider calling for advice if you are struggling with career issues. These types of overtures keep your network active and ensure people will remember you. Develop and maintain a list of people for whom you have worked and send an update to each person on that list each time you start a new job. LinkedIn is particularly useful here, as it prompts you to be in touch with people when they have work anniversaries or change some aspect of their profile.

Moving Forward Through the Cycle: Reassessment

At the conclusion of your externship, reassess your career goals in light of your experience. Consider the following questions: Would you like to work long term for this employer? Would you like to work in this field of law? Have your short-term or long-term goals changed as a result of the externship? What are those goals now? See Chapter 28 On Finishing Strong, for more about ending your externship.

Reflect on what you will need to pursue your current career goals. Identify your strengths and the areas for improvement based on your placement experience. Did you obtain the skills, knowledge, experience, and connections you addressed in your goals memorandum at the beginning of the externship? How will you fill the gaps?

Reassess the transferable skills you need to develop for your job search. Return to the information-gathering section described earlier in the chapter in light of your experience in your externship. Interview attorneys, explain the experience you have gained, and find out what else you still need to do to achieve your career goals.

Examine which aspects of your externship experience made you happy. Were there times in your externship where time flew by? What did you learn about the areas of law that do or do not interest you? What else did you learn from the experience that may affect your goals? This may include practice area, venue, type of practice, your own propensities, the importance of working with clients, etc.

Explore the areas of your work that need improvement. For example, if you had difficulties with completing assignments, consider what part you played in this issue. Could you have asked for more clarity in assignments or guidance on your progress? Could you have managed your time more efficiently? Did you have similar problems in any previous work experiences? What changes do you need to make? Should you ask for assistance in making these changes?

> **Exercise 26.9** List the three aspects of your externship you most enjoy and the three aspects you least enjoy. Can you extrapolate what you would look for in future positions? In what ways?

Many students consider staying at a placement for a second semester, in the hope of increasing the possibility of being hired for full-time employment. While this may be an effective strategy for some students, there are also drawbacks. First, it limits the number of attorneys you will meet and who will get to know your work; second, it limits the skills and knowledge you build because you are working in the same field.

—Supervising Attorney, U.S. Government Agency, Office of General Counsel

Conclusion

Most lawyers who participated in externships while in law school will tell of the sometimes subtle and often profound influence the experience had on their career paths. Generally, career plans evolve over time, and the externship is a crucial part of the learning process.

Keep your eye on your ultimate career goals and the skills, knowledge, values, and experiences sought by the employers for whom you might want to work. Doing so will enrich your externship by ensuring you take full advantage of your experience. Many of the skills you are learning in your externship—reflection, narrative storytelling, understanding your audience, presentation skills, effective advocacy, critical thinking, networking, communication, and self-assessment—can help you to build the bridge between your externship and your ultimate career.

ENDNOTES

1   Nancy Levit & Douglas O. Linder, The Happy Lawyer: Making a Good Life in the Law 96–100 (2010).

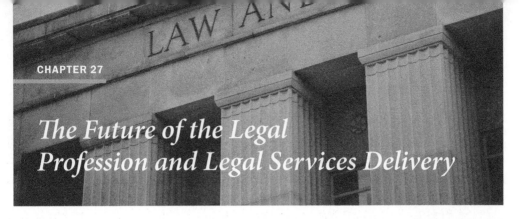

The Future of the Legal Profession and Legal Services Delivery

LEAH WORTHAM

> *. . . The times they are a-changin'.*
>
> –Bob Dylan

- "2018: The year Axiom becomes the world's largest legal services firm." That is a 2013 prediction by Eric Chin on the Beaton Capital blog. Time will tell how close the prediction comes to truth. Note the phrasing "legal services firm." The "What We're Not" section of Axiom's 2015 website says "We're not a law firm but we don't mind . . . [because] we were actually built on the premise that the current law firm model is broken so we don't mind being something completely new and different."

- In an initial public offering statement filed with the SEC in 2012, LegalZoom, a company offering automated on-line legal document assembly and pre-paid legal service plans, reported that they had served 2 million customers in the previous ten years, earned $156.1 million in revenue in 2011, and that their software was used to create 20% of the California limited liability companies established in 2011.

- LawHelp Interactive, a free automated-document-assembly program, developed with support from the U.S. Legal Services Corporation Technology Innovation Grant program, reported their software was used to create 2.3 million legal documents between 2005–2015.

- In 2007, the Australian law firm, Slater & Gordon (S&G), became the first law firm to sell publicly-traded shares and be listed on a stock exchange. S&G self-describes as a "consumer law firm" with a substantial personal injury practice along with areas of law used by individuals and small businesses including family, real estate conveyancing, estate planning, criminal law, and business litigation. By 2015, S&G had expanded from 400 staff in 15 offices in Australia when they "went public" to 1400 staff in 80 locations. When the U.K. followed Australia's lead to allow non-lawyer ownership of law firms, S&G obtained an alternative business structure (ABS) license allowing outside investment in their U.K. ventures and acquired law firms there such that by spring 2015 they had 3800 staff in 27 locations in the U.K.

· Leonard Jacoby & Stephen Meyers opened their first law office in California in 1972 and were pioneers in the "legal clinic" movement to run storefront offices offering lower and often flat fee arrangements for routine legal services through routinization, automation, and use of non-lawyer staff. They also challenged California bar restrictions on lawyer advertising and were the first U.S. firm to run a television ad. In 2013, J&M announced a joint venture with a London private equity and law firm to pursue expansion to give "the public, especially lower and middle income clients, access to affordable quality representation" saying they were pursuing a growth strategy in the U.K. because their "ability to raise capital necessary to serve the public is severely restricted in the US by an outdated rule of professional conduct." In 2011, J&M filed lawsuits in three U.S. states challenging state bar rules against non-lawyer ownership and investment as unconstitutionally preventing them from raising capital needed for investment in technology and expansion.

The anecdotes above are a sampling of winds of change in the legal profession and legal services market that are discussed in this chapter. If you read more about "future stuff," you likely will see the term NewLaw. NewLaw is often contrasted to "BigLaw," a shorthand way of describing the historical organization of large law firms with a pyramid structure of partner income largely dependent on the hourly billing of associates and paralegals. George Beaton's book, NEWLAW NEW RULES: A CONVERSATION ABOUT THE FUTURE OF THE LEGAL SERVICES INDUSTRY, is cited in the Further Resources section of this chapter. Many of the differences in the "old" ways of working, though, also apply to smaller firms and legal work done outside law firms. Jordan Furlong, editor of the well regarded Law21 blog, says NewLaw "describe[s] any model, process, or tool that represents a significantly different approach to the creation or provision of legal services than what the legal profession traditionally has employed." This means "not just law firm models, but also new legal talent combinations, legal service managers, and technology that both changes how lawyers practice and places the power of legal service provision in clients' hands."

Part One of this chapter describes evolution in the legal market and a difference in thinking about legal services "vertically" versus "horizontally." Thinking "vertically" refers to a lawyer providing a series of made-to-order prescriptions for particular clients. Thinking "horizontally" refers to seeking commonalities among client problems within an area of law, developing standard processes for recurring problems, and using such processes to help meet client needs more cheaply and simply. Part One also discusses the difference in conceiving legal practice as what lawyers do as opposed to what clients need—helping clients use the law to achieve their goals. Part Two describes five factors pressing change in the nature of law practice. Part Three expands on the snapshots in the chapter's opening with fuller case studies that illustrate changes in delivery of legal services and highlight the impact of the five factors pressing change. Part Four examines what this information suggests for people entering the profession and how your externship can help you map out your place in this changing world.

QUESTION TO CONSIDER

As you read the chapter, think about how it connects (or does not) with things you observe in your placement, see in the media, or otherwise have come across. What additional variables seem to be in the mix by the time you are reading? The Further Resources section at the end of the chapter suggests blogs and websites where updated information is likely to be available, and new ones appear frequently.

Part One: Changing Conceptions of Legal Service Provision

Most discussions of the future of delivery of legal services refer to Richard Susskind at some point. During his law studies in the U.K. in the 1980s, Susskind started focusing on the impact of technology on the practice of law and the legal system when few others were looking at this in any depth. Susskind wrote a trilogy of books cited in Further Resources at the end of the chapter: THE FUTURE OF LAW, TRANSFORMING THE LAW, and THE END OF LAWYERS. His latest book, TOMORROW'S LAWYERS: AN INTRODUCTION TO YOUR FUTURE, focuses directly on helping law students and new lawyers find satisfying careers in the rapidly changing legal world. Unlike those assailing an oversupply of law graduates, Susskind believes most of law school training will remain useful and important in coming years but cautions that those who flourish in the future legal world will need to embrace new technologies and look for new methods to help people with their legal problems. This means that lawyers will need to add additional skills and knowledge to traditional legal training, use that training in different ways, and consider combining legal services with services offered by other kinds of professionals and providers. In TOMORROW'S LAWYERS, Susskind predicts "fundamental shifts" in the legal profession by 2015-2018 and "by 2035 . . . that the legal profession will have changed beyond recognition."

One of Susskind's most-cited ideas is an evolutionary path in legal services he traces through five stages that can be visualized as a left-to-right continuum: (1) "bespoke," meaning individualized, built from scratch; (2) standardized; (3) systematized; (4) packaged; and (5) commoditized.

Bespoke, a term more common in the U.K. than the U.S., refers to something made-to-order, hand-crafted for a particular person. The British refer to the bespoke, "Savile Row suit"—one-of-a-kind made to a person's specific measurements with the client's choice of fabric, lapel width, cut, and so on. Susskind points to lawyers' oral advocacy in court as the classic "bespoke" service, although even then, lawyers may have approaches or even lines that they repeat in similar kinds of cases. Applied to another type of practice, in a bespoke approach to contract, each contract would begin with a blank sheet of paper with no use of "standard terms" or patterning on past similar contracts.

Standardization refers to the way lawyers have for years distilled experience with a category of matters into guides about process (e.g., checklists or procedure manuals for a type of case) or substance (e.g., past bodies of text such as standard form documents, templates, or "banks" of past research memos or briefs). Think, for example, of formbooks and practitioner handbooks on a particular area of law, which often include checklists of standard client questions or alternative causes of action with their required elements. Before computers, books of this type or firm pleading banks existed in hard copy and later migrated to electronic form for faster retrieval.

Systematization uses technology to take standardization a step further by having the computer, rather than a person, make judgments on how to modify, combine, or create documents based on input such as facts and client goals for a particular matter. This means innovations like automatic-document-assembly systems, interactive checklists, and software that can suggest the appropriate next step on a project. Systematizing requires marrying experience in an area of law practice with information-technology knowledge to identify possible decisions and alternative paths of action based on inputted information. Computers, of course, are only as good as their programming, but properly programmed, the computer will not absent-mindedly skip a step that needs to be checked or language that must be included in a contract.

Packaged refers to moving beyond systematized tools designed for internal law firm use to those that can be used by clients directly. Rather than providing the client with the product of the firm's systematization of an area of legal work, the firm produces a product that can be used directly by the client without intermediation by a firm lawyer. LegalZoom and RocketLawyer provide this kind of service for a flat fee to their individual and small business clients. The large international accounting firms and British law firms have been particularly innovative in designing products for the corporate market. Susskind describes the evolution of Abacus, somewhat like a TurboTax for corporate tax forms, from an internal product used by the Deloitte accounting firm to a product sold to in-house corporate departments for preparation of their own tax forms.

For another example, see aosphere, developed as an affiliate of Allen & Overy, a major British law firm, http://www.aosphere.com, which describes itself on its 2015 web as follows:

> aosphere LLP (formerly Derivative Services LLP) specializes in providing user-friendly access to complex legal information for institutions large and small. We use our expertise in all aspects of derivatives trading and key compliance issues like shareholding disclosure, marketing restrictions and cross border data transfers to provide subscription products which help you to reduce legal, regulatory and operational risk. Our secure data management system allows you to manage your bespoke legal documents alongside your aosphere subscriptions offering a seamless, one-stop solution to risk reduction.

The final stage in the continuum is **commoditization.** Commodities are commonly defined as products traded with little differentiation in quality so price competition can be fierce. If there are a sufficient number of competing products that cannot be differentiated, the price can be driven down to the cost of producing an additional unit, which for software is next-to-nothing, although the cost of creating the system originally may have been considerable. Those needing to generate revenue from legal expertise generally worry about how to add value so their service is still profitable. This reduction in price, however, also opens up opportunities for thinking about access to legal service for the many who have not been able to buy legal services in the market. In Susskind's words, "commoditization will be fundamental in radically increasing access to justice for those who cannot currently afford legal services."

The remaining Parts of this chapter identify ways in which developments in the delivery of legal services and the legal services market up and down the income spectrum relate to the continuum from bespoke service to commodity. This includes providing legal services with a more predictable and finite cost, finding cheaper ways to solve legal problems, and disaggregating legal components of a matter to reduce cost or assign tasks to providers with the best expertise for the purpose. As discussed in Part Two, clients along the income spectrum also may benefit from the previously-described forms of alternative legal service or from more traditional bespoke representation being offered in a multidisciplinary (MDP) practice combining legal service with other needs in forms of "one-stop-shopping."

The remainder of this chapter also highlights how, all along the income scale, clients experience frustration with lawyers who see legal services delivery as about the lawyer rather than the client. Chapter 15 on the client relationship discusses varying paradigms of the lawyer-client relationship. Other chapters in this book also focus on the client-lawyer relationship, particularly when lawyer and client come from different cultural, socio-economic, or other groups with different power levels in the society. See particularly Chapter 6 on Navigating Cultural Difference and Chapter 20 on Criminal Justice Lawyering. Perhaps surprisingly, given their seemingly stronger position in relation to their lawyers, corporate clients also express considerable frustration with their lawyers' understanding of their needs, communication with them, and failure to focus adequately on cost-effective solutions for their objectives.[1]

In a 2015 blogpost, Paul Lippe, ABA Journal columnist and founder and CEO of Legal OnRamp,[2] related an interesting depiction of NewLaw. He described a presentation slide created by a large, international London-based firm. The slide depicted the legal services world with clients in the middle and various innovations in legal service delivery surrounding it, his firm being just one of many in orbit around the client.[3] He commented that, when showing the slide to large U.S. firms, many seemed quite surprised that a law firm would depict a major law firm as just one of the options available to the corporate clients they serve.

Richard Susskind is among many speakers to legal audiences who invoke the parable of executives of a major power tool company being shown a picture of an electric drill and being asked if this is what their company sells. When they venture, "yes," trainers replace the slide with one of a beautifully-drilled hole, proclaiming THAT is what customers want to buy.[4] Paul Lippe frames the problem as a "dangerous belief . . . that law is primarily about the reasoning processes—the credentials and intentions of the lawyer—as opposed to the outcome for the client, the processes and systems to deliver that outcome, and the overall impact for society: lawyer-centric rather than purpose-centric."[5]

Some may see the previous description of the client-lawyer relationship as reflecting a common law system "instrumental" paradigm of client control of decision making, which is different from that in at least parts of continental Europe and elsewhere in countries with civil law systems. In civil law systems, lawyers may be described as a "free" or "liberal profession" making decisions about how client matters should be handled with more independence from clients than a lawyer in the U.S.[6] Within the U.S. system, a focus on what clients want and need is not meant to imply that lawyers should be merely "hired guns," and there are no ethical constraints or space for lawyers to consider their own values in the ways they conduct their careers. Chapter 9 on Professionalism, Chapters 10–13 on ethical issues, Chapter 15 on Client Relationships, and Chapter 24 on Professional Identity and Formation discuss limits on lawyer conduct in assisting clients and the need for lawyers to consider their own values in constructing a professional identity that will guide their choice of client, type of work, and many decisions they make as lawyers.

Lawyers may forget, to their and their clients' peril, that clients do not seek to use law so lawyers can practice skills they learned in law school. Instead, clients hire lawyers to achieve what clients need and want in their personal or corporate lives. Societies, too, should seek a fair and accessible system that helps people and entities go about their lives and businesses within fair legal bounds, with respect for human rights, with an equitable system for resolving disputes, and with the state performing its public functions like adjudication of criminal allegations and allocation of punishment in a just manner. These client and societal objectives do not include, as an end in itself, providing employment for lawyers to continue functioning as they historically have functioned. And, as the opening quote suggests, a number of factors are now converging so the times for lawyers and legal services delivery are "a changin"—and quickly in many respects.

Part Two: Five Factors Pressing Change

This part identifies five factors pressing change upon lawyers and the legal services market. The first is pressure to make the cost of legal services cheaper and more predictable. The second is technology: the changes it permits in how lawyers reach potential clients and deliver services and the new types of services and ways of working that technology enables. The third is globalization, accelerated by technology, which allows people, business entities, tangible and intangible goods, and ideas to cross national borders much more easily than in the past. This fuels a fourth factor: pressure for change in the regulation of legal professions and the delivery of legal services. The fifth is changing demographics, which refers to shifts in the age cohort, gender, ethnic, and cultural background composition of those who comprise the legal profession and legal service consumers.

Cost

Most law students and lawyers probably recognize that low- and middle-income people generally find billed-by-the-hour, market-rate legal services beyond their means. Small- and medium-sized businesses, without their own internal legal staffs, also often hesitate to contact law firms for much day-to-day work like review and drafting of contracts or advice on legal compliance, assuming a lawyer will be too expensive. Gillian Hadfield and Jamie Heine note that the U.S. uses considerable public funds to investigate public health questions like incidence of disease, effectiveness of various interventions, and the distribution of medical services. Yet there is no National Institute of Legal Health to track the public legal health of our citizens and little systematic information on the percentage of the legal services market used by individuals versus large institutional clients.[7] Extrapolating from available data, they estimate that only about 35% of the $289 billion in U.S. expenditures for legal services serve individuals. Faced with a legal problem, Americans often simply do nothing, or, if a court appearance cannot be avoided, appear pro se.

While many individuals and small businesses find the cost of legal services out of reach, large institutional clients also have been aggressively seeking lower and more predictably-priced legal services as well. In the boom years through 2006, law firms serving these clients regularly charged by the hour and were able to collect hefty bills with expensive time-based rates, even for inexperienced new associates. Then came the economic downturn of 2007—with ripple effects in rescinded associate offers, layoffs, and some firm closures and bankruptcies. Corporate management increasingly sought to concentrate resources on functions directly related to profit and relentlessly cut costs for functions deemed peripheral to the production and marketing of the goods or services bringing in revenue. So corporate general counsel often found themselves under pressure to cut their budgets, particularly for outside counsel, in the same way other "back-office" corporate functions like human resources and financial management also were being pressed.

Today there are similarities along the full income spectrum of potential clients, from individuals to large corporations, regarding ways to make legal services more accessible and convenient as well as less expensive.

The hourly-billing system that prevailed in much of law practice at least since the 1950s when it became the norm, is now losing some of its dominance. Some types of services for clients at the lower end of the income spectrum for years commonly have been offered through other arrangements: the contingent fee system for personal injury cases; flat fees for matters like basic incorporation documents, immigration, individual bankruptcy, uncontested divorce, and some criminal matters.

In recent years, corporate and other entity clients also have entered percentage contingent fee arrangements and other kinds of "alternate" fee arrangements, e.g., a "success fee" with a percentage on top if a previously-agreed bench mark if "success" is achieved. Pressures for predictable flat fees have moved up the client income scale as well. Many of the innovators discussed in this chapter offer forms of flat-fee arrangements.

Likewise, ideas about "unbundled" legal services and "limited legal representation" also began in large part in discussions of making legal services more available and affordable: pro bono "advice only" clinics; hotlines; disaggregating components of legal service, e.g., retaining a lawyer only for settlement discussions or some drafting rather than representation on the full matter. Today, new entities compete with law firms for aspects of corporate clients' legal matters by offering cheaper and often more effective solutions with technology such as computerized document review. One hears increasingly about unbundling and decomposing legal services with lawyers being retained only for segments of a matter along the full spectrum of types of clients. In an ABA JOURNAL blog post, Paul Lippe estimates that the "unbundled segment" of the legal services market is growing at about 40% year after year while the law firm sector "is flat, or growing at very most 4% per year."[8]

Jordan Furlong, a prominent commentator on legal services delivery, gives examples of the do-it-yourself era in which lawyers biggest competitors up and down the income spectrum often are their clients.[9] The Chief Judge of New York reported that in 2010 more than 95% of people appeared pro se in New York courts when facing eviction, a consumer credit matter, or child support action.[10] This chapter opened with statistics on LegalZoom's growth and has competitors like RocketLawyer nipping at its heels. Shake, a tablet-based contract-drafting application pitched toward small businesses, reported being used for more than $1 million in contracts through September 2013. Furlong reports that 46% of U.S. corporate law departments decreased spending on outside counsel in 2013 while 42% planned to add in-house lawyers.

Technology

Technology presses change in the way legal services are marketed and delivered. It also is part of the "solution" to the previously described more-for-less challenge.

One of the most visible impacts of technology on the legal services market has been the advent of e-discovery firms, which allow outsourcing of document review resulting in a negative economic impact on law firms that depended on a significant amount of revenue coming from legions of young lawyers and paralegals spending days going through boxes of paper. Technology also enables outsourcing for other purposes, whether subcontracting legal research to a lower-cost country or to a provider in a part of the United States with lower office and labor costs, or "insourcing" by setting up their own "back offices" in less costly parts of the U.S. or abroad.

Communication and secure data and document-sharing options allow teams of providers to collaborate on different aspects of a project without being physically in the same office, city, or even country. This increased accessibility assists coordination of a project into components with the work apportioned among providers who can do a particular component most cost effectively, e.g., a law firm working in tandem with an e-discovery business or another entity doing data analysis. It also enables corporate counsel to contract with teams of experienced lawyers assembled for their particular expertise with a time-limited commitment rather than incurring the expense of hiring additional employees. Small firms can collaborate to assemble teams who can handle bigger projects with more experience, person-power, and diversity of knowledge than any firm alone.

Technology enables forms of sharing and crowd sourcing. At the institutional client end of the spectrum, Cisco's General Counsel led the creation of Legal OnRamp, an initiative for in-house legal departments and invited law firms to create a limited-access website where participants could share legal information and solutions to cut costs and enhance quality. Eversheds, a major British Law Firm, created SHINE (Sharing In-House Expertise) with similar objectives of collaboration among in-house counsel. For individual clients or small businesses, websites already exist where people discuss the legal solutions they have used and share other information.

Cloud computing now offers data storage, and many providers offer firms a menu of software and computer services for their practices, which can be covered by a monthly fee and reduce the firm's IT costs to only the expense of procuring and maintaining their staff's computers and other digital devices. A 2011 survey found that even at that time one in five law firms said they were using "software-as-a-service" (SaaS). SaaS eliminates the expense of servers, licensing software, and retaining staff who keep abreast of developments and maintain a data system. The reduction in need for capital investment can assist solo or small practices in entering and competing in the market against larger firms.

The opportunity to communicate by email, text message, and forms of audio and video conference allow the growth of "virtual law firms" where lawyers can work from wherever they are able to connect to the Internet and avoid the overhead expense of offices. On the client side, of course, this arrangement also means avoiding lost work time and struggling in traffic to get to a lawyer's office during business hours. Software for virtual law firms offer clients 24/7 access to documents, billing information, and a payment portal that allows clients to buy legal services in the same manner as other consumer goods. A website can provide basic information about an area of law of interest and include a series of questions regarding the client's particular situation, e.g., specifics related to constructing a will that the client can fill out on line at 2:00 a.m. with answers in a form easily downloaded and used by the firm. Clients can check on-line to see if a draft of their document is ready to view and log on to check on the status of their bill and pay. To protect the security of client information and ensure confidentiality, a virtual law practice requires a secure client Web space accessible only with a user name and secure password, commonly called a client portal.[11]

A pre-paid legal insurance company with enough subscribers can staff a phone app that allows insured members and their families to access a lawyer for advice any time, day or night. In the event of an auto accident or a question about a contract, this services would be available.

On-line dispute resolution is another often-mentioned technological innovation that can benefit those seeking cheaper and more accessible services. Examples as this book goes to press include Modria, FairOutcomes, and Cybersettle.

Using big data is a current hot topic in many fields. A February 2015 Forbes article describes Lex Machina, a service provider that aggregates data to evaluate contested patents and inform patent litigation strategy. Founder, Josh Becker, assembled a team to develop a machine-learning system to interpret legal filings and create a database of patent cases going back to 2000. As described in Forbes, this use of technology allows companies to "handicap[] law firms based on their win-loss records before specific judges with specific procedural maneuvers, so in-house attorneys can determine who [sic] to hire."[12] Becker calls this "Moneyball law" after the Michael Lewis book and the resulting movie that described Oakland A's Billy Beane's use of statistics in managing a baseball team. Lex Machina is reported to be planning an expansion into copyright and trademark law and the rest of federal civil litigation and giving its service free to federal judges.

Susskind also stresses the great preventive and risk management potential in legal knowledge technology that is "embedded" in systems and processes, so detecting actions that would be problematic for clients does not depend on human recognition and awareness. Another February 2015 FORBES article describes a $73 million contract Axiom recently signed with what it describes as "one of the world's largest" global banks.[13] Axiom will create a process that monitors thousands of the bank's master trading agreements on items like many-page contracts governing swaps and derivatives. The system will set up an audit trail that technologically flags any clause that deviates from standard contract terms to determine if it needs to be referred to the bank's lawyers or other staff to assess legality and risk.

In addition, technology has implications for lawyer oversight. A major rationale for lawyer regulation has been the need to protect the public. Some argue now that web-accessible public reviews by past clients provide a more timely and effective way to hold lawyers accountable and ascertain quality than our current licensing and slow and cumbersome discipline system. In addition, just as we have become used to various websites that allow price comparison of many products and services, some forecast an increasingly efficient electronic legal marketplace allowing price comparison for legal services.

Globalization

In 2009, then ABA President Carolyn Lamm created the E2020 commission to review possible changes in the Model Rules of Professional Conduct, and regulatory approaches more generally, focusing on technology and globalization as the two major factors driving change.

One future, and indeed present, consequence of globalization is the degree to which border-crossing has become a part of more and more lawyers' work—in large firms serving multinational corporations and also in smaller firms or organizations whose primary clients are individuals or small- and medium-sized businesses. Many people living in the U.S. have family members living elsewhere, own or inherit property outside U.S. borders, or buy and sell goods abroad. Most lawyers need some appreciation for the ways in which other countries' legal systems may function differently from ours. Enhanced skills for working with people from varying backgrounds also has become increasingly important. See Chapter 5 on Effective Communication and Professional Relationships and Chapter 6 on Navigating Cultural Difference.

Technology has eased travel and communication, which make possible many border-crossing modes of law practice that would have been unthinkable even a few years ago. The options for providers of components of unbundled legal services need not be impeded by geography. Eerily while working on this chapter, the following email popped into the author's inbox: "I'm Sagar, Assistant Manager-Business Development of XXX, a legal outsourcing company in New Delhi, India, offering legal, paralegal, and administrative support solutions to law firms and attorneys. . . ." The message ended with "Would you be interested in referring our services or sending us a small project to gauge the quality and efficiency of our support services?"

Traditionally national (or state) restrictions on offering legal services maintained a degree of local control of lawyers and the delivery of legal services (or from a critical perspective such regulation shielded of lawyers from outside competition). As discussed further in the next section, regulatory change, entwined with competitive market pressures, is causing many of these restrictions to loosen or fall. Not only lawyers, law firms, and client matters cross borders—so also do regulatory trends.

Pressures for Regulatory Change

Various forms of "deregulation" of lawyers and the legal services market are under active consideration, or have already occurred, around the globe as highlighted in the following paragraphs:

- Deregulation can narrow the scope of activities reserved to lawyers, a/k/a limiting the lawyer's monopoly or narrowing the reach of forbidden "unauthorized practice of law" (UPL). This can occur through expanding areas in which non-lawyers can work by creating new regulated professions, such California's legal document assistants or Washington state's limited license legal technician. Some advocate moving to a completely deregulated market where providers only would be restricted by the usual commercial speech standard of truthfulness about credentials and services offered.

- Deregulation can increase movement toward a national bar freed from the strictures of state licensing in a federal system like the U.S. and liberalize the ability of legal professionals qualified in another country to become licensed to practice across national borders. Relying on a string of U.S. cases in the 1980s that struck down residency requirements, the European Union has reduced considerably barriers to lawyers in one country practicing in another.

- Deregulation can broaden the freedom to advertise and market legal services, which generally is already the case in the U.S. but still is highly restricted in many other countries.

- Deregulation can end the restriction of ownership and management of law firms to licensed lawyers, opening up new possibilities: offering law firms as publicly-traded companies; permitting private equity investment; and encouraging existing companies, such as retail chains, to add legal services as an additional item for sale.

- Deregulation can allow lawyers to provide legal services in a multidisciplinary practice (MDP) setting, in which legal services are offered along with other professional services and those other professionals share management, control, and ownership with lawyers.

The U.S. is already a relatively deregulated, market-based regime in some respects. First, it offers greater access to become a licensed lawyer than in some other countries. Of course bar entry generally entails an expensive legal education, passing the relevant state bar exam, and clearing the state's moral character process. Statistics bear out, however, that even if people are unsuccessful on an initial try at the bar exam, most J.D.s from ABA-accredited schools end up being admitted if they persist. In practical terms, admission to law school is the gate to enter the bar. Unlike some other countries, state bars and the U.S. state and federal governments do not operate in ways that severely limit the number of people admitted to practice or require a substantial apprenticeship period after academic training in law.

Second, the U.S. is also quite liberal with regard to advertising, marketing, and price competition, although these changes did not come from bar regulators' initiatives. The Supreme Court held in a series of cases that, by-and-large, advertising in the public media is commercial speech protected by the First Amendment as long as it is not false and misleading. Lawyer advertising is still heavily restricted in much of the rest of the world.

With regard to price competition, U.S. lawyers are subject to antitrust laws. The Supreme Court in *Goldfarb v. Virginia,* 421 U.S. 773 (1975), struck down the "learned profession" exemption to the antitrust laws and forbade a minimum-fee schedule imposed by a bar association. By contrast, such minimum fees and agreed-upon fee scales are still common practice in many other parts of the world.

Beginning with *Piper v. New Hampshire,* 470 U.S. 274 (1985), the Supreme Court also decided a series of cases on state bar residency requirements, greatly enhancing the ability of lawyers to move among states and be licensed in multiple jurisdictions. Nevertheless, the U.S. state-based system of lawyer licensing and regulation restricts to some degree a fully competitive U.S. market place for legal services.

Despite these developments, the U.S. is significantly less liberal in other respects than a number of other countries. The definition of activities reserved to licensed lawyers is much broader in the U.S. than in many other countries. U.S. jurisdictions commonly define the practice of law as anything that involves application of facts in a particular matter to law and enforce the reservation of the practice of law through "unauthorized practice of law" (UPL) rules. Many other countries do not include legal advice or much transactional and regulatory work in the definition of reserved activities. In some countries, the lawyer monopoly is limited to court work and preparation of particular documents.

Much attention currently is focused on regimes' rules about who can own, manage, control, and share profits in entities that offer legal services, either alone or in combination with other professional services. ABA Model Rules 1.5(e) and 5.4 (d), followed by almost all U.S. jurisdictions, restrict non-lawyer ownership or management of any entity "authorized to practice law for a profit" and sharing of fees with non-lawyers.[14] Model Rule 5.4(d) explicitly forbids partnerships with non-lawyers. Model Rule 5.7 lays out a set of rules for what lawyers must do if they provide or control an organization that provides "law-related services" in conjunction with or related to the legal services the lawyer is offering.

Two important keywords in this debate are alternative business structures (ABS) and multidisciplinary practices (MDP). ABS refers to the possibility for law firms or other entities offering legal services to be owned by non-lawyers and to raise capital through devices like public stock offering or private equity investment. MDP refers to offering legal services in conjunction with other professional services with people from those other professions in positions of management and profit sharing

Much current attention regarding the ABS and MDP debate is focused on dramatic changes in this regard made first in Australia and then the United Kingdom. These changes regarding ownership, management, and service delivery were driven by national studies expressing concern that their lawyer regulation regimes were not adequately serving the public in making quality legal services affordable as well as a desire for their legal services sectors to be competitive in the global marketplace.

Similar changes have been recommended in Canada, Singapore, and Hong Kong. Laura Snyder's January 2015 ABA JOURNAL article on ABS developments in the U.K., which is cited in Further Resources, gives ABS examples from some of the 386 entities granted ABS licenses from the first granted in 2012 through December, 2014. Schillings was a law firm concentrating on privacy and defamation. With its ABS license, it combined with a cybersecurity business to offer legal services along with risk consulting and cybersecurity services related to reputation defense and has a non-lawyer as a partner and chief operating officer. MyHomeMove and Kings Court Trust are consumer services firms with a common shareholder, Smedvig Capital, a private equity firm. Both have an online platform designed to handle volume. Both employ lawyers but have CEOs who are not lawyers. MyHomeMove offers a fixed fee service for U.K. consumers for the title search and contract exchange process to buy a home along with a case management system for reviewing documents on line; offices with evening and weekend opening hours; and contact by email, text message, or phone as the client prefers. Kings Court Trust's website offers "fair, fixed and transparent pricing for all our estate administration services."

Additional regulatory changes in the Australian and U.K. regimes also have garnered considerable attention in the U.S. and elsewhere. These countries have shifted from a bar "self-regulation" model to a "co-regulation" model, meaning that the bar's authority for setting conduct standards and enforcement mechanisms has moved from the bar to a government entity. In both countries, the government delegated back some authority in a shared regulation scheme, though one where the delegation can be revoked. Some Australian states have pioneered what is often termed shifting from an *ex post* to an *ex ante* system of discipline and quality control. An *ex post* system seeks to protect the public by punishing rules violations after they occur. An *ex ante* system puts systems in place that are designed to prevent substandard service from occurring at all. This also entails a shift from correctives focused on individual lawyers to a press to create firm-wide quality control structures to lessen the risk of employees deviating from good practice standards.

Like most other countries, the U.S. discipline system currently operates in a quasi-criminal framework. The admitting jurisdiction's rules of professional conduct provide the "criminal code." An entity in the state is charged with receiving, investigating, and prosecuting complaints. Major ABA Commissions in 1970 (Problems and Recommendations in Disciplinary Enforcement—the "Clark Commission") and 1992 (Commission on Evaluation of Disciplinary Enforcement—the "MacKay Commission") decried the state of U.S. lawyer discipline, and considerable improvements were made in staffing and transparency. Despite improvements, most observers would agree that the process is somewhat hit-or-miss and slow. The disciplinary process can take a long time and may leave behind many harmed clients before a dishonest or repeatedly incompetent lawyer is removed from practice or even sanctioned at all. The inefficiency and perceived ineffectiveness of this system in protecting clients has prompted calls for a more proactive and entity-based system in the U.S. as well.

Unlike many other countries, the U.S. has an array of civil remedies available to clients injured by lawyer conduct, including malpractice, third-party injury actions, breach of fiduciary duty, and disqualification motions for conflicts of interest. While the discipline system focuses almost totally on the conduct of individual lawyers, civil liability and disqualification have firm-wide fiscal consequences; so, by necessity, firms must focus on the conduct of all employees. Most large law firms and many smaller ones pay a lot of attention to trends in liability and devise practice management systems to avoid liability. Often such risk management efforts are recommended and supported by their insurers. Some might say that this looking-over-the-firm's-shoulder regime, focused on civil liability, disqualification, and insurer risk management, offers more effective quality-control than the formal discipline system.

Australia and the U.K. have, in varying ways, put in place official systems focused at the firm level: encouraging and in some ways requiring firms to structure management systems for matters such as protecting confidentiality, avoiding conflicts of interest, meeting required deadlines, handling of client money and property, and providing competent representation. Their systems also include requirements for firm-level client complaint receipt and response with oversight from an outside entity to assure such complaints are taken seriously. In New South Wales, where Sydney is located, Australian firms that wish to operate as limited liability corporations must do an annual self-assessment of how fully they comply with a set of ten "appropriate management systems." The consequence for non-compliance is not discipline, but rather assistance from the bar in becoming fully compliant.[15] A 2008 study of New South Wales firms found a "dramatic lowering in complaint rates" after implementing the self-assessment system.[16]

Demographic Shift

The previous section on globalization discussed the impact of recent immigration to the United States. People who are first- and second-generation in this country may have ties abroad to family or property, which could entail a need for legal help. Many relatively new U.S. residents will be familiar with and have connections to other countries and cultures, which can enhance their interest and ability to undertake border-crossing commercial ventures as business clients and as members of the legal profession well-equipped for a more globalized legal services market.

This section concentrates on the generational shift in those who will be the lawyers and potential clients of the future: how characteristics of those who now comprise most of the law school student bodies and recent profession entrants relate to trends discussed in this chapter.

First, though, a word about another still-large U.S. age cohort. The baby boom generation born between 1946 and 1964 comprised almost 25 % of the U.S. population in 2011 when the oldest turned 65. Boomers continue to be well represented in the senior ranks of the legal profession. Future lawyers may want to think about the legal services needs that will be generated as this population bulge ages. A 2012 U.S. Census study projects that by 2030 more than 20% of the U.S. population will be over 65 as compared with 13% in 2010 and 9.8% in 1970.

The group after the boomers is called generation X with its birthdate boundaries ranging from 1961–1965 at the start and 1976–1981 as end dates. This section concentrates on the next cohort, millennials, because most law students now and for at least some years to come will be from this group. Note though that some of the legal service innovators described in Part Three are from generation X and exhibit preferences for technological innovation, seeking better ways to do things and more flexible workplaces, and have a bent for entrepreneurship, which will be discussed in relationship to millennials in the following paragraphs.

Starting birthdates for millennials vary from 1977 to 1982, with end dates ranging from 1999 through the mid-2000s. Although sometimes referred to as the "echo baby boom," this generation is even larger than the boomers. The Bureau of Labor Statistics estimates that in 2025 people born between 1981 and 2000 will be about 44% of the workforce. Those of you born between 1980–2000 (plus or minus a few years) will play a predominant role in what happens in the legal profession and legal services market of the future: as the majority of current law students; as an already substantial group of young lawyers; as age mates beginning to move into positions in businesses that involve interacting with legal problems and lawyers; and as millennials making life changes that may generate legal needs, e.g., buying houses, having children, starting businesses.

The following discussion looks at possible implications of research about millennials in relation to the other drivers of change discussed in this chapter and the ways that lawyers and clients for that age group may function in the changing legal services market. The generalizations discussed refer to ways that the millennial age cohort differs from prior generations and does not mean that everyone in the age group shares the particular traits identified. Because many current readers of this chapter fall within the "millennial" range, this section often addresses "you" directly.

The starting point for discussing millennials is almost always technology. We are all familiar with the "digital native" cliché, and indeed most people in the millennial cohort have used digital devices since childhood. Communication through social media is common. You and your contemporaries may be more frequent social media users than older generations, although, of course, there are always exceptions. Commenters on generational differences often cite the expectation of younger people for quick access to information at the moment one wants it, which growing up with Google has generated.

In addition, some evidence supports millennials' preferences for visual presentation of information—think of the explosion of innovative information graphics—and multi-media resources. Many of you are probably used to creating and manipulating pictures and graphics, making videos, and other visual representations for work, school, or pleasure. Making big data analysis useful often depends on visual ways to make the results understandable. The Internet presence of many new-type legal service providers looks very different than traditional lawyer websites.

Workplace consultants advise that younger workers are quick to look for better and faster ways to do things, particularly through technology. As a result, you may be less wedded to a "bespoke" conception of legal service delivery and more open to other opportunities on Susskind's continuum described in Part One. Given evidence of millennials' interest in promoting social good, your age cohort may find commoditization's pressure to reduce the cost of service to zero to be more an opportunity than a threat than some past generations of lawyers.

Much is written also about your interest in social entrepreneurship—finding new ways to achieve the common good through technology and through market-based solutions. The following section describes a number of innovations in access to justice spurred by the Legal Services Corporation Technology Initiative Grants. It seems likely that people from the millennial cohort have been major players in these projects.

Whether because of use of different teaching methods in prior education or the collaboration possibilities offered by technology, millennials are said to be more interested in teamwork and have less of the individualist preference for solitary work than previous generations of lawyers. Thus you may be more adaptable to working on matters where tasks are allocated among service providers and coordinated through technology.

Surveys of millennials and their predecessors in generation X, as well as anecdotal workplace information, evidence a greater priority for adequate time for the family, friends, and other personal dimensions of life than may have been demanded by earlier generations. This chapter already has discussed pressure on hourly billing against the client need/desire for cheaper and more predictable legal services costs. Hourly billing also often is identified as a major obstacle to making law firms more family friendly and amenable to a balanced life. Many corporations have made changes more supportive of work-life balance by basing increased responsibility, compensation, and advancement on results achieved rather than "face-time" in an office and number of working hours recorded. A law firm where compensation depends on hours billed to clients and where partner compensation in large part is determined by profit from associate-billing to clients can be antithetical not only to client desires for cost predictability and efficiency but also to a results-based metric of merit, which also can help to provide adequate time and flexibility to meet lawyers' family and personal needs. See Chapter 25 on Work & Well-being.

Articles about millennials in the work place often also cite your interest in flexibility as to workplace and structure. Teleworking offers lawyers flexibility and also reduces the need for impressively decorated law offices in high-per-square-foot cost areas of cities. A June 21, 2015 article in the WASHINGTON POST, *End of the Corner Office: D.C. Law Firm Designs its New Space for Millennials,* describes the move of the Washington office of Nixon Peabody, a firm with more than 700 lawyers in offices in 16 cities, to new office space redesigned with the preferences of millennials in mind. This redesign includes identical-size offices for partners, associates, and paralegals with other spaces for "curling up with a laptop and informal places to run into colleagues." The article points out how economics played an important role in convincing non-millennial partners to give up their corner offices: the impact of the 2008 financial crisis and "newly cost-conscious clients." The new space is about one-third lower in size and commensurate cost. Identical offices also mean fewer move complications when promoting lawyers to partner or bringing in lateral partners. The increasing number of millennials and the desire to retain satisfied, productive firm members and employees creates a significant economic consideration for firms.

Survey data suggests the millennial cohort includes many people with an entrepreneurial bent who are interested in starting their own businesses. Your age cohort also is described as confident, optimistic, and open to change—all useful characteristics in looking for new and better ways to do things including in creating your own enterprises.

In the 2015 book produced by the ABA Standing Committee on Professionalism, THE RELEVANT LAWYER: REIMAGINING THE FUTURE OF THE LEGAL PROFESSION and cited in Further Resources, law professor Lucille Jewel writes about "Indie Lawyering," a different characterization of solo and small-firm lawyers serving individual clients. Professor Jewel uses the term "indie," first applied to music and movie producers working independently from mass-media film and music companies. Applied to the legal profession, she describes this as a "new style of lawyering that uses technology to connect the individual practitioner with individual clients in order to solve legal problems collaboratively in a community-centered way." She discusses how this style of lawyering relates to several "contemporary cultural trends": interest in social enterprise; the sharing economy; the growth of Do-it-Yourself culture; interest in bespoke, artisan, hand-crafted products with Internet marketing allowing producers to cross geographical boundaries to match producers with those interested; and "long-tail markets," meaning niche markets for items with too few customers in a geographic area, though possibly a viable market when connected through the Internet. Her chapter points out the ways the current ethics rules prohibiting direct solicitation, multijurisdictional practice, and interdisciplinary practice are impediments to these forward-thinking initiatives.

As previously discussed, cloud-computing services offer storage and also monthly leasing of software and IT support. This type of service lowers the cost to individuals and small firms striking out in new ventures without the kinds of equipment and staffing costs that might have been needed in the past. Nonetheless, there are challenges. Developing innovative ways to work may require capital investment in process analysis and technology. As previously noted, U.S. ethical rules require lawyer ownership and management of for-profit entities engaged in the practice of law. The partnership or professional corporation model limits law firms to raising funds by capital contribution from partners or lines of credit. In addition, the current U.S. model is criticized for impeding long-range planning and investment because the necessary funds would be a reduction in partner/owner income.

Finally, the millennial cohort is more ethnically and culturally diverse than previous generations, and surveys show you to have more familiarity with and openness to people of differing backgrounds, which, again, is an advantage in a more globalized legal world.

> **Exercise 27.1** Make a list of the traits attributed to millennials that are mentioned in this chapter. Consider the advantages the traits offer for reorganizing the way legal services are offered to meet the challenges of cheaper and more accessible services, with more predictable cost, and that cross geographic boundaries. Consider what these generational differences may mean both to what your contemporaries can offer as legal services providers and how your age mates may act as clients: what marketing to them would be effective and what they would want from a service provider.

> Which of these traits do you think you hold at least to some degree? What might they suggest for your career and your life more generally?

Part Three: Stories From NewLaw

So far, this chapter has described changes in the legal profession in general terms, offering multiple perspectives and frameworks for understanding that change. This section tells several stories that illustrate these changes.

Axiom Law: What "Not a Law Firm" Looks Like

The Axiom law story begins in 1999 with Mark Harris, a 29-year-old associate who was bored in his job at a major New York law firm and quit. He teamed up with an MBA to launch Axiom in 2000. Their original venture focused on hiring former law firm and in-house lawyers for temporary assignments with corporations on particular projects with defined time frames—working at the client's office or remotely. This niche was not the contract-lawyering business in which firms bring on recent graduates for short high-volume projects like document review. The original Axiom venture used lawyers with significant expertise in various areas of law. This "secondment," the lending of large-firm lawyers to corporate clients, has been a relatively common part of retainer agreements in Europe. Axiom offered a variation on this service.

Axiom later started to develop what they call "tech-enabled legal services," employing not only lawyers but also IT professionals, process analysts, and management consultants. The Axiom Law website includes a number of case studies of technology and process analysis to various types of legal matters for business clients. The following is an example of one of Axiom's early retainers of this type.

In 2011, Kraft Food, a major multinational company, spun off their North American grocery business and divided into two new companies. The company had over 40,000 contracts. The separation required, at the least, changing the name of the contracting party and determining which contracts would go to which company. As with many companies founded in a pre-digital age, Kraft had no central data base of their contracts. As a first phase, Axiom's team loaded all commercial agreements into a contract management system, gathered related information not in the contracts themselves, and considered the impact of the spinoff on the agreements. They then prepared a proposal for how the contracts could be renegotiated with billing on a fixed-fee-per-agreement structure. Axiom completed the first phase in 35 days while traditional law firms with which Kraft consulted told them the project could not be completed within the time frame needed for the transaction. Axiom was then hired again for the second phase of notification and renegotiation of the new contracts. At the end of the project, the new companies had contracts in one place and a 90-page "playbook" systematizing basic types of agreements and giving standard guidance. This document defined the roles and responsibilities of legal and non-legal employees involved in the company's contracting process with guidelines for negotiation and defined processes and templates for the workflow for varying types of contracts.

More recently, Axiom reports entering a $73 million contract with a large global bank to monitor mass trading agreements including complex contracts on instruments like swaps and derivatives. The "embedded legal system" they designed flags any clause that deviates from standard contract terms so a determination can be made on the need for a legal and risk-assessment review. Mary Schapiro, former chair of the Securities and Exchange Commission and Financial Industry Regulatory Authority, joined Axiom's board of directors saying the firm was offering a solution to the kinds of problems in the financial industry she and other drafters of Dodd-Frank were trying to fix with the law—firms realizing and taking responsibility for risk exposure. Dodd-Frank was the major legislation passed in 2010 to restructure the U.S. financial regulatory system in response to the financial crises of 2007–10.

By 2015, Axiom is said to be approaching $200 million in revenue with clients from at least half of the Fortune 100 companies. Axiom and some other fixed-fee competitors sometimes are referred to as competing for "mid-level, day-to-day corporate work" as contrasted to the "bet-the-company" matters for which corporate clients still may be willing to pay top dollar for "bespoke" advice. Axiom's July 2015 website proclaims, "With over 1300+ employees across 3 continents, we experience a nerdy excitement from improving the way legal, compliance and contracts work is done."

Axiom presents themselves as explicitly "not a law firm." Current U.S. ethics rule would not permit them to identify as a law firm because their funding and management structures include people who are not lawyers. Because Axiom is retained directly by corporate general counsels, they may be termed support to "the lawyers" and avoid running afoul of U.S. unauthorized practice rules.

LegalZoom: Another Not-a-Law-Firm

In 2001, two more restless law firm associates, Brian Lee and Brian Liu, teamed with a web developer to launch LegalZoom (LZ), an automated-document-assembly company. With unfortunate timing, the dot-com-bubble burst dried up venture capital just as they were launching. They raised the first $250,000 in capital from friends and family, and subsequently other investors came in. While LZ engendered charges of unauthorized practice of law (UPL) from some state bar regulators and from some former customers, LegalZoom, with its deep pockets of capital investment, aggressively defended and sometimes preemptively brought their own actions to stave off UPL challenges to their services.

LegalZoom announced a public stock offering for August 2012, but it was withdrawn just before it was to commence. The LZ snapshot opening this chapter reports statistics from the public offering statement. The press reported various speculations on the factors that might have caused LegalZoom to determine they would not receive their desired stock price in a public offering. Harking back to the five stages of legal services delivery in Part Two, Richard Granat, a frequent commenter on e-lawyering issues, cited the difficulties in maintaining a profit margin with commoditized legal services driving prices toward zero and the heightened competition from small firms that had begun offering comparable prices with the addition of built-in service from an attorney.[17]

Because of the U.S. ethical rules prohibiting partnering with non-lawyer-owned entities, in the U.S., LegalZoom only could offer forms of prepaid legal service plans or referrals to attorneys, not a package integrating their automated forms with attorney review and advice. In the fall of 2012, LZ launched in the U.K., teaming with QualitySolicitors, a network of firms serving individuals and small businesses. In February 2014, Permira, a European private equity fund, acquired $200 million in equity in LegalZoom. In December 2014, LegalZoom acquired an ABS license in the U.K. In LegalZoom's announcement of its plans with the U.K. ABS license, they cited the "broader freedom" the ABS scheme gave to teams with lawyers than they have under current U.S. rules.

Legal Services Corporation: Harnessing Technology to Expand Access to Justice

U.S. state and federal courts are flooded with self-represented people who are unable to pay a lawyer. Civil legal services called "legal aid" programs and the U.S. Legal Services Corporation (LSC), the federal funder of civil poverty law assistance, daily face the consequences of unaffordable legal services. People within these organizations have collaborated to achieve perhaps even more visible progress in technology application than what one sees in the private practice of law.

In 1998, LSC convened a "summit" on the use of technology to improve access to justice with representatives of legal services organizations and court personnel. This conference developed ideas for what became the LSC Technology Initiative Grant

(TIG) program, which commenced operation in 2000. Since then, TIG has awarded $46 million in grants to leverage technology to widen access to legal services for low-income people. The TIG web page, http://tig.lsc.gov, provides a wealth of information and links to resources created by legal services programs and state and location governments, sometimes in partnership with nongovernmental organizations and community groups and with commercial technology companies, which can be used by legal service program professional staff, pro bono lawyers, and people navigating legal processes themselves.

Three major areas of innovation have resulted. The first is LSC's creation of an Internet platform where people can be directed to websites linking them to legal aid programs in their locale and to government websites with legal information and court forms. The U.S. map on the home page of the LSC/TIG site links relevant state resources including information for all 50 states, D.C., and the U.S. territories on things like locations of LSC-funded offices, pro bono opportunities for lawyers who would like to volunteer, and access to useful information on many aspects of the law. Some state resources include Live Chat options to ask questions about the resources; others provide legal information with easy-to-follow visuals or explanatory videos.

The second innovation is LawHelp Interactive (LHI) developed and maintained by ProBono Net, which created automatic-document-assembly programs to be used by legal aid staff, pro bono lawyers, and self-represented people on a range of legal needs. The LSC/TIG site reports that, between 2005 and 2015, 2.3 million legal documents were generated using the LHI system. LHI received the InnovAction Hall of Fame award in 2010 from the College of Law Practice Management. Their website provides links to a number of other innovations in legal services delivery as well. http://collegeoflpm.org/innovaction-awards/innovaction-hall-of-fame.

A third innovation is the A2J Clinic Project, which took the automated-document-assembly project a step further by linking law students in clinics to expert poverty law providers to create automatic-document-assembly programs for particular types of legal problems, while also simplifying the interface so they can be navigated more easily by clients and the people assisting them. For more information, see Ronald Staudt's 2009 article in Further Resources as well as material and links on the LSC/TIG website.

The A2J Clinic project, as well as another LSC TIG grantee, were named 2014 finalists for the Hague Institute for the Internationalization of Law's (HiiL's) 2014 Innovating Justice Awards. These awards seek to promote ideas and initiatives to encourage justice sector innovation. HiiL's website http://www.innovatingjustice.com/

also is a useful place to look for an overview of often-technology-enabled innovations happening around the world.

A review of the program for the January 2015 TIG 15th anniversary conference, http://tig.lsc.gov/2015-tig-conference-session-materials, and the accompanying slide decks and videos, show many innovations going on in legal services programs and they also reflect ways technology may be integrated in legal services delivery more generally.

> **Exercise 27.2** Review the 2015 session topics below (or those on the LSC website from a more recent conference) and think about which are relevant to the management of and delivery of services by for-profit law firms or in-house counsel's offices as well.
>
> ### Client Information and Service
>
> - *WriteClearly & ReadClearly:* free plain language tools to assure that legal service websites and materials are easily understandable to clients;
> - Using Drupal open source website content management for legal services public information;
> - Top Ten Tips for Building Effective Websites;
> - Experience with on-line intake systems;
> - Using gaming to help self-represented parties understand what they need to do;
> - Exploring Technology Options to Better Service Self-Represented Litigants;
> - On-line triage systems on phones or websites;
> - How Native Mobile Applications Can Reach Broader Audiences, taking note that since February 2014 applications developed for mobile devices have surpassed desktop internet usage;
> - Mobile Innovations for Clients: optimizing content for mobile websites, SMS text campaigns to deliver legal information and referral options;
> - Community and Client Outreach for Technology Tools to Promote Legal Access: Videos, Text Campaigns, Social Media, and More;
> - A2J Author Course Project that teaches clinical students how to create document assembly projects for self-represented litigants.
>
> ### Recruiting and Supporting Pro Bono Lawyers
>
> - Pro Bono in a Box: A "turnkey" project for recruiting pro bono lawyers,

automated documents, continuing legal education outlines, and so on to marshal volunteer lawyers;

- App Ready Idea in Search of Developers: Brainstorming next steps to put checklists for client interviews and limited scope representation by pro bono "lawyer for the day" projects in a mobile application that can be accessed easily when needed, e.g., when interviewing the client and in the courthouse;

- Engaging Pro Bono Attorneys in Virtual Law Practice;

- Innovative Pathways to Pro Bono: Using Technology to Expand the Role and Impact of Volunteers including tapping into "volunteer technologists, designers and others in the private sector with an interest in access to justice."

Effective Internal Management of Legal Services Programs

- Considering How Automated Forms Can Improve Lawyer Effectiveness;

- Using data visualization tools such as maps, graphs, and charts to make data useful and accessible;

- Designing a data analysis program and partnering with research institutions in developing it;

- Using project management approaches in legal services programs;

- Using Agile software to manage teams and projects;

- Developing procurement processes for selection of hardware and software including best ways to identify and evaluate vendors and strategies for system implementation;

- Choosing technology systems;

- Providing data security;

- Using expert systems as tools for document automation, surveys, instruments, and forms;

- Using SharePoint Online for managing collaborative work;

- Using Phone Systems 2015: recent trends in call center, VoIP technology, and best practices to upgrade a legacy phone system;

- Identifying Case Management System User Groups;

- Using Google Fusion to create multi-dimensional maps for internal management use and public information including combining data from different sources;

- Using VMware for communications, human resources, accounting, and systems.

Slater & Gordon: The First Publicly-Traded Law Firm in the World

Slater & Gordon was established in Melbourne, Australia in 1935. The firm had a long-standing connection with the Australian trade-union movement. Over the years, the firm specialized in personal injury work mixed with consumer cases and other matters of concern to individuals. Because Australia does not permit contingent fees and has a "loser pay" rule, the U.S. model for a low- or moderate-income person bringing a plaintiff's action does not directly apply. S&G developed and heavily advertised a "no-win, no-fee" model to provide a mechanism for people without funds to bring a lawsuit and obtained a trademark for the phrase.

While much of their business was high-volume, relatively-low-value personal injury cases, the firm also took on some large high-profile cases. For example, S&G won the first successful asbestos case in Australia 1985. High-profile tort cases also can incur significant expenses, and by the late 1980s, the firm was losing money with its then sole proprietor interested in retirement. A partner group bought him out for $1 million Australian dollars (A$1 million). The 1990s brought several successful highly publicized cases: an A$500 million settlement for 300 people who became HIV-positive after being given contaminated blood in childbirth or surgery and a settlement for 30,000 landowners in Papua, New Guinea for damages caused by waste from a nearby mine.[18] While the firm's finances improved, S&G wanted to expand and found the traditional methods of law firm investment unsatisfactory for their needs.[19]

As a public company, one can find on the Internet S&G's original 2007 prospectus, Annual Reports and other information about activities, announced strategy, financial data, and other filings with the Australian Stock Exchange. In summer of 2015, S&G's share price plummeted after an announcement of the U.K. Financial Conduct Authority's investigation of Quindell, whose personal services division S&G had acquired in March 2015 for $A1.2 billion, and S&G's June 29 filing with the Australian Stock Exchange regarding two accounting errors in past financial statements by S&G's audit firm. The S&G stock price on the Australian stock exchange at its initial offering in May 2007 was A$1 per share. The share price had risen as high as $A7.85 in April 2015 but was trading at $A3.42 as this chapter was going to press in August 2015 after the previously-stated developments.

Jacoby & Myers: Challenging U.S. Restrictions on Non-Lawyer Ownership

Similar to Axiom's birth with a frustrated 29-year-old lawyer, Jacoby & Meyers (J&M) was conceived when law school section mates 28-year-old Leonard Jacoby and

29-year-old Stephen Meyers met again by chance at a consumer law conference in 1972. Jacoby had been in private practice since law school. Meyers had started his career representing migrant farm workers at California Rural Legal Assistance and then moved to a firm where he was litigating class-action consumer law cases. They formulated the vision of "neighborhood clinics" where middle-income or low-income people not poor enough to qualify for free services could find legal help that was accessible both as to price and convenience.

J&M opened their first office in Van Nuys, California in September 1972. By the mid-1980s they had 300 lawyers in 150 offices in six states with a peak of 329 lawyers in 1989. They located in shopping centers, had evening and weekend hours, offered flat fees, were the first law firm to take credit cards, and created standard protocols and forms for things like intake interviews and commonly-used pleadings. Much initial drafting was done by paralegals. Specialists in often-handled areas of law, such as bankruptcy, personal injury, and criminal law, were hired to cover several offices, rather than the firm operating on a "general practitioner" model under which many of the solo lawyers and small firms serving lower and middle-income people commonly worked. Standard fees were established, and clients were given a written estimate of fees upon retention.

When the firm commenced, lawyers were forbidden from advertising in public media including newspapers, radio, and television. When opening the initial Van Nuys office garnered considerable local news and television coverage with interviews of the young founders, the California Bar alleged that their talking openly with the press about their new model for legal services was tantamount to forbidden advertising and charged them with an ethics code violation. J&M responded to the charges with a claim of infringement on their First Amendment rights to free speech and the public's right to be informed. J&M prevailed in the California Supreme Court just a month before the previously-mentioned *Bates* case treating lawyer advertising as protected commercial speech was decided by the U.S. Supreme Court. The day after the *Bates* case was decided, J&M ran a full-page advertisement in the Los Angeles Times and shortly thereafter became the first lawyers to advertise on television.

By the mid-1990s, J&M's original legal clinic model had become less economically viable, perhaps in large part because they were victims of their success. Many new lawyers entered the market between the 1970s and 1990s, and others adopted J&M's cost-cutting innovations. J&M shifted focus to personal injury work and created a form of franchising with an organizational structure of affiliated offices.

Fast forward to this decade when, against the backdrop of regulatory changes in the U.K. and Australia, in May 2011, J&M filed lawsuits in New York, New Jersey, and Connecticut challenging the respective state rules against non-lawyer investment in law firms. The complaint filed in the New York's Southern District Federal Court challenged that state's Rule 5.4 forbidding non-lawyer ownership of entities providing legal services on a for-profit basis on the following five grounds:[20] (1) violation of freedom of speech, "the fundamental right of access to the courts," several other rights, and "the right of collective associations to secure [such] rights" under the 1st and 14th Amendments, (2) void for vagueness under the 1st Amendment and the Due Process clause of the 14th Amendment because of its ambiguity about "precisely **which** types of 'ownership interests' . . . might run afoul of Rule 5.4's proscription," (3) a forbidden burden on interstate commerce brought under the "dormant" aspect of the Commerce Clause, (4) a violation of 14th Amendment substantive due process, and (5) a violation of the 14th Amendment Equal Protection Clause. In November, 2012, the 2nd Circuit granted leave to J&M to amend their complaint to cure an objection to standing and remanded the case to the district court for a ruling on the merits on New York's Rule 5.4 as well as various other New York statutes that prohibit non-lawyer investment in law firms.[21] On July 15, 2015, New York's Southern District dismissed the complaint, rejecting all the grounds set out above.[22] Given J&M's persistence in litigation thus far, it seems likely that this decision on the merits may be appealed.

While the U.S. litigation was proceeding, J&M pursued their quest to expand and take in outside capital through a different route as well: like LegalZoom and Slater and Gordon, they pursued operations in the United Kingdom. In 2013, they created a joint venture, J&M Europe Limited, with MJ Hudson, a London-based private equity and corporate law firm, with the announced intention of looking for targets for expansion in the U.K. and Europe. In a 2014 interview, Gabe Miller, then CEO and General Counsel of J&M, said they were considering alternative forms of affiliation other than direct acquisition of law firms including becoming a "branded affiliate" where a firm could use J&M's marketing, technological, and administrative support or a "referral sponsor," pooling referrals across a network of firms.[23] While in 2013 J&M announced they were likely to seek an ABS license in the U.K., it appears they had not done so by 2015.

> **Exercise 27.3** These case studies offer different pictures of the future from varying corners of the legal market. Choose one of these stories and assess how it fits on the continuum of legal delivery models described in Part I of this Chapter and illustrates the pressures for change described in Part II. Do you approve of these

innovations? Can you think of other ways to innovate that are not described here? What would you need to do to become an innovator yourself?

Crystal-Ball Gazing

Predicting the future in the rapidly changing world of legal services delivery is difficult. One of William Hubbard's primary initiatives as ABA President from August 2014–2015 was creation of a Commission on the Future of Legal Services. A September 2014 ABA JOURNAL article describes the commission's task as identifying "the most innovative practices being used around the country to deliver legal services, as well as more theoretical ideas, and to develop a blueprint for fostering innovations in the legal system that will improve access to justice."[24] Hubbard went on to say, "If we don't change, the profession as we know it will go away. We have to deliver legal services with more accessibility and less complexity using the tools available to us or we put ourselves at risk of becoming obsolete."

The fortunes of the entities in our case studies have waxed and waned over the research and writing of this chapter and likely will have taken new twists and turns by the time you are reading. At press, Axiom appears to be going strong. In statements regarding the ABA Future of Legal Services Commission, ABA President William Hubbard looks to LSC's work for useful models to harness technology to close the access to justice gap.

In Laura Snyder's previously-cited ABA JOURNAL on ABS in the U.K., she features LegalZoom and Jacoby and Myers as "using the U.K. as a place to develop new models for legal services . . . [that they] both intend, in time, to deploy . . . outside the U.K." LegalZoom, though, faces stiff competition in the U.S. and challenges in how to add services to their commoditized model to make it profitable. Jacoby and Meyers announced bold European expansion plans in 2013 including a possible ABS application, but by August 2015, had not applied and seemed to still be "considering" what to do in the European market. Their lawsuit challenging non-lawyer ownership rules had just been dismissed on the merits.

Slater and Gordon, which had experienced enormous growth since going public in 2007, and, with a large U.K. acquisition in March 2015 would have been the largest provider in the personal injury market in the U.K., hit a significant snag with the previously-described accounting controversy. Likely those who oppose repeal of non-lawyer ownership and investment in law firms will point to S&G's recent problems as representative of reasons to retain the ban. On the other hand, as a publicly-traded company, S&G's activities and regulatory and financial status are much more transparent than information about Axiom, LegalZoom, and Jacoby and Meyers. Like other privately-held companies and law firms configured as partnerships or limited liability corporations, clients and the public do not have easy access to much information about the entity's financial health. Some predict the U.S. will follow the countries allowing ABS and MDP structures, but many in the American bench and bar continue to oppose such a change.

> **Exercise 27.4** Look at the ABA Commission on the Future of Legal Services website. What recommendations does it make? At the time you are reading this chapter, have any of them come to fruition? Does the push to liberalize U.S. rules on non-lawyers owning and sharing management of firms seem to be accelerating or receding? Those who oppose U.S. changes to permit MDP and ABS argue that lawyer's independent professional judgment and other core values of the profession are likely to be compromised. Look at examples of this debate in the American Bar Association, U.S. state bars, other countries considering the change, in scholarly literature, or in the lawyer and popular press and formulate your own point of view.

Part Four: What Does This Mean for You?

This chapter seeks to provide a window on the changing legal profession and legal services delivery landscape so you can think about implications for your future and the kind of opportunities you may want to pursue in this changing world. Further Resources at the end of the chapter gives sources offering greater depth on some topics and selected blogs and websites for information that will be current at the point you read this chapter.

As discussed in Part One, much of lawyers' traditional vision of law practice, starting with law school, is as a bespoke, start-from-scratch-with-individually-tailored-service operation. Nonetheless, for decades there have been form books, made more efficient by word processing; practitioner handbooks; pattern jury instructions; and so on. Well-run law offices maintained banks of past pleadings and briefs for matters and issues that were likely to recur. Lawyers developed client questionnaires for information normally needed for a particular type of matter. Nevertheless, technology has opened the door for automation to move directly from data entry through steps of analysis and document preparation to determination of next steps. Once tasks are disaggregated and systematized, those that cannot be computerized may be accomplished more cheaply by people with less than three years of expensive law school education. Technology also allows aggregation of massive amounts of data for such purposes as accurate prediction of outcomes or monitoring and legal-compliance system review like Axiom is providing to the international banking client's work on derivatives.

This chapter outlined ways these innovations in technology and other forms of systematization and disaggregation of legal work can respond to the need for cost-effective legal services along the full client spectrum: corporate client pressure to reduce legal bills; prices small businesses and middle-income clients will consider affordable; and ways to make legal information and access to the legal system possible for people who cannot pay lawyers at all. Technology offers options for providing legal services to clients in ways that are more convenient for them and hence more attractive. As lawyers find ways to systematize legal services delivery and use data analysis for legal problem solving, this opens options for lawyers to earn at least some of their living by "packaging" those systems for clients' own use. If U.S. regulatory strictures are relaxed, lawyers also can combine with other service providers to provide a set of "one-stop" services to clients, such as combining estate planning with other services of concern to older people and their families, or combining advice on various types of legal compliance with other services needed by self-employed clients and small businesses.

> **Exercise 27.5** Pick an area of law practice in which you have an interest. This may include the practice at your placement this semester (including judging), the practice at a law firm where you have worked, or your dream practice. Do some research on the ways in which firms, agencies, or courts handle your area of interest. Look at advertisements and web pages and consider how the lawyers market their services. Consider innovations that seem to be out there already. Then sketch out a new model for running the same practice. Think about ideas that move the practice model further along the continuum from a "bespoke" to a "commoditized" practice. Consider how cost-savings, technology, globalization, or generational change might suggest different approaches. If you run up against a regulatory barrier, such as unauthorized practice or non-lawyer ownership, identify how removing the barrier would unlock the potential in your proposal. Above all, do not worry about being "realistic." Innovation and change begin with those who dream beyond current boundaries.

If, as many predict, the United States allows forms of non-lawyer ownership of legal services providers, this could result in multiple providers operating under regional or national "brand names" that specify practices and procedures designed to reduce cost and assure uniform quality. Consider how this might look quite different from the current

U.S. model of a number of individual practitioners operating somewhat autonomously as solos or in small firms who currently provide most services to individuals and small businesses if those clients seek legal services.

What does this changing world, and potential for even more change during your career, suggest for where you are now—a law student in an externship? Generally one cannot think about how to do something more efficiently without understanding well what the "something" is. Technology professionals alone cannot design an estate-planning diagnostic or a system to see if legal instruments being entered throughout a corporation vary from the approved norm. Technology expertise must be joined with deep knowledge of the law, both as it is on the books and as it functions in the relevant part of the legal system. By doing an externship, you are taking an important step in acquiring knowledge-of-practice expertise in an area of law practice.

Look for ways to learn beyond the four corners of what you are assigned. Assume you have been asked for a legal research memo. Consider what you can gain in knowledge about the practice area beyond improvement in your research and writing skill. What do you know or can you learn about how the lawyer decided that assignment was needed? What use will be made of the memo? What information do lawyers in your placement use to make predictions about outcomes that guide the strategies they pursue and the client advice they give? Is there data that could be collected and analyzed to deepen the foundation for educated guesses about the future? Did your supervising lawyer suggest models or places to start that would have allowed you to build on work already done? If not, where do you think such models exist? A legal information professional, either at your law school library or placement firm library, should be able to assist you in creating a method for finding information or sources for possible starting points. If talking to someone outside the firm, see Chapter 11 on ways to seek advice from others without compromising client confidentiality.

Think generally about the systems your placement has, or lacks, to save time and insure uniform quality. How is technology used? What tasks do lawyers, secretaries, and other people without a law degree perform? Do you see ways in which technology and delegation of tasks could be more effective? For more insight into practice structure see Chapter 14 on the lawyering process, which includes a suggested practice audit.

Within your area of law practice, can you think of service niches with potential clients who could benefit from such services but are not seeking them? What are the possible reasons they are not seeking these services? What other professional service needs logically accompany the type of service your office is providing? What combinations might allow one-stop-shopping that would be useful to clients?

Consider what skills you have from prior education and experience: in technology, marketing, team leadership, project analysis, or another profession that could be combined with law in a multidisciplinary service provider. Do you have other skills relevant to future trends in the legal profession? Think about ways such skills could be valuable in areas of law practice that appeal to you.

Law schools vary in how much of what is going on in the rapidly changing world of law practice and legal services delivery comes into your classes. Watch the list of speakers coming to your law school. Attend speaker events and ask questions about changes they observe. Think about speakers you might suggest be invited by student organizations or the law school administration. Find other opportunities to talk with lawyers you meet about what is changing in their areas of practice.

As you listen in class, read, and complete assignments, think about whether there is an underlying, or overt, assumption that lawyering is, and should remain, an individually-tailored-solution-for-each-matter. Some of law school's educational approach is intentionally "bespoke": write from scratch, do not use a form, do your own original research, do not trust secondary sources. Valid educational reasons exist for bottom-up training, and relying on the work of others always requires an assessment of the reliability of that work product. These messages, however, may solidify a worldview that encourages lawyers to see all matters as unique and unpredictable, thus diverting attention from time- and cost-saving approaches that look for the repetitive and predictable aspects of an area of practice.

Individual characteristics and life situations of clients—both individuals and entities—are important to recognize and acknowledge in working with them. That, however, is not inconsistent with looking for commonalities in legal problems clients may face in an area of law, what law relates to the problem, and common approaches to consider in getting what many clients want and need regarding the problem. In your law school courses, ask yourself what kinds of problems in this practice area are likely to recur and how some standardization, systematization, and packaging of solutions might help clients find solutions more simply and cheaply. Think also about how government agencies, the judiciary, or other entities with which people and businesses interact can adjust their ways of working so that work product and processes are smoother and less frequently become "legal problems."

As Paul Lippe, CEO of Legal OnRamp put it in a FORBES 2014 interview, lawyers generally "believe that the complexity that matters is complexity of reasoning, rather than complexity of information and organization."[25] As an example, he cites a project mapping thousands of documents a bank had created with multiple forms of living will language, revealing eight different ways the same clause was expressed—"eight different ways to navigate the same road to Aunt Sally's. Most lawyers imagine that 'bespoke' drafting is a good thing; but for the bank as a whole, simplification and standardization are much better." Think about how law schools mirror, and perhaps shape, that worldview and consider what an alternative perspective on the subjects you study would look like.

Develop a system for staying abreast of developments in the legal services market that may be relevant to types of work you are interested in pursuing. Many of the blogs listed in Further Resources also provide a "Blogroll" taking you to additional sites and directing you to new ones that might be worth checking regularly. To stay current, set up a news feed using one of the many web-based news readers like Netvibes or follow the blogs on Facebook or other social media. Look at websites of firms that seem to be offering legal services in new ways and service providers creating products to help lawyers do so or offering services competing with those of lawyers.

As you work on your career choices, recognize that the very definition of what it means to be "lawyer" and to "practice law" is undergoing profound change. Various observers of the legal world have come up with lists of new types of law jobs that may exist in the future or already exist and likely togrow.[26] In reading this list, consider which of these jobs sound interesting to you, in light of your own preferences about role, subject matter, risk tolerance, and personal well-being.

- *Legal Process Engineer:* someone who uses legal research, analysis, and experience to capture the substance in an area of law and practice that technology needs to navigate.

- *Legal Technologist:* people with training who build a career on creating systems to make the practice of law more efficient and the legal system more accessible. Richard Susskind points out that much of the technology work thus far has been done by IT people who found their way into the legal world or by lawyers with a penchant for computers.

- *Legal Hybrid:* lawyers who themselves have or acquire the training to provide some multidisciplinary service a client needs.

- *Legal Process Analyst:* people with experience and training in the unbundling of tasks in a matter by separating their components and having the ability to determine a reliable and cost-effective provider for each task.

- *Legal Project Manager:* someone who carries out the next step after legal process analysis—allocating work to providers, overseeing the contractual arrangements, monitoring task completion, overseeing quality, and pulling services together for the client. Robert Denney's December 2014 version of his semi-annual "What's Hot and What's Not" compilation report identifies project management, including management of projects being handled within the firm, as important to produce "efficiency, fee transparency, client value and profits" and says it should be "a top concern of most law firms" but observes many lawyers have not yet acknowledged it or lack the necessary skill set.

- *Online Dispute Resolution (ODR) Practitioner:* practitioners who can advise clients on how to use ODR and assist in doing so as needed.

- *Legal Management Consultant:* someone who helps in-house legal departments function most effectively.

- *Legal Risk Manager:* someone who helps clients avoid risk. Susskind uses the analogy of a client preference for a "fence at the top of the cliff to an ambulance at the bottom."

- *Contract or Litigation Analyst:* someone who identifies key elements in large collections of legal documents.

- *Privacy Professional:* someone who does compliance work on increasing regulation regarding privacy in business and government.

- *Regulatory Compliance Lawyer:* someone specializing in compliance in a particular area—akin to the privacy professional, though in other fields.

- *Alternative Litigation Funder:* someone who locates third-party funding for cases (as well as those working in the litigation-funding companies themselves).

- *Professionalism or Client Relations Coordinator:* someone who oversees retainers and fee arrangements with clients and serves as a liaison with clients regarding their concerns.

- *Pricing Specialist:* someone who works with firm management on fee arrangements as well as negotiating them with clients and making judgments regarding discounting. Robert Denney's December 2014 "What's Hot and What's Not" reports that probably more than 50% of the largest 200 firms in the U.S. have created a pricing director position while mid-size firms often have added this responsibility to that of the chief operating officer.

· *Lawyer Coach:* someone who coaches pro se litigants in their own representation.

· *Internal Investigations Lawyer:* lawyers who specialize in handling internal investigations for clients (often former prosecutors).

One additional important role, which likely will never go away or be replaced by a computer, is the *Expert Trusted Advisor*: a lawyer who can combine deep law and practice knowledge in a field with sensitivity to a matter's context, whether that be a corporate merger or a marriage dissolution. The trusted advisor can communicate concern, empathy, and understanding for the client's situation, see strategy options, and lay out choices effectively for the client along with an experience-based assessment of possible outcomes of each choice.

Some lawyers default to saying that "of course that's what MY area of practice requires, so I will never become obsolete." That reflexive reaction, though, ignores the reality that attention to the emotional and relational dimensions of law practice are not inconsistent with analyzing whether legal tasks can be disaggregated and assessed to see what can be done more quickly, cheaply, and effectively through technology or by less-highly-educated workers. Such analysis can reduce costs and response time and also can free up lawyer time and energy for the more creative, human relations dimensions of law practice. Of course, if one is stuck in hours billed as the metric of a for-profit law practice, less lawyer time means less income, so this forward-thinking approach requires consideration of alternative fee structures and ways to expand the client base by offering accessibly-priced legal services to people who are not now using lawyers at all for those matters.

Some of the jobs above are specific to private law practice. Others are functions that also need to be performed for local, state, and federal governments and courts to create and maintain systems to help individuals and small businesses navigate their legal questions and problems more cheaply and accessibly than one-on-one-bespoke advice from a lawyer.

Self-help assistance, unbundling, and other such efforts sometimes are dismissed as second (or maybe third, fourth, or tenth) class justice for low-income people, which will divert attention from the need for more lawyers to serve those who cannot pay. Indeed, many problems facing poor people are legally complex and require at least as much or more talent and creativity as those of the wealthy. A more constructive way of thinking about these ideas may be triage—separating out what is simple enough to be self-navigated or handled with the help of someone less-expensively trained than a lawyer as opposed to more complex matters requiring lawyer time and thought.

The following closing exercise gives a framework for thinking about the division of tasks into those where technology and trained non-lawyers can meet some legal needs versus those which require a lawyers' training and experience as well as a person-to-person connection with a lawyer. It is meant to stimulate your thinking about ways to thrive in the legal environment you are likely to face.

> **Exercise 27.6** Jordan Furlong suggested the following exercise for lawyers in the December 2014 end-of-year post on his Law21 blog. You do not yet have experience as a practicing lawyer to draw on, but you can use your externship, other job and clinical legal experiences, your time in law school, and extrapolate from your other work, volunteer, and professional experiences. Below is a version adapted a bit to the law student perspective.
>
> Make three columns on a piece of paper or a computer.
>
> Furlong's first column is "everything you love about being a lawyer." As a student, consider everything about your legal experience thus far that you love—and at least what you like a lot. Consider your experiences with legal work, law school courses, and law school co- and extra-curricular activities. Think also about why you came to law school and what your greatest passions were in pre-law school experiences. Consider specifically what it is you liked about these experiences in law school and before. Furlong observes that lawyers probably will identify in this column the parts of lawyering "most closely associated with actual people and actual service," the parts "least susceptible to automation and outsourcing."
>
> The second column for lawyers is what you "really don't like about being a lawyer: what bores you, discourages you, upsets you, gets put off or rushed through because the thought of facing it makes you question your career choice." Furlong observes that some of this work may be unavoidable, but much of it is "amendable to change, systematization or outsourcing to more appropriate providers." Computers are good at tedious, repetitive, boring work—and they do not get frustrated by it. Neota Logic is a New York firm that has created a no-code platform so lawyers and other professionals can develop automated applications for areas of law, risk management, and so on. They describe their work as "building robots and destroying dumb jobs—the ones lawyers don't do cost-effectively at scale, and really don't or shouldn't want." What

work do you see at your placement, in other legal jobs, or as tasks you have done in law school that software could be programmed to do or could be done by others without requiring three years of legal education?

The third column is for "everything you wish you could do as a lawyer"—the help you want to provide, the people you wish to serve, the "insights and assistance and improvements" that you would want to see happen in the provision of legal services.

Then synthesize the first and third columns to consider possibilities for a legal career. From Furlong: "Take the second column and look for ways to move these items off your desk and ideally, out of your practice altogether, into the waiting arms of a growing array of specialists who will do them for you, and do them better than you." (Perhaps some of you with an entrepreneurial bent will think about how to create and improve those services as well.)

The exercise echoes a message running throughout many chapters in this book: becoming an actor rather than acted upon and, as Furlong puts it, "accepting the things we cannot change and moving swiftly in the direction of those we can."

FURTHER RESOURCES

Books & Articles

George Beaton, NewLaw New Rules: A Conversation about the Future of the Legal Services Industry (2013).

Raymond H. Brescia, Walter McCarthy, Ashley McDonald, Kellan Potts, & Cassandra Rivais, *Embracing* Disruption: *How Technological Change in the* Delivery *of Legal Services Can Improve Access to Justice*, 78 Alb. L. Rev. 553 (2014/15).

James E. Cabral, Abhijeet Chavan, Thomas M. Clarke, John Greacen, Bonnie Rose Hough, Linda Rexer, Jane Ribadeneyra & Richard Zorza, *Using Technology to Enhance Access to Justice*, 26 Harv. J. of L. & Tech. 243 (2012).

David Galbenski & David Barringer, Legal Visionaries: How to Make Their Innovations Work for You, 27 Interviews (2013).

David Galbenski, Unbound: How Entrepreneurship is Dramatically Transforming Legal Services Today (2009).

Richard S. Granat, *eLawyering for a Competitive Advantage—How to Earn Legal Fees While You Sleep*, http://apps.americanbar.org/dch/thedl.cfm?filename=/EP024500/relatedresources/eLawyering_for_Competitive_Advantage.pdf (last visited Feb. 25, 2015).

GILLIAN K. HADFIELD & JAMIE HEINE, LIFE IN THE LAW-THICK WORLD: THE LEGAL RESOURCE LANDSCAPE FOR ORDINARY AMERICANS, IN BEYOND ELITE LAW: ACCESS TO CIVIL JUSTICE FOR AMERICANS OF AVERAGE MEANS, (S. Estreicher & J. Radice (eds.) (forthcoming 2015).

Luz E. Herrera, *Training Lawyer-Entrepreneurs*, 89 DENV. U. L. REV. 887 (2012).

Nick Robinson, *When Lawyers Don't Get All the Profits: Non-Lawyer Ownership of Legal Services, Access, and Professionalism* (Harvard Law Sch. Program on the Legal Profession, Research Paper No. 2014–20), http://papers.ssrn.com/sol3/papers.cfm?abstract_id=2487878.

Laura Snyder, *Flexing ABS*, 101 A.B.A.J. 62 (2015).

Brittany Stringfellow Otey, *Millennials, Technology, and Professional Responsibility: Training a New Generation in Technological Professionalism*, 37 J. LEGAL PROF. 199 (2013).

REINVENTING THE PRACTICE OF LAW: EMERGING MODELS TO ENHANCE AFFORDABLE LEGAL SERVICES (Luz Herrera ed., 2014).

Ronald W. Staudt, *All the Wild Possibilities: Technology That Attacks Barriers to Access to Justice*, 42 LOY. L.A. L. REV. 1117 (2009).

RICHARD SUSSKIND, TOMORROW'S LAWYERS: AN INTRODUCTION TO YOUR FUTURE (2013). Susskind is also the author of THE FUTURE OF LAW: FACING THE CHALLENGES OF INFORMATION TECHNOLOGY (1996), TRANSFORMING THE LAW: ESSAYS ON TECHNOLOGY, JUSTICE AND THE LEGAL MARKETPLACE (2000), and THE END OF LAWYERS: RETHINKING THE NATURE OF LEGAL SERVICES (2008), but TOMORROW'S LAWYERS distills much of what is likely of most concern to law students and recent graduates from the previous books in a short, readable paperback.

THE RELEVANT LAWYER: REIMAGINING THE FUTURE OF THE LEGAL PROFESSION (Paul A. Haskins ed., 2015).

Richard Zorza, *Some First Thoughts on Court Simplification: The Key to Civil Access and Justice Transformation*, 61 Drake L. Rev. 845 (2013).

Blogs

Legal Rebels, http://www.abajournal.com/legalrebels.

Adam Smith, Esq., http://adamsmithesq.com.

Attorney at Work, http://www.attorneyatwork.com.

eLawyering Blog, http://www.elawyeringredux.com.

FutureLawyer, http://www.futurelawyer.com.

3 Geeks and a Law Blog, http://www.geeklawblog.com.

Blog: Random Academic Thoughts (RATs), John Flood Home Page, http://www.johnflood.com/blog.

Law21, http://www.law21.ca.

Neil Rose, Legal Futures, http://lawyerwatch.wordpress.com.

legalfutures, http://www.legalfutures.co.uk/neil-rose.

Legaltech News, http://www.legaltechnews.com.

Neota Logic, http://blog.neotalogic.com.

Robert Denney Associates, Inc., http://www.robertdenney.com (publishes twice-a-year reports on "what's hot and what's not" in the legal profession).

Future Law Office 2010: Redefining the Practice of Law, Robert Half Legal, http://www.roberthalf.com/legal/future-law-office (last visited, Aug. 4, 2015): Annual Future Law office report on trends affecting the legal field plus articles on various other developments in law practice.

ENDNOTES

1   Clark D. Cunningham, *What Do Clients Really Want From Their Lawyers?*, 2013 J. Disp. Resol. 143 (2013).

2   Legal OnRamp was created to facilitate sharing of legal information and solutions among corporate general counsel toward better outcomes and reduced costs.

3   Paul Lippe, *Firms of the Future Must Orbit Around the Client*, A.B.A. J., (March 25, 2016), http://www.abajournal.com/legalrebels/article/firms_of_the_future_must_orbit_around_the_client/.

4   RICHARD SUSSKIND, TOMORROW'S LAWYERS: AN INTRODUCTION TO YOUR FUTURE 157–58 (2013). The actual source seems to be a classroom admonition from Harvard Business School Professor Theodore Levitt, Clayton M. Christensen, Scott Cook, & Taddy Hall, *Marketing Malpractice: The Cause and the Cure*, HARV. BUS. REV. 1 (2005).

5   David J. Parnell, *Paul Lippe Of Legal OnRamp: Every Legal Department Will Seek To "Cisco-ify" Themselves*, FORBES (April 21, 2014, 11:50 AM), http://www.forbes.com/sites/davidparnell/2014/04/21/paul-lippe-of-legal-onramp-on-the-legal-market-david-parnell/.

6   *See generally*, JOHN HENRY MERRYMAN & ROGELIO PÉREZ-PERDOMO, THE CIVIL LAW TRADITION (3d. 2007);JOHN LEUBSDORF, MAN IN HIS ORIGINAL DIGNITY (2001) (regarding France).

7   GILLIAN K. HADFIELD & JAMIE HEINE, LIFE IN THE LAW-THICK WORLD: THE LEGAL RESOURCE LANDSCAPE FOR ORDINARY AMERICANS, IN BEYOND ELITE LAW: ACCESS TO CIVIL JUSTICE FOR AMERICANS OF AVERAGE MEANS, (S. Estreicher and J. Radice (eds.)) (forthcoming 2015).

8   Paul Lippe, *Firms of the Future Must Orbit Around the Client*, (Mar. 26, 2015) http://www.abajournal.com/legalrebels/article/firms_of_the_future_must_orbit_around_the_client/.

9   Jordan Furlong, *Who's Your Biggest Competitor*, LAW21 (Aug. 7, 2014), http://www.law21.ca/2014/08/whos-biggest-competitor/.

10   *Id.* (citing Hadfield & Heine, supra note 7).

11   Richard S. Granat & Stephanie Kimbro, The Future of Virtual Law Practice, in THE RELEVANT LAWYER: REIMAGINING THE FUTURE OF THE LEGAL PROFESSION 83, 84–88 (Paul A. Haskins ed. 2015).

12   Daniel Fisher, *Stanford-Bred Startup Uses Moneyball Stats To Handicap Judges, Lawyers*, FORBES (Feb. 2, 2015, 7:00 AM), http://www.forbes.com/sites/danielfisher/2015/02/02/stanford-bred-startup-uses-moneyball-stats-to-handicap-judges-lawyers/.

13   Daniel Fisher, *Legal-Services Firm's $73 Million Deal Strips the Mystery from Derivatives Trading*, FORBES, (Feb. 12, 2015, 8:50 AM) http://www.forbes.com/sites/danielfisher/2015/02/12/legal-services-firms-73-million-deal-strips-the-mystery-from-derivatives-trading/.

14   ABA MODEL RULES OF PROF'L CONDUCT r. 1.5(e) & 5.4(d) (1983).

15   Christine Parker, Tahlia Gordon, & Steve Mark, *Regulating Law Firm Ethics Management: An Empirical Assessment of an Innovation in Regulation of the Legal Profession in New South Wales*, 37 J. OF LAW & SOC. 466 (2010).

16   *Id.* at 493.

17   Richard Granat, *LegalZoom's Achilles' Heel: Free Legal Forms*, E-LAWYERING BLOG (Aug. 4, 2012), http://www.elawyeringredux.com/2012/08/articles/free-law/legalzooms-achilles-heel-free-legal-forms/.

18   Richard Lloyd, *Market Force: The Money*: AM. L.., Dec. 1, 2008, at 98. "In 2007 Australia's Slate & Gordon became the first law firm in the world to go public. Others have been slow to follow, but as a regulator says, 'once you allow it, it's pretty hard to put it back in the box.'"

19   *See* Andrew Grech & Kirsten Morrison, Slater & Gordon: *The Listing Experience*, 22 GEO. J. LEGAL ETHICS 535 (2009) by the Managing Director and General Counsel and Company Secretary of S&G regarding the circumstances bringing S&G to seek outside investment and the choice of public listing among other alternatives.

20   Amended Complaint, Jacoby & Meyers, LLP v. Presiding Justices, 847 F.Supp.2d 590 (S.D.N.Y. 2012) (No. 11 Civ. 3387), remanded, 488 Fed. App'x. 526 (2d Cir. 2012) (No. 12-1377), as amended, (Jan. 9, 2013).

21   Jacoby & Meyers, LLP v. Presiding Justices, 488 F. App'x 526 (2d Cir. 2012), as amended (Jan. 9, 2013).

22   Jacoby & Meyers, LLP v. Presiding Justices, No. 11-CV-03387-LAK, 2015 U.S. District LEXIS 92041 (S.D.N.Y. July 15, 2015).

23   Neil Rose, *Jacoby & Meyers Lays Out Twin-Track Approach to UK Expansion,* LEGALFUTURES (Feb. 27, 2014), http://www.legalfutures.co.uk/latest-news/jacoby-meyers-lays-twin-track-approach-uk-expansion; Neil Rose, *From "America's Most Familiar Law firm Brand" to the UK's? Jacoby & Meyers Unveils ABS Plan,* LEGALFUTURES (Aug. 9, 2013, 12:05 AM), http://www.legalfutures.co.uk/latest-news/from-americas-most-familiar-brand-to-uks-jacoby-meyers-unveils-abs-plan.

24   James Podgers, *Urgent Business: New ABA President William Hubbard is Committed to Closing the Gap in Legal Services Delivery for the Poor and Moderate-Income People*, A.B.A. J., Sept. 2014, at 62.

25   David J. Parnell, *Paul Lippe Of Legal OnRamp: Every Legal Department Will Seek To "Cisco-ify" Themselves*, FORBES (April 21, 2014) http://www.forbes.com/sites/davidparnell/2014/04/21/paul-lippe-of-legal-onramp-on-the-legal-market-david-parnell/.

26   These suggestions combine ones made by Susskind, *supra* note 4 and Stephanie Francis Ward, *15 Fairly New Legal Industry Jobs and 6 More You May See Soon*, A.B.A. J. (Sept. 30, 2013), http://www.abajournal.com/legalrebels/article/what_new_legal_services_jobs_have_emerged_in_the_last_five_years.

On Finishing Strong: Looking Back and Looking Forward

SUSAN L. BROOKS & ALEXANDER SCHERR

*To look backward for a while is to refresh the eye,
to restore it and to render it fit for its prime
function of looking forward.*

—Margaret Fairless Barber

*You can't connect the dots looking forward;
you can only connect them looking backwards.*

— Steve Jobs

A s you finish up your externship, we encourage you to focus on three things: (1) creating a positive ending; (2) assessing the learning you have accomplished, including how it fits into the bigger picture of the career goals as discussed in Chapter 26; and (3) planning how you will integrate your externship experience into your remaining time in law school or whatever your next steps may be.

Finishing Strong

Every work experience, including your externship, has a beginning, middle, and ending. Most of the chapters of this book have explored at length how to navigate successfully the beginning and middle phases. In this chapter we suggest you take time to plan and to carry out your ending with a similar level of thoughtfulness. The kind of ending you create will affect your how you view your externship overall. It also can have a significant influence on whether you leave a positive impression on your supervising attorney, which in turn may affect the role your externship plays in your future career development. Understandably, your investment in finishing strong will depend on whether and to what extent you enjoyed your externship and viewed it as worthwhile. Regardless of whether you have thoroughly enjoyed your externship or cannot wait for that final day, we suggest you put some effort into creating a positive ending.

A positive ending has at least two important dimensions: one that affects your own understanding and plans for the future and another that affects how your placement remembers you and can contribute to your future career. First, we want to address how to foster long-term connections with the people with whom you have worked.

Lawyers tend to be a close-knit community, and those connections may extend beyond where you might imagine. You may find lawyers at your placement who can help you take the next step, or they can be a roadblock to a future job prospect if you leave them with a negative impression, whether you list them as a reference or not. We encourage you to expect any lawyer or judge with whom you have worked to be interested in your progress. We suggest you try to leave a positive impression and pave the way for future contact. It is almost always advisable to try to build bridges rather than to risk burning them.

To finish strong we recommend taking the following steps. While many of these recommendations are also listed in Chapter 26 on Career Planning, they are well worth repeating:

- Make sure your supervising attorney is aware of your last day well in advance.

- Make sure you have a clear understanding of your supervising attorney's expectations for the work that needs to be completed before you leave. This may include transfer memos to the file for whoever might handle your cases or projects next.

- Find out if your supervising attorney would like to mark the end of your externship some way. This could mean a final sit-down meeting or perhaps going out for lunch or coffee.

- Regardless of whether you are able to have a more significant way of marking your ending, try to schedule an exit interview with your supervising attorney if possible (even if it is only 15 minutes).

- Be sure to express appreciation and gratitude for your supervising attorney's time and mentorship, both orally and in writing. You might consider sending a handwritten note or a letter rather than an e-mail message.

· Record the contact information for your supervising attorney and anyone else at your placement with whom you had a successful working relationship, and make a point of staying in touch.

There are several other things that are useful to do at the end of your externship. You may recall some of these from previous chapters as well.

Create a portfolio of your written work. Place in a separate folder any writing you did in the externship that you can retain, consistent with the applicable norms of privacy and confidentiality at your placement. With the permission of your supervising attorney, you may be able to use one or more of these writings as samples of your work for prospective employers. Place a cover sheet on any sample you intend to circulate stating clearly that you have obtained permission to use the document as a writing sample. This eliminates potential issues of confidentiality and demonstrates your professionalism to the reader.

Talk to your supervising attorney about whether he or she is willing to be a reference for you in the future. In some instances you may want to request a general letter of reference, addressed "To whom it may concern." Usually, however, you simply want some assurance the attorney is willing, sometime in the future, to write a targeted letter of reference for you when you request it. Even if you are uncertain whether your supervising attorney is willing to act as a reference—say, maybe you thought the externship did not go as well as you had hoped—it is worthwhile to discuss this issue so you will have realistic expectations. There is always a chance your supervisor thinks more highly of your work than you imagine and simply may not be an expressive communicator or attuned to giving appreciative feedback.

Ask your supervising attorney for a detailed evaluation. Your externship teacher and your school's program may require every supervising attorney to complete a detailed written evaluation the attorney will share with you in person as a matter of course. If not, you may want to request some form of detailed evaluation, written or otherwise. You may want to give a list of the all of the work you have completed to your supervising attorney to help prepare for this type of evaluation. Detailed feedback from your supervising attorney can be highly useful to assess your learning experience and what you gained from your externship.

Assessing Your Externship Experience

A detailed evaluation from your supervising attorney is one way you can begin to assess your externship experience. Assessment can help you make informed decisions related to your professional development going forward. As your externship comes to a close, it is useful to review your experience and consider what you have learned and how you might build on it for the future. You might think of this as a kind of individualized strategic planning process. A strategic planning model can help you to tease out what you have learned, which includes thinking about how you can apply your learning going forward and identifying areas you now know you want to explore further based upon your externship experience.

Throughout this book, one goal has been for you to see the value of thinking positively and optimistically. For instance, Chapter 5 on Effective Communication and Professional Relationships introduced you to a model called Appreciative Inquiry (AI), where the emphasis is on figuring out what is going well and doing more of it, rather than what is wrong and how to fix it. This strengths-oriented approach is supported by the research presented in Chapter 25 on Work and Well-being about the benefits of positive psychology and adopting a growth mindset. The creators of AI developed a model for strategic planning called SOAR, Strengths, Opportunities, Aspirations, and Results.

To apply SOAR to your externship, we advise you to take a systematic look at all of the written materials you have created during your externship. These may include

- your learning goals and objectives;

- timesheets;

- journal entries;

- legal documents you created;

- readings for your externship seminar, together with seminar discussions and your experience of any in-class exercises;

- written feedback or evaluations you have received from your supervising attorney, your externship professor, or your peers.

You also might create a list of the skills you learned or improved during the externship. Consider also the list of lawyering skills from Shultz and Zedeck, from the NCBE study, and from the MacCrate Report. See Appendix I on different ways to describe what lawyers do. You may find that your descriptions of skills fit into more than one category. Many skills you learn in law school cut across a number of contexts.

Finally, in addition to assessing your skills, review your insights into the practice where you have worked during your externship, the people who work there, and the kinds of issues they address. You may have written about many of these things in earlier journals. What lawyering have you observed that you want to emulate? What kinds of conduct and attitude in your supervisors and co-workers did you like and admire? What kinds of cases or issues drew your interest and even your passion? Even if you did not like or admire everything about your placement, identifying discrete and particular things that struck you positively can be useful for your future plans.

After reviewing all this, make a chart with columns for each of the four categories below, and fill it in with this guidance:

Strengths

What were the strengths of your externship experience? Here, you can start with your self-assessment, though be sure to consider the varying dimensions of your externship. What professional and personal strengths did you exhibit? What were your supervisor's strengths? Your externship teacher's strengths? What other positives can you identify related to the nature of your work experience and the skills and subject matter you succeeded in learning?

Opportunities

On the flip side of every setback or negative experience lies an opportunity. If you received negative feedback about your research or writing skills during your externship, you have a renewed opportunity to focus on improving those skills. If you found it difficult to communicate with your supervising attorney or with others at your placement, you have an opportunity to focus more of your efforts on how you can communicate more effectively in the future. This positive reframing is an example of adopting a "growth mindset," an approach discussed in several previous chapters, including Supervision, Communication, and Work and Well-being. Adopting a growth mindset by reframing your challenges as opportunities will set you up for success in your future efforts to address whatever challenges you identify.

Aspirations

As you step away from your externship, have your "big-picture" goals changed or become more solidified? Maybe you have now decided you are passionate about public service, even if you are not sure what exact path will lead you there. Maybe you now see you want to position yourself to be able to take a position working in-house at a corporation or non-profit entity.

Results

What concrete and specific takeaways can you identify from your externship experience? What tangible work products did you create? Now is also a good time to re-visit your initial goals and the specific tasks you anticipated might help you to achieve them. Compare your supervisor's evaluation to your own self-evaluation. Look again at the 26 characteristics of effective lawyers identified by Shultz and Zedeck, the list of skills and abilities in the NCBE study, and the MacCrate Report list of knowledge, skills, and values. See Appendix I for more discussion of these studies. Make sure you give yourself credit for both more and less tangible results.

The SOAR model is a practical way to organize what you have learned, focus your memory of it, and integrate your learning into plans for the future. It represents another chance to strengthen your capacity to reflect on experience and guide your professional growth accordingly. For some students, this ability comes naturally, while others need to work consciously on applying past experience to the future. We encourage you to think of the SOAR model as an affirmative way to bridge the transition between your experience at your placement and your future. See also Chapter 8 on Reflection and Writing Journals for a discussion of summary journals.

Looking Forward

Re-entry/Transition

Now that you have spent some time assessing what you have accomplished, consider your next steps. What will you be doing after you finish this externship: returning to being a law student on a full-time basis; graduating and taking a bar exam? You may be shifting from working a significant number of hours each week outside the classroom to taking a full array of more traditional classes. It can be challenging to move away from the excitement and intensity of working on real problems with real lawyers. Returning to more traditional classes may offer opportunities to integrate lessons learned in your placement in ways that deepen your learning of doctrinal subjects. For instance, if you were a judicial extern for a family court judge, consider how your lived experience of family law might inform your study of family law in a more traditional class. Perhaps you now have a greater appreciation of the extent to which some matters cannot be captured in casebooks. For instance, from your time in court, you may have observed how non-legal dimensions of family law play a role in the proceedings. You can discuss in class the ways in which the parties' emotions toward each other often influence whether or not they are able to resolve a case in a more or less adversarial manner.

What steps might you take to prepare yourself for the transition and keep the momentum going from your externship? How might you integrate your newly gained knowledge and experience with the classroom learning you are about to undertake? If you are moving rapidly toward graduating and taking the bar, how can you maximize what you have gained from your externship to help you succeed in those efforts?

Your "Elevator Speech"

As discussed in Chapter 26, it is useful to make some written notes for a concise, two-minute (or less) summary of your externship. The elevator speech refers to something you can use to explain or present in the length of an elevator ride. Crafting this short talk means you have a carefully thought out description that may come in handy at networking events, in casual conversation with someone you meet, or in answering a question at a formal interview. Although an interviewer probably will know about your externship from your resume, your ability to capture the value of your experience in a sound-bite may take you a lot further in a job interview than what is written on your resume. Think of your speech as something you would like professional contacts or potential employers to know about you regardless of what questions they ask.

The results from your SOAR chart can offer a good starting point. You also may want to refer back to your time sheets and journal entries for a detailed picture of what you did during your externship.

After you write your short externship description, it is also important to try to be prepared for a range of questions you may be asked by prospective employers that may or may not relate directly to your elevator speech. For instance: What do you see yourself doing in ten years? Why are you interested in real estate/public interest law/ tax planning? What did you enjoy most about your externship? What would you do differently the next time you began a research project? What can I tell you about this firm/agency/position?

Learning to Learn From Experience

Consider what you have learned about learning from experience through your externship. Did your approach to learning from experience change in any way during the externship? Are you more attentive to your surroundings now that you have observed attorneys and worked on real problems? Do you make more of an effort to record your reactions to events? Are you more able to translate your insights and reactions into valuable learning and plans for the future? Stated simply, has your capacity for reflection and for guiding your own professional development increased?

What have you learned about the ways you learn best? If you now believe that you learn best by doing, describe what you mean by that. Are there any things that you learn best by seeing someone else do them first, or do you prefer to give things a try on your own? What are the limits of learning by doing? Have you struck a different balance between the ways law school teaches you to learn: reading, discussion, writing, and now experience and reflection?

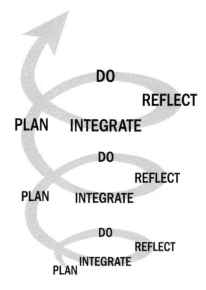

Remember the chart about the learning cycle we presented to you in Chapter 1. How do you understand it differently now, after you have had both experience and the opportunity to reflect on what you have learned? Has your capacity for planning, reflection and integration strengthened over the course of the semester? If so, how has this affected the way that you do the things you do?

Conclusion

As you conclude your externship, you are beginning the next cycle of experiential learning. Through your individualized strategic planning process, you have reflected on your externship in ways that can help you identify and target new goals and objectives as you move forward. We hope this book has contributed to your ability to gain more from your experiences through all phases of the experiential learning cycle: in effect, to increase your ability to learn from practice and transfer what you learn to new situations you will face. We encourage you to use your enhanced knowledge of how to learn from practice throughout your professional career. And we wish you success and happiness in all of your future endeavors!

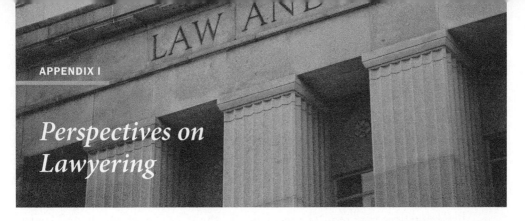

Perspectives on Lawyering

ALEXANDER SCHERR

T his appendix summarizes four important studies of legal education and law practice from 1992 through the present day: the MacCrate Report, the Carnegie Report, a study by Marjorie Shultz & Sheldon Zedeck, and a study by the National Conference of Bar Examiners. Many chapters in this book refer to these studies. This appendix describes the genesis of each study and highlights conclusions referred to in other chapters in this book.

Appendix 1.1: The MacCrate Report

The MacCrate Report was the result of multi-year study conducted by a special committee of the American Bar Association. See ABA TASK FORCE ON LAW SCHS. & THE PROFESSION: NARROWING THE GAP, LEGAL EDUCATION AND PROFESSIONAL DEVELOPMENT—AN EDUCATIONAL CONTINUUM (1992). In general, the MacCrate Report addresses the transition that young lawyers make from law school to the practicing bar. The name of the special committee expresses one of the committee's primary goals: to explore how to "narrow the gap" between a law school education and the requirements of active practice. The Report represents a benchmark in efforts to align what law schools teach with what the legal profession requires.

The Report has three main parts. Part I explores the "Profession for Which Lawyers Must Prepare," and includes descriptions of recent changes in lawyers and legal services, the diversity of practice settings at that time, and the organization and regulation of the profession. Part II sets out a "Vision of the Skills and Values" which it recommends young lawyers acquire, and includes a specific statement of ten "skills" categories and four "values" categories. Part III traces an "Educational Continuum Through Which Lawyers Acquire Their Skills and Values." This part follows the path of legal training from pre-law through law school through the transition to practice and professional development after law school. The Report ends with a statement of six principal recommendations.

Part II of the Report proposes a specific set of skills and values for all lawyers; perhaps not surprisingly, this Part has prompted a large volume of reaction and commentary since the Report's publication. This Part identifies the skills and values which, in the Committee's view, a young lawyer should strive to acquire and, by extension, which both law schools and the legal profession should seek to teach. While recognizing that specialized practices may require specific skills, the Report suggests that all lawyers share these skills and values.

> [C]ompetent representation of a client still requires a well-trained generalist— one who has a broad range of knowledge of legal institutions and who is proficient at a number of diverse tasks. This is so because any problem presented by a client . . . may be amenable to a variety of types of solutions of differing degrees of efficacy; a lawyer cannot competently represent or advise the client or other entity unless he or she has the breadth of knowledge and skill necessary to perceive, evaluate, and begin to pursue each of the options. Id., at 124.

This list of skills and values includes ten categories of "fundamental lawyering skills" and four categories of "fundamental values of the profession." Each category includes several sub-listings, and each sub-listing includes further discussion of the relevant skill or value. The Report encourages use of these listings as a vehicle for organizing resources and as a basis for discussing and refining skills and values within the profession. The Report discourages the use of these listings as a standard for a law school curriculum, as a measure of law schools in an accreditation process, as a statement of the minimum performance to avoid malpractice, and as a source for bar examinations.

Fundamental Lawyering Skills

- *Skill 1: Problem Solving*

  In order to develop and evaluate strategies for solving a problem or accomplishing an objective, a lawyer should be familiar with the skills and concepts involved in:

  - 1.1 Identifying and Diagnosing the Problem
  - 1.2 Generating Alternative Solutions and Strategies
  - 1.3 Developing A Plan of Action
  - 1.4 Implementing the Plan
  - 1.5 Keeping the Planning Process Open to New Information and New Ideas

- *Skill 2: Legal Analysis and Reasoning*

In order to analyze and apply legal rules and principles, a lawyer should be familiar with the skills and concepts involved in:

- · 2.1 Identifying and Formulating Legal Issues
- · 2.2 Formulating Relevant Legal Theories
- · 2.3 Elaborating Legal Theory
- · 2.4 Evaluating Legal Theory
- · 2.5 Criticizing and Synthesizing Legal Argumentation

- *Skill 3: Legal Research*

In order to identify legal issues and to research them thoroughly and efficiently, a lawyer should have:

- · 3.1 Knowledge of the Nature of Legal Rules and Institutions
- · 3.2 Knowledge of and Ability to Use the Most Fundamental Tools of Legal Research
- · 3.3 Understanding of the Process of Devising and Implementing a Coherent and Effective Research Design

- *Skill 4: Factual Investigation*

In order to plan, direct, and (where applicable) participate in factual investigation, a lawyer should be familiar with the skills and concepts involved in:

- · 4.1 Determining the Need for Factual Investigation
- · 4.2 Planning a Factual Investigation
- · 4.3 Implementing the Investigative Strategy
- · 4.4 Memorializing and Organizing Information in an Accessible Form
- · 4.5 Deciding Whether to Conclude the Process of Fact-Gathering
- · 4.6 Evaluating the Information That Has Been Gathered

■ *Skill 5: Communication*

In order to communicate effectively, whether orally or in writing, a lawyer should be familiar with the skills and concepts involved in:

- 5.1 Assessing the Perspective of the Recipient of the Communication
- 5.2 Using Effective Methods of Communication

■ *Skill 6: Counseling*

In order to counsel clients about decisions or courses of action, a lawyer should be familiar with the skills and concepts involved in:

- 6.1 Establishing a Counseling Relationship That Respects The Nature & Bounds of a Lawyer's Role
- 6.2 Gathering Information Relevant to the Decision to Be Made
- 6.3 Analyzing the Decision to Be Made
- 6.4 Counseling the Client About the Decision to Be Made
- 6.5 Ascertaining and Implementing the Client's Decision

■ *Skill 7: Negotiation*

In order to negotiate in either a dispute-resolution or transactional context, a lawyer should be familiar with the skills and concepts involved in:

- 7.1 Preparing for Negotiation
- 7.2 Conducting a Negotiation Session
- 7.3 Counseling the Client About the Terms Obtained From the Other Side in the Negotiation and Implementing the Client's Decision

■ *Skill 8: Litigation and Alternative Dispute-Resolution Procedures*

In order to employ—or to advise a client about—the options of litigation and alternative dispute resolution, a lawyer should understand the potential function and consequences of these processes and should have a working knowledge of the fundamentals of:

- 8.1 Litigation at the Trial-Court Level
- 8.2 Litigation at the Appellate Level

- 8.3 Advocacy in Administrative and Executive Forums

- 8.4 Proceedings in Other Dispute-Resolution Forums

■ *Skill 9: Organization and Management of Legal Work*

In order to practice effectively, a lawyer should be familiar with the skills and concepts required for efficient management, including:

- 9.1 Formulating Goals and Principles for Effective Practice Management

- 9.2 Developing Systems and Procedures to Ensure that Time, Effort, and Resources Are Allocated Efficiently

- 9.3 Developing Systems and Procedures to Ensure that Work is Performed and completed at the Appropriate Time

- 9.4 Developing Systems and Procedures for Effectively Working with Other People

- 9.5 Developing Systems and Procedures for Efficiently Administering a Law Office

■ *Skill 10: Recognizing and Resolving Ethical Dilemmas*

In order to represent a client consistently with applicable ethical standards, a lawyer should be familiar with:

- 10.1 The Nature and Sources of Ethical Standards

- 10.2 The Means by Which Ethical Standards are Enforced

- 10.3 The Processes for Recognizing and Resolving Ethical Dilemmas

Fundamental Values of the Profession

■ *Value 1: Provision of Competent Representation*

As a member of a profession dedicated to the service of clients, a lawyer should be committed to the values of:

- 1.1 Attaining a Level of Competence in One's Own Field of Practice

- 1.2 Maintaining a Level of Competence in One's Own Field of Practice

- 1.3 Representing Clients in a Competent Manner

■ *Value 2: Striving to Promote Justice, Fairness, and Morality*

As a member of a profession that bears special responsibilities for the quality of justice a lawyer should be committed to the values of:

- · 2.1 Promoting Justice, Fairness, and Morality in One's Own Daily Practice
- · 2.2 Contributing to the Profession's Fulfillment of its Responsibility to Ensure that Adequate Legal Services Are Provided to Those Who Cannot Afford to Pay for Them
- · 2.3 Contributing to the Profession's Fulfillment of its Responsibility to Enhance the Capacity of Law and Legal Institutions to Do Justice

■ *Value 3: Striving to Improve the Profession*

As a member of a self-government profession, a lawyer should be committed to the values of:

- · 3.1 Participating in Activities Designed to Improve the Profession
- · 3.2 Assisting in the Training and Preparation of New Lawyers
- · 3.3 Striving to Rid the Profession of Bias Based on Race, Religion, Ethnic Origin, Gender, Sexual Orientation, or Disability, and to Rectify the Effects of These Biases

■ *Value 4: Professional Self-Development*

As a member of a learned profession, a lawyer should be committed to the values of:

- · 4.1 Seeking Out and Taking Advantage of Opportunities to Increase His or Her Knowledge and Improve His or Her Skills
- · 4.2 Selecting and Maintaining Employment That Will Allow the Lawyer to Develop as a Professional and to Pursue His or Her Professional and Personal Goals

Appendix 1.2: The Carnegie Report

Over the course of a decade or more, the Carnegie Foundation has sponsored a program entitled "The Carnegie Foundation for the Advancement of Teaching's Preparation for the Professions." This program has resulted in a series of reports comparing education in different professions, including medicine, nursing, engineering, preparation of clergy, and law. Published in 2007, the report on legal education has achieved a high profile and has had an impact similar to that of the MacCrate Report. William M. Sullivan, et al., Educating Lawyers: Preparation for the Profession of Law (2007) (the "Carnegie Report.")

Organized in five chapters, the Carnegie Report discusses three different domains of preparation for law students in law school: intellectual and cognitive, including knowledge of doctrine and process and legal analysis; expert practice, including acquiring core skills of lawyering and strengthening the capacity for decision making; and identity and purpose, including the formation of professional identity. The first chapter lays out these core domains, which it describes as the "three apprenticeships" of intellect, expert practice, and identity and purpose. Chapters 2–4 explore each of these apprenticeships in turn, providing descriptive detail about each, including illustrations from specific schools studied in the report. The book concludes with a series of recommendations for improving how law schools encourage these apprenticeships.

The Carnegie Report has become known in significant part for its focus on the three apprenticeships, described in more detail in the following paragraphs:

Apprenticeship of Intellect and Cognition: This apprenticeship refers to the development of doctrinal knowledge and the capacity for legal analysis. The Carnegie Report explores this development by focusing on and critiquing what it describes as the "signature pedagogy" of legal education, the Socratic method or "case dialogue." The Report assesses the purposes of this method and its impact on students' understanding of the landscape of the law. It assesses certain gaps in what "case dialogue" can and cannot provide, including direct experience with clients and a focus on ethical substance. It describes the methodology in action, including application of law to facts, adjustment for varying degrees of student preparation, the problem of legal indeterminacy, and the use of the interpretive tools of policy analysis. It ends with a critique of exclusive reliance on this method, with comparisons to other professions.

Apprenticeship of Expert Practice: This apprenticeship refers to the development of both behavioral competencies and decision-making capacity, through the use of a wider range of teaching methods, including simulations, clinics, and externships. The Report describes and assesses several of the barriers to implementing more practice-based education in law schools. It revisits the apprenticeship concept to place it at "the heart of education," including in this discussion interactions between expert attorneys and students through face-to-face contact. It stresses the integration of intellectual and practical concerns through repeated opportunities for practice including the handling of discrete problems and exercising related competencies. It describes how this methodology works in several ways: teaching the theory of the case; integrating cognition and practice through legal writing; the teaching of negotiation skills; the focus on developing legal judgment, including expertise; and the potential of clinical teaching.

Apprenticeship of Identity and Purpose: This apprenticeship refers to the development of a young lawyer's understanding of the lawyer's role both as a representative and as a public citizen. It also implicates the connection between that role and the student's own ethical, moral, and political values. The Report roots its discussion of this apprenticeship in what it describes as unease about whether the legal profession as a whole and individual practitioners have lost a sense of overarching purpose to their work as lawyers. It discusses the moral development of young lawyers, both in specifically ethical terms and in moral and political terms, and identifies several different methods for helping law students navigate the tension between legal analysis and moral action and reaction. It describes how law schools already try to encourage this apprenticeship, both through "mandatory" courses in professional responsibility and through other "pervasive" methods for integrating all three apprenticeships in a single educational experience. It assesses different ways in which classroom, simulation, clinical, and field placement courses can advance integration of the three apprenticeships.

The Carnegie Report ends with a series of observations about legal education:

- Law schools provide rapid socialization into the standards of legal education.

- Law schools rely heavily on one signature pedagogy to accomplish their socialization process.

- The signature pedagogy has both valuable strengths and unintended consequences.

- Assessment of student learning remains underdeveloped.

- Legal education approaches the challenge of improvement only incrementally rather than comprehensively.

- The Report concludes with a strong recommendation that law schools take what it terms as an "integrative model" for reform. This model suggests that the teaching of legal doctrine and analysis continue and encourages training in lawyering abilities, including responsibility for clients alongside an emphasis on how student identity, values, and personal preference can come into harmony with the fundamental purposes of the legal profession.

Appendix 1.3: Lawyering Effectiveness Factors—The Shultz & Zedeck Studies

Another perspective on lawyering arose from an effort to help law school admissions offices identify more accurately those applicants with the greatest promise for success, both in law school and as practitioners. Berkeley law professors Marjorie M. Shultz and Sheldon Zedeck conducted several studies designed to specify certain characteristics of "lawyering effectiveness" and to assess how well those characteristics might predict performance in law school and in practice. Marjorie M. Shultz & Sheldon Zedeck, *Predicting Lawyer Effectiveness: A New Assessment for Use in Law School Admission Decisions*, CELS 2009 4TH ANNUAL CONFERENCE ON EMPIRICAL LEGAL STUDIES PAPER 18 (July 31, 2009) (available at SSRN: http://ssrn.com/abstract=1442118 or http://dx.doi.org/10.2139/ssrn.1442118). See also Marjorie M. Shultz & Sheldon Zedeck, *Predicting Lawyer Effectiveness: Broadening the Basis for Law School Admission Decisions*, 36 LAW & SOC. INQUIRY 620 (2011); Kristen Holmquist, Marjorie Shultz, Sheldon Zedeck, & David Oppenheimer, *Measuring Merit: The Shultz-Zedeck Research on Law School Admissions*, 63 J. LEGAL EDUC. 565 (2013).

The Shultz & Zedeck studies have two salient features. First, the studies identity 26 different "lawyering effectiveness factors," derived from multi-year interviews and surveys. Second, the studies assess how those factors help assess "merit" in the admissions process for law schools:

> In deciding who passes through that portal, law schools . . . should care not just about academic proficiency but also about potential professional competence. Despite acknowledging important overlap between the skills of attaining high law school grades and those of high quality professional performance, . . . additional elements related to professional performance should be considered when selecting students for admission. Commentators had long critiqued the LSAT as too narrow, but—during 60 plus years of LSAT use—no persuasive additions or alternatives had emerged. Id., at 565–566.

The Shultz & Zedeck studies relied on social science studies relating to organizational psychology and employment testing. One of their stated goals was "to predict effective professional performance"; another was "to reduce or eliminate racial and ethnic disparities in law school admission testing." Id.

The studies derived the lawyering effectiveness factors through a multi-year survey of law students, law faculty, and practicing lawyers. Conducting both individual and group interviews, the authors asked questions such as the following: "If you were looking for a lawyer for an important matter for yourself, what qualities would you most look for? What kind of lawyer do you want to teach or be?" *Predicting Lawyer Effectiveness: a New Assessment*, supra, at 25. Based on the resulting interviews, the authors distilled the following list of "26 Effectiveness Factors."

Lawyering Effectiveness Factors

1. *Analysis and Reasoning*: Uses analytical skills, logic, and reasoning to approach problems and to formulate conclusions and advice.

2. *Creativity/Innovation*: Thinks "outside the box," develops innovative approaches and solutions.

3. *Problem Solving*: Effectively identifies problems and derives appropriate solutions.

4. *Practical Judgment*: Determines effective and realistic approaches to problems.

5. *Providing Advice & Counsel & Building Relationships with Clients*: Able to develop relationships with clients that address client's needs.

6. *Fact Finding*: Able to identify relevant facts and issues in case.

7. *Researching the Law*: Utilizes appropriate sources and strategies to identify issues and derive solutions.

8. *Speaking*: Orally communicates issues in an articulate manner consistent with issue and audience being addressed.

9. *Writing*: Writes clearly, efficiently, and persuasively.

10. *Listening*: Accurately perceives what is being said both directly and subtly.

11. *Influencing & Advocating*: Persuades others of position and wins support.

12. *Questioning and Interviewing*: Obtains needed information from others to pursue issue/case.

13. *Negotiation Skills*: Resolves disputes to the satisfaction of all concerned.

14. *Strategic Planning*: Plans and strategizes to address present and future issues and goals.

15. *Organizing and Managing (Own) Work*: Generates well-organized methods and work products.

16. *Organizing and Managing Others (Staff/Colleagues)*: Organizes and manages others' work to accomplish goals.

17. *Evaluation, Development, and Mentoring*: Manages, trains, and instructs others to realize their full potential.

18. *Developing Relationships within the Legal Profession*: Establishes quality relationships with others to work toward goals.

19. *Networking and Business Development*: Develops productive business relationships and helps meet the unit's financial goals.

20. *Community Involvement and Service*: Contributes legal skills to the community.

21. *Integrity & Honesty*: Has core values and beliefs; acts with integrity and honesty.

22. *Stress Management*: Effectively manages pressure or stress.

23. *Passion & Engagement*: Demonstrates interest in law for its own merits.

24. *Diligence*: Committed to and responsible in achieving goals and completing tasks.

25. *Self-Development*: Attends to and initiates self-development.

26. *Able to See the World Through the Eyes of Others*: Understands positions, views, objectives, and goals of others.

In a 2011 report on their study, the authors grouped these 26 factors into 8 different groupings that offer perspective on the relationships between the factors:

- *Intellectual and Cognitive*: Analysis and Reasoning; Creativity and Innovation; Problem Solving; Practical Judgment.

- *Research and Information Gathering*: Researching the Law; Fact Finding; Questioning and Interviewing.

- *Communications*: Influencing and Advocating; Writing; Speaking; Listening.

- *Planning and Organizing*: Strategic Planning; Organizing and Managing One's Own Work; Organizing and Managing Others.

- *Conflict Resolution*: Negotiation Skills; Able to See the World Through the Eyes of Others.

- *Client and Business Relations*: Networking and Business Development; Advising Clients.

- *Working with Others*: Developing Relationships within the Legal Profession; Evaluation, Development, and Mentoring.

- *Character*: Passion and Engagement; Diligence; Integrity/Honesty; Stress Management; Community Involvement and Service; Self-Development.

Predicting Lawyer Effectiveness: Broadening the Basis, supra, at 651–653, Table 8.

Appendix 1.4: Testing Skills and Abilities for Newly Licensed Lawyers—The NCBE Study

The National Conference of Bar Examiners (the "NCBE") is a private nonprofit business that develops licensing tests for bar admission and provides character and fitness services to state bars across the country. The NCBE develops the licensing tests that most applicants for bar admission take, including the Multistate Bar Exam, the Multistate Essay Exam, the Multistate Performance Test, the Multistate Professional Responsibility Exam, and the Uniform Bar Exam. It also provides assistance to those who grade the various exams that it distributes, offers study aids for law students, and helps state bar examiners with character and fitness evaluations for state bars. NAT'L CONF. BAR EXAMINERS, https://www.ncbex.org/about/ (last visited July 30, 2015).

As part of its effort to ensure that its testing products meet the needs of a licensing examination, the NCBE commissioned a multi-year study to determine the tasks, areas of knowledge, and the skills and abilities most widely recognized as significant for a newly-licensed lawyer. Steven S. Nettles & James Hellrung, *A Study of the Newly Licensed Lawyer* (July 2012), linked at http://ncbex.org/publications/ncbe-job-analysis/ (last visited July 30, 2015). This study sought to provide the NCBE with current and reliable information on the knowledge and the abilities that young lawyers would require after admission to the bar. It sought to answer the question, "which tasks, knowledge domains, skills, and abilities are significant to the newly licensed lawyer?" The results would help to define "the content domain that may be used as a basis for preparation of licensing examinations offered by the NCBE." Id.at 3.

The NCBE study developed a list of knowledge domains and common skills and abilities for newly licensed lawyers through an interview process with 26 newly licensed lawyers, experienced lawyers, and judges. The content of these interviews was then reduced to a list of tasks, knowledge domains, and skills and abilities. These lists of domains and skills/abilities were further refined through review of job logs from 43 newly admitted lawyers that tracked the lawyer's daily activities for a period of seven days. An initial draft list of 922 total list items was reduced to a statement of 329 tasks, 86 knowledge statements, and 36 skills and abilities. The study then created a survey instrument containing these statements, with knowledge domains and tasks listed in no particular order. The researchers distributed the survey to a group of over 20,000 newly licensed lawyers, those who had received their bar licenses within the previous three years. 1,669 of the respondents produced usable survey responses.

Those surveyed were asked to rank the skills/abilities list by their significance to their work as a newly licensed lawyer, from "0-not expected" to "4-extremely significant." This resulted in a ranking of the list of skills and abilities from most significant to least significant. The following list presents the list of skill/abilities from those found most significant to those found least significant.

1. Skill/Ability 2: Written communication
2. Skill/Ability 29: Paying attention to details
3. Skill/Ability 10: Listening
4. Skill/Ability 1: Oral communication
5. Skill/Ability 3: Professionalism
6. Skill/Ability 19: Using office technologies (e.g. word processing and email)
7. Skill/Ability 16: Critical reading and comprehension
8. Skill/Ability 17: Synthesizing facts and law
9. Skill/Ability 8: Legal reasoning
10. Skill/Ability 26: Organizational skills
11. Skill/Ability 21: Knowing when to go back and ask questions
12. Skill/Ability 27: Interpersonal skills
13. Skill/Ability 13: Working within established time constraints
14. Skill/Ability 24: Issue spotting
15. Skill/Ability 18: Decisiveness
16. Skill/Ability 25: Answering questions succinctly
17. Skill/Ability 15: Judgment

18. Skill/Ability 22: Computer skills

19. Skill/Ability 5: Electronic researching

20. Skill/Ability 31: Diligence

21. Skill/Ability 9: Advocacy

22. Skill/Ability 7: Fact gathering and evaluation

23. Skill/Ability 36: Consciousness of personal and professional limitations

24. Skill/Ability 32: Planning and strategizing

25. Skill/Ability 23: Information integrating

26. Skill/Ability 12: Working collaboratively

27. Skill/Ability 20: Negotiation

28. Skill/Ability 11: Resource management

29. Skill/Ability 28: Interviewing

30. Skill/Ability 33: Courtroom presence

31. Skill/Ability 35: Creativity

32. Skill/Ability 30: Attorney client privilege—document reviewing

33. Skill/Ability 34: Trial skills

34. Skill/Ability 4: Legal citation

35. Skill/Ability 14: Jury selection

36. Skill/Ability 6: Non-electronic researching

Id. at 313. The study includes other lists of tasks and knowledge domains, ranked generally by significance, but also ranked by the practice area, practice size, and other dimensions of practice for the newly admitted lawyers who responded to the survey.

Appendix II

Permanent Weblinks

This book contains many web links, some of which may have expired by the time you read this book. To give you permanent access to each link, this Appendix provides permanent links to each of the links in the book. Where a page is no longer available at the link cited in the text, this Appendix provides an alternate "available" link. Note that it may happen that the permanent link has also become unavailable. We apologize for this inconvenience and encourage you to use your most reliable web search engine to find the document.

Chapter 3—Learning from Supervision

Page 58

THE EFFECTIVE LAW STUDENT SUPERVISION PROJECT

> *Original:* https://www.griffith.edu.au/criminology-law/effective-law-student-supervision-project
>
> *Permanent:* https://perma.cc/3WLD-L3C4

Chapter 4—Observation

Page 82

Greg Guest et al, COLLECTING QUALITATIVE DATA: A FIELD MANUAL FOR APPLIED RESEARCH (2013)

> *Original:* http://www.sagepub.com/upm-data/48454_ch_3.pdf
>
> *Permanent:* http://perma.cc/7HYR-75SV

Council for Court Excellence, COMMUNITY OBSERVATION OF THE UNITED STATES DISTRICT COURT FOR THE DISTRICT OF COLUMBIA (Aug. 2004)

> *Original:* http://www.courtexcellence.org/uploads/publications/2004USDistCtFinalReport.pdf
>
> *Permanent:* http://perma.cc/5P45-U7UQ

DC Coalition Against Domestic Violence, DC COURT WATCH (2006)

> *Original:* http://dcsafe.org/wp-ontent/uploads/2010/10/Court_Watch_Report_Apr072.pdf
>
> *Permanent:* http://perma.cc/56LR-VZR3

Chapter 5—Effective Communication and Professional Relationships

Page 87

Mark Pagel, *How Language Transformed Humanity*, TED (July 2011)

> *Original:* http://www.ted.com/talks/mark_pagel_how_language
> _transformed_humanity
>
> *Permanent:* http://perma.cc/M78S-TNJ7

Page 95

Amy Cuddy, *Your Body Language Shape Who You Are*, TED (June 2012)

> *Original:* http://www.ted.com/talks/amy_cuddy_your_body_language
> _shapes_who_you_are
>
> *Permanent:* http://perma.cc/LH5U-ZPZ5

Page 96

Ron Guttman, *The Hidden Power of Smiling*, TED (Mar. 2011)

> *Original:* http://www.ted.com/talks/ron_gutman_the_hidden_power
> _of_smiling
>
> *Permanent:* http://perma.cc/M78S-TNJ7

Page 99

VIRTUS, CORE VALUES PROJECT

> *Original:* http://www.virtusinc.com/wp-content/uploads/2009/11/core-values-worksheet.pdf
>
> *Permanent:* https://perma.cc/U4BJ-A26U

Page 104

Big Think, DANIEL GOLEMAN DISCUSSES EMOTIONAL INTELLIGENCE, YouTube (April 23, 2012)

> *Original:* https://www.youtube.com/watch?v=Y7m9eNoB3NU
>
> *Permanent:* http://perma.cc/KJ3K-6RVL

Body Language Quiz, BERKELEY UNIVERSITY OF CALIFORNIA: GREATER GOOD (last visited Dec. 6, 2015)

> *Original:* http://greatergood.berkeley.edu/ei_quiz/
>
> *Permanent:* http://perma.cc/355E-FNV5

Page 108

Nicole Black, *How Can Lawyers Better Communicate With Their Clients?*, MYCASE BLOG (Aug. 21, 2012)

> *Original:* http://www.mycase.com/ blog/2012/08/how-can-lawyers-better-communicate-with-their-clients/
>
> *Permanent:* http://perma.cc/9VBF-R4B4

Mark Pagel, *How Language Transformed Humanity*, TED (July 2011)

> *Original:* http://www.ted.com/talks/mark_pagel_how_language_transformed_humanity?language=en
>
> *Permanent:* http://perma.cc/6KRD-HSPH

THE HAVEN: A CENTRE FOR TRANSFORMATIVE LIVING (last visited Dec. 6, 2015)

> *Original:* http://www.haven.ca
>
> *Permanent:* http://perma.cc/N7TA-ET3N

Amy J. C. Cuddy et al., *The Benefits of Power Posing Before a High-Stakes Social Evaluation* (Harvard Bus. Sch., Working Paper No. 13-027, 2012)

> *Original:* http://nrs.harvard.edu/urn-3:HUL.InstRepos:9547823
>
> *Permanent:* http://perma.cc/E5TA-BST4

Page 109

Denali Tietjen, *Mindfulness Meditation Benefits More Than the Mind*, BOSTON.COM (June 4, 2014)

> *Original:* http://www.boston.com/health/2014/06/04/mindfulness-meditation-benefits-more-than-the-mind/crdobytPKLDVhfRcCWkZ2M/story.html
>
> *Permanent:* http://perma.cc/W4C2-PMZ3

Chapter 6—Navigating Cultural Difference

Page 125

PROJECTIMPLICIT

> *Original:* https://implicit.harvard.edu/implicit/
>
> *Permanent:* http://perma.cc/G5LJ-H55Q

Page 149

MTV's Look Different

Original: www.lookdifferent.org

Permanent: http://perma.cc/D2EM-CNAV

Page 150

Microaggressions: More than Just Race, Psychology Today (Nov. 17, 2010)

Original: https://www.psychologytoday.com/blog/
microaggressions-in-everyday-life/201011/microaggressions-more-just-race

Permanent: https://perma.cc/H2WZ-V5SA

National Center for State Courts, Strategies to Reduce the Influence of Implicit Bias

Original: http://www.ncsc.org/IBstrategies

Permanent: http://perma.cc/83CQ-N7HV

Chapter 7—Bias in the Legal Profession

Page 156

Cate Matthews, *He Dropped One Letter In His Name While Applying For Jobs, and the Responses Rolled In*, The Huffington Post Black Voices (Sep. 2, 2014)

Original: http://www.huffingtonpost.com/2014/09/02/jose-joe-job-
discrimination_n_5753880.html?ncid=fcbklnkushpmg00000047&ir=Black+Voices

Permanent: http://perma.cc/S4HT-6CF3

David Binder Research & MTV, DBR MTV Bias Survey Summary 2 (April 2014)

Original: http://cdn.lookdifferent.org/content/studies/000/000/001/DBR_MTV_
Bias_Survey_Executive_Summary.pdf

Permanent: http://perma.cc/RZS4-35PD

Page 198

Gender and Racial Fairness State Links, National Center for State Courts

Original: http://www.ncsc.org/Topics/Access-and-Fairness/Gender-and-Racial-
Fairness/State-Links.aspx?cat=Gender%20Fairness%20Task%20Forces%20
and%20Reports

Permanent: http://perma.cc/L3GA-YAQJ

ABA COMM'N ON WOMEN IN THE PROFESSION, VISIBLE INVISIBILITY: WOMEN OF COLOR IN FORTUNE 500 LEGAL DEPARTMENTS (2012)

> *Original:* http://www.americanbar.org/content/dam/aba/administrative/diversity/next_steps_2011.authcheckdam.pdf

> *Permanent:* https://perma.cc/5GGQ-NYH6

Page 199

Yassmin Abdel-Magied, *Beat Your Bias, Question Your First Impression*, TEDxSOUTHBANK, (January 2015)

> *Original:* https://www.youtube.com/watch?v=vbHkh_faQu8

> *Permanent:* https://perma.cc/AEE8-F7V7

Mellody Hobson, *Color Blind or Color Brave*, TED (Mar. 2014)

> *Original:* http://www.ted.com/talks/mellody_hobson_color_blind_or_color_brave

> *Permanent:* http://perma.cc/8CJ5-47NH

TEDx Talks, *Immaculate Perception: Jerry Kang at TEDxSanDiego*, YOUTUBE (2013)

> *Original:* https://www.youtube.com/watch?v=9VGbwNI6Ssk

> *Permanent:* http://perma.cc/WLG6-42E6

Vernā Meyers, *How to Overcome Our Biases? Walk Boldly Toward Them*, TED (Nov. 2014)

> *Original:* https://www.ted.com/talks/verna_myers_how_to_overcome_our_biases_walk_boldly_toward_them

> *Permanent:* http://perma.cc/CWR9-6R9Y

How to Tell People They Sound Racist, ILL DOCTRINE (Jul. 21, 2008)

> *Original:* http://www.illdoctrine.com/2008/07/

> *Permanent:* http://perma.cc/Z94M-3XM5

Human Rights Campaign, *Lana Wachowski Receives the HRC Visibility Award*, YOUTUBE (Oct. 24, 2012)

> *Original:* https://www.youtube.com/watch?v=crHHycz7T_c

> *Permanent:* http://perma.cc/SZ76-L2CW

Stella Young, *I'm Not Your Inspiration, Thank You Very Much*, TED (Apr. 2014)

> *Original:* https://www.ted.com/talks/stella_young_i_m_not_your_inspiration_thank_you_very_much

> *Permanent:* http://perma.cc/4MKB-QQLJ

Page 200

Dr. Arin N. Reeves, *Written in Black & White-Exploring Confirmation Bias in Racialized Perceptions of Writing Skills in Yellow Paper Series* (Nextions Original Research, 2014)

> *Original:* http://www.nextions.com/wp-content/files_
> mf/14151940752014040114WritteninBlackandWhiteYPS.pdf

> *Permanent:* http://perma.cc/8CCU-WE9P

Karen M. Richardson, *Report of the Eighth Annual NAWL National Survey on Retention and Promotion of Women in Law Firms*, NATIONAL ASSOCIATION OF WOMEN LAWYERS (Feb. 25, 2014)

> *Original:* http://www.nawl.org/p/bl/et/blogid=10&blogaid=56

> *Permanent:* http://perma.cc/R6HY-4TFA

AMERICAN BAR ASSOCIATION COMMISSION ON WOMEN, A CURRENT GLANCE AT WOMEN IN THE LAW (February 2013)

> *Original:* http://www.google.com.au/url?sa=t&rct=j&q=&esrc=s&s
> ource=web&cd=2&ved=0CCIQFjAB&url=http%3A%2F%2F-www.
> americanbar.org%2Fdam%2Faba%2Fmarketing%2Fwomen%2Fcurrent_
> glance_statistics_feb2013.authcheckdam.
> pdf&ei=g_XuVJbbKI_q8AWttoH4Bw&+usg=AFQjCNFshK0ILzdpbwxdHAEynldhlA8hJw

> *Available:* http://www.americanbar.org/dam/aba/marketing/women/current_
> glance_statistics_feb2013.authcheckdam.pdf

> *Permanent:* http://perma.cc/5KEC-TX7V

2012 Representation of United States State Court Women Judges, NATIONAL ASSOCIATION OF WOMEN JUDGES

> *Original:* http://www.nawj.org/us_state_court_statistics_2012.asp

> *Permanent:* http://perma.cc/LE29-5Z7E

Women in the Federal Judiciary: Still a Long Way to Go, NATIONAL WOMEN'S LAW CENTER (Nov. 18, 2015)

> *Original:* http://www.nwlc.org/resource/
> women-federal-judiciary-still-long-way-go-1

> *Permanent:* http://perma.cc/S5ZW-8YSX

Judicial Facts and Figures 2013, UNITED STATES COURTS (last updated Sep. 30, 2013)

> *Original:* http://www.uscourts.gov/Statistics/JudicialFactsAndFigures/judicial-facts-figures-2013.aspx

> *Permanent:* http://perma.cc/2V8E-X5PC

DAVID B. ROTTMAN ET AL., NATIONAL CENTER FOR STATE COURTS, PERCEPTIONS OF COURTS IN YOUR COMMUNITY: THE INFLUENCE OF EXPERIENCE, RACE, AND ETHNICITY (Mar. 25, 2003)

> *Original:* https://www.ncjrs.gov/pdffiles1/nij/grants/201356.pdf

> *Permanent:* http://perma.cc/REU6-ZNC7

NALP Bulletin, *LGBT Representation Up in 2012*, NATIONAL ASSOCIATION FOR LAW PLACEMENT (Jan. 2013)

> *Original:* http://www.nalp.org/lgbt_representation_up_in_2012

> *Permanent:* http://perma.cc/Y48L-ZRU6

NALP Bulletin, *Reported Number of Lawyers With Disabilities Remains Small*, NATIONAL ASSOCIATION FOR LAW PLACEMENT (Dec. 2009)

> *Original:* http://www.nalp.org/dec09disabled

> *Permanent:* http://perma.cc/26LE-QZ4S

ABA COMMISSION ON MENTAL & PHYSICAL DISABILITY LAW, ABA DISABILITY STATISTICS REPORT (2011)

> *Original:* http://www.americanbar.org/content/dam/aba/uncategorized/2011/20110314_aba_disability_statistics_report.authcheckdam.pdf

> *Permanent:* http://perma.cc/R33M-XD6A

Page 201

ABA PRESIDENTIAL INITIATIVE COMMISSION ON DIVERSITY, DIVERSITY IN THE LEGAL PROFESSION: THE NEXT STEPS (Apr. 2010)

> *Original:* http://www.americanbar.org/content/dam/aba/administrative/diversity/next_steps_2011.authcheckdam.pdf

> *Permanent:* http://perma.cc/2RQC-CWWR

MODEL RULES OF PROF'L CONDUCT r. 8.4 (AM. BAR ASS'N 2011)

> *Original:* http://www.americanbar.org/groups/professional_responsibility/publications/model_rules_of_professional_conduct/rule_8_4_misconduct.html

> *Permanent:* http://perma.cc/N3AH-5W7E

Bankr. D. Ariz. R. 1000-1

> *Original:* http://www.azb.uscourts.gov/rule-1000-1
>
> *Permanent:* http://perma.cc/Z3WS-58HQ

Ariz. LRCiv

> *Original:* http://www.azd.uscourts.gov/sites/default/files/local-rules/LRCiv%20 2014.pdf
>
> *Permanent:* http://perma.cc/6FFW-FZNV

Press Release, Ark. Judicial Discipline & Disability Comm'n (Aug. 6, 2014)

> *Original:* http://www.state.ar.us/jddc/press_releases.html
>
> *Permanent:* http://perma.cc/6T3E-X7QB

Model Standards of Conduct for Mediators Standard II.B.1 (Am. Bar Ass'n, Am. Arbitration Ass'n, & Ass'n Conflict Resolution 2005), available at

> *Original:* http://www.americanbar.org/groups/dispute_resolution/policy_ standards.html
>
> *Permanent:* http://perma.cc/P9HZ-XC2X

Chapter 9—Professionalism

Page 238

Honesty/Ethics in Professions, Gallup Historical Trends (Dec. 8-11, 2014)

> *Original:* http://www.gallup.com/poll/1654/honesty-ethics-professions.aspx
>
> *Permanent:* http://perma.cc/R2RT-YSSL

Page 239

Stacey Barchenger & Andrew Ford, *Judge Challenges Attorney to Courtroom Brawl*, USA Today (June 3, 2014, 7:45 AM)

> *Original:* http://www.usatoday.com/story/news/nation/2014/06/03/ judge-attorney-courtroom-fight/9901631/
>
> *Permanent:* http://perma.cc/N49S-87K9

Angry judge reprimanding second year law student

>*Original:* https://www.youtube.com/watch?v=vO4G55uTMvM
>
>*Permanent:* https://perma.cc/68V6-LA85

Page 241

AMERICAN BAR ASSOCIATION COMMISSION ON PROFESSIONALISM, ". . . . IN THE SPIRIT OF PUBLIC SERVICE:" A BLUEPRINT FOR THE REKINDLING OF LAWYER PROFESSIONALISM (1986)

>*Original:* http://www.abanet.org/cpr/professionalism/Stanley_Commission_Report.pdf
>
>*Permanent:* http://perma.cc/AP7S-A3G3

Page 252

Lawyers Who Lead by Example 2014 Awards, N.Y.L.J. (Oct. 2014)

>*Original:* http://nylawyer.nylj.com/adgifs/specials/101414LifetimeAchievers/2014_1014ssLifetimeAchievers.html?et=editorial&bu=New%20York%20Law%20Journal&cn=20141014&src=EMC-Email&pt=Special%20Report
>
>*Permanent:* http://perma.cc/4RZC-22HN

Staff Writers, *12 True Legal Heroes Law Students Should Look To*, BEST COLLEGES ONLINE (Mar. 20, 2012)

>*Original:* http://www.bestcollegesonline.com/blog/2012/03/20/12-true-legal-heroes-law-students-should-look-to/
>
>*Permanent:* http://perma.cc/QD24-YMEE

Page 258

Center for Professional Responsibility, AMERICAN BAR ASSOCIATION

>*Original:* http://www.americanbar.org/groups/professional_responsibility.html
>
>*Permanent:* http://perma.cc/W9VR-6JY3

AMERICAN BOARD OF TRIAL ADVOCATES

>*Original:* www.abota.org
>
>*Permanent:* http://perma.cc/3D2G-MDC7

Center for the Study of Ethical Development, UNIV. OF ALA. (2015)

>*Original:* http://ethicaldevelopment.ua.edu/
>
>*Permanent:* http://perma.cc/FNH4-JJN7

JAMES M. WICKS ET AL., N.Y. STATE BAR ASS'N COMMERCIAL AND FED. LITIG. SECTION, SOCIAL MEDIA ETHICS GUIDELINES (June 9, 2015)

> *Original:* https://www.nysba.org/Sections/Commercial_Federal_Litigation/ Com_Fed_PDFs/Social_Media_Ethics_Guidelines.html
>
> *Permanent:* http://perma.cc/JH95-U25R

RONALD. C. MINKOFF, A.B.A. STANDING COMMITTEE ON PROFESSIONALISM, REVIVING A TRADITION OF SERVICE: REDEFINING LAWYER PROFESSIONALISM IN THE 21ST CENTURY (2009)

> *Original:* http://www.americanbar.org/content/dam/aba/migrated/cpr/ professionalism/century.authcheckdam.pdf
>
> *Permanent:* http://perma.cc/YU6D-WCN2

Page 262

AM. BAR ASS'N CTR. PROF. RESPONSIBILITY, MODEL RULES OF PROFESSIONAL CONDUCT

> *Original:* http://www.americanbar.org/groups/professional_responsibility/ publications/model_rules_of_professional_conduct/model_rules_of_ professional_conduct_table_of_contents.htm
>
> *Permanent:* https://perma.cc/EY5C-NLRB

Chapter 10—Ethical Issues in Externships: An Introduction

Page 273

National Institute on Alcoholism and Alcohol Abuse, *Alcohol Facts and Statistics*

> *Original:* http://pubs.niaaa.nih.gov/publications/AlcoholFacts&Stats/ AlcoholFacts&Stats.htm
>
> *Permanent:* https://perma.cc/QR82-L968

Centers for Disease Control and Prevention, Fact Sheet, *Alcohol Use and Your Health*

> *Original:* http://www.cdc.gov/alcohol/fact-sheets/alcohol-use.htm
>
> *Permanent:* https://perma.cc/A7CQ-KYP7

Page 274

Am I Alcoholic Self Test, NATIONAL COUNCIL ON ALCOHOL AND DRUG ABUSE, INC. (2015)

> *Original:* https://ncadd.org/learn-about-alcohol/alcohol-abuse-self-test
>
> *Permanent:* https://perma.cc/XPJ5-4FEQ

Original: https://ncadd.org/get-help/take-the-test/am-i-drug-addicted

Permanent: http://perma.cc/MYU6-3ZFJ

Page 277

Substance Abuse and Mental Health Tool Kit for Law Students and Those Who Care About Them

Original: http://www.americanbar.org/content/dam/aba/migrated/lsd/ mentalhealth/toolkit.authcheckdam.pdf

Permanent: https://perma.cc/SK5S-PGYJ

Know Your Rights: Workplace Sexual Harassment, AMERICAN ASS'N UNIV. WOMEN

Original: http://www.aauw.org/what-we-do/legal-resources/ know-your-rights-at-work/workplace-sexual-harassment/#strategies

Permanent: http://perma.cc/W4NL-W3P7

National Council on Alcoholism and Drug Dependence, *Am I Drug Addicted?*

Original: http://www.americanbar.org/groups/lawyer_assistance.html

Permanent: http://perma.cc/4RUT-AH76

Page 278

Todd Essig, *When 'Study Drugs' Kill (Part 1): How Ambition Becomes Adderall Addiction*, FORBES (Feb. 10, 2013, 1:31 PM)

Original: http://www.forbes.com/sites/toddessig/2013/02/10when-study-drugs- kill-part-1-how-ambition-becomes-adderall-addiction/

Permanent: http://perma.cc/9EJA-E2MS

Todd Essig, *When Study Drugs Kill (Part 2): Reducing the Risks From Brain Doping*, FORBES (Feb. 10, 2013, 1:31 PM)

Original: http://www.forbes.com/sites/toddessig/2013/02/10when-study-drugs- kill-part-2-reducing-the-risks-from-brain-doping/

Permanent: http://perma.cc/U7LY-JCH6

Chapter 12—Ethical Issues in Externships: Conflicts of Interest

Page 302

State Rules Comparison Charts, AM. BAR ASS'N CTR. FOR PROF'L RESPONSIBILITY

Original: http://www.americanbar.org/groups/professional_responsibility/policy/rule_charts.html

Permanent: http://perma.cc/BN7S-Q953

N.Y. GEN. MUN. LAW § 800-809 (2009)

Original: https://www.osc.state.ny.us/localgov/pubs/gmlposter.pdf

Permanent: https://perma.cc/8W7K-RWUV

Supplemental Standards of Ethical Conduct for Members and Employees of the Securities and Exchange Commission, 5 C.F.R. § 4401

Original: http://www.gpo.gov/fdsys/pkg/CFR-2012-title5-vol3/pdf/CFR-2012-title5-vol3-part4401.pdf

Permanent: http://perma.cc/7FBF-3Z9W

Page 311

Statement of Law Deans Concerning Stimson Remarks, BALKINIZATION

Original: http://balkin.blogspot.com/2007/01/statement-of-law-deans-concerning.html

Permanent: https://perma.cc/5DUX-PHLZ

Page 330

Stephen Jones, *The Case for Unpopular Clients*, WALL STREET J. (Mar. 13, 2010)

Original: http://www.wsj.com/articles/SB10001424052748703625304575116250512434096

Permanent: http://perma.cc/LN8Z-HZNS

In re Formal Advisory Opinion 10-1, 741 S.E.2d 622 9 (Ga. 2013)

Original: http://www.gabar.org/barrules/handbookdetail.cfm?what=rule&id=557

Permanent: https://perma.cc/manage/create

Brian Baxter, *John Edwards, A Man of Many Lawyers, Shuffles Legal Team Once Again*, AM. LAW DAILY (Mar. 23, 2012)

Original: http://www.amlawdaily.typepad.com/amlawdaily/2012/03/Edwards-legal-team.html

Permanent: http://perma.cc/F4C7-ND8R

Page 331

Charter of Core Principles of the European Legal Profession and Code of Conduct for European Lawyers, Jonathan Goldsmith, responsible editor (The Council of Bars and Law Societies of Europe, 2013)

> *Original:* http://www.ccbe.eu/fileadmin/user_upload/NTCdocument/EN_CCBE_CoCpdf1_1382973057.pdf
>
> *Permanent:* http://perma.cc/9GCL-PYBE

American Bar Association, ABA Formal Opinion 09-455: Disclosure of Conflicts of Information When Lawyers Move Between Law Firms (Oct. 8, 2009)

> *Original:* http://iardc.fastcle.com/EdutechResources/resources//bytopicid/24414/ABA%2009-455.pdf
>
> *Permanent:* http://perma.cc/R5PP-Y6VF

Chapter 13—Ethical Duties in Externships: Duties to Tribunals and Third Parties

Page 356

Rules of the Delaware State Courts, Del. State Cts.

> *Original:* http://courts.delaware.gov/Rules/?DLRPCwithComments_Oct2007.pdf
>
> *Permanent:* http://perma.cc/R5XU-8S6M

Chapter 14—Learning About Lawyering

Page 395

Blind Men and an Elephant, Wikipedia

> *Original:* https://en.wikipedia.org/wiki/Blind_men_and_an_elephant
>
> *Permanent:* https://perma.cc/6PLT-H93L

Page 396

Cognitive Bias, Wikipedia

> *Original:* https://en.wikipedia.org/wiki/Cognitive_bias
>
> *Permanent:* https://perma.cc/NFS5-547H

List of Cognitive Biases, Wikipedia

> *Original:* https://en.wikipedia.org/wiki/List_of_cognitive_biases
>
> *Permanent:* https://perma.cc/L5AS-PX8V

Marjorie M. Shultz & Sheldon Zedeck, *Predicting Lawyer Effectiveness: A New Assessment for Use in Law School Admission Decisions*, CELS 2009 4th Annual Conference on Empirical Legal Studies Paper 18 (July 31, 2009)

> *Original:* http://ssrn.com/abstract=1442118
>
> *Permanent:* http://perma.cc/3Q8U-BHCZ

Steven S. Nettles & James Hellrung, Nat'l Conf. Bar Examiners, A Study of the Newly Licensed Lawyer (July 2012)

> *Original:* http://ncbex.org/pdfviewer/?file=%2Fdmsdocument%2F56
>
> *Permanent:* http://perma.cc/XZK8-K4JU

NCBE Job Analysis, Nat'l Conf. Bar Examiners (2015)

> *Original:* http://ncbex.org/publications/ncbe-job-analysis/
>
> *Permanent:* http://perma.cc/E83Y-ZYJ5

Bayesian Inference, Wikipedia

> *Original:* https://en/wikipedia.org/wiki/Bayesian_inference
>
> *Permanent:* https://perma.cc/QZP7-KQ7J

Cognitive Obstacles: Why Distractions Can Improve Creativity and Problem-Solving, Why We Reason (Nov. 14, 2015)

> *Original:* http://whywereason.com/tag/shane-frederick/
>
> *Permanent:* http://perma.cc/5NKC-6EZR

Conjunction Fallacy, Wikipedia

> *Original:* https://en.wikipedia.org/wiki/Conjunction_fallacy
>
> *Permanent:* https://perma.cc/C93U-TPWG

Chapter 15—Client Relationships

Page 426

Nat'l Ass'n of Law Placement, Class of 2013 National Summary Report (July 2014)

> *Original:* http://www.nalp.org/uploads/NatlSummaryChartClassof2013.pdf.
>
> *Permanent:* http://perma.cc/ZF67-RUK2

AMERICAN CIVIL LIBERTIES UNION

> *Original:* https://www.aclu.org
>
> *Permanent:* https://perma.cc/9ZCE-PW4H

Judicial Selection in the States: *Georgia*, NAT'L CTR. FOR ST. CTS.

> *Original:* http://www.judicialselection.us/judicial_selection/index.cfm?state=GA
>
> *Permanent:* http://perma.cc/W44P-ZJBE

Boundaries, WASH. ST. BAR ASS'N (2015)

> *Original:* http://www.wsba.org/Resources-and-Services/
> Lawyers-Assistance-Program/Self-Care/Boundaries
>
> *Permanent:* http://perma.cc/S45N-8LHQ

Chapter 16—Collaboration and Teamwork

Page 428

California Western Scholarly Commons, Teamwork1, YouTube (Feb. 28, 2015)

> *Original:* https://www.youtube.com/watch?v=Rjxqbv3pS90
>
> *Permanent:* http://perma.cc/JN5B-QYGX

Page 429

California Western Scholarly Commons, *Teamwork2*, YOUTUBE (Feb. 28, 2015)

> *Original:* https://www.youtube.com/watch?v=2TlnqEBTTJY
>
> *Permanent:* http://perma.cc/JCR4-93CU

Page 430

Candy Chang, STREET VENDOR GUIDE

> *Original:* http://candychang.com/street-vendor-guide/
>
> *Permanent:* https://perma.cc/3CTE-CSSJ

California Western Scholarly Commons, *Teamwork3*, YOUTUBE (Feb. 28, 2015)

> *Original:* https://www.youtube.com/watch?v=79ztf5_XT0I
>
> *Permanent:* http://perma.cc/9FUW-H5ZG

The Value of Teamwork in the Non-profit Sector

> *Original:* https://www.youtube.com/watch?v=79ztf5_XT0I
>
> *Permanent:* http://perma.cc/PUW4-2F9E

Center for Urban Pedagogy

> *Original:* http://welcometocup.org/
>
> *Permanent:* https://perma.cc/8BXL-YS6E

Page 431

Commons: Village pump/Copyright, WIKIPEDIA

> *Original:* http://commons.wikimedia.org/wiki/Commons:Village_pump/Copyright
>
> *Permanent:* http://perma.cc/AWW9-N628

Page 435

California Western Scholarly Commons, *Forming*, YOUTUBE (Feb. 28, 2015)

> *Original:* https://www.youtube.com/watch?v=PF59v6Of1-s
>
> *Permanent:* http://perma.cc/5ZZZ-XA5S

Page 436

California Western Scholarly Commons, *Norming*, YOUTUBE (Feb. 28, 2015)

> *Original:* https://www.youtube.com/watch?v=7-RN7AK_6VM
>
> *Permanent:* http://perma.cc/L9LW-63UC

California Western Scholarly Commons, *Storming*, YOUTUBE (Feb. 28, 2015)

> *Original:* https://www.youtube.com/watch?v=By1iNhnfuBM
>
> *Permanent:* http://perma.cc/G5FX-ZU6L

Page 439

California Western Scholarly Commons, *Dialogue1*, YOUTUBE (Feb. 28, 2015)

> *Original:* https://www.youtube.com/watch?v=lFgNy_fAvn8
>
> *Permanent:* http://perma.cc/PZ6Y-BAJN

Page 440

California Western Scholarly Commons, *Dialogue2*, YOUTUBE (Feb. 28, 2015)

> *Original:* https://www.youtube.com/watch?v=HogmhLqXmlI
>
> *Permanent:* http://perma.cc/XYS4-KY2F

Page 441

Team-Based Learning Collaborative (2013)

> *Original:* www.teambasedlearning.org
>
> *Permanent:* http://perma.cc/3UTL-6CFV

Team Builders Plus

> *Original:* www.Teambuildinginc.com
>
> *Permanent:* http://perma.cc/WK22-8EMJ

Page 442

California Western Scholarly Commons, *Teamwork4*, YouTube (Feb. 28, 2015)

> *Original:* https://www.youtube.com/watch?v=hLWB7RAw43I
>
> *Permanent:* http://perma.cc/2SAY-U95H

Ben Klayman, *GM Top Executives Spared in Internal Report on Safety Failure.* Reuters (June 5, 2014, 10:31 PM)

> *Original:* http://www.reuters.com/article/2014/06/06/
> us-gm-recall-idUSKBN0EG1KI20140606
>
> *Permanent:* http://perma.cc/6XHX-PPTP

Victor Li, *Lex ink.1 Tackles How Collaboration May Help Firms Stay Relevant During Flux*, ABA J. (June 1, 2014 7:50 AM)

> *Original:* http://www.abajournal.com/magazine/article/
> lexthink.1_tackles_how_collaboration_may_help_firms_stay_relevant_during
>
> *Permanent:* http://perma.cc/6TRA-TX6K

What Skills Are Required To Become A Lawyer?, Ultimate L. Guide

> *Original:* http://www.ultimatelawguide.com/careers/articles/what-skills-are-
> required-to-become-a-lawyer.html
>
> *Permanent:* http://perma.cc/H6SF-86KV

International Academy of Collaborative Professionals

> *Original:* https://www.collaborativepractice.com/
>
> *Permanent:* https://perma.cc/TR7V-PHXQ

Thomas L. Friedman, *How to Get a Job at Google*, N.Y. Times (Feb. 22, 2014)

> *Original:* http://www.nytimes.com/2014/02/23/opinion/sunday/friedman-how-
> to-get-a-job-at-google.html
>
> *Permanent:* http://perma.cc/XD3V-QANW

Chapter 17—Writing for Practice

Page 465

GRAMMAR GIRL

Original: http://www.quickanddirtytips.com/grammar-girl

Permanent: http://perma.cc/3DNE-3HXU

Research Guides, GA. ST. L. LIBR.

Original: http://libguides.law.gsu.edu/

Permanent: http://perma.cc/83EE-V924

LADY (LEGAL) WRITER

Original: http://ladylegalwriter.blogspot.com/

Permanent: http://perma.cc/XS78-7ARQ

LAWPROSE

Original: http://www.lawprose.org/blog

Permanent: http://perma.cc/3EPQ-59RP

Articles, LEGAL WRITING PRO

Original: http://www.legalwritingpro.com/articles/

Permanent: http://perma.cc/5TUG-DMKK

THE (NEW) LEGAL WRITER

Original: http://raymondpward.typepad.com/newlegalwriter/

Permanent: http://perma.cc/3ZYU-5QGB

WORDRAKE

Original: http://www.wordrake.com/writing-tips/

Permanent: http://perma.cc/6SWZ-2ZT7

iWriteLegal, APPLE APP STORE

Original: https://itunes.apple.com/us/app/iwritelegal/id561864315?mt=8

Permanent: https://perma.cc/LY94-4Z9F

Chapter 18—Making Presentations

Page 488

Chris Anderson, *How to Give a Killer Presentation*, Harv. Bus. Rev. (June 2013)

> *Original:* https://hbr.org/2013/06/how-to-give-a-killer-presentation
>
> *Permanent:* https://perma.cc/LCN6-H86H

Presentation Zen

> *Original:* www.presentationzen.com
>
> *Permanent:* http://perma.cc/F6HK-4HVX

Chapter 19—Judicial Externships

Page 513

Debra Cassens Weiss, *Federal Judge to Time Lawyers in 9/11 Trial 'Like a Speed Chess Match*,' A.B.A. J. L. News Now (April 28, 2011, 1:24 PM)

> *Original:* http://www.abajournal.com/news/article/
> federal_judge_to_time_lawyers_in_9-11_trial_like_a_speed_chess_match/
>
> *Permanent:* http://perma.cc/8ZRR-WXZ9

Page 517

Tony Mauro, *Sotomayor Says Lack of Diversity is 'Huge Danger' for Judiciary*, The BLT: The Blog of LegalTimes

> *Original:* http://legaltimes.typepad.com/blt/2013/11/
> sotomayor-says-lack-of-diversity-is-huge-danger-for-judiciary
>
> *Available:* http://legaltimes.typepad.com/blt/2013/11/sotomayor-says-lack-of-
> diversity-is-huge-danger-for-judiciary.html
>
> *Permanent:* http://perma.cc/LYA6-QFAL

Page 524

Institute for the Advancement of the American Legal System, Quality Judges Initiative

> *Original:* http://iaals.du.edu/initiatives/quality-judges-initiative/
> implementation/judicial-performance-evaluation
>
> *Permanent:* https://perma.cc/9LCZ-HDYY

Page 527

Radio Television Digital News Ass'n.

> *Original:* http://rtdna.org

> *Permanent:* http://perma.cc/K9DX-2SE3

U.S. Cts.

> *Original:* www.uscourts.gov

> *Permanent:* http://perma.cc/X8H4-4J42

Page 529

David B. Rottman, et al., Nat'l Ctr. for State Courts, Perceptions of the Courts in Your Community: The Influence of Experience, Race and Ethnicity: Final Report (2003)

> *Original:* https://www.ncjrs.gov/pdffiles1/nij/grants/201302.pdf

> *Permanent:* https://perma.cc/S68K-9LMV

Page 530

Eileen Patten, *The Black-White and Urban-Rural Divides in Perceptions of Racial Fairness*, Pew Res. Ctr. FactTank (Aug. 28, 2013)

> *Original:* http://www.pewresearch.org/fact-tank/2013/08/28/the-black-white-and-urban-rural-divides-in-perceptions-of-racial-fairness/

> *Permanent:* http://perma.cc/E33X-B4KU

Page 531

Nat'l Ctr. for St. Cts.

> *Original:* http://www.ncsc.org

> *Permanent:* http://perma.cc/F3FA-DPQS

Page 538

Herbert B. Dixon, Jr., *The Evolution of a High-Technology Courtroom*, Future Trends in State Courts 28 (2011),

> *Original:* http://www.ncsc.org/~/media/Microsites/Files/Future%20Trends/Author%20PDFs/Dixon.ashx

> *Permanent:* http://perma.cc/LSV3-HGV8

Page 542

Federal Judicial Center, Ethics for Federal Judicial Law Clerks
(4th ed. 2013)

> *Original:* http://www.fjc.gov/public/pdf.nsf/lookup/Maintaining-Public-Trust-4D-FJC-Public-2013.pdf/$file/Maintaining-Public-Trust-4D-FJC-Public-2013.pdf
>
> *Permanent:* http://perma.cc/K4DJ-WUKA

Page 543

Ethics Resource Guide, Nat'l Ctr. for St. Cts.

> *Original:* http://www.ncsc.org/Topics/Judicial-Officers/Ethics/Resource-Guide.aspx
>
> *Permanent:* http://perma.cc/G5VK-S5V6

Judicial Conference of the United States, *Code of Conduct for Judicial Employees*

> *http://www.uscourts.gov/rulesandpolicies/codesofconduct/codeconductjudicialemployees.aspx*
>
> *Permanent:* SEE COMMENTS

Page 544

Nat'l Ctr. for St. Cts., CourTools

> *Original:* http://www.courtools.org/
>
> *Permanent:* http://perma.cc/9EH6-6VSR

2010 Judicial Conference of the United States Committee on Court Administration and Case Management, *Civil Litigation Management Manual,* U.S. Cts. (2nd ed. 2010)

> *Original:* http://www.uscourts.gov/FederalCourts/PublicationsAndReports/CivilLitigationManagementManual.aspx
>
> *Permanent:* http://perma.cc/5RBE-2QY6

Robert C. LaFountain et al., Examining the Work of State Courts: An Overview of 2012 State Trial Court Caseloads, Nat'l Ctr. for St. Cts. (2014)

> *Original:* http://www.courtstatistics.org/~/media/Microsites/Files/CSP/NCSC_EWSC_WEB_NOV_25_14.ashx
>
> *Permanent:* http://perma.cc/QZ8U-XK8F

Judicial Selection and Retention Resource Guide, Nat'l Ctr. for St. Cts.

> *Original:* www.ncsc.org/topics/judicial-officers/judicial-selection-and-retention/resource-guide.aspx
>
> *Permanent:* http://perma.cc/8QW6-EMN2

N.Y.C. Bar Ass'n Council on Jud. Admin., Judicial Selection Methods in the State of New York: A Guide to Understanding and Getting Involved in the Selection Process (Mar. 2014)

> *Original:* http://www2.nycbar.org/pdf/report/uploads/20072672-GuidetoJudicialSelectionMethodsinNewYork.pdf
>
> *Permanent:* http://perma.cc/BVU9-MTXW

Page 545

Am. Bar Ass'n Coalition for Just., Judicial Selection: The Process of Choosing Judges (June 2008)

> *Original:* http://www.americanbar.org/content/dam/aba/migrated/JusticeCenter/Justice/PublicDocuments/judicial_selection_roadmap.authcheckdam.pdf
>
> *Permanent:* http://perma.cc/T3XR-VWBL

U.S. Chamber Institute for Legal Reform, *Promoting "Merit" in Merit Selection, A Best Practices Guide to Commission-Based Judicial Selection*

> *Original:* http://ilr.iwssites.com/uploads/sites/1/meritselectionbooklet.pdf
>
> *Available:* http://www.instituteforlegalreform.com/uploads/sites/1/meritselectionbooklet.pdf
>
> *Permanent:* http://perma.cc/927V-7A2P

N.Y. St. Bar. Ass'n Jud. Selection, Judicial Diversity: A Work in Progress (Sept. 2014)

> *Original:* http://www.nysba.org/judicialdiversityreport/
>
> *Permanent:* http://perma.cc/RT3S-35F8

Judicial Performance Resources, Am. Bar. Ass'n Jud. Division

> *Original:* http://www.americanbar.org/groups/judicial/conferences/lawyers_conference/resources/judicial_performance_resources.html
>
> *Permanent:* http://perma.cc/XBR7-9MLY

Am. Bar Ass'n, Black Letter Guidelines for the Evaluation of Judicial Performance (Feb. 2005)

> *Original:* http://www.americanbar.org/content/dam/aba/publications/judicial_division/jpec_final.authcheckdam.pdf

> *Permanent:* http://perma.cc/XE5K-RWWA

Page 546

Research & Resources, Nat'l Consortium on Racial and Ethnic Fairness in the Courts

> *Original:* http://www.national-consortium.org/Research-and-Resources.aspx

> *Permanent:* http://perma.cc/79PY-J5AM

Mark Soler, Reducing Racial and Ethnic Disparities in the Juvenile Justice System, *in* Trends in State Courts: Special Focus on Juvenile Justice and Elder Issues 27 (Carol R. Flango et al. eds., 2014)

> *Original:* http://www.ncsc.org/~/mdia/Microsites/Files/Future%20Trends%20 2014/2014%20NCSC%20Trends%20Report.ashx

> *Permanent:* http://perma.cc/HE5D-MZG4

Steve Leben, The Procedural-Fairness Movement Comes of Age, *in* Trends in State Courts: Special Focus on Juvenile Justice and Elder Issues 59 (Carol R. Flango et al. eds., 2014)

> *Original:* http://www.ncsc.org/~/media/Microsites/Files/Future%20Trends%20 2014/2014%20NCSC%20Trends%20Report.ashx

> *Permanent:* http://perma.cc/GP59-HS6W

Public Trust and Confidence Resource Guide, Nat'l Ctr. for St. Cts.

> *Original:* http://www.ncsc.org/topics/court-community/public-trust-and-confidence/resource-guide.aspx

> *Permanent:* http://perma.cc/JY2S-D8DJ

Long Range Plan for Information Technology, U.S. Cts.

> *Original:* http://www.uscourts.gov/uscourts/FederalCourts/Publications/2014-IT-long-range-plan.pdf

> *Permanent:* http://perma.cc/KP8P-2VPJ

Technology in the Courts Resource Guide, NAT'L CTR. FOR ST. CTS.

> *Original:* http://www.ncsc.org/Topics/Technology/Technology-in-the-Courts/Resource-Guide.aspx
>
> *Permanent:* http://perma.cc/HP2V-NWWB

James J. Sandman & Glenn Rawdon, Technology Solutions for Increased Self-Representation, *in* TRENDS IN STATE COURTS: SPECIAL FOCUS ON JUVENILE JUSTICE AND ELDER ISSUES 55 (Carol R. Flango et al. eds., 2014)

> *Original:* http://www.ncsc.org/~/media/Microsites/Files/Future%20Trends%20 2014/2014%20NCSC%20Trends%20Report.ashx
>
> *Permanent:* http://perma.cc/EA87-3FS3

Page 547

Social Media and the Courts Network, NAT'L CTR. FOR ST. CTS.

> *Original:* http://www.ncsc.org/Topics/Media/Social-Media-and-the-Courts/Social-Media/Home.aspx
>
> *Permanent:* http://perma.cc/TK2F-84V6

Joyce Cram, Elder Court: Enhancing Access to Justice for Seniors, *in* TRENDS IN STATE COURTS: SPECIAL FOCUS ON JUVENILE JUSTICE AND ELDER ISSUES 77 (Carol R. Flango et al. eds., 2014)

> *Original:* http://www.ncsc.org/~/media/Microsites/Files/Future%20Trends%20 2014/2014%20NCSC%20Trends%20Report.ashx
>
> *Permanent:* http://perma.cc/KBX9-3PGV

Page 548

AMERICAN BAR ASSOCIATION, JUDICIAL DIVISION, TRIAL ATTORNEY EVALUATION OF A JUDGE

> *Original:* http://www.americanbar.org/content/dam/aba/migrated/jd/lawyersconf/performanceresource/survey/trial_court_attorney.pdf
>
> *Permanent:* https://perma.cc/UXZ7-HCHA

Page 553

DAVID B. ROTTMAN ET AL., NAT'L CTR. FOR ST. CTS., PERCEPTIONS OF THE COURTS IN YOUR COMMUNITY: THE INFLUENCE OF EXPERIENCE, RACE AND ETHNICITY, FINAL REPORT 105 (Jan. 31, 2003)

> *Original:* https://www.ncjrs.gov/pdffiles1/nij/grants/201302.pdf
>
> *Permanent:* https://perma.cc/4J2R-G4PY

Chapter 20—Criminal Justice Law Placements

Page 563

U.S. Attorney's Manual tit. 9-27.000 (Dec. 2014)

Original: http://www.justice.gov/usam/usam-9-27000-principles-federal-prosecution#9-27.001

Permanent: http://perma.cc/X4DM-C5PV

Page 586

Innocence Project

Original: http://www.innocenceproject.org/

Permanent: http://perma.cc/Y4HZ-TBRH

Page 603

Gideon's Promise

Original: http://gideonspromise.org/

Permanent: http://perma.cc/XW2J-6E36

National Right to Counsel Committee, Justice Denied: America's Continuing Neglect of Our Constitutional Right to Counsel (Apr. 2009)

Original: http://www.constitutionproject.org/documents/justice-denied-america-s-continuing-neglect-of-our-constitutional-right-to-counsel/

Permanent: http://perma.cc/HK3Y-CA6V

Chapter 21—Public Interest Lawyering

Page 625

Equal Justice Works

Original: http://www.equaljusticeworks.org/

Permanent: http://perma.cc/45JE-QEL4

Nat'l Legal Aid and Defender Ass'n

Original: http://www.nlada100years.org/

Permanent: http://perma.cc/M5QW-6CCY

Pub. Serv. Job Directory

Original: https://www.psjd.org/

Permanent: https://perma.cc/FF9U-QLNL

Chapter 22—Public Service Lawyering

Page 643

Careers in Federal Government, Pub. Serv. Job Directory

    Original: http://www.psjd.org/Careers_in_Federal_Government

    Permanent: http://perma.cc/N5XG-4F5X

PSJD, The Federal Legal Employment Guide, 2015-2015

    Original: https://www.psjd.org/getResourceFile.cfm?ID=75

    Available: https://www.psjd.org/2015_-_2016_Federal_Legal_Employment_Guide_%28FLEG%29

    Permanent: http://perma.cc/QF8X-N9TM

Page 644

    Original: http://www.americanbar.org/content/dam/aba/administrative/market_research/lawyer-demographics-tables-2014.authcheckdam.pdf

    Permanent: http://perma.cc/9VG5-4F8N

Chapter 23—Transactional Lawyering

Page 655

Sonia Sotomayor, *Diversity and the Legal Profession*, C-SPAN Video (Aug. 26, 2010)

    Original: http://www.c-spanvideo.org/program/295200-1

    Permanent: http://perma.cc/6PB9-5KUS

Page 656

Mind Tools Editorial Team, *Emotional Intelligence: Developing Strong "People Skills,"* Mind Tools

    Original: http://www.mindtools.com/pages/article/newCDV_59.htm

    Permanent: http://perma.cc/AVU4-KCDL

Page 683

    University of Denver Sturm College of Law, Externship Handbook

    Original: http://www.law.du.edu/documents/legal-externship-program/ExternshipHandbook.pdf

    Permanent: https://perma.cc/K4P6-NUBX

Chapter 25—Work & Well-being

Page 701

Authentic Happiness, U. OF PENN.

> *Original:* https://www.authentichappiness.sas.upenn.edu/
> *Permanent:* https://perma.cc/8YMM-Q5VM

Page 719

NEW YORK CITY BAR ASSOCIATION, *Cheat Sheet*

> *Original:* http://www.nycbar.org/images/stories/diversity/thecheatsheet.pdf
> *Permanent:* https://perma.cc/279Q-AQLU

Page 720

Repayment Plans, FED. STUDENT AID

> *Original:* https://studentaid.ed.gov/sa/repay-loans/understand/plans
> *Permanent:* https://perma.cc/GB2B-3P9C

Page 721

Ronald C. Kessler et al., *Age of Onset of Mental Disorders: A Review of Recent Literature*, 20 CURRENT OPINIONS IN PSYCHIATRY 359 (July 2007)

> *Original:* http://www.ncbi.nlm.nih.gov/pmc/articles/PMC1925038/
> *Permanent:* http://perma.cc/SB7N-SZP4

Major Depressive Disorder, INTERNET MENTAL HEALTH

> *Original:* http://www.mentalhealth.com/home/dx/majordepressive.html
> *Permanent:* http://perma.cc/7JBG-9W8S

Page 722

Directory of Lawyer Assistance Programs, AM. BAR ASS'N.

> *Original:* http://www.americanbar.org/groups/lawyer_assistance/resources/lap_programs_by_state.html
> *Permanent:* http://perma.cc/39FM-6BKB

DAVE NEE FOUNDATION

> *Original:* http://www.daveneefoundation.com/
> *Permanent:* http://perma.cc/G4AM-27KD

Lawyers With Depression

> *Original:* http://www.lawyerswithdepression.com/
>
> *Permanent:* http://perma.cc/YCZ7-CD4U

Anderson Cooper, *Mindfulness*, CBS News: 60 Minutes (Dec. 14, 2014)

> *Original:* http://www.cbsnews.com/news/
> mindfulness-anderson-cooper-60-minutes/
>
> *Permanent:* http://perma.cc/B7FA-TB4T

The Mindful Lawyer

> *Original:* http://themindfullawyer.com/
>
> *Permanent:* http://perma.cc/P6B2-KE8M

Barbara Frederickson, *Love—A New Lens on the Science of Thriving*, YouTube (Aug. 23, 2012)

> *Original:* https://www.youtube.com/watch?v=ZxoPLtRnxZs
>
> *Permanent:* https://perma.cc/FDE6-LLMM

Larry Richard, What Makes Lawyers Tick?

> *Original:* http://www.lawyerbrainblog.com/
>
> *Permanent:* http://perma.cc/WYZ5-CT4M

Page 723

Wake Forest Baptist Med. Ctr., *Proper Sleep a Key Contributor to Health, Well-Being*, ScienceDaily (Jan. 22, 2014)

> *Original:* http://www.sciencedaily.com/releases/2014/01/140122153606.htm
>
> *Permanent:* http://perma.cc/9GAC-DCAM

Mental Health Foundation, Sleep Matters: The Impact of Sleep on Health and Wellbeing (Jan. 2011)

> *Original:* http://www.mentalhealth.org.uk/publications/sleep-report/
>
> *Permanent:* http://perma.cc/BSB3-ACN5

Jennifer Soong, *The Secret (and Surprising) Power of Naps*, WebMD Magazine

> *Original:* http://www.webmd.com/balance/features/
> the-secret-and-surprising-power-of-naps
>
> *Permanent:* http://perma.cc/8QMA-9P7R

Tony Schwartz, *More Vacation is the Secret Sauce*, Harv. Bus. Rev. (Sept. 6, 2012)

> *Original:* http://blogs.hbr.org/2012/09/more-vacation-is-the-secret-sa/
>
> *Permanent:* http://perma.cc/YWV6-96VQ

Alcohol Facts and Statistics, Nat'l Inst. On Alcohol Abuse and Alcoholism (Mar. 2015)

    Original: http://www.niaaa.nih.gov/alcohol-health/ overview-alcohol-consumption/alcohol-facts-and-statistics

    Permanent: http://perma.cc/LMQ2-9QB9

Ronald C. Kessler et al., *Age of Onset of Mental Disorders: A Review of Recent Literature*, 20 Current Opinions in Psychiatry 359 (July 2007)

    Original: http://www.ncbi.nlm.nih.gov/pmc/articles/PMC1925038/

    Permanent: http://perma.cc/K3FS-4CHR

Major Depressive Disorder, Internet Mental Health

    Original: http://www.mentalhealth.com/home/dx/majordepressive.html

    Permanent: http://perma.cc/2GJN-J9PD

Page 724

N.Y. St. Bar. Ass'n, Special Committee On Balanced Lives in the L. Final Rep. (Mar. 7, 2008)

    Original: http://www.nysba.org/WorkArea/DownloadAsset.aspx?id=26859

    Permanent: http://perma.cc/J55X-FDT2

Heidi Burgess, *Transformative Meditation*, U. Colo. Conflict Res. Consortium (1997)

    Original: http://www.colorado.edu/conflict/transform/tmall.htm

    Permanent: http://perma.cc/MMJ5-LHDM

Staff, Ctr. for Ct. Innovation

    Original: http://www.courtinnovation.org/staff

    Permanent: http://perma.cc/RRF9-3FQ8

Donison Law Firm

    Original: http://www.donisonlaw.com/

    Permanent: http://perma.cc/6R8C-95SH

Law Office of Janelle Orsi

    Original: http://www.janelleorsi.com/

    Permanent: http://perma.cc/Z4JB-5V9C

Andrew Strickler, *Flex Time Beats Cash in Legal Recruiting, Survey Finds*, LAW360
(May 30, 2013, 6:13 PM)

> *Original:* http://www.law360.com/articles/446009/
> flex-time-beats-cash-in-legal-recruiting-survey-finds
>
> *Permanent:* http://perma.cc/D47K-2TLT

Chapter 27—The Future of the Legal Profession and Legal Services Directory

Page 759

AOSPHERE: ALTERNATIVE SOLUTIONS FOR LEGAL RISK MANAGEMENT

> *Original:* http://www.aosphere.com
>
> *Permanent:* http://perma.cc/CYE9-ZS8R

Page 779

Technology Initiative Grant Program, LEG. SERVS. CORP.

> *Original:* http://tig.lsc.gov
>
> *Permanent:* http://perma.cc/K3VS-ZU7E

InnovAction Hall of Fame, C. OF L. PRAC. MGMT.

> *Original:* http://collegeoflpm.org/innovaction-awards/innovaction-hall-of-fame
>
> *Permanent:* http://perma.cc/6SBC-JS9G

INNOVATING JUSTICE

> *Original:* http://www.innovatingjustice.com/
>
> *Permanent:* http://perma.cc/YD5N-77B7

Page 780

Technology Initiative Grant Program, LEG. SERVS. CORP.

> *Original:* http://tig.lsc.gov/2015-tig-conference-session-materials
>
> *Permanent:* http://perma.cc/35K2-MN2M

Page 795

RICHARD S. GRANAT, ELAWYERING FOR A COMPETITIVE ADVANTAGE (2008)

> *Original:* http://apps.americanbar.org/dch/thedl.cfm?filename=/
> EP024500/relatedresources/eLawyering_for_Competitive_Advantage.pdf
>
> *Permanent:* http://perma.cc/N9ND-E7NV

Nick Robinson, When Lawyers Don't Get All the Profits: Non-Lawyer Ownership of Legal Services, Access, and Professionalism (Aug. 27, 2014) (Harv. L. Sch. Program on the Legal Prof., Research Paper No. 2014–20)

>*Original:* http://papers.ssrn.com/sol3/papers.cfm?abstract_id=2487878
>
>*Permanent:* http://perma.cc/D77D-X248

Page 796

Legal Rebels, Am. Bar. Ass'n

>*Original:* http://www.abajournal.com/legalrebels
>
>*Permanent:* http://perma.cc/YS4D-79U5

Adam Smith, Esq.

>*Original:* http://adamsmithesq.com
>
>*Permanent:* http://perma.cc/257X-753K

Att'y at Work

>*Original:* http://www.attorneyatwork.com
>
>*Permanent:* http://perma.cc/7NCB-BRSH

eLawyering Blog

>*Original:* http://www.elawyeringredux.com
>
>*Permanent:* http://perma.cc/5MH3-5YNW

FutureLawyer

>*Original:* http://www.futurelawyer.com
>
>*Permanent:* http://perma.cc/3FUB-AX9G

3 Geeks and a Law Blog

>*Original:* http://www.geeklawblog.com
>
>*Permanent:* http://perma.cc/C4LJ-UAFL

Blog: Random Academic Thoughts (RATs), John Flood Home Page

>*Original:* http://www.johnflood.com/blog
>
>*Permanent:* http://perma.cc/FP9R-6DWA

Law21

>*Original:* http://www.law21.ca
>
>*Permanent:* http://perma.cc/U9T4-Y8K4

LAWYER WATCH

> *Original:* http://lawyerwatch.wordpress.com
>
> *Permanent:* http://perma.cc/NE4U-8LKG

Neil Rose, LEGAL FUTURES

> *Original:* http://www.legalfutures.co.uk/neil-rose
>
> *Permanent:* http://perma.cc/M65P-6KFS

LEGALTECH NEWS

> *Original:* http://www.legaltechnews.com
>
> *Permanent:* http://perma.cc/E2ZK-H4EP

NEOTA LOGIC

> *Original:* http://blog.neotalogic.com
>
> *Permanent:* http://perma.cc/7EZ2-XPCF

ROBERT DENNEY ASSOCIATES, INC.

> *Original:* http://www.robertdenney.com
>
> *Permanent:* http://perma.cc/HPU7-RJ5R

Future Law Office 2010: Redefining the Practice of Law, ROBERT HALF LEGAL

> *Original:* http://www.roberthalf.com/legal/future-law-office
>
> *Permanent:* http://perma.cc/6T9X-3XHS

Page 797

Paul Lippe, *Firms of the Future Must Orbit Around the Client,* AM. BAR. ASS'N LEGAL REBELS (Mar. 26, 2015, 1:55 PM)

> *Original:* http://www.abajournal.com/legalrebels/article/firms_of_the_future_must_orbit_around_the_client/
>
> *Permanent:* http://perma.cc/UC8V-NZHG

David J. Parnell, *Paul Lippe of Legal OnRamp: Every Legal Department Will Seek to "Cisco-ify" Themselves,* FORBES (Apr. 21, 2014, 11:50 AM)

> *Original:* http://www.forbes.com/sites/davidparnell/2014/04/21/paul-lippe-of-legal-onramp-on-the-legal-market-david-parnell/
>
> *Permanent:* http://perma.cc/WV59-DAF5

Paul Lippe, *Firms of the Future Must Orbit Around the Client*, AM. BAR. ASS'N LEGAL REBELS (Mar. 26, 2015, 1:55 PM)

> *Original:* http://www.abajournal.com/legalrebels/article/firms_of_the_future_must_orbit_around_the_client/
>
> *Permanent:* http://perma.cc/B2T9-AWZA

Jordan Furlong, *Who's Your Biggest Competitor?*, LAW21 (Aug. 7, 2014)

> *Original:* http://www.law21.ca/2014/08/whos-biggest-competitor/
>
> *Permanent:* http://perma.cc/HV2L-S22F

Daniel Fisher, *Stanford-Bred Startup uses Moneyball Stats to Handicap Judges, Lawyers*, FORBES (Feb. 2, 2015, 7:00 AM)

> *Original:* http://www.forbes.com/sites/danielfisher/2015/02/02/stanford-bred-startup-uses-moneyball-stats-to-handicap-judges-lawyers/
>
> *Permanent:* http://perma.cc/AA92-WRSY

Daniel Fisher, *Legal-Services Firm's $73 Million Deal Strips The Mystery From Derivatives Trading*, FORBES (Feb. 12, 2015, 8:50 AM)

> *Original:* http://www.forbes.com/sites/danielfisher/2015/02/12/legal-services-firms-73-million-deal-strips-the-mystery-from-derivatives-trading/
>
> *Permanent:* http://perma.cc/LF3R-ZDX3

Richard Granat, *LegalZoom's Achilles' Heel: Free Legal Forms*, ELAWYERING BLOG (Aug. 4, 2012)

> *Original:* http://www.elawyeringredux.com/2012/08/articles/free-law/legalzooms-achilles-heel-free-legal-forms/
>
> *Permanent:* http://perma.cc/N8M2-2JKX

Page 798

Neil Rose, *From 'America's Most Familiar Law Firm Brand' to the UK's? Jacoby & Meyers Unveils ABS Plan*, LEGALFUTURES (Aug. 9, 2013)

> *Original:* http://www.legalfutures.co.uk/latest-news/from-americas-most-familiar-brand-to-uks-jacoby-meyers-unveils-abs-plan
>
> *Permanent:* http://perma.cc/5SKC-B4HH

Neil Rose, *From "America's Most Familiar Law firm Brand" to the UK's? Jacoby & Meyers Unveils ABS Plan*

> *Original:* http://www.legalfutures.co.uk/latest-news/
> from-americas-most-familiar-brand-to-uks-jacoby-meyers-unveils-abs-plan
>
> *Permanent:* https://perma.cc/8B6Q-ZTLU

David J. Parnell, *Paul Lippe Of Legal OnRamp: Every Legal Department Will Seek To "Cisco-ify" Themselves*, Forbes (Apr. 21, 2014, 11:50 AM)

> *Original:* http://www.forbes.com/sites/davidparnell/2014/04/21/
> paul-lippe-of-legal-onramp-on-the-legal-market-david-parnell/
>
> *Permanent:* http://perma.cc/263R-34LC

Stephanie Francis Ward, *15 Fairly New Legal Industry Jobs and 6 More You May See Soon*, Am. Bar Ass'n Legal Rebels (Sept. 30, 2013, 9:57 PM)

> *Original:* http://www.abajournal.com/legalrebels/article/
> what_new_legal_services_jobs_have_emerged_in_the_last_five_years
>
> *Permanent:* http://perma.cc/YWX4-EV4Z

Page 815

Marjorie M. Shultz & Sheldon Zedeck, *Predicting Lawyer Effectiveness: A New Assessment for Use in Law School Admission Decisions*, 4th Annual Conference on Legal Studies (July 31, 2009)

> *Original:* http://dx.doi.org/10.2139/ssrn.1442118
>
> *Permanent:* http://perma.cc/3E6K-5WRG

Page 818

Nat'l Conf. Bar Examiners

> *Original:* https://www.ncbex.org/about/
>
> *Permanent:* https://perma.cc/98WY-FEXT

Steven S. Nettles & James Hellrung, *A Study of the Newly Licensed Lawyer*

> *Original:* http://ncbex.org/publications/ncbe-job-analysis/
>
> *Permanent:* https://perma.cc/C7VK-DE88

Index

This index includes names of people mentioned, quoted, and whose works are excerpted as well as concepts and entities referenced in the text. It does not include references to Further Resources and Endnotes, which appear at the end of most chapters.